MEMOIRS OF THE MUSEUM OF ANTHROPOLOGY
UNIVERSITY OF MICHIGAN
NUMBER 9

STUDIES IN THE ARCHEOLOGICAL HISTORY OF THE DEH LURAN PLAIN
The Excavation of Chagha Sefid

By

FRANK HOLE

Contributions by
M. J. Kirkby, Colin Renfrew

ANN ARBOR
1977

© 1976 Regents of The University of Michigan
The Museum of Anthropology
All rights reserved

Printed in the
United States of America

ISBN 978-1-949098-43-3 (paper)

ISBN 978-1-949098-73-0 (ebook)

CONTENTS

List of Figures v
List of Tables viii
List of Plates xi
Preface xiii
Acknowledgements xiii

Part 1. General Discussion

  I. Research Objectives and Strategy
     Introduction 1
     Synopsis of previous results 3
     Research strategy 8

  II. Principal Results and Implications
     Introduction 10
     The transition from the Mohammad Jaffar to the Sabz phase 10
     Origins and implications of the Choga Mami Transitional 12
     What happened to the original settlers? 16
     The Deh Luran sequence 17
     Eras and strategies of subsistence 18
     Assessment of developments throughout western Iran 19
     Major research problems remaining 21

  III. The Ages and Characteristics of the Phases
     Estimated ages of the phases 24
     Remarks on radiocarbon dating 27
     Summary of the phases 28

Part 2. Excavation and Analysis

  IV. Stratigraphy and Architecture
     Methods of excavation 41
     Depositional history—west trench 46
     Depositional history—Area B 79
     Architectural features 86

  V. Burials
     Prehistoric burials 91
     Intrusive burials 93

  VI. Pottery
     Introduction 94
     The pottery sequence 97
     Stone, plaster and asphalt vessels 139

  VII. Chipped Stone Artifacts
     Introduction 148
     Tool types 151

VIII. Other Artifacts
    Introduction 196
    Grinding and pounding tools 200
    Miscellaneous stone artifacts 208
    Miscellaneous artifacts 216
    Bone artifacts 219
    Matting and basketry 223
    Figurines and objects of lightly baked clay 226
    Ornaments 236
    Copper 245

Bibliography 246

Appendix 1: Land and Water Resources of the Deh Luran and Khuzistan Plains
            by *M.J. Kirby*, University of Leeds 251

Appendix 2: The Later Obsidian of Deh Luran—The Evidence of Chagha Sefid
            by *Colin Renfrew*, University of Southhampton 289

FIGURES

1. Topographic map of Chagha Sefid with the excavations in Areas A, C, D and B indicated . . . 42
2. Section through site along south profile of excavation. 43
3. Chagha Sefid, about 1.5 km southwest of Deh Luran 44
4. An erosional gully cut into sterile sands and gravels at the base of Chagha Sefid before settlement began 48
5. Profile of south side of Area A pit showing the successive stratigraphic zones 49
6. Zone A2, Ali Kosh Phase. Remnant of a mud brick house 51
7. Zone A3, Ali Kosh Phase. Remnants of two fireplaces in the corners of rooms 52
8. Zone A3, Ali Kosh Phase. Details of fireplace 53
9. Zone A4, Early Sefid Phase. Burials and disturbed clusters of bones with overlying walls dotted 54
10. Zone A4, Early Sefid Phase. Remnants of rooms lying above burials 55
11. Profile of east end of pit in Area A. 56
12. Zone C, Event 1, Late Sefid Phase. A rectangle of stones with a plaster basin at one end. . . . 58
13. Zone C, Event 1, Late Sefid Phase. Courtyard or room paved with stones 60
14. Zone C, Event 2, Late Sefid Phase. Large mud brick platform 61
15. Zone C, Event 3, Early Surkh Phase. Paved floor or courtyard with adjacent plaster-floored rooms 62
16. Zone C, Events 3-4, Early Surkh Phase. Open area is filled with rock, ash and trash and the entire area is eroded 63
17. Zone C, Event 4, Early Surkh Phase. Final building of pavement on leveled structures of Event 3. 64
18. Zone C, Event 5, Early Surkh Phase. Brick pavement or small platform built over former paved area. 65
19. Zone C, Event 6, Early Surkh Phase. Final Structure discernible in Area A 66
20. Zone D1, Surkh Phase. Large stones partially outline the brick platform of Zone C. 68-69
21. Zone D3, Surkh Phase. Complex of stone-founded rooms. 70
22. Zone D4, Surkh Phase. Partial rebuilding of Zone D3 rooms and addition of a plastered floor work area with plaster basins 71
23. Zone E1, Surkh Phase. Remains of a multi-room house unit 72
24. Zone F, Surkh Phase. Corner of large brick platform 73
25. Zone F, Late Surkh Phase. Profile, reconstruction of brick platform 74
26. Zone F, Late Surkh or Choga Mami Transitional Phase. Trace of brick wall is Choga Mami Transitional age, remnants of wall west of platform are probably of Late Surkh Phase age . . . 76
27. Zone G1, Choga Mami Transitional Phase. Remnants of two large work rooms adjacent to the brick platform, and two small rooms 76-77
28. Zone G2, Choga Mami Transitional Phase. Rebuilding of the structure of Zone G1 78-79
29. Zone H, Choga Mami Transitional Phase. Room of long, finger-impressed mud bricks with a plaster basin inside 80

30. Zone I, Sabz Phase, Traces of a room largely destroyed when the plaster kiln was built 81
31. Zone I, Sabz Phase. Section through oven along east profile of Area D 82
32. Zone J, Sabz Phase and intrusive plaster kiln of uncertain age 83
33. Profile of Area B showing stratigraphic zones 84
34. Area B. *a.* Zone C, Sefid Phase. *b.* Upper levels, probably Sefid Phase. 85
35. Burials 7, 8, 9, 4, and 10 92
36. Burials 1 and 2 (intrusive) 93
37. Jaffar Painted. Mohammad Jaffar Phase 102
38. Jaffar Plain. Sefid Phase 105
39. Khazineh Red. Early Sefid Phase 108
40. Khazineh Red. Later Sefid Phase 109
41. Khazineh Red. Early Surkh Phase 110
42. Khazineh Red. Late Surkh Phase and Choaga Mami Transitional 111
43. Sefid Red-on-Cream. Sefid Phase, varieties A, C 115
44. Sefid Red-on-Cream. Sefid, Surkh Phases, varieites A, B 116
45. Sefid Red-on-Cream. Sefid Phase 117
46. Sefid Black-on-Cream. Sefid, Surkh Phases 119
47. Sefid Black-on-Red. Sefid Phase 123
48. Sefid Black-on-Red. Surkh Phase 124
49. Sefid Burnished Plain. Later Sefid Phase 128
50. Susiana Black-on-Buff. Sabz, Choga Mami Transitional phases 130
51. Susiana Black-on-Buff, Plain Buff and Miscellaneous. Sabz, Choga Mami Transitional, Surkh and Sefid phases 131
52. Sialk Black-on-Red. Choga Mami Transitional, Surkh phases 140
53. Sialk Black-on-Red. Choga Mami Transitional, Surkh phases 141
54. Sherds with white paint. Surkh, Choga Mami Transitional, Sefid phases 144
55. Stone, plaster and asphalt bowls. Choga Mami Transitional, Surkh, Sefid phases 146
56. Chipped stone tool types 161
57. Drills and reamers 163
58. Reamers, blades and pointed pieces 164
59. Various chipped stone tool types 165
60. Plain sickles 167
61. Sickles 168
62. Blade, round end scrapers 170
63. Flake, round end scrapers 171
64. Blades and miscellaneous end scrapers 172
65. Blades 174
66. Used blades 175
67. Notched, truncated blades 176

FIGURES vii

68.	Backed, notched blades	177
69.	Notched flakes	179
70.	Used flakes, notched flakes	180
71.	Denticulate flake scrapers	181
72.	Denticulate flake scrapers, bifacially chipped flake	182
73.	Burins, bifacially chipped picks and flake, scaled flake	183
74.	Bullet cores	189
75.	Blade cores, variety *a*	190
76.	Blade cores, variety *b*	191
77.	Blade cores, variety *c*	192
78.	Flake cores	193
79.	Flake cores	194
80.	Saddle-shaped grinding slabs	202
81.	Saddle-shaped grinding slabs, trough metate	203
82.	Boulder mortars, shaped and polished stone	204
83.	Boulder mortars	205
84.	Mortars	206
85.	Handstones	207
86.	Shaped and polished stones	214
87.	Miscellaneous ceramic objects	218
88.	Bone objects	222
89.	Animal figurines	228
90.	Human figurines	229
91.	Stalk and T-shaped figurines	230
92.	Miscellaneous ornaments	239
93.	Map for the Khuzistan Plain, Iran	252
94.	The Deh Luran area: rivers and alluvial fan patterns	256
95.	The Deh Luran area: surface stoniness	257
96.	The Deh Luran area: depth of dissection	258
97.	The Deh Luran area: salinity of soils	259
98.	The Deh Luran area: vegetation zones	260
99.	The Deh Luran area: the overall pattern of environment	262
100.	Upper Khuzistan: the overall pattern of environment	264
101.	Upper Khuzistan: principal physiographic zones and features	265
102.	Upper Khuzistan: present agricultural land use	267
103.	Correlation between monthly evaporation and monthly mean temperatures	270
104.	Accumulated water surplus for dry farming at 150 m elevation in Deh Luran and Khuzistan areas	271
105.	Chemical composition of Khuzistan rivers at various stages of flow	273

106. Relationships between meander wavelength and bankfull discharge for U.S. rivers and for Khuzistan rivers ... 274
107. Upper Khuzistan: sites for which air photograph measurements of present and former meander characteristics have been analyzed ... 275
108. Sequence of river courses in Khuzistan, based on freshness and wavelength of meander patterns ... 277
109. Upper Khuzistan: Sasanian or Early Islamic canal lines ... 278
110. Relationship between bankfull discharge and drainage area for Khuzistan rivers today ... 280
111. Total aggradation of the main plains level since dates shown ... 282
112. The obsidian trade in Western Asia, c. 7500-5500 B.C. ... 291
113. The obsidian trade in Western Asia, c. 5000-3000 B.C. ... 292
114. Blade widths from the Sefid phase at Chagha Sefid ... 298
115. Percentage of obsidian in the chipped stone industry at Chagha Sefid ... 115
116. Number of pieces of chipped stone and of obsidian per cubic meter at Chagha Sefid in successive phases and stratigraphic zones ... 302
117. Phase-by-phase variation in the percentage of obsidian in the chipped stone industry at four sites in Deh Luran ... 305
118. Phase-by-phase variation in the number of pieces of chipped stone and of obsidian per cubic meter at four sites in Deh Luran ... 306
119. The percentage of group 1g obsidian in the total obsidian industry in successive phases at Ali Kosh and Chagha Sefid ... 308

TABLES

1. Radiocarbon dating of phases in Deh Luran ... 11
2. Radiocarbon dates from sites in Deh Luran and nearby ... 25
3. Ages of the phases in Deh Luran ... 27
4. Volume of deposit excavated at Chagha Sefid ... 46
5. Percentages of rim sherds of each type by stratigraphic zone ... 96
6. Percentages of rim sherds of each type by cultural phase ... 97
7. Total sherds of each type by stratigraphic zone ... 98
8. Percentages of sherds of each type by stratigraphic zone ... 99
9. Total sherds of each type by cultural phase ... 100
10. Percentages of sherds of each type by cultural phase ... 100
11. Jaffar Painted sherds by stratigraphic zone ... 104
12. Jaffar Painted sherds by cultural phase ... 104
13. Jaffar Plain sherds by stratigraphic zone ... 106
14. Jaffar Plain sherds by cultural phase ... 106
15. Khazineh Red sherds by stratigraphic zone ... 113
16. Khazineh Red sherds by cultural phase ... 114
17. Sefid Red-on-Cream and Sefid Painted by stratigraphic zone ... 120

18. Sefid Red-on-Cream and Sefid Painted by cultural phase	121
19. Sefid Black-on-Cream by stratigraphic zone	122
20. Sefid Black-on-Cream by cultural phase	122
21. Sefid Black-on-Red by stratigraphic zone	126
22. Sefid Black-on-Red by cultural phase	127
23. Sefid Burnished Plain by stratigraphic zone	129
24. Sefid Burnished Plain by cultural phase	129
25. Susiana Black-on-Buff vessel forms by stratigraphic zone	135
26. Susiana Black-on-Buff vessel forms by cultural phase	136
27. Susiana Black-on-Buff design styles by stratigraphic zone	137
28. Susiana Black-on-Buff design styles by cultural phase	138
29. Susiana Plain Buff by stratigraphic zone	139
30. Susiana Plain Buff by cultural phase	139
31. Sialk Black-on-Red by stratigraphic zone	142
32. Sialk Black-on-Red by cultural phase	143
33. Miscellaneous sherds by stratigraphic zone	145
34. Miscellaneous sherds by cultural phase	145
35. Sherds of stone, plaster and asphalt by stratigraphic zone	147
36. Sherds of stone, plaster and asphalt by cultural phase	147
37. Percentages of chipped stone tool types at Ali Kosh, Chagha Sefid and Tepe Sabz	149
38. Chipped stone raw materials by cultural phase	150
39. Chipped stone tool types by stratigraphic zone	152
40. Chipped stone tool types by cultural phase	153
41. Flint chiped stone tool types by stratigraphic zone	154
42. Flint chipped stone tool types by cultural phase	155
43. Obsidian chipped stone tool types by stratigraphic zone	156
44. Obisidan chipped stone tool types by cultural phase	157
45. Crystal chipped stone tool types by stratigraphic zone	158
46. Crystal chipped stone tool types by cultural phase	159
47. Number and percentage of core types at Ali Kosh, Chagha Sefid and Tepe Sabz	184
48. Cores and debitage to chipping debris at Ali Kosh, Chagha Sefid and Tepe Sabz	185
49. All chipping debris by cultural phase	186
50. Chipping debris by raw material and stratigraphic zone	187
51. Chipping debris by raw material and cultural phase	188
52. Grinding and pounding tools at Ali Kosh, Chagha Sefid and Tepe Sabz	198
53. Grinding slab types by stratigraphic zone	209
54. Grinding slab types by cultural phase	210
55. Handstones, pounders and pestles by stratigraphic zone	211
56. Handstones, pounders and pestles by cultural phase	212

57. Miscellaneous stone artifacts at Ali Kosh, Chagha Sefid and Tepe Sabz 213
58. Miscellaneous stone artifacts by stratigraphic zone 216
59. Miscellaneous stone artifacts by cultural phase 217
60. Miscellaneous artifacts at Ali Kosh, Chagha Sefid and Tepe Sabz 219
61. Miscellaneous artifacts by stratigraphic zone 220
62. Miscellaneous artifacts by cultural phase 221
63. Bone artifacts by stratigraphic zone 224
64. Bone artifacts by cultural phase 225
65. Mats and basketry by stratigraphic zone 226
66. Mats and basketry by cultural phase 226
67. Figurines at Ali Kosh, Chagha Sefid and Tepe Sabz 227
68. T-shaped figurines by stratigraphic zone 231
69. T-shaped figurines by cultural phase 232
70. Stalk figurines by stratigraphic zone 233
71. Stalk figurines by cultural phase 234
72. Figurines by stratigraphic zone 235
73. Figurines by cultural phase 236
74. Lightly baked clay objects by stratigraphic zone 237
75. Lightly baked clay objects by cultural phase 238
76. Ornaments at Ali Kosh, Chagha Sefid and Tepe Sabz 240
77. Labrets by stratigraphic zone 241
78. Labrets by cultural phase 241
79. Bead styles at Ali Kosh, Chagha Sefid and Tepe Sabz 242
80. Ornaments by stratigraphic zone 243
81. Ornaments by cultural phase 244
82. Indicator plants for vegetation mapping 261
83. Synthetic rainfall records 268
84. Estimated open-water evaporation 268
85. Excess of rainfall over crop water needs 269
86. Areas irrigable by major rivers in Upper Khuzistan and Deh Luran 272
87. Meander wavelengths for Khuzistan rivers 276
88. Obsidian analyses from Ali Kosh and Tepe Sabz 290
89. Trace element composition of the obsidian analyzed 294
90. Quantities of obsidian recovered from successive phases at Chagha Sefid 295
91. Quantities and weight of obsidian waste, Zone B2, Sefid phase 296
92. Frequency of grey obsidian in successive phases at Chagha Sefid 299
93. Changes through time in the Deh Luran obsidian industry 300
94. Obsidian in area A (Zone B2, Sefid phase) 304

PLATES
(Pages 315–369)

1. Chagha Sefid from the south early in the autumn (1a) and from the northwest after crops have begun to grow (1b).
2. Chagha Sefid from the west.
3. View of Deh Luran at the base of the mountains in early October (3a) and January (3b).
4. Flash flooding on the Ab-i-garm (4a) and its effects (4b).
5. The initial 3x5 meter pit in Area A (5a) and the main trench (5b).
6. Areas A, C, and D linked into a continuous step trench.
7. The gully cut into the sterile soil under the archeological deposits in Area A.
8. A brick walled room in Zone A3 and its fireplace.
9. Burial No. 4 (9a) and the plaster floor of Zone A4 (9b).
10. Event No. 1 of Zone C.
11. The lower platform in Zone C.
12. The platform in the early Surkh phase being exposed.
13. The brick walls against the side of the platform.
14. Events No. 3 (14a) and 4 (14b) in Zone C.
15. Events No. 4 (15b) and 5 (15a) in Zone C.
16. Zone D1.
17. Zone D1.
18. Platform (18a), Zone D1; oven (18b,c), Zone D3.
19. Zone D4.
20. Initial pit in Area C.
21. Platform in Zone F.
22. Platform in Zone F.
23. House adjacent to platform in Zone G1.
24. Houses in Zone H (24a) and I (24b).
25. Oven (25a) and kiln (25b) in Zone I.
26. Plaster basin, Zone C (26a-d); plaster basin, Zone E1 (26e); basin, Zone D4 (26f).
27. Basins and ovens, various phases.
28. Burials No. 5 (28a), 3 (28b), 4 (28c,d).
29. Burials No. 7, 8, 9.
30. Burial No. 7.
31. Burials No. 7 (31a), 5 (31b).
32. Burial No. 10 (32a); burial of dog and basket (32b,c).
33. Burial No. 1, 2.
34. Susiana Black-on-Buff, open bowls.
35. Susiana Black-on-Buff, open bowls.

36. Susiana Black-on-Buff, open bowls.
37. Susiana Black-on-Buff, open bowls.
38. Susiana Black-on-Buff, hemispherical bowls, miscellaneous bowls.
39. Susiana Black-on-Buff, miscellaneous bowls.
40. Susiana Black-on-Buff, miscellaneous bowls and jars.
41. Susiana Black-on-Buff, miscellaneous bowl sherds.
42. Susiana Black-on-Buff, pots, basin, pedestal.
43. Susiana Black-on-Buff, miscellaneous unique bowls.
44. Susiana Black-on-Buff, jars, handles, spouts.
45. Ground stone tools from Chagha Sefid.
46. Grinding and pounding tools.
47. Grinding and pounding tools.
48. Grinding and pounding tools.
49. Miscellaneous stone artifacts.
50. Miscellaneous stone artifacts.
51. Miscellaneous artifacts.
52. Asphalt and other artifacts.
53. Bone tools.
54. Miscellaneous ornaments and other artifacts.
55. Miscellaneous ornaments and other artifacts.

PREFACE

This report consists of contributions that deal collectively with the archeological history of Deh Luran. These studies supplement, and in some cases change, conclusions that we had reached in our previous report (Hole, Flannery, and Neely, 1969). As will be seen in this volume, the essentials of a stratigraphic history of Deh Luran have been revealed through a combination of excavations and surface reconnaisance for a span that begins more than 10,000 years ago and continues up to nearly the present day. The sequence is unique in southwest Asia both for its long duration and for the details concerning environment, settlement patterns, subsistence, and cultural dynamics. Although we do not pretend that we have completed all the necessary research in this area, the effectiveness of conducting highly specific projects, directed toward the solution of well-defined problems within a limited area, has been amply demonstrated. With this essential background we can now plan and carry out further studies of similar specificity that will carry us farther along in our understanding of the processes involved in the establishment of domestication and its subsequent development.

The excavation of Chagha Sefid was the central focus of our work in 1968-1969; the other studies are contributory to it and to the series of studies that we hope to carry out in the future. Responsibility for the work was divided as follows. I was responsible for organization of the overall project, and for the excavation of Chagha Sefid and the subsequent analysis of the material. Michael and Anne Kirkby carried out studies of water and land resources and of modern land use on the Deh Luran and Upper Khuzistan plains. James Neely directed the survey of Deh Luran and the analysis of material. Jane Renfrew made botanical collections in and around Deh Luran and did the analysis of seeds recovered in the excavation. Colin Renfrew aided in various aspects of the work and did the analysis of obsidian. Jane Wheeler Pires-Ferreira participated in excavation and survey and began her analysis of the fauna in the field.

It was originally intended that all of the specialist studies be included in this volume. However, because of the time-consuming, detailed analyses which are necessary to complete some of them, and because of the bulk of text and illustrative material needed to support them, the studies of seeds and animal bones, the survey of ancient settlements on the Deh Luran plain, and of modern land use will appear separately and later. When it became clear that firm completion dates could not be expected for any of these studies, I decided to publish the strictly archeological material and the reports by Colin Renfrew and Michael Kirkby which had been completed in 1973. With the exception of a few additional references, the text has not been altered substantially since then.

ACKNOWLEDGEMENTS

To bring an archeological project to a successful conclusion requires an enormous amount of work, much of it routine and tedious. It is a task which requires an unusual commitment of hard work from the members of the team who are responsible for the fieldwork, the subsequent analysis, and the preparation of manuscripts for publication. For their support and help, I owe a special debt of gratitude to all of the persons and organizations listed below.

The National Science Foundation, through a grant (NSF GS 2194) to Rice University, provided the basic funding in spite of severe financial cuts that year in the Foundation's overall budget in support of archeology. Rice University, through the Research Sponsor's Fund, administered by then President, Kenneth S. Pitzer, awarded a grant to enable the participation of Michael and Anne Kirkby, who made fundamental contributions to the project. Additionally, Rice University provided laboratory space and other support without which it would have been impossible to complete the analysis in the years that have elapsed since our return from the field.

Permission to carry out the fieldwork was graciously granted by the Ministry of Culture and Arts of Iran under the Directorship of Mr. A. A. Pourmand. Mr. Mohammad Khorramabadi, Director of Excavations, was very helpful in his understanding of the special requirements of our multi-faceted project and in assigning two representatives of the Archeological Service, Mssrs. Azimzadeh and Memar Reza Zahedani, to work with us in their official capacities. Mr. Khorramabadi also kindly arranged for permission to take certain material to the United States for study, thus greatly facilitating the analysis.

Owing to a cut by the National Science Foundation in our proposed budget, we were unable to bring graduate students from the United States to work on aspects of the project. This left us short of supervisory personnel, a need that was fortunately met through the presence in Iran for variable lengths of time of well-trained and capable persons who volunteered to work on the project. These persons included the following graduate students: Lynn Berry Fredlund, University of Colorado; Robb Gibbs, University of Michigan; Elizabeth Carter, University of Chicago; and Harvey Weiss, University of Pennsylvania. Fredlund and Gibbs worked on the excavation, Carter on the survey of Deh Luran and on various other aspects of our work throughout the season, and Weiss on the survey of Khuzistan.

Dr. Jean Perrot, head of the French Archeological Mission at Susa, kindly provided us with two members of his staff, Nathalie Berset and Pierre de Miroschedji, who worked primarily with James Neely on the survey of the Deh Luran plain.

For some weeks in the spring, Anne Hechle worked with us on the survey of Khuzistan, illustrating artifacts from the excavation and helping with the survey itself. Others who visited us and contributed to various aspects of the work are John Hansman, Donald Whitcomb, and Henry Wright. Hansman provided us with useful information on Islamic chronology and on the ancient irrigation systems of Khuzistan. Whitcomb worked with James Neely for some days and obtained valuable information for us on the recent uses of ancient mills. Wright, who was conducting his own survey, stayed at our house in Dizful and provided highly useful information on and help with problems of Uruk chronology in connection with the survey of Deh Luran.

Official members of the staff included Barbara Hole, who took charge of the domestic arrangements and kept the daily processing of artifacts flowing smoothly. She also did the flotation of seed samples and tutored Bobby and Steve, our boys, who gave up a year of formal schooling to participate in the project in excavation, on survey, and in photography. Bonnie Laird, a student at Rice University, worked on the excavation and carried out the analysis of ceramics that were picked up on the survey of Khuzistan. The other official members of the staff each have chapters of their own in this report.

One can hardly think of working in Iran without the help and friendship of many persons whose primary interests are quite apart from archeology. Alan Craig, of Khuzistan Water and Power Authority, and his wife Padma provided us with continual hospitality during our sojourns into town from Deh Luran. In addition, Alan's unparalleled knowledge of Khuzistan and of the resources to make it intelligible, were continually proffered and gratefully received by us all.

Nor should we fail to mention Mr. Rashidian, an old friend who manages the guest house for Khuzistan Water and Power Authority in Andimeshk and who has been instrumental over the years in helping us arrange for goods and services, and in offering most welcome and useful advice.

Our thanks also go to Dr. Jean Perrot who welcomed us to the chateau at Susa and enabled some members of our team to work there.

Following return of the artifacts to the United States, I have been greatly aided in sorting and counting by Theodore Henderson, Ed Koehler, Ted McDonald, Michael and William O'Brien, and Eddie Schorr. Helping with typing and in many of the details in the preparation of the manuscript was Mary Margaret Williamson. Barbara Burger and William O'Brien helped with photography of the artifacts, and Heather Blanton traced the architectural drawings.

Frank Hole
Houston, Texas
January, 1973

Part 1. General Discussion

I

RESEARCH OBJECTIVES AND STRATEGY

INTRODUCTION

The Chagha Sefid project had its birth during the analysis of material derived from excavations at Ali Kosh and Tepe Sabz in 1963. At that time we recognized an archeological discontinuity in our chronological sequence and wanted to find a site that would bridge, and hence inform us about the nature of, that gap. At the time, we wrote that "no drastic, catastrophic breaks occur in the segment [of the sequence] we have recovered.... We do not know whether it will be necessary to intercalate another phase between Mohammad Jaffar and Sabz.... What eludes us still is a clear cut picture of its [Sabz Phase] origins" (Hole, Flannery and Neely, 1969:5, 358).

We were inclined at the time to view most changes in sequences as indigenous, although we did recognize the possibility that sites in nearby Iraq, which were under excavation while we wrote the report, might have some bearing on the origins of the Sabz Phase (Ibid.:358). What was abundantly clear was the important change in subsistence that appeared with the Sabz Phase, a change that saw the introduction of hybrid cereal grains and hybrid races of domestic cattle and dogs. We considered these changes as more important—as far as the later course of prehistory in the region is concerned—than the changes in ceramics which also signaled the Sabz Phase.

The problem on which we concentrated, therefore, was relatively simple: to determine the nature of the transition between Mohammad Jaffar and Sabz. In order to accomplish this goal we needed to find a suitable site, one in which we thought transitional material would be preserved. Our previous surveys of the plain had suggested that Chagha Sefid had material of both the Mohammad Jaffar and Sabz phases, a situation we did not find at either Ali Kosh or Tepe Sabz. Thus we reasoned that if transitional material existed, it would most probably be found at this site.

After arriving in Deh Luran we carried out an intensive surface collection of the site to determine where material of suitable age might be found accessible to excavation. Following analysis of the surveyed material by James Neely, we selected areas in which to dig, and the excavation of the entire range of material from Mohammad Jaffar to Sabz occupied my attention full-time for nearly five months. Analysis of the material derived from the excavation has fully confirmed our impressions in the field that we had a complete sequence, and it has enabled us to state with precision what factors were involved in the abrupt changes in economy that had been first recognized in our previous work.

Interpretations have been greatly aided by the results of excavations at three important sites in Iraq, Choga Mami, Tell es-Sawwan, and Umm Dabaghiyah, which have been published in preliminary form since our last report was written. These studies include both standard archeological evidence and, more importantly, preliminary studies of flora and fauna which are crucial to our interpretations of changes in subsistence. Our interpretations have also been aided by the opportunity, which additional field work afforded, to visit Jaffarabad, under excavation by the French Mission in Iran, Chogha Mish, an American project, and Sialk and Giyan where we obtained comparative collections of sherds.

SYNOPSIS OF PREVIOUS RESULTS

The Prehistory and Human Ecology of the Deh Luran Plain should be consulted for complete details of our previous work. As the present project focused on clarifying the nature of one segment of the sequence, it is useful to repeat our summary of the differences between the Mohammad Jaffar and Sabz phases. This summary is taken from a report in which Hole and Flannery (1968) distinguished two basic and temporally distinct patterns of subsistence: the era of dry farming and caprine domestication, and the era of early irrigation farming and cattle domestication.

The Era of Dry Farming and Caprine Domestication

This era was characterized in the following way (Hole and Flannery, 1968:166):

(1) There are *permanent villages*, either of mud-brick or mud-walled houses, apparently occupied year-round by groups of ca. 50-100 persons who farmed and collected local wild resources. This settlement type is unknown so far in south-west Iran prior to cereal domestication.[1] (2) In addition, there are *semi-permanent seasonal camps or villages*, occupied either by a group of 50-100 persons during a planting-and-harvesting season, or by a 'herding unit' (a term adapted from Barth, 1961) sent out seasonally from a permanent village for the purpose of pasturing flocks. These sites may have remains of wooden structures or, occasionally, no detectable structures at all. Possibly, the permanent village may have developed out of the semi-permanent seasonal camp, judging by the evidence from Tepe Guran. It is worth noting, however, that semi-permanent encampments were not discontinued after permanent settlement began, but became a functionally-specific settlement type. (3) *Pastoral camps in caves*, evidently occupied seasonally by herding units from permanent villages (at lower elevations?), are a third kind of settlement. As open-air settlements became increasingly permanent, butchering stations ceased to exist, and base camps in caves may have become a settlement type specific to herding, analogous to the semi-permanent village. However, on the basis of present evidence, we would suggest that pastoral camps in caves were made by herding units who remained in the area for shorter periods.

On ethnographic analogy alone, we would predict that there should be a fourth settlement type, which we have so far been unsuccessful in locating. These would be *transitory camps* made by herding units enroute from one valley to another; convenient rock shelters along the annual routes of transhumance taken by Iranian herders today would be worth surveying for this postulated settlement type.

Note that at this time period we have no evidence of anything approaching true 'pastoral nomadism', which was no doubt a later development, probably linked to the rise of the large sedentary societies on which nomads are ultimately dependent. Between 10,000 and 5500 B.C. our evidence suggests nothing more than seasonal transhumance.

[1] However, permanent villages with substantial architecture which seem to pre-date the local domestication of cereals do occur in other parts of the Near East, e.g., Tell Mureybat (van Loon, 1966).

As a late representative of the era of dry farming and caprine domestication, the Mohammad Jaffar Phase marks the base line from which we postulated a subsequent phase which we hoped to find in further excavation (Ibid.:177-181).

The Mohammad Jaffar Phase saw innovations in subsistence, architecture, and artifacts. The villagers of this phase lived in houses whose foundations were built of river pebbles, with some use of larger cobbles and even river boulders. Above these foundations, the walls were of clay-slab bricks, plastered with mud; a few crumbled wall fragments indicate that in some cases this plaster was painted with red ochre. The walls were up to a metre thick, and floors were of stamped mud or clean clay, covered with over-two, under-two reed or clubrush mats.

A thousand years or more of agriculture had preceded this phase, and the carbonized plant remains reflect the changed land surface of this part of the Deh Luran plain. Emmer wheat and two-row hulled barley were still virtually the only crops known. But practices of fallowing and grazing had removed a great deal of the natural vegetational cover in the vicinity of the site, and its place was taken by pasture plants like plantain, mallow, vetch, oat grass, and canary grass (Helbaek, personal communication). In particular, the area had seen an increase in the woody perennial legume *Prosopis*, a plant related to American mesquite and known to the Arabs as *shauk*. The fleshy pods of this plant are edible, and the discarded seeds (which are not eaten) appeared in carbonized form by the hundred in Mohammad Jaffar Phase middens. Adams (1965, 5) points out that *shauk* tends to increase with cultivation because it matures so late in the year that it competes hardly at all with winter-sown crops, and hence does not suffer the fate of winter-maturing weeds.

Farming in the Mohammad Jaffar Phase, while obviously successful, required careful weeding and a reasonable fallowing system, which had altered the landscape to a noticeable degree. Similar problems must have beset the herdsman as he sought to find adequate pasture for his flocks in a region where the amount of land given over to cultivation was on the increase. For herding was also expanding, to judge by the animal bones, and sheep along with it. Sheep were outnumbered by goats at the start of the Mohammad Jaffar Phase, but gaining on them rapidly by 5500 B.C. In later periods, they were to overtake and pass them by a wide margin, becoming the most common domestic animal of prehistoric and early historic Khuzistan (Adams, 1962, 115). Sheep, after all, have a panting mechanism which enables them to survive better than goats under the hot climatic regime of the steppe (Schmidt-Nielsen, 1964, 99).

Osteologically, both the sheep and the goats of the Mohammad Jaffar Phase can be considered as highly domesticated. Some goats had already begun to exhibit the helically-twisted or 'corkscrew' horn core of modern Iranian domestic goats, although most individuals preserved the straight, medially-flattened, or quadrangular horn core cross-section. The male sheep of this period had the 'goat-like' horn core cross-section typical of some domesticates, and not the anteriorly-broad cross-section of wild Luristan sheep, while females were probably hornless. The Mohammad Jaffar villagers still liked to eat their goats and sheep at the tender stage, and only about 40 per cent of the herd reached the age of 3 years.

Mohammad Jaffar Phase hunters brought down gazelle, onager, aurochs, and wild pig, seemingly using projectiles whose heads were barbed with backed and diagonal-ended microliths set in asphalt. As in earlier periods, piles of onager and aurochs bones are accompanied by the flint pebble choppers, flint blades, and scarred 'slicing slabs' which were probably used in butchering. Cut marks near tendon attachments show that limbs were disarticulated with flint blades; most bones show no evidence of burning, while a few are charred, as if some haunches had been roasted over hot coals. The villagers continued their use of winter water birds, and fished for catfish and some carp, as well as collecting crabs, water turtles, and freshwater mussels. As the grazing of domesticated animals increased, it would have reduced the amount of forage available for the wild ungulates; no real decrease in the number of such animals is noted in the Mohammad Jaffar refuse, but it may be significant that more small mammals seem to have been eaten in this period. Fox, hedgehog, and wild cat were included in the diet. Large canids were rarely eaten, and there is no evidence yet for the domestic dog.

The Mohammad Jaffar villagers continued to produce flint blades in the same remarkable quantity as in preceding phases; more than a hundred sickle blades were recovered from levels of this period. An innovation was the practice of trimming sickle blades so that they would fit into a particular slot in the handle, a custom that was to become common in later phases. Drills, reamers, and end-scrapers made either on blades or on flakes were also tools typical of the period. It may be that many of the drills, reamers and scrapers were for use in making wooden tools which have not been preserved; others, like some of the bone awls and needles, may have been for perforating hides. Some two per cent of the chipped stone from this phase was obsidian.

The most striking innovation in the field of containers was pottery, which made its first appearance in the Mohammad Jaffar Phase (pl. XV). The pottery of this period was soft, friable, and predominantly chaff-tempered, made of clay which differed but little from that used in previous periods to make figurines. The techniques used to finish and decorate the surface were not so far removed from those used in wall-surfacing: a smoothing or burnishing of the clay, in some cases followed by a coating of red ochre. The tempering material, chaff, was a by-product of grain threshing. Several of the vessel shapes are shared by stone bowls of the same period. The pots themselves could easily have been baked in an oven like that used for centuries previously to roast grain or bake figurines. In other words, although pottery appears rather abruptly in the Mohammad Jaffar Phase, virtually all the concepts needed to manufacture it had already existed previously in south-western Asia: clay working, smoothing and ochre-painting of clay, firing, and container forms. We do not know where this type of pottery, introduced into the Deh Luran plain early in the Mohammad Jaffar Phase, was first manufactured. It seems likely, however, based on the Guran excavation, that a less complex assemblage preceded the association of three types that we found in the Mohammad Jaffar Phase (Mortensen, 1964).

Three pottery types which have chronological significance have been defined for the Mohammad Jaffar Phase. These are (1) Jaffar Plain, a buff, chaff-tempered ware with pinkish firing clouds; (2) Jaffar Painted, which is identical to Jaffar Plain except for the addition of geometric designs in fugitive red-ochre paint; and (3) Khazineh Red, a chaff-and-grit-tempered ceramic with a soft red slip, which may be burnished on certain vessels.

Khazineh Red is one of the troublesome Iranian red wares referred to by Young (1966, 235) which probably have more to do with the availability of suitable clays than they do with any particular ceramic tradition that has cultural-historical implications (cf., Matson, 1965, 206-207). It begins at ca. 6000 B.C. in the Mohammad Jaffar Phase as a minor part of the ceramic assemblage, and increases steadily through time, reaching peak frequency between 5000-4500 B.C. (see fig. 10). Not until after 4000 B.C. is it fully replaced by harder and more salmon-red pottery of Susa A type. We tried to divide Khazineh Red into subtypes, and eventually concluded that its changes through time were so gradual as to make this unfeasible. Two of these changes were a steady increase in grit temper relative to chaff, and a decrease in frequency of burnished vessels.

The Mohammad Jaffar folk also made lightly-baked clay figurines in great numbers. Most appeared as fragmentary cylinders, broken limbs and torsos, but there was at least one recognizable human figure depicted in a squatting position with hands on knees—the kind frequently referred to as a 'mother goddess'. A number of stalk- or T-shaped figurines may have been highly stylized human figures also.

When an adult male died during the Mohammad Jaffar Phase, his body was taken outside the house and buried in semi-flexed position on its left side, facing west. No evidence of mat-wrapping was detected on the burials we found, but red ochre appeared in some graves and at least one individual seems to have had a basket (with perishable foodstuffs?) at the shoulder. The individual was accompanied by his articles of personal adornment, including as many as three or four turquoise beads. At the hips were traces of his beaded G-string and bell-shaped artifact showing continuity in male ornaments with the preceding phase (pl. XIVb).

Ali Kosh was a village of approximately 100 persons during this period. On the basis of our surface collections, it is possible that there were two other small villages in the 300-square-kilometre Deh Luran plain at that time; this will, of course, have to be confirmed by future excavations. We might therefore tentatively estimate the population density of the plain as no greater than 1.0 person per square kilometre. This still represents quite an increase over the Paleolithic density estimated for Khorramabad.

The Mohammad Jaffar people participated in an ever-widening trade network at this time, although the *amount* of material exchanged was fairly small, and there is no evidence of a medium more sophisticated than balanced reciprocity. They had obsidian from eastern Turkey, turquoise possibly from north-eastern Iran, specular hematite which may have come from Fars, and sea shells from the Persian Gulf. The designs on their pottery, made in red ochre, show some relationship to designs on the contemporary pottery at Tepe Guran in Luristan (Mortensen,

1964, fig. 18) and Tepe Sarab in southern Kurdistan (Braidwood, 1960). The dimple-based, hole-mouth vessels of red burnished pottery suggest jars from Guran (Mortensen, 1964, 117-18) and from Tepe Sialk, on the high Iranian Plateau (Ghirshman, 1938, 14-15), and the deep, convex-walled vessels in plain buff and fugitive ochre-painted buff are reminiscent of those in Guran (Mortensen, 1964, fig. 16C), in Jarmo (Braidwood and Howe, 1960) and in Hajji Firuz Tepe in Azarbaijan (Young, 1962). Ties with sites on the alluvial lowlands are much less clear; however, Joan Oates reports (personal communicaton) finding sites with Jarmo-like material near Mandali in eastern Iraq. Sites with Hassuna material are probably younger than the Mohammad Jaffar Phase and in any case, have quite different total assemblages of artifacts.

The Era of Early Irrigation and Cattle Domestication

The next adaptive pattern, revealed by our work at Tepe Sabz, showed a transformation of the subsistence economy and considerable changes in artifacts. For this reason we postulated a gap in our chronological sequence. To underscore the differences and to summarize the data we again reproduce the relevant sections from our preliminary report (Hole and Flannery, 1968:181-182).

> Midway through the sixth millenium, peoples in certain areas of southwestern Iran went through a rapid and crucial transition which was to set them clearly on the path toward population expansion and urban life. The three major innovations of that period were (1) the beginnings of competent irrigation, (2) the beginnings of cattle domestication, and (3) the use of a full range of cereals improved either by mutation or hybridization. Our evidence suggests that irrigation was still a small-scale affair, and cattle may have been used solely or mainly for food at this time. But 2000 years later, more sophisticated irrigation and the cultivation of improved cereals with the cattle-drawn plough carried some peoples in south-western Iran to the threshold of civilization.
>
> This transition was not a major factor in the highlands of Luristan. In the Valley of Khorramabad, for example, our carbonized plant samples from the site of Bog-i-No (Young, 1966, 238), radiocarbon dated (probably very conservatively) to 4250 B.C., show no evidence of irrigation. It may be that people in the well-watered valleys of the oak-pistachio woodland belt did not feel the need for irrigation, and retained the old dry-farming pattern long after those in more arid regions had made the transition. The mountain peoples did, however, accept the domestic ox.
>
> The area with the strongest evidence for early irrigation is the Upper Plains of Khuzistan. Adams (1962, 110) predicted this five years ago when he observed that northern Khuzistan's underlying gravels, good drainage, adequate rainfall, and easily-diverted streams probably facilitated the transition from dry-farming to irrigation. The Upper Plains is a region where the natural rainfall (ca. 300 millimetres) probably lessened the chance of crop failure during early attempts at irrigation; it is also a zone where there are incentives for irrigation, because the latter technique makes it possible to extend cultivation south to the 200 millimetres isohyet, and even beyond, greatly increasing the area farmed.
>
> There are two lines of evidence for early irrigation. One is the evidence used by Adams (1962), which consists of observing the distribution pattern of sites with regard to fossil stream channels. Assuming that early irrigation was limited to breaching the natural levees of small streams, alignments of prehistoric sites along the fossil beds of formerly aggrading watercourses in areas at (or below) the limits of rainfall cultivation suggests irrigation. This line of reasoning led Adams to the conclusion that agriculture in the Susiana *a* period was mainly dependent on rainfall, while site distributions from later periods (Susiana, *b, c*) more strongly indicate irrigation (Adams, 1962, 112-113).
>
> The other line of evidence concerns the size of seeds of flax or linseed (*Linum bienne*), which are found in the carbonized state in prehistoric sites. Helbaek's studies (1960, 193) indicate that dry-farmed flax, dependent on rainfall alone, has a seed length range of 3.29-4.03 millimetres. By contrast, seeds from flax grown by means of irrigation in the hot alluvial lowlands of Mesopotamia are the largest known, measuring 4.39-6.20 millimetres. Helbaek's study of our plant remains from the Deh Luran plain indicates that irrigation of flax (and presumably other plants as well) began in our Sabz Phase (5500-5000 B.C.), which is equivalent to Susiana *a* (Helbaek, 1966, 351 and personal communication).

Along with the change in subsistence we also postulated a change in settlement pattern (Ibid.:182-183).

> (1) There are *permanent villages, irrigation-oriented*, which in the words of Adams (1962, 113) occur 'grouped along the margins of shallow fossil valleys that are still traceable at intervals on the alluvial land surface', or in other localities where artificial water control can be practised. (2) In addition, there are *permanent villages, dry-farming oriented*, which 'are so located that irrigation would not have been possible in their vicinities without the great irrigation works which are known only to have been constructed much later' (ibid., 112). (3) We have also located *pastoral camps in caves* from this same period; these seem to have been occupied by herding units engaged in seasonal transhumant movements from the steppe-piedmont (or lower valleys) to Luristan. One pastoral camp of this period, found in Kunji Cave, had remnants of 'huts' or 'pens' with dry-laid stone walls, not unlike those often constructed by shepherds in the area today. (4) *Craft-specialist villages*, at least some of which engaged in metallurgy, constitute another settlement type. The recently-investigated site of Tall-i-Iblis, where abundant remains of smelting were found, is an example of this type (Caldwell, 1966). Some of these sites are located on the western edge of the central Iranian Plateau where copper sources are available, and other examples will undoubtedly appear as archeological investigation of this region proceeds. For example, copper in some quantity characterized the lowermost levels of Tepe Sialk (Ghirshman, 1938), which is located at no great distance from

the Anarak copper lode (Wertime, 1964). Should Sialk be reinvestigated, this aspect of its economic pattern would be worth checking.

We strongly suspect other settlement types from this period, but these have not been investigated by us. For example, in Mesopotamia during the latter part of this era, sites like Eridu (Lloyd, 1948) evidently served as *temple centres* for the surrounding countryside, and our surveys in Khuzistan found hints that such centres may also appear in south-western Iran at the same time. Such temple sites suggest the presence of local centres to which large groups of villages were oriented, and indicate that full understanding of economic and political organization in Khuzistan and southern Mesopotamia cannot be obtained merely by excavating small villages, no matter how carefully.

Although most permanent villages of this era still remained in the range of 1-2 hectares, by the end of the era at least some had reached 5 hectares or more. Unfortunately, we have had no opportunity to investigate these larger sites; it would be interesting to know if they contain a wider range of activity areas, diversified residences, and more evidence of craft activities (with their associated tools) than smaller villages of the same period.

Our oldest evidence for the change to irrigation farming and cattle domestication was found in the Sabz Phase, stratigraphically the lowest deposits we found in the site of Tepe Sabz (Ibid.:184-188).

Although Neely's 1963 trench at Tepe Sabz produced abundant architectural evidence from later periods at the site, the Sabz Phase deposits he exposed were limited to midden or midden-filled courtyard. Hence we know little about the Sabz Phase houses except that reed or club-rush mats were used on the floors, and the doors evidently swung on circular stones which had been perforated to serve as a pivot. These recall the 'door pivot stones' from Jarmo (Braidwood and Howe, 1960, 43).

Fortunately, despite their scarcity of wall stubs, the Sabz Phase middens were rich in artifacts, charred seeds, animal bones, carbonized sheep and goat dung, and charcoal left from tamarisk fires, adding up to quite a bit of information on village subsistence patterns.

The people of the Sabz Phase planted free-threshing hexaploid bread wheat as well as emmer. They had hulled six-row barley, which was to become with time the most successful cultivated cereal of the Mesopotamian lowlands (Helbaek, 1960). In addition, they raised two-row hulled barley, lentils, vetch, vetchling, and the irrigated flax already mentioned. They also left behind almonds which may have been gathered wild on the slopes of the nearby mountains.

Accompanying this agricultural development came a shift in settlement pattern. Instead of occupying areas near ancient swamp margins, many sites of the phase (including Tepe Sabz itself) are located where they could take advantage of small streams coming down off the mountains to the north. Many of these areas are low-lying, and flood seasonally from rainfall run-off. These seasonally inundated areas could easily have been used for irrigation with only a minimum of diversion or enlargement of the natural drainage network of the plain.

But not all Sabz Phase villages used irrigation; as pointed out by Adams (1962, 112), some villages of this period in Susiana proper were located in situations where irrigation could not have been practised. Artificial water control during the Sabz Phase may have been only an insurance policy against a bad year, a supplement to rainfall farming. Its implications for the future of lowland steppe agriculture, however, are obvious.[1]

The principal tools of the Sabz Phase were plain blades, and sickle blades which had been trimmed to fit into particular slots in a handle. Equipment for composite hunting tools included crescent-shaped microliths, while use of items like drills, reamers, and scrapers had begun to taper off. We do not yet know whether or not this decrease in hide-working tools is related to the increase in spindle whorls and the growing of irrigated flax, a situation which suggests that woven wool or plant fibre may have been replacing leather for certain items. Generally speaking, the change in flint also suggests a shift away from a preoccupation with hunting.

Although they made a few stone bowls with simple or 'beaded' rims, like their Mohammad Jaffar predecessors, the villagers of the Sabz Phase had entered into a tradition of pottery-making which, though changing gradually through time, was to characterize Khuzistan for the next two thousand years. They still made oval bowls and hole-mouth jars of soft, chaff-tempered Jaffar Plain pottery, but they had virtually ceased to produce Jaffar Painted ware. They still made Khazineh Red bowls with simple or beaded rims, but grit particles now constituted a greater part of the temper than previously. In addition, the Sabz potters had begun to make a hard, sand-tempered pottery, Susiana Plain Buff, which was far sturdier and less friable than anything seen in the Mohammad Jaffar Phase (pl. XV). It appears to have been fired at a higher temperature than the soft, chaff-tempered wares of the Mohammad Jaffar Phase—possibly even in a true kiln—and although still handsome, it represented a clear technological advance. Susiana Plain Buff was made into oval basins (like the oval bowls in chaff-tempered pottery), deep convex-based bowls (like their chaff-tempered counterparts), small hemispherical bowls with simple or beaded rims (like their stone counterparts), hole-mouth jars with dimple bases, and several new shapes—perhaps the most distinctive being a bowl supported by a short pedestal.

Appearing for the first time in this phase, also, were numbers of vessels of this same grit-tempered yellowish-buff ware to which designs had been added with paint: this type we called Susiana Black-on-buff. Most designs were geometric, and the paint used was an iron oxide or peroxide, like red ochre, but fired at such a temperature that it almost always turned tawny brown or greyish-black, rather than red. Moreover, except in the case of a few reddish variants (possibly accidental), it was not fugitive. The paint was applied in a broad-line, free-hand manner, with a great deal of individualism, yet the vessels have a more professional quality about them than those

---

[1] We were told by farmers of the Deh Luran plain that without irrigation they get a crop only two to three times in 5 years. Adams (1962, 110) says that in Khuzistan in general, dry farming yields an average of 410 kilograms of wheat per hectare, while irrigation yields 615 kilograms (about 9 bushels an acre).

of the Mohammad Jaffar Phase. At the same time, they lack the standardization and extremely precise painting of later phases in the sequence.

Vessels in Susiana Black-on-buff included large oval basins with black bands at rim and base, or deep, convex-based bowls whose exteriors were covered with painted designs: herringbones, chevrons, vertical panels of wiggly-line motifs, checkerboards, screens, or crosshatching. There were bowls on pedestal bases, some of which had little triangular or diamond-shaped 'windows' cut in them. A few small bowls with incurved rims were covered with designs which resembled knotted cords or basketry; some of which were so densely painted that the design, instead of appearing in black on a buff background, appeared as buff designs in a black field. This technique of 'reserve' or 'negative' decoration was to increase in the Khazineh Phase. Close relationships are seen with the pottery of basal Jaffarabad (= Susiana *a*), and in a more general way with earliest Eridu (Oates, 1960), Samarra and Matarrah (Braidwood et al., 1952).

Materials of the Sabz Phase (= Susiana *a*) are widespread in Khuzistan, but lie principally north of the isohyet indicating 300 millimetres of rainfall. The farmers were competent at irrigation, but they preferred to stay within the area where rainfall farming was possible, an area still sparsely-enough inhabited so that there was room for many villages. In the Deh Luran plain, there were at least six villages of this phase, each containing perhaps 100 persons. This would give us an estimated population density of 2 persons per square kilometre. Adams' survey in Susiana proper found 34 villages which have deposits dating back to this period, of which only two (Jaffarabad and Chogha Mish) have been excavated. Most are in the neighbourhood of one hectare in size, but a few may have been considerably larger—we have verbal reports that Chogha Mish, for example, may have been a sizeable settlement already in the Sabz Phase. A conservative estimate for the population of Susiana proper at this time period would, therefore, be 3,400 persons.

We do not know yet whether or not the Sabz Phase was an indigenous development from the Mohammad Jaffar Phase. Numbers of artifact types bridge the gap between the two phases, but there are also striking differences. Certain pottery types, ornaments, and tools continued into the Sabz Phase, but the whole aspect of the chipped stone industry changed drastically, and new tools and economic plants appeared in significant quantity. Were the tools which show continuity merely those which were of wide distribution throughout the steppe in the early sixth millennium, or do they really indicate a local origin for the Sabz Phase?

Only future excavations will be able to solve the problem of the extent to which the Sabz Phase is native to Khuzistan. If indeed it consists, in part, of an influx of new peoples, our guess would be that the area most likely to contain its origins is the adjacent Tigris River steppe of north-east Mesopotamia. In the latter region, sites like Tell es-Sawwan (El-Wailly, 1963, 1964) had already assumed unprecedented proportions and evidently included the residence of important persons whose status was expressed in the form of rich burial equipment. Our limited exposure of the Sabz Phase revealed no high status graves, but the agricultural complex we recovered is identical to that of Tell es-Sawwan (Helbaek, 1964, 1966), which suggests that both areas lie within the same farming province.

RESEARCH STRATEGY

As a general principle, I have chosen to work on problems that can be resolved in a season's work. Although this limits what one can plan to do, it ensures that well-defined tasks can be completed and, following complete analysis, that they will provide a firm base on which to build future research. The series of projects is basically cumulative. We have deliberately attempted to advance quickly in our knowledge by eliminating as much redundancy as possible. This has been accomplished both by limiting our work to relatively small operations and by completing the analysis of material before we return to the field. Only in this way, it seems to me, can we hope to know well enough where we have been to enable us to propose and carry out work that will advance us a step farther toward our goal of understanding both the events and the dynamics of developing agriculture and animal husbandry in Deh Luran.

The initial choice of Deh Luran as the base of our operations was partly accidental. We found there the kinds of things—long sequences, and remains of seeds and bones—that we could use to investigate the problems of early agriculture. Once started in this region it was logical to continue to build upon the base of knowledge that we had already gained. Thus, with three projects we have been able to accurately define a sequence some 4000 years long and to begin to understand the processes involved in the major changes that we record within this sequence.

M. Kirkby's research into land use throughout the full range of history of the Deh Luran plain, as well as other studies, to be published later of the flora, fauna, and settlement patterns of the area, are directed toward these goals. It has now become very clear that although the sequence in Deh Luran is unique in many respects, it is similar in others to developments elsewhere in southwest Asia. It will be out of the knowledge gained from a series of similar regional studies that we will eventually be able to piece together the complicated mosaic of factors that led first to the urban civilizations of Elam and Sumer and eventually to the modern political systems of the area today. Such long-range goals, it seems to me, are best approached through a series of well-defined projects such as this.

In view of our conclusions about major differences in subsistence patterns in the Mohammad Jaffar and Sabz phases, a logical step was to excavate a site that would shed some light on how this transformation came about. Although these matters are discussed in more detail in Part 2, it is useful at this point to give a brief resume of the manner in which we approached the problem.

Chagha Sefid contains a longer sequence than we actually dug. We did not dig post-Sabz Phase deposits because we were primarily interested in the manner in which the Sabz Phase developed. In view of our findings, however, it seems desirable in the future to continue the excavation through to the terminal occupation of the site in the Uruk Period. The reasons for this are given later in more detail but basically they relate to intrasite variation, which becomes a crucial issue when we consider the cultural dynamics of agricultural development on the Deh Luran plain.

As in previous years, our primary concern was with minute changes in stratigraphy and the recovery of carbonized seeds and the very small flint artifacts, sherds, and the like that characterize sites of this period. In order to accomplish these goals it was necessary to excavate at a very slow pace and to screen all material carefully. As a consequence, we were unable to make broad horizontal exposures of architecture of any given phase. Nevertheless, by these means we were able to document the changes we were looking for and to satisfy our immediate objectives.

Our previous work had demonstrated the advantages of digging relatively small trenches into sites in order to determine their stratigraphic successions and the associations of artifacts and subsistence remains with the strata. Accordingly, we followed nearly the same procedure in excavating Chagha Sefid. After selecting various areas on the site for our initial soundings, we eventually selected the west side of the site for intensive excavation (for fuller discussion see Chapter IV, Stratigraphy and Excavation). We dug a trench 45 meters long which cut through about 18 meters of deposit vertically. The trench was excavated in a series of steps, with a deep pit at the lower end which reached virgin soil under the site. This trench enabled us to obtain a stratigraphic series from the Ali Kosh Phase through the Sabz Phase, with three new phases intervening between the Mohammad Jaffar and Sabz. Thus we were able to bridge the gap we had previously recognized.

II

PRINCIPAL RESULTS AND IMPLICATIONS

INTRODUCTION

It is customary to present one's conclusions at the end of the analysis but this practice needlessly breaks up the continuity of presentation for readers who wish to obtain a rapid overview before they attempt to digest the substance of the detailed analysis. It is assumed that archeologists who are specially interested in the details of our findings and in particular aspects of the analysis and interpretation will study the relevant portions of this report. These persons, as well as those who are less interested in the particulars, will find a reading of the remaining sections more meaningful if they have a clear conception of the nature of the results, their implications, and the problems that need immediate work.

The present section is chiefly interpretive in that it discusses the reasons for the conclusions. A summary of the substantive results, and a discussion of the nature of the new phases and their dating, is also included. For reference to the strata excavated in each phase and the relative chronology, see Table 1.

THE TRANSITION FROM THE MOHAMMAD JAFFAR TO THE SABZ PHASE

Our principal objective in digging Chagha Sefid was to determine the nature of the disconformity in the Deh Luran sequence which appeared between the Mohammad Jaffar and Sabz phases. Before we began the excavation we considered three possible causes of the disconformity. These are stated below as hypotheses, along with their test implications, and our conclusions.

Hypothesis: There is a gap in the sequence which must be filled with material as yet undiscovered.
Discussion: Prior to excavation we had determined that a gap existed. Nevertheless, an apparent but not real disconformity could have resulted from a misinterpretation of the evidence. This would have happened if parallel but different contemporary traditions occurred in separate sites on the Deh Luran plain, accounting for the apparent lack of continuity in ceramics and subsistence activities. Therefore, it seemed best to test the null hypothesis that there was no gap in the sequence.
Evidence which will reject the null hypothesis:
    a. Accurate radiocarbon dates which show that the Sabz Phase is always later than Mohammad Jaffar and that there is an interval between the two such that they cannot be considered contemporary or even immediately successive.
    b. Discovery of previously unknown material stratigraphically above the Mohammad Jaffar and below the Sabz Phase.

Conclusions: The excavation of Chagha Sefid provides evidence in radiocarbon dates and in new material which is stratigraphically between the Mohammad Jaffar and Sabz phases. Therefore, we reject the null hypothesis, and the hypothesis that there is a gap is supported.

The excavation of Chagha Sefid demonstrated that new material occurs between the Mohammad Jaffar and Sabz phases. It remained to determine its origin. There were two possibilities: either it was a local development or it was introduced from outside the Deh Luran plain. These possibilities also can be stated as hypotheses.

Hypothesis: The gap can be filled with a phase or phases which show development of a kind that can be explained through purely local changes.
Evidence which will reject the hypothesis:
    a. An abrupt change in artifacts or subsistence in all sequences which may be found developing from Mohammad Jaffar to Sabz.
    b. Clear-cut evidence at some point in the

Table 1

PHASES IN DEH LURAN RELATED TO RADIOCARBON DATES AND TO APPROXIMATELY EQUIVALENT ARCHEOLOGICAL DEPOSITS AT OTHER SITES.[1]

Dates x 1.03 1950	Deh Luran Phase	Ganj Darreh	Ali Kosh	Tepe Guran	Jarmo	Sarab	Chagha Sefid	Tell es-Sawwan	Choga Mami	Tepe Sabz	Jaffarabad
3000 200 400 600	Susa A										●
800 4000 200 400 600 800	Bayat									●	
5000	Mehmeh Khazineh Sabz C. M. Trans.								●	●	
200 400 600 800	Surkh Sefid						●	●			
6000 200 400 600	Mhd. Jaff.		●	●		●	●				
800 7000 200 400 600 800	Ali Kosh Bus Mordeh		●	●			●				
8000 200 400 600 800 9000	?	●	●								
200 400 600 800 10000 200 400 600 800 11000		● ● ●									

[1] Strata excavated in each site are indicated by cross-hatching.

sequence of new artifacts or subsistence whose priority elsewhere is certain and for which a mode of transmission into Deh Luran can be found.

Conclusion: As we discuss fully below, our excavation provides evidence of both types and we consequently reject this hypothesis.

Hypothesis: There was an intrusion from outside Deh Luran at some time between the Mohammad Jaffar and Sabz phases which brought in new material.

Discussion: Having established that local development cannot account for the changes, we are left with this alternative. In effect it is the converse of the preceding hypothesis. Under the circumstances, it is difficult to reject the hypothesis; rather we find evidence that strongly supports it. Nevertheless, had we found evidence of the following kind we would have rejected this alternative.

Evidence which will reject the hypothesis:
   a. There is no other area in which the "new" material occurs earlier than in Deh Luran.
   b. There is no means of transmitting any new material to Deh Luran nor any mechanism for its adoption.
   c. In a sequence which is stratigraphically and chronologically complete, there are changes which can be attributed to local stylistic and technical innovation that enables us to regard them as transitional between the Mohammad Jaffar and Sabz phases.

Conclusions: The excavations of Choga Mami and Tell es-Sawwan provide evidence of a long development of the elements that are introduced into Deh Luran considerably later than in Iraq. The mechanism of population expansion and emigration working through adaptive advantage (or cultural dominance) is suggested below as a means for the introduction of the new material. The excavation of a complete sequence shows the essential discontinuity that we had recognized earlier. Thus we cannot reject this hypothesis and conclude on present evidence that the Sabz Phase had its origins in the Choga Mami Transitional which intruded into Deh Luran after a long period of development as the Samarran in Iraq.

ORIGINS AND IMPLICATIONS OF THE CHOGA MAMI TRANSITIONAL

From the standpoint of cultural dynamics, the Choga Mami Transitional is the most interesting phase because it records the inception of a major shift in the economic orientation of people living in Deh Luran. As discussed above and in more detail below, the most reasonable interpretation of the appearance of this material is that it came from nearby Iraq. The reasons are:

(1) Samarran, which is antecedent to the Choga Mami Transitional, occurs in eastern Iraq but not in Deh Luran or in any other site in Iran that has yet been excavated or recognized on survey.

(2) The Choga Mami Transitional is a late development of the Samarran, as is seen at Choga Mami.

(3) Based on surface finds in the Mandali region, the Samarran intrudes on a local sequence of material that appears similar to the Sefid Phase in Deh Luran. The nature of the intrusion is not known, but it seems certain that Samarran does not develop out of the local traditions there. Rather, it appears that Samarran is an outgrowth of the Hassunan, at least in northern Mesopotamia.

(4) Thus there is a long tradition leading from Hassunan through Samarran and ultimately to the Choga Mami Transitional in eastern Mesopotamia which does not occur in Deh Luran. The tradition in Deh Luran is separate and distinct; it is closely related to that of the mountain regions of western Iran and eastern Iraq rather than of the steppelands of northern Mesopotamia.

(5) The intrusion of the Choga Mami Transitional was probably an actual movement of people, judging from the ceramics, the domestic cattle and dogs, the hybrid races of grains and irrigation, and the particular form of impressed bricks and the composition of floors, all of which are marked departures from previous tradition in Deh Luran.

(6) Finally, even primitive irrigation with improved grains greatly enhances the amount and reliability of yields from a suitable environment relative to what is possible with dry farming. Thus the potential for significant population increase is available at some favored sites. Other areas such as the Deh Luran plain, which are underpopulated for this new technology, are an open invitation to settlement and exploitation by peoples employing better techniques.

This evidence suggests the possibility of actual migration from Iraq but in no way proves it. The explanation of population expansion is suggestive. It is, however, an unproven hypothesis. The implication is that populations of Samarran and later of Choga Mami Transitional peoples spread into regions that were environmentally favorable to irrigation agriculture as the density of population in any one locale became too great. Such an expansion, I suggest, was accomplished even at the cost of displacing a local population from its traditional settlements. This could have happened through invasion and conquest of territory, through mutual agreement, or through the judicious exodus of the indigenous population in Deh Luran. In view of the basic differences in subsistence strategies which allows dry farmers and herders to exploit a much wider landscape, with no appreciable differences in yield, than irrigation farmers the latter two possibilities appear to be most likely.

The circumstances in Deh Luran at the time of Choga Mami Transitional may be analogous to those described by Barth in Swat Pakistan (Barth, 1956). Swat, an area of considerable environmental diversity, was occupied originally by the Kohistanis, who practiced agriculture and transhumant herding. Depending on a subsistence base of one crop annually along with transhumance, the Kohistanis are able to maintain stable villages over any part of the territory. This situation seems reasonably similar to that of the early villagers in Deh Luran (Hole, Flannery and Neely, 1969). Within the last 200 years, however, Pashto-speaking Pathans have moved into the area and taken over much of the land formerly occupied by Kohistanis. The Pathans differ from the Kohistanis principally in practicing two-crop agriculture and the limit of their expansion corresponds with the terrain where this is possible. The strong hierarchical organization of the Pathans depends on their being able to produce a considerable agricultural surplus; this is possible through year-round farming. The Kohistanis also have advanced agriculture and irrigation but depend economically as much on herding as on cereal grains. "By having two strings to their bow, so to speak, the Kohistanis are able to wrest a living from inhospitable mountain areas which fall short of the minimal requirements for Pathan occupation (Barth, 1956:1082)." While the Kohistanis are organized into politically separate village districts of 400-2000 persons, the Pathans are reported to have been able to muster 15,000 fighting men. A clear case of expansion by a politically dominant group at the expense of the weaker is thus indicated.

There remains a third group, the Gujars who are principally herders and who have recently become politically dependent upon either the Pathans or Kohistanis, depending on where they reside. Their subsistence requirements are met by small-scale farming in fields at high altitudes or by trading animal products. The Gujars sometimes do wage labor for either group and tend herds on contract.

Concluding his analysis, Barth (1956:1088) lists four factors that determine settlement in Swat Pakistan.

(1) The distribution of ethnic groups is controlled not by objective and fixed 'natural areas' but by the distribution of the specific ecologic niches which the group, with its particular economic and political organization, is able to exploit. In the present example, what appears as a single natural area to Kohistanis is subdivided as far as the Pathans are concerned, and this division is cross-cut with respect to the specific requirements of the Gujars.
(2) Different ethnic groups will establish themselves in stable co-residence in an area if they exploit different ecologic niches, and especially if they can thus establish symbiotic economic relations, as those between Pathans and Gujars in Swat.
(3) If different ethnic groups are able to exploit the same niches fully, the militarily more powerful will normally replace the weaker, as Pathans have replaced Kohistanis.
(4) If different ethnic groups exploit the same ecologic niches but the weaker of them is better able to utilize marginal environments, the groups may co-reside in one area, as Gujars and Kohistanis in West Kohistan.

The modern situation in Swat North Pakistan, of course, differs from that in Deh Luran in the sixth and seventh millenia in the following ways: physical environment, political organization—Swat is more highly stratified, and agricultural technology, which appears to be more highly developed, including two-cropping and use of the plow. Nevertheless, the essential components of mixed agriculture and herding on the one hand, and irrigation agriculture on the other, exist in Deh Luran. Our data now suggest that the Deh Luran plain was occupied originally by people who followed broad spectrum subsistence strategies based at different times on varying proportions of agriculture, herding, collecting and hunting. The population on the plain was small and probably seasonal, moving into the lower ranges of the Zagros during the summer when pastures on the plain had dried or were depleted. In short, this was a subsistence pattern regulated to a large extent by the needs of animals and the need of people for animal protein. In terms of land use, it was an extensive rather than intensive adaptation which depended for its success upon diverse techniques of subsistence that helped buffer annual irregularities in the supply of any one component, and also upon seasonal mobility.

Owing to the vagaries of rainfall, agriculture on the plain is undependable, but this problem can be eased through irrigation, with the yields considerably increased over dryfarming, thereby enabling farmers to produce more food from a smaller acreage. At the same time irrigation represents an investment in particular plots of land and the increased yields require greater storage capacity, thus limiting mobility, though certainly not excluding it for all of the population.

Historic accounts of Sumer suggest strongly that "given the economic complex of grain/caprine within the environment of Mesopotamia, a specific intensity of land use is most productive" (Meadow, 1971:153). And, moreover, given this mode of production, the most effective land tenure arrangement was the relatively large communal "estate" which controlled sufficient land to ensure proper fallowing and could provide labor for working the land. Since Sumerian times at least, this has been the predominant form of landholding in Mesopotamia and, by extension, may have been characteristic of some periods in Deh Luran.

Archeological evidence that this mode of land use may have existed in much earlier times comes chiefly from Tell es-Sawwan (Al-A'dami, 1968; Abu Al-Souf, 1968) and Choga Mami (Oates, 1969). Both sites were well established at the time of the Choga Mami Transitional incursion into Deh Luran that we have described. At Tell es-Sawwan large houses within a walled enclosure seem to have been the traditional residences for large family groups and perhaps served as storage centers as well. The use of irrigation is attested through plant remains at both sites and a canal at Choga Mami. At the latter site, similarly large, multi-room houses were also found. At the same time in Deh Luran, the residential structures are certainly less permanent and appear in our limited exposure to be those of relatively small family groups. In fact, the total resident population of Ali Kosh and Chagha Sefid may have been only a small fraction of that which lived at Sawwan. These data accord well with our picture of relatively dispersed settlement at these two sites attuned to extensive exploitation of a broad area rather than the nucleated settlements necessary for the intensive use of a smaller area.

In this regard it is useful to note the land use studies carried out on the Deh Luran plain by the Kirkbys. In surveying both the natural environment of the plain and the use made of it by modern peoples, it became clear to them that

> the present restricted area of farming is correlated with the considerable use of the Deh Luran plain for winter wet-season sheep and goat grazing ... Winter dry farming or winter grazing appear to be merely mutually exclusive alternative uses of available land. (Kirkby and Kirkby, 1969:5)

This interpretation is based upon the fact that the best grazing occurs on the land on which cereal grains grow best by dry farming. Irrigation allows the planting of land that is not necessarily also best for grazing, and it provides an opportunity for the separation of farming from herding activities. Once the higher and more dependable yields of irrigation agriculture were recognized it would be a simple step to remove most of the herding to the margins of the plain and the significantly better pastures in the mountains. Such a physical separation would have benefited farming and herding by keeping animals out of the fields and by allowing them to graze in cooler, lusher pastures. It is notable how much larger the animals kept by nomads today are than those kept year-round in Deh Luran. That this procedure may have become necessary is suggested by the increase in the number of agricultural villages after the introduction of irrigation. Removal of grazing land through farming and an increase in the number of people to feed may have forced herders to seek pastures elsewhere. However, as agricultural practices became more skillful, subsistence turned more to the cereals for protein with a corresponding lesser dependence on animals. Thus the stage was set for use of domestic animals largely for emergency rations, for ceremonial purposes, and for their secondary products: milk and its derivatives, wool, hair and skins. Although this is the modern pattern of animal use, its origin is not at all certain. The archeological evidence is suggestive but not conclusive. Our primary data are the substantially smaller quantities of animal bones (both wild and domestic) found in the phases after irrigation was introduced. We may add that at Chagha Sefid itself, some 90 percent of the bones were those of the caprines, suggesting a heavy dependence on herding even before irrigation was introduced to the plain. Moreover, at Chagha Sefid there was little evidence of hunting, a striking contrast with Ali Kosh, suggesting that some specialization of subsistence among villages was already in progress. The location of Chagha Sefid at the base of the mountains, with ready access to upland pastures, may well have been the deciding factor in this apparently early specialization. Chagha Sefid itself, on a perennially flowing spring that is capable of providing irrigation water, was thus a logical place for new settlers and for a separation of farming from herding.

Although this reconstruction of possible events has focused on Deh Luran, it is possible to put it in larger perspective. Before 6000 B.C., western Iran and many of the valleys of the Zagros were inhabited by people who practiced dry farming and herding, the proportions of the two and the permanence of the settlements varying in accordance with local environmental factors. At this time the density of population seems to have been very low and the villages are all located in areas that could be dry farmed. By 6000 B.C., we have evidence of people living in the steppelands at the base of the Zagros; some of these took advantage of rivers that flow off the mountains to irrigate their crops. Some of the earliest evidences of this come from Tell es-Sawwan and Choga Mami, both in Iraq. At both sites hybrid races of cereals are present although at the moment it cannot be determined how these were developed or introduced. The two factors of improved grains and irrigation resulted in unusually large and dependable yields. The effects of these innovations are clear in the large size of the walled settlement, the richness of grave goods and the evidence of much craft activity at Tell es-Sawwan. It is reasonable to think that increased yields led to an increase in the population which would ultimately have caused emigration to similar locales. Such a spread of peoples and culture seems to be documented in the intrusion of Choga Mami Transitional ceramics into Deh Luran. The spread continued farther south, still along the steppelands, at least as far as Khuzistan, where the same ceramics are found at Chogha Mish and other sites. Recently, similar ceramics have been found on the Mesopotamian plain itself where irrigation must have been necessary (Adams and Nissen, 1972:174-175).

The spread of these peoples into areas like Deh Luran that were already occupied may have led to a major reorientation of the traditional subsistence patterns. By analogy with the circumstances at Swat, I postulate a shift in settlement of the indigenous Deh Luranis to camps or villages away from the irrigated fields. Thus the potential yield from the Deh Luran plain was considerably increased through specialization effected by the separation of herding and dry farming from irrigation agriculture. What is important is the possibility of symbiotic relations between the two groups and the effect it had on overall populations in the steppelands and the establishment of new dry farming villages in mountain valleys previously not used for that purpose. Our surveys suggest that population did increase rapidly with the advent of irrigation and considerable numbers of villages were founded in the mountains (e.g., in the Khorramabad Valley area, which is one of the upland summer pastures of transhumant peoples from the Deh Luran area today). Again by analogy with Swat, we may postulate that some of these villages were founded by herders who planted crops for harvest in the late spring and summer rather than in the winter as had been their custom in the hot lowlands.

The emphasis on irrigation in this discussion should not be misconstrued. As Adams (1962) has pointed out, and as seems logical, dry farming and irrigation may have been carried out in close proximity simultaneously; the crucial variable would be available water and dependability of rainfall. It seems reasonable to think that early dry farmers on the Khuzistan steppe depended more upon animal sources of protein than they did on cereals, principally because of the extreme variability in crop yields from year to year. Since the carrying capacity of the steppes for animals is severely limited, the important factor in the growth of population must have been irrigation. One may also postulate that although some of the excess population of villages using irrigation was probably forced to engage in lower intensity dry farming and transhumance, the overall effect was an increase in population, through more effective use of the available environmental niches. After an initial rapid increase, the population remained relatively stable on the lowland steppe until the end of the Ubaid period some 1000 years later.

The hypothetical reconstruction of a migration into Deh Luran which is suggested above appears to conform to available evidence. One can, however, devise some tests of the hypothesis. It can be rejected if any of the following conditions are met:

a. Populations in sites of the two traditions are of the same size and residential stability.

b. Populations in sites of the two traditions have the same degree of wealth and similar levels of social differentiation.
c. There is no change in the size or structure of the sites following the appearance of the Choga Mami Transitional into Deh Luran.
d. There is no "wave of advance" (Ammerman and Cavalli-Sforza, 1973) of the kind one would predict with population expansion.

Clearly we do not have enough data to determine whether any of these conditions is satisfied in either Deh Luran or in eastern Iraq. Still, the available evidence points to quite substantial houses and large sites in Iraq as opposed to smaller houses and sites in Deh Luran. Moreover, the houses themselves in the latter region point to patterns of seasonal transhumance. It is difficult, at the present time, however, to assess the size of the populations. What seems indicated at Sawwan is an increase in the local population from level I in which only two houses are found, to level III in which more than 10 were occupied. What is significant there, as well, is that the earliest houses are of the same modular size and design as the later. Thus, it is a distinct possibility that local expansion of the population accounts for the enlargement of that village.

Equally important is the abundant evidence at Sawwan of high quality goods that are largely reserved for the deceased, and of the apparent emphasis on the long-term use of cemeteries. These facts suggest both much greater wealth than in Deh Luran and much greater permanence of residence, generally associated with fixed property rights and probably with corporate land holding.

The Samarran arrives at the Mandali area somewhat later than at Sawwan itself, and arrives still later in Deh Luran, in the form of the Choga Mami Transitional. My present assessment of early examples of Susiana *a*, as it is found at Jaffarabad and at Fazali, is that it too developed out of the same tradition, but quite likely somewhat later than in Deh Luran. There, too, there is evidence of its intrusive nature. Our preliminary assessment of the number of sites of different ages in Khuzistan suggests an eight-fold increase with the advent of Susiana *a*. Even allowing for some error, population increases can hardly be doubted. Thus, a gradual movement of people southward along the front of the Zagros Mountains, in response to population pressure, seems indicated.

Taken collectively, therefore, the various lines of evidence imply that the hypothesis cannot be rejected.

WHAT HAPPENED TO THE ORIGINAL SETTLERS?

If we assume that our interpretation up to this point has been correct, we can ask what happened to the original peoples who had lived on the plain. As suggested earlier, there are several possibilities, two of which are considered below.

Hypothesis: There was a separation of the two groups, each of which adopted different strategies of subsistence.

Discussion: The implication is that the two strategies of subsistence are not strictly compatible and that separation enables a more efficient use of the resources and results in greater productivity overall. The original settlers emphasized extensive use of the plain with wet area farming and seasonal transhumance. The Choga Mami Transitional/Sabz Phase people emphasized permanent settlements in their irrigated fields, intensive use of the land, the production of surpluses, and storage. When separated, the two patterns of subsistence are complementary.

Evidence which would reject the hypothesis:
a. Herding continues in the same apparent frequency after the Choga Mami Transitional and there are no differences in the animals themselves (e.g., age-sex distribution, size) that might suggest that they were maintained under different conditions and used for different purposes.
b. No evidence of transhumant peoples with typical Deh Luran style artifacts (Surkh, Choga Mami Transitional or Sabz Phase) can be found.
c. The settlement pattern at the site, as regards form of houses, size and type of rooms, burials, etc. remains constant after the Choga Mami Transitional.
d. The biology of skeletal populations shows considerable similarity before and after the Choga Mami Transitional.

Conclusions:

On presently available evidence we cannot reject the hypothesis. This may be principally because we lack the requisite data. Neither the excavation at

Chagha Sefid nor the one at Tepe Sabz is large enough to demonstrate essential changes in the pattern of settlement. Nor are there data on physical type, and such data would not necessarily be expected to show differences. Similarly, there is no evidence at the time of this writing to suggest differences in the structure of the faunal populations. Nevertheless, it is striking how few bones occur after the Choga Mami Transitional, strongly suggesting a different diet than had characterized the area previously.

Hypothesis: The newcomers to the plain and the original settlers both continued to use Chagha Sefid, the former year-round and the latter seasonally.

Discussion: Such a pattern may be more realistic for the time we are considering, when the intensity of land use overall was considerably less than it was in later times. Indeed one can see such a practice today in many villages which are occupied year-round by farmers and seasonally by transhumant peoples who often erect their black tents over the walls of abandoned mud brick houses.

Evidence which would reject the hypothesis:
   a. Extensive excavation of Choga Mami Transitional and Sabz Phase deposits reveals no intrasite variation in the type of architecture, size of structures, evidence of storage and the like which would suggest simultaneous occupation by people of different traditions and practices.
   b. There is a disappearance of products that are typically derived from mountain regions where transhumant peoples are likely to travel seasonally.
   c. There is a change in the populations of the animals or in their basic skeletal characteristics such that they cannot be regarded as primarily derived from the stock of transhumant pastoralists.
   d. There is no longer any evidence of the traditional Deh Luran artifacts, but rather a total replacement of types.

Conclusions:

At the present time we do not have adequate data for rejecting or even adequately assessing the second hypothesis. On the contrary, what little evidence we do have suggests continuity of the local tradition along with new elements. For example, we see the continued use of Khazineh Red pottery which is a typical Deh Luran product not found in Iraq. This ware, which began in the Mohammad Jaffar Phase, is found throughout the Deh Luran sequence in spite of the introduction of Susiana Buff wares in the Choga Mami Transitional, which are made of different clays and with different techniques than the red wares. Additionally, we have data that suggest a pattern of transhumance into the mountains, both sherds of Deh Luran types found in caves, and products that come from the mountains: almonds, obsidian, copper and certain kinds of flint found at Chagha Sefid itself. Needless to say, we cannot be sure that the ceramics were made or used by people who lived seasonally in a village with irrigation agriculture. Nor can we rule out exchange or trade between farmers and herders to account for the presence of mountain resources on the plain. The similarity of the remaining artifacts over wide areas is too great to decide questions of continuity of local traditions. Perhaps the best test of the coexistence of parallel traditions will come from a study of settlement patterns as further excavations and survey are completed. Thus, although we can point to continuing contact of the Deh Luranis with the Central Zagros, we cannot specify the nature of these relationships.

THE DEH LURAN SEQUENCE

One of the most important results of the three excavations on the Deh Luran plain is that they have given us an accurate picture of changes through time. This is important insofar as strategy of excavation and the value of the results for others are concerned. It would not have been necessary to remark on this specifically except that in conversation with various colleagues I have frequently been asked whether I think the trenches were large enough to have provided an adequate sample. The reason for the question is obvious when our work is viewed in the context of normal digs in Southwest Asia where far larger areas are routinely exposed. My answer has always been an unequivocal "yes" and the reasons for it can be conveniently summarized.

Hypothesis: Our sample has been large enough to have given us an accurate picture of changes in artifacts throughout the phases. In this instance it is the null hypothesis, that our sample has not given us an

accurate picture of the changes, that we wish to test.
Evidence which will reject the null hypothesis:
   a. The changes we find are consistent with evidence elsewhere.
   b. There is non-random, patterned change in the occurrence of artifacts.

Conclusions:

The evidence suggests that we should reject the null hypothesis. Changes found elsewhere are paralleled (although in shorter segments of the entire span) elsewhere, and there is a patterned change in the artifacts that enables us to seriate the material so that changes match the relative stratigraphy. What is more, this seriation enables us to predict with a high degree of accuracy what "should" be found in the phases that intervene between Mohammad Jaffar and Sabz. Although the supporting evidence is impressive, it is more to the point that we cannot reject the original hypothesis; therefore, I feel that we do have an accurate picture of artifactual changes in Deh Luran throughout the sequence.

We can go somewhat farther with this assessment, however. At present we have no unexplained disjunctions of the kind we found in our previous work. I consider the evidence for an intrusion into a developing Deh Luran sequence during the Choga Mami Transitional to be unchallenged. No other similar disjunction occurs in the entire sequence of phases. The radiocarbon dates are not in themselves very useful since they are not precise enough for our purposes. Far better, in my view, is the stratigraphic evidence. Indeed, I have evaluated the radiocarbon dates on the basis of stratigraphy rather than the other way around.

There is another aspect to the question of whether enough has been dug, however. This concerns whether we have found all of the range of variation that exists in any phase. There is no reason to think that we have, as I note in discussing ceramics and as is evident in architecture. Still less are we certain that we have an accurate picture of intersite variation. The differences in subsistence between contemporary phases at Ali Kosh and Chagha Sefid is fair warning that there will be other surprises of this kind. Still, we can point to the patterning in the occurrence of artifacts as evidence that we have the essential outline of changes that we sought.

"ERAS" AND STRATEGIES OF SUBSISTENCE

When we postulated two distinct "eras" of production, dry farming and irrigation agriculture, we were suggesting stages in an overall development without claiming that all people in Southwest Asia participated in the second era. Even with this disclaimer, however, it seems necessary to postulate other variants, not as eras but rather as adaptive strategies. In retrospect, we should have done this initially (Hole and Flannery, 1968).

The importance of designating sets of adaptive strategies rather than stages of development or eras is emphasized by our work in Deh Luran, where one can see more clearly than elsewhere what kinds of variations are actually present. There seems to be little doubt that dry farming was used by most if not all of the earliest farmers, nor is there doubt that caprine domestication was a component of the strategy. What has now become apparent, however, is the different emphases that were placed on these two aspects of subsistence, and on hunting and gathering. There are two major factors to consider: (1) the immediate locale and its potential with respect to wild and domestic resources and (2) the ability of the people to take advantage of the resources. The latter is clearly tied to techniques available and is consequently somewhat dependent on time: hence our "eras." The former, on the other hand, depends on both natural and cultural factors: the local environment, and the size and ability of the local populations. What is a good strategy for a population of one size with certain technical capabilities, may not be appropriate even with the same techniques if the population is significantly larger or smaller. In order to sort out the dynamics of any local developmental sequence we need to have some means of assessing these kinds of variables.

As a suggestion for future consideration, it seems necessary to postulate a wider set of adaptive strategies than was implied in our earlier summary. Just how these should be expressed is less important than our recognition that they exist and collectively compose the cultural mosaic of Southwestern Asian prehistory. We have not found any villages which appear to have depended solely on cereal grains while there are sites where herding is well attested and where agriculture is not manifest. These are probably seasonal camps of agriculturalists. In recent times there have been nomadic peoples who themselves do no farming and depend on trade with villagers for their cereals. One important problem is the consideration of the point at which such an adaptive strategy developed, and under what circumstances. There remains the possibility as well that there are groups of hunters and perhaps peoples who herd animals that we do not presently think of as domestic, namely gazelles or even deer. And finally, we should consider the possibility that there were people who subsisted chiefly on the collecting of wild plants—cereals, acorns, almonds, and pistachios—along with some hunting, long after domestication was well advanced.

It is well known, also, that shellfish collecting and fishing were locally important, especially in southern Mesopotamia, and this may have been supplemented with some farming, and gathering of dates, edible reeds and the like.

When we consider farming itself, it is the amount and predictability of the yield that is of overriding importance in determining what proportion of the diet can be sustained by the effort. In Deh Luran farming was certainly precarious even under better hydrologic conditions than today, principally because of the timing of rainfall or runoff. In more predictably wetted areas, farming could be relied upon much more as a staple, with a corresponding lesser dependence on animals, and perhaps with a greater population density.

Irrigation agriculture had two major effects: (1) it permitted more predictable yields and probably higher yields, and (2) it encouraged greater residential stability because of the value of particular plots of land and because of the requirements of storage.

The important differences between the two methods of farming derive from the potential of irrigation. With irrigation, crops could be planted in new, highly fertile areas; it was a technique that responded rapidly, through greatly increased yields, to changes in technology (hybrid grains, canals, hoeing, draft animals) and in social organization (cooperative labor on canals, management of large plots with sufficient fallowing, and the accumulation of surpluses which literally could be fed back into the system to amplify the technological and social gains).

With the advent of specialization, manifest especially in the potential of irrigation, subsidiary strategies could be accommodated which were heretofore effectively precluded. In particular, and most relevant to the Deh Luran scene, is the separation from the agricultural villages themselves of most herding functions and the production of the secondary byproducts of the animals. Such animals as remain in the villages may be more for ceremonial than for subsistence use. In any case, as the eating of meat becomes rarer because of the increase in populations and the consequent increase in the value of animals, the stage is set for the emergence of groups who employ animals more for their secondary products, which can be exchanged, than for their value as elements of the diet.

What we should look for archeologically are variations on these alternate types of subsistence, without locking onto the facile assumption that there is one set of patterns that characterizes any very large region. Indeed, as more work is done, it is increasingly apparent that there is no single line of development; rather there is a very complex anastomosing network of interrelationships which collectively comprise the elements out of which the urban civilizations of southern Mesopotamia were to arise.

ASSESSMENT OF DEVELOPMENTS THROUGHOUT WESTERN IRAN

The excavation of Chagha Sefid is notable for the information it provides on adaptive strategies in use from the earliest times in Deh Luran. Our latest results enable us to glimpse intracultural variation and, taken together with results of similar excavations outside Deh Luran, they enable us to gain further perspective on subsistence strategies and their effect on subsequent cultural development. It is now clear, based on work at these sites, along with Michael Kirkby's review of environmental factors, that from the earliest settlements, precise and effective strategies of land use had been worked out. In illustration, I shall review evidence from the Zagros area.

Contrary to what one might have supposed (cf. Reed, 1969:367), among the earliest evidence we have of settlements are sites in which animal husbandry played an important, if not the sole role, in domestic subsistence. Zawi Chemi, Ganj Darreh and perhaps Asiab all have much evidence of herding, although the first two sites also have numbers of grinding stones reported. That this pattern continues is evident at both Guran where the lowest strata have evidence of herding but no grinding stones, and Sarab which appears to be a herding camp. These two sites are especially interesting in that they are both in areas where dry farming is carried out today, areas where farming settlements seem to have been a later development than herding camps. On the Deh Luran plain itself, our work at Ali Kosh suggests a winter occupation by herding peoples who were doing some planting, and the evidence at Chagha Sefid points even more strongly to the herding activity, even at the expense of hunting.

Thus, although we do not have detailed evidence from all the sites mentioned, it now seems highly probable that herding is at least as old as farming in the Zagros and that very soon after the establishment of farming, elements of the population were detached at least seasonally from their parent farming villages. What is presently uncertain is whether fully distinct strategies were followed by any of the people whose remains we have excavated so far.

For people who had been oriented toward hunting, a shift to herding seems to imply few substantial changes in the way of life except perhaps a greater concentration on a few species. On the other hand, the extensive use of vegetable foods cannot be demonstrated at all for the Zagros during the Pleistocene, and botanical evidence suggests that cereals were not present in quantities that were economically important. In any event, the tending of plots and the conversion of cereals into palatable foods represent significant changes from the pattern of life and from the diet that we reconstruct for Pleistocene hunters.

Aside from herding camps, there is also good evidence for mixed agriculture and herding as at Jarmo, one of the few sites in the Zagros where domestic pigs are found. Of all the sites so far dug this is perhaps closest to Childe's prototype of the self-sufficient village farming community. It is situated in an optimum environment for dry farming, fuel, and wild food resources, so that year-round residence, based on very local resources, appears to be a logical adaptive strategy.

Other sites show considerably less evidence of year-round occupation and appear to be base camps where agriculture is practiced and where herding is a seasonal component of the strategy. Such sites would be Ali Kosh, Chagha Sefid and the later part of Guran. While any of these sites might have been used year-round, the subsistence suggests otherwise; heavy dependence on caprines implies seasonal movement out of Deh Luran, and Flannery has suggested that wider ranging subsistence was in effect at Guran following the introduction of agriculture.

Until final reports are available on most of these sites the patterns of activities suggested above must be considered tentative, but they do imply that there is no simple pattern that describes all sites of any given age or even of any given local phase of culture. At a minimum, the differences in subsistence in the Ali Kosh Phase at Ali Kosh and Chagha Sefid illustrate this point very well. The implication must be, as Michael Kirkby has suggested, that different parts of the Deh Luran plain were suitable for different strategies of land use. Although we cannot reconstruct the land surface during the Ali Kosh Phase, by analogy with modern conditions it is evident that the best grazing is not necessary where agriculture is most easily practiced. Thus we surmise that the specific features of the plain were different at the two sites and that the two populations adopted different strategies to exploit them.

It seems absolutely necessary to have similar studies of the Kermanshah plain where Braidwood's survey teams found the greatest concentration of early sites outside of Khuzistan itself (Braidwood, 1960). Strangely, this area did not see the development of any very large early prehistoric sites; thus the importance of understanding the strategies of land use is emphasized.

Future research should be directed toward determining what characteristics of topography, soil, precipitation, elevation and vegetation were related to different kinds of sites and to local developments. At the moment we have no way to determine what patterns of alluviation and incision were present in any of the upland valleys where sites have been excavated. M. Kirkby's analysis suggests that the geologic processes upland were reflected in the lowland areas, but that different processes were active simultaneously in the two broad regions. The wave of alluviation and sedimentation, for example, moved downslope, resulting in equilibrium conditions more like the present far earlier in the upland valleys than on the Khuzistan plain system.

For this reason it may be possible to plot early sites in large plain systems like Kermanshah, which are known from surface survey, with respect to specific environments that are still visible today. A tentative attempt in this direction was made by Flannery and myself, using assessments that had been made in the field as to the ages of sites and plotting these against a soil map. A striking differential distribution of sites with respect to soils was revealed. As nearly as we can assess the situation today, it does look as if there is a close relation between particular local circumstances and the pattern of settlement and subsequent development of cultures.

MAJOR RESEARCH PROBLEMS REMAINING

The results of our work at Chagha Sefid suggested several projects that might be undertaken next. One of these, which was completed in 1973, was a study of the pastoral nomads of the region. Briefly, this work shows that typical nomad camps were in use in upper Khuzistan and probably in Deh Luran also by the time of the Sefid Phase (Hole, 1974, 1975). This study also resulted in information on modern nomads which will help us interpret our archeological findings more accurately. Finally, we now have a substantial body of information on patterns of transhumance, subsistence practices and the management of livestock which will be of great aid in helping us recover evidence of developments in animal domestication.

On the Deh Luran plain itself, we need to investigate some sites and phases much more extensively to determine the extent of intrasite variation and to get accurate information on the sizes and composition of settlements. It will be especially useful to do this for the Surkh, Choga Mami Transitional and Sabz Phases so that we can see just what kinds of changes were introduced. This should enable us to assess whether there was a bifurcation of the populations and whether indigenous Deh Luranis adopted separate subsistence strategies.

It is also necessary to examine separate sites of the same age to determine more accurately the nature of specific adaptations to local circumstances. This may entail a sampling of the Deh Luran plain itself in the attempt to determine the nature of the lake/marsh and the courses of the major rivers, especially the Dawairij.

The nature of the relations among sites likewise need investigation. We have found alabaster objects in Ali Kosh that are apparently identical to those found in graves at the bottom of Tell es-Sawwan. In Chagha Sefid, we found one sherd of Hassuna or early Samarran type and in both areas are objects of cold hammered copper. These suggest a network of exchange, the nature of which is by no means clear, that links the Zagros sites to those on the Mesopotamia plain as far north as Sawwan. As more information becomes available on the distribution of sea shells, and possibly other traded materials, we should be able to gain a more accurate impression of the relations among widely separated sites.

In this connection it will be useful to carry out detailed studies of burials and skeletal analysis. Sawwan appears to be an ideal site at which to study a skeletal population, and additional digging in contemporaneous sites in Deh Luran should produce a large enough series to test the hypothesis that different populations existed in these two regions. It may also be possible, as in the instance of the Ali Kosh Phase at Ali Kosh, to determine whether there is a significant difference in age, sex, status or morphology between skeletons whose interments are different: seated and flexed, as opposed to extended. The question of status or cultural differences with respect to cranial deformation and grave goods should also become clearer if a much larger sample is excavated in Deh Luran.

The relation of developments in Deh Luran to those in Khuzistan is also of great interest. Limited evidence suggests that there was an early village occupation in Khuzistan (Hole, 1974, 1975; Kantor, 1974) which was also truncated by a later Samarran-like intrusion, which has been grouped with the Susiana *a* there. The only excavated site which spans the transition is Choga Mish where a series of pottery (Archaic 1 and 2) precedes Susiana *a*. As yet the details of the transition are not reported. Both Jaffarabad and Boneh Fazili have ceramics in their earliest levels which combine elements of Choga Mami Transitional and Susiana *a*. It is not clear whether the two "phases" can be stratigraphically separated at either site. Thus, although it cannot be demonstrated at this time that a separate Choga Mami Transitional exists in Khuzistan, it is clear that a local "Archaic," equivalent to the Deh Luran Mohammad Jaffar, Sefid and Surkh phases is succeeded by the Susiana Buff wares. This implies a disjunction in the sequence, perhaps of the same kind we find in Deh Luran. If this is the case it is of great importance in any study of the dynamics of developing agriculture. At the moment the limited evidence points to a lowland rather than to a highland origin for the intrusive group which brought buff ware pottery, irrigation and hybrid grains into Deh Luran and Khuzistan.

The question of the origin of the Samarran complex is likewise not clear. This is a problem that needs to be investigated primarily in Iraq, if our hypothesis that it occurred later in Iran is correct. The basic issue is whether it has its origin in the Hassunan, with which it apparently overlaps slightly in distribution in northern Mesopotamia or whether it has a more southerly origin. The assumption that it represents a movement southward can hardly be demonstrated to be universally correct at the present time and, in fact, there is some contradictory evidence. This evidence derives from the Samarran/Choga Mami Transitional sherds found by Adams near Warka and from the fact that Samarran sites are almost all south of those with Hassuna material. This problem must be investigated in relation to particular hydrologic circumstances on the Mesopotamian plain, and to an entirely different set of subsistence strategies from those we find in the sites oriented toward the Zagros. In particular, we should look for a riverine adaptation, the hunting of gazelles and pigs and possibly the use of cattle. If M. Kirkby is right, there is also the possibility of doing some dry farming in selected areas. In short, there may be a quite independent development in southern Mesopotamia which later spread north, called the Samarran, along the Tigris and Zagros front. We should keep in mind that sea shells turn up with great frequency in Zagros sites, shells which may well have been transmitted through contacts of the Mesopotamian plainsdwellers with Zagros herders who wintered in places like Khuzistan and Deh Luran.

The question of cattle domestication remains cloudy, especially since the animals occur only in low frequencies in Zagros sites, yet they are found domesticated as early as the Samarran in the lowland. The presence of cattle in lowland sites of the Levant suggests that they may have been at home in marshy areas and along the major rivers of the Mesopotamian plain, as well as in Anatolia. If this is the case, then their domestication could very well have taken place in Mesopotamia.

Most authors have discounted the possibility that gazelles were domesticated but there is no good reason to do so. They are relatively tractable animals and well-adapted to hot desert steppes. Their occurrence in high frequency in early villages like Mureybit and even in the earliest part of Guran only points to the possibility. Assuming that they were tended, their demise as domesticates may have had more to do with their limited potential for secondary products than with their basic incompatibility with domestication. Field studies of these animals are needed to determine their adaptability to herding, the effects of breeding on size, their durability in transhumance, etc.

A subject about which we know very little is craft specialization. Çatal Hüyük, Çayönü, Sawwan, Beidha and Sialk all have some evidence of manufacturing of local resources, possibly for commercial distribution. At the very least, Çatal Hüyük and Sawwan show a very high degree of technical and artistic competence which it is hard to believe was solely for internal consumption. Indeed, the alabaster objects found at Ali Kosh argue to the contrary and it is not the least bit certain that it was in Sawwan itself that the objects were crafted. In fact, the burials at Ali Kosh in which these objects were found are almost certainly earlier than even the lowest levels of Sawwan. Moreover, there is no published evidence from Sawwan to suggest that crafts were produced at that site. Workshops have so far only been identified at Beidha and Çayönü but at neither of these places is there evidence of the production of luxury goods.

One must conclude that there was a much more active intercourse among sites than has hitherto been suggested and, equally importantly, that the sites which contain the craftsmen have not yet been identified. Such sites, at the moment, are not suggested by what we know about the Zagros front; certainly nothing in Deh Luran hints at the possibility. It is obviously necessary, however, to have the raw materials, and these are available along the Zagros rather than the Mesopotamian plain itself. What is needed immediately is a study of the alabaster objects and an attempt to determine their geologic source.

At Sawwan the wall partially enclosing the site is considered by the excavators to be a defensive structure and they report finding sling missiles embedded in it. Whatever the true nature of the wall may be, this site is unique in the area as known in having a wall at all, although a "guard tower" has been reported at Choga Mami. Trenching of contemporaneous sites in Deh Luran and in Khuzistan to discover whether similar structures are present, along with a careful analysis of their construction and association with domestic architecture, may help determine their function. The hypothesis that wealthy farmers were subject to raiding by their more mobile and less affluent contemporaries is attractive but unproven. In fact, direct evidence of conflict of any sort cannot be found until early historic times. Perhaps it is more realistic to consider that walls merely enclose a domestic social space and separate it from the fields beyond.

If I am correct, the Choga Mami Transitional, the Samarran, and Susiana *a* all indicate irrigation agriculture and cattle domestication. If this is true, then there remains the strong probability that contemporary dry farmers lived, at least for some time, close by. There is no particular reason why their ceramics should show the same changes; thus there is a possibility that there may be some overlap in the chronology of sites which have quite different ceramics. The same is true for purely hunting and gathering peoples. Certainly when the first village in Deh Luran was founded in the Bus Mordeh Phase, the area was highly suitable for hunters. Of these we have no direct traces, and it is scarcely possible that groups of these people did not persist in the area until long after farming and even irrigation agriculture were established.

At this stage of our research we thus have a background of information which includes an accurate relative chronology, a body of data on subsistence strategies and, to a lesser degree, cultural practices, and the beginnings of important studies in geomorphology and land use. Against this background we can now focus clearly on research projects that can be carried out rapidly and efficiently to test certain hypotheses and to fill in important areas of information. We have reached the point in our study of this area where we can solve problems concerning the processes of cultural development and it is to this end that we shall direct our future investigations.

III

THE AGES AND CHARACTERISTICS OF THE PHASES

ESTIMATED AGES OF THE PHASES

The period with which we have been concerned in Deh Luran extends over some 4000 years and has been subdivided into 10 phases. The relative chronology of these phases is certain both from our work in Deh Luran and from other sites where segments of the sequence have been excavated. Purely stratigraphic relationships, however, do not tell us very much about the absolute time that should be assigned to any phase nor about the absolute calendric dates of the phases. For the latter information we must turn to radiocarbon dating, which itself is subject to limitations that make it presently impossible to assign accurate calendric dates to most of our phases. The exception to this is the Bayat and Mehmeh phases which fall within the time that has been adjusted to conform with tree-ring dates. Since we cannot project these adjustments back to include our entire sequence, I have presented only the radiocarbon dates and their correction with the half life of 5730 years (Table 1).

Some 63 radiocarbon dates are available from sites whose deposits bear a close relation to the Deh Luran sequence; 36 of these are from Deh Luran itself. Of that total, 31 are useful in assessing the ages of our phases. Dates which do not conform to the known stratigraphy or sequence of phases are not included in Table 1. Table 2 represents the entire list of dates.

Ten sites, including the three from Deh Luran, are considered in this assessment: Ganj Darreh, Ali Kosh, Tepe Guran, Jarmo, Sarab, Chagha Sefid, Tell es-Sawwan, Choga Mami, Tepe Sabz, and Jaffarabad. The strata which have been dug in each of these sites are shown in Table 1, along with the radiocarbon dates.

Ganj Darreh provides the oldest dates and, although the material has not been described in detail yet, it is preceramic in the usual sense and is clearly older than any reasonable date for our earliest phase in Deh Luran. This site, taken together with Zawi Chemi and Shanidar B1, suggests a long period antecedent to settlement in Deh Luran during which poeple were herding either sheep or goats in mountain pastures. The importance of these sites to the Deh Luran sequence is largely in showing that settlement on the margin of the plains is in no way to be considered the first settled life with animal husbandry or cereal domestication.

The Bus Mordeh Phase is not known for certain outside of Ali Kosh although we await with interest the studies of Asiab and Ganj Darreh to see how they may relate to this phase. A single radiocarbon date (of three available) is reasonable and places the phase back to about 8200 B.C., or possibly as much as 1000 years later than the founding of Ganj Darreh.

Somewhat more secure is the dating of the Ali Kosh Phase which is represented at Ali Kosh, Chagha Sefid, and probably Tepe Guran and Jarmo, although the latter two sites do not have useful dates. There are 6 dates from the Deh Luran sites, 3 of which are reasonable. These suggest an interval between 7200 and 6400 corrected radiocarbon years B.C. for the phase. This dating also corresponds with a date of 6712 corrected radiocarbon years B.C. from Tepe Guran, and Braidwood's estimate of about 6750 B.C. for the earlier deposits at Jarmo, although the dates from the latter site are not very informative (Braidwood, 1975:127).

The Mohammad Jaffar Phase is typologically equivalent to the upper part of Jarmo and the middle levels of Guran. Regional differences in ceramic styles make such an equation somewhat arbitrary and this is compounded by the fact that, except at Chagha Sefid and possibly Guran, there is nothing later than this

Table 2

RADIOCARBON DATES FROM DEH LURAN AND NEARBY AREAS

Site	Phase	Zone	Date in C-14 Years	Years B.C. (Date x 1.03 - 1950)	Sample No.	Comment
TS	Bayat	A1	6050 ± 140	4382	I-1499	OK
TS	Bayat	A1	6170 ± 200	4405	SI-203	OK
TS	Bayat	A2	6060 ± 200	4292	SI-204	OK
TS	Bayat	A2	5700 ± 250	3921	SI-205	OK
TS	Bayat	A2	5860 ± 230	4085	I-1503	OK
TS	Bayat	A3	5770 ± 120	3993	SI-156	OK
TS	Bayat	A3	6060 ± 140	4292	I-1502	OK
TS	Bayat	A3	6070 ± 100	4302	UCLA-750A	OK
TS	Mehmeh	B1	5410 ± 160	3622	I-1500	too young
TS	Mehmeh	B3	6470 ± 160	4714	I-1493	OK
TS	Khazineh	C1	7460 ± 160	5734	I-1501	too old
TS	Khazineh	C3	6925 ± 200	5183	UCLA-750B	OK
TS	Khazineh	C3	7200 ± 1000	5466	SI-206	too old
TS	Sabz	D	6740 ± 190	4992	I-1497	too young
TS	Sabz	D	9050 ± 160	7372	UCLA-750C	too old
CS	Surkh	F	7730 ± 110	6012	UGa 291	too old
CS	Sefid	C1	8000 ± 710	6290	UGa 293	OK
CS	Sefid	C1	8040 ± 90	6331	UGa 297	OK
CS	Sefid	B2	9530 ± 145	7866	UGa 310	too old
CS	Sefid	B2	11270 ± 90	9658	UGa 300	too old
CS	Sefid	A4	9690 ± 100	8031	UGa 295	too old
CS	Mhd. J.	SB/A	8085 ± 145	6378	UGa 302	OK
CS	Mhd. J.	SB/A	8760 ± 165	7073	UGa 296	too old
AK	Mhd. J.	A2	7220 ± 160	5487	I-1495	too young
AK	Mhd. J.	A2	7820 ± 190	6105	I-1494	OK
AK	Ali K.	B1	7740 ± 600	6022	SI-207	too young
AK	Ali K.	B1	8100 ± 170	6393	I-1491	too young
AK	Ali K.	B2	8250 ± 175	6548	H-O-1845	OK
AK	Ali K.	B2	7770 ± 330	6053	H-O-1848	too young
AK	Ali K.	B2	8425 ± 180	6728	H-O-1833	OK
AK	Ali K.	B2	8850 ± 210	7166	Shell 1174	OK
CS	Ali K.	A1	8760 ± 150	7073	UGa 294	OK
CS	Ali K.	A1	10425 ± 145	8788	UGa 305	too old
AK	Bus M.	C2	9900 ± 200	8247	UCLA-750D	OK
AK	Bus M.	C2	7380 ± 180	5651	I-1489	too young
AK	Bus M.	C1	7670 ± 170	5950	I-1496	too young
GD		B	10838 ± 98	9213	P. 1486	OK
GD		B	10860 ± 170	9236	GaK 994	OK
GD		C	11189 ± 196	9575	P-1485	OK
GD		D	10918 ± 100	9296	P-1484	OK

Table 2 (Cont'd)

Site	Phase	Zone	Date in C-14 Years	Years B.C. (Date x 1.03 - 1950)	Sample No.	Comment
GD		E	12350 ± 150	10771	GaK 807	too old?
G	(Sefid)	H	7760 ± 250	6043	?	OK
G	(Ali Kosh)	U	8410 ± 200	6712	?	OK
S	(Mhd. Jaff./		7644 ± 89	5923	P-467	OK
S	Sefid)	4	7605 ± 96	5883	P-465	OK
S		5	7955 ± 98	6245	P-466	OK
es-S	Samarran	III	7299 ± 86	5568	P-856	OK
es-S	Samarran	I	6808 ± 82	5062	P-857	too young
es-S	Samarran	I	7456 ± 73	5730	P-855	OK
CM	CM Trans		6846 ± 182	5100	BM-483	too young
Jaff	Susa A	1		3268	TUNC 3	OK
Jaff	Susa A	2		3375	TUNC 4	OK
Jaff	Susa A	2		3458	TUNC 5	OK
Jaff	Susa A	2		3450	TUNC 6	OK
Jarmo	(pottery)	II2	5266 ± 450	3474	C-744	too young
Jarmo	?	PQ14	9040 ± 250	7361	W-607	too old
Jarmo	?	N18	11200 ± 200	9586	W-665	too old
Jarmo	?	PQ14	11240 ± 300	9627	W-657	too old
Jarmo	(pottery)	II4	8830 ± 200	7145	W-651	too old
Jarmo	(aceramic)	II5	6695 ± 360	4946	C-743	too young
Jarmo	(aceramic)	I7a	7950 ± 200	6238	W-652	too young
Jarmo	(aceramic)	17	6606 ± 330	4854	C-742	too young
Jarmo	(aceramic)	I7	6707 ± 320	4958	C-113	too young

Key to sites: (TS) Tepe Sabz, (AK) Ali Kosh, (CS) Chagha Sefid, (GD) Ganj Darreh, (G) Guran, (S) Sarab, (es-S) Tell es-Sawwan, (CM) Choga Mami, (Jaff) Jaffarabad.

Note: Pottery occurs in the upper part of Jarmo and it is considered to be of about the same age as Mohammad Jaffar and earlier than Sarab. The contexts of Jarmo PQ14 and N18 are not given but in this assessment they are assumed to have ceramics; consequently the dates appear to be too old.

phase at any of the sites mentioned. Two radiocarbon dates out of four from Deh Luran are useful and suggest a range between 6400 and 6100 B.C. The Jarmo dates are not useful but a determination from Tepe Guran falls within this range.

The Sefid Phase is evidenced only at Chagha Sefid but I suggest that its chronological counterparts in the Zagros may be seen in the uppermost levels of Tepe Guran and in Sarab. The Sarab dates are 6200 to 5900 B.C. and two dates (out of 5) from Chagha Sefid are about 6300 B.C. Thus I tentatively place the range of this material at 6300 to 5900 B.C. in Deh Luran.

The Surkh Phase, found only at Chagha Sefid, has no useful dates, although one which I judge to be too old, has been run. The phase can be dated best by the phases which are known to be stratigraphically earlier and later, namely the Sefid and the Choga Mami Transitional. Assuming that the Sefid Phase ends at 5900 B.C. and that the Choga Mami Transitional is slightly later than the Samarran (which I judge to be contemporary with the Surkh), then the Surkh Phase should date between 5800 and 5400 B.C. Dates from Tell es-Sawwan, of Samarran age, fall in this range. It is known from Choga Mami that the Choga Mami Transitional is a terminal variant of the Samarran.

A single date from the Choga Mami Transitional

Table 3
APPROXIMATE AGES OF THE PHASES IN DEH LURAN AND THEIR RELATION TO PERIODS DESIGNATED IN OTHER AREAS

	Years B.C. (Date x 1.03 - 1950)	Northern Mesopotamia	Southern Mesopotamia	Khuzistan
Bayat	4400-3900	Ubaid	Ubaid 4	Susiana *d*
Mehmeh	4800-4400	Ubaid	Ubaid 3	Susiana *c*
Khazineh	5000-4800	Ubaid	Ubaid 2	Susiana *b*
Sabz	5200-5000	Halaf	Ubaid 1	Susiana *a*
Choga Mami Transitional	5400-5100	Halaf	?	?
Surkh	5900-5400	Samarra/Halaf		Choga Mish "Archaic"
Sefid	6300-5900	Hassuna		
Mohammad Jaffar	6400-6100	Jarmoan		
Ali Kosh	7200-6400	Jarmo (preceramic)		
Bus Mordeh	8200-7200	Karim Shahirian		

from Choga Mami itself is considered too young to actually date this "phase"; it is 400 years younger than the date from Tell es-Sawwan III. There are no dates from Chagha Sefid. I estimate the overall range of this distinctive period to be 5400 to 5100 B.C. In Deh Luran itself it may have lasted only a century or so but in the absence of sufficient deposits at Choga Mami, its length of development cannot be stated with accuracy. It is possible that the ceramic traditions in Deh Luran and the Mandali area diverged at this time, making precise correspondences difficult.

There are no new data on the remaining phases that have been found in Deh Luran. Nevertheless, in view of the fact that our previous listing was not corrected in accord with the newly known half life of C-14, it is useful to review the other phases. We have no useful dates for the Sabz Phase although it is certain that it followed immediately upon the Choga Mami Transitional and is a development of it. I estimate its range now to be about 5200 to 5000 B.C. This is considerably at variance with our previous estimate, which was based on ignorance of the substantial deposits between the Sabz and Mohammad Jaffar phases.

A single Khazineh date of 5183 (out of three dates) provides our only estimate for this phase. I estimate the range now to be between 5000 and 4800 B.C. The standard deviation of the date mentioned carries it well within these limits.

For the Mehmeh Phase we have two dates, one of which seems suitable. I estimate the range now to be between 4800 and 4400 B.C.

We are on the most secure ground when we reach the Bayat Phase, for which all eight dates are closely clustered and reasonable. The range is between 4400 and 3900 B.C. We can compare this range with dates from Jaffarabad for Susa A which is later than the Bayat (= Susiana *d*). Four dates from that site fall in the range 3500-3200 B.C.

Table 3 presents the latest estimates for the ranges of the various phases and suggests their archeological equivalents elsewhere.

REMARKS ON RADIOCARBON DATING

There are a number of conventions employed by archeologists in the listing of radiocarbon dates and in interpreting their significance. In our previous report we simply listed the dates as given by the laboratories. Since that time it has become conventional to correct the dates in accord with the longer half life. For that reason Table 2 gives corrected as well as uncorrected dates. In *Radiocarbon* dates are listed uncorrected, and archeologists should follow this practice also although it is sometimes not done, as in the case of the Tehran dates for Jaffarabad. The correction is to multiply the dates by 1.03, a relatively simple procedure, yet in reviewing dates for other areas it has become apparent that some archeologists have multiplied by another constant. The importance of publishing the original, uncorrected dates is thus emphasized.

Table 1 uses corrected dates with bars to suggest one standard deviation. Some authors prefer to draw bars the length of two standard deviations in order to increase the probability that the dates actually fall within the range shown on their charts. I have chosen not to do this because I think we can be more precise when we use both stratigraphic and radiocarbon evidence. Should others wish to employ the more conservative method, the list of dates in Table 2 provides the data.

The dates for the phases in Table 3 are the best estimate possible now. It should be clear, however, that the boundaries are not precise and that some degree of overlap can be expected. This overlap may in fact occur when more accurate dates are available for the Deh Luran sequence, and it is probable when we correlate sites that are widely separated geographically. There is no theoretical reason, for example, why the Mohammad Jaffar or Ali Kosh phases should have begun or ended at the same time in different areas. The Mohammad Jaffar Phase is defined as the first in which a characteristic type of pottery occurs and it ends when we have evidence of changes in the ceramics. There is no reason to expect that pottery was introduced at all sites even within a span of 200 years and changes in the ceramics may have more to do with local factors than with overall trends. A case in point is the truncation of the Surkh Phase; in other areas this phase may have lasted considerably longer than it did at Chagha Sefid.

It remains to comment on radiocarbon dating in general. It is well known that the dates do not accurately represent calendar years in the range of time we are dealing with. The correction most often used today is the MASCA correction which suggests that radiocarbon dates at 3000 B.C. are about 550 years too young. Thus, the Bayat Phase is older than shown on Table 1. However, since there is no way at present to determine what correction should be applied to dates of 4000 B.C. and earlier, I have not made any correction at all. The dates should give an idea of the relative magnitude of the ages although the accuracy of this is not known. Promising research in the correlation of radiocarbon dates with varves (Tauber, 1970; Stuiver, 1970) seems to show that there is not a linear relationship of time with age of the kind demonstrated over the last 3000 years of the tree-ring chronology. It is suggested that the oldest dates will not be as far removed from the younger ones as they seem now, which would fill in some of the apparent chronological gaps. In view of the uncertainty in these correlations, I have not presented the possible corrections.

SUMMARY OF THE PHASES

This review of the phases follows the pattern we adopted in our previous reports (Hole and Flannery, 1968; Hole, Flannery and Neely, 1969) and it is assumed that readers are familiar with them. Rather than dealing with all of the phases in Deh Luran, we will concentrate here only on those that occur at Chagha Sefid. As well as delineating the characteristics of each phase, this summary will also compare and contrast contemporaneous deposits in Chagha Sefid and Ali Kosh.

With our long sequence it is now possible to be very precise about some of the trends in artifacts, architecture, and subsistence. Aside from ceramics and architecture, however, there are few things found in the new phases which were not found in our previous work. It is certain, as an examination of the tables which summarize the findings on artifacts will show, that the new phases in Chagha Sefid relate more closely to the earlier Mohammad Jaffar and Ali Kosh than they do to the later Sabz through Bayat phases. It will be useful in this section, therefore, to group the phases so that these similarities will be emphasized.

A major disjunction in the traditional Deh Luran sequence occurs with the Choga Mami Transitional which can now be seen to be an early stage of the Sabz/Susiana development that we found at Tepe Sabz. In spite of this change, there is a demonstrable continuity in artifacts throughout the entire sequence. The reasons for this appear to be twofold: first, continuity is strongly correlated with an irreducible minimum set of tools for hunting, butchering and food processing, and second, in other artifacts such as ornaments, there is considerable similarity throughout the region that includes eastern Iraq and the Zagros mountains. Thus foreign elements entering Deh Luran are reflected largely in changes in subsistence, in ceramics, and probably in architecture and settlement pattern.

Rather than abrupt changes, we find evidence of shifting emphases in the importance which various artifacts were accorded in each phase. For example, the proportion of plain blades throughout the sequence declines rapidly from its peak in the Bus Mordeh. This decline is independent of any "cultural" changes and it probably reflects a progressive shift in activities.

Ali Kosh through Surkh Phases

The pattern of settlement and subsistence in these phases at Chagha Sefid is similar to what we found at Ali Kosh. During this interval, roughly 7200-5400 B.C., we are still within the era of dry farming and caprine domestication with small settlements that are characterized by some degree of transhumance. Considering these phases as a group, there is much more evidence of herding at Chagha Sefid than there is at Ali Kosh, indicating specific differences between contemporaneous sites. It also seems apparent that there is considerably less hunting and gathering in the economy of the settlers at Chagha Sefid. Nevertheless, the subsistence strategies in all the phases mentioned are based on a combination of dry farming and herding at both sites. It is the importance of these pursuits relative to each other and to hunting and gathering that differs.

To some degree these different emphases probably relate to specific environmental differences in the immediate surroundings of the sites. This is a matter that will be discussed in detail by Michael Kirkby in Appendix I. Although it is impossible to be very specific about the physical locale of Chagha Sefid with respect to the surface features of the plain, it has been determined that Ali Kosh was situated near a seasonal or permanent marsh. Thus at that site the settlers were able to take advantage of a variety of water resources that are not evident at Chagha Sefid. There is a good possibility, therefore, that the latter site was in a more steppe-like environment, a conclusion that seems to be supported by the plant remains. What is abundantly clear is that the large concentrations of wild leguminous plants that were found at Ali Kosh are not present. On the other hand, specific steppe plants, such as *Prosopis*, which appeared only in the Mohammad Jaffar Phase at Ali Kosh, are found throughout at Chagha Sefid. M. Kirkby has suggested a progressive change in the environment at Ali Kosh which saw the marsh shrinking and steppe vegetation entering.

Under prehistoric conditions the plain saw continual annual flooding as water from the mountain slopes was distributed through a series of shifting, braided channels. Conditions for primitive agriculture could hardly have been better, as the farmers were able to take advantage of locally wet spots for planting their crops. Nevertheless, productive crops depend as much on the timing of precipitation and water flow as they do on the total amount available. In an area of low rainfall and dramatic fluctuations in the timing and amount of precipitation annually, farming is somewhat precarious even under conditions of flooding and aggradation, and during these early phases crops were a supplement to the diet rather than a dependable staple.

We have no way to accurately estimate the sizes of the local groups or their degree of permanence. The mud-brick houses at Ali Kosh appear to be somewhat more substantial than the structures at Chagha Sefid in the Ali Kosh Phase, but the very restricted exposures of each are hardly sufficient to permit definitive statements on this point. There are no extensive exposures of architecture until the late Sefid and Surkh phases. Although the rooms were founded on stone they appear to have had walls and roofs of perishable material. There is very little evidence of the use of mud brick walling, except as spacers and a few courses of capping over the stones. In all, the domestic architecture looks very insubstantial and quite likely was occupied only seasonally.

At Chagha Sefid there is evidence that the settlement shifted somewhat over the surface of the mound. Thus one can hardly use the overall surface area to calculate the total population. We did not systematically sample the site to determine the periods during which various parts were occupied, nor would this have given us a realistic estimate of the total number of persons resident. My overriding impression is that the population was small and that its size may have varied considerably from year to year, if our reconstruction of the pattern of life is accurate.

During the dry farming era there is no suggestion in either dwellings or in burials at either site of differences in status. Personal ornamentation is common on burials at Ali Kosh, and less so at Chagha Sefid, but the differences are not striking and the same kinds of ornaments occur in both sites. The finely made alabaster phallus and "bells" at Ali Kosh are evidence of access to finely made crafts but the significance of this is hard to assess at the present time.

What we see in general during this era is a picture of people who are practicing a combination of farming, herding, hunting and gathering in proportions that probably relate more to local circumstances than to fundamental differences among villagers in their ways of life.

That these people had contacts with other areas is certain. What is not certain is the nature of these contacts. Among products derived from the mountains are obsidian, copper, turquoise, basalt, and the cereal grains themselves. Contact with neighboring lowland regions is seen in the alabaster objects, sea shells and stray sherds. Still, the immediate geographic sphere within which these people operated seems restricted (on the basis of ceramics) largely to the Zagros and perhaps the Mandali plain in eastern Iraq. Interestingly, there are quite noticeable differences in ceramics in Khuzistan itself, at least in the limited quantity that I have been able to see. Tentatively I would postulate that the Saimarreh/Karkheh river system roughly bounds the limits of Deh Luran style artifacts to the south and east. To the north and west, similar material is found as far as Jarmo, near Sulamaniyah.

ALI KOSH PHASE
7200–6400 B.C.

Deposits of this phase have now been excavated at Ali Kosh and at Chagha Sefid, thus providing us with information on intersite variation, and serving to confirm our previous stratigraphic sequence. As nearly as we can tell, there is no occupation at Chagha Sefid earlier than the Ali Kosh Phase, although there remains a possibility that such an occupation might be found under a part of the site which we did not examine. We did not dig a great deal of this phase at Chagha Sefid and this may account for the lack of certain kinds of artifacts, although, in general, the assemblages are very similar.

Chagha Sefid seems to have been occupied somewhat later than Ali Kosh, although in both instances the sites were placed upon the sterile sands and gravels of the Pleistocene surface of the plain. Following M. Kirkby's analysis, we can surmise that settlers at Chagha Sefid chose a well-drained and slightly elevated surface on which to settle. From the start the people constructed houses of mud or mud brick, founded directly on sterile soil. These structures consisted of rectangular rooms, on the order of 2x3 meters in area, arranged in clusters. We do not have the complete plan of any of these houses, and no features were found in place on the floors. In some instances, roasting or parching ovens were set into the corners of the rooms, and, rarely, floors were plastered.

The style of the structures in the two sites is somewhat different, as can be readily seen by comparing the plans (Fig. 6; Hole, Flannery and Neely, 1969:Fig. 10). The extent to which these are real differences, however, remains to be determined by more extensive digging. These differences will be discussed more fully below.

Preliminary study of the animal bones indicates that the people at Chagha Sefid were much more oriented toward herding than their counterparts at Ali Kosh. This difference is also seen in the rarity of hunted or collected animals at Chagha Sefid, where it appears that domestic animals provided the bulk of the meat diet. At this time there is no evidence of domestication other than of the caprines, who comprise up to 95 percent of the faunal remains.

Seeds also show some differences in the two sites, although the crops are basically similar. The staple cereal diet was provided by emmer wheat and barley, but at Chagha Sefid, there are significant quantities of 6-row barley, along with the 2-row variety. According to Helbaek (1969) 6-row barley requires more water and is especially suited to irrigation agriculture on the Deh Luran plain. The presence of this crop can probably be explained by the local hydrology. At places on the prehistoric plain, natural run-off via the braided distributaries would have approximated the conditions of irrigation. Such places may have existed around Chagha Sefid and not around Ali Kosh.

At the same time it is clear that the settlers were collecting *Prosopis*, a steppe plant that is related to dry conditions as well as to grazing. Its use is not apparent at Ali Kosh until the Mohammad Jaffar Phase, again very likely pointing to specific differences in local environments. The villagers at Chagha Sefid were also bringing foods back from the mountains, as the presence of almonds attests. Wild legumes were also collected, although not in the quantity that we found at Ali Kosh.

Although the chipped stone tool kit is based on small blades and is both numerous and varied, it shows some differences from that at Ali Kosh. The most apparent difference is that there are relatively fewer blades at Chagha Sefid, even though these tools are still twice as numerous as all other tools combined; at Ali Kosh they were nearly five times as numerous. Obsidian, which was found to be about two percent of the chipped stone at Ali Kosh, is about one percent at Chagha Sefid.

The grinding stones are of the same types at both sites, but there is somewhat less variation in style at Chagha Sefid. A basic inventory of metates, manos, pestles, pounders and hammerstones, used in the preparation of food is present. The remainder of the artifacts shows the same pattern: there are no types at Chagha Sefid that are not found at Ali Kosh, but the quantity and variety of types at the former site is somewhat less than at Ali Kosh. Certain of these differences are probably related to very specific activities. For example, at Ali Kosh we found numerous pebble choppers associated with the butchering of animals. The animals at Chagha Sefid were more often cut apart rather than chopped and this may reflect the more common hunting of large game at Ali Kosh. Differences of this sort are interesting in regard to varying strategies of subsistence but they can hardly be considered fundamental in the overall developments in Deh Luran.

MOHAMMAD JAFFAR PHASE
6400–6100 B.C.

Our exposure of this phase was limited at Chagha Sefid because our primary interest was in linking it with later material. Accordingly, James Neely dug well into Mohammad Jaffar Phase deposits in Area B and then terminated that part of the excavations. Although it was assumed that this material would also turn up in the main trench, this proved not to be the case.

The Mohammad Jaffar material at Chagha Sefid which has been excavated is apparently somewhat later than the variety found at Ali Kosh. This seems clear from an examination of the ceramics, although the possibility of some differences between these roughly contemporaneous sites should not be disregarded. Still there is enough evidence of similarity to justify calling both assemblages Mohammad Jaffar.

As a matter of record it should be noted that on our reexamination of Ali Kosh in 1969, we found sherds on the surface after the very heavy winter rains which suggest that the site did have a later Mohammad Jaffar and even a Sefid Phase occupation on it. If this is the case, most of the traces have since been eroded so that few if any of them remain intact for excavation. It is also clear now that the few "foreign-looking" wares in a basically Mohammad Jaffar style are of a type we call Sefid Painted, a late Mohammad Jaffar ware. We also found a few early buff wares (Hole and Flannery, 1962) which can now be related to the Choga Mami Transitional Phase at Chagha Sefid.

At neither site is there enough architecture to give a good impression of its characteristics. It seems very likely, however, that the practice of founding walls on rows of stones began at this time. In other respects we can only assume that the houses were similar to those found in the Ali Kosh and Sefid phases.

The Mohammad Jaffar Phase is distinguished principally by the occurrence of ceramics for the first time in our sequence. In all cases these wares are relatively friable, chaff-tempered and often painted with designs in fugitive red ochre. In overall composition, the wares at the two sites are similar but there are some specific differences that we attribute to chronological differences between the two sites. Most striking is the relative lack of Khazineh Red at Chagha Sefid; this can hardly be attributed to differences in time since it was very abundant at Ali Kosh and at Chagha Sefid in the Sefid Phase. It is most likely to be explained by the very small exposure at Chagha Sefid which did not give us an adequate sample of the contents of this phase.

More likely to be chronological are the differences in the shapes of the vessels and the introduction of Sefid Painted. The earliest ceramics in western Iran are usually flat-bottomed, but at Chagha Sefid we find a higher proportion of rounded bottomed vessels than at Ali Kosh. This is taken to be a normal development that is paralleled elsewhere. We also note a change in the technique and style of painting. Sefid Painted consists of Mohammad Jaffar shapes and designs but the surfaces of the vessels have a cream slip on which red paint is applied. The paint on these well-fired wares is not fugitive and the designs are much sharper and brighter looking than the earlier varieties. During the Mohammad Jaffar Phase the designs are in the style of the other ceramics, but during the Sefid Phase there are notable differences, thus establishing a convenient point at which to divide the sequence.

At Chagha Sefid we find the same general set of stone tools as before and again the proportion of plain blades at Chagha Sefid is about half of what it is at Ali Kosh. Still, blades at Chagha Sefid are three times as numerous as all other tools. Somewhat surprising is the rapid jump in the proportion of obsidian, which now accounts for about eight percent of the chipped stone; at Ali Kosh it was nearly 2 percent. Colin Renfrew (Appendix II) suggests that the two sites had differential access to a limited supply of obsidian although the evidence may also reflect the fact that we are dealing with a later aspect of the phase at Chagha Sefid. Supporting this latter contention is the fact that trapezoidal geometrics account for one percent of the tools, whereas they were not found in situ in deposits at Ali Kosh.

There is presently no report on the seeds from this phase at Chagha Sefid, but a review of the circumstances at Ali Kosh is useful. We had surmised that the quality of the land surrounding that site was deteriorating as evidenced by the presence of steppe vegetation, particularly *Prosopis*. Michael Kirkby suggests that this may reflect gradually changing hydrologic conditions as the wave of alluviation encroached upon the site and the marsh gradually dried up. In other words it may have been natural factors rather than land use that were reflected in the presence of these plants. In any case, it now seems apparent that Ali Kosh was not entirely abandoned after the Mohammad Jaffar Phase, but, because of erosion, the extent to which it was occupied later cannot be determined with any accuracy.

SEFID PHASE
6300–5900 B.C.

This phase, found only at Chagha Sefid, is a direct development out of the Mohammad Jaffar and is defined chiefly by its characteristic ceramics.

Both Jaffar Plain and Khazineh Red continue from previous phases and to these are added four new types: Sefid Red-on-Cream, Sefid Black-on-Cream, Sefid Burnished, and Sefid Black Painted. The earlier Sefid Painted has run its course by this time. We find in the Sefid Phase that Khazineh Red assumes the proportion that we had anticipated it would from our findings at Ali Kosh and Tepe Sabz. As the sample of material from this phase is large, and at least half of the amount dug is in midden, I feel that we have an excellent idea of the total range of variation among these types.

There are also notable differences in architecture. In particular, we find that buildings and rooms are now founded almost exclusively on stone. This is not true in the earliest traces of Sefid Phase architecture, but by its terminal period, all buildings are founded on stone. The earliest traces of buildings continue in exactly the same tradition as those of the Ali Kosh Phase at Chagha Sefid. However, above a three meter accumulation of midden, we find late Sefid Phase houses founded on stone and in a somewhat different architectural pattern.

Although the traces of this architecture are not very extensive, there is repeated use of a complex that includes a paved area surrounded by small rectangular rooms, some of whose floors are plastered. In spite of the apparent effort entailed in constructing the pavements and wall foundations, there is little evidence of brick architecture above them. The evidence clearly seems to suggest the use of perishable walling and roofing, except in the lowermost courses. Rectangular rooms about 2-3 meters by 3-4 meters are suggested by the remains we have. Another feature that recurs throughout the upper Sefid and Surkh phases is the plaster basin. These implements are most often set into what look like open corridors, although some are found within rooms as well. It is not clear just how these basins were used, although some kind of food processing is suggested.

Within the houses we continue to find the large oval roasting pits or parching ovens set into the corners of rooms. Similar ovens are found at nearly every site of this general period. Somewhat surprising is the lack of any small hearths of the type that might have been used for cooking and heating.

The most striking architectural features are the brick platforms. There are two of these, one each in the Sefid and Surkh phases. These platforms are built of large mud bricks up to a height of about 1.5 meters. The example in the Sefid Phase is about 7 by 10 meters. As far as we can determine at this time, this structure was free-standing in the vicinity of the multi-room houses and oriented the same as the houses.

Although the settlement pattern can hardly be definitively determined on the basis of our present exposures, they suggest a community of small, multi-room houses separated from one another by corridors about two meters wide, with larger open spaces and middens nearby. In the midst of these was a free-standing brick platform. Considerable permanence in residence is implied by the frequent rebuildings of the same structures. In the case of the house with plastered floors, it looks very much as if plaster was renewed on an annual basis. This would be expected if the superstructure were removed annually during transhumant treks.

Most of the artifacts show continuity with preceding phases, but the first real change in chipped stone occurs at this time. This is seen chiefly in the rarity of the various geometric forms that characterized earlier phases. In their place we find that trapezoidal geometrics are now the common form of projectile tip. We also find for the first time a number of implements chipped from crystal, although this material is always rare. Plain blades continue their decline; they are now only about twice as numerous as other tools, and obsidian has dropped to 5 percent. Actually obsidian occurs in variable quantities in the different subsegments of the Sefid Phase and is 7 percent in the last; it is rarely found thereafter.

SURKH PHASE
5900–5400 B.C.

Villagers of the Surkh Phase continued to use the relatively small, stone-founded, multi-room houses, but also had considerably larger rooms. These latter, up to 5 meters long and nearly 3 meters wide, stand in sharp contrast to the small rooms, which are usually no more than 2x3 meters. At least some of these rooms contain fireplaces and plaster basins, suggesting that they are for domestic purposes. If this is so it leaves in doubt the uses of the other rooms which are clustered together in groups of four to six. We are severely hampered in our interpretation by the facts that material was not left in the rooms and that floors could not be recognized.

The general pattern of settlement continues to suggest, as it did in the Sefid Phase, a series of closely-spaced housing units separated by narrow corridors and midden areas. Again there is no trace of permanent superstructures over the stone foundations, and there is considerable evidence of repeated rebuildings on the same general plans as the mound accumulated.

Continuing previous tradition we find both fireplaces, now with flat stone bases, and plaster basins. Both of these are sometimes found inside rooms, although basins often occur in corridors outside the houses.

Especially noteworthy in this phase are the brick pavements and the platform, which is similar to the one in the Sefid Phase. The brick pavements appear to be about room-size and are sometimes built on or within the confines of rooms. These occur in several styles. The earliest is made of normal wall bricks, while the later ones are of elongate, cigar-shaped bricks. Our exposures are too small to suggest how they relate to the overall configuration of the house units.

The large brick platform, found in the late Surkh Phase was, like its earlier counterpart, apparently free-standing. Unlike the earlier version, it was built first of a core of soft, ashy mud bricks and then capped over with dense yellow clay bricks. Nothing in association with either structure gives a clue as to its use.

Architecturally there is little to distinguish the

Sefid and Surkh phases; rather their most striking characteristics—the use of stone foundations and the platforms and pavements—appear to separate both these phases from the earlier Mohammad Jaffar, Ali Kosh and Bus Mordeh. Platforms occur in both phases and it is likely that pavements would also be found in the Sefid if enough area were excavated. In both there are plaster basins and fireplaces, the latter set into the corners of rooms.

Most clearly distinguishing the two phases are the ceramics. At this time Khazineh Red makes up 84 percent of all sherds. There are no new types, but Sefid Red-on-Cream and Sefid Burnished are no longer found. Thus the number of types in use drops from six to four. This change is not absolutely abrupt, as can be seen in the analysis of the pottery. What the present figures reflect are relative proportions of the occurrence of sherds throughout the zones that make up the Surkh Phase. Certain types which are found in the Sefid Phase and which occur in small numbers in the early Surkh Phase collectively make up less than one percent of the total Surkh Phase wares; consequently they are said to be no longer present.

It is useful to consider the changes in proportions of the types. Jaffar Plain, which in the Sefid Phase was 6 percent, has now increased to 10 percent. This increase is spurious in the sense that there are more types in the Sefid Phase and consequently any single type is likely to be a smaller part of the total than it is in the Surkh Phase. This is especially true of this particular ware because all of the other types are red wares, often, in contrast with Jaffar Plain, breaking into very small pieces. The other types, however, do show trends that we would expect. Khazineh Red increases from 57 percent in the Sefid Phase to 84 percent, Sefid Black-on-Cream drops from 8 to 4 percent and Sefid Black Painted from 7 to 2 percent.

Vessels themselves have a tendency to become larger as time passes. This is especially noticeable after the Mohammad Jaffar Phase and is seen in the very large spouted vessels found in the Sefid and Surkh phases, although, of course, small containers continue to be used.

Among the chipped stone tools, the trends established earlier continue in the Surkh Phase. Plain blades are now little more than half of the chipped stone, obsidian has dropped to one percent, and there is still some crystal. New types, truncated sickles and backed blades, both of which will gain in popularity in succeeding phases, make their first appearance. Trapezes are still the only form of geometric found.

The remaining inventory of tools is very much like the Sefid Phase. The major exception is that there are no longer any shallow basin or trough metates, nor are there combination rolling handstones and pestles. In view of the great numbers of grinding stones that were found in wall foundations, these omissions are probably an accurate reflection of the tools in use at the time. Thus, once again, we see a general decline in the types of implements employed for household activities. By this time the tool inventory was near to the minimum necessary if the people were to continue their mixed agricultural and pastoral economy.

Choga Mami Transitional and Sabz Phases

With these phases we see a fundamental change in subsistence practices which we have characterized as the "era of irrigation agriculture and cattle domestication." At Chagha Sefid we still do not have definitive evidence of this change because of the relatively small exposures at our disposal; however, such practices are attested to at Choga Mami itself and at Tepe Sabz. This change to an apparent emphasis on farming at the expense of herding is reflected in a marked decline in the amount of meat consumed, from both domestic and wild stock. In view of the history of this region, stretching from the late Pleistocene, this shift in diet is remarkable indeed, and presages modern conditions in which most villagers live nearly exclusively on cereals, supplemented with dairy products and minor amounts of meat.

To be sure such a change may be of only local importance at this time if we consider Southwest Asia as a whole; yet the overall increases of population that are evidenced by the multiplicity of small villages may, even by this time, have strained the limits of the area to regenerate sufficient livestock to maintain the human populations. A far higher proportion of an area's potential can be realized by first replacing inedible plants with domesticated cereals, and then taking animals out of competition for the edible plants which man can consume more efficiently directly. To pass them through an animal intermediary is to lose much of the potential energy, however palatable the final product may be.

One can view a shift toward intensive farming, with the use of improved races of grains, which are more productive than their primitive counterparts, and the systematic use of artificially channeled water to supplement the irregular winter rainfall, as a successful device to increase the yield from the environment. The effects of this change should be noticeable in population increases and, depending on local circumstances, probably in changes in the accumulation and consumption of wealth, and in settlement pattern and social organization.

The central assumption that we make is that quite different social arrangements are enabled by the two subsistence orientations: mixed dry farming, herding and extensive consumption of meat; and irrigation agriculture with increasing emphasis on cereals rather than animals in the diet. The fundamental difference comes about largely in the implied specialization which places a very high value on one component of the diet. If this component fails, the people are in a much more dangerous situation than if they had retained the "two strings to their bow" and had been able to fall back upon consumption of ample herds. Such a system also puts higher priority on land of a particular type and quality and, along with the requirements of storage, these facts suggest the desirability of permanent and substantial residence. Finally, efficient, intensive agriculture is seasonally labor intensive, both for the maintenance of fields and canals, and in the harvesting and threshing of the yields. Perhaps the use of cattle in agriculture for trampling fields, plowing, and threshing should also be considered here. These various factors collectively suggest that multi-family, landholding cooperatives are a logical, if not necessary, organization.

Historic documents, as well as limited archeological data, point toward a form of "landed estate," the latter evidence taking us back to Samarran times when large, multi-room, multi-family(?) houses and storerooms were characteristic. To a somewhat lesser degree this is shown at Choga Mami where the houses are only slightly smaller. The implications of these presumed shifts in diet, social organization, and land tenure are obvious in any consideration of the emergence of urbanism little more than a millenium later.

What remains unclear, assuming this suggested pattern to have been widespread in locally favorable places, is what is happening concomitantly in areas where dry farming is both possible and productive and where high mountain pastures are available and perhaps not yet fully exploited. Modern excavations have tended to ignore sites that would be relevant to this problem.

As far as Deh Luran itself is concerned, it appears that some portions of the plain were suitable for the kind of intensive agricultural economy I have described. Both Chagha Sefid and Tepe Sabz have substantial remains of this era, although neither has been dug extensively. There is also evidence of other sites at this time, the most noteworthy of which is Musiyan, the largest site on the plain.

In discussing the results of our excavations I raised a number of hypotheses which might account for our archeological evidence and concluded that irrigation and intensive farming entered the local scene with the Choga Mami Transitional. Still in question is what happened to the original population. Did they adopt the artifacts and life style of the people from eastern Mesopotamia? Did they abandon sites where intensive cultivation could be practiced and continue their previous methods of dry farming and herding elsewhere on the plain? Did they give up farming and use the plain only seasonally as fully transhumant herders who entered into symbiotic relations with the newly settled irrigation agriculturalists? Were the locals annihilated totally, or forced completely out of the area, leaving no tangible traces? There are many possibilities of this kind which remain matters for future investigation. Whatever the outcome may be, we have an important instance of cultural dynamics evidenced in the sites on the Deh Luran Plain.

CHOGA MAMI TRANSITIONAL
5400–5100 B.C.

The name of this phase is unfortunately cumbersome, yet it accurately fulfills the criteria of naming phases: that they refer to local circumstances and that they be recognizable in their artifacts. The term is derived from Joan Oates' work at Choga Mami and was suggested to me by her for what I had called the "pre-Sabz Phase" in my preliminary assessment of the site (Hole, 1969). This phase is presently recorded only at Choga Mami and at Chagha Sefid among the excavated sites in Deh Luran, but it is found in surface collections near Warka (Adams and Nissen, 1972:174-175), and my surface collections from Susiana suggest similar material at several sites. Nevertheless, the most conspicuous resemblances are to be found in the three sites first mentioned. This apparent widespread distribution is most remarkable and is presently susceptible to different interpretations.

The phase is clearly distinguished by its ceramics which are basically a form of buff ware, notable for its gritty texture and relatively crude geometric designs. There is an evident antecedent to it in the Samarran in northern Mesopotamia, but not in Deh Luran, nor in southern Mesopotamia. In Deh Luran alone, apparently, there is also a ware, Sialk Black-on-Red, which is very similar to wares from the eponymous site which our group picked up on the surface. Interestingly, at Sialk itself there are buff wares in the same deposit (Sialk I, which are reminiscent of the general class of Samarran ceramics.

Our exposure at Chagha Sefid is too small to make the association of all the types of pottery absolutely certain, since the possibility of mixtures of various types cannot be entirely ruled out. Nevertheless, there seems to be a high proportion of Khazineh Red, some Jaffar Plain, a low proportion of Sefid Black-on-Cream and the Susiana Black-on-Buff with the characteristic designs of this phase, Susiana Plain and some Sialk Black-on-Red. Thus we see an increase in types from four to six with the appearance of the Choga Mami Transitional.

At Choga Mami there is little red ware; this always appears to be a specifically Iranian trait, a point that has been made by various authors in describing the entire Susiana sequence. What we seem to have is the intrusion of ceramics derived from Iraq and their addition to the local inventory of wares which continues from the previous phases.

The second striking change with this phase is seen in the architecture. We have already mentioned the use of cigar-shaped bricks in the Surkh Phase for pavements, but not, so far as we can tell, for houses themselves at that point. Similar bricks are found in the Samarran at both Choga Mami and Sawwan. With the Choga Mami Transitional, however, we find the use of finger impressed cigar-shaped bricks and these are found also at Choga Mami at the same time.

What is more impressive than the similarity in bricks at the two sites, however, is the presence, for the first time in our Deh Luran sequence, of substantial brick houses. Now we have walls standing a meter or more high, walls of rooms that are not founded on rows of stones. Thus both the style of architecture and its implied permanence changes dramatically from previous phases. As only one room, which is probably part of a multi-room structure, has been dug so far, we cannot offer any evidence in support of other settlement similarities.

The chipped stone tools show some changes as well, for the first time really presaging the Sabz Phase. This is seen primarily in the proportion of retouched and used flakes which now exceeds that of retouched and used blades. This is an indication of the trend toward sloppier chipping techniques, and also reflects the lesser importance of activities that go with the extensive use of blades. Evidence of subsistence suggests that the broad spectrum farming, herding, hunting and collecting that characterizes earlier periods required far more blades. As time passes we find fewer and fewer of these implements, a fact which is likely related to a gradually changing emphasis in basic subsistence and in the uses to which animals are put. Plain blades are now about one half of all tools, there is a little obsidian, and trapezes continue to be the only geometrics. To an even greater extent than in the Surkh Phase we see a reduction in the variety of ground stone and other tools. In a sense this is truly a transitional phase in that we find the last uses of naturalistic figurines, most ornaments and some of the artifacts associated with butchering.

Although the data on fauna and seeds are not yet available, a preliminary study of the bones suggests the presence of domestic cattle and dogs, and a dog painted on a sherd is further evidence. These species have also been reported from Tell es-Sawwan. Seeds from Sawwan, Choga Mami and Tepe Sabz all indicate the use of hybrid races of the cereals and strongly suggest the practice of irrigation. Even without adequate samples of seeds from Chagha Sefid, there is scarcely reason to assume a different agricultural orientation.

SABZ PHASE
5200–5000 B.C.

With the Sabz Phase we have in all likelihood the local crystallization of an irrigation adaptation. No longer can we consider it transitional. As far as we can tell there were no further fundamental changes in the subsistence, although adjustments were made to accommodate a changing environment or other circumstances.

The Sabz Phase is revealed in our excavation at Chagha Sefid in only the fragmentary remains of a stone-founded house and a few cubic meters of material in situ. Nevertheless, characteristic Sabz Phase ceramics clearly overlie those of the Choga Mami Transitional and these herald the onset of the Sabz Phase.

By this time the Sefid wares have run their course although there is still some Jaffar Plain and Khazineh Red. Predominant, however, is the Susiana Black-on-Buff, with lesser quantities of Susiana Plain Buff and Sialk Black-on-Red. The latter type does not occur at Tepe Sabz and more extensive excavation of the deposits at Chagha Sefid may reveal that the few sherds of this type were intrusive from the underlying levels. The Sabz pottery is noted for its gritty feel, although it is fired harder than the earlier ware and sometimes has designs "burned" into the clay through overfiring.

For a complete description of the characteristics of this phase readers should refer to Hole, Flannery and Neely (1969:354-358). Although at Chagha Sefid our material is limited, there are some notable changes from earlier phases. First there is a great reduction in tool types. This tendency has been noted in earlier phases but it amounts to a near discontinuity at this time. This raises the question of whether some material in the Choga Mami Transitional may have been redeposited. That this is probably not the case is suggested by Mortensen's (1973) study of the flints from Choga Mami. Essentially the same material was found there that we report from Chagha Sefid. Thus the abrupt change with the advent of the Sabz Phase underscores the crystallization of new ways. It is a culmination of trends, yet it is also a rapid termination of the lingering traces of former practices. From this time onward, indigenous flint chipping is more remarkable for its crudity than for its quality. To some degree this must reflect a lessened demand for blades with the new subsistence practices; however, the fact that "imported" blades occur in the Mehmeh and Bayat phases suggests that craftsmen who could produce the desired product were no longer available locally.

In other categories of artifacts, much the same thing is seen. Figurines essentially disappear and there are few ornaments. On the other hand chipped and polished celts (hoes?) become common, as do spindle whorls and perforated stones (loom weights? digging stick weights?).

With the limited material at our disposal we are able to perceive trends through time and to see how certain new agricultural requirements are met through the invention and perfection of tools like hoes. As well, we may be getting the first glimpses of specialization in crafts like weaving, ceramics and possibly others. Until we have dug extensively enough to recover the plans of settlements and have been able to study intrasite variation, we shall have only the most ephemeral glimpses. I think we now know what to look for and we have the techniques which will enable us to recover and analyze data from crucial periods. Until we have done so it is fruitless to speculate further on the wider implications of our data.

Part 2. Excavation and Analysis

IV

STRATIGRAPHY AND ARCHITECTURE

Chagha Sefid is an impressive mound visible from nearly any point on the Deh Luran plain if the weather and light are good (Pl. 1). Its first recorded mention is on the French map of the Deh Luran plain (Gautier and Lampre, 1905:Fig. 94), although there is no record that it was archeologically tested during the seasons of work at Musiyan, Mohammad Jaffar (Ali Kosh) and Khazineh. Neither did the French work at Farukhabad, the highest site in the western portion of the plain. This neglect by French workers may have reflected the control of part of the plain by the Wali of Pusht-i-Kuh whose fort, built in 1908 (Lorimer, 1908:17), lies in ruins today atop Chagha Sefid and gives the site an added elevation that gleams white on a sunny day.

The roughly oval mound has maximum dimensions today of about 165 by 120 meters. Its shape is at least in part due to erosion of the west side by a channel that floods seasonally after heavy rains (Fig. 1 and Pl. 2). Examination of the banks of this channel reveals architecture and artifacts; thus it is clear that the prehistoric site was somewhat more extensive than it appears today. Today the site covers a little more than 2 hectares of surface. The mound rises some sixteen meters above the present land surface and is topped by the white plastered fort that gives the site its name. We now know that the base of the site is 3.5 to 5 meters below the modern surface (Fig. 2). Our excavation totaled about 18 meters in vertical depth, all of which is prehistoric. The top of the site may have been planed off and in some places filled to provide a suitable base for the building of the fort.

While the site is large in comparison with other prehistoric sites on the plain, it is not large when one considers that it was occupied for an estimated 3500 years. Assuming continuous occupation it took about 240 years to accumulate each meter, approximately the same rate as at Ali Kosh but considerably faster than at Tepe Sabz. As we shall discuss later, the rate of accumulation is related to the nature of the houses and the size of occupation.

Chagha Sefid lies a little more than 1.5 kilometers southwest of the town of Deh Luran which sits at the lower end of the alluvial fan that was always the site of the largest settlements in historic times (Fig. 3, Pl. 3). In this location adequate water, albeit brackish and sulphurous, is perennially available in the Ab-i-Garm to support a modest population and some irrigation of crops. The alluvial fan is well-drained, enabling farmers to subsist today by a combination of dry farming and flood water irrigation (Pl. 4), combined with fallowing. This seems to have been the practice during prehistoric times as well—thus the area around Chagha Sefid has seen agriculture on a nearly continuous basis for some 9000 years.

Except for work done in connection with building the fort in the early 1900s, there appears to have been no recent human disturbance of Chagha Sefid. As nearly as we can tell from surface material the site was not occupied after the early Uruk period, about 3500 B.C.

METHODS OF EXCAVATION

Excavation Techniques

In order to achieve comparability with our results of 1963 we followed basically the same techniques of excavation, the principal difference being that we were able to expose much larger portions of the site horizontally than we had done at either Ali Kosh or at Tepe Sabz. (For a full discussion, the reader is referred to Hole, Flannery and Neely, 1969:23-27.) Our procedures were tailored to the goals we had set: to attempt to complete the early stratigraphic se-

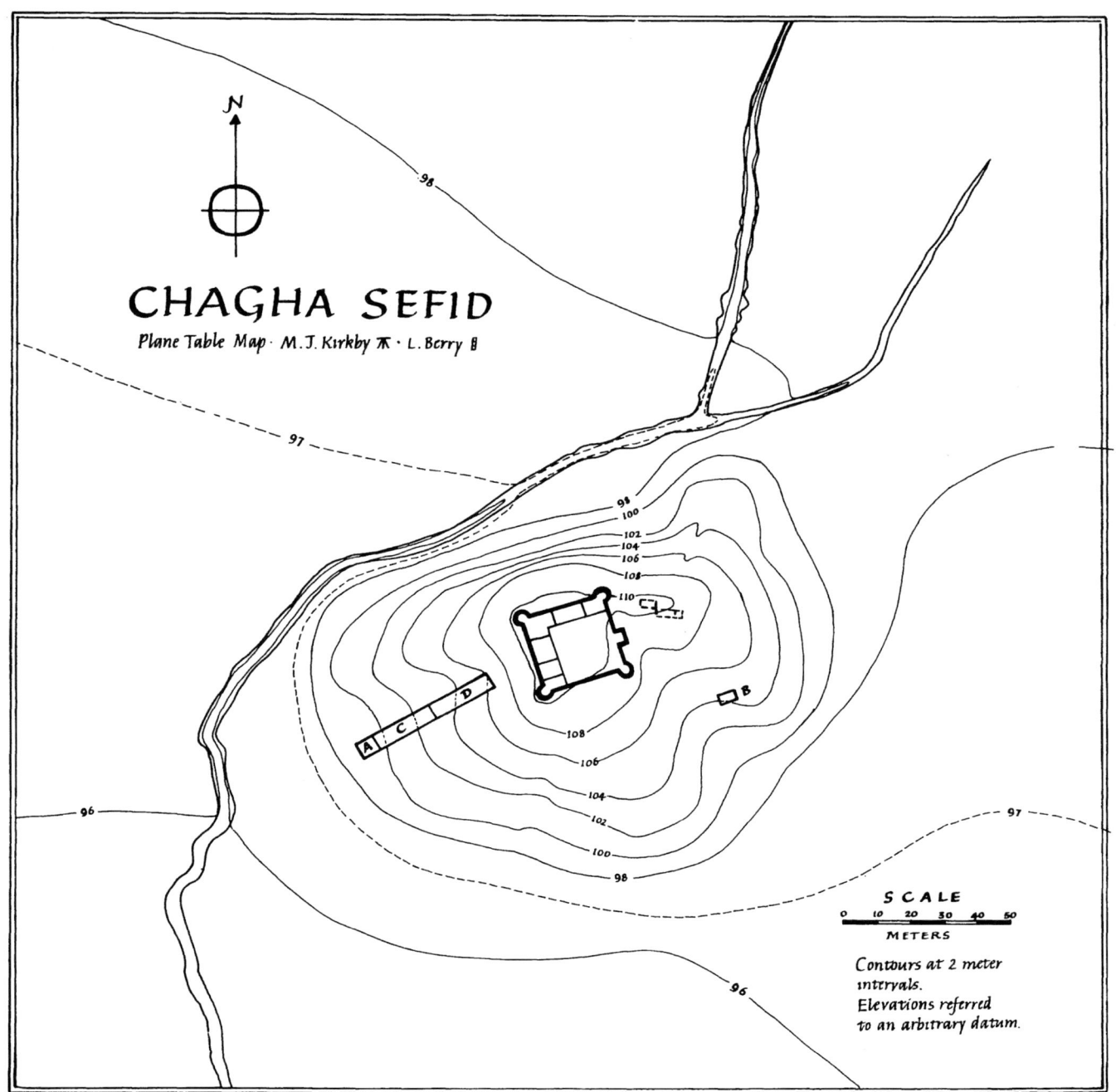

Fig. 1. Topographic map of Chagha Sefid with the excavations in Areas A, C, D and B indicated. The fort on top is largely in ruins.

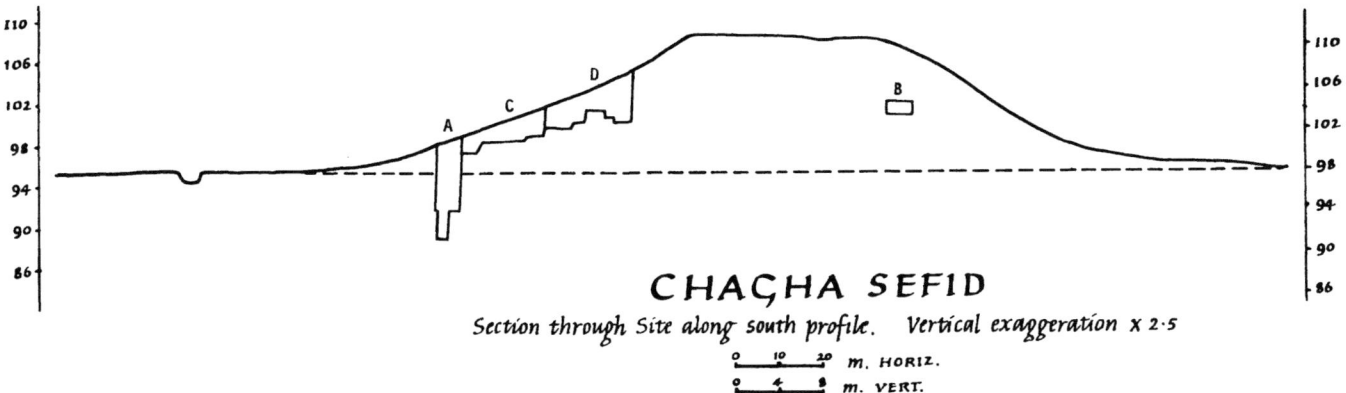

Fig. 2. Section through site along south profile of excavation. The total length of the trench is 45m. Note slope of modern land surface toward the west.

quence and to document in as fine detail as possible the changes between the Mohammad Jaffar and Sabz phases.

Initially we carried out an intensive surface survey of the mound to determine where we might find material of suitable age. We knew from previous surveys in 1961 and 1963 that the site probably contained the material we sought but we were not sure exactly where on the site we should dig. Based on the systematic survey in 1968 we chose two areas, A and B, on the west and south sides respectively, in which to put our initial pits. Since we did not know what kind of remains we would find we elected to begin with small pits (3 x 5 meters) and to enlarge them if the need arose. Neely was in charge of Area B and I was in charge of Area A and, later, Areas C and D.

Our previous experience had demonstrated that digging in one meter squares by arbitrary units of 10-20 centimeters was effective in that it enabled us to readily find the elusive traces of mud walling and also facilitated the recovery and recording of the thousands of small pieces of flint and pottery. When walls or other features were discovered we were then able to proceed systematically to expose them, making use of the one-meter squares to aid in the assignment of digging and in recording but not allowing them to detract from the goal of exposing contemporaneous material horizontally. Rather than digging in alternate squares, as we had done in 1963, we usually dug in adjacent squares, moving systematically over the area.

In view of our experience with mud architecture at Ali Kosh and Tepe Sabz, it may seem surprising that we found relatively little mud walling intact at Chagha Sefid. The problems of finding mud walling in this particular environment remain as described before (Hole, Flannery and Neely, 1969:24) but the simple fact is that most of the walls had been severely eroded by man or nature before new buildings were installed. Fortunately most of the structures had stone foundations but it is probably this same factor of erosion that prevented our finding more walls intact. It appears that stone from earlier foundations was frequently reused in later buildings and in consequence any bricks that lay above were destroyed. In cases where stones were not used under the walls we were often able to find the lower courses of bricks even when the superstructures of the buildings had been leveled. Only rarely did we find bricks in place above the stone foundations. There is no evidence that the stone-founded buildings in the Sefid and Surkh phases ever had solid superstructures. As we discuss later, most of these rooms were probably walled and roofed with poles and thatch or matting.

The system of using one-meter squares also enabled us to move efficiently ahead with test pits to preview the strata to come. Finally, the system was well-adapted to the capabilities of the workmen, who were organized into teams of three: a pickman, a dirt carrier and a screener. Since a large portion of our artifacts were recovered from the screen, it would have been impossible to attempt associational analysis of the artifacts with one another and with the fea-

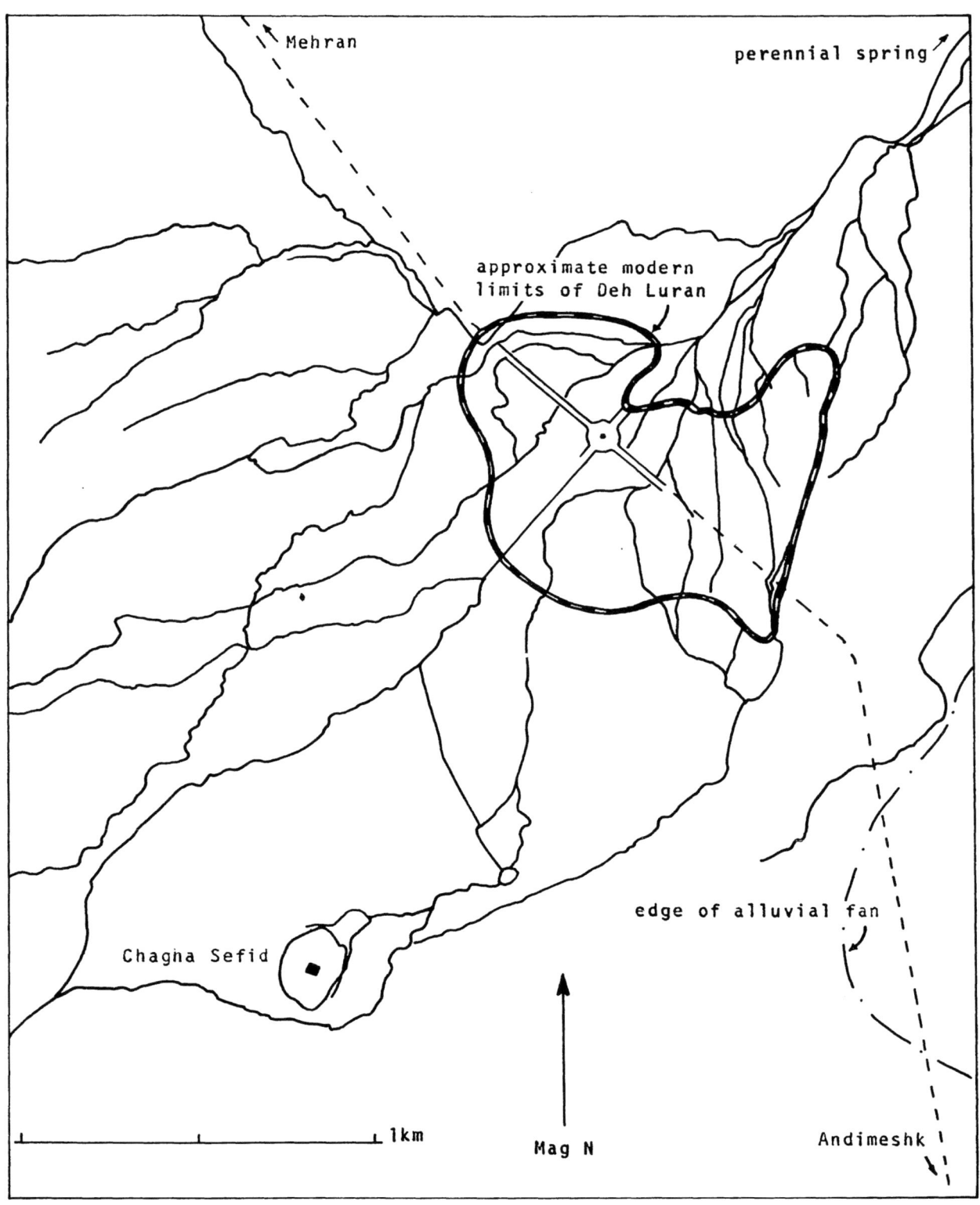

Fig. 3. Chagha Sefid is about 1.5 km southwest of Deh Luran. Water from the perennial spring and seasonal runoff are used to irrigate fields around the site. The courses of the ephemeral streams are changed regularly as they are directed toward planted fields.

tures unless we had strict control over where they came from. This was readily achieved through using one meter squares and teams of men who were responsible for only one such unit each.

Unlike the situation in some excavations, we operated with relatively few supervisors who were often too busy directing and recording the operations to do much digging themselves. We dug only when unusual care was needed or when there was some stratigraphic question that we could only understand by doing the work ourselves. In this way we had two or, rarely, three supervisors working with a total of 6 pickmen and about a dozen other persons on the site. The crews were not large, yet the pace of the work strained the supervisory staff to its fullest unless the digging was in pure midden or was a routine clearing of intrusive material.

The size of our excavation was both useful and detrimental to efficient supervision. When a supervisor was occupied with recording features, drawing profiles, or digging, he could assign his pickmen to a less sensitive area, thus ensuring that the work continued without sacrificing control. Nevertheless, the length of the excavation (ultimately 45 meters) made it necessary to do a lot of walking up and down hill to keep track of what was being done. Fortunately the workmen, although they had been for the most part totally unschooled in digging, were quick to recognize features of interest and to either stop work when they occurred or to call us. Considering the shortage of staff I think we worked out an effective compromise: our work proceeded more slowly than we would have liked, but under the control that we determined was necessary.

The Areas of Excavation

Area A. Opened initially as a 3 x 5 meter pit (Pl. 5a), when we hit stone wall foundations just below the surface we expanded the pit to 5 x 6 meters, and maintained that size down to the bottom, some 7 meters below the surface of the mound. This pit served to link our newly found Sefid Phase with the Mohammad Jaffar and preceramic phases at the bottom of Chagha Sefid.

Area B. Excavated by James Neely with the assistance of Nathalie Berset before he began his survey of the plain, this pit never exceeded 3 x 5 meters (Pl. 1b). After finding Sefid Phase material near the surface, Neely proceeded down until he had a good stratigraphic overlap with the Mohammad Jaffar Phase.

Area C. This area was opened with a 3 x 5 meter pit some 20 meters up-slope from Area A in an attempt to find material of Sabz Phase to which we might tie the Sefid Phase ceramics found below (Pl. 5b). The finding of stone wall foundations led us to open this pit to 5 x 6 meters and later to extend it the total 20 meter length so that we could relate the stratigraphy to our pit in Area A.

Area D. When Area C proved not to have Sabz Phase material as we moved up-slope another 20 meters (Pl. 5b) and opened a 2 x 2 meter pit. This exposed a historic plaster kiln (Pl. 25b) and in order to find any early material we had to enlarge the pit to 5 x 6 meters. When Sabz Phase material was found we continued digging and eventually dug out the entire 20-meter length of the trench, thus linking it with Area C.

In all we dug a trench 45 meters long and 5 meters wide on the west side of the site (Pl. 6). The total depth of deposits uncovered in this modified step trench was 18 meters, including the 3 meter deep erosional gully at the bottom of the site. Much of the material removed from the trench, especially in its upper reaches, was disturbed by erosion and by the digging of later prehistoric peoples. Nonetheless, substantial traces of architecture were found along the entire trench and the stratigraphic relationships of the structures were readily apparent.

In all the excavation areas we opened only a total of 240 square surface meters of deposit or slightly less than one percent of the total surface of the site, and considerably less of the total volume. An estimated 536 cubic meters of deposits with good stratigraphic context were excavated. (Table 4 gives the volume excavated in each zone and phase.)

Stratigraphic Zones and Cultural Phases

As a result of this long stratigraphic sequence we were able to divide the site into a series of zones that was based on stratigraphic and architectural changes. The material from each of these zones (and its subdivisions) was analyzed separately and forms the basis of our discussion of the changes in the sequence.

Table 4
VOLUME (IN CUBIC METERS) OF DEPOSIT
EXCAVATED AT CHAGHA SEFID

Area	Zone	Volume	Phase	Volume
SD	J	2.30	Sabz	3.60
SD	I	1.30		
SD	H	20.80	Choga Mami Transitional	83.90
SD	G2	20.70		
SD	G1	42.40		
SD	F	48.90	Surkh	206.50
SD, SC	E2	27.90		
SD, SC	E1	40.70		
SC	D3	9.60		
SC	D2	31.40		
SC	D1	13.90		
SC	C2	34.10		
SA	C1	43.70	Sefid	148.90
SA	B2	63.90		
SA	B1	30.30		
SA	A4	11.00		
SB	C	7.50	Mohammad Jaffar	22.50
SB	B	9.00		
SB	A	6.00		
SA	A3	17.15	Ali Kosh	70.60
SA	A2	19.45		
SA	A1	34.00		
			Total	536.00

Following analysis of the material we were then able, as we did in 1963 (Hole, Flannery and Neely, 1969:27-28), to group the zones into cultural phases, each of which is characterized by a particular assemblage of material: architecture, artifacts, seeds and bones. In this way we have defined 3 new phases in the Deh Luran sequence that fit between the Mohammad Jaffar Phase as found at Ali Kosh and the Sabz Phase as found at Tepe Sabz.

We are under no illusions that we have discovered all the variations within each phase nor are we certain we have divided them in a final form. Only further excavation of contemporary sites will tell us whether any of the sites we have dug is "typical" and whether there are major variations in, or additions to, the inventory of material that we have found in our rather restricted exposures. Nevertheless, as we document in the discussions of artifacts, the evidence for essential continuity is impressive and there are no longer any disjunctions in the sequence to be accounted for.

The excavation of a site whose strata lie so closely on top of one another presents problems in analysis that are difficult to control. We know, for example, that material is often brought from the surface to the base of the site through the action of burrowing rodents and this factor has probably been operative throughout the occupation of the site. Thus, this factor alone will inevitably cause mixing of deposits that appear to be undisturbed. Often it is possible to trace rodent burrows but this is not always the case. Also, in this site as in almost all others, the prehistoric inhabitants dug into earlier deposits for mud, for bricks, and stones for wall foundations and for burial pits. These factors inevitably introduce older material into later deposits and later material into older strata. The extent of this kind of mixing is probably not severe, especially when one treats the occurrence of various types of artifacts as percentages. In the delineation of phases I have assumed that any mixing which I was unable to detect is *relatively* unimportant but this assumption can only be tested by finding deposits that are unequivocally undisturbed. Such contexts would be found most often in sites where material is preserved on floors, especially in burned rooms. In the absence of burned rooms, and even of floors in the usual sense, I have treated material within the confines of rooms and between layers of rooms as contemporaneous. The zones are thus distinguished by building or midden layers and the material found in the layers is considered representative of these zones.

DEPOSITIONAL HISTORY — WEST TRENCH

The Sterile Surface of the Plain

Perhaps as early as the first settlement at Chagha Sefid, the Mehmeh and Dawairij rivers had begun a process of alluviation that continued until around 2000 B.C. Under these conditions the water table was several meters higher than today and the plain was subject to more widespread flooding through a series of braided, unstable, and frequently shifting river courses that tended to produce a broad, fan-shaped area of relatively high water table near the mountains.

Although the date of the inception of this regime of alluviation is uncertain, it is clear that the three sites we have dug (as well as Choga Mami in Iraq and Tula'i in Susiana) have similar sediments underlying them directly below the first occupations. These sediments, consisting of layers of white sand, heavy clay and gravel, suggest deposition under quite different conditions than characterize the plain today. Today, save on the alluvial fan at the town of Deh Luran, there are 3-6 meters of fine grained alluvium above the basal sands and gravels, which is now being cut by the seasonal channels that drain toward the perennial rivers. These rivers are now incised 5-10 meters below the surface of the plain. A basic change in the character of sedimentation is evident soon after each of the sites was founded if we assume that the villagers derived the mud for their house walls from the immediate vicinity of the site. Our evidence for the use of clay walling is found at the base of Ali Kosh, the earliest of the sites. After that time, fine grained mud and midden soils were used for bricks and the mud surfacing of walls.

It seems reasonable, although it is not yet proven, that the sites were each founded on sandy knolls which afforded a relatively well-drained base for houses, but allowed access to wetter depressed areas next to the site for agriculture and to mud for construction. If this is the case, the sediments under the sites remained as depositional relicts of a period of rapid stream flow that left bank sands and point bars scattered across the plain, long after the sedimentary regime had been basically altered. Unfortunately the cycles of erosion and alluviation cannot be dated with any accuracy for the period before occupation of the plain. For further discussion of the sedimentary history of the plain see Appendix I, on land and water resources, by Michael Kirkby.

Zone A

Immediately underlying the first traces of occupation are a series of sterile sands, clays and gravel, layers into which there was cut a steep-sided channel (Figs. 4, 5, Pl. 7). This appears to be the erosional head of an intermittent channel like those that can be seen today above the town of Deh Luran on the alluvial fan.

Four zones were distinguished in the lowermost portion of Area A. These four zones were regarded as a distinct stratigraphic unit bounded below by the sterile surface of the plain and above by a sharply contrasting black ashy midden (Fig. 5). Each of the zones, numbered one to four from bottom to top, has traces of mud brick architecture and eroded earth from mud walls. Within this series there is no appreciable change in the architecture or in the nature of the deposits. It was only after we had completed the analysis of the artifacts that it became apparent that Zones A1-3 pertain to the Ali Kosh Phase, while Zone A4 is Sefid Phase and consequently culturally a part of the Zone B midden. Zone A thus misses an important segment of the known sequence, the Mohammad Jaffar Phase, which we found represented intact only in Area B.

Approximately 4 meters of deposit including the channel cut are in Zone A, but only about 1.75 meters if we discount the cut. Of this amount, about 80 cm is Zone A4.

ZONE A1, ALI KOSH PHASE

The slope of the midden and clay deposits that lie over the sterile sand suggest that the first settlement lay to the southeast of our pit in Area A. The midden rapidly filled the channel, leveling the surface before houses were built in Zone A2 (Fig. 5). The channel contains both rich midden and fragments of mud brick walls, but no coherent architecture. This suggests that old house debris was deliberately thrown into the cut on top of the initial midden filling to level the depression (Pl. 7). Additional filling of low places was accomplished with sands and gravels on the northern side of our pit. Thus Zone A1 contains the oldest material we excavated but much of it is not in situ, having been redeposited when this portion of the site was leveled during the Ali Kosh Phase.

In digging the fill from the wadi we found numerous small sherds of pottery of assorted ages which had been brought down from the surface by burrowing rodents. The major source of intrusion is a burrow some 8 meters below the present surface of the site, a situation analogous to that at Ali Kosh where we found living rodents who had burrowed and brought sherds down some 7 meters to the original plain surface. The types of pottery found in this zone

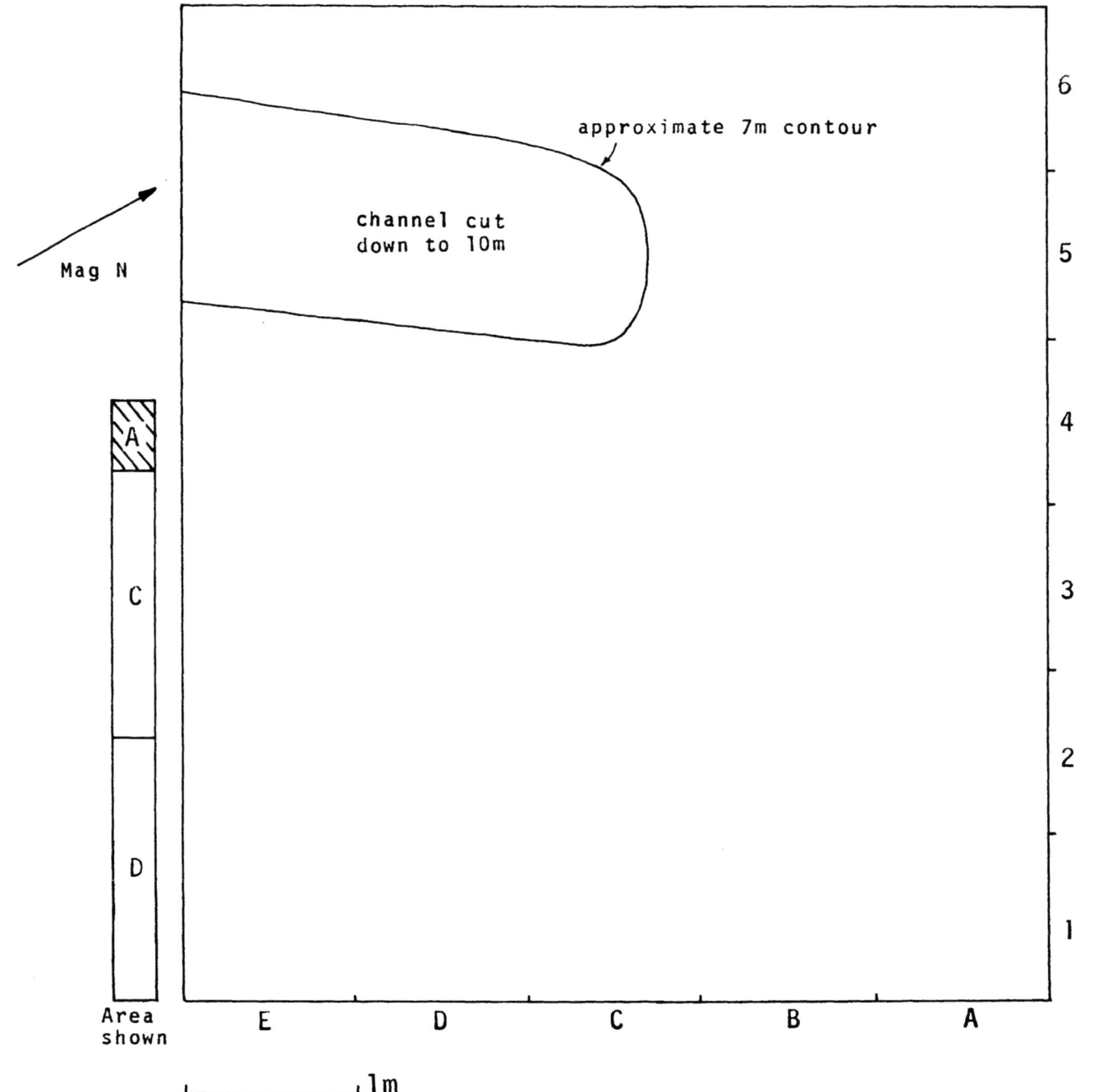

Fig. 4. An erosional gully cut into sterile sands and gravels at the base of Chagha Sefid before settlement began. During the initial occupation of the site the gully was filled with midden and brickbats to approximate the level of the original land surface, which occurred in Area A at a depth of 7m below the modern surface.

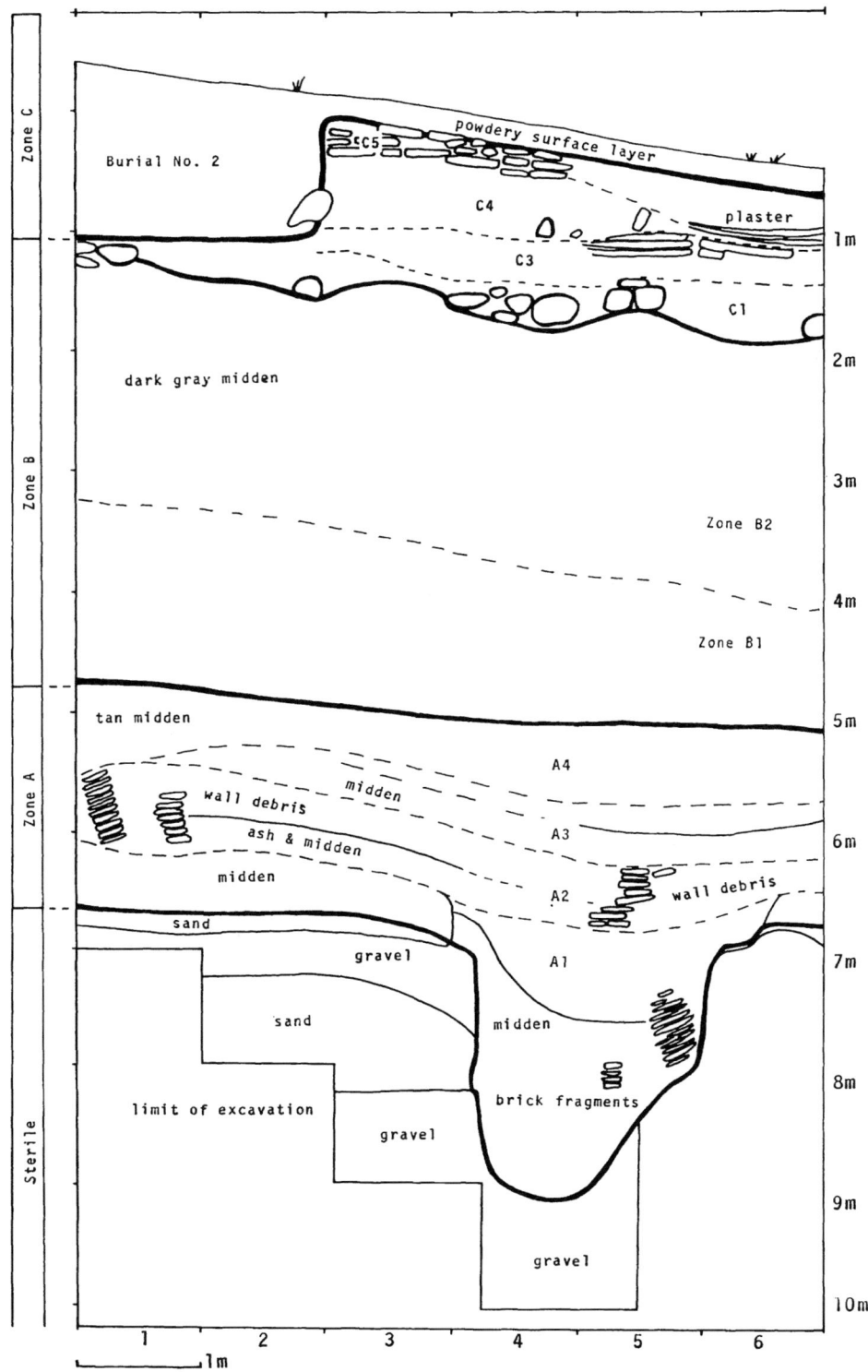

Fig. 5. Profile of south side of Area A pit showing the successive stratigraphic zones. Details in Zone C are greatly simplified for clarity. The erosional gully at the base of the site cuts 3m into sterile sands and gravels.

are clearly derived from the surface rather than from, for example, the midden in Zone B. As well as Sefid and Surkh Phase sherds, there were a few Susiana Black-on-Buff and Uruk examples.

ZONE A2, ALI KOSH PHASE

After the midden had been leveled, a brick house was built whose only intact wall stubs remained in the southwest corner of the excavation, although fragments of bricks from this structure are scattered in the southeast end of the excavation (Fig. 6). The buff bricks are of two sizes: 5 x 15 x 95 cm and 5 x 15 x 30 cm. The interior of the walls was covered with a layer of mud slightly darker than the bricks. Slumping of the wall into the channel no doubt contributed to the degradation of the walls. Walls stand a maximum of 60 cm high and the interiors of the abandoned rooms were filled with midden. No floors could be detected.

Following abandonment of the structure the area was allowed to erode until a relatively level surface was once again available on which to build another house.

ZONE A3, ALI KOSH PHASE

The eroded walls of Zone A2 left a high point in the southeast corner of our excavation and the walls of Zone A3 were built on a level surface adjacent to the old walls. Zone A3 includes the building, erosion and rebuilding of structures in the same location.

1) First mud brick walls were laid to form a corner in the northeast part of the excavation (Fig. 7, 8a). Inside the corner, flat stones for the base of a fireplace were laid (Fig. 8a, Pl. 8b) and the floor inside the walls was plastered, the edge of plaster curving up against the walls (Fig. 8b, Pl. 8d). This construction is about 30 cm higher than the walls in Zone A2.

2) The walls of the lowermost fireplace were then destroyed to make way for the later version which we found in considerably better condition (Fig. 8b, Pl. 8a,c). The final fireplace had walls of buff clay with gray mortar which were heavily burned during use. The bottom of the fireplace was lined with pebbles. The shape of the top could not be determined because of erosion.

3) Along with other walls whose traces have largely disappeared, another fireplace was laid in square A6 (Fig. 7) and it too was destroyed to make way for a final construction.

ZONE A4, SEFID PHASE

Our analysis of the artifacts suggests that the area we dug was not occupied during the Mohammad Jaffar Phase but there is no visual evidence of a prolonged abandonment in the interface between zones A3 and A4. Rather the two are separated by a thin ashy layer that covers the entire area of our excavation. The deposits above the ash (Zone A4) contain ceramics.

Following the abandonment of the houses in Zone A3, three burials were placed in the debris that resulted from the collapsing and eroding of the walls. Evidence that the area was not used for houses for a considerable time is seen in the fact that the burials were interred serially (Fig. 9). The evidence for this is burial No. 7 whose left leg and arm were cut when the pit was dug for burial No. 8. Burial No. 9 was undisturbed and of uncertain age relative to the other two (Pl. 29). Burial No. 4 was also placed in eroded wall debris in the northwest corner of our excavation (Fig. 9, Pl. 9a). This burial had been considerably disturbed and consisted of a detached skull and a thoracic section placed on flat rocks of a former fireplace. Other redeposited bones (burials No. 5, 6) were found outside the area of the previous houses. The skulls of Nos. 5 and 6 did not come from burials 4, 7, 8 or 9, each of which had its own skull, so they must have been removed from other, nearby, disturbed burials.

Although the primary burials (Nos. 7, 8, 9) were situated in the corner of the house in Zone A3, it is probable that there is no special significance to this fact; the burials were simply put into convenient mounds of earth. Above the burials, however, we find houses of Zone A4 which were built essentially over the same location as the houses in Zone A3. Thus the burials lie below the corners of these houses (Figs. 9, 10). Although one might suppose that the burials were placed beneath the floors of these houses, in view of the extensive disturbance of the skeletons and the fact that they lie partly below the walls themselves, it seems more likely that the bodies

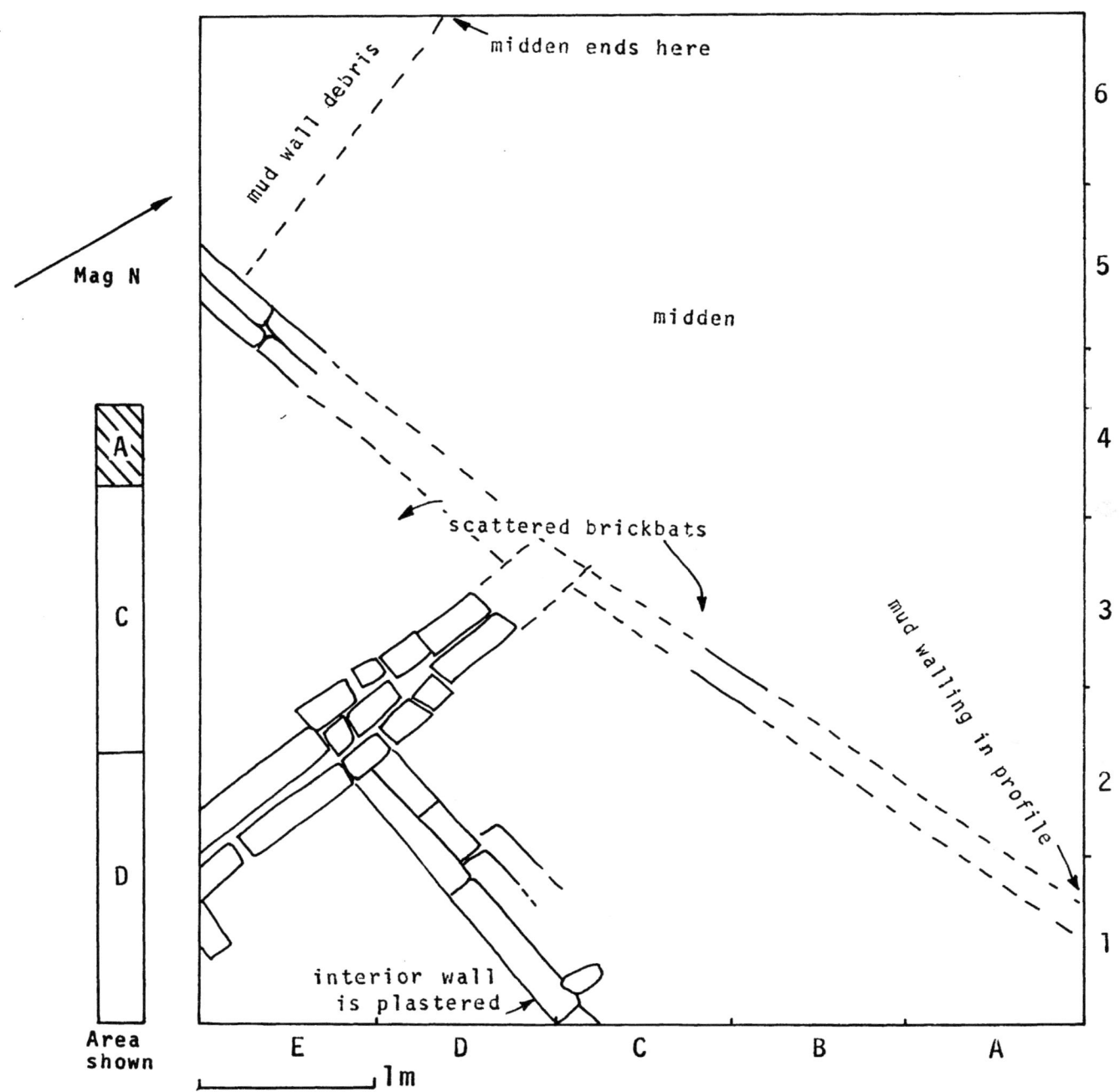

Fig. 6. Zone A2, Ali Kosh Phase. Remnant of a mud brick house.

were inadvertently covered and partially excavated while the house of Zone A4 was being built. In any case, there is no evidence for pits descending from the floors of the Zone A4 houses.

The structures in Zone A4 which lie 25-50 cm above the burials consist of traces of mud walling on essentially the same plan as the houses of Zone A3. There are also traces of mud bricks in the southeast corner of the excavation and remnants of a floor which was replastered several times in the northwest corner (Fig. 10, Pl. 9b). The traces of architecture are truncated over most of the pit by midden which must have accumulated shortly after the houses were abandoned. It also seems likely that some of the mud

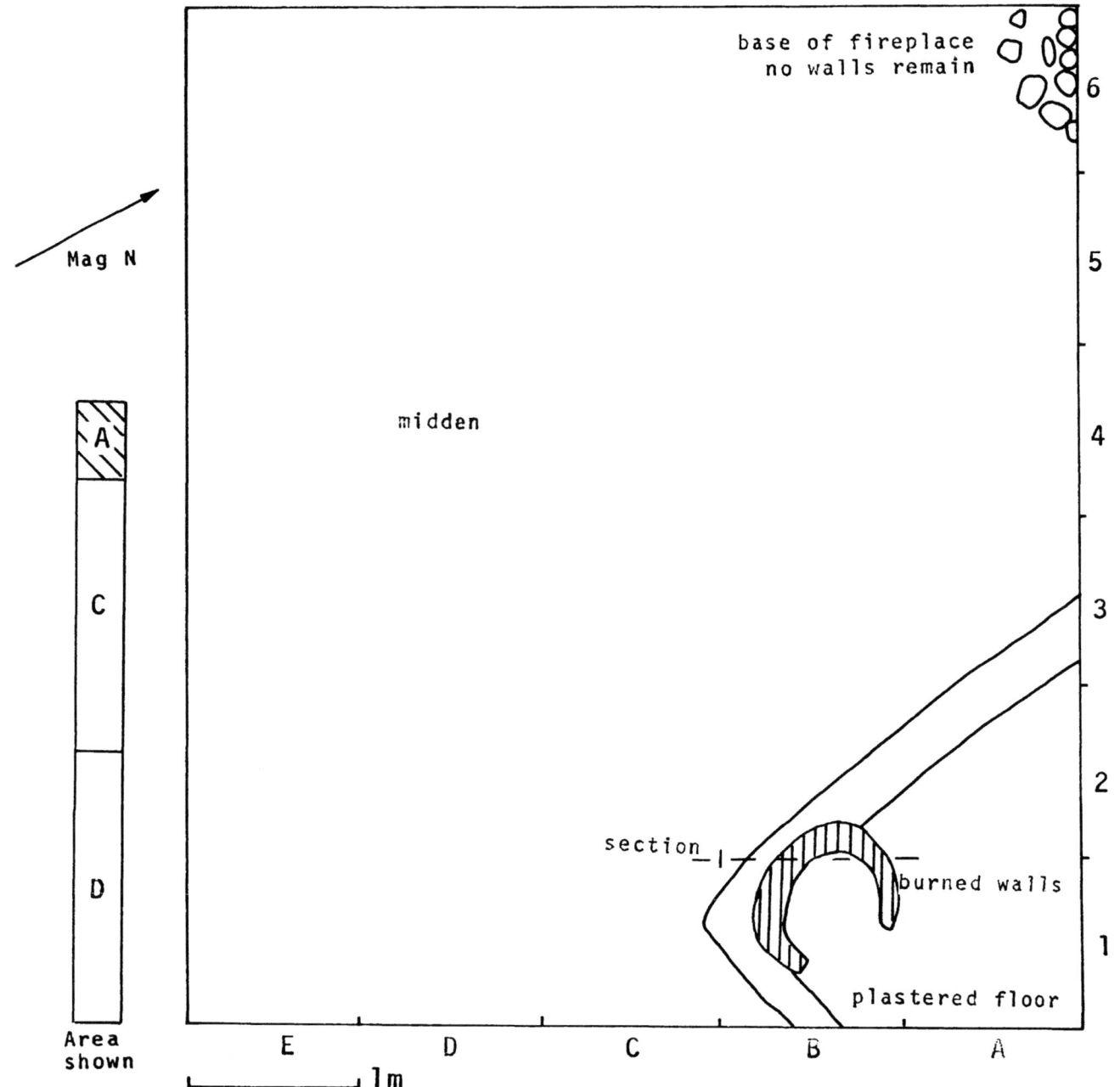

Fig. 7. Zone A3, Ali Kosh Phase. Remnants of two fireplaces in the corners of rooms. For details, see Fig. 8.

walling was taken for use elsewhere on the site while some simply eroded away.

After our analysis of the artifacts it seems apparent that Zone A4 accumulated after a substantial interval during which the part of the site that we call Area A was not occupied. It is during this interval that we find the Mohammad Jaffar Phase developing, as revealed in our exposure in Area B. From the evidence there, as well as at Ali Kosh, we know the phase to have lasted several hundred years. This interval in Area A is marked by the erosion of the houses of Zone A3 but only to a slight degree by the accumulation of artifacts from the Mohammad Jaffar Phase (Fig. 11). Although the deposits of Zone A4

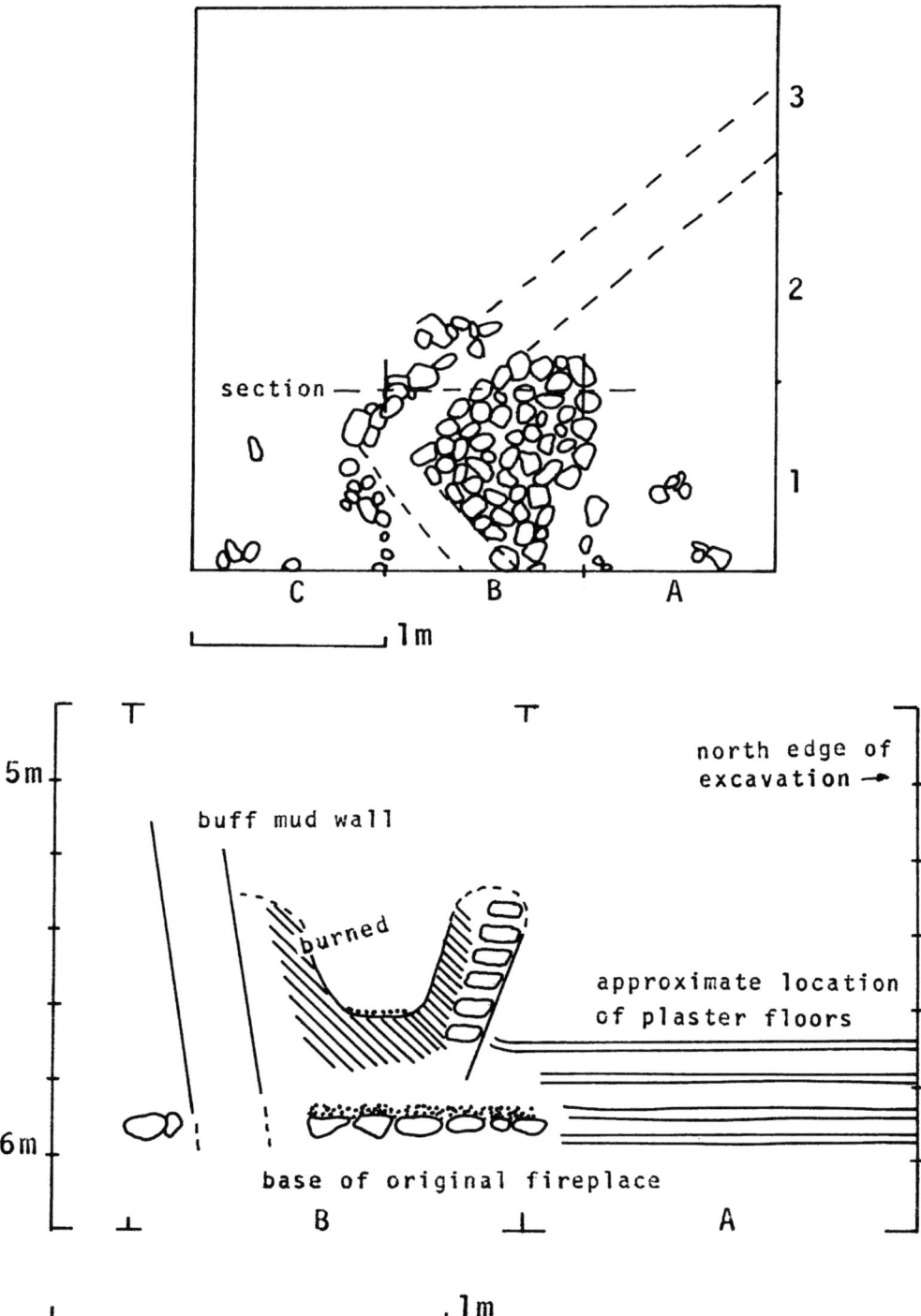

Fig. 8. Zone A3, Ali Kosh Phase. *a.* Detail of base of original fireplace. *b.* Section through fireplace showing rebuildings. Fireplace appears narrow because of the location of the section. (Scale enlarged for clarity)

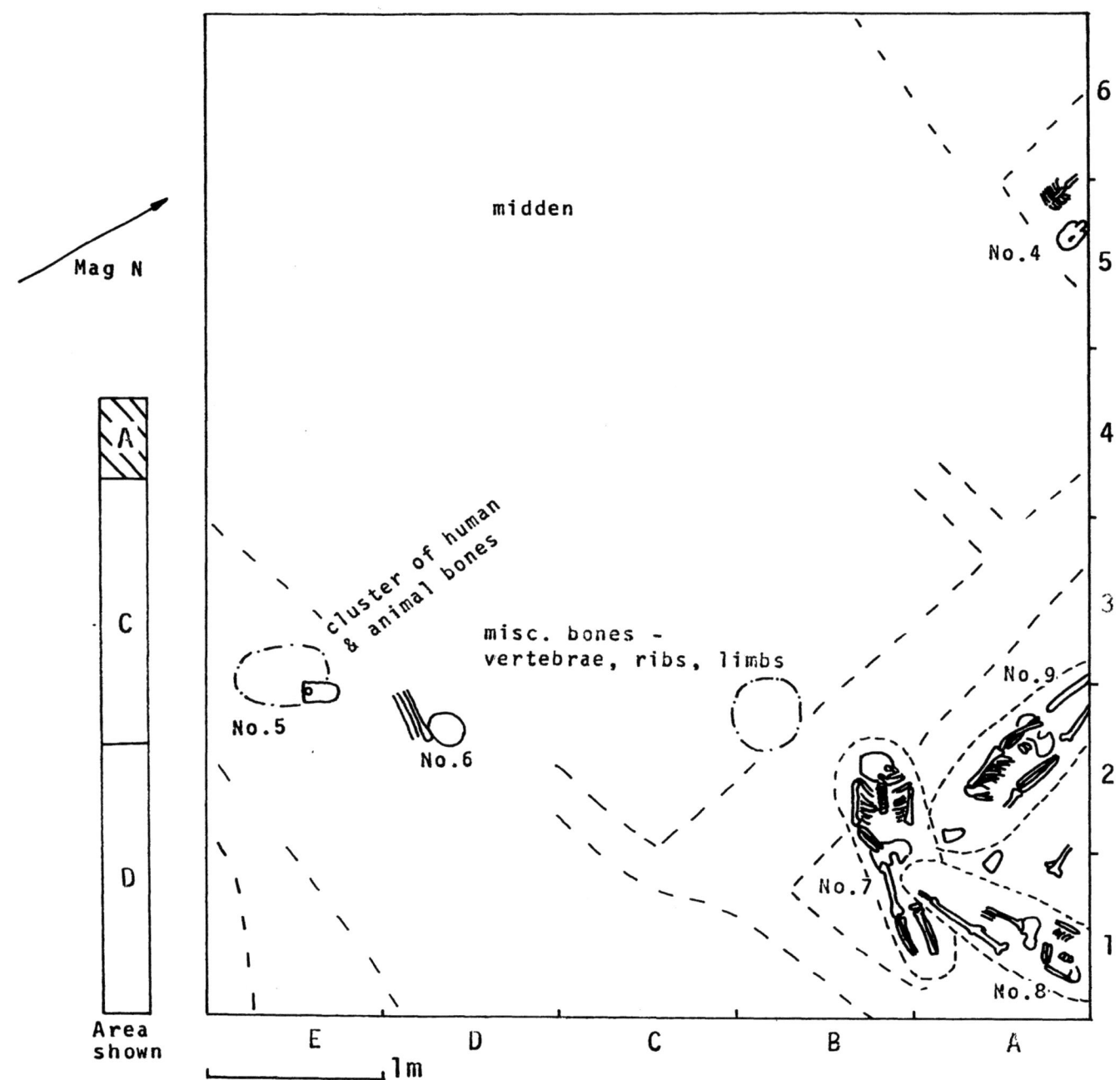

Fig. 9. Zone A4, Early Sefid Phase. Burials and disturbed clusters of bones with overlying walls dotted. (See Fig. 10.)

are assigned to the Sefid Phase, the burials may very well pertain to the Mohammad Jaffar Phase, a point about which we cannot be certain in the absence of accompanying artifacts. For a fuller discussion of the burials, see Chapter V.

Zone B

The 3 meters of midden that comprise this zone began to accumulate only after the houses of Zone A4 had eroded down nearly to their bases; conse-

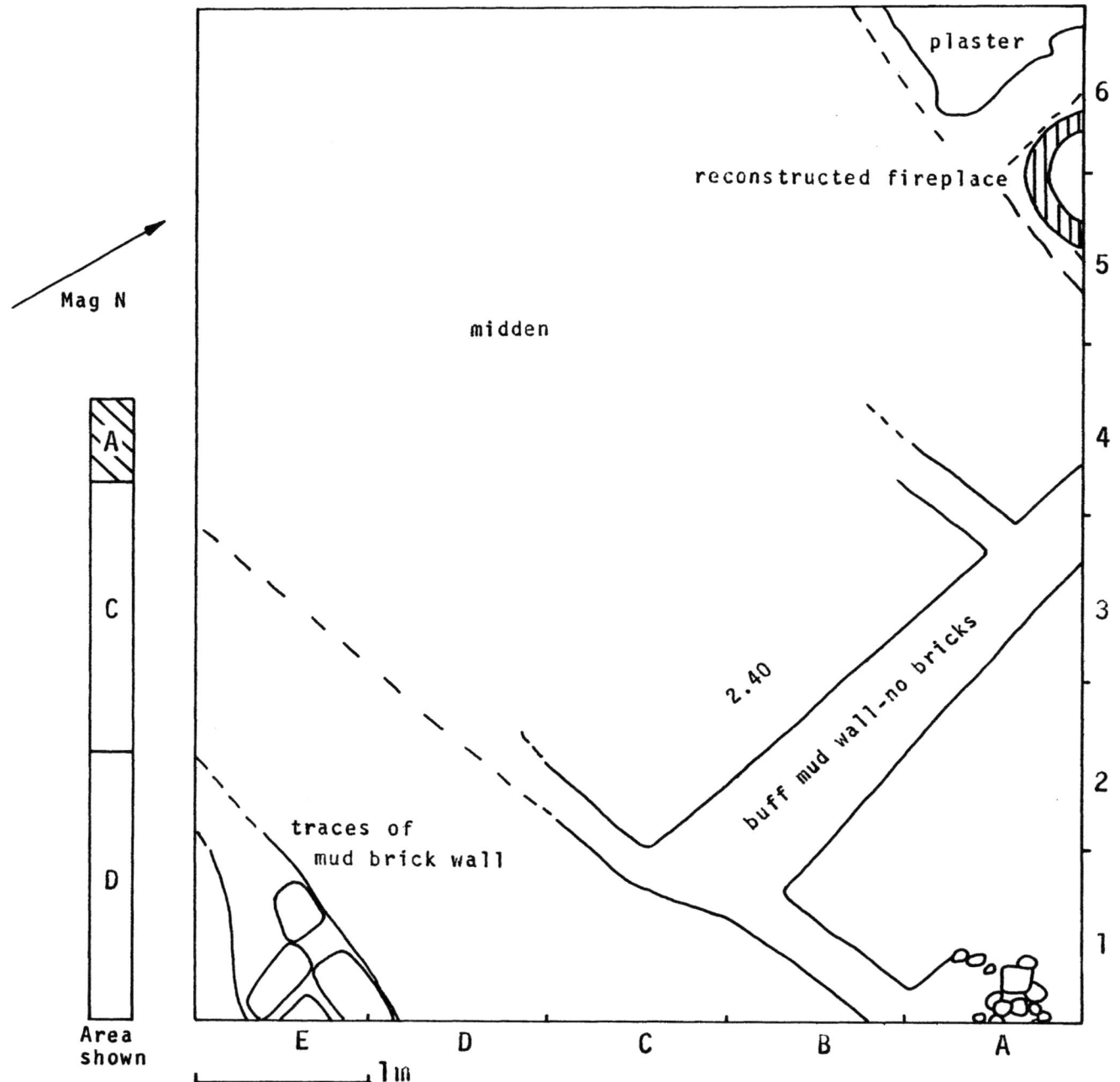

Fig. 10. Zone A4, Early Sefid Phase. Remnants of rooms lying above burials.

quently the depositional history is broken by an interval of unknown duration. In view of the similarity in the artifacts of A4 and B1, however, it seems unlikely that a very substantial time elapsed. It seems rather that the focus of housing on the site shifted from the area occupied in Zone A4 to one nearby and slightly higher up the mound. Thus the area that had been occupied was now covered by midden. Zone B consists exclusively of midden whose layers slope, like the surface of the site today, to the west. This suggests that the center of the site was the focus of settlement throughout. Within the midden no layer could be traced across the entire thirty square meters. For this reason, a rough division, based on the most

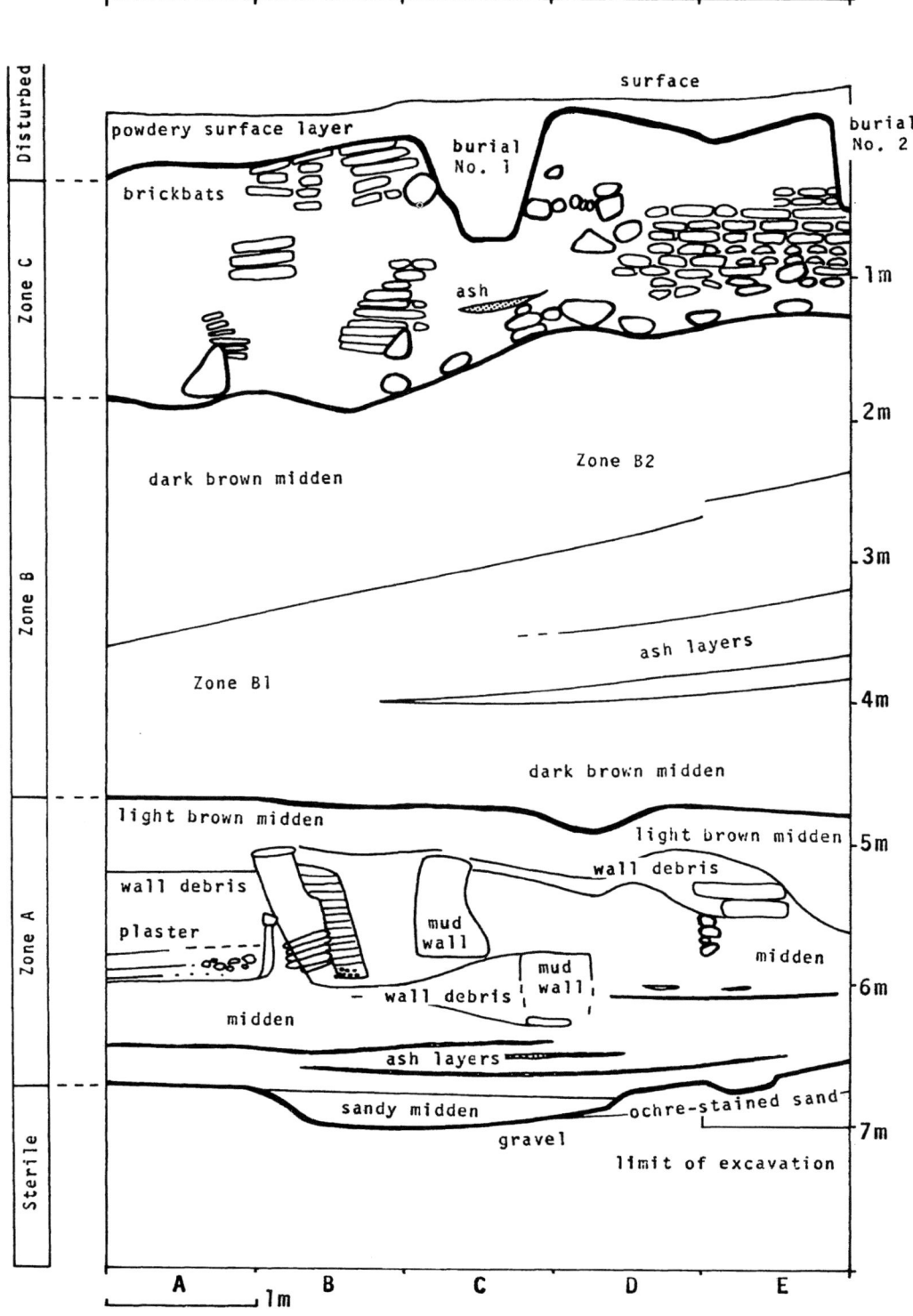

Fig. 11. Profile of east end of pit in Area A. Note the uneven surface of Zone B2 on which houses were built in Zone C.

STRATIGRAPHY AND ARCHITECTURE

distinctive layers, was made to provide a basis for comparing artifacts from the lower and upper portion of the midden.

ZONE B1, SEFID PHASE

The deposit of black, organic midden lies directly above the eroded remnants of Zone A4 and consists of steeply sloping ash beds that dip toward the northwest and then thin out toward the west (Fig. 11). No features were seen, although the deposit was rich in pottery, bone, and other artifacts.

ZONE B2, SEFID PHASE

A continuation of the midden consisted of sloping layers of ash and dirt. In the top of the midden are the remains of a fireplace and some redeposited bones that we attribute to Zone C. The upper part of the midden was as rich in artifacts as the lower, a characteristic we find generally true in middens, in contrast to areas that have substantial architectural remains and consequently a high proportion of relatively sterile earth.

Zone C

Zone C is a complex set of superimposed structures that lie closely on top of one another; the floors of these structures are intact only in small fragments, and rooms were filled with trash to level the surface for the next structure. Consequently, although we can determine the sequence of building events, it is not possible to separate the artifacts that go with any particular building. Thus, though we have a series of construction events distinguished stratigraphically, the artifacts have been simply divided into a lower component from areas A and C and an upper component from Area C. These are designated zones C1 and C2 on the tables showing the occurrence of artifacts.

Although Zone C is divided for analysis into two parts, C1 and C2, assigned to the late Sefid and early Surkh phases respectively, there is no sharp break between the two. The decision to divide Zone C was made on the basis of ceramics; several types found in zones B and C1 disappear in Zone C2, although the remaining types show an unbroken continuity. This portion of the sequence illustrates very well the arbitrary nature of phase designations when sequences are not interrupted. Our analysis conforms to what one would expect theoretically if he had a continuum: namely, that the types of pottery in use gradually and almost imperceptibly change unless there is a rapid introduction of "foreign" wares such as we see in the Choga Mami Transitional levels above the Surkh deposits. In defense of the decision to assign the deposits in Zone C to separate phases, however, is the fact that one can use the knowledge that certain types disappear as a refinement in relative dating of ceramics that are found elsewhere, especially on the surfaces of surveyed sites.

The fact that deposits of this zone occurred in both areas A and C enabled us to get a fuller set of architecture than from any of the other zones in Area A. Nevertheless, because this zone lies close to the surface in each area, and is consequently disturbed to varying depths, the amount of material we recovered is somewhat less than might be expected. Although the foundation stones were preserved to just below the surface in Area A, the fill around them was heavily disturbed by erosion and intrusive pits. For this reason, artifacts pertaining to the later construction events, and documenting the beginning of the Surkh Phase, were taken from the deposits associated with the architecture that extended into Area C.

Notable in Zone C and succeeding zones is the fact that nearly all walls are founded on large stones, either derived directly from near the mountains or from broken and worn grinding stones. Indeed it seems that when grinding stones broke while a house was in use they were piled outside the walls, a practice that may have led to their deliberate use as foundation stones.

EVENT 1, LATE SEFID PHASE

Apparently cut into the midden of Zone B is the base of a fireplace and bones representing burial No. 3 (Fig. 12, Pl. 28). Directly above this, also cut into the top of Zone B2 was a mud-lined, plastered basin standing 50 cm high whose base is at the level of, and adjacent to, the redeposited bones of burial No. 3. Although we cannot be certain that the burial was disturbed when the basin was built, this seems prob-

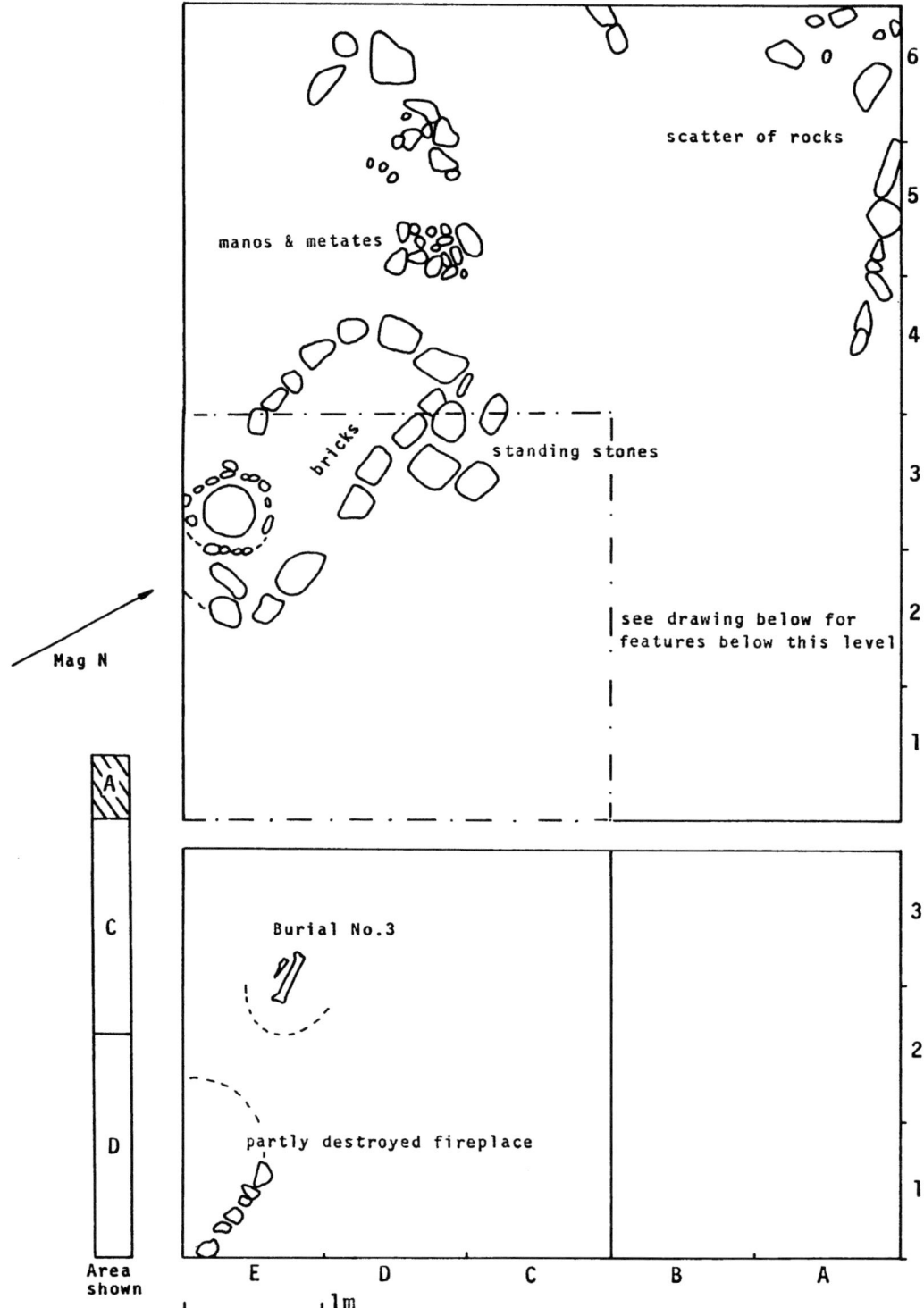

Fig. 12. Zone C, Event 1, Late Sefid Phase. A rectangle of stones with a plaster basin at one end lies directly over the redeposited bones of burial No. 3.

able. Associated with the basin and nearly level with its top is a rectangle of stone whose interior was paved with mud bricks (Fig. 12 and Pl. 10). This rectangle is about 40 cm above the level of the burial and fireplace. To the north of the rectangle are four stones standing on end: two mortars, a mano and a polished stone of uncertain function (Fig. 12, Pl. 13). Although the rectangle appears to have been an isolated unit on a surface that is otherwise scattered with trash (Fig. 12), it may have been constructed as an integral part of the stone pavement which appears to have been a courtyard (Fig. 13) or paved room that lay around and partially over the rectangle. If this is the case, the scatter of trash on the same level as the rectangle (i.e. directly on the midden) merely reflects the initial shift from midden deposition to house construction. Owing to the pressure of soil and stones above, the area of the rectangle may have subsided somewhat relative to the entirely paved area surrounding it. The instability of the loosely compacted underlying midden is well illustrated in Figure 11.

EVENT 2, LATE SEFID PHASE

Built on top of the midden of Zone B2 in Area C is a large platform of soft, gray ashy mud brick that was probably quarried out of the earlier B2 midden (Fig. 14). These bricks contained a high proportion of charred grain whose presence was evident to our pickmen even before we recognized the bricks themselves.

At the earliest, the platform is contemporary with Event 1 although it was not possible to establish the sequence with certainty owing to disturbance during later periods and severe damage done to our profiles in one of the heavy downpours that repeatedly plagued our work. Allowing for the natural slope of the mound it appears that the platform lies on essentially the same level as the stone foundations of Event 1 although nearly 3 meters to the east of them (Pl. 11). Moreover, both the platform and the stone foundations have the same orientation. It is clear that in terms of the artifactual—if not necessarily the architectural—sequence the two features are contemporary.

The platform itself is about the same size as the late Surkh Phase example in Zone F. Our estimate of the size is 7 x 10.3 meters, assuming the corners are square. It stands about 1.8 meters high and is founded on large stones. The bricks, which appear the same throughout, measure 60 x 30 x 10 cm and are made of dark gray ashy mud (Pl. 11a).

Since the platform lay very close to the surface of the mound its upper levels were somewhat disturbed. Later construction also cut into the platform (Fig. 15, Pls. 11,12). Adding to our difficulties in finding it and determining its characteristics was heavy rain that was rapidly absorbed by the soft ashy bricks, turning much of the upper layers into a mushy goo that had to be cleared away and discarded. Thus it was not until we had stripped off some of the upper layers of bricks that we realized we were digging through bricks rather than midden. Once they were recognized, however, it became easy to trace them and the better preserved lower layers were exposed across the entire platform, enabling us to reconstruct its size and shape accurately (Pl. 12a,b).

It remains to be seen in further excavation whether the platform served as the foundation of a structure. It is certain from our experience after rains that the platform would not have provided a useful floor for an open area; thus there is a possibility it may have been covered in some manner. In contrast, the platform in Zone F was capped by dense yellow-clay bricks that absorbed far less water, although clearly erosion would have been a problem with it as well.

EVENT 3, EARLY SURKH PHASE

A rebuilding of the stone pavement of the first construction and the addition of plaster-floored rooms gives us our most complete architectural remains of Zone C. The walls of part of this architectural complex cut into the platform of Zone C2, and are consequently later than it (Fig. 15, Pl. 13). The plan shown in Figure 15 represents a series of rebuildings of the same structures. The number of rebuildings is suggested by the 23 layers of plaster on the floor of the room at the west end of the excavation.

Basically the complex consists of a stone-paved courtyard with plastered and presumably covered rooms adjacent to it (Fig. 15, Pl. 14a). The pavement

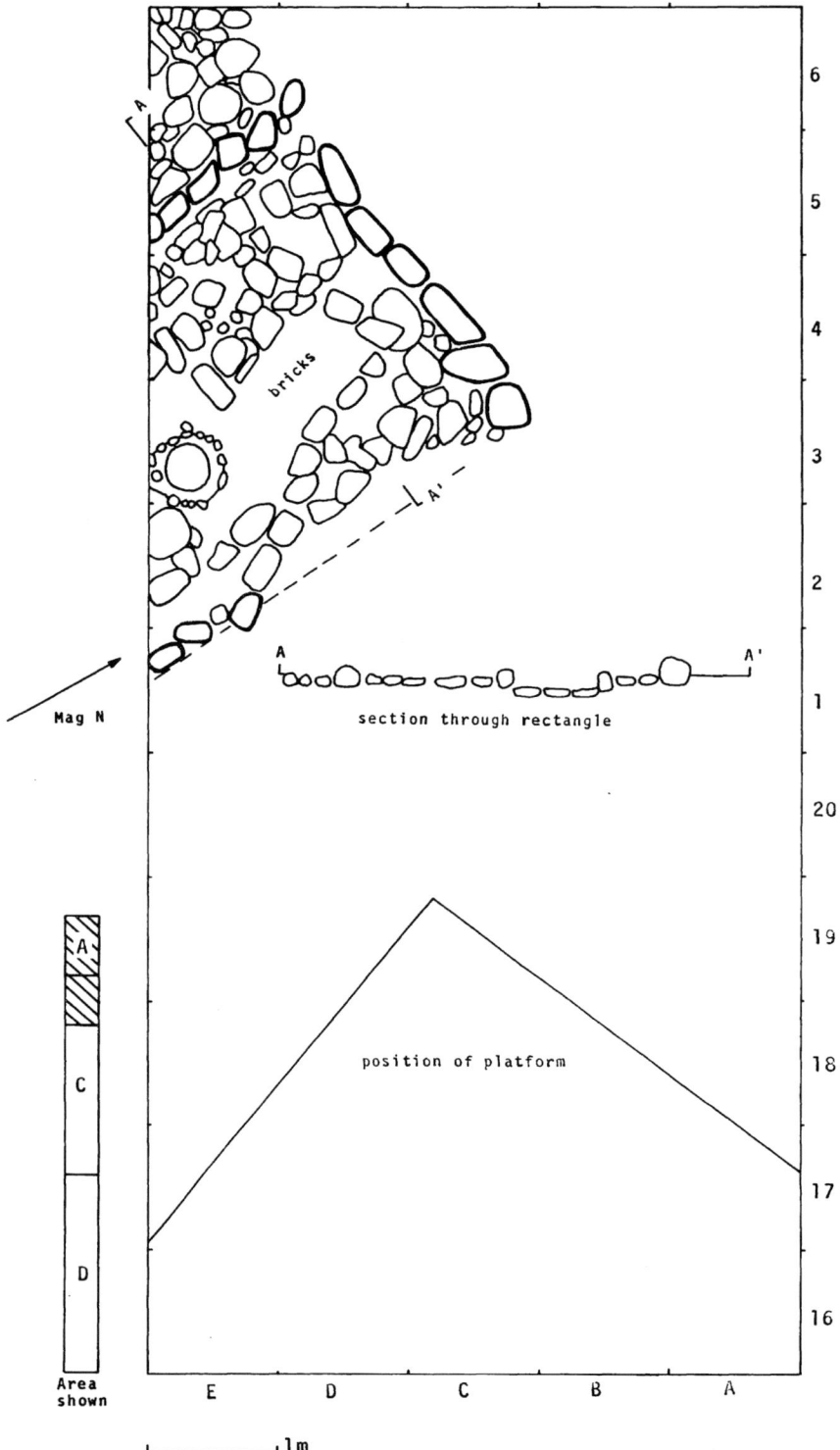

Fig. 13. Zone C, Event 1, Late Sefid Phase. Courtyard or room paved with stones. This unit overlies the features shown in Fig. 12.

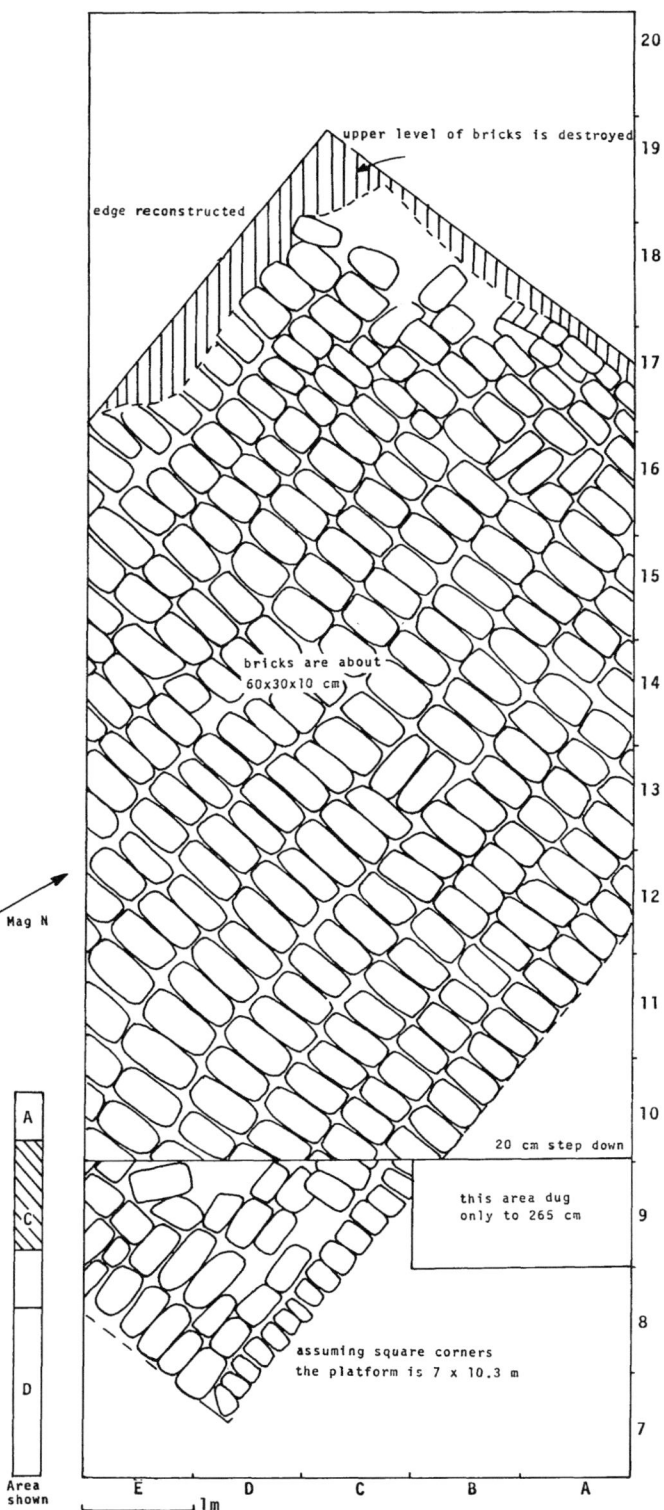

Fig. 14. Zone C, Event 2, Late Sefid Phase. Large mud brick platform.

represents an accumulation of another 20-30 cm above the similar structure in Event 1. In Figure 15 we see a section across the pavement and plastered rooms showing how the wall foundations supported low(?) mud brick walls. During the use of these structures broken pieces of grinding stones were piled against the bases of mud walls which were exposed to the outside (Pl. 13b,c).

An open, unplastered area with a plaster basin lies alongside the paved courtyard. Since this area was repeatedly filled with stones and other trash including ash it was presumably unroofed and exposed. The fill in this area may be interpreted as either an attempt to control mud or as part of leveling as the rebuildings raised the area. This filling eventually covered parts of the walls adjacent to the open corridor (Fig. 16).

EVENT 4, EARLY SURKH PHASE

Built on the broken walls of Zone C3 and on the trash thrown among and over them is a new layer of paving 20-30 cm thick that partially overlies the structures below. Basically, however, it is a set of structures very close in plan to those below. As this level lies near the surface of our excavation much of the remains were eroded and distrubed by later quarrying (Fig. 17, Pl. 14b).

EVENT 5, EARLY SURKH PHASE

The only traces of architecture preserved were in Area A and the adjoining southeast corner of Area C. There is at this time a complete abandonment of the previous architectural complex and the building of a pavement of plano-convex mud bricks that measure some 20 x 15 x 6 cm (Fig. 18, Pl. 15). The pavement or platform itself measures about 4 meters on a side and is about 60 cm high as nearly as we are able to reconstruct it. It was not founded on stones. The platform was disturbed by the pit of burial No. 2 and the house of Event 6, the surrounding areas were disturbed by the pit of burial No. 1 and various pitting and erosion (figs. 4, 18). Both burials are historic.

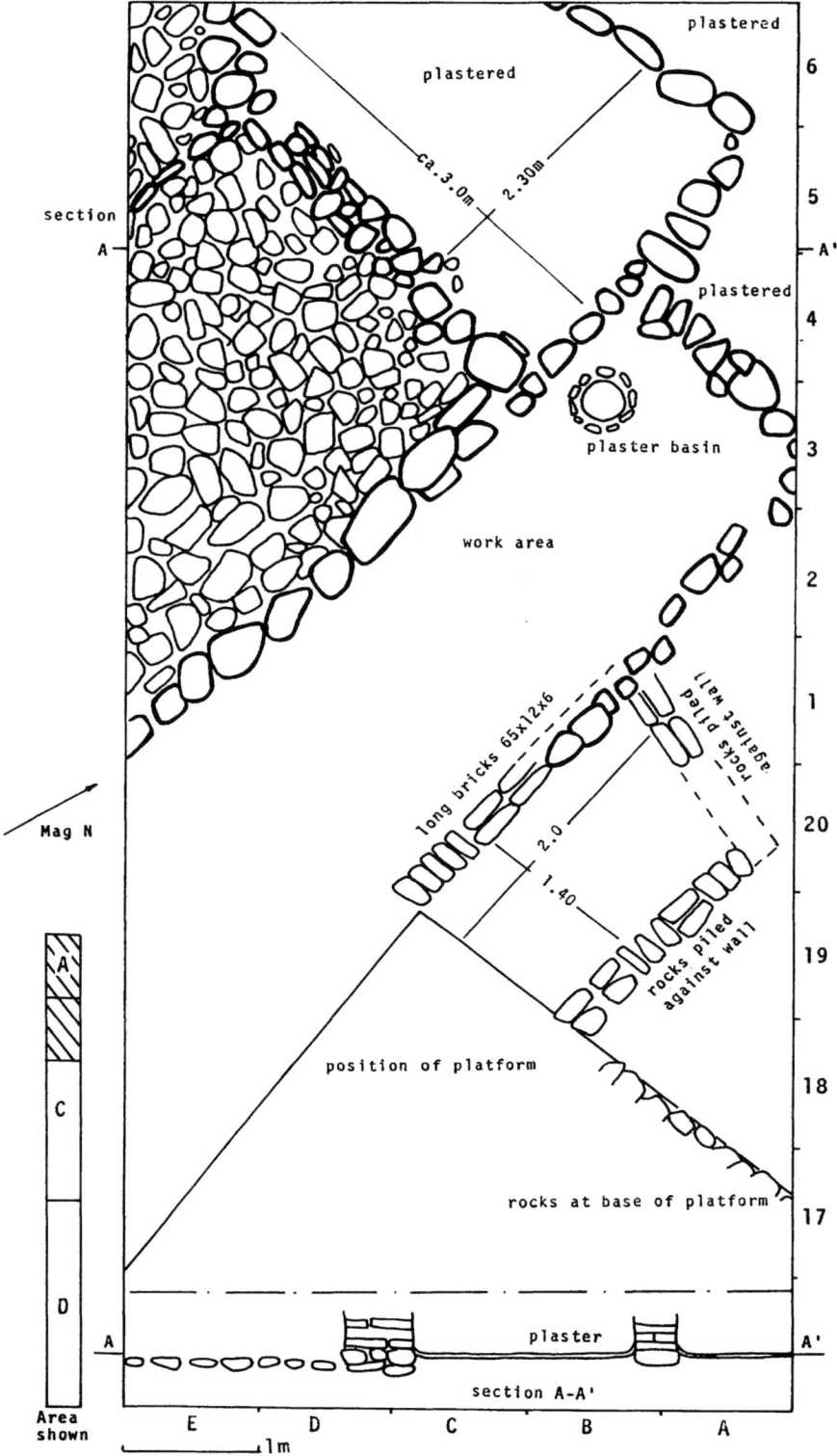

Fig. 15. Zone C, Event 3, Early Surkh Phase. Paved floor or courtyard with adjacent plaster-floored rooms. Note how brick platform of Event 2 is used as rear wall of small room. Area between stone paved area and brick platform is apparently open. A section through the paved area and plaster floors is at the bottom of the drawing.

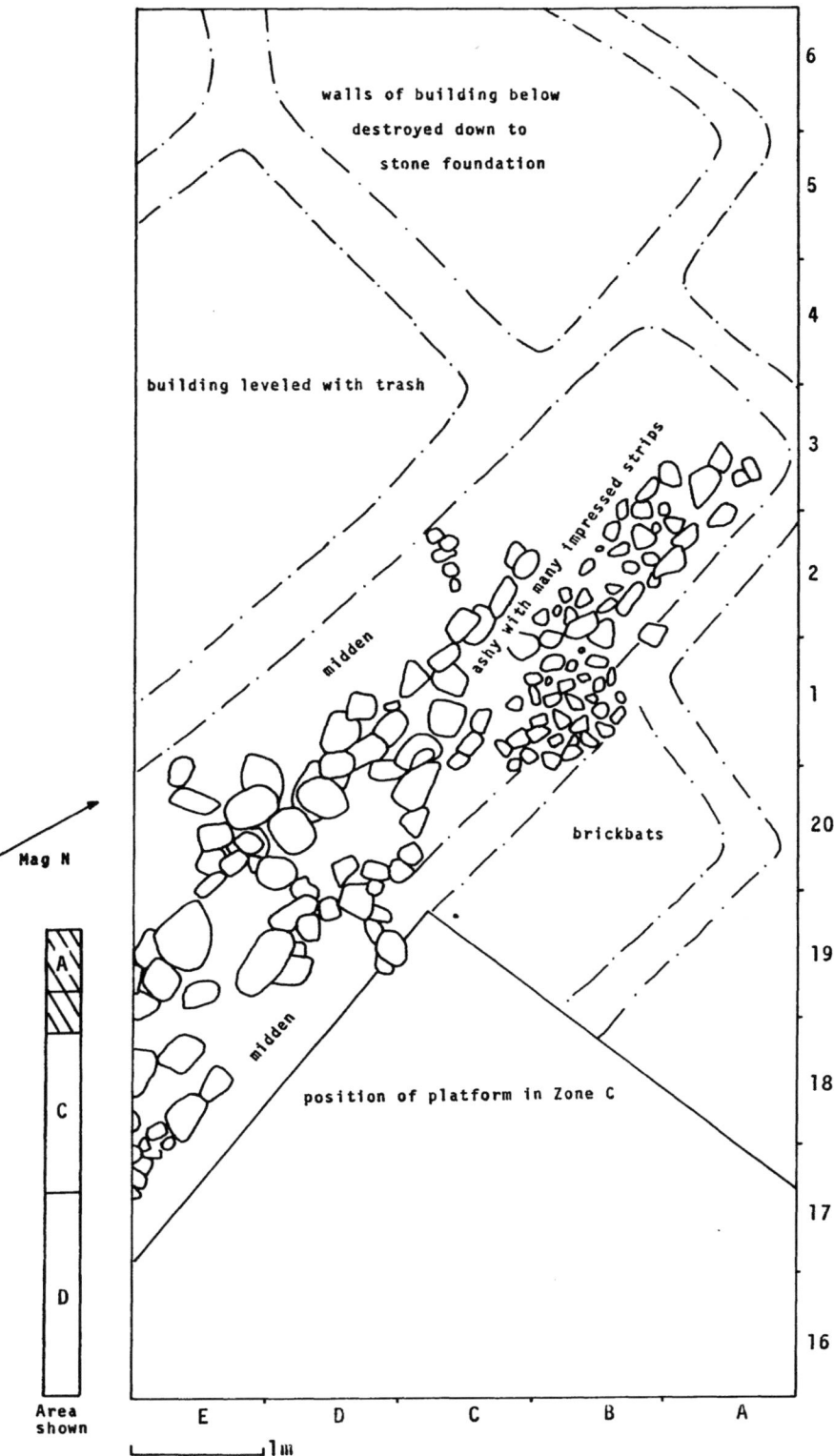

Fig. 16. Zone C, Events 3-4, Early Surkh Phase. Open area is filled with rock, ash and trash and the entire area is eroded.

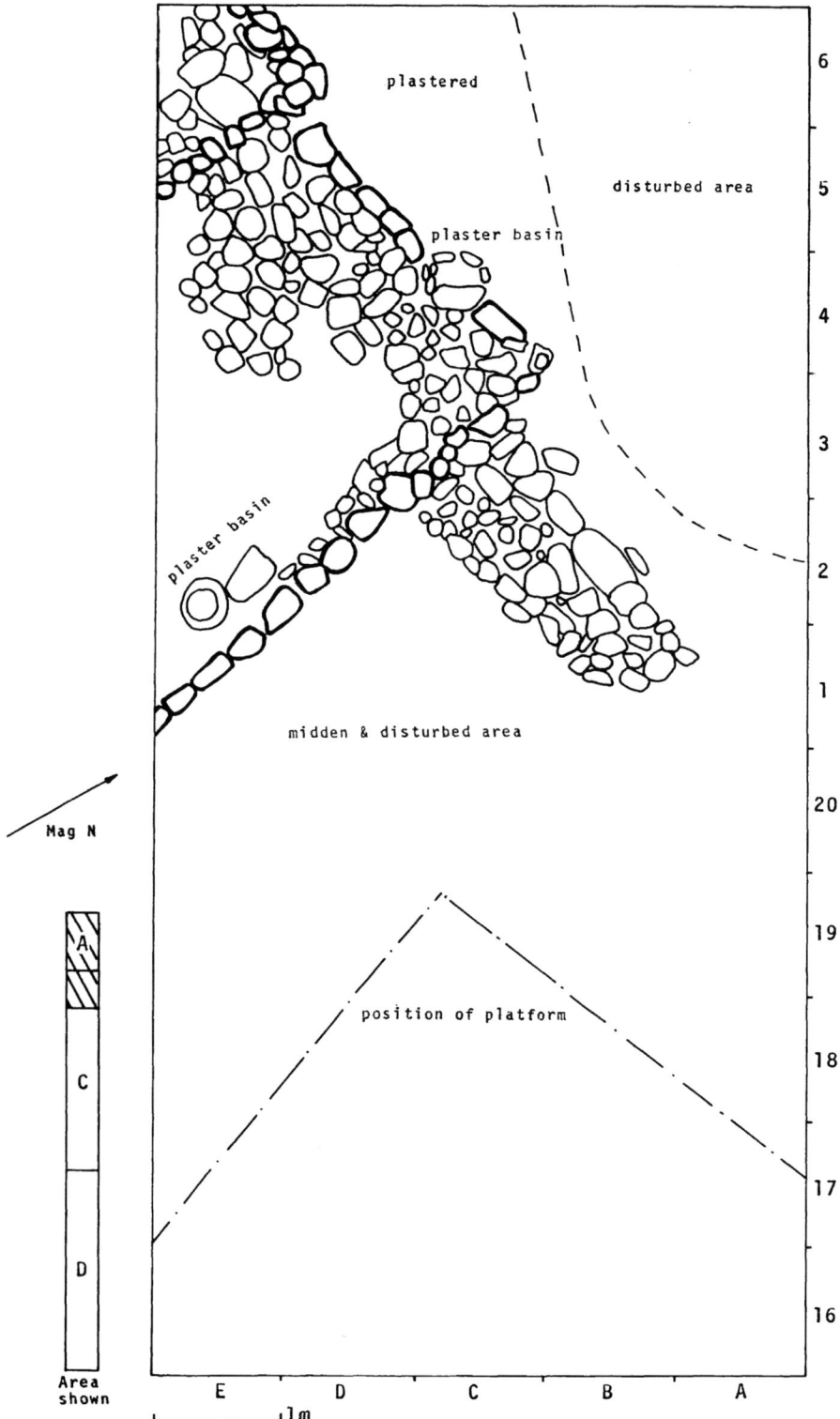

Fig. 17. Zone C, Event 4, Early Surkh Phase. Final building of pavement on leveled structures of Event 3.

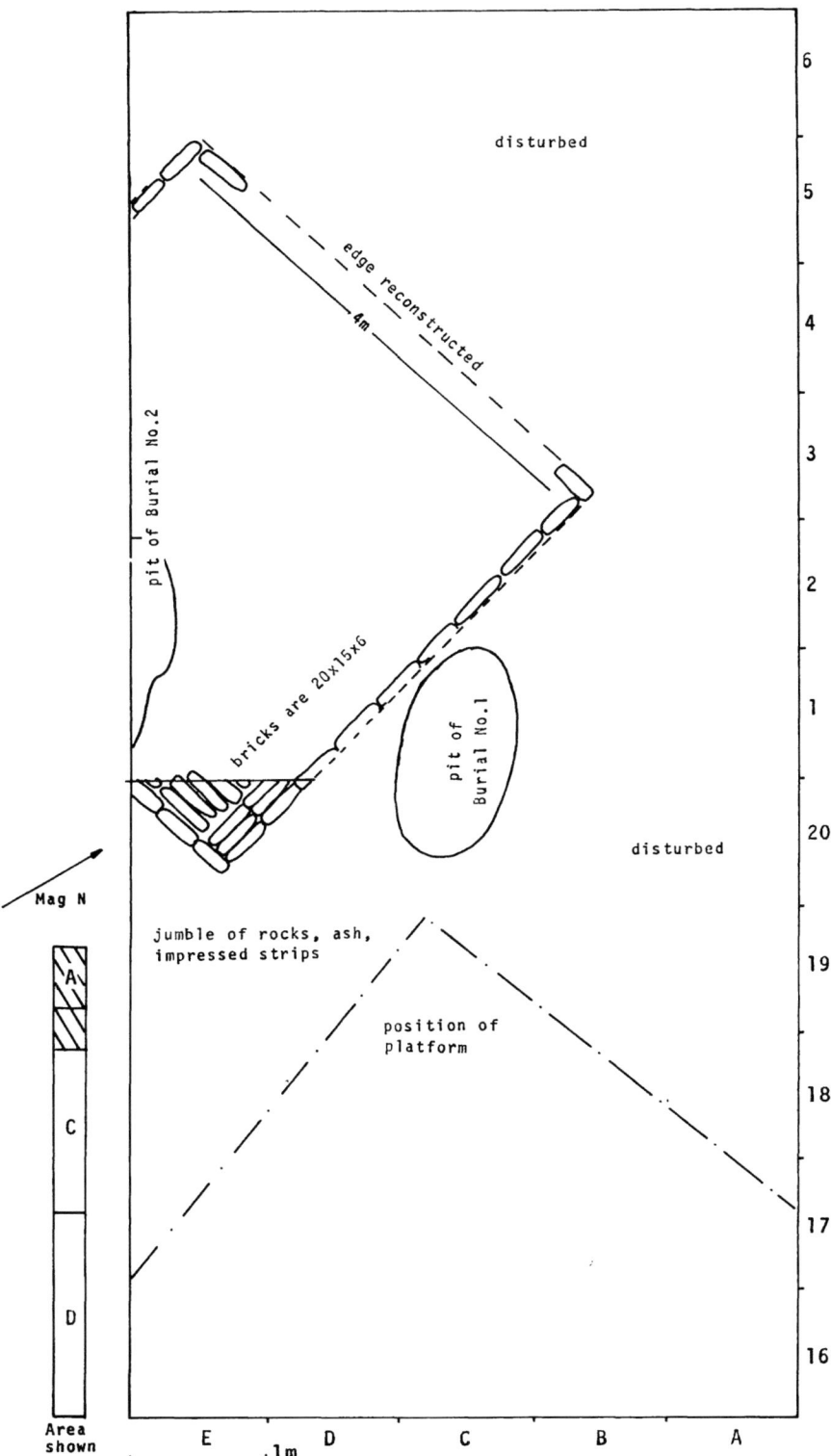

Fig. 18. Zone C, Event 5, Early Surkh Phase. Brick pavement or small platform built over former paved area. Disturbance of this stratum which lies near the surface prevented tracing any related architecture.

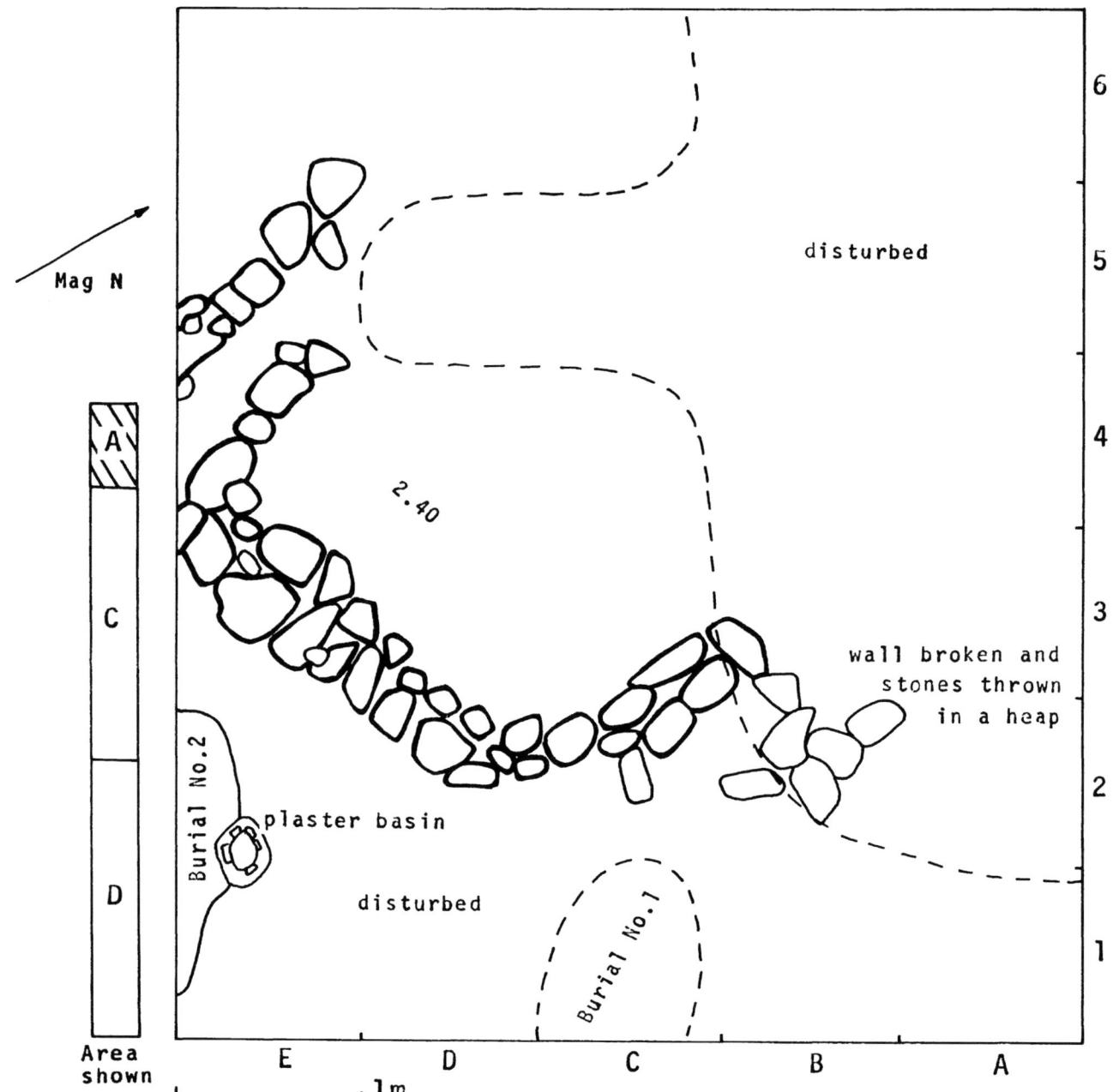

Fig. 19. Zone C, Event 6, Early Surkh Phase. Final structure discernible in Area A.

EVENT 6, EARLY SURKH PHASE

The final substantial construction attributed to Zone C lies partially atop the brick pavement. In its construction, most of the underlying pavement was destroyed. Event 6 is a stone-founded building which itself was largely destroyed by later disturbances (Fig. 19). The remains consist solely of wall foundations which were set partially into the underlying brick pavement and which rest nearly on the stone pavement of Event 4. The plaster basin alongside burial No. 1 is probably associated with this room.

Zone D

Occurring only in Area C, the architecture ascribed to this zone lies above the mud brick platform of Zone C2 and higher than any of the structures of Zone C. Although there is relatively little fill between rebuildings in Zone D it was possible to separate artifacts from each of the stages for purposes of analysis.

ZONE D1, SURKH PHASE

The areas immediately adjacent to the large mud brick platform had been filled with trash to the top of the platform before the first new structure was built. This structure, whose southwest wall lay on the edge of the platform, extended beyond the platform and also lay on the trash-filled upper portion of Zone C (Fig. 20, Pl. 16a). The nature of this building is not clear: large rocks outline the southwest wall and two intersecting walls but the "floor" is littered with small rocks and brickbats and is pocked with hollows that are filled with trash (Pl. 16b). The south and northeast walls are of smaller stones lying atop the edge of the platform. It may be that this entire area was open and used partly as a dump.

To the east are house walls consisting of small rectangular rooms or open areas (Pl. 17a). One of these areas contains two plaster basins and apparently the remains of an oven against the south wall (Pl. 17b). Adjacent to this, to the east, is a brick pavement about 3 x 3.5 meters in extent, founded on rocks (Pl. 18a). The bricks in the pavement, measuring 60-80 x 12-14 x 8 cm resemble those found later in Zone F. No trace of walls enclosing the pavement was found.

Other architectural traces are fragmentary but suggest two or three more rectangular rooms, one of which has the base of a fireplace set alongside its wall.

The reconstruction in Figure 20 is based on the alignment of large foundation stones; however, much of the area was littered with piles of rock that had evidently been toppled from the walls or placed in the area as fill prior to the building of the next layer of structures. In some cases the actual sequence of building is somewhat in doubt (Pl. 17a,b). For example, the room containing the basins has two rows of "foundation" stones along one wall. Both of these are on the same level yet they could hardly have been contemporary unless the innermost had fallen off the outermost when the room was abandoned. Adding to the difficulty is the fact that the same general outline for walls was used repeatedly so that the new foundation stones lie almost immediately above the older. Neither is the interpretation aided by the fact that subsidence of the underlying strata has caused some shifting in the absolute levels of the walls which, for the most part, seem to slope down toward the west, following the contour of the site. Finally, no plastered floors were used, nor were we able to pick up hard-packed surfaces that might have served in their stead.

ZONE D2, SURKH PHASE

This consists essentially of a leveling of the entire area through its use as a trash dump. Midden and trash accumulated to a depth of 30-50 cm during this time. Possibly some rebuilding of portions of the previous structures was undertaken but this is not certain. What is clear is that the area did not have newly built rooms for some time.

ZONE D3, SURKH PHASE

The area of the former workroom with the plaster basins was used again; perhaps it had never been completely abandoned, but at this time only one basin was in use (Fig. 21). Additionally, a series of stone-founded rooms were built and an oven with clay walls and a stone-lined base was installed (Fig. 21, Pl. 18b,c), probably in the corner of a room, although the extent of our excavation did not allow us to determine this. Figure 21 shows walls that are approximately contemporary, although there is some ambiguity about this. The walls shown are contemporary in a purely stratigraphic sense, but some may represent rebuilding within the same area. At any rate they do not form a coherent architectural unit. The problem of recognizing structures in this zone is the same as described above for Zone D1. Following abandonment of these rooms, 20-30 cm of midden and wall debris covered the area.

ZONE D4, SURKH PHASE

The final architecture of Zone D consists of a partial rebuilding of the walls of Zone D3 and the

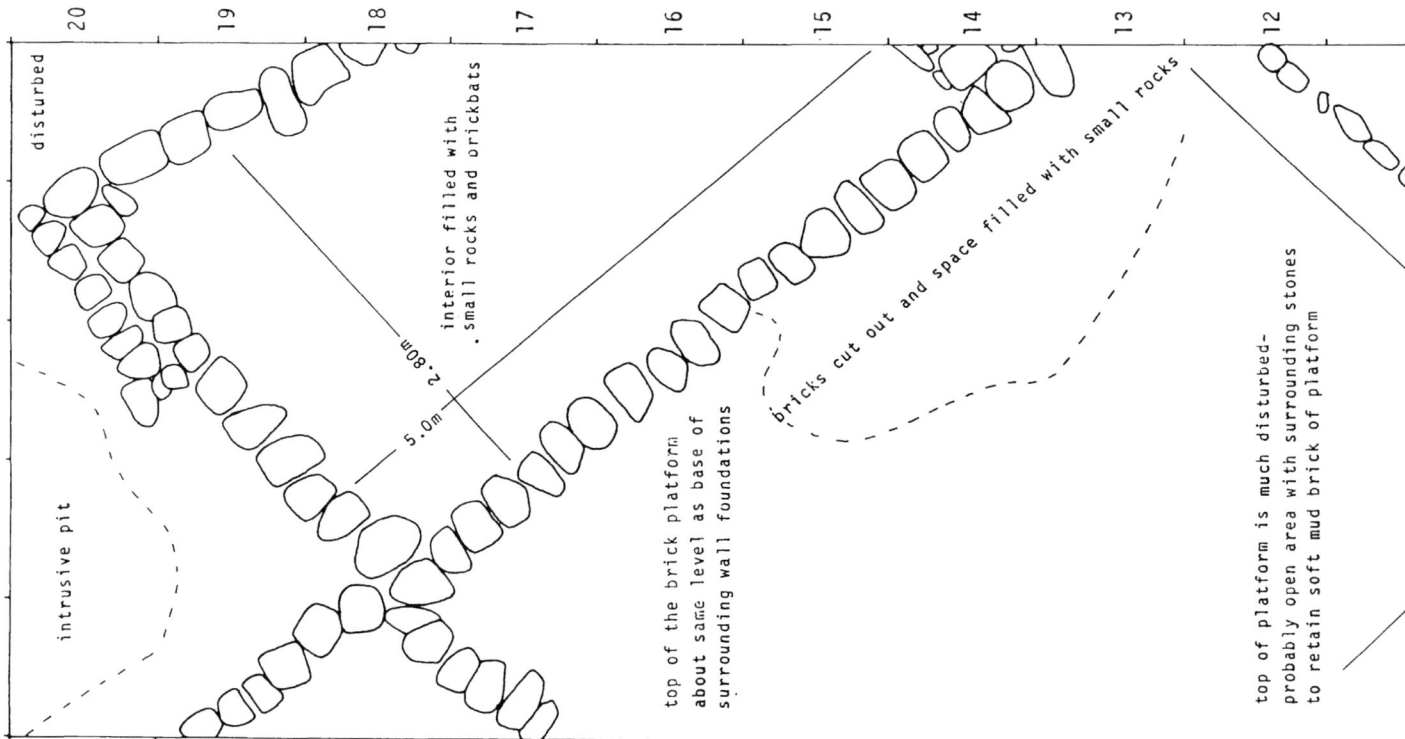

Fig. 20. Zone D1, Surkh Phase. Large stones partially outline the brick platform of Zone C. Except for the workroom, the nature of the structures is uncertain.

addition of a new work area that consisted of a plastered floor into which basins were set (Fig. 22). By this time the previous work area was used as a midden. It could not be determined whether the work area was covered, although the north edge of the plastered floor butts against a row of stones set on edge. These stones are much smaller than is typical for foundations. The remaining edges of the plaster were disturbed by rocks and other debris when the area was used later as a dump.

A somewhat unusual feature is the plaster basin set at one end of a stone walkway (Fig. 22, Pl. 19). It looks as if the stones form a path to the basin although they may have served as the foundation of a partial wall screening the work area from the trash-midden outside.

Zone E

Although much of the architecture in this zone was disturbed in rebuilding, an exposure 10 meters long was obtained in Zone E2. There is no apparent discontinuity with the style of architecture of Zone D, but this zone represents a new set of buildings set farther to the east and about 20 cm above the houses of Zone D.

ZONE E1, SURKH PHASE

From the fragments remaining it appears that the architecture in this zone is basically the same as described for Zone E2: a complex of small, multi-room structures. Zone E1 shows an area about 5 meters wide that was probably an open court. It contained remains of several plaster basins, some of which were rebuilt many times. There was, as well, a general scattering of gravel and other trash, including extensive ash deposits which collapsed during the heavy rains while we were digging, leaving the balk between areas C and D a morass of mud (Pl. 20b).

ZONE E2, SURKH PHASE

In spite of the loss of critical profiles because of the rain, it appears that the extant structures on the west end of our exposure had been robbed of many of their stones. The principal complex consists of three rooms founded with stone (Fig. 23, Pl. 21a). The two smaller rooms are 3.0 x 2.50 meters and

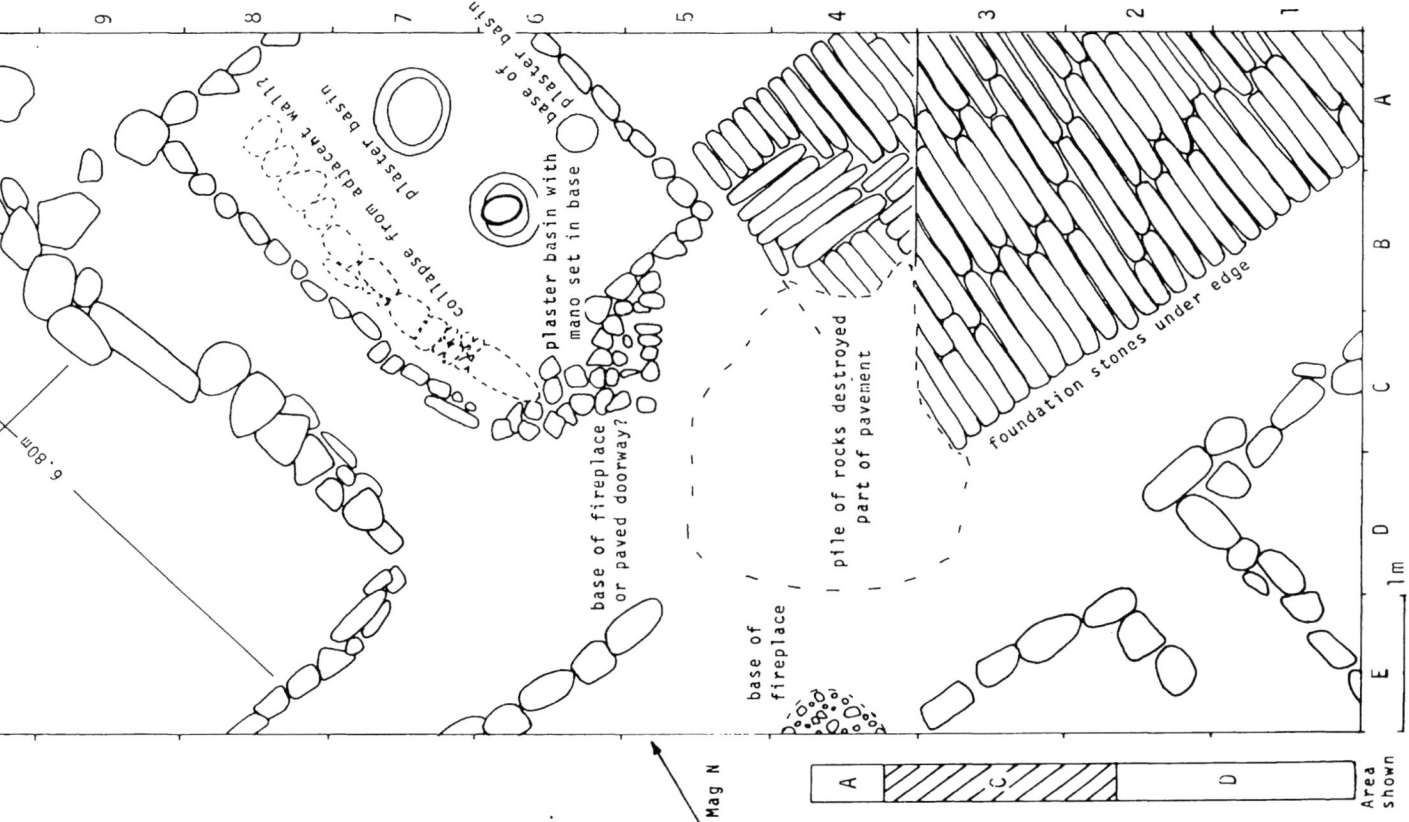

2.60 x 1.80 meters in the north-south, east-west dimensions respectively. The larger room, apparently at a right angle and adjacent to the smaller rooms, is about 4.80 meters in its east-west dimension but its full extent north-south could not be determined. The floor of this room may have been partially paved with flat stones (Pl. 20a). The entire rectangular unit with four or more rooms inside thus measures at least 5 meters east-west and more than 7 meters north-south.

To the west of this complex is a courtyard or corridor about 2.5 meters wide which contained plaster basins and refuse. A parallel complex of rooms appear to lie west of the corridor but it lies too close to the surface of the site for its character to be ascertained (Pl. 21a).

Still another wall to the southeast of the first complex suggests another set of rooms. In the corridor between buildings was a single basin. This feature was not excavated since the squares where it is probably preserved lay under a step in our trench.

There was nothing intact in the structures nor were there "floors." This is a consistent feature of the buildings at Chagha Sefid and is probably a result of the severe denudation of the structures between each phase of rebuilding. In consequence, although house rooms and work areas can be deduced on architectural grounds, there is no possibility of doing an analysis of the association of certain artifacts with the areas.

In contrast with most of the other architecture in the site, brick filler walls were sometimes used between stone walls and not just overlying them (Fig. 23).

A fragmentary burial was found in the southeast corridor, possibly having been put down while the area was not in use for domestic dwellings. The burial seems to have been disturbed in the building of later houses.

Zone F, Surkh Phase

Stratigraphically this zone consists of a large mud brick platform and the traces of architecture that are on the same level as its base (Figs. 24, 25, 26, Pls. 21, 22). It appears that the platform was built as a freestanding structure against which brick buildings

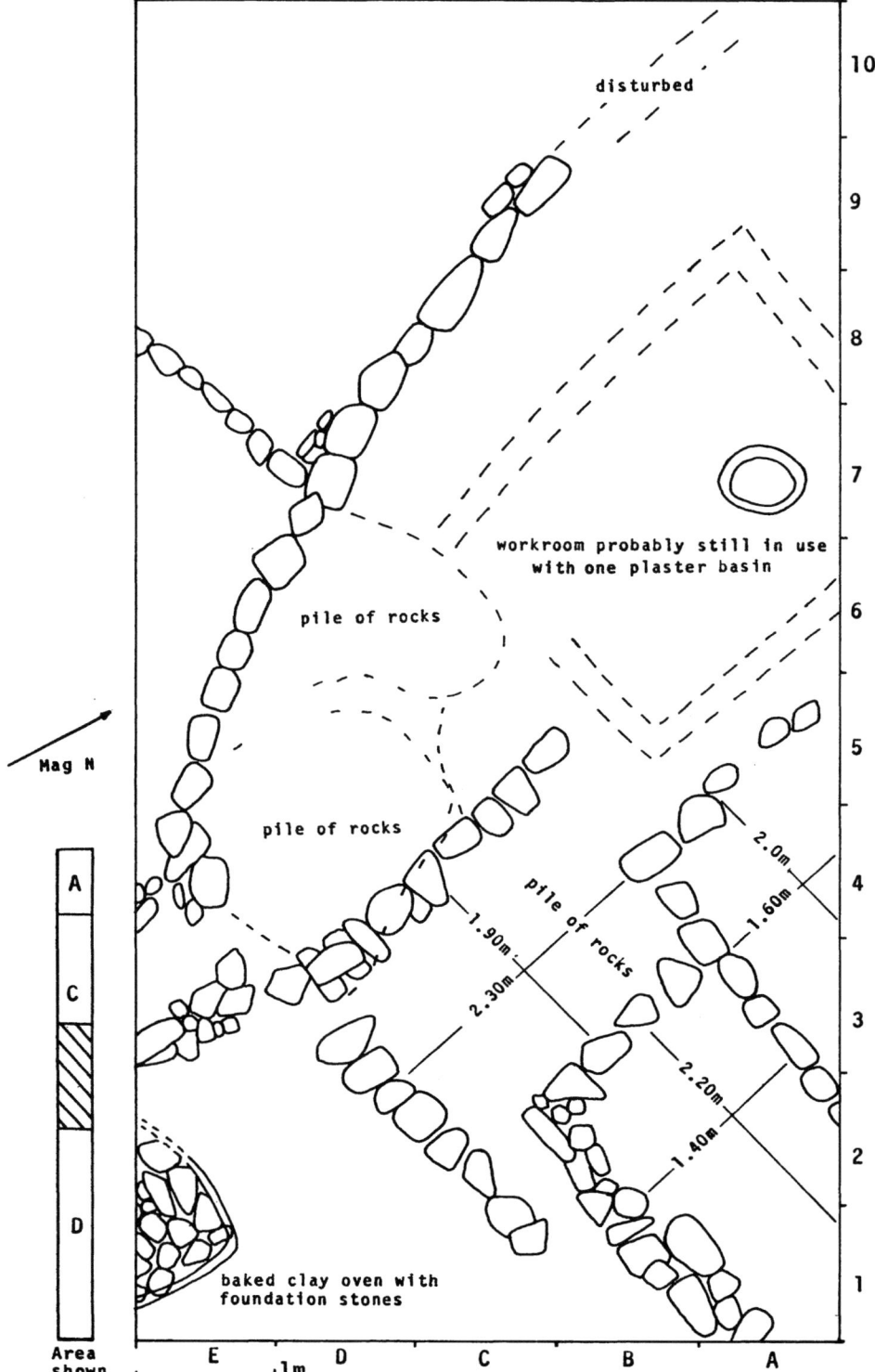

Fig. 21. Zone D3, Surkh Phase. Complex of stone-founded rooms. Stratum was badly disturbed and contemporaneity of all rooms is not assured.

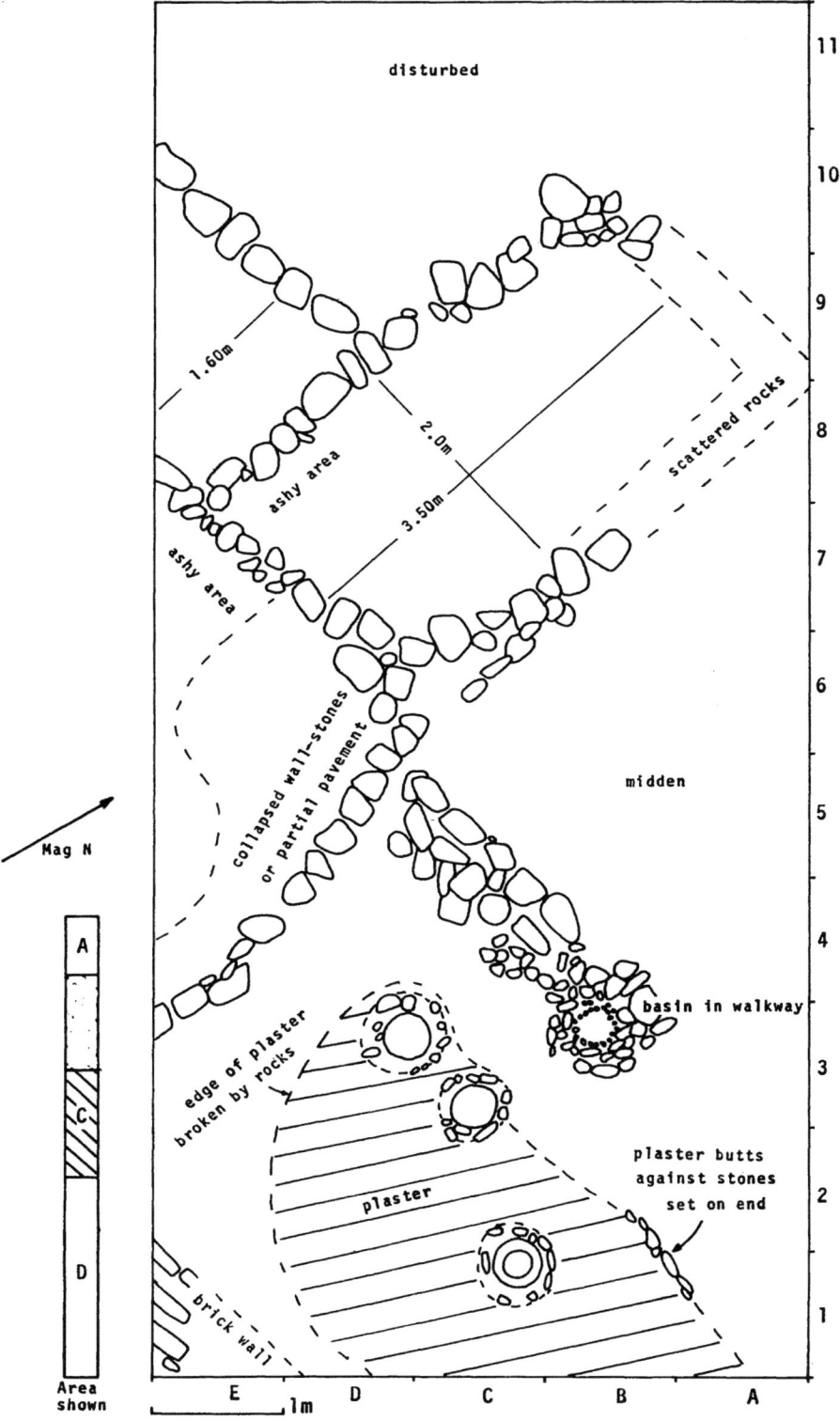

Fig. 22. Zone D4, Surkh Phase. Partial rebuilding of Zone D3 rooms and addition of a plastered floor work area with plaster basins. The area surrounding the plaster was badly disturbed by piles of rocks.

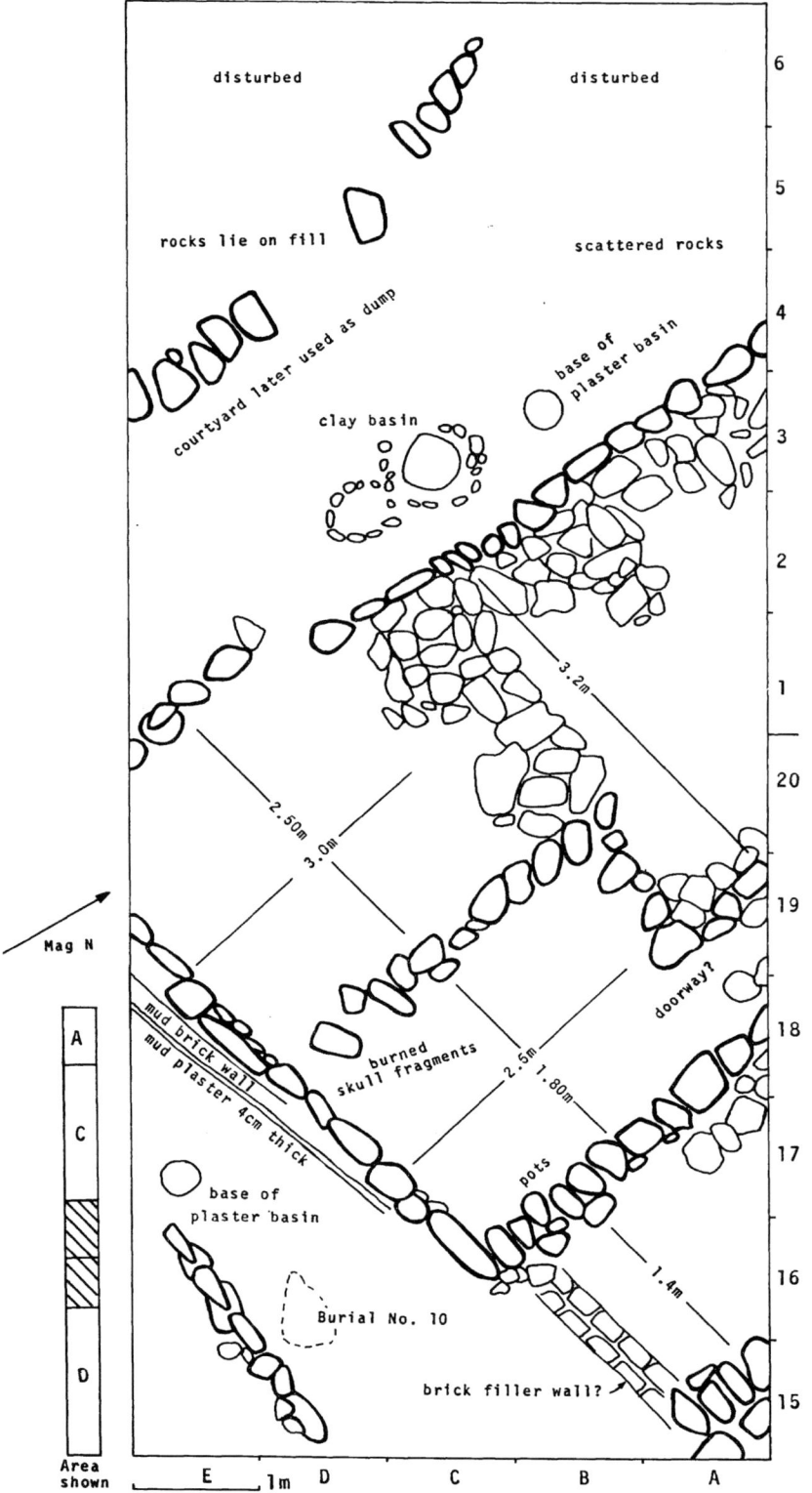

Fig. 23. Zone E1, Surkh Phase. Remains of a multi-room house unit separated from other rooms by open corridor work areas with plaster basins.

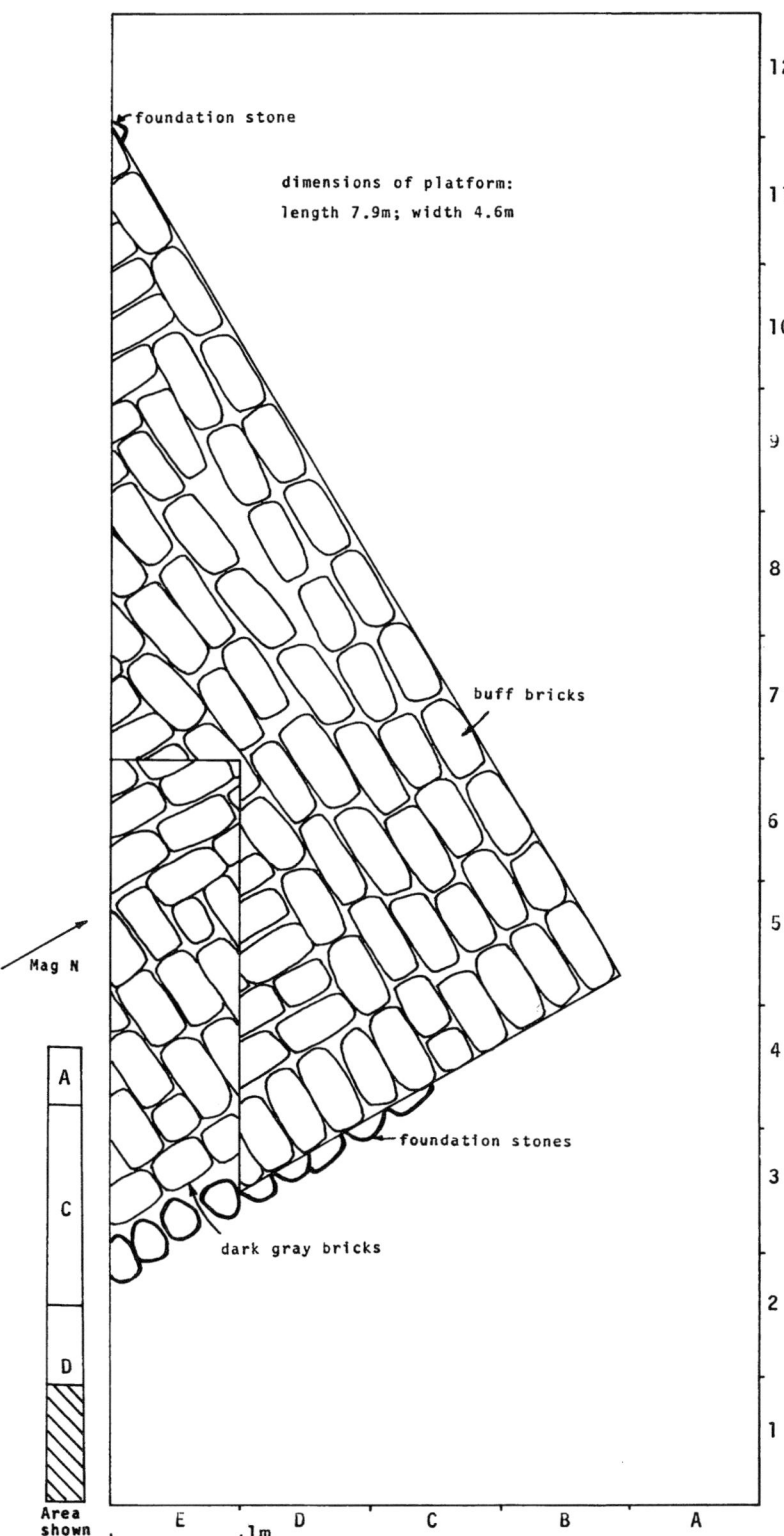

Fig. 24. Zone F, Surkh Phase. Corner of large brick platform. Trench cut into platform revealed inner core of soft, dark gray bricks. Outer core is dense buff clay bricks.

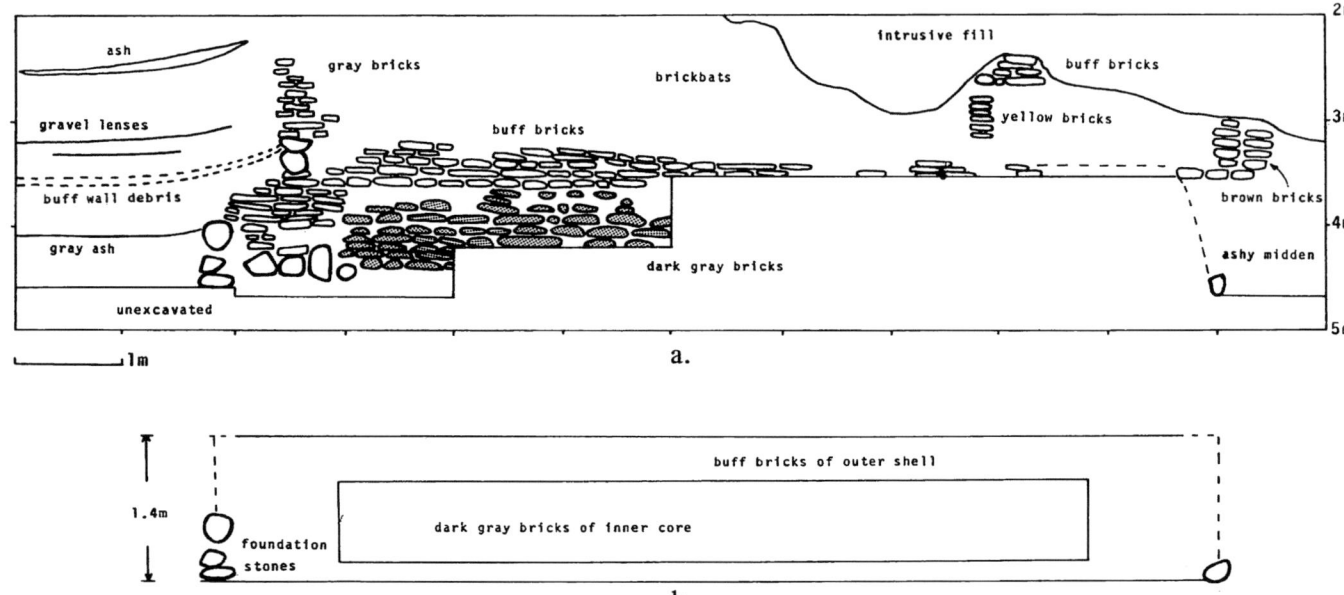

Fig. 25. Zone F, Late Surkh Phase. *a.* Profile through brick platform along south side of excavation. *b.* Approximate dimensions and shape of platform reconstructed.

were later placed (as they had been against the platform in Zone C). Strictly speaking there are no deposits that can be assigned to the time of the construction of the platform because we did not systematically dig out its foundations and the surrounding area, except within the confines of the trench. Thus, if the platform was freestanding, we have nothing more than incidental droppings in its immediate vicinity to indicate its age. Nevertheless, it is clear that the structures built into and against the base of the platform, although later than the platform, are of late Surkh Phase. In respect to their inferred dimensions and basic method of construction, the platforms in zones F and C are essentially the same.

Inasmuch as we have only one corner of the platform, we cannot determine its size with absolute accuracy; however, by analogy with the earlier platform, we would judge it to have been rectangular and at least 7 by 10 meters horizontally. If this is the case, however, the long dimension of the platform may have been oriented east-west rather than north-south as in Zone C.

Both platforms are founded on a single row of large rounded stones which were, in some cases, more than one course high (Fig. 24). The basic difference between the two structures is in the capping. The example in Zone F is capped with bricks of yellow clay which are considerably heavier and more durable than the interior core of soft, black, ashy bricks. In both platforms the black bricks were of the same size.

In neither platform is it possible to determine whether the sides, which stood about 1.5 meters, were vertical or slightly battered. Verticality is only certain up to the height of the foundation stones at the east end.

We determined the construction technique by cutting a trench one meter wide into the platform from the east side along our south profile (Fig. 25, Pl. 21). This cutting went down to the base of the platform and showed it to have been built on top of Surkh Phase material; the few sherds incorporated in the bricks themselves are also of Surkh Phase. The black bricks had been quarried from a Surkh Phase midden. The interior core was built some 6-7 layers thick and then capped and faced with heavy yellow clay bricks to a depth of 5-6 layers.

Owing to disturbance of the upper part of the platform by erosion and later buildings it was not possible for us to determine whether it had served as the base for a structure or whether it had simply had a flat, unadorned top. In any case, there was no evidence that it had once had a stone-founded structure on it except for the later Choga Mami Transitional building which cut into the upper edge of the platform when it had already been nearly buried by the accumulating deposits around it (Figs. 26,27). The area adjacent to the platform is nearly devoid of coherent architecture. To the west on the same level as the base of the platform is a scatter of brickbats, burned plaster, and stones, along with a small fragment of a brick pavement similar to the one found in Zone D (Fig. 26). To the east, after some 50 cm of Surkh Phase midden had accumulated, the corner of the platform was cut to provide a foundation for a brick wall and a plaster basin was set into the corner of the platform (Pl. 22). The nature of the room against the platform is not clear; its "floor" consists of a layer of gravel and eroded sherds. Outside of the wall to the south a midden consisting of finely bedded layers of ash and dirt accumulated, much of it probably washed off the platform itself. This midden has the look of a partially water-laid deposit (Pl. 21a).

Zone G

Two major stages of building are found in these deposits, each using the edge of the Zone F platform as a base against which to build. In each case the horizontal exposure of architecture is more than 5 by 15 meters. Two distinct kinds of structures appear to be represented in each.

ZONE G1, CHOGA MAMI TRANSITIONAL PHASE

Lying directly above the brick wall foundation that had been cut into the platform is a building consisting of two small brick-walled rooms whose orientation conforms to the platform against which they were built. It is likely that the underlying brick structure (Fig. 26) is the first structure of this phase but the few artifacts in association with it are not diagnostic of the Choga Mami Transitional. The general alignment of the walls is the same as that of the room in Zone F. Part of the exterior wall was broken and is reconstructed in Fig. 27. Another segment of the same wall seems to have been repaired with stones that bridge a one-meter gap to the next brick wall. None of these walls was founded on stone. The interior of the irregularly-shaped larger room has a "floor" of ash and gravel, plaster and sand. Outside of the room to the south, the area remains a finely layered midden.

The west end of the room was closed with a brick wall whose traces at this level consisted only of brickbats filling an area about a meter wide between the house and the large stone-founded room.

Of distinctly different form and size is the large stone-founded building whose walls are oriented with the platform into whose side they were partially built. This area saw an accumulation of 50 cm of midden before the walls were built. Inside the room is a basin (Pl. 23a,b) and the base of a fireplace (Pl. 23c) essentially identical to the ones found in earlier zones. The fireplace was broken and survived only in fragments above its base of flat stones. Disturbance in the rebuilding of Zone G2 apparently destroyed the west end of this structure.

A similar rectangular unit partially survives still farther to the west. Again founded on large stones, this structure contains the remains of two plaster basins. The north wall has an interior facing of clay bricks while the eastern wall is carefully faced with smaller stones to present a smooth facade (Fig. 27).

The two large rooms may not have been covered and may have served as open courtyard work areas. There are no domestic structures immediately adjacent to either so far as we were able to see.

ZONE G2, CHOGA MAMI TRANSITIONAL PHASE

This is basically a rebuilding, some 60 cm higher, of the large stone-founded room (Fig. 28). In the northwest corner is a plaster basin and adjacent to it the skull and leg bones of a dog, along with the remains of a basket (Pl. 32). The east end of the room was filled with bricks and lies now at the same level as the top of the Zone F platform. Stones underlying the south wall of the room are partially collapsed over the top of the platform.

The one meter wide wall at the east end stood one meter high on a level with the foundation stones and partially overlying some of the earlier ones. The bricks in this wall measure 80 x 10 x 10 cm and are finger impressed, with the furrows on the top side, marking a departure from earlier bricks but consistent with our findings in Zone H.

The top of the platform itself may have been used

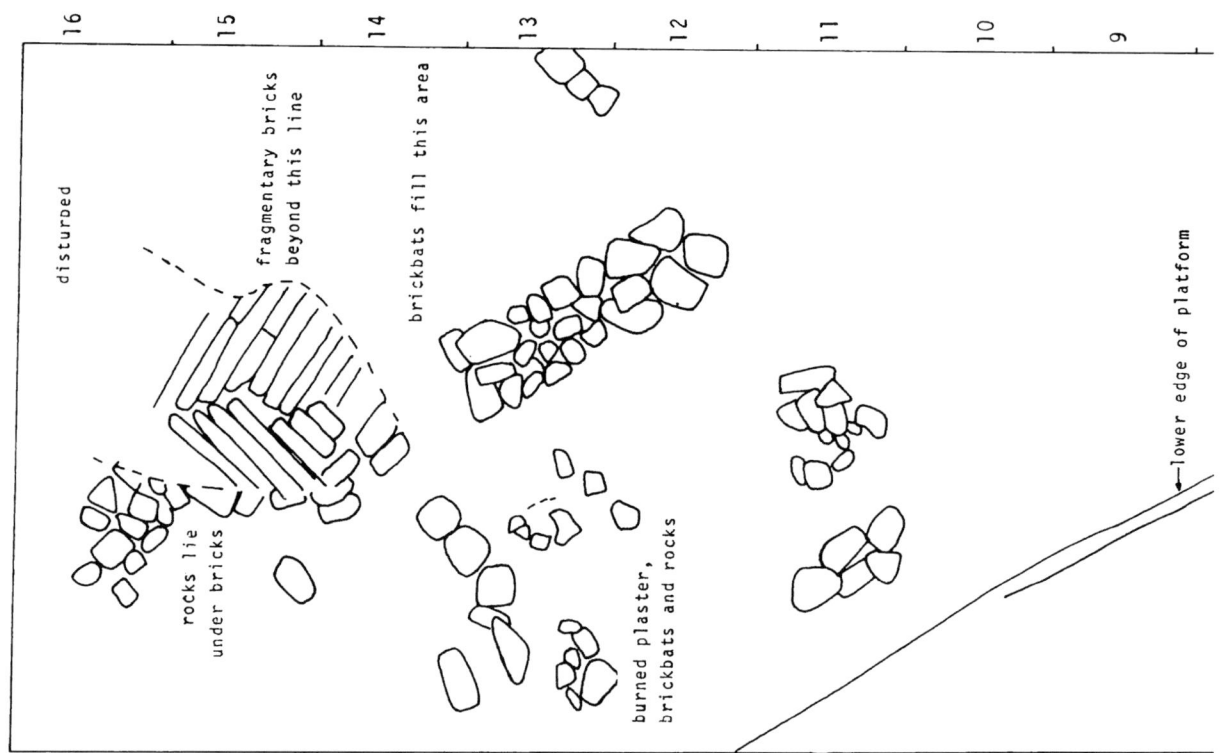

Fig. 26. Zone F, Late Surkh or Choga Mami Transitional Phase. Trace of brick wall cut into edge of platform is probably of Choga Mami Transitional age. Scattered remnants of walls to the west of the platform are probably of Late Surkh Phase age. Entire stratum is highly eroded.

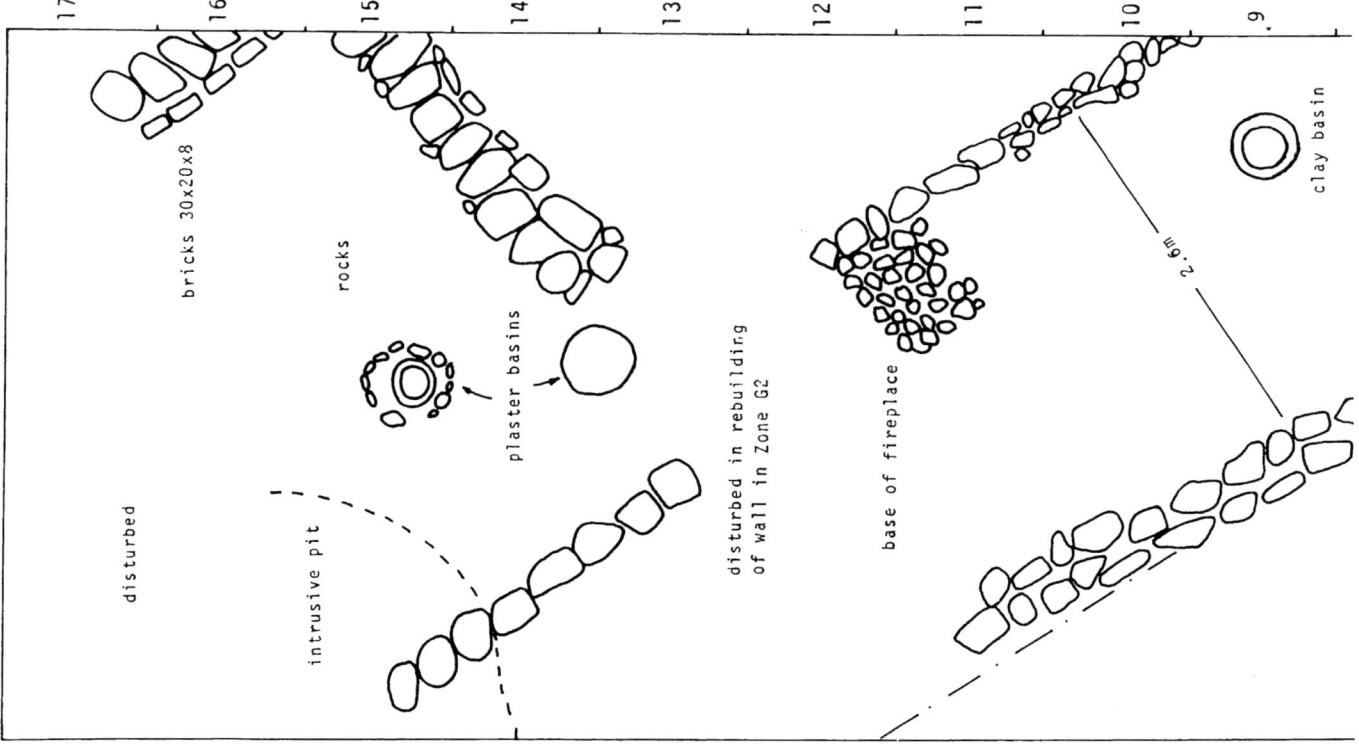

Fig. 27. Zone G1, Choga Mami Transitional Phase. Remnants of two large open(?) work rooms adjacent to the brick platform, and two small brick-walled rooms.

STRATIGRAPHY AND ARCHITECTURE

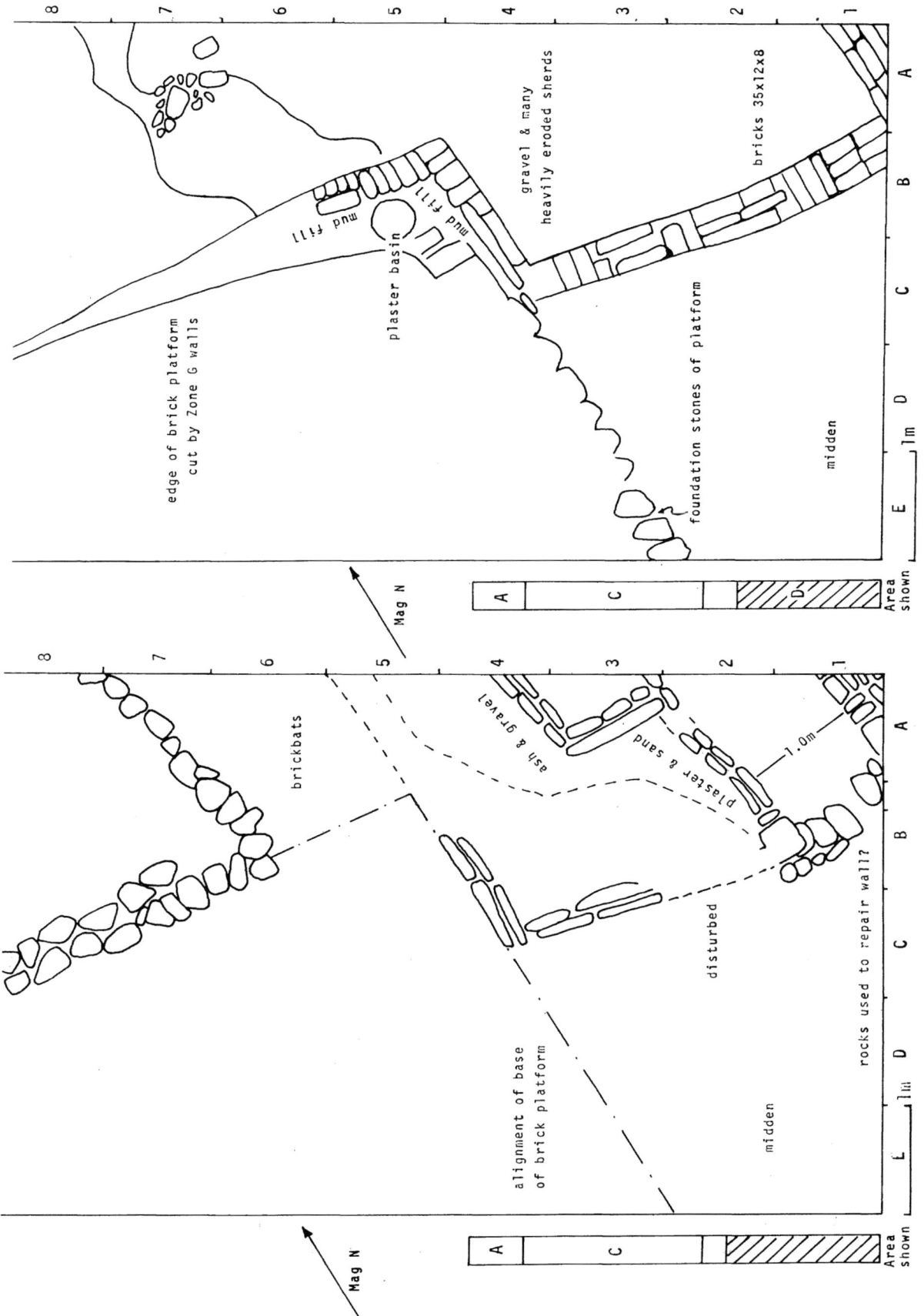

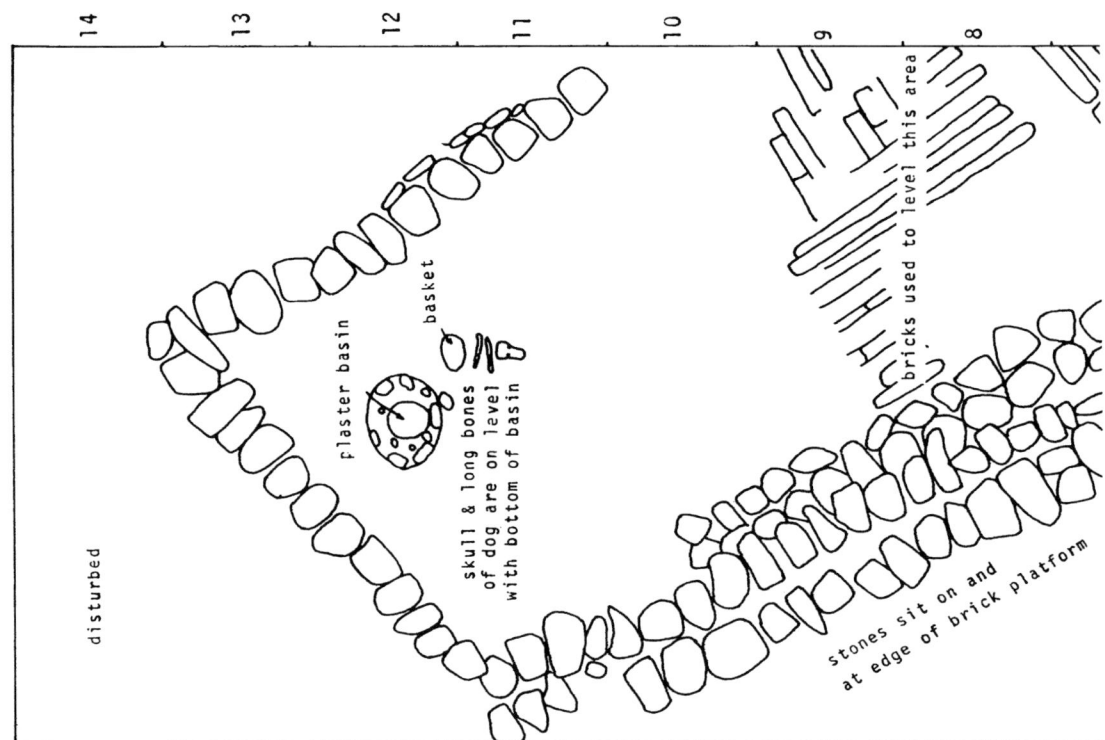

Fig. 28. Zone G2, Choga Mami Transitional Phase. Rebuilding of stone-founded room and of the brick walled structure of Zone G1.

at this time, judging from the line of stones along its east edge. If that was the case it was probably an open courtyard. Since most of the surface of the platform was disturbed we could not definitely assign any of the material found above it to Zone G2.

East of the platform and again built against it was another small room with a thin mud brick wall about 50 cm above the G1 walls. Inside there were layers of gravel, heavily eroded sherds and brickbats. Outside, the finely layered midden continued to accumulate.

By the end of Zone G2 the surface of the site in the area exposed by our trench was essentially flat. The platform was no longer standing above the rest of the area and even the interiors of rooms were leveled with brickbats to prepare the way for the next stage of building.

Zone H, Choga Mami Transitional Phase

This is the uppermost layer in Area D that contains an essentially complete plan of a room (Fig. 29) although the upper portion of the structure was destroyed during the excavation for the kiln and ash pit in Zone J. Still, the southwest wall of the house stood about one meter high. The room shown in Fig. 29 is nearly one meter above the room of Zone G2.

In contrast with many of the walls in Chagha Sefid, this one was constructed solely of bricks without stone foundation. The uppermost brick layers, which had slumped somewhat toward the east, or interior of the room, were unusually long; intact examples are 1.60–2.60 m in length and 15 cm wide and high. The "bricks" were probably formed partly in place as the courses were laid. Bricks from the lower courses were smaller: about 75 x 15 x 15 cm.

Outside the wall, to the west, was a stack of broken manos and metates, probably laid against the base (on a level with the top of the platform in Zone F) to help prevent erosion (Pl. 24a). West of the wall itself, however, the strata were badly disturbed by intrusive material because of the proximity of these levels to the surface of the site.

The room circumscribed by the walls measured 2.40 m north-south and 1.40 m east-west. To the south of this room was midden, a feature we found in all the lower levels as well. Inside the room was a truncated plaster basin, rocks lying next to it, and a pile of fire-cracked rocks in the southwest corner of

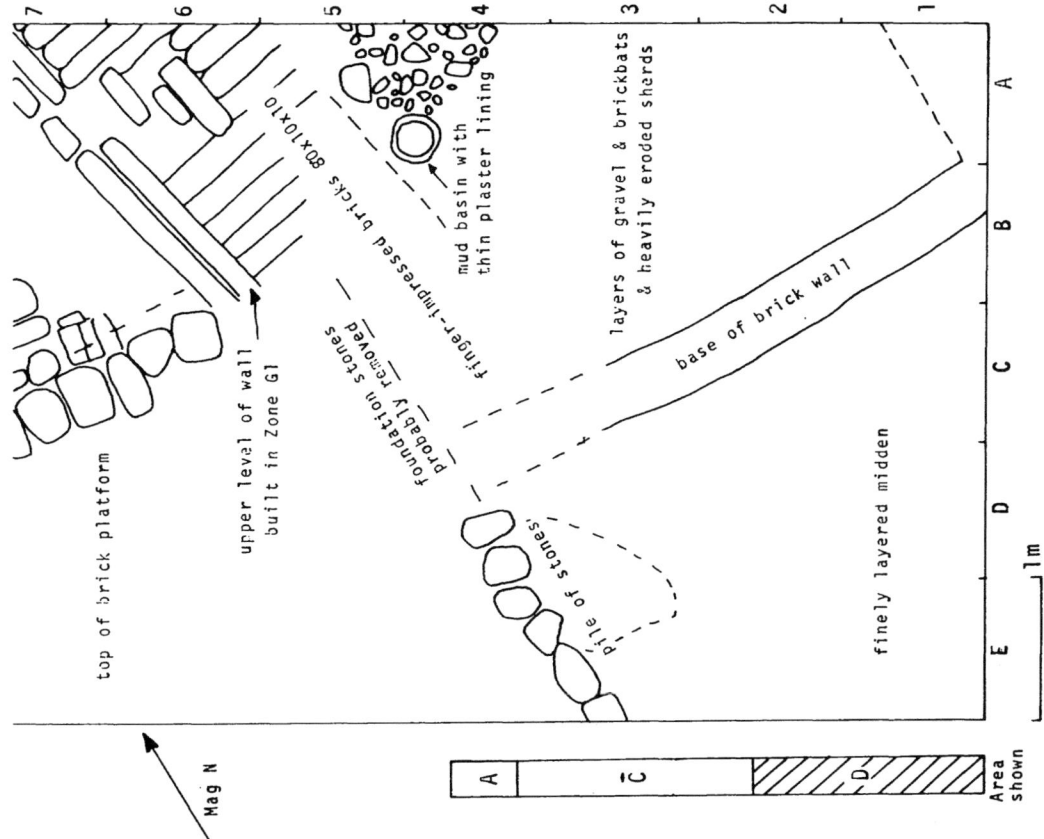

the room. Thus, while the remains are severely denuded, it appears that this was a workroom.

The line of bricks that formed the north wall continues along the top of the edge of the platform. Unfortunately this area was badly disturbed and contains nothing in context. The area considered useful for analysis is only 5 x 5 meters.

The walls of the house had all slumped badly, leaving brickbats lying on the ground outside the walls. Following the slumping, the house was covered with trash from an adjacent area. While this material is clearly somewhat later than the house, it lies stratigraphically under the structures in Zone I and can be considered essentially contemporary with the house.

Zone I, Sabz Phase

The uppermost traces of prehistoric walls occur in this zone although they were cut and partly removed by the excavation for the kiln (Zone J) and its associated ash pit (Fig. 30, Pl. 24b). These walls are about 60 cm above the brick-walled room of Zone H. Additionally there is a mud-walled oven whose top was severely eroded and whose interior was filled with bricky trash and ash of later periods (Fig. 31). This oven appears to go with the stone walls.

When we began the excavation of Area D we put in a 2 x 2 meter pit to see whether the strata were of the Sabz Phase. Immediately upon opening the pit we found early forms of a black-on-buff pottery which we recognized as Sabz Phase wares, and the top of the kiln (Pl. 25a). The work area was rather small considering the size of the kiln and when we found a small portion of stone wall cutting diagonally across squares DE 1-2, we removed it. In the process we also inadvertently removed part of a burial pit containing a newborn infant whose presence was not discovered until we cleaned and mapped the south profile. The date of the burial is uncertain although it lies stratigraphically under well-defined, but featureless, buff layers that go down about 120 cm (Fig. 30). There were no artifacts found with the burial.

More extensive remains of contemporary stone walls were found adjacent to the kiln (Pl. 24b). When the latter feature had been removed it was apparent

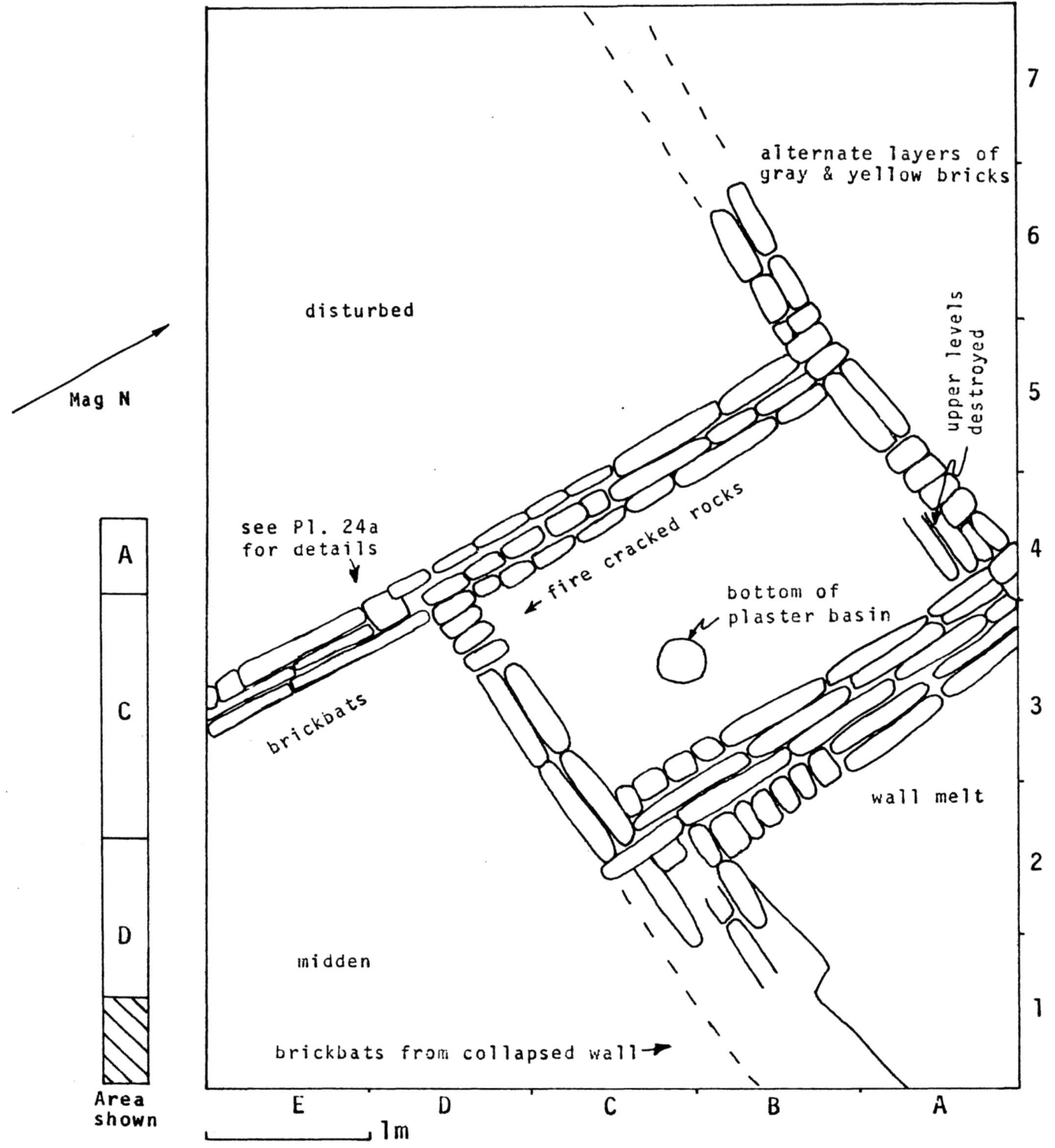

Fig. 29. Zone H, Choga Mami Transitional Phase. Room of long, finger impressed mud bricks with a plaster basin inside.

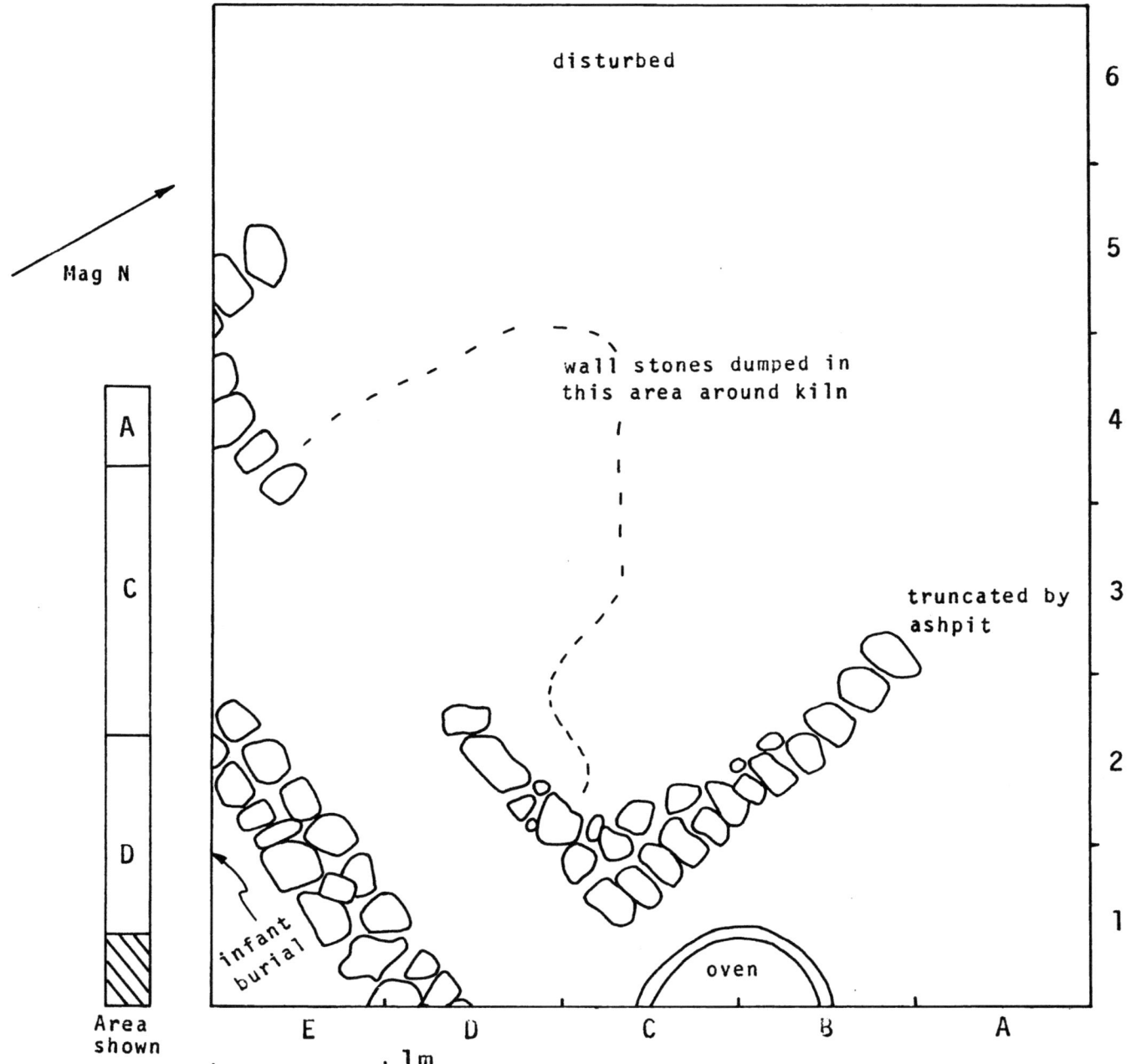

Fig. 30. Zone I, Sabz Phase. Traces of a room which was largely destroyed when the plaster kiln was built (see Fig. 32).

that the wall had been partly excavated to accommodate the kiln and that most of the interior of the structure had been removed during digging for the ash pit. The oven which we see in profile (Fig. 31, Pl. 25a,b) was probably situated in a courtyard outside the rooms indicated by the two stone foundations. There were no traces of bricks above either of the stone foundations; apparently the walls were denuded by surface erosion and then covered with Mehmeh Phase and later debris from structures higher up the side of the mound. The stone walls lie on top of the brick structure found in Zone H and in approximately the same orientation.

Relatively little intact material can be assigned to

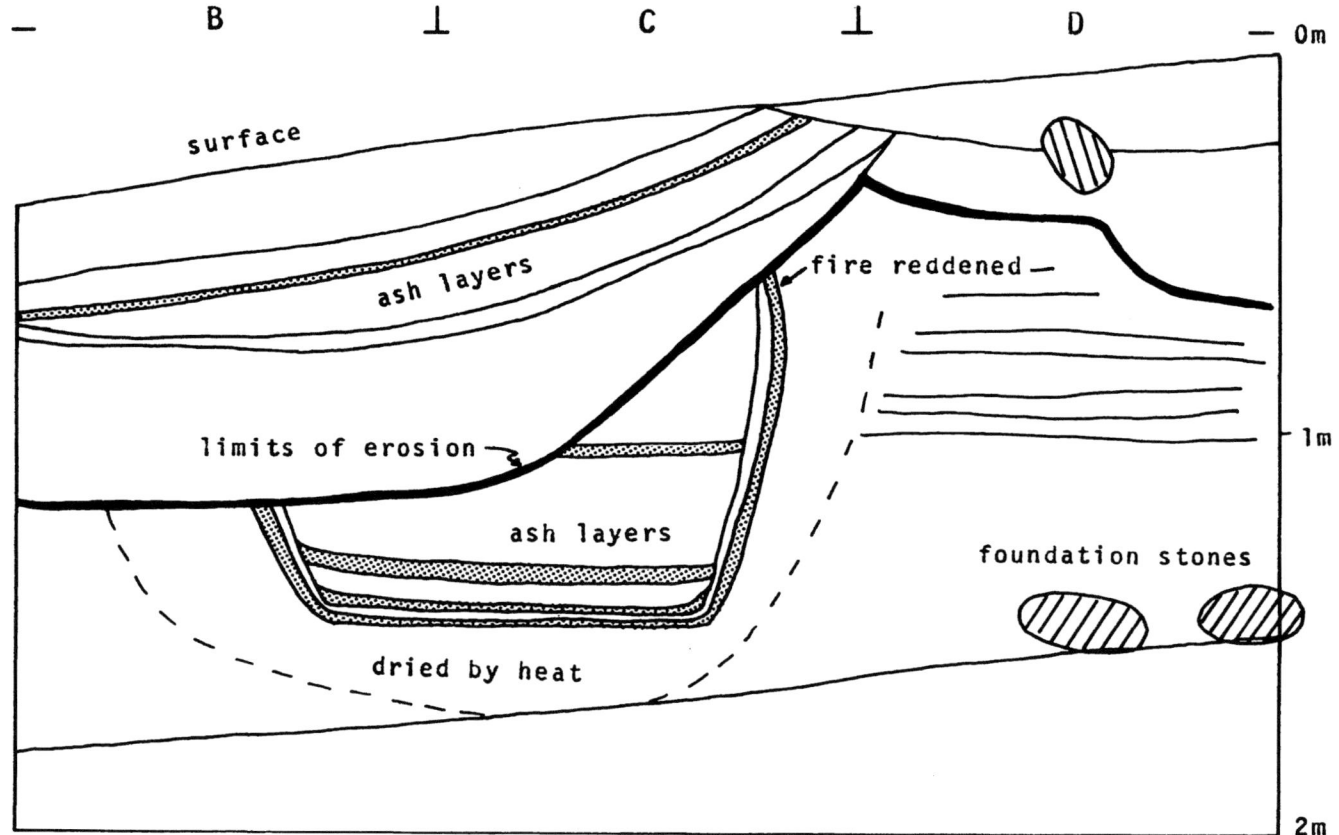

Fig. 31. Zone I, Sabz Phase. Section through oven along east profile of Area D. House wall seen in Fig. 30 is shown here as foundation stones.

Zone I although it is fair to assume that many of the Sabz Phase sherds found in the vicinity of the kiln and ash pit pertain to this zone.

Zone J, Sabz Phase

The final construction in Area D was a plaster kiln and its associated ash pit to the north of the oven (Fig. 32, Pl. 25b). The kiln and pit disturbed most of the 5 square meter area we opened initially in Area D; consequently there is very little material less than 180 cm down that can be considered in undisturbed context and in parts of the area disturbance goes down to 260 cm.

The age of the kiln is uncertain and without radiocarbon dating may not be determinable. It was filled with ashy material that contained sherds of Mehmeh and Bayat phases, but it is a distinct possibility that the oven was used when the fort atop the site was built and then was covered over by earth moved downslope by erosion after the top of the site had been leveled.

It is noteworthy that a plaster kiln of the same type and proportions was in use in Deh Luran while the excavations were going on. The lateness of such kilns is thus assured; what is uncertain is their antiquity. The abundance of plastered basins suggests that the art of burning lime was known during the prehistoric occupation of the site, but no kilns have come to light that are contemporary with the basins. The lack of plastered walls and floors suggests that lime plaster was not produced on a large scale.

DEPOSITIONAL HISTORY — AREA B

Supplementary to the main excavation on the west side was a small pit called Area B on the south side of Chagha Sefid. This pit was dug simultaneously with the beginning of Area A and was used to determine which would be the most suitable for extensive

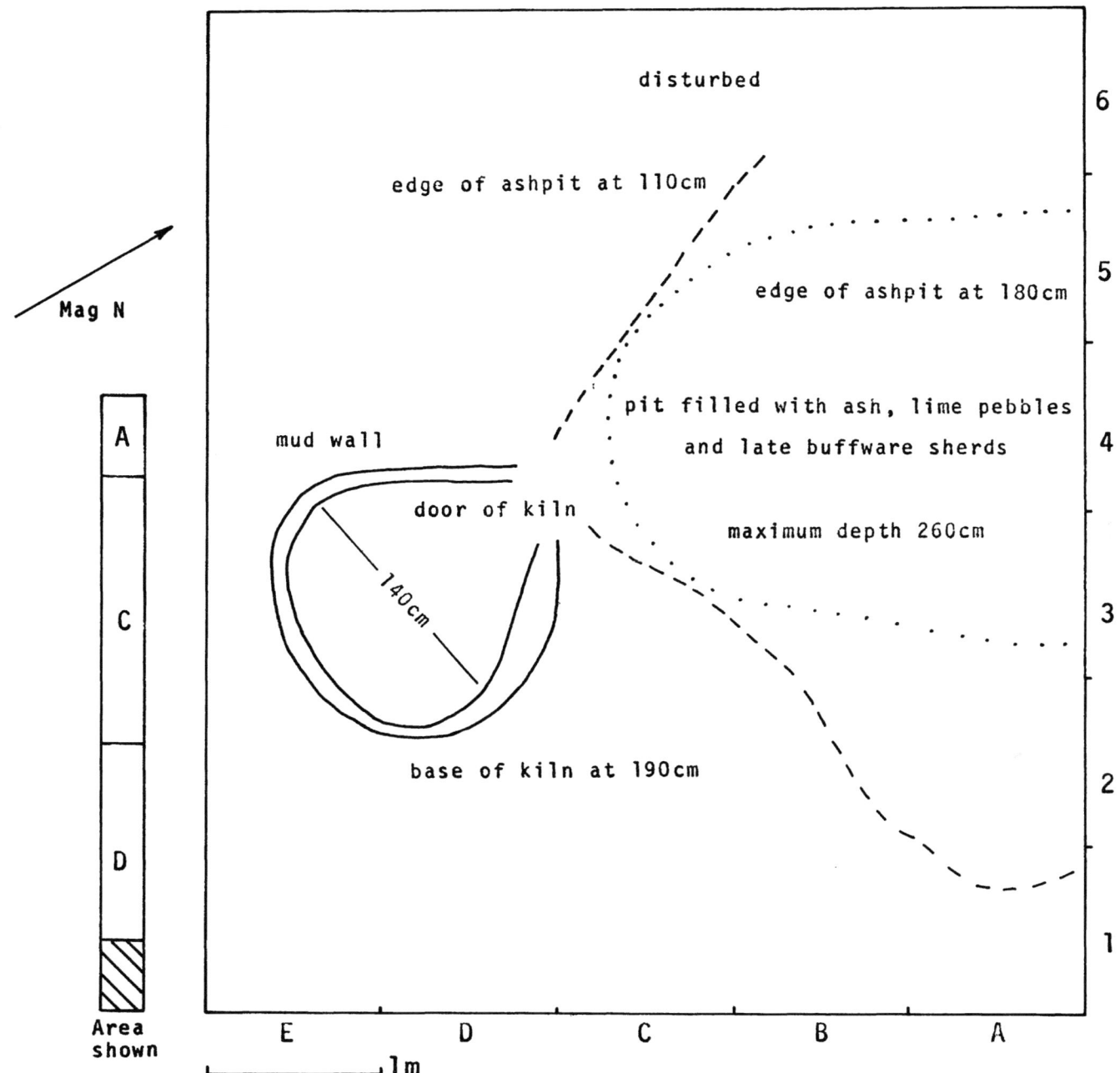

Fig. 32. Zone J, Sabz Phase and intrusive plaster kiln of uncertain age. Strata of Zone J are intact only in squares E1, E2 and D1.

excavation. James Neely was in charge of the work, which consisted of digging a 3 x 5 meter pit down into Mohammad Jaffar Phase levels (Fig. 33). At this point the work was terminated as the exposure in Area A with its wall foundations seemed more promising. Also figuring in our decision was the fact that prevailing winds made work very difficult on the east side where dust continually swirled around the pit.

The pit in Area B is about on a level with the brick platform in Zone F. This means that the Sefid and Mohammad Jaffar deposits on that side of the site are about four meters higher than their counterparts in Area A. This difference in absolute elevation

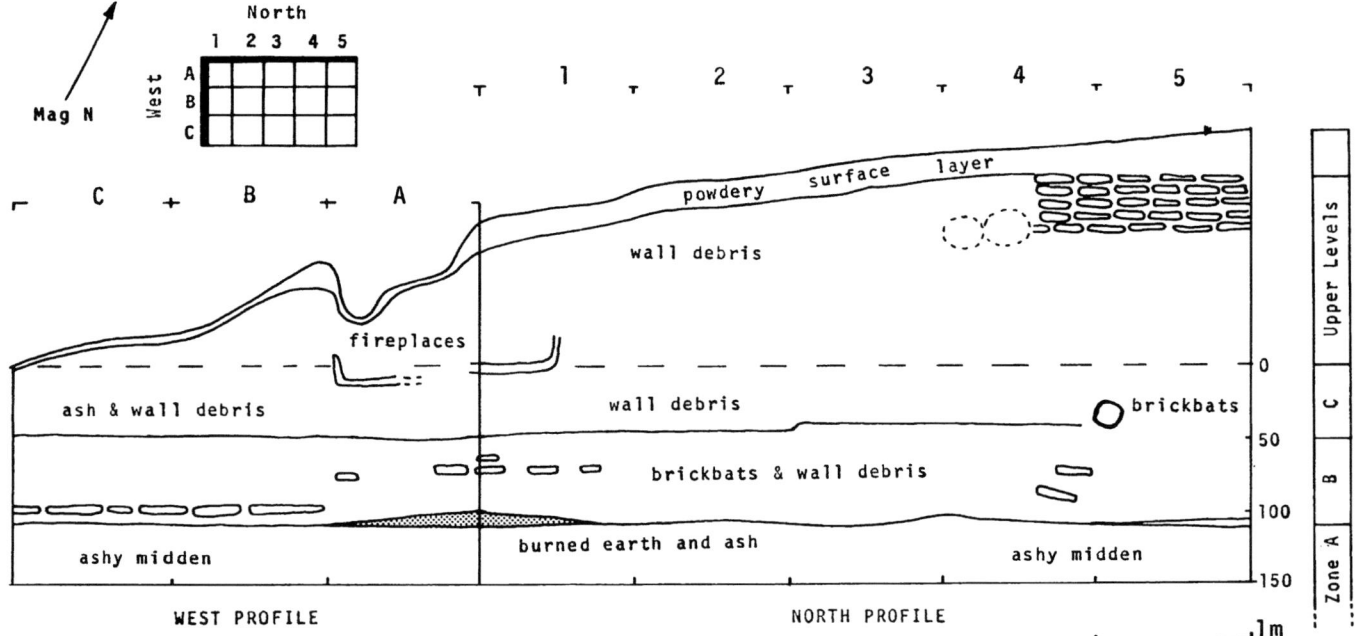

Fig. 33. Profile of Area B showing stratigraphic zones.

reflects both the slope of the plain itself and the fact that settlement tended to be located near the central rather than the peripheral parts of the mound.

Stratigraphically, three zones were discerned in a total useful depth of about 1.5 meters. Since the mound sloped steeply and was eroded where we dug, there was very little in the upper levels (Fig. 33). Only after a considerable amount of surface material had been removed was it possible to expose the 15 squares across the entire pit. This point then became the datum from which other measurements were taken. The sequence below this datum, beginning with the lowermost levels, consists of three zones defined stratigraphically.

Zone A, Mohammad Jaffar Phase

This zone, 110-150 cm below datum, consists solely of ashy midden. We attribute these deposits to the Mohammad Jaffar Phase.

Zone B, Mohammad Jaffar Phase

This zone, 50-110 cm below datum, consists chiefly of eroded wall debris. Although no coherent architecture was seen, the zone contained numerous brickbats. These deposits contain material of Mohammad Jaffar Phase.

Zone C, Mohammad Jaffar Phase

This zone consists of material 0-50 cm below datum. Although separated from the stratum of Zone B by a clearly defined interface between wall debris and midden, the material found here is also of Mohammad Jaffar Phase. The only architectural feature is a burned clay fireplace that was rebuilt once on a slightly different plan (Fig. 34a). By analogy with similar features in the main trench the fireplace here was probably adjacent to a wall, although the latter may have lain outside our excavation. The fireplaces were roughly oval and perhaps as much as 1.5 meters long, with sides and floors of baked clay. Although the sides had been badly broken, in one place the wall of the uppermost fireplace stood 30 cm high. As nearly as we can tell the sides were vertical.

Upper Levels

Above the well stratified layers of building debris and ash we found chiefly midden and brickbats. In

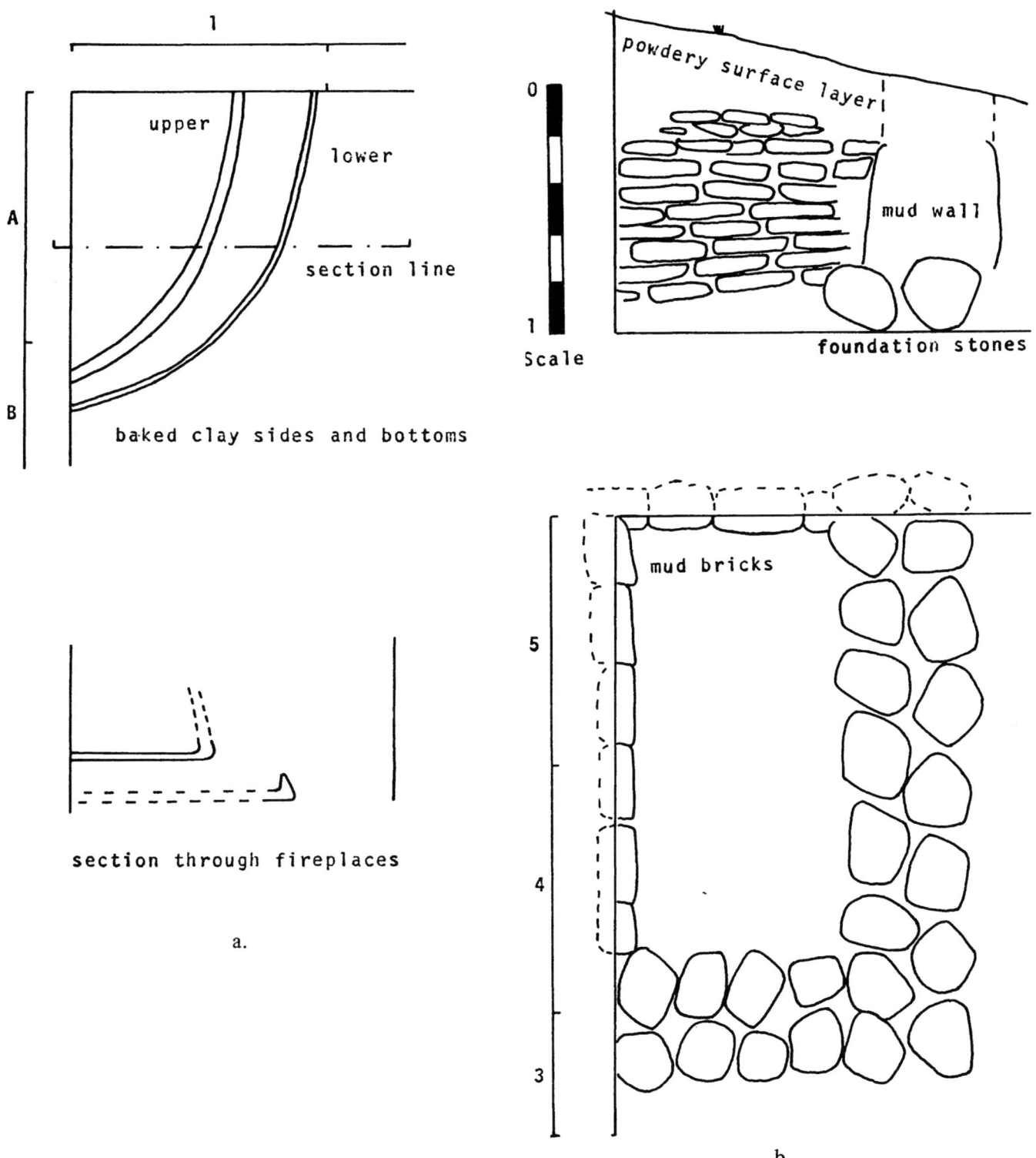

Fig. 34. Area B. *a.* Zone C, Sefid Phase. Plan and section of two fireplaces. *b.* Upper levels, probably Sefid Phase. Plan and section of stone-founded, mud walled room with possible bin in corner.

the uppermost corner of the pit stands the stone foundation of the corner of a structure that had a brick structure, possibly a bin, 1.60 x .85 m set inside. The outer walls of the structure were of packed mud over the foundation stones while the bricks of the bin are of well-formed, unbaked clay, approximately 30 x 20 x 8 cm. Because of the amount of intrusive material near the surface we could not determine the age of this structure although it seems most likely to be of the Sefid Phase.

ARCHITECTURAL FEATURES

The series of zones has revealed successive portions of architectural units and the repeated occurrence of certain features which have not been discussed in detail in the preceding pages. The nature of the buildings themselves and the techniques of their construction, as well as those of basins and fireplaces are discussed below.

Architectural Units

Because of the narrow excavation, which did not expose any single architectural unit in its entirety, little can be said about the typical units. Our best exposure is in Zone E1 (Fig. 23) where a multi-room structure separated by about two meters from other structures is partly exposed. One can project the wall lines to obtain a reasonable guess as to the nature of the remainder of the unit but this will naturally remain only a guess. The nearest parallels come from Choga Mami which has extensive remains of Samarran age and from Mureybit where a house in Level XIV looks very similar to the ones at Chagha Sefid (van Loon, 1968:Fig. 6). At Choga Mami the separate house units consist of 8-12 small rooms of mud brick with heavy buttresses at the intersections of the walls. Only by extending our excavation laterally some 5-10 meters could we hope to determine whether any of the buildings in Chagha Sefid are of the same general style.

The lack of building debris and of more than a few courses of bricks in any of the pre-Choga Mami Transitional rooms suggests that the superstructures may have been made of perishable material. A review of the literature shows that a good many early villages had houses with stone foundations and, apparently, pole or thatch superstructures. In the early (PPNA) levels at Beidha, Kirkbride (1968:266) has found clear evidence of such wall members, and, toward the end of the site's occupation, a change in architecture to full stone walls without supporting posts. Mortensen (1964: Fig. 10) has described a similar change from wooden huts to bricked houses at Guran, and reeds and posts were used at Mureybit (van Loon, 1968:273). The fact that many early villages have traces only of stone wall foundations lends support to the idea that perishable superstructures were common. For example, Munhatta and Mallaha, like Chagha Sefid, have stone foundations lying directly upon stone foundations, with little of the intervening material one would expect had there been full mud brick walls above the stones.

Ethnographic literature provides some useful analogs to this practice. Edelberg (1966/67) describes seasonal dwellings of nomads in Luristan which are pole and thatch or tent structures with stones outlining the bases. Such structures are erected anew each year on the old foundations. He also describes animal "barns" with heavy center posts and peaked roofs that rest on ridge poles and stone walls. Another study (Nissen, 1968) of a village in southern Iraq suggests a similar method of construction. The lower course of walls was made of packed mud inside of which bundles of reeds were placed vertically and arched across the top. The roof was then made of matting placed over the arches, giving the houses the appearance of elongate domes. Thus there is good reason to think that many of the structures at Chagha Sefid and at other villages consisted of temporary shelters of the type erected today largely by transhumant peoples. Moreover, it may be that some of the larger stone enclosures at Chagha Sefid were used primarily for the keeping of animals rather than for human residence.

The earliest houses in southwest Asia seem to have been small, isolated, round structures that were replaced with rectangular house units by the time Deh Luran was settled, and in the Levant by the time of PPNB. The latter type of structure lends itself very well to multiplication as more space is needed for living, storage or the keeping of animals. It is striking how small rooms within a single house unit often are. Rooms of 1.5 x 1.5 m are relatively common and might be considered bins for storage except for evidence at Beidha (Kirkbride, 1966:24-25) and Çayönü (Braidwood et al., 1971:1239) that they were used as small workshops for craft activities. Although such use may have been common at some sites it is by no means certain that small rooms invariably housed such activities. The little rooms are too small for adults to sleep in comfortably and in the absence of evidence of crafts it seems more likely that they were storage bins. Such rooms are seen at Chagha Sefid (Fig. 21) in association with larger rooms, but one has the distinct impression that most living was done out of doors at this site, as it is in modern villages in the area except during inclement weather. Unfortunately we have no useful information about the function of any of the rooms because they were all cleaned of usable artifacts upon their abandonment, and trash was thrown in from unknown contexts.

Bricks, Wall Construction, and Platforms

Bricks are used in the earliest constructions in Deh Luran, in contrast with the situation at sites like Tepe Guran where some form of wooden hut apparently preceded the use of clay. Perhaps this is merely a reflection of the unavailability of wood in Deh Luran since rude shelters of that material seem to have been made throughout most of human history.

The bricks found at Ali Kosh and Tepe Sabz have been described in our earlier report; there are significant differences in Chagha Sefid. The Ali Kosh Phase bricks at the two sites are of different types. At Chagha Sefid, long, narrow bricks (95 x 15 x 5 cm), were used in rows of two. At Ali Kosh, however, the bricks were the full width of the wall (Hole, Flannery and Neely, 1969:Pls. 10c, 9b) and apparently were cut as blocks out of the fine grained sediments surrounding the site. In common at the two sites is the use of simple mud walling without prior forming of bricks.

Mohammad Jaffar Phase construction is not attested at Chagha Sefid, nor are the Sefid, Surkh and Choga Mami Transitional at either Ali Kosh or Tepe Sabz.

Sefid Phase architecture sees the use of mud walling and a few traces of rectangular bricks (ca. 50 x 20 x 10 cm) in Zone A4 (Fig. 10). No other brick walling is found in this phase, but the first use of stone-founded walls is attested. The use of stone foundations was seen as early as the Mohammad Jaffar Phase at Ali Kosh although the single example is somewhat enigmatic, occurring as it did very close to the surface. We (Hole, Flannery and Neely, 1969: Fig. 12) thought at the time that the pebble layer was the base of a wall, but it now seems more likely that the adjacent stones were the foundation and that the pebbles were a pathway alongside the wall. In any case, we have not found similar layers of pebbles under any walls in Chagha Sefid. Instead we usually find a single row of large stones on which bricks were laid (see Fig. 15).

Once the technique of using foundation stones was invented, it persisted to this day in areas where stone is readily available. Nonetheless, *some* walls were not founded on stone in the Late Surkh, in Choga Mami Transitional and in phases at Tepe Sabz. Perhaps these walls were not directly subjected to erosion.

The most complete departure from known types of bricks is found in the large brick platforms of the late Sefid and Surkh phases. Striking in both instances is the use of very soft, black, ashy bricks as the core of the platform. Although we found no overlying denser bricks in the Sefid Phase example, it is clear from our experience with rain that the soft bricks readily absorb water and would be virtually useless as an exposed surface. Ashy bricks were found incorporated into some walls at Ali Kosh and they occur as well in the brick pavement in Zone C of Chagha Sefid, but are not found at the latter site in house walls, where their lack of cohesive compaction would tend to cause slumping.

The platform in Zone F shows the use of dense buff clay bricks of the same size as the interior ashy bricks (ca. 60 x 30 x 10 cm). Whereas the ashy bricks of the core are plano-convex, probably because of slumping after their initial shaping, those of the outer core are nearly rectangular and straight-sided, reflecting their greater density and cohesion.

Another departure from our previous results is found in the brick pavements. The one in Zone C (Fig. 18) is about 4 meters on a side and no more than 60 cm high. The bricks in this structure measure 20 x 15 x 6 cm. A similar pavement, also about 60 cm thick, is found in Zone D1, Surkh Phase. It measures about 3 x 3.5 meters but the bricks are elongate and set with alternate courses at right angles. The bricks are generally 60-80 x 12-14 x 8 cm, although shorter ones are found, especially at the corners. In contrast with the earlier pavement, this one is founded on stones along the edge. A fragment of another pavement of this type, with the bricks laid in a herringbone pattern, is in Zone F, later Surkh Phase (Fig. 26).

One use to which the pavements may have been put is suggested by Nissen (1968) who surveyed a recently abandoned village and elicited from an informant the uses and names of architectural features. Along with each house complex was a sleeping platform "measuring from 2-8 sq. m and being ca. 1.50 m high . . . During summertime the entire family normally slept here, everyone seeking to take advantage of the cooling wind and elevation" (Nissen, 1968:109). Elevated platforms are used by villagers today, although they are often built on mud walls or entirely of wood. The important point is that an elevated, outdoor place to sleep is desirable in hot weather when there is little air circulation at ground level.

The uses of the large brick platforms remain obscure. They are larger than seems necessary for sleeping but their use as an elevated gathering place is certainly not precluded. An habitual feature of Near Eastern villages is a place in which men gather and in which guests can be received. Ordinarily these are rooms in houses, especially of the richer members of the community. In colder or inclement weather, and when sufficient material for spanning wide rooms is available, it is reasonable to have these rooms indoors. However, in summer on the Deh Luran plain it is distinctly desirable to have greater circulation of air, especially in a shaded place. As a suggestion, I submit that the large platforms may have been such meeting places and may have been covered with a light framework of poles and matting, while the bricks themselves were covered with matting.

With the Choga Mami Transitional we find another kind of brick, this time elongate with furrows in the upper surface created by running the fingers in 2-3 rows along the length of the wet clay. Such bricks are found in the wall or filler in Zone G2 (Fig. 28) and in the room above in Zone H (Fig. 29). These bricks are about 80 x 10 x 10 cm. Similar bricks were used in Samarran buildings of Choga Mami although it is not stated whether they were furrowed (Oates, 1969:116). In the Choga Mami Transitional at Choga Mami, steps leading to a platform were built of *libn* which "was marked with 3 deep grooves or fingermarks along the top" (Oates, 1969:121).

Although floors as such were rarely found, in the Choga Mami Transitional levels we found surfaces paved with gravel and sherds. Significantly, villagers in Choga Mami were doing the same thing at the same time. "We think that the sherds may have been laid to improve the drainage of floors and walls immediately above, just as a modern soak-away is packed with fragments of brick" (Oates, 1969:126). It should be noted as well that during this phase the structures at Chagha Sefid, in contrast with those found in earlier zones, were not laid on stone foundations.

Plaster Basins

Some of the most commonly occurring features in the Sefid and later phases are the plastered basins which are associated with open (courtyard?) areas and stone-founded or stone-walled brick rooms (Pls. 26, 27). Many of these basins were sufficiently intact to give a good idea of their overall size and of the technique of construction. Surviving examples stand some 30-40 cm high and are roughly 40-60 cm in diameter at the top. The bases may be either large stones (Pl. 27c) or simply a heavy layer of plaster (Pl. 26b,d). The walls, often supported with a casing of stones, are then built of clay, with an interior facing of plaster; rims are capped with stones. It appears that the basins were set into floors, probably protruding some distance above them. As the levels of the floors rose the basins were replastered, and the walls built higher, sometimes a dozen or more times.

We cannot be certain how these basins, which formed a deep mortar-like utensil with an interior that was hard as stone, were used. Because the plaster was impervious to water they could have held liquids, although their use as mortars for the grinding of grain or other vegetable foods (legumes, acorns, etc.) seems more likely (R. L. Solecki, 1969:993). If this was the case, large wooden pestles were probably employed. Today one sees wooden mortars and pestles in use (Löffler and Friedl, 1967:Fig. 65) and the plaster basins may have been their functional counterparts, used in the absence of suitable logs (which would have been difficult to cut and hollow out with the stone tools found at the site, even if wood had been available locally).

Mud Basins

Similar in style but different in construction and overall size are basins lined with fine layers of unfired mud or clay (Pls. 26f, 27e). These basins would not have been suitable for use with liquids and their durability under pounding is likewise questionable. In other respects they appear similar to plastered basins except that surviving portions suggest that they were not as deep. Again the tops are lined with stones and the openings were probably at or near the level of the floors into which they were set.

Basins of both kinds often occur with piles of stones around them, possibly indicating some association between the two. However, as the piles of stones include fragments of manos, metates, and unshaped stones, it seems more likely that these stones were placed alongside the basins to fill the holes into which they were put and to provide a solid dry surface around them. If this is the case the stones are not directly related to the way the basins were used.

The fact that basins often occur in groups indicates that the areas continued to be used for the same purpose through several stages of rebuilding. In many instances these areas appear to have been open. In only a few instances were the areas around the basins plastered or obviously paved with stones.

The closest approximation to the plaster basins at Chagha Sefid appears to be at Bouqras (de Contenson and van Liere, 1966:Pl. 11, No. 6) where a basin is set into a plastered floor. In this instance the top of the basin is flush with the surface of the floor. There are no details of the construction of the basin itself. Similar features are not reported at other sites.

In view of the availability of stone at Chagha Sefid, it seems unlikely that the plaster basins were used for the same purposes as the contemporary stone mortars. Roughly analogous in size to the plaster basins are the standing mortars found in several Natufian sites (e.g., Mallaha, El Wad, Nahel Oren), but whether they are to be considered functionally different from the contemporaneous low mortars at these Natufian sites is questionable.

Fireplaces

The only form of fireplace appears to be the large, generally stone-based enclosure with vertical clay walls, usually set into the corner of a room. Examples of these are found as early as the Ali Kosh Phase at Chagha Sefid and Ali Kosh (although those at the latter site, with sides of mud bricks, did not have stone bases) and continue to be used through the early Sabz Phase at Chagha Sefid. None was found in the excavation of Tepe Sabz.

Although most examples were broken down to the base, the surviving forms (Figs, 7, 8, 34, Pls. 8, 25a, 27a) clearly show a similarity in size and construction throughout. It appears that the walls are about 20-40 cm high and the total interior area is about one meter across. One example from Zone A3, Ali Kosh Phase has an apparently open side but this may be the result of breaking. No example with walls intact was excavated completely enough to determine whether it had an open side.

Judging from the position of the fireplaces with respect to walls, some were placed inside rooms. Some of the examples are associated with plastered floors although others (e.g., Fig. 23) may have been in open courtyards. Unfortunately walls and floors were not preserved sufficiently to determine whether any of the examples was out of doors. What does seem clear is that there is no consistent positioning of the fireplaces in a particular corner and, very clearly, most rooms do not have them. From the lack of fireplaces inside rooms we can deduce that little heating was done. Our exposure is too small to tell whether fireplaces served more than one house.

Although all of the fireplaces showed evidence of burning, there were no sticks or large pieces of charcoal remaining in any of them. It is possible, in view of this, and in view of the notable lack of charred wood in the site, that dung, grass, or shrubby plants were the common fuel.

The fireplaces are relatively deep, lending some support to the idea that they may have served as ovens, although the facts that none of the sides curve in substantially and that there is no trace of roofing material suggests that they were open at the top.

With this arrangement it would be possible to roast meat by building a fire inside and removing the ashes before the meat was placed inside. If the meat was then covered to prevent loss of heat it would cook at least on the bottom and sides. In instances where ash and bones were found near fireplaces, especially at Ali Kosh (Hole, Flannery and Neely, 1969:Fig. 11c) this may have been the practice.

An equally plausible use of the ovens is to parch grain. This has been suggested by several authors (e.g., Braidwood et al., 1953:526; Helbaek 1969: 402). In this case, after the floor of the oven had been heated and the ash removed, grains would be spread out to roast, thus rendering the glumes easier to remove when the grains were finally cracked or ground.

There is no suggestion that the ovens were used in the firing of ceramics although this use is not precluded. We did not find the usual masses of kiln wasters that one would expect in the immediate vicinity of a ceramic kiln. As yet no obvious ceramic kiln has yet been described from any contemporary site in southwest Asia.

Without going into an exhaustive listing, we can say that most early villages have similar fireplaces/ovens. Indeed, one may say that they are a nearly (there are none at Beidha [Kirkbride, 1966:16]) universal feature in these villages, varying only slightly in their construction. From Anatolia through the Levant they ordinarily have bases of plaster, often used to cement a layer of pebbles. In the Zagros they have either simple baked clay bases or flat stones underlying the firebox. Ordinarily, too, when the sides are preserved, they appear to have been between 20 and 50 cm high, sometimes slightly incurving, but more often vertical. The forms vary from circular to oval, and the long dimensions are in the range of one to two meters.

Although the evidence for this is much less secure, such fireplaces appear to disappear by the post-Sabz Phase range of time. Is it only coincidence that in Deh Luran their disappearance coincides with the introduction of free-threshing grains and the apparent drop in the quantity of meat in the diet?

As a final comment, the use of the ovens for roasting suggests a possible use for the enormous numbers of ceramic strips that were found in the Sefid and Surkh phases. These strips were usually found in large concentrations of ash and the strips themselves are often heavily coated with calcined ash and fired relatively hard, even harder than contemporary pottery. The context, such as it is, suggests that they are objects of mundane utility that were exposed differentially to firing: they range from scarcely fired to very well baked.

Assume that a fireplace was heated for the roasting of meat. By the nature of the construction of the ovens, the upper parts of the meat would not cook very well since the heat was concentrated at the bottom and along the sides of the oven. A way to cook the meat through would be to cover it with a layer of material that would hold the heat. Still better would be to cover the meat with a layer of material that could itself be heated without damage to the meat. If ceramic strips had been packed on and around the meat to a depth of, say, 5-10 cm, it would have been a simple matter to build a fire on top of the strips, thus heating them thoroughly and cooking the meat from the top down. The relatively loose packing of the strips would ensure the escape of steam and they would be easy to remove when the roasting was done. Moreover, in such a use, some of the strips would become well fired, while others would be only slightly affected by the heat, and some might become coated with the calcined ash that was often found on the strips. When the meat was done, the strips could be simply discarded in the nearest convenient midden.

Such an explanation accounts for the observed characteristics of the ceramic strips, although it does not exclude more obvious solutions, namely, placing stones atop the meat, or building a covered oven. Without experimentation it is difficult to determine which of these alternatives would yield the best results. Whatever their use may have been, ceramic strips enjoyed only a brief popularity.

V

BURIALS

Ten burials or portions of burials, two of which are of recent age, were found in the excavation. The remainder are prehistoric as is attested by the condition of the bones and their context within prehistoric strata.

PREHISTORIC BURIALS

Eight skeletons or clusters of bones have been given burial numbers but only four of these are in articulated or semi-articulated condition. With the exception of burials No. 3 and 10, all are in Zone A4, Sefid Phase. Nevertheless, owing to the degradation of the land surface in that area following its abandonment, the age of the burials is not certain. This is a matter that is discussed in the chapter on stratigraphy. The burials are no earlier than late Ali Kosh Phase, but they may be of Mohammad Jaffar Phase or early Sefid Phase. If we accept the evidence from Ali Kosh of burial practices in the Ali Kosh and Mohammad Jaffar phases as indicative, it seems most likely that the burials are of Sefid Phase. The reasons for this are that at Ali Kosh, Ali Kosh Phase burials are usually in a seated position, wrapped in matting and wearing beads and pendants (Hole, Flannery and Neely, 1969:Figs. 105, 106, 107), while those of the Mohammad Jaffar Phase are flexed and also have ornamentation (Hole, Flannery and Neely, 1969:Figs. 108, 109). In both cases red ochre is evident on the bones and in the Ali Kosh Phase cranial deformation was practiced.

The burials in Zone A4 at Chagha Sefid show traces of ochre and were probably placed on mats but in an extended position and without ornaments. The skulls show extreme cranial deformation. The sample size in Zone A4 is small, only one burial remaining nearly intact, so that the evidence can hardly be considered definitive. The orientation of the Chagha Sefid burials is different from those at Ali Kosh with the exception of burial 30 at Ali Kosh, which is extended alongside the seated burials (Hole, Flannery and Neely, 1969:Fig. 105). Whether these differences signify temporal changes in the habits of Deh Luran populations or whether they indicate that contemporary villages had different burial practices cannot be determined at this time.

The most complete burials are Nos. 7, 8, and 9 (Fig. 35a, Pl. 29), three bodies laid on their backs in a completely extended position with arms along the sides or crossed over the pelvis. These represent separate and sequential interments as indicated by disturbance of the bones. Burial No. 7 is the first. Burial No. 9 was probably placed in next, its pit cutting into the left arm of burial No. 7. The final interment is No. 8 whose pit cut into the left femur of No. 7 and probably also displaced the skull and upper right arm of No. 9. Later digging seems to have disturbed burial No. 8 as well, but this digging was probably in connection with the house whose corner lies directly above the burials.

This little cluster of skeletons illustrates very well the lack of standardization in orientation. The head of No. 7 is toward the west, No. 9 was headed toward the south and No. 8 toward the northeast. The one intact skull shows deformation (Pls. 30a,b, 31a).

No ornaments accompanied these burials; however, traces of matting were found under the skeletons and the bones showed traces of red ochre.

In the same zone is burial No. 4, consisting of a skull lying upside down, a rib cage with two arm bones lying in it, and a large piece of the pelvis, along with a few other small pieces of broken human bone (Fig. 35b, Pl. 28c,d). This skeleton, evidently of a child, was covered with red ochre. Among the human bones are a great many pieces of caprine bone. The ensemble was lying on a pavement of flat stones, probably the base of a fireplace which in turn seems to have been contained within the corner of a mud brick room. By the time the skeleton was placed on the stones all traces of ash, as well as fragments of the sides of the fireplace, had been eroded or removed. Thus, although the skeleton was placed on a bed of stones it appears to have been a secondary deposition of skeleton and caprine bones which were not originally associated with the fireplace. Most likely the bones were placed in the convenient mound of earth left after the walls of the former structure had collapsed.

In the same zone are burials 5 and 6. No. 5 is a deformed skull found lying upside down in a pile of caprine bones (Pl. 28a). Next to the skull was a femur, and half of the jaw lay 40 cm away from the skull. Pieces of arms, legs and vertebrae were scattered and mixed with the caprine bones. The entire skeleton except for hand and foot bones appears to be present, although the collection was in very fragile condition. There was no trace of a pit, nor any associated artifacts.

Burial No. 6 consists of a skull and two femurs. The skull was broken in antiquity. There was no trace of a pit, nor any associated artifacts.

In reconstructing the events, it appears most likely that the various bodies were interred in the top of the Zone A3, Ali Kosh Phase deposits, sometime after occupation had moved to another part of the site. When the area was reoccupied by buildings in Zone A4, the builders of these structures unearthed some of the bodies and reinterred them nearby. There is a good possibility that this portion of the west slope of the mound was used for burials in the late Mohammad Jaffar or early Sefid phases.

Later in the Sefid Phase we find burial No. 3, consisting only of the head of a femur, a femur, a metapodial, a calcaneus, a talus and a fragment of scapula (Pl. 28b). This burial was probably unearthed when the plaster basin that begins the construction events of Zone C was set into the ground. There is no question that these bones are of Sefid Phase age although there are no artifacts in direct association. The deposits below and above are late Sefid Phase.

Burial No. 10 is that of a child, in Zone E1 of the late Surkh Phase (Fig. 35c, Pl. 32a). The remains are of the left side only. The skeleton is represented by

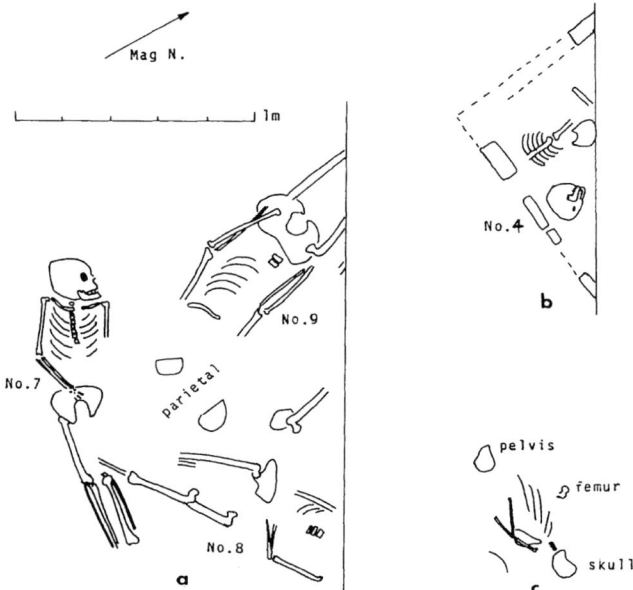

Fig. 35a. Burials 7, 8, 9, Zone A4, Sefid Phase deposits. Three extended burials placed in the following sequence: first No. 7, second No. 9, and third No. 8.

35b. Burial No. 4, Zone A4, Sefid Phase deposits. Disarticulated skeleton of a child placed, along with caprine bones, on the degraded remains of a fireplace which was inside the corner of a room.

35c. Burial No. 10, Zone B1, Sefid Phase. Disturbed burial of a child. Only the left side of the body is partially intact. The skull is represented by a parietal fragment, the body by the left side of the torso, while a pelvis fragment lies nearby.

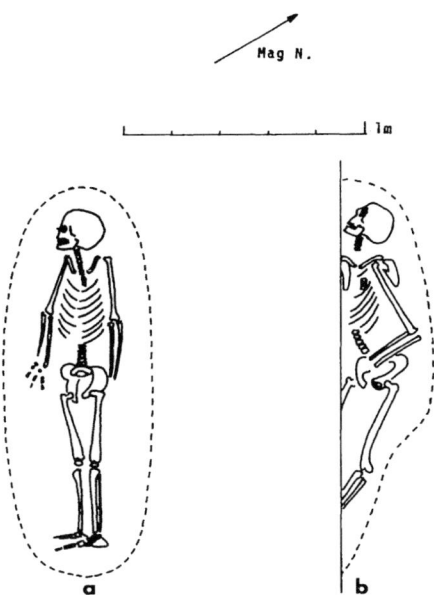

Fig. 36a. Burial No. 1, Intrusive. Extended skeleton lying in a pit dug from the surface some two meters into deposits of Sefid Phase.

36b. Burial No. 2, Intrusive. Extended skeleton lying in pit dug from the surface some two meters into deposits of Sefid Phase. The skeleton is slightly twisted owing to a contraction of the burial pit caused by the presence of a plaster basin which was not removed when the pit was dug.

one parietal, a pelvis fragment, ribs, some vertebrae and the left arm and shoulder blade. A carnelian bead was found near the body in the shallow burial pit which contained numerous charred seeds. The bones are stained with red ochre.

Also in Zone E1 were a number of other bones which were recovered in the faunal collections. Portions of three burned and cut skulls, totalling 34 fragments, (Fig. 23) came from the ashy fill on the floor of the room adjacent to burial No. 10. Along the east wall of this room were sherds of several red ware vessels. Other fragments, some burned, lay near the burial in the corridor between the rooms. These fragments include teeth, other skull fragments, and a vertebra. It seems clear that the bones came from several disturbed burials and were simply incorporated into trash that filled the remains of the rooms.

INTRUSIVE BURIALS

Two burials in well defined pits dug from the surface into Sefid Phase deposits are very similar to burials which had iron ornaments found in the top of Ali Kosh. In both instances at Chagha Sefid the bones are in excellent condition. Neither had diagnostic artifacts in association. The bodies were extended with the heads toward the northwest. Burial No. 2 had a large metate place upside down over the skull but there were no other associated artifacts (Pl. 33b-d). The left ulna had been fractured and had healed. The burial pit was only slightly larger than the skeleton and was dug down about two meters. The body lay slightly on one side, perhaps because the pit could not be dug entirely straight because of the presence of the plaster basin (Fig. 36b, Pl. 33c).

Burial No. 1 (Fig. 36a, Pl. 33a) was extended on the back with the arms alongside the body. The head points toward the northwest and, like burial No. 2, the face looks to the south.

The similarity in orientation of these skeletons with those found at Ali Kosh is striking (Hole, Flannery and Neely, 1969:Fig. 110).

VI

POTTERY

INTRODUCTION

In our excavation at Chagha Sefid, we recovered more than 41,000 pot sherds. Because the deposits consisted largely of midden and eroded remains of houses, we found few whole pots and relatively few sherds that could be reconstructed from rim to base. Much the same situation obtained at Ali Kosh and Tepe Sabz. In order to make our analysis comparable with our previous results, we followed exactly the same procedure: we screened all material that was in good stratigraphic context and saved all sherds. After the excavation was completed we counted body sherds that could not be reconstructed and discarded them, returning to Houston all rims and those body sherds that had either enough curvature to permit some reconstruction, or painted decoration. The analysis that follows is, therefore, based on counts of body sherds by the types designated below, and re-examination of all sherds returned to Houston. Our previous analyses had demonstrated the merit of this method for documenting the changes in a long sequence. The present analysis was carried out in exactly the same fashion and has resulted in the addition of three more phases to our ceramic sequence.

Our earlier work had defined seven pottery types; to this list we add six more, each of which is given a binomial designation that refers to the site or phase in which the type is best known, and to the basic characteristics of the type, e.g., Sefid Red-on-Cream. Within many of the types are "varieties" that are based on a combination of vessel form and design. These are analogous to the bowl "types" defined by us previously for the type Susiana Black-on-Buff.

For each stratigraphic zone, a count was made of the number of pot sherds of each type, and on the basis of this we calculated the percentage which each type constituted of the total sherd count for that zone. By observing the presence or absence of types as well as the relative abundance of each type, we were able to divide our stratigraphic sequence into phases. The procedure is illustrated in Tables 5-8. To explain this procedure, I quote directly from our previous report (Hole, Flannery and Neely, 1969:106).

> Such percentages come from counts of sherds, not whole vessels. They should in no way be considered a reflection of the "real" proportion which certain types of pottery constituted in typical households of each cultural phase. To give only one example of the difficulties encountered, we know of no way to tell sherds of unpainted ("plain") vessels apart from sherds from unpainted areas on otherwise decorated ("black-on-buff") vessels. Hence many sherds from the unpainted bases of Susiana Black-on-Buff bowls were undoubtedly classified as Susiana Plain Buff. Still another problem is that large bowls may break into more sherds than small bowls. We are not extremely concerned with such problems because, presumably, any archeologist working in the Deh Luran plain in the future will encounter the same difficulty; any percentages he calculates from sherds alone will be skewed in the same way ours are, which means that his results should be roughly comparable with ours.

Typology

Each of our pottery types consists of vessels characterized by a particular paste, surface treatment, decoration, and range of shapes, which occurred during a specific period within a specific geographical area. Each pottery type has a specifiable "life span," a fact which is made clear by reference to Tables 5-8. We may take Jaffar Painted as a convenient example. The name Jaffar refers to the fact that this ware has its greatest frequency during the Mohammad Jaffar Phase. It is distinguished from Jaffar Plain by having painted designs and by having a different "life span." At Chagha Sefid, Jaffar Painted accounts for 55 percent of all sherds in the oldest deposits of the Mohammad Jaffar Phase. Thereafter it declines in frequency to 33 and 22 percent through the remainder of that phase and down to 7 and 1 percent in zones of the early Sefid Phase. At this time Jaffar Painted has run its course.

One important difference should be noted between our present and our previous analyses. Some of the types at Chagha Sefid can only be recognized when diagnostic sherds are present; not all sherds of these types can be distinguished. For example, Sefid Black Painted is basically Khazineh Red that has black paint applied to the upper body in solid bands or panels. Lower body sherds and bases of this type can only be recognized when they have some black paint on them. If the paint is not present the sherds must be classified as Khazineh Red. Thus, especially in the Surkh Phase, when less paint was applied to these vessels, most of their sherds are counted as Khazineh Red. This obviously presents a problem in analysis when we depend upon percentages to illustrate changes through time. Since rim sherds can invariably be classified accurately, I calculated the relative proportions of rims of each type, as well as of total sherds, to see whether my breakdown into phases would be affected. Comparison of Tables 6, 8, 9, 10 shows that the same results are obtained by either method, although the absolute percentages are different. Thus the basic procedure we have followed in our work in Deh Luran is demonstrated to be a useful and accurate tool for analysis of changes.

As a further aid to understanding, brief definitions of the terms we will use in describing our pottery types are given below, as they appear in our previous publication (Hole, Flannery and Neely, 1969:110-111).

Terms Used in Analysis

Paste: The clay, along with any natural inclusions, from which the vessels were made. (Often referred to as "fabric" in Near East reports.)

Temper: Non-plastic particles added to the clay by the potter, usually in order to increase the porosity of the paste so that shrinking and warping during drying will be minimized.

Temper size: We follow Shepard (1956:118) in restricting "coarse temper" to particles over 0.5 mm. in diameter, and "fine temper" to particles under 0.25 mm in diameter, with "medium temper" particles occupying the 0.25 to 0.5 mm range.

Surface Treatment: The final touches applied to the outside of the vessel by the potter before firing.

Wet-smoothing: The wiping of the surface of the newly-made pot with wet hands or a piece of fabric before firing.

Burnishing: The rubbing of leather-hard pottery with a hard implement, such as stone, to close the surface pores of the clay.

Checking: The flaking-off of particles of the vessel surface.

Crazing: A network of fine cracks on the surface of a vessel.

Slip: A fine solution of well-cleaned clay applied to the surface of a vessel (See Colton, 1953:39-40; Shepard, 1956:191-93).

Wash: A very thin, watery slip.

Self-slip: If the paste is fine, wet-smoothing the surface will cause the finer particles to rise to the surface, and the result will be much the same as if a slip had been applied. The difficulty of telling the difference between a slip and self-slip has been discussed previously (See Braidwood and Braidwood, 1960:33-34).

Carbon streak: A dark line seen in the cross-section of sherds from a vessel which did not oxidize completely when fired. (Usually referred to as a "dark core" in American reports.)

Firing cloud: A discolored blotch on the vessel surface, caused by contact with burning fuel or another vessel during firing.

Smudging: A blackening of the vessel surface caused by carbon or tarry combustion products.

Hardness: We measured the hardness of the Deh Luran pottery by means of Moh's scale, which, although in common use, is at best a rough test. Moh's scale provides a set of ten minerals, ranked in hardness from 1 (talc) to 10 (diamond). For example, if a sherd can be scratched by fluorite (hardness of 4) but not by calcite (hardness of 3), and if the sherd itself will scratch calcite, its hardness must be between 3 and 4 (see Shepard, 1956:114 and Table 4).

Color: Color of the paste and surface of Deh Luran pottery was measured against 196 color chips provided by the Munsell Soil Color Charts, the standard most commonly in use throughout the United States and Europe (Munsell, 1961). The Munsell charts divide color into three attributes—hue, value, and chroma—so that any given color chip can be designated by a number (e.g., 5YR 6/4) and name (e.g., "reddish brown"). The charts have the advantage of standardizing color terms for pottery and facilitating comparisons.

Vessel Forms: Our pottery drawings are reconstructions of nearly all the shapes in which the prehistoric pottery of Deh Luran appeared. The illustrations should in turn make clear the definitions of vessel form used in the text of the report.

Decoration: Paint applied in designs or in solid panels.

Techniques of Pottery Manufacture in the Prehistoric Sequence

Chaff or straw and grit (principally sand) were the most commonly used tempering materials at Chagha Sefid, as well as in the rest of the Deh Luran plain. Before the Choga Mami Transitional, virtually all pots had some chaff or very finely chopped straw temper,

Table 5

PERCENTAGES OF RIM SHERDS OF EACH TYPE
by Stratigraphic Zone

Phase	Zone Area	Zone	Jaffar Painted	Jaffar Plain	Khazineh Red	Sefid Painted	Sefid Red-on-Cream	Sefid Black-on-Cream	Sefid Burnished	Sefid Black-on-Red	Susiana Black-on-Buff	Susiana Plain Buff	Sialk Black-on-Red	Total Rims
Sabz	SD	J									97		3	35
	SD	I			6					20	66	6		15
Choga Mami Transitional	SD	H			18						71	1	8	70
	SD	G2		1	36						52	1	8	61
	SD	G1		5	70					2	14		8	134
Surkh	SD	F		3	91					2	1		1	257
	SC, SD	E2		6	76			3		14				114
	SC, SD	E1		1	86			5		7				254
	SC	D3		5	73			5		17				87
	SC	D2		5	81			5		7				338
	SC	D1		2	82			5		8				175
	SC	C2		6	82			4		8				248
Sefid	SA	C1		2	70	1	5	3	9	8				703
	SA	B2		3	49		13	12	9	13				2,574
	SA	B1	2	12	40	1		26	1	4				1,165
	SA	A4	38	6	38		6	13						16
Mohammad Jaffar	SB	C	10	70	20									10
	SB	B	44	55										36
	SB	A	72	28										83
Ali Kosh	SA	A3												10
	SA	A2												2
	SA	A1												14
	Total Rims		113	351	3,605	24	684	555	315	572	151	4	27	6,401

although the paste may have been sandy as well and included some grit.

Pots are, with few exceptions, smoothed and in many cases slipped as well. Only one type, Sefid Burnished, is consistently burnished to a high luster, although an occasional pot of other types may be burnished. All of the vessels found at Chagha Sefid are handmade—or so we infer from the unevenness of their sides, their asymmetry, and the lack of complicated profiles. None of the pottery shows any sign of having been coiled, although some Susiana vessels were built in sections, as their breaking at the joints illustrates.

As before, we find the earliest paint to be fugitive,

Table 6

PERCENTAGES OF RIM SHERDS OF EACH TYPE
by Cultural Phase

Phase	Jaffar Painted	Jaffar Plain	Khazineh Red	Sefid Painted	Sefid Red-on-Cream	Sefid Black-on-Cream	Sefid Burnished	Sefid Black-on-Red	Susiana Black-on-Buff	Susiana Plain Buff	Sialk Black-on-Red	Total Rims
Sabz			2					6	88	2	2	50
Choga Mami Transitional		2	49					1	38	1	8	265
Surkh		4	83			4		8				1,473
Sefid	1	5	50	1	15	11	8	10				4,458
Mohammad Jaffar	60	39	1									129
Ali Kosh												26
Totals	113	351	3,605	24	684	555	315	572	151	4	27	6,401

readily rubbing off on one's hands. This is a red-ochre paint that characterizes Jaffar Painted vessels. By the Sefid Phase, although red paint was still used, it was applied in such a way that it remains permanent, and black paints were also used. Both the red and black are derived from iron oxides. With the appearance of the Susiana wares, black became the predominant color, although its hue varies greatly from reddish to tawny or chocolate brown to black, evidently as a result of differences in firing. In general the early Susiana wares lack the crisp, deep black designs of the later wares (post-Sabz Phase).

A small series of sherds has white paint, often along with either black or red paint. These sherds are listed separately. White paint is rarely seen and is difficult to achieve. The paint has not been analyzed for its mineral composition.

THE POTTERY SEQUENCE

The eleven major pottery types distinguished at Chagha Sefid appeared in the following order, from earliest to latest:

Jaffar Painted
Jaffar Plain
Khazineh Red
Sefid Painted
Sefid Red-on-Cream
Sefid Black-on-Cream
Sefid Burnished
Sefid Black Painted
Susiana Black-on-Buff
Susiana Plain Buff
Sialk Black-on-Red

Three types—Jaffar Painted, Jaffar Plain, and Khazineh Red—appeared together in the Mohammad Jaffar Phase at Ali Kosh and at Chagha Sefid. At Chagha Sefid we also find the beginning of Sefid Painted in the later zones of the Mohammad Jaffar Phase.

The Sefid Phase sees the demise of Jaffar Painted and Sefid Painted, and the introduction of Sefid Red-on-Cream, Sefid Black-on-Cream, Sefid Burnished, and Sefid Black Painted.

The Surkh Phase has only four types: Jaffar Plain, Khazineh Red, Sefid Black-on-Cream, and Sefid Black Painted. The painting and the vessel forms of the latter type change from the Sefid to Surkh phases.

The Choga Mami Transitional is distinguished by the introduction of Susiana Black-on-Buff and

Table 7

TOTAL SHERDS OF EACH TYPE
by Stratigraphic Zone

Phase	Zone Area	Zone	Jaffar Painted	Jaffar Plain	Khazineh Red	Sefid Painted	Sefid Red-on-Cream	Sefid Black-on-Cream	Sefid Burnished	Sefid Black-on-Red	Susiana Black-on-Buff	Susiana Plain	Sialk Black-on-Red	Total Sherds
Sabz	SD	J									76		3	79
	SD	I		1	5						18	2		26
Choga Mami Transitional	SD	H		19	54		1	2		3	124	4	15	222
	SD	G2		34	122			1			87	57	10	311
	SD	G1	1	93	707		1	21		4	52	28	27	934
Surkh	SD	F	3	182	1,036		4	32		8	12	8	11	1,296
	SC, SD	E2	1	108	756			15		17		1		898
	SC, SD	E1		189	1,532	7	7	83		21	1	1		1,841
	SC	D3	2	34	206	1		27		15				285
	SC	D2	4	236	2,150	3		132	3	33				2,561
	SC	D1	3	74	733			64		15				889
	SC	C2	1	102	1,413	1		51		30				1,598
Sefid	SA	C1	6	113	4,050	12	46	52	95	70				4,444
	SA	B2	10	350	10,324	91	1,527	1,237	1,890	1,481				16,910
	SA	B1	97	1,222	2,419	161	1,618	988	905	401				7,811
	SA	A4	13	92	29	1	26	3	1	2				167
Mohammad Jaffar	SB	C	36	104	25	4								169
	SB	B	104	184	16	9		1						314
	SB	A	342	264	9	4			2					621
Ali Kosh	SA	A3	2	10	18		7	2	1	4				44
	SA	A2			17		1			1				19
	SA	A1		26	67		21	6	3	9				132
	Totals		625	3,437	25,691	294	3,259	2,717	2,900	2,114	370	101	66	41,571

Susiana Plain Buff. The former has designs nearly identical to those found at Choga Mami. Also beginning in this phase is Sialk Black-on-Red, while sherds of Jaffar Plain and Khazineh Red continue to appear.

Our final phase, the Sabz Phase, marks a continuation of the Susiana sequence, with the addition of typical vessels painted in the Sabz style, along with Sialk Black-on-Red and Jaffar Plain and Khazineh Red, types that go throughout the sequence.

Along with changes in the types characteristic of each phase, we find changes in the shapes of the pots themselves. These changes are not striking, however, as the dominant vessel form in the Mohammad Jaffar,

Table 8
PERCENTAGES OF SHERDS OF EACH TYPE
by Stratigraphic Zone

Phase	Zone Area	Zone	Jaffar Painted	Jaffar Plain	Khazineh Red	Sefid Painted	Sefid Red-on-Cream	Sefid Black-on-Cream	Sefid Burnished	Sefid Black Painted	Susiana Black-on-Buff	Susiana Plain	Sialk Black-on-Red	Total Sherds
Sabz	SD	J									96		4	79
	SD	I		3	20						70	7		26
Choga Mami Transitional	SD	H		8	25			1		1	55	1	4	222
	SD	G2		10	40						27	18	3	311
	SD	G1		10	76			2			6	3	3	934
Surkh	SD	F		15	79			3			1		1	1,296
	SC, SD	E2		12	84			2		2				898
	SC, SD	E1		10	83			5		1				1,841
	SC	D3		12	72			9		5				285
	SC	D2		9	84			5		1				2,561
	SC	D1		8	82			7		2				889
	SC	C2		7	89			3		2				1,598
Sefid	SA	C1		3	91		1	1	2	2				4,444
	SA	B2		2	62		10	8	11	8				16,910
	SA	B1	1	16	31	2	21	13	11	5				7,811
	SA	A4	7	55	18		16	1						167
Mohammad Jaffar	SB	C	22	62	14	3								169
	SB	B	33	58	5	2								314
	SB	A	55	42	1									621
Ali Kosh	SA	A3												44
	SA	A2												19
	SA	A1												132
	Totals													41,571

Sefid and Surkh phases is the hemispherical bowl whose walls range from incurving to slightly outleaning. Nevertheless, slight changes in these vessels, along with changes in size and in the form of the base, do enable us to define chronological changes. Only in the latter two phases, with the appearance of the Susiana wares, do we have striking differences in the vessel forms.

The Mohammad Jaffar Phase has the shapes that remain basic throughout the sequence. Nearly all vessels are a form of hemispherical bowl with either simple or beaded rims. In this phase the bowls have slightly out-turned rims, usually with concave bases although a few of the earlier flat-based examples, some with a thickened "heel" at the wall-base juncture, are found. Additionally we find a few hole-

Table 9

TOTAL SHERDS OF EACH TYPE
by Cultural Phase

Phase	Jaffar Painted	Jaffar Plain	Khazineh Red	Sefid Painted	Sefid Red-on-Cream	Sefid Black-on-Cream	Sefid Burnished	Sefid Black-on-Red	Susiana Black-on-Buff	Susiana Plain	Sialk Black-on-Red	Total Classified Sherds	White Paint on Misc. Types	Other
Sabz		1	5						94	1	3	105		
Choga Mami Transitional	1	146	883		2	24		7	263	89	52	1,467	6	
Surkh	14	925	7,826	12	11	404	3	139	13	10	11	9,368	20	2
Sefid	126	1,777	16,822	265	3,217	2,280	2,891	1,954				29,332	3	1
Mohammad Jaffar	482	552	50	17		1	2					1,104		
Ali Kosh												195		
Totals	625	3,437	25,691	294	3,259	2,717	2,900	2,114	370	101	66	41,571		

Table 10

PERCENTAGES OF SHERDS OF EACH TYPE
by Cultural Phase

Phase	Jaffar Painted	Jaffar Plain	Khazineh Red	Sefid Painted	Sefid Red-on-Cream	Sefid Black-on-Cream	Sefid Burnished	Sefid Black Painted	Susiana Black-on-Buff	Susiana Plain	Sialk Black-on-Red	Total Sherds
Sabz		1	5						90	2	2	105
Choga Mami Transitional		10	60			2			18	6	4	1,467
Surkh		10	84			4		1				9,368
Sefid		6	57		11	8	10	7				29,332
Mohammad Jaffar	44	50	5	2								1,104
Ali Kosh												195
Totals	625	3,437	25,691	294	3,259	2,717	2,900	2,114	370	101	66	41,571

mouth and carinated vessels, some examples of pedestals and spouts and some miniature pots.

The Sefid Phase continues the same tradition, although the hemispherical bowls tend to be more straight sided and range farther toward outleaning than in the preceding phase. New are tab handles standing vertically on rims, possible tripod legs, and nose lugs. Some vessels have plastic decoration.

Basically a continuation of the preceding phases, the Surkh Phase sees increased use of handles, especially with fenestration, more pedestals, and large jars. Hemispherical bowls tend toward hole-mouth in the Surkh Black Painted series, in contrast to their more open form earlier.

The Choga Mami Transitional and the succeeding Sabz phases see the introduction of large, shallow open bowls with carinations, the typical form of the early buff wares. The Khazineh Red, however, maintains previous tradition with hemispherical and hole-mouth bowls.

The Sabz Phase has increased use of pedestals, basins and jars, along with a series of sharply carinated vessels in Sialk Black-on-Red. Some of the latter are evidently rectangular.

The details of the changes noted above can be seen in the figures illustrating each type.

Illustrations

The ceramics are illustrated by photographs and drawings. Extensive use is made of photographs for the Susiana wares in order to convey an accurate impression of the quality of these pots, which are quite distinct from the slipped and often untempered Susiana wares of post-Sabz phases. Most of the earlier wares, because of the fugitive designs and low contrast between painting and background, did not lend themselves to photographic illustration.

Each type is illustrated with one or more figures (line drawings) or plates (photos). The drawings illustrate the entire range of variation within a type and are grouped stratigraphically when possible. An attempt was made to reconstruct vessels and when this was not possible, suggested reconstructions are indicated by dashed lines. The actual extent of the sherds from which reconstructions were made is indicated by the solid lines on the right hand side of the section.

In instances where designs are clearly repetitive in panels, they have been entirely reconstructed. When there is doubt whether the design is repetitive, the extent of the actual sherd is shown.

Diameters of vessels at the rim are indicated in centimeters. When there is a range of variation in rim form, wall angle and diameter, a series of rim sherds of the same shape of vessel is placed inside or alongside a reconstructed form.

When profiles of sherds are to the right of the sherd, the sherd shows a design on the outside of the vessel. When profiles are to the left, the sherd shows an interior design. In instances where the profile is between two views of the same sherd, the one on the left is always the outside and the one on the right is always the inside.

Unfortunately it is not possible to convey the quality of painting very well in simple black and white line drawings; our photographs help in this regard, but we have no satisfactory solution for the early painted wares. Red paint is shown as black if it is on a red ware vessel, or as a dotted texture if it occurs along with white or black paint or cream slip.

The scale is indicated on each figure. Line drawings of reconstructed vessels are at a scale of either 1:4 or 1:2½. Drawings of sherds, and photographs are at a scale of either 1:2½ or 1:1.

TYPE: Jaffar Painted (Fig. 37)

Sample: 625

Temporal distribution: Mohammad Jaffar and Sefid phases, with a few stray sherds appearing in the Surkh Phase. Although we had suspected the type went out of use at the end of the Mohammad Jaffar Phase (Hole, Flannery and Neely, 1969:117) it is now certain that at least some vessels were in use in the later Sefid Phase.

Appearance: Jaffar Painted is similar to Jaffar Plain with the addition of designs painted with fugitive red. It is important to note that whereas at Ali Kosh the forms of the two types were identical, Jaffar Painted at Chagha Sefid retains the earlier convex-walled bowl form that is not found in the Jaffar Plain vessels.

Paste: Identical to that of Jaffar Plain.

Temper: Mainly chaff.

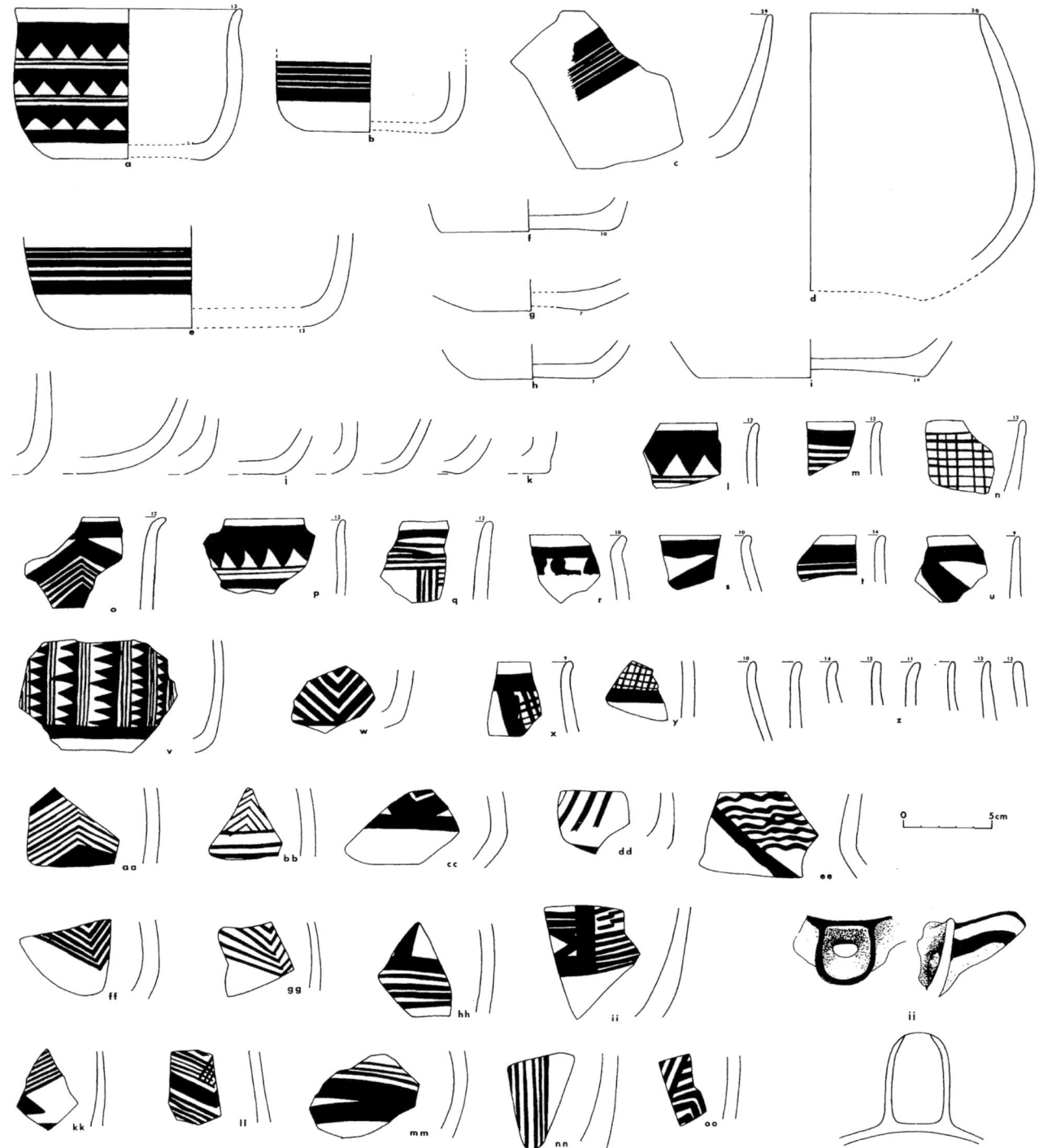

Fig. 37. Jaffar Painted. The entire range of variation in vessel forms and designs. Zones of the Mohammad Jaffar Phase.

Color: The paste is identical in color to Jaffar Plain, rarely having poorly-fired gray cores.

Surface treatment: Identical to Jaffar Plain.

Decoration: Except for an occasional red band around the interior of the rim, all designs are external. The paint is made from red ochre and is usually fugitive.

VESSEL FORMS

Convex-walled bowls: These vessels are nearly identical in form to the comparable vessels from Ali Kosh (Hole, Flannery and Neely, 1969:Fig. 44), but they differ from the common bowl form of the Jaffar Plain series at Chagha Sefid. The chief difference from the Ali Kosh bowls may be in the forms of the bases. Unfortunately only a few bases were found; of these some are clearly concave like the Jaffar Plain (Fig. 37*f,g,h,i*), while others are apparently flat like some of those found at Ali Kosh (Fig. 31*a,b,e,l*). Only one "heel" base was found (Fig. 37*k*); this form is commonly found at Jarmo and Sarab on similar wares.

The 10 examples of trough spouts are identical to those found at Ali Kosh and to those found in the Jaffar Plain (Fig. 37*ii*).

With few exceptions, all measurable rims are 10-16 cm in diameter. One example (Fig. 37*c*) is 29 cm, but this appears to be an isolated and rare instance of a large vessel. One vessel is oval (Fig. 37*v*).

Decoration is similar to that found at Ali Kosh, consisting of geometric designs, usually arranged in horizontal panels. Typically, the body of the vessel is treated as a unit; rows of zig-zags, chevrons, or triangles encircle the body as a continuous horizontal band. Two instances of vertical design mark the only deviations from this pattern (Fig. 37*v,nn*). Usually the horizontal decorative band is delimited by a firm, thick line at top and bottom. The upper line runs just below the rim, while the lower line marks the juncture with the base, the latter rarely being painted.

By far the most common designs are horizontal ziz-zags or chevrons (Fig. 37*o,w,aa-cc,ff,gg,kk,ll*). Other common designs are panels of filled triangles between horizontal bands (Fig. 37*l,p*), and cross-hatching (Fig. 37*n,x,y*). Less common are wavy lines (Fig. 37*dd,ee*) and horizontal panels of bands with irregular elements set into them (Fig. 37*r,ii*).

In all, the designs are very similar to those from Ali Kosh (Hole, Flannery and Neely, 1969:Fig. 44). It is now clear that a few aberrant sherds from Ali Kosh which were attributed to Jaffar Painted are, in fact, Sefid Painted (Hole, Flannery and Neely, 1969: Fig. 44:*i,m,p,q*). Additional surface collections at Ali Kosh in 1969 produced others of this type. It now seems apparent that a small and eroded component of this phase is present at Ali Kosh.

Jar (Fig. 37*ee*): A body sherd from the juncture of the body and neck of a large jar came from the Sefid Phase deposit in Area B. This sherd has an irregular wavy-line design, probably set into a large pendant triangle. No rim sherds of jars were found.

Hole-mouth bowl (Fig. 37*d*): One example of a hole-mouth bowl whose exterior was entirely covered with fugitive red paint was taken from a mixed context. This vessel is identical in paste and surface treatment to the remainder of the Jaffar Painted, but in form and "decoration" unique. (Although no base was found in the same context, a base that may have come from a similar vessel was found in another mixed context (Fig. 37*i*). Both sherds have the same appearance, size and texture although the slope of the base does not match that of the wall. The base, which is convex, has fugitive red paint entirely covering it.) In a tentative reconstruction, the vessel, which has a rim diameter of 20 cm, stood 18 cm high.

TYPE: Jaffar Plain (Fig. 38)

Sample: 3,437

Temporal distribution: Mohammad Jaffar through Choga Mami Transitional. Too few sherds of any type were found in Sabz Phase deposits to state whether Jaffar Plain occurs there; however at Tepe Sabz this type was found in low frequency through the Khazineh Phase.

Appearance: A hand-made, poorly fired, friable undecorated ware. Like analogous plain wares from Ali Kosh, Jarmo and other early villages, it is primarily chaff-tempered, with a dark unoxidized core and a buff surface blotched with reddish or grayish firing-clouds.

Paste: Porous, and pitted as a result of the burning-out of vegetal fibers.

Temper: Almost exclusively chaff-tempered although small pieces of grit are sometimes found.

Table 11

JAFFAR PAINTED SHERDS AT CHAGHA SEFID
by Stratigraphic Zone

Phase	Zone Area	Zone	Convex-walled Bowls with Direct Rims	Jar Sherds	Spouts and Fragments	Body Sherds	Total Sherds
Sabz	SD	J					
	SD	I					
Choga Mami Transitional	SD	H					
	SD	G2					
	SD	G1					1	1
Surkh	SD	F				3	3
	SC, SD	E2				1	1
	SC, SD	E1					
	SC	D3				2	2
	SC	D2				4	4
	SC	D1				3	3
	SC	C2				1	1
Sefid	SA	C1	5			1	6
	SA	B2	6			4	10
	SA	B1	18		2	77	97
	SA	A4	6			7	13
Mohammad Jaffar	SB	C	1		1	34	36
	SB	B	16	1	2	85	104
	SB	A	60		5	277	342
Ali Kosh	SA	A3	1			1	2
	SA	A2					
	SA	A1					
	Totals		113	1	10	501	625

Color: The paste is usually buff, rarely with a gray carbon streak. The surface, where not covered by reddish or gray firing-clouds, varies from light brown (7.5YR 6/4 on the Munsell scale) and light reddish brown (5YR 6/4) to pink (5YR 7/4), tan, or buff.

Surface treatment: With a few exceptions, all vessels were smoothed. True burnishing occurs only on the Burnished Wares which are described later. In some instances a thin wash of the same clay as the paste may have been used, to judge from the cracking and peeling of some of the surfaces.

Decoration: None.

VESSEL FORMS

Because this ware is extremely friable, it was difficult to reconstruct many rim to base profiles; it is clear, however, that the predominant shape is that of the open bowl with a concave base. The series of shapes is somewhat different from that found at Ali Kosh, a fact which, taken along with the presence of other types not found in Mohammad Jaffar Phase deposits there, suggests that for the most part we have a later version of this ware at Chagha Sefid. In particular, we have none of the convex-walled bowls which were the most common form at Ali Kosh, nor have we any carinated vessels.

Open bowls (Fig. 38*k,n,o*): Except for the miniature vessels, none of these could be reconstructed, but they all appear to have either relatively straight sided or slightly outleaning walls. The sides of the vessels

Table 12

JAFFAR PAINTED SHERDS AT CHAGHA SEFID
by Cultural Phase

Phase	Convex-walled Bowls with Direct Rims	Jar Sherds	Spouts and Fragments	Body Sherds	Total Sherds
Sabz					
Choga Mami Transitional				1	1
Surkh				14	14
Sefid	35		2	89	126
Mohammad Jaffar	77	1	8	396	482
Ali Kosh	1			1	2
Totals	113	1	10	501	625

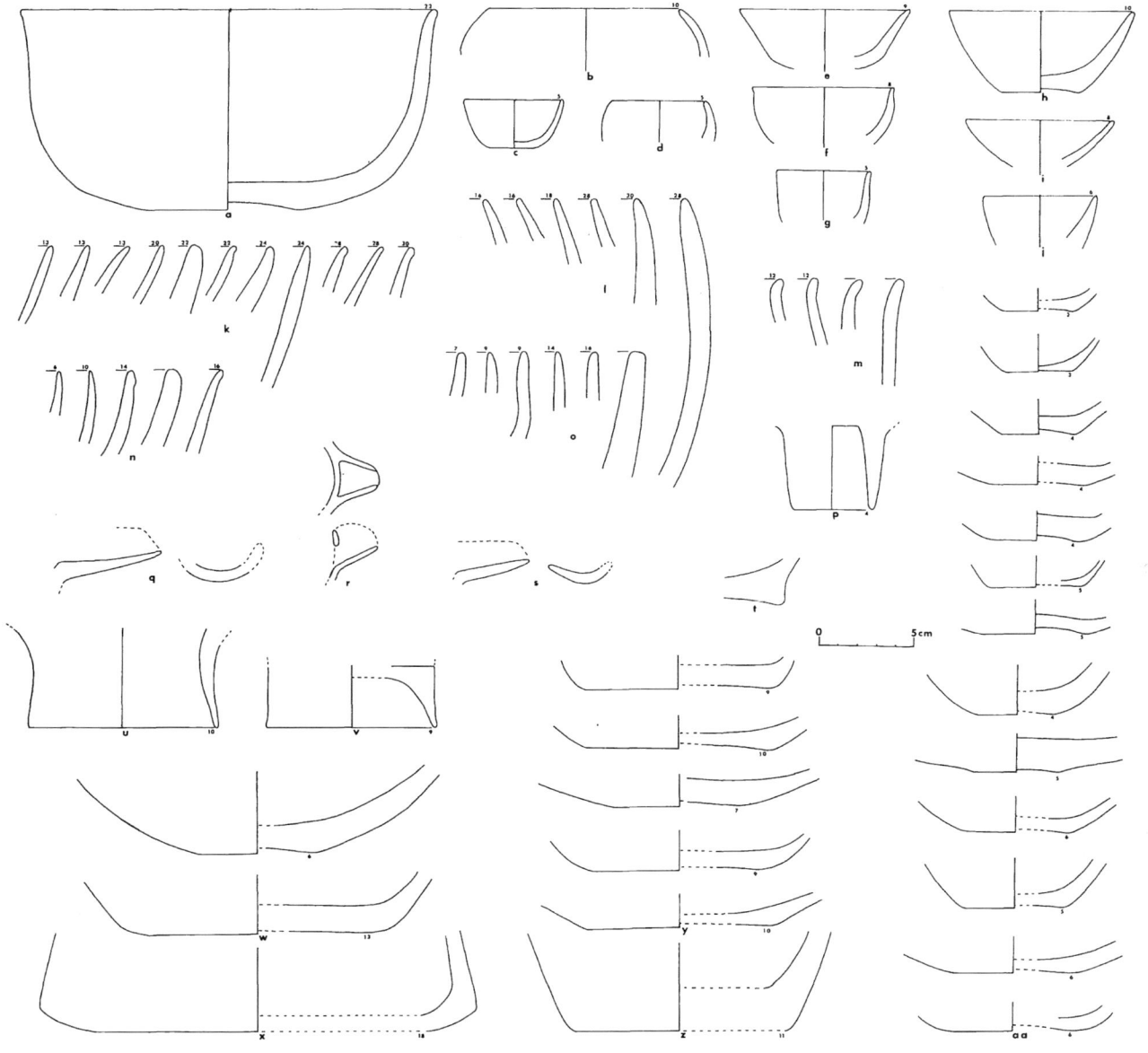

Fig. 38. Jaffar Plain. The entire range of variation in vessel forms. Zones B1, B2, and C1, Sefid Phase.

have a slightly curved or straight profile down to the base which is concave in all but two instances (Fig. 38c,z). The bases are usually well-formed and because of the concavity could be easily measured; the diameters of the concave bases range from 9.5 to 3.5 cm. The range of variation is shown in Fig. 38w,y,aa.

Rims are simply rounded or have a slight bevel on the interior; a few are slightly flaring. Rim diameters could be measured on a high proportion of the pieces although some inaccuracy is expected because their surfaces were not always carefully smoothed nor are the vessels exactly round. The larger bowls have diameters ranging from about 20 to 30 cm, while a smaller series clusters between 10 and 16 cm. The heights of the bowls could not be determined accurately although a matching of rims with bases suggests heights of up to 20 cm for the larger bowls and up to 7 to 8 cm for the smaller.

The flat based bowls (Fig. 38c,z) are like those

found at Ali Kosh (Hole, Flannery and Neely, 1969: Fig. 43:*w,x*), and probably represent an earlier form of this ware than was common at Chagha Sefid. The same conclusion holds for the single "heel" base (Fig. 38*t*), a form common in the Ali Kosh vessels (Hole, Flannery and Neely, 1969:Fig. 43*s-v*).

Some of the bowls had simple trough spouts with straps bridging the opening along the line of the rim. None of the examples was complete, although from the fragments it is clear that they follow the same form as spouts on other types of vessels found at Chagha Sefid (Fig. 38*q,r,s*) and the spout from Ali Kosh (Hole, Flannery and Neely, 1969:Fig. 43*o-r*).
Miniature vessels (Fig. 38*c,d,f,g*): Seven small bowls, essentially like the larger series of open bowls except in size, have rim diameters ranging from 5-8 cm and stand less than 5 cm high. Rim sherds of this size are rare and such vessels probably constituted a small component of the total assemblage at any time.
Hole-mouth jars (Fig. 38*b,d,l*). Only four rim sherds of this form were found. Two vessels, with rim diameters of 5 and 10 cm are shown partially reconstructed (Fig. 38*b,d*).
Pedestal bases (Fig. 38*p,u,v*): Three of the four examples are illustrated. The pedestals have basal diameters ranging from 4 to 9 cm and stand from 3.5 to 5.5 cm high. Although these were presumably bases for open bowls we found no examples from which a complete reconstruction could be made. No pedestals were found at Ali Kosh.

Table 13
JAFFAR PLAIN SHERDS AT CHAGHA SEFID
by Stratigraphic Zone

Phase	Area	Zone	Open Bowls with Direct Rims	Open Bowls with Beaded Rims	Hole-mouth Bowls	Pedestals	Spout Fragments	Body Sherds	Total
Sabz	SD	J							
	SD	I						1	1
Choga Mami Transitional	SD	H						19	19
	SD	G2		1			1	32	34
	SD	G1	3	3				87	93
Surkh	SD	F	6	2				174	182
	SC, SD	E2	7					101	108
	SC, SD	E1	4				2	183	189
	SC	D3	4					30	34
	SC	D2	17	3			2	214	236
	SC	D1	5			1		68	74
	SC	C2	11	2	2			87	102
Sefid	SA	C1	19		1		7	86	113
	SA	B2	70	2	1	2	9	266	350
	SA	B1	141				17	1,064	1,222
	SA	A4	1		1			90	92
Mohammad Jaffar	SB	C	7					97	104
	SB	B	20					164	184
	SB	A	23	1			1	239	264
Ali Kosh	SA	A3						10	10
	SA	A2							
	SA	A1						26	26
	Totals		338	14	4	4	39	3,038	3,437

Table 14
JAFFAR PLAIN SHERDS AT CHAGHA SEFID
by Cultural Phase

Phase	Open Bowls with Direct Rims	Open Bowls with Beaded Rims	Hole-mouth Bowls	Pedestals	Spout Fragments	Body Sherds	Total
Sabz						1	1
Choga Mami Transitional	3	4			1	138	146
Surkh	54	7	2	1	4	857	925
Sefid	231	2	2	3	33	1,506	1,777
Mohammad Jaffar	50	1			1	500	552
Ali Kosh						36	36
Totals	338	14	4	4	39	3,038	3,437

TYPE: Khazineh Red (Figs. 39-42)

Sample: 25,691

Temporal distribution: Throughout the sequence with the maximum frequency in the Sefid and Surkh phases.

Appearance: A relatively coarse red ware, handmade, with a wide range of color variation due to inconsistent firing or accidental refiring over cooking fires. In many instances slip has come off portions of the pots, especially in the Surkh Phase when a sandier paste was used; these vessels are often very friable.

Paste: The paste varies from fine to coarse, the latter occurring principally on the thicker vessels. The paste is usually sandy in texture.

Temper: Chaff was the usual temper but after the Sefid Phase, when a sandier paste was used, the chaff is less noticeable; evidence of its use consists of tiny holes in the paste that have remained after the chaff burned out. On the thicker vessels fine grit was also used as a tempering agent.

Color: Both the core and surface colors are highly variable; gray or purple firing clouds are common. Up to half of the sherds, especially the thicker examples, have a dark gray or black unoxidized core. On the Munsell scale, the surface color ranges from weak red to pink (10R 5/3 to 7.5YR 7/4) with the majority of sherds falling within the light red range (2.5YR 6/6 to 5YR 6/6). Aside from the gray or black interior, the typical core color is reddish brown (5YR 6/4 or 6/6).

Surface treatment: All of the vessels are smoothed but few were burnished. Red slip appears to have been applied on most, if not all, of the vessels, a fact that is obvious when the slip has come off leaving a light colored undersurface visible. It is only on vessels on which the slip was worked well into the undersurface that the paint has remained firmly in place.

Decoration: None of these vessels is painted although spouts, handles and nose lugs occur.

VESSEL FORMS

Although vessel forms are limited, there are distinct temporal differences throughout the site as well as differences with our findings at Ali Kosh and Tepe Sabz. In the Mohammad Jaffar Phase we found few sherds of this ware, a surprising finding in view of the fact that Khazineh Red accounted for about 50 percent of all sherds in the Mohammad Jaffar Phase at Ali Kosh. Moreover, there are few hole-mouth vessels at Chagha Sefid, although they were the most common vessel form of this ware at both Ali Kosh and Tepe Sabz. At Chagha Sefid, in the Sefid Phase, where we had more than 16,000 sherds, or nearly seven times as many of this ware as in the entire sequence at Ali Kosh and Tepe Sabz, the vessels fall within a narrow range of hemispherical and open bowls, as described below. The same situation prevails through the sequence at Chagha Sefid except that base forms change and there are pedestal bases, legged vessels, carinated bowls, jars and various handles in the Surkh and Choga Mami Transitional phases.

Hemispherical bowls with beaded rims (Figs. 39*a,e-h,r*; 42*c,m,n*). This is a common form that is represented in the Mohammad Jaffar Phase at Ali Kosh (Hole, Flannery and Neely, 1969:Fig. 45*e-g*), but which disappears by the Sabz Phase. At Chagha Sefid we find that this vessel form declines in frequency from 31 percent in the Sefid Phase to 21 percent in the late Surkh. We have no useful data from the Mohammad Jaffar, Choga Mami Transitional or Sabz phases at Chagha Sefid. The earlier forms, in the Sefid and early Surkh phases, have concave bases but the bases later include a few rounded bottoms (Figs. 40*f*; 42*j*). In all phases the rim diameters are most commonly (49 out of 77 examples) between 16 and 30 cm; the range is from 6 to 30 cm.

Hemispherical bowls with direct rims (Figs. 39*b,s-v,q*; 40*q-t*; 41*e*). The most common vessel form, it is represented by 85 out of all the measurable rims of Khazineh Red. We did not separate this form from the bowls with incurved rims or the open bowls in our previous report. The number of examples available for study from Chagha Sefid allowed us to separate a group whose vessel walls are essentially vertical. This form declines in frequency from a high of 40 percent in the Sefid Phase to 25 percent in the later Surkh Phase. The range of rim diameters is between 8 and 32 cm, with most examples (55 out of 85) falling between 11 and 20 cm.

Hemispherical bowls with incurved, direct rims (Figs. 39*b*; 41*d*; 42*s*): Bowls with slightly incurving rims. The rim diameters range from 6 to 30 cm, with 25 out of 33 measurable examples falling between 16

Fig. 39. Khazineh Red. Vessel forms in zones B1 and B2, early Sefid Phase.

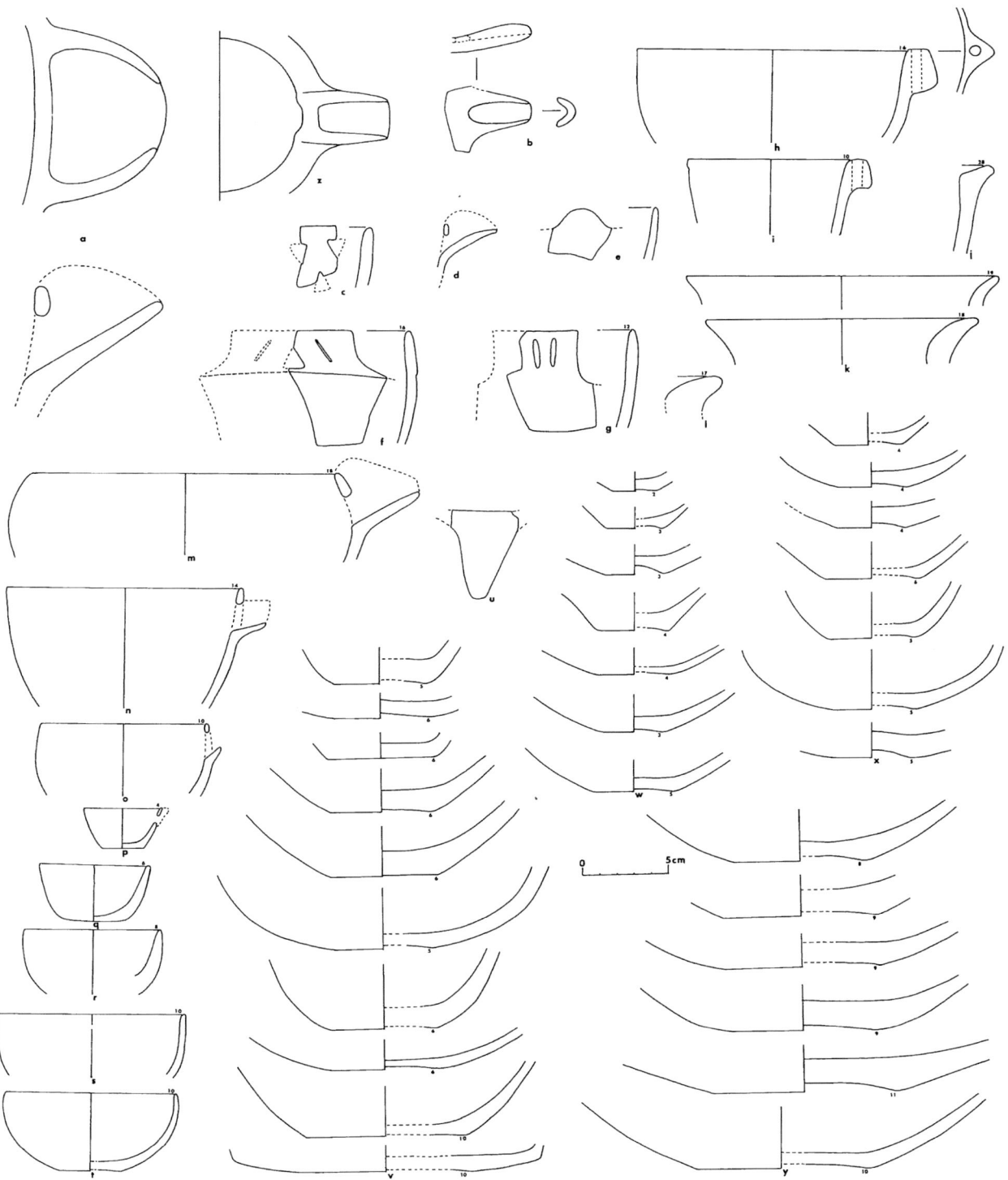

Fig. 40. Khazineh Red. Vessel forms in zones B2 and C1, later Sefid Phase.

Fig. 41. Khazineh Red. Vessel forms in zones C2 through D2, early Surkh Phase.

POTTERY

Fig. 42. Khazineh Red. Vessel forms in zones E, F, late Surkh Phase and Zone G, Choga Mami Transitional.

and 30 cm. These vessels are commonly found in the Mohammad Jaffar Phase at Ali Kosh (Hole, Flannery and Neely, 1969:Fig. 45a-d), but relatively rarely in the Sabz and later phases. At Chagha Sefid this form reaches a peak in the early Surkh Phase.

Carinated bowls (Figs. 39d; 42k,l,o): Only four carinated bowls were found; their rims range between 17 and 23 cm.

Open bowls (Figs. 39i,j,k-q; 41a,d-f,o,r,w-z; 42d,e,i,j): Open bowls can be regarded as part of a continuum that grades into hemispherical bowls; open forms have outleaning walls. This type, which begins in the Mohammad Jaffar Phase at Ali Kosh (Hole, Flannery and Neely, 1969:Fig. 45n-o) in low frequency, gradually increases in proportion through the sequence at Chagha Sefid. Out of 53 measurable examples, 33 are between 16 and 30 cm in diameter. The range is from 10 to 38 cm.

Hole-mouth bowls (Fig. 41b): Eighty-nine sherds of hole-mouth bowls could be identified; no entire vessel was reconstructable. Rims of this form were found in the Mohammad Jaffar Phase at Ali Kosh (Hole, Flannery and Neely, 1969:Fig. 46). At Chagha Sefid the first trace of this form appears in the early Sefid Phase, but they are more typical of the late Surkh Phase. All examples are between 16 and 28 cm in diameter.

Jars (Figs. 40j,l; 41m,n; 42a,b): There were 13 measurable examples of jars with heavy, everted rims. These examples, which are scattered throughout the sequence, range from 17 to 28 cm. One example, from Zone F (late Surkh Phase), may have had a flat base (Fig. 42a,b); otherwise the overall forms of these vessels could not be determined. It is likely that they were relatively straight sided, as body sherds of globular jars were not found.

Spouted vessels (Figs. 40a,b,d,m-p,z; 41g,k,q; 42t): Although many spout fragments were found throughout Chagha Sefid, only eight examples had a sufficient amount of rim attached to permit an estimate of their diameters and forms. Spouts were attached to either incurved hemispherical or straight sided bowls. The smallest example is on a vessel only 4½ cm in diameter while the largest spouted vessel is estimated to be about 46 cm. The other examples are between 9 and 18 cm. Three varieties of spouts can be distinguished. Most common is the trough spout with high sides (Figs. 40a,d,m,n; 41k,q; 42t). In all cases there is a strap across the rim. Examples range from 2 to 8 cm in length. Two examples of trough spouts without high sides come from the early Surkh Phase (Fig. 40o,p). The third variety is a very shallow, elongate trough. Rims were not attached to either example of this (Figs. 40b; 41q).

Handles (Figs. 40c,e,f,g; 41p,f; 42f,g): Plain tab (Fig. 40e; 41p) and fenestrated tab handles are found on some hemispherical bowls beginning in the late Sefid Phase. Reconstructed examples are shown in Figures 40f,g; 41f. When tab or fenestrated handles are added to bowls they are often thicker than the rim of the vessel. Examples which illustrate this are shown in Figures 41l; 42f,g.

Pedestal bases (Figs. 41h,i; 42p): There are two pedestal bases, both from Zone D of the middle Surkh Phase; they measure 6 and 7 cm in diameter and the one measurable example stands 2 cm high. A possible pedestal in Zone F, late Surkh Phase is shown reconstructed in Fig. 42p.

Legs (Figs. 40u; 41c,j): Fragments of legs were found throughout. One reconstructable example from the late Surkh Phase shows a tripod support 4½ cm high, probably for an open bowl (Fig. 42g). Other examples range in height from 4½ to about 7 cm.

Nose lugs (Fig. 40h,i): Two hemispherical bowls with diameters of 9½ and 16 cm have vertically perforated nose lugs set onto the rim.

Sefid Wares

Four types of pottery are grouped as Sefid Wares: Sefid Red-on-Cream (with a variety called Sefid Painted in the tables), Sefid Black-on-Cream, Sefid Black-on-Red, and Sefid Burnished Plain. Collectively these compose the majority of sherds of the Sefid Phase and all have their major, if not sole, time of production during the Sefid Phase. The types thus constitute a convenient and easily recognizable marker for the Phase. At the same time it should be recognized that Sefid Red-on-Cream begins in the late Mohammad Jaffar Phase, while Jaffar Plain and Khazineh Red both constitute substantial proportions of the total sherd count in the Sefid Phase and provide continuity with the Mohammad Jaffar Phase. Each Sefid type has its own series of vessel forms, so that collectively they make up a varied set of household utensils. In spite of the large number of sherds we found, there were few reconstructable vessels; indeed,

Table 15

KHAZINEH RED SHERDS AT CHAGHA SEFID
by Stratigraphic Zone

Phase	Area	Zone	Bowls with Beaded Rims	Bowls with Direct Rims	Hole-mouth Bowls	Carinated Bowls	Jars	Spouts and Fragments	Handles	Pedestals	Legs	Nose Lugs	Body Sherds	Totals
Sabz	SD	J												
	SD	I	1										4	5
Choga Mami Transitional	SD	H	8	4	1			1					40	54
	SD	G2	8	14	0								100	122
	SD	G1	50	38	5	1		2					611	707
Surkh	SD	F	107	95	27		3	14	2		3		785	1,036
	SC, SD	E2	32	43	12			8	1				660	756
	SC, SD	E1	95	97	26	2		10					1,302	1,532
	SC	D3	34	29	1			4					138	206
	SC	D2	101	167	2		1	15	2	1	1		1,860	2,150
	SC	D1	60	82	1		1	8		1	2		578	733
	SC	C2	72	131	1		1	17			2		1,189	1,413
Sefid	SA	C1	194	289	11		5	27	4				3,523	4,053
	SA	B2	230	1,033	1	1	2	55			1	2	8,999	10,326
	SA	B1	17	450	1			20					1,931	2,419
	SA	A4	1	5									23	29
Mohammad Jaffar	SB	C		2									23	25
	SB	B						2					14	16
	SB	A											9	9
Ali Kosh	SA	A3		4									14	18
	SA	A2		2									15	17
	SA	A1		6				1					60	67
	Totals		1,009	2,492	89	4	13	184	9	2	9	2	21,875	25,691

it is often difficult with the small rim sherds to get an accurate estimate of diameter or even of the form of the bowl. The drawings show the forms of the common containers and the range of variation in measurable rims.

It is not possible to distinguish lower body sherds of Sefid Red-on-Cream from those of Jaffar Plain. For this reason the total counts of the former will be somewhat lower than is actually the case. Too, it is sometimes impossible to distinguish between Sefid Red-on-Cream and Sefid Black-on-Cream, when the red paint is very dark.

Table 16

KHAZINEH RED SHERDS AT CHAGHA SEFID
by Cultural Phase

Phase	Bowls with Beaded Rims	Bowls with Direct Rims	Hole-mouth Bowls	Carinated Bowls	Jars	Spouts and Fragments	Handles	Pedestals	Legs	Nose Lugs	Body Sherds	Totals
Sabz		1									4	5
Choga Mami Transitional	66	56	6	1		3					751	883
Surkh	501	644	70	2	6	76	5	2	8		6,512	7,826
Sefid	442	1,777	13	1	7	102	4		1	2	14,476	16,825
Mohammad Jaffar		2				2					46	50
Ali Kosh		12				1					89	102
Totals	1,009	2,492	89	4	13	184	9	2	9	2	21,878	25,691

TYPE: Sefid Red-on-Cream (Figs. 43-45)

Sample: 3,259 plus 294 "Sefid Painted"

Temporal distribution: Principally Sefid Phase although this type begins in the late Mohammad Jaffar Phase as a continuation of the typical painting of that phase.

Appearance: This type probably represents a series of improvements in the manufacture of the Jaffar wares although it is usually easily distinguished from them by the surface treatment and design elements.

Paste: Relatively compact but porous and pitted as a result of burning out of vegetal fibers.

Temper: All are chaff tempered with occasional small pieces of grit as accidental inclusions. In general the chaff is less obtrusive than in the Jaffar wares.

Color: The paste, like that of Jaffar Plain and Painted, is buff. While cores may be dark gray on the thicker pieces, thinner sherds are fired to a uniform buff throughout. The unpainted interiors are 5YR 6/3 to 10YR 7/3. Designs are various shades of red, the intensity depending largely on the thickness of the paint and the firing. The range is 2.5YR 4/4 to 10R 3/4 to 10R 4/8.

Surface treatment: The vessels are all slipped, especially on the outside where cream slip is used as a base for the painted design. Interiors are ordinarily slipped, usually with cream, although red was used in some instances, especially on the decorated series. In the Surkh Phase black paint in part replaces the red.

Decoration: A series of 294 sherds (Sefid Painted variety) has linear geometric designs in a "developed" Mohammad Jaffar style and various curvilinear and free-standing design elements. Most of these sherds were very small and it was not possible to reconstruct an entire vessel nor to determine rim diameters. It is probable that some of these sherds are parts of the vessels that compose the majority of Sefid Red-on-Cream. There are some 3,259 sherds of the latter, most of which appear to have the red paint confined to the upper portion of the vessels. A thin red band often runs around the inside of the rim. The interiors and the lower bodies are covered with a cream colored slip. In all cases the red slip may be, but rarely

POTTERY

Fig. 43. Sefid Red-on-Cream. Painted varieties A and C which are basically a development out of Jaffar Painted. Zones B and C1, Sefid Phase.

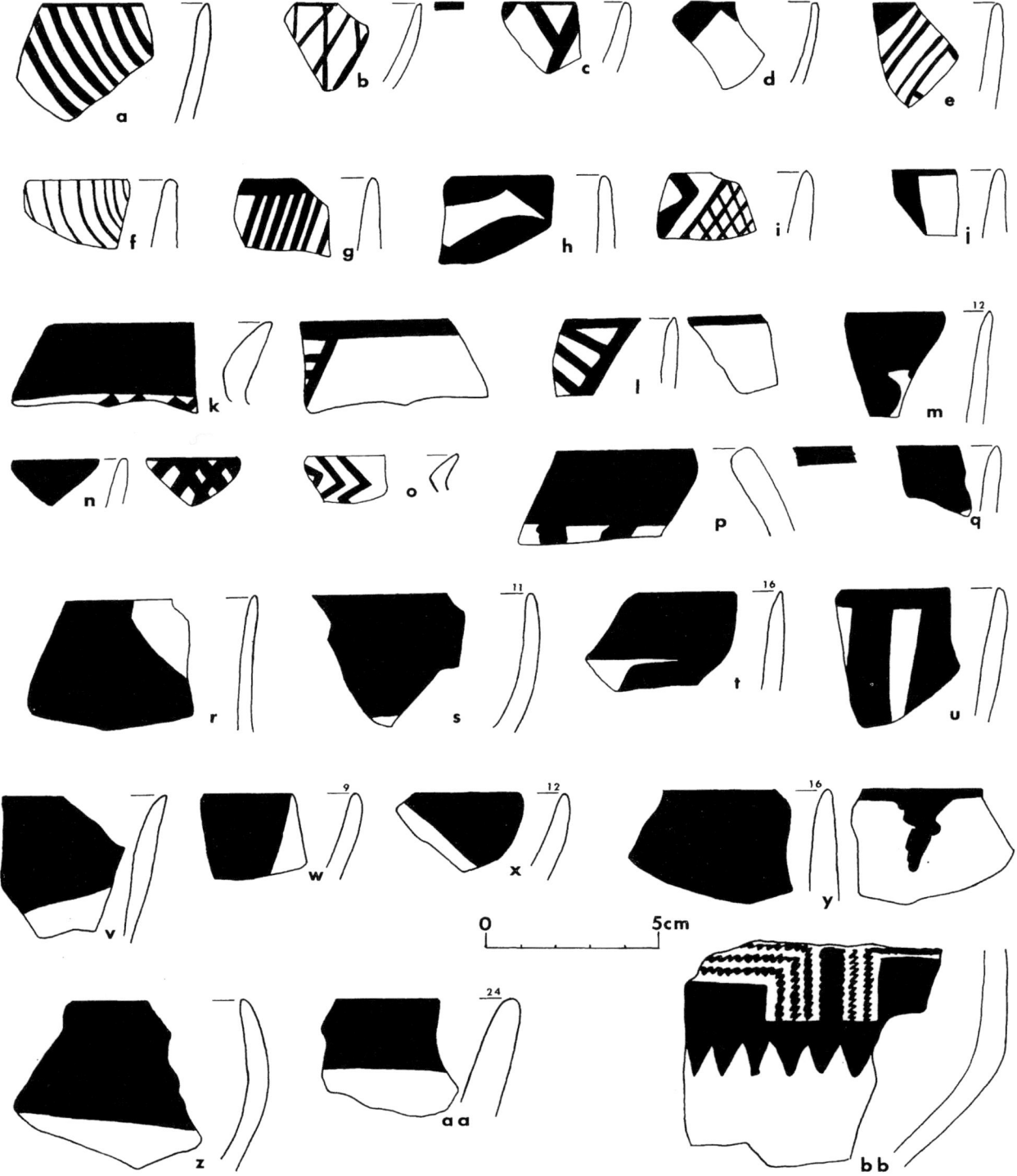

Fig. 44. Sefid Red-on-Cream. Painted varieties A, with developed Mohammad Jaffar designs, and B, with broad maroon bands. Zone B, Sefid Phase except *l,n,u,bb,* Surkh Phase.

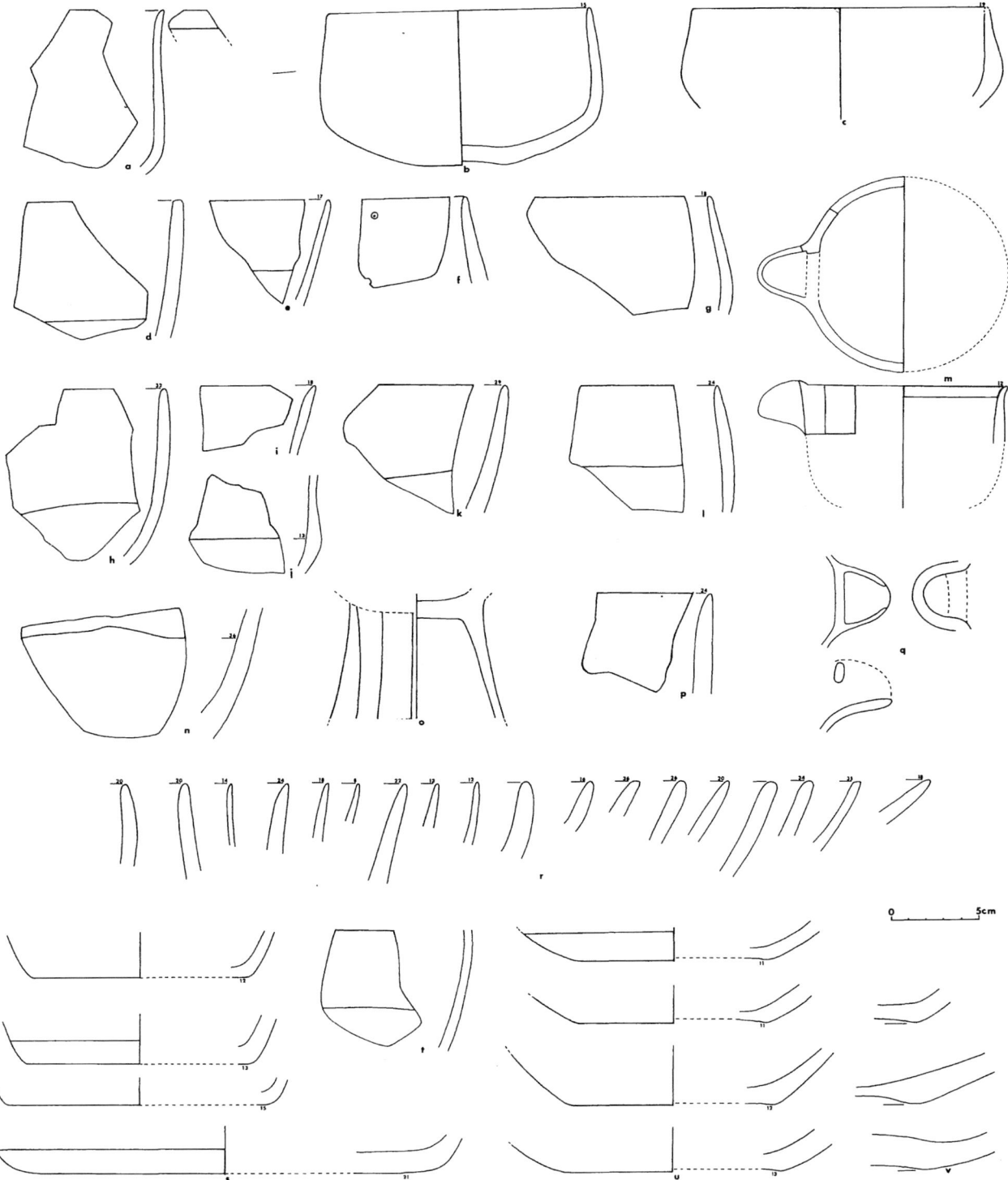

Fig. 45. Sefid Red-on-Cream. Range of variation in vessel forms. All zones B1 and B2, Sefid Phase.

is, fugitive although it has often flaked off where chaff burned out of the paste.

SEFID PAINTED VARIETY

This small group of decorated sherds is from a variety of vessels, most of them small. It can be expected, although not proven, that some of these sherds are from vessels illustrated in the group that has solid panels of red on the outside as the principal decoration (Figs. 44, 45). This variety begins in the late Mohammad Jaffar Phase and is thus earlier than the bulk of the Sefid Red-on-Cream.

Most of the sherds are from bodies of painted vessels; rim sherds are very small. There are no reconstructable vessels. Therefore, we describe only the range of design elements for this group, although the few rim sherds suggest that all came from either small hemispherical or straight-sided bowls.

Variety A—A continuation of the Jaffar Painted tradition of closely-spaced lines and triangles (Fig. 43 *j-z*) which grades into more curvilinear open variations (Figs. 43*b,e,g-i*; 44*a-i*). The paint is usually bright red on a cream slip. A few sherds have black paint (Fig. 44*bb*) and deeper hues of red. Interiors are either cream or red.

Variety B—Swirling broad maroon lines on a yellow-cream slip (Fig. 43*c,f*; 44*h,m-x*).

Variety C—Isolated design elements, usually red dots on a cream slip or open linear loop designs (Fig. 43*a,d*).

VESSEL FORMS OF SEFID RED-ON-CREAM (INCLUDING THE SEFID PAINTED VARIETY)

Convex-walled bowls (Fig. 44*z*; 45*c,g*): Vessels that appear to be identical in shape to convex-walled bowls of the Jaffar wares occur in low frequency. Measurable examples had rim diameters of 12 to 19 cm. On these vessels the paint on the outside may go all the way to the base or stop at about the point where the side of the vessel curves toward the base.

Straight sided bowls (Figs. 44*a,e,f-j,m,q,r,t,u,y,aa*; 45*a,b,d,h,l,p*): More abundant than the convex-sided bowls are those with relatively straight sides. Measurable rims range from 14 to 20 cm. The overall heights of these vessels could not be determined. Paint often occurs only on the upper portion of the vessel, terminating about at the point where the side turns toward the base. Below the paint the vessels have cream colored slip. Many vessels, however, seem to have paint all the way to the base; indeed the sides of all the bases illustrated are painted. A rim sherd of a straight sided vessel with a slightly everted rim was broken at the junction of a spout. This vessel has been reconstructed in Figure 45*m*. The form of the spout follows that of other contemporary spouts.

Open bowls (Figs. 44*b-d,s,v-x*; 45*e,r*). The most common form of vessel is the bowl with slightly outleaning sides. None of the vessels is open like those of the Susiana series, nor do any have painting other than a band inside the rim. Diameters range from 13 to 36 cm.

Bases (Fig. 45): The bases in zone B1 are flat (Fig. 45*s*), while those of B2, with one exception, are slightly concave (Fig. 45*u,v*). Diameters of bases range from 13 to 24 cm for the flat variety while the concave bases range from 11.5 to 13 cm. Bases of vessels whose sides are not painted down to the base are not included here. It is possible that some of the Jaffar Plain bases are from these bowls.

Spouts (Fig. 45*m,q*): Several fragments of spouts and one reconstructable example were found. All spouts of the Sefid Phase appear to be of the same style: trough-shaped with a strap across the spout approximately in line with the rim. Spouts are painted red on the outside and have a red band across the top of the strap. Insides of spouts are covered with cream slip.

Pedestal (Fig. 45*o*): A reconstructable pedestal with broad vertical stripes comes from Zone B2. The pedestal in its broken form stands 7.5 cm high and apparently supported a large open bowl.

Jars (Fig. 44*k,o*): Two sherds of jars were found, one with an apparent neck diameter of 20 cm (Fig. 43*o*). The other, though too small to measure, is clearly from a much smaller vessel.

Hole-mouth bowl (Fig. 44*p*): One thick sherd is of a hole-mouth vessel whose diameter could not be measured.

TYPE: Sefid Black-on-Cream (Fig. 46)

Sample: 2,717

Temporal distribution: Principally Sefid and Surkh phases, although sherds of this type are found as late

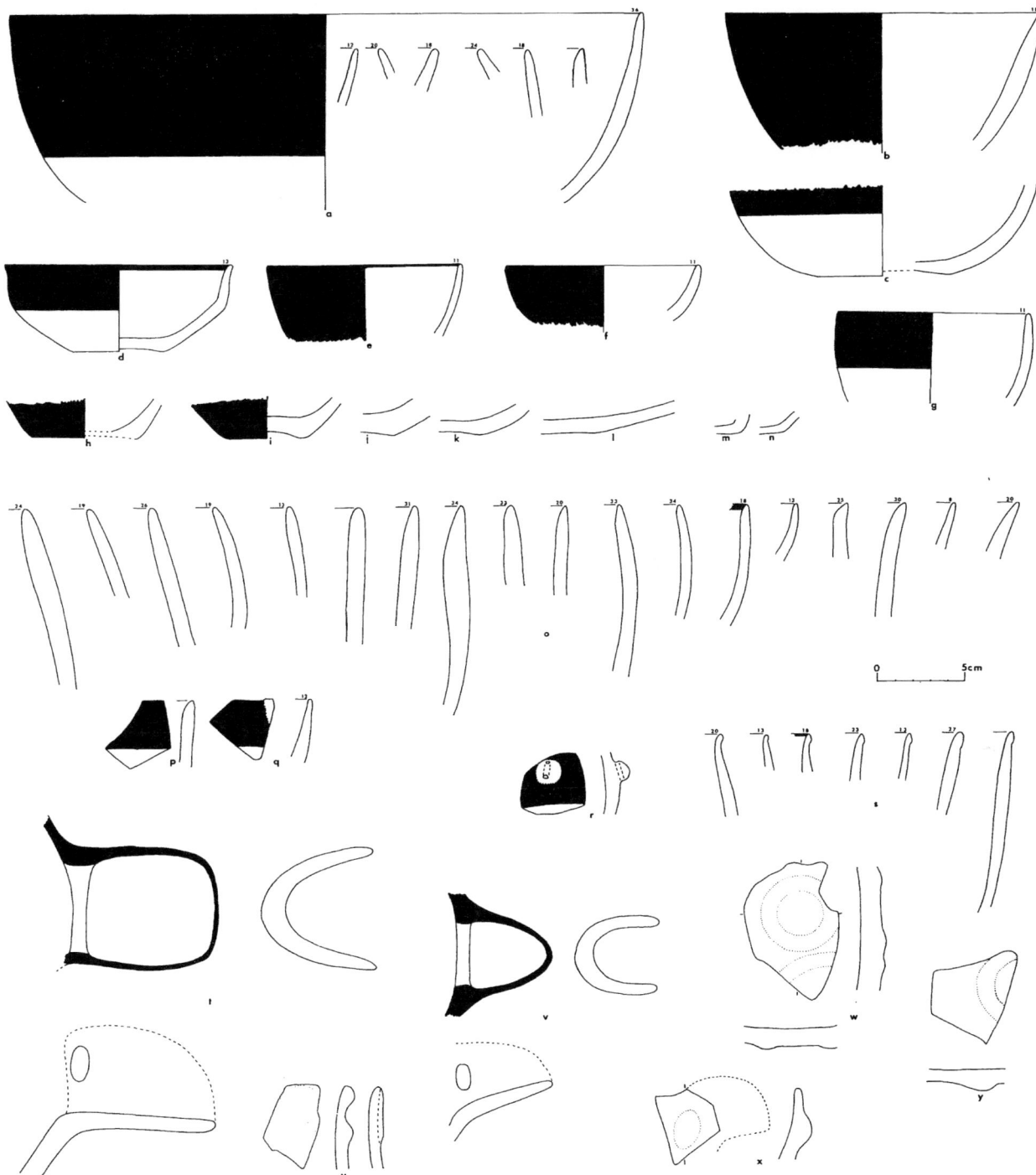

Fig. 46. Sefid Black-on-Cream. Vessel forms in Zone B, Sefid Phase except *r*, Zone D1, Surkh Phase.

Table 17

SHERDS OF SEFID RED-ON-CREAM AND SEFID PAINTED AT CHAGHA SEFID
by Stratigraphic Zone

Phase	Zone Area	Zone	Sefid Red-on-Cream					Sefid Painted							Painting Style		
			Beaded Rims	Direct Rims	Spouts & Handles	Body Sherds	Total Sherds	Direct Rims	Hole-mouth Jars	Jars	Sherds of Spouts	Sherds of Pedestals	Body Sherds	Total Sherds	Style A	Style B	Style C
Sabz	SD	J															
	SD	I															
Choga Mami Transitional	SD	H				1	1										
	SD	G2															
	SD	G1				1	1										
Surkh	SD	F				4	4										
	SC, SD	E2															
	SC, SD	E1				7	7	1					6	7	3		3
	SC	D3											1	1	1		
	SC	D2											3	3	1		2
	SC	D1															
	SC	C2											1	1			1
Sefid	SA	C1	1	38	1	6	46	4	1	1			6	12	4	2	
	SA	B2	5	227	11	1,284	1,527	8				1	82	91	61	17	13
	SA	B1	8	300	10	1,300	1,618	10			2		149	161	152	4	3
	SA	A4			1	25	26						1	1	1		
Mohammad Jaffar	SB	C															
	SB	B															
	SB	A															
Ali Kosh	SA	A3		2		5	7						4	4	4		
	SA	A2				1	1						9	9	9		
	SA	A1		2		19	21						4	4	4		
	Totals		14	570	22	2,653	3,259	22	1	2	2	1	266	294			

as Choga Mami Transitional. Rim sherds are confined to the Sefid and Surkh Phases.

Appearance: Similar to Sefid Red-on-Cream except that Black-on-Cream vessels have considerably more painting on the outside. In this sense they are like the Sefid Black-on-Red wares, although there is a considerable difference in shapes of vessels between these two types. Flecks of paint have often popped off where calcium exploded.

Paste: Relatively compact but porous and pitted as a result of burning out of vegetal fibers.

Temper: All are chaff tempered with occasional small pieces of grit as accidental inclusions. Pieces of calcium are included as grit.

Table 18
SHERDS OF SEFID RED-ON-CREAM AND SEFID PAINTED AT CHAGHA SEFID
by Cultural Phase

Phase	Sefid Red-on-Cream					Sefid Painted							Painting Style		
	Beaded Rims	Direct Rims	Spouts & Handles	Body Sherds	Total Sherds	Direct Rims	Hole-mouth	Jars	Sherds of Spouts	Sherds of Pedestals	Body Sherds	Total Sherds	Style A	Style B	Style C
Sabz															
Choga Mami Transitional				2	2										
Surkh				11	11	1					11	12	5		6
Sefid	14	566	22	2,615	3,217	22	1	1	2	1	238	265	218	23	16
Mohammad Jaffar															
Ali Kosh		4		25	29						17	17	17		
Totals	14	570	22	2,653	3,259	22	1	2	2	1	266	294			

Color: The paste is buff, like that of Jaffar Plain and Painted, and is usually fired throughout although dark cores remain on the thick sherds. The surface under the paint appears to be simply smoothed paste. Interiors and lower body sherds show a range of color resulting from firing differences. Although the overall appearance is pale brown, great variation may exist on the same sherd. Firing clouds may be red (10R 4/8) and the interiors are generally 7.5YR 6/4, light brown, to 7.5YR 7/6, reddish yellow, on the Munsell scale. In some instances the interior has a red slip and looks like Khazineh Red.

Surface treatment: Surfaces are smoothed and probably self-slipped although a small proportion have red interiors that probably result from slipping or from firing.

Decoration: Painted decoration is confined to black panels on approximately the upper two thirds of the vessels. The interiors of the rims are not painted. Several instances of plastic decoration, most likely around spouts, were also found.

VESSEL FORMS

Hemispherical bowls (Fig. 46*a-c,e-g,p,q*): All rim sherds are of bowls that have slightly incurving, straight sided or slightly outleaning sides. Except when sherds are large enough to measure the diameter, it is not possible to accurately tell what the precise angle of the rim is. Nevertheless, it is clear that basically one form of vessel occurs in this type. Measurable examples range from 11 to 36 cm in diameter. Since most bases of this type are counted as Jaffar Plain, except when they are still attached to the rims, we have relatively few examples that are definitely from vessels of this type. It is likely, however, that most of the bases are concave (see Fig. 46*c,h-k*). Nearly all rims are either simple rounded direct or slightly beveled to the interior. Only 9 rims out of the total 555 are beaded. One vessel is carinated (Fig. 46*d*).

Spouts (Fig. 46*t,v,x*): The common form of deep trough spout with a strap bridging the opening at the rim is the only type found on this ware.

Plastic decoration (Fig. 46*v,w,x,y*): Several examples of concentric rings of clay applied to the bodies of vessels were found but none is completely intact. Double rings seem to be the most common, while one oval lump was found attached to the edge of a spout fragment (Fig. 46*x*).

Perforated lug (Fig. 46*r*): One example of a lug was found on an upper body sherd from Zone D, Surkh

Phase. The lug is an appliqued button of clay with a hole pierced vertically.

TYPE: Sefid Black-on-Red Ware (Fig. 47-48)

Sample: 2,114

Temporal distribution: Sefid through Surkh and possibly Choga Mami Transitional phases.

Comment: This is basically Khazineh Red pottery which has black paint on a portion or all of the exterior, and sometimes a band around the inside of the rim as well. Unless a vessel could be reconstructed from sherds lying together, sherds from the lower body and base have probably been counted as Khazineh Red. This problem is less serious in the Sefid Phase when body sherds with both black paint and a portion of the red background were common. In the Surkh Phase, however, paint is almost exclusively confined to a narrow band around the rim; thus body sherds of this type could not be distinguished from Khazineh Red. In view of this, the most accurate reflection of the proportions of this type are seen in the rim sherd counts alone (Table 21).

Appearance: Like Khazineh Red, this is a relatively coarse red ware with a wide range of color variations, and solid panels or bands of black applied to the upper portions of the pots.

Paste: The same as Khazineh Red

Temper: The same as Khazineh Red

Color: Except for the black paint, the colors are the same as Khazineh Red.

Surface treatment: Vessels are smoothed and

Table 19
VESSEL FORMS IN SEFID BLACK-ON-CREAM AT CHAGHA SEFID
by Stratigraphic Zone

Phase	Area	Zone	Beaded Rim Bowls	Direct Rim Bowls	Sherds of Spouts	Body Sherds	Total Sherds
Sabz	SD	J					
	SD	I					
Choga Mami Transitional	SD	H				2	2
	SD	G2				1	1
	SD	G1				21	21
Surkh	SD	F				32	32
	SC, SD	E2		3		12	15
	SC, SD	E1		11		72	83
	SC	D3		4		23	27
	SC	D2	2	17		113	132
	SC	D1	1	9	1	53	64
	SC	C2	3	7		41	51
Sefid	SA	C1		20		32	52
	SA	B2		314	17	906	1,237
	SA	B1	3	156	8	821	988
	SA	A4		2		1	3
Mohammad Jaffar	SB	C					
	SB	B				1	1
	SB	A					
Ali Kosh	SA	A3		1		1	2
	SA	A2					
	SA	A1		2	1	3	6
		Totals	9	546	27	2,135	2,717

Table 20
VESSEL FORMS IN SEFID BLACK-ON-CREAM AT CHAGHA SEFID
by Cultural Phase

Phase	Beaded Rim Bowls	Direct Rim Bowls	Sherds of Spouts	Body Sherds	Total Sherds
Sabz					
Choga Mami Transitional				24	24
Surkh	6	51	1	346	404
Sefid	3	492	25	1,760	2,280
Mohammad Jaffar				1	1
Ali Kosh		3	1	4	8
Totals	9	546	27	2,135	2,717

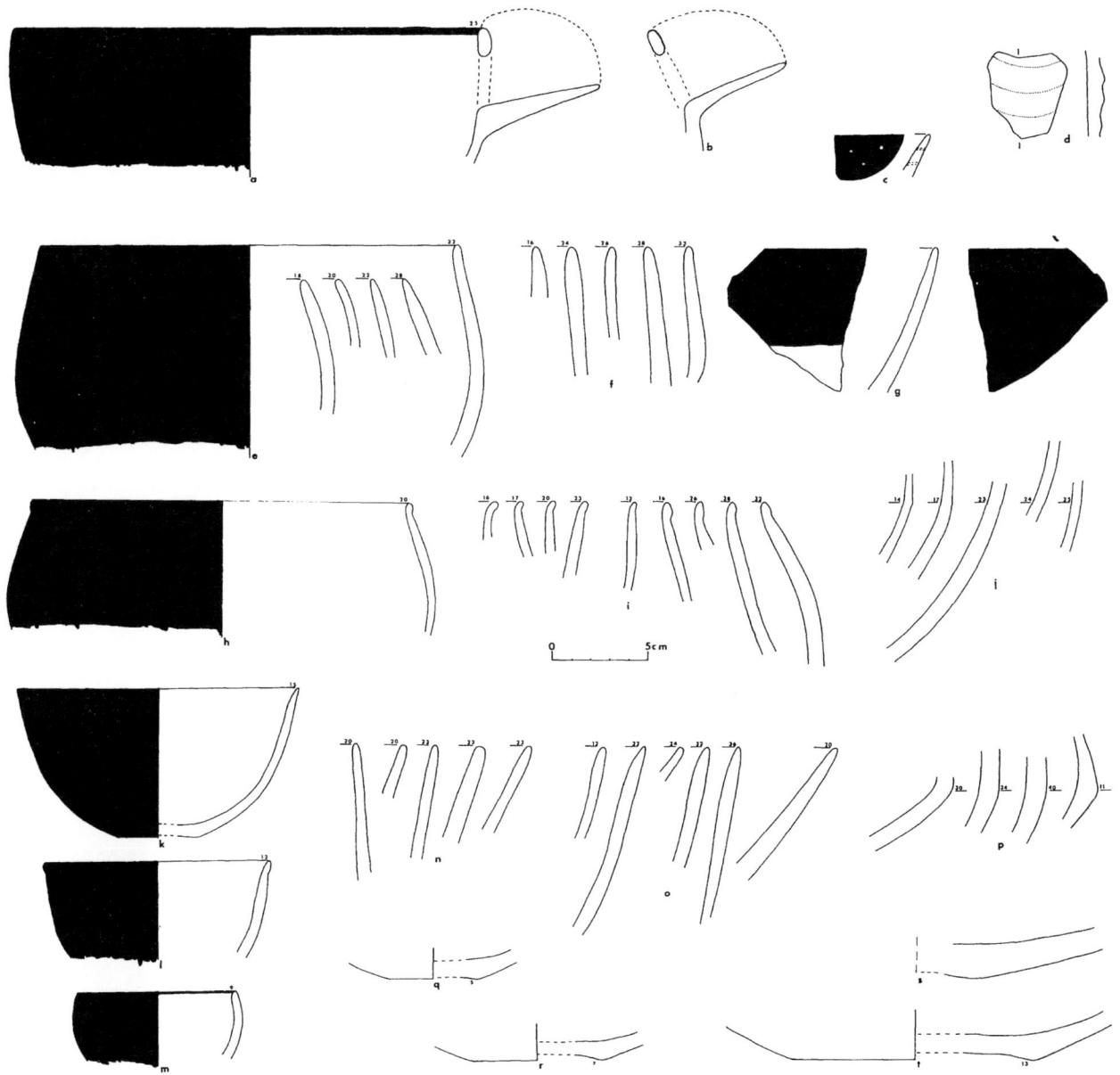

Fig. 47. Sefid Black-on-Red. Vessel forms in Zone B, Sefid Phase.

slipped. Red slip is applied inside and out and the rims or portions of the upper body are painted black.

Decoration: With two exceptions, decoration consists solely of black bands on and around the rims or upper portions of the vessels. Rarely the insides are partially painted black as well. Two examples have solid black pendant triangles around the exterior of hole-mouth bowls. One spout has a crude linear design.

VESSEL FORMS

Vessel forms change considerably, as does the decoration, from the Sefid to the Surkh Phase. The Sefid Phase has a narrow range of hemispherical bowls with slightly incurving or vertical sides, along with slightly open bowls, two of which are carinated. Many of the sherds are too small to permit an accurate determination of either the shape or the

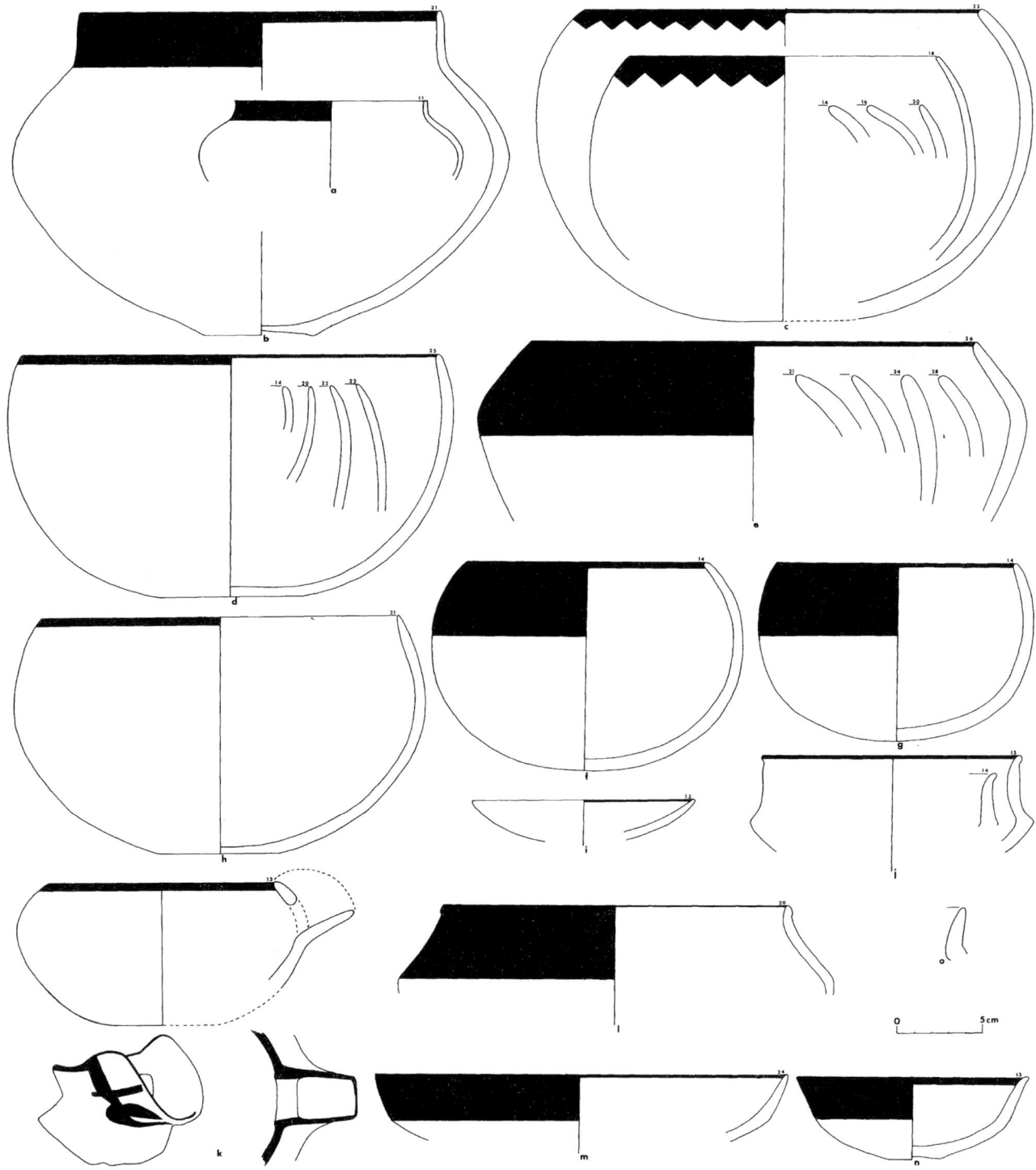

Fig. 48. Sefid Black-on-Red. Vessel forms in zones of the Surkh Phase.

diameter; therefore the counts in Table 21 merely indicate whether the rims are beaded, direct, or of hole-mouth vessels. Small sherds of jars with direct rims cannot be distinguished from sherds of hemispherical bowls. In the Surkh Phase the predominant form is that of the hemispherical bowl with incurving rims which grades into hole-mouth vessels. Additionally we find a few carinated bowls and a few jars, one of which was nearly intact.

Hemispherical bowls with incurving direct rims: Four hundred and sixty-four out of 572 rim sherds have direct rims; of these a high proportion curve inward. The vessels in the Sefid Phase are distinguished from those of the Surkh Phase in two ways: the walls are more nearly vertical (compare Figs. 47*e,f,n,o* and 48*c,d,g,h*) and the paint on the outside covers the entire outside in the Sefid Phase (Fig. 47*k*). In the Surkh Phase the vessels are more globular and the paint is confined to a band around the rim (Fig. 48*g,h*), usually including a band on the inside. Interior bands are rare on Sefid Phase vessels. Rim diameters in the Sefid Phase range from 8½ to 32 cm; those in the Surkh Phase from 7 to 25 cm. All bases found in the Sefid Phase are concave (Fig. 47*k,q-t*), whereas flat and round bases are present in the Surkh Phase (Fig. 48*c,d,g-h*).

Hemispherical bowls with incurving beaded rims (Fig. 47*h,i*): These vessels are confined to the Sefid Phase; later beaded rims are from either straight sided or slightly outleaning vessels. Measurable rims show a range of 17 to 20 cm. Paint on these vessels apparently covers the entire outside and is confined to a narrow band across the top of the rim on the inside.

Open bowls with direct and beaded rims (Figs. 47*l,o*; 48*i*): Reconstructable vessels of this form in the Sefid Phase (Fig. 47*k*) can be considered an extension of hemispherical bowls with straight sides. The range of variation in rim diameter is 12 to 20 cm. One example from the Surkh Phase in area D is a shallow bowl with a narrow black band around the direct rim (Fig. 48*i*).

Hole-mouth bowls. One-fourth of the rims in the Surkh Phase are of hole-mouth bowls, although it appears that none has an extremely constricted mouth. These vessels grade into hemispherical bowls. Measurable rims range between 14 and 23 cm in diameter and restorable examples stand from 13 to 20 cm high. Two vessels had black pendant triangles painted below the rim on the outside (Fig. 48*c*); the other examples had black paint on approximately the upper one third of the vessel. Bases of restorable examples are round (Fig. 48*e,f*).

Carinated bowls with beaded and direct rims (Fig. 48 *j,m,n*): Both examples from the Sefid Phase have direct rims and paint down to the carination; their rims are 13½ and 24 cm in diameter. The one vessel from Zone B2 which is intact has a concave base (Fig. 48*n*). The examples from the Surkh Phase are much more sharply carinated (Fig. 48*j*). These examples have only a narrow black band around the rim. In addition to the examples illustrated, most of the 20 other beaded rims from the Surkh Phase are probably of similar vessels. Measurable examples range from 14 to 23 cm.

Jars (Fig. 48*a,b*): One entirely restorable jar is from Zone E of Area D. It has a vertical neck 21 cm in diameter and the vessel stands 20 cm high (Fig. 48*b*). A rim sherd of a similar vessel with a diameter of about 11 cm is from the same zone (Fig. 48*a*). One sherd of a large jar with a thick, slightly outleaning neck is also from Zone F of Area D (Fig. 48*o*). The diameter of this vessel could not be measured.

Spouts: In all, 53 spouts and fragments of spouts were recovered, some of which are illustrated (Figs. 47*a,b*; 48*k*). In the Sefid Phase all spout fragments are large and indicate that deep trough spouts with a strap across the rim were used on hemispherical bowls. From the Surkh Phase similar but smaller spouts also occur on hemispherical bowls (Fig. 48*k*). The reconstruction is based on the spout itself, although the actual bowl to which it was attached was not found. The rim diameter was measured from the bridging strap and a small portion of rim still present on the sherd.

Lug: One sherd has a lug pierced with a horizontal hole.

Molded sherd (Fig. 47*d*): One body sherd has concentric rings molded into it. By analogy with similar sherds found in the Black-on-Cream ware, this decoration was probably applied near a spout on the upper portion of the vessel. Vessels with similar plastic decoration are found at Umm Dabaghiyeh (Kirkbride, 1972:Pl. xi).

Perforated sherd (Fig. 47*c*): One sherd of a small open bowl with a direct rim has three small holes drilled through near the rim after the sherd was fired. These holes are much smaller than the usual "mend"

Table 21

VESSEL FORMS IN SEFID BLACK-ON-RED WARES AT CHAGHA SEFID
by Stratigraphic Zone

Phase	Area	Zone	Beaded Rims with Black Band	Beaded Rims with Black Sides	Direct Rims with Black Band	Direct Rims with Black Sides	Hole-mouth with Black Band	Jars	Spout Fragments	Body Sherds	Total Sherds
Sabz	SD	J									
	SD	I									
Choga Mami Transitional	SD	H	2		1						3
	SD	G2									
	SD	G1			1		2	1			4
Surkh	SD	F			5		1	1	1		8
	SC, SD	E2	4		5		7	1			17
	SC, SD	E1	1		8		9		2	1	21
	SC	D3			4		11				15
	SC	D2	4		12		9		8		33
	SC	D1			11		4				15
	SC	C2	3		14		3		10		30
Sefid	SA	C1	7			22	26		4	11	70
	SA	B2	2	7		335	3		24	1,110	1,481
	SA	B1				44			4	353	401
	SA	A4								2	2
Mohammad Jaffar	SB	C									
	SB	B									
	SB	A									
Ali Kosh	SA	A3				1				3	4
	SA	A2								1	1
	SA	A1				1				8	9
	Totals		23	7	61	403	75	3	53	1,489	2,114

holes that are commonly found on sherds of all types at Chagha Sefid.

Bases (Fig. 47*q-t*): It is only in the Sefid Phase that we found bases separate from reconstructable vessels. In these instances the black paint extended down to the base and sometimes covered the entire base as well. An exceptionally large example measures 13 cm in diameter while others are typically smaller, in the

Table 22

VESSEL FORMS IN SEFID BLACK-ON-RED WARES
by Cultural Phase

Phase	Beaded Rims with Black Band	Beaded Rims with Black Sides	Direct Rims with Black Band	Direct Rims with Black Sides	Hole-mouth with Black Band	Jars	Spout Fragments	Body Sherds	Total Sherds
Sabz									
Choga Mami Transitional	2		2		2	1			7
Surkh	12		59		44	2	21	1	139
Sefid	9	7		401	29		32	1,476	1,954
Mohammad Jaffar									
Ali Kosh				2				12	14
Totals	23	7	61	403	75	3	53	1,489	2,114

5 to 7 cm range. Bases in the Surkh Phase can be round, flat or concave (Fig. 48). Concave examples measure 6-7 cm in diameter.

TYPE: Sefid Burnished Plain (Fig. 49)

Sample: 2,900

Comment: Sefid Burnished Plain was not recognized as a distinct type while we were in the field carrying out the initial sorting and discarding of body sherds. In consequence, some sherds of this type that were found in post-Sefid Phase deposits were probably counted as Jaffar Plain. Nevertheless, it is clear that Sefid Burnished Plain is predominantly restricted to the Sefid Phase. The fact that only three rim sherds of this type occurred in later deposits is a clear indication of its restricted temporal distribution.

Temporal distribution: Confined to the Sefid Phase.

Appearance: It is well-burnished, hard-surfaced soft ware. Although distinct in appearance from Jaffar Plain, these vessels are made of the same paste and have the same basic shapes and sizes. As Jaffar Plain declines in frequency, Sefid Burnished Plain takes its place.

Paste: Essentially the same as Jaffar Plain, the paste is porous and pitted as a result of the burning-out of vegetal fibers.

Temper: The majority of sherds are wholly chaff-tempered, although pieces with fine grit tempering occur.

Color: The cores are ordinarily fired throughout and no grey or black cores were noted except on the thickest bases. Exterior colors vary from 5YR 4/4, reddish brown, 5YR 4/6, yellowish red, 5YR 7/6, reddish yellow, to 7.5YR 6/6, reddish yellow to 10YR 5/8, yellowish brown and 10R 6/8, light red.

Surface treatment: In some instances surfaces appear to have been slipped but this effect may have resulted from the burnishing itself which covered the entire vessel, inside and out. Burnish marks are rare; the surfaces were carefully smoothed to eliminate them.

Decoration: None.

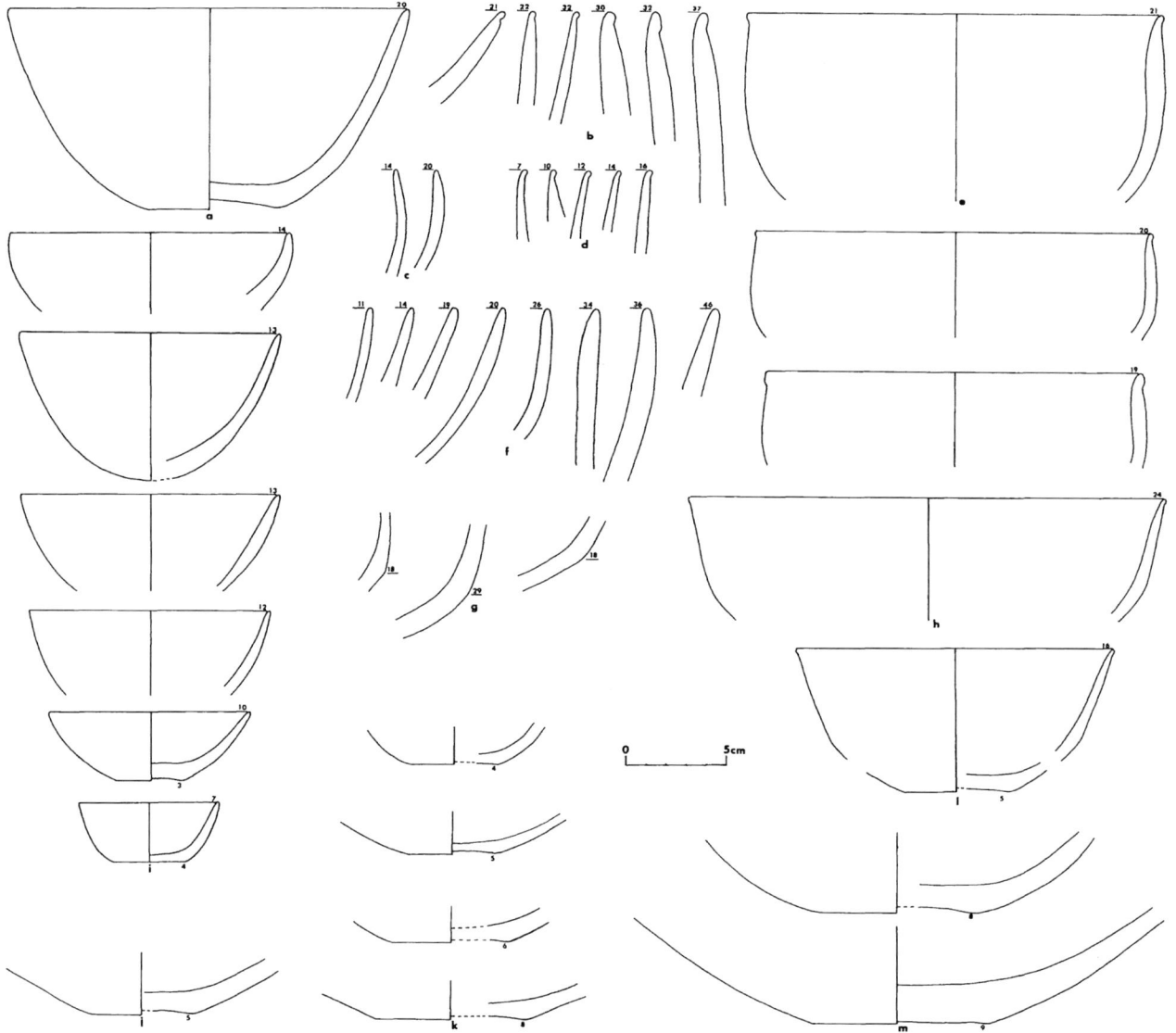

Fig. 49. Sefid Burnished Plain. Range of variation in vessel forms. Zones B2 and C1, later Sefid Phase.

VESSEL FORMS

Open bowls (Fig. 49*a,c,f,i,k,l*): Most vessels are of this form with either a pronounced beaded rim or a simple direct rim. Bases, with one exception (Fig. 49 *i*), are concave. Rim diameters of bowls with direct rims range from 7-46 cm; those with beaded rims range from 12 to 32 cm. Some examples of vessels with beaded rims are carinated (Fig. 49*l*).

Hemispherical bowls with beaded rims (Fig. 49*b,d,e*): These vessels are of the same shape as comparable bowls of Khazineh Red and Jaffar Painted and Plain. The bases are apparently concave.

Bases (Fig. 49): With the one exception noted above, all bases are concave. The range of variation is illustrated (Fig. 49*j,k,m*). Diameters of bases range between 8½ and 13½ cm.

TYPE: Susiana Black-on-Buff (Figs. 50-51; Pls. 34-44)

Sample: 370 sherds (plus 97 examples out of context)

Temporal distribution: Choga Mami Transitional through Bayat Phases and later.

Appearance: Identical to Susiana Plain Buff with the addition of designs painted in black on a smoothed but probably not slipped surface.

Paste: Identical to Susiana Plain Buff with a hardness range of 2 to 4 on Moh's scale with most sherds in the 3 to 4 range. The clay is well compacted, showing no laminations or contortions. The pots were fired throughout without gray carbon cores although some color differences over the surface of single pots occurred as a result of differential firing.

Temper: Without exception the early buff wares are sand tempered and almost invariably have a gritty feel. The sand grains seldom exceed .25 mm in diameter.

Color: In most cases surface color is identical to the core color. On the Munsell scale colors range from 10YR 7/3-4 (very pale brown) to 2.5Y 8/1 (white) to 5Y 8/3 (pale yellow). Many sherds appear darker to the eye than indicated in the range given above; this results from heavy applications of paint that make the bodies appear darker than they are.

A group of 22 sherds has a pink core with what appears as a buff slip. According to Matson (1971: 66) sherds that have a white skin on a pink body result from the migration of soluble salts to the surface as the pot is drying. On firing these salts react with iron in the clay leaving a white surface that is often mistaken for slip.

Surface treatment: Surfaces, especially the outside, are smoothed but there is no evidence of slipping, burnishing or polishing. The interiors of some vessels

Table 23

VESSEL FORMS IN SEFID BURNISHED PLAIN AT CHAGHA SEFID
by Stratigraphic Zone

Phase	Zone Area	Zone	Beaded Rims	Direct Rims	Sherds of Spouts	Body Sherds	Total Sherds
Sabz	SD	J					
	SD	I					
Choga Mami Transitional	SD	H					
	SD	G2					
	SD	G1					
Surkh	SD	F					
	SC, SD	E2					
	SC, SD	E1					
	SC	D3					
	SC	D2	3				3
	SC	D1					
	SC	C2					
Sefid	SA	C1	26	37		32	95
	SA	B2	80	148	2	1,660	1,890
	SA	B1		17	1	887	905
	SA	A4				1	1
Mohammad Jaffar	SB	C					
	SB	B					
	SB	A				2	2
Ali Kosh	SA	A3		1			1
	SA	A2					
	SA	A1	3				3
	Totals		112	203	3	2,582	2,900

Table 24

VESSEL FORMS IN SEFID BURNISHED PLAIN AT CHAGHA SEFID
by Cultural Phase

Phase	Beaded Rims	Direct Rims	Sherds of Spouts	Body Sherds	Total Sherds
Sabz					
Choga Mami Transitional					
Surkh	3				3
Sefid	106	202	3	2,580	2,891
Mohammad Jaffar				2	2
Ali Kosh	3	1			4
Totals	112	203	3	2,582	2,900

Fig. 50. Susiana Black-on-Buff. *a,b,* open bowls, variety A; *c,d,* open bowls, variety B; *f,* open bowls, variety C; *g,j,* unique open bowls; *d,e,r,* open bowl interiors; *h,* miscellaneous bowls, variety A; *m,* miscellaneous bowls, variety D; *i,* basin; *k,l,n-r,* pedestals. *h,i,k,p-r,* out of context; *j,m,o,* Sabz; *a-g,l,n,* Choga Mami Transitional.

Fig. 51. Susiana Black-on-Buff, Plain Buff and Miscellaneous. *a*, miscellaneous bowls, variety B; *b,d*, jars; *c,e,f*, open bowls, variety D; *h*, base sherd. Susiana Plain Buff: *i,j*, "Sabz pots"; *k*, basin. Miscellaneous: *l*, Black rim plain ware bowl; *m*, Crude plain ware bowl; *g*, Hassuna incised. *a,c,d,e,f*, out of context; *k*, Sabz; *b,j*, Choga Mami Transitional; *h,i,l,m*, Surkh; *g*, Sefid.

are very roughly finished and retain traces of a scraping tool.

Decoration: Almost exclusively linear designs are present on the pots described in this report. The color varies with the thickness of the paint and the degree of firing. The paint on some vessels is vitrified but this is exceptional. Grayish hues predominate although the color range on the Munsell scale is 2.5YR 9 (black) to 10YR 2/2 (very dark brown) to 10YR 5/2 (grayish brown). It will be obvious in the illustrations that the intensity of the painted lines varies inversely with the grittiness of the surface on which they were painted. Sherds that were better smoothed and well-fired have crisp black lines.

VESSEL FORMS

Open bowls: The most common vessel form among the early Susiana Black-on-Buff pots is the open bowl which has a variety of exterior and interior designs. As a form of vessel it has obvious continuity with our previous types 13, 14 and 15 which are found in the Sabz and later phases (Hole, Flannery and Neely, 1969:144-150, Figs. 54, 56, 57, 59).

Three new varieties found in good archeological context have been identified, and sherds of one other new variety were recovered from a less secure context. It it likely that the latter variety is somewhat later in time than the uppermost levels of our excavation. A fifth variety was previously found in the Sabz Phase. The varieties of open bowls are distinguished by the decorative motif although together they form a homogeneous group that is readily distinguishable from later bowl types. In general, the designs are similar and in some cases identical to designs found on Samarran Transitional sherds at Choga Mami (Oates, 1969:136-138, Pl. 32). These vessels denote the diffusion of a design style as well as of a type of pottery (here the oldest Susiana Black-on-Buff).

Variety A – The chief distinguishing feature is a series of closely set narrow wavy lines on the interior just below the rim. This design motif is regarded as *the* defining characteristic since outside designs vary somewhat. Additionally there is a horizontal black band on top of and usually on either side of the rim (Fig. 50a,b; Pl. 34a,b,d,f) and two or more bands some distance below the rim on the outside (Fig. 50a; Pl. 34a,d,f) or various combinations of diagonal lines or XX's on the exterior (Fig. 50b).

Variety B – Inside the vessel are pendant triangles filled either with simple lines (Fig. 50c; Pl. 35a,d-h) or a combination of lines and dots (Fig. 50d; Pl. 35 b,c). The outsides are characterized by large XX's (Fig. 50c,d; Pl. 35f,g), although some horizontal bands or diagonal lines also appear.

Variety C (Fig. 50f; Pl. 34c,e,g) – The final new variety found in good context has the following characteristics: First, the insides have vertical sets of three or four lines pendant from the rim. In some cases the sets of lines are connected by horizontal lines. Second, the outsides have the same array of XX's or diagonal lines found on other varieties of open bowls.

Variety D (Fig. 51c,e,f) – Four sherds found out of context are included as a distinct variety because of their similarity to sherds found in Samarran contexts elsewhere. They have a series of horizontal zig-zag lines inside the rims. The outsides of the bowls are decorated like the others in this series.

Variety E (Pl. 36c,d,e) – A small group of Sabz-like sherds whose drafted lines on the inside are frequently finer than on the usual early open bowls and which show considerable use of reserve decoration. The outsides are clearly in the Sabz style (Pl. 36a,b) (cf. Hole, Flannery and Neely, 1969: Figs. 49,50).

Unique examples (Fig. 50g,j; Pl. 37a-g,i) – While most of these sherds were not found in good context they have the same paste and design characteristics as other open bowls. It is probable that these relate to slightly later deposits than we excavated in Chagha Sefid but the sherds are included to extend the range of variation of our early bowls; this may prove useful for purposes of comparison.

Open bowl interiors – It is difficult to tell which of the varieties of bowls had decorated bases although one vessel illustrated in Fig. 50d; Pl. 35a (variety B) had the ∫∫∫ design under the pendant triangles. Other base sherds showing this same design are shown on Fig. 50r; Pl. 36f,h,i. These vessels were apparently flat-bottomed.

Other free-standing designs on the bases of bowls include birds (Pl. 36h) and geometric designs (Pl. 36l, m). One sherd (Fig. 50e; Pl. 36o) shows that the geometric design (a stylized "bucrania") is apparently in the center of the base with the bird design arranged symmetrically around it.

A final group of sherds has concentric rings on the interior. These designs are generally the same as on Miscellaneous bowls, variety C, where they were found on the outside. Since these sherds have no designs on the outside it is difficult to tell to which variety of bowls they may pertain. Some sherds are from pedestaled bowls (Pl. 36f,j,k).

The similarity of these designs to sherds illustrated from the Choga Mami Transitional is striking (Oates, 1969:Pl. 32:Nos. 2-4, 6-8).

Miscellaneous open bowl sherds: While these are clearly from open bowls they cannot be assigned to one of the varieties described above. An unusual example is illustrated (Pl. 37j).

Hemispherical bowls (Pl. 38a-l): These vessels most closely resemble "types" 2, 3, 6 in our 1969 report. Reconstructed vessel forms are shown in Fig. 50. Although our sample is not large it will be clear from a comparison of Pl. 38a-l with Hole, Flannery and Neely, 1969:Fig. 52 that we have a quite different set of design elements on pots of basically the same shape. This is not unexpected since we have an older Susiana Black-on-Buff than we found at Tepe Sabz. As compared with Tepe Sabz we most strikingly lack the more open designs with lozenges, diagonals and hatchured diamonds (Hole, Flannery and Neely, 1969:Fig. 52c,f,i). By contrast we have predominantly a horizontal motif of closely spaced black bands with the light background in reserve.

The rim sherds are too small to permit accurate

estimation of the diameters or, in most cases, heights of the vessels; however none of the measurable examples falls outside the range given for the Tepe Sabz sherds: rim diameters 14-18 cm with heights of 4-9 cm.

Painted designs, except for a black line inside the rim on the more open vessels, are confined to the outside. The base and lower part of the bowls are unpainted so that the design appears as a horizontal panel.

Miscellaneous bowls (Pl. 38*m-x*): Intermediate in form between the closed hemispherical bowls and the open bowls is a large series of bowls which have no direct design counterparts in the later phases in Deh Luran, although in form they most closely resemble bowl "type" 1. This group comprises a wide range of forms and sizes, from vessels whose sides are nearly vertical to those that slope outward (the most common form). The somewhat outleaning veseels may also be sway-backed, probably as a result of the pot slumping before it had completely hardened. The entire range of variation in shape and size is shown in Figs. 50-51.

Since there is marked variation in both form and design we have distinguished varieties that constitute relatively consistent groupings.

Variety A — When the rims are present it is evident that the most common motif consists of a ladder-like design running horizontally below the rim (Fig. 50*h*; Pl. 38*n,o,q,s,t-x*; 39*a-h*), while the mid-section of the vessel has closely-spaced wavy lines or bands. The lower panel terminates at or near the basal curvature leaving the lower portion of the bowls unpainted. The more open vessels sometimes have either a series of short pendant lines or loops inside the rim. Sherds of similar vessels that do not have the wavy line motif are shown in Pl. 38*m,p,r*.

These bowls are relatively large; measurable rims range from 20 to 30 cm while the heights are between 6.5 and 9 cm. Thickness at mid-body averages 1 cm.

Variety B — This characteristic set of vessels, many of which are sway-backed in profile with outleaning rims is distinguished by a motif of closely spaced vertical lines running horizontally around the bowl just below the rim (Fig. 51*a*; Pl. 39*i-m,p,q*; 40*a-i*). Inside the rim are wavy lines, tasseled triangles, pendant short lines and one free-standing element (Pl. 39*j*; 40*d,e,i*). The body designs are variable but often consist of ⟨⟨⟨ (Pl. 40*d*) or hatchured diamonds arranged horizontally between bands of black lines (Pl. 39*i-k*). One pot, found out of context, was restorable (Fig. 51*a*).

Based principally on the restorable vessel and on the lack of distinctive base sherds it seems evident that the bases were rounded. The range of variation in rim diameter is 28 to 32 cm while heights range from 8.5 to 9.5 cm.

Variety C — Most of these vessels are slightly sway-backed in shape although there is considerable variation.

All have a series of black lines encircling the neck and body (Pl. 40*j-r*). The lowermost ring marks the junction of the rounded base and the body (Pl. 40*m*). Often there is a slight carination at the base. The rims are all outleaning and, with one exception, have a black line with short, pendant lines on the inside (Fig. 51*a*).

While the pattern of designs on all the vessels is the same, three distinct groups of design elements within the overall pattern can be distinguished.

1. Vessels whose bodies have a band of XXX's framed by the horizontal bands (Pl. 40*m-r*).
2. Vessels whose bodies have a series of vertical lines connecting two or more of the horizontal bands (Pl. 41*a-h*).
3. Vessels whose bodies have a series of ⟨⟨⟨ between horizontal bands (Pl. 41*i-k*). On larger sherds these can be seen to combine with other motifs that make up separate horizontal panels (Pl. 41*i,j*).

Variety D — These are the "Sabz pots" described in Hole, Flannery and Neely, 1969:Fig. 50 which are characteristic of the Sabz Phase. The few sherds of this type that we found are very similar to those from Tepe Sabz. The rim sherds all have the dense cross-hatching commonly found in Tepe Sabz (Hole, Flannery and Neely, 1969:Fig. 50*e*) and the body sherds for the most part also show the use of reserve decoration (Fig. 50*m*; Pl. 42*a-i,k*).

Unique examples of bowls (Pl. 43*a-h*): The remainder of the bowl sherds show unique designs. In shape, size and quality of painting they fit well within the miscellaneous bowl category. Body sherds of other bowls that could not be assigned a particular variety are shown in Pl. 43*i-t*.

Jars: Few jar sherds were found although there are some restorable examples of short, squat jars that give an indication of the range of variation (Fig. 51*b, d*). Rims of similar jars with ladder designs are shown in Pl. 44*a-d*. Also found are high necked jars with rings encircling the neck (Pl. 44*e*), with flaring rims (Pl. 44*f,g*) and with flat horizontal rims (Pl. 44*h,i*).

Basins (Fig. 50*i*; Pl. 42*j*): A few sherds have designs and forms that are similar to the Sabz Phase basins at Tepe Sabz (Hole, Flannery and Neely, 1969:Fig. 49). At Chagha Sefid there were not enough sherds to reconstruct the size of the vessels.

Pedestals: Reconstructed examples (Fig. 50*n-p*) show that the pedestals are same as we found previously at Tepe Sabz in the Sabz Phase (Hole, Flannery and Neely, 1969:Fig. 51*a-f*). Both closed and fenestrated examples are in the Chagha Sefid collection (Pl. 42*l-t*).

Spouts and handles — No reconstructable vessels with spouts or handles were found; however, by analogy with red ware examples, it is likely that some of the hemispherical bowls were equipped with spouts while handles are more likely found on the open bowls. The two spouts are simple troughs; one has evidence of the use of straps (Pl. 44*l-m*). The handles are simple tabs that probably stood vertically on the rims of bowls (Pl. 44*i,k*). Similar examples from Tepe Sabz are illustrated in Hole, Flannery and Neely, 1969:Fig. 53.

TYPE: Susiana Plain Buff (Fig. 51*k,m*)

Sample: 101

Temporal distribution: Late Surkh(?), and Choga Mami Transitional through Bayat phases, and later.

Appearance: In the earlier report (Hole, Flannery and Neely, 1969:124-125) we described the entire range; here we are concerned only with Sabz and Choga Mami Transitional sherds, which differ from the bulk of the later Susiana Plain Buff in having a sandier paste.

Paste: Compact and, in the later phases of our sequence, made up of very well-cleaned clay. It is fired buff throughout, with gray carbon streaks. Hardness on Moh's scale ranges between 2 and 5, with most sherds falling between 2 and 4 (Hole, Flannery and Neely, 1969:124).

Temper: Changes through time can be detected. During the Sabz Phase, nearly all sherds have a sandy texture caused by the inclusion of coarse grit or sand. Eroded sherds of this phase have surfaces liberally dotted with sand grains averaging 0.5 mm in diameter. Through time, fine grit gradually replaces coarse grit, and during the Mehmeh and Bayat phases sandy-textured sherds are largely confined to large basins and deep bowls. In all sand-tempered sherds, the temper is well distributed throughout the paste (Hole, Flannery and Neely, 1969:124).

Color: The surface color ranges from pale greenish-buff (the majority) to a pale green, pale yellow, and pale orange. The green, yellow, and orange sherds are confined to the well-fired, very finely-made bell shaped bowls. On the Munsell scale, the range is from 2.5Y 4/2 to 10YR 8/6. All of the vessels are thoroughly fired, and the cores are essentially the same color as the exterior (Hole, Flannery and Neely, 1969:126).

Surface treatment: The exterior surfaces are smooth although the pottery has a sandy feel. Interiors are sometimes rougher and have linear scratches from the scraping done during the shaping of the vessel.

Decoration: None.

VESSEL FORMS

Open bowls: Sixteen base sherds and no rims, suggesting that for the most part these belong to Susiana Black-on-Buff vessels. This suggestion is supported by the fact that open bowls do not occur in Plain Buff at Tepe Sabz until the Khazineh Phase.

"Sabz pots" (Fig. 51*i,j*): Two sherds of an unpainted version of the Black-on-Buff Sabz pot which is found in the Sabz Phase. The one sherd found in Zone F was doubtless out of context.

Large basins (Fig. 51*k*): Two rims and 6 body/base sherds of basins were found in Choga Mami Transitional strata. The basins closely resemble those found at Tepe Sabz (Hole, Flannery and Neely, 1969:127-128:Fig. 47:*b,c,d*). One restorable rim to base sherd is about 14 cm high and has a diameter of about 48 cm.

TYPE: Sialk Black-on-Red (Figs. 52-53)

Comment: The name reflects the fact that these rare wares resemble a series of pottery found in Sialk I_2 along with a series of black-on-buff wares that

Table 25
VESSEL FORMS IN SUSIANA BLACK-ON-BUFF AT CHAGHA SEFID
by Stratigraphic Zone

Phase	Zone Area	Zone	Rims and Bodies of Open Bowls	Rims and Bodies of Hemispherical Bowls	Rims and Bodies of Miscellaneous Bowls	Sherds of Jars	Rims of Basins	Sherds of Pedestal Bases	Sherds of Spouts	Sherds of Handles	Body Sherds Not Classified by Form	Total Sherds
Sabz	SD	J	17	5	36	3	1	3			11	76
	SD	I	2	2	12	1			1			18
Choga Mami Transitional	SD	H	41	2	43	1	1	2	1	2	31	124
	SD	G2	38	1	23	4			1		20	87
	SD	G1	16		14	3		2			17	52
Surkh	SD	F			5	1			1		5	12
	SC, SD	E2										
	SC, SD	E1			1							1
	SC	D3										
	SC	D2										
	SC	D1										
	SC	C2										
Sefid	SA	C1										
	SA	B2										
	SA	B1										
	SA	A4										
Mohammad Jaffar	SB	C										
	SB	B										
	SB	A										
Ali Kosh	SA	A3										
	SA	A2										
	SA	A1										
		Totals	114	10	134	13	2	7	4	2	84	370

resembles the varieties found in the Choga Mami Transitional at Chagha Sefid (Ghirshman, 1938:15-16). Although the illustrations in the Sialk report are somewhat ambiguous as to type, we collected a series of sherds from the North Mound at Sialk in 1969; it is on the basis of this comparison that we have named our wares after Sialk, the first site at which they were reported and, until our work at Chagha Sefid, the only site where they were reported excavated. It seems significant that the black-on-red pottery occurs contemporaneously with the black-on-buff wares of Samarran derivation at both sites. It is likewise significant that no sites intervening between Deh Luran, at the base of the Zagros, and Sialk, at the edge of the plateau, seem to have these wares.

Table 26

VESSEL FORMS IN SUSIANA BLACK-ON-BUFF AT CHAGHA SEFID
by Cultural Phase

Phase	Rims and Bodies of Open Bowls	Rims and Bodies of Hemispherical Bowls	Rims and Bodies of Miscellaneous Bowls	Sherds of Jars	Rims of Basins	Sherds of Pedestal Bases	Sherds of Spouts	Sherds of Handles	Body Sherds Not Classified by Form	Total Sherds
Sabz	19	7	48	4	1	3	1		11	94
Choga Mami Transitional	95	3	80	8	1	4	2	2	68	263
Surkh			6	1			1		5	13
Sefid										
Mohammad Jaffar										
Ali Kosh										
Totals	114	10	134	13	2	7	4	2	84	370

Sample: 66 (plus 13 examples out of context)

Temporal distribution: Late Surkh through early Sabz phases.

Appearance: a hand-made, low-fired, friable ware of poorly cleaned, chaff tempered clay. The core is sometimes unoxydized.

Paste: Compact but pitted from the burning out of chaff fibers.

Temper: Predominantly chaff with some small grit inclusions. The clay has very fine grains of sand that give the surface a slightly gritty feel.

Color: A wide range of color, partly resulting from firing problems. One sherd may exhibit the entire range of color variation. The darker reds are 10R 4/6, while the lightest surfaces are 10YR 7/2 or about the same as the Susiana Buff. Exteriors and interiors of the same sherd sometimes show both extremes, possibly in some cases as a result of one surface being slipped.

Surface treatment: The exteriors of all vessels are smooth and many have a thick red slip.

Decoration: All vessels have designs painted in black and a few have white paint as well. Most of the designs are laddered lines or densely cross-hatched areas which give the effect of reserve decoration.

VESSEL FORMS

Although the sample is small there are enough examples to indicate a number of vessel forms. There is no reason to believe, however, that we have found anything approaching the range of variation of this type.

Open bowls (Fig. 52a-c,e): These are like the Susiana Black-on-Buff bowls in form. Examples are restricted to the late Surkh and Choga Mami Transitional phases. The 3 measurable rims are 18, 22 and 30 cm in diameter. Some of the vessels appear to be very shallow open bowls. The designs are similar to those found on Susiana Black-on-Buff open bowls, variety B, which are contemporary (cf. Fig. 50).

The exteriors seem to be decorated with no more than a black line at the rim while all the insides feature pendant triangles filled with laddered lines (Fig. 52a). Some body sherds suggest that the interiors of the bases may also have had linear decoration (Fig. 53d). None of these sherds was large enough to reconstruct.

Carinated bowls (Fig. 52k): The carinated bowl is in the form that goes back to Mohammad Jaffar times. The rim is slightly everted, a sharp carination occurs

Table 27
DESIGN STYLES ON SUSIANA BLACK-ON-BUFF OPEN BOWLS AT CHAGHA SEFID
by Stratigraphic Zone

Phase	Zone Area	Zone	Style A	Style B	Style C	Style D	Style E	Unique Rims	Bases	Bases	Interior Rings	Miscellaneous	Total Open Bowl Sherds
Sabz	SD	J	2	7			2				2	4	17
	SD	I		2									2
Choga Mami Transitional	SD	H	2	20	4		1	1		1	9	4	42
	SD	G2	3	14	1		1		7	3	5	14	48
	SD	G1	11	1				1	1	2	1	2	19
Surkh	SD	F											
	SC, SD	E2											
	SC, SD	E1				Occurs out of stratigraphic context							
	SC	D3											
	SC	D2											
	SC	D1											
	SC	C2											
Sefid	SA	C1											
	SA	B2											
	SA	B1											
	SA	A4											
Mohammad Jaffar	SB	C											
	SB	B											
	SB	A											
Ali Kosh	SA	A3											
	SA	A2											
	SA	A1											
		Totals	18	44	5		4	2	8	6	17	24	128

about midway on the body and the base is probably rounded. Base sherds of this type would be plain red and consequently recorded simply as Khazineh Red.

The carination is marked by a black line above which are panels of decoration with laddered lines, rings of bands and a 3-pronged design element arranged in paired rows between the bands. The rims have groups of 3 to 4 pendant lines inside and out.

One vessel has a rim diameter of about 18 cm; the restoration is based on isolated rim sherds and on a

Table 28

DESIGN STYLES ON SUSIANA BLACK-ON-BUFF
OPEN BOWLS AT CHAGHA SEFID
by Cultural Phase

Phase	Style A	Style B	Style C	Style D	Style E	Unique Rims	Bases	Bases	Interior Rings	Miscellaneous	Total Open Bowl Sherds
Sabz	2	9				2			2	4	19
Choga Mami Transitional	16	35	5	Out of context only		2	2	8	6	15	20	109
Surkh											
Sefid											
Mohammad Jaffar											
Ali Kosh											
Totals	18	44	5			4	2	8	6	17	24	128

large body sherd which is broken just below the rim.
Straight sided bowls: Thirteen sherds of bowls with simple direct rims (Fig. 52*f,j,l*), sometimes slightly outflaring (Fig. 52*d,g,h,i*), had densely drafted designs on the exterior and simple bands or loops on the inside of the rim. The exterior designs consist of a panel delimited by heavy black lines containing a pattern based on cross-hatching (Fig. 52*f,j,l*). One example from a mixed context also has a white line. No examples were large enough to permit reconstruction.
Hole-mouth bowls: Three sherds of hole-mouth bowls constitute the sample of this vessel form. The diameters of the larger sherds suggest bowls of 16 cm to about 27 cm diameter. Two designs are panels of cross-hatching and one has heavy chains of diamonds arranged horizontally (Fig. 53*i,j,k*).
Hemispherical bowls (Fig. 53*a-c,f*): Two sherds plus 2 out of context have slightly incurving simple direct rims. Three measurable examples have diameters of 15 and 18 cm. The exterior designs consist of chains of diamonds arranged horizontally and of cross-hatching and laddered lines.

Miscellaneous Sherds

Hassuna incised (Fig. 51*g*): One sherd of a globular jar made of sandy paste buff ware, with a horizontally arranged linear design, has a panel of fingernail incisions at the junction of the body and neck. The diameter of the neck is approximately 16 cm. This sherd appears to be Hassuna incised, a ware that is contemporary with the Sefid Phase deposit in which this sherd was found. This is the only example of the ware at Chagha Sefid. Hassuna incised pottery is commonly found in northeast Iraq and doubtless was imported from that area.

Black Rim Plain Bowl (Fig. 51*l*): Made of a paste similar to Khazineh Red, this vessel is probably simply a Surkh Black Painted Red that did not receive the usual red slip. The shape, size and painting are identical to the usual bowls of this ware in the Surkh Phase.

Crude Plain Bowl (Fig. 51*m*): An unusual vessel that may not be contemporary with the deposits in which it was found is a coarse, chaff tempered plain ware with a flattened rim and apparently a flat base. No other sherds in the excavation match this example, which is from Zone F, Late Surkh Phase.

White-on-Red Sherds (Fig. 54)

Sample: 29

Temporal distribution: Chiefly Surkh and Choga Mami Transitional phases.

Appearance: White paint was used on red ware vessels of several types: Sefid Red-on-Cream, Khazineh Red, Surkh Black Painted Red Ware, and Sialk Black-on-Red. There are so few of these sherds that they are illustrated together to show the range of variation. These are not considered a separate type.

Decoration: White paint was applied in linear designs, often geometric, on the red slipped surface of vessels. Often the white paint was used in combination with black.

VESSEL FORMS

Jars are the most common vessels on which white paint occurs. Six examples of such vessels with white lines on the inside of the neck are illustrated (Fig. 54*b,d,g,p,u,y*). Four of these jars are Surkh Black

Painted Red wares (Fig. 54b,p,u,y); the others are Khazineh Red.

Open or straight sided bowls account for three rims; on two of these white paint occurs only on the outside (Fig. 54h,i,r,s). Three carinated vessels all have white designs on the insides and no designs at all on the outside (Fig. 54m). Hole-mouth or hemispherical bowls are represented by four rims (Fig. 54 a,e,f,n). The white paint consists of a simple line around the band on two of these (Fig. 54e,n), an inverted V on one (Fig. 54f) and a similar zigzag design on the outside with pendant lines on the inside of the fourth example (Fig. 54a). The remainder are body sherds of bowls and jars.

STONE, PLASTER AND ASPHALT VESSELS

Stone Bowls

Sample: 30 sherds in context and 9 other examples
Temporal distribution: Throughout the sequence.

Sherds of stone bowls are rare at Chagha Sefid and although most are too fragmentary for accurate reconstruction, some indication of rim and base form can be obtained. Sixteen sherds are of gypsum while the remainder are of limestone, marble and sandstone. A

Table 29

VESSEL FORMS IN SUSIANA PLAIN BUFF
AT CHAGHA SEFID
by Stratigraphic Zone

Phase	Zone Area	Zone	Rims of Basins	Bodies and Bases of Basins	Rims of Sabz Pots	Bases of Open Bowls	Body Sherds	Total Sherds
Sabz	SD	J						
	SD	I				1	1	2
Choga Mami Transitional	SD	H	1	3				4
	SD	G2	1	1		13	42	57
	SD	G1		1		1	26	28
Surkh	SD	F	1	1	1		5	8
	SC, SD	E2					1	1
	SC, SD	E1					1	1
	SC	D3						
	SC	D2						
	SC	D1						
	SC	C2						
Sefid	SA	C1						
	SA	B2						
	SA	B1						
	SA	A4						
Mohammad Jaffar	SB	C						
	SB	B						
	SB	A						
Ali Kosh	SA	A3						
	SA	A2						
	SA	A1						
	Totals		2	6	2	16	75	101

Table 30

VESSEL FORMS IN SUSIANA PLAIN BUFF
AT CHAGHA SEFID
by Cultural Phase

Phase	Rims of Basins	Bodies and Bases of Basins	Rims of Sabz Pots	Bases of Open Bowls	Body Sherds	Total Sherds
Sabz				1	1	2
Choga Mami Transitional	2	5		14	68	89
Surkh		1	1	1	7	10
Sefid						
Mohammad Jaffar						
Ali Kosh						
Totals	2	6	2	16	75	101

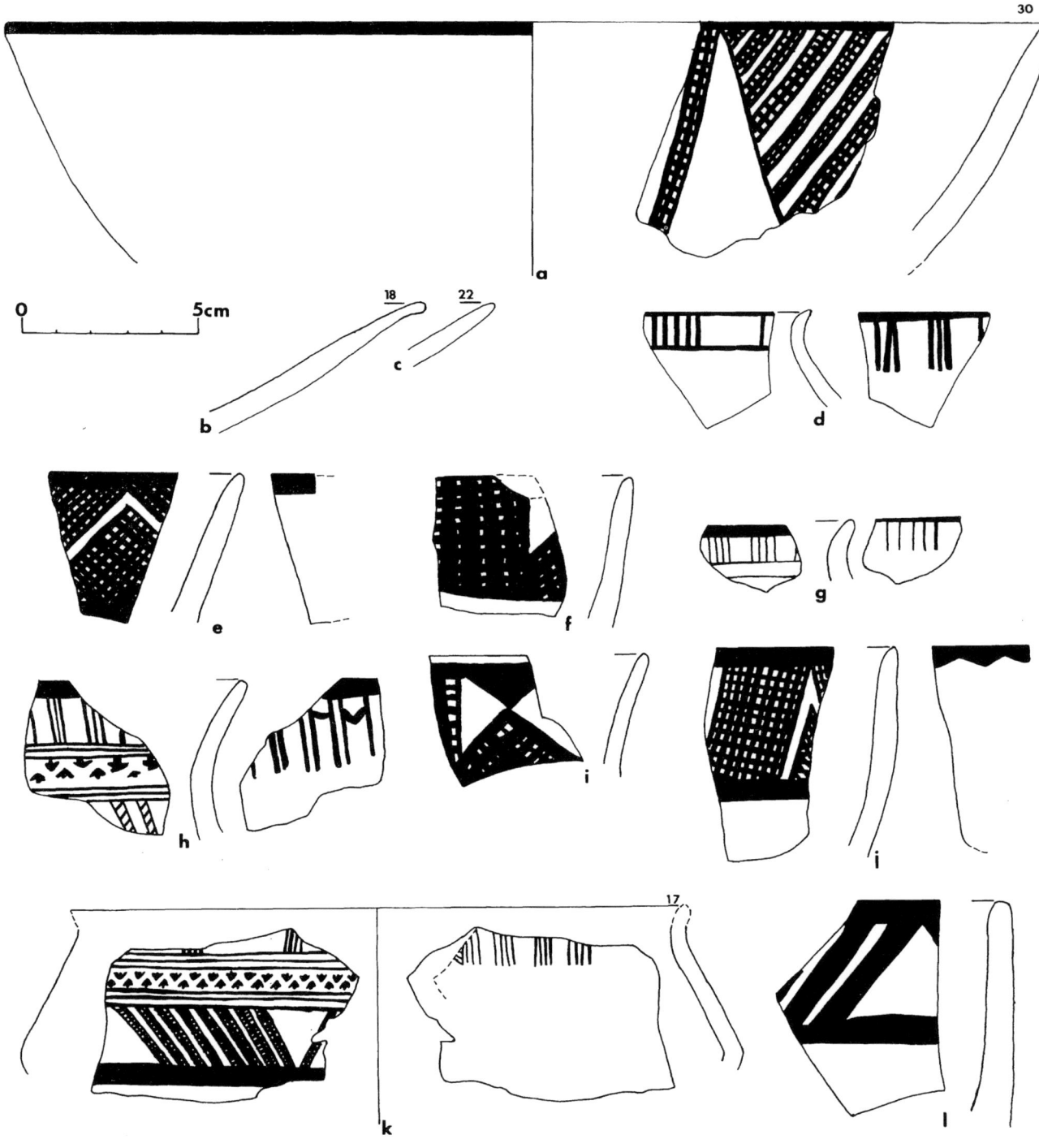

Fig. 52. Sialk Black-on-Red. *a-c,e,* open bowls; *f,j,l,* straight-sided bowls; *d,g,h,i,* flaring rim bowls; *k,* carinated bowl. *b,c,f,* out of context; *a,d,e,k,* Choga Mami Transitional; *i,j,l,* Surkh.

POTTERY

Fig. 53. Sialk Black-on-Red. *a-c,f,* hemispherical bowls: *i-k,* hole-mouth bowls; *d,* interior design; *e,g,h,* miscellaneous body sherds. *b,c,j,l,* out of context; *a,d,e,g,k,* Choga Mami Transitional; *f,h,i,* Surkh.

Table 31

VESSEL FORMS IN SIALK BLACK-ON-RED AT CHAGHA SEFID
by Stratigraphic Zone

Phase	Zone Area	Zone	Rims of Open Bowls	Sherds of Open Bowls	Rims of Carinated Bowls	Sherds of Carinated Bowls	Rims of Straight Sided Bowls	Rims of Other Bowls	Rims of Hole-Mouth Bowls	Rims of Hemispherical Bowls	Miscellaneous Body Sherds	Total Sherds
Sabz	SD	J					1				2	3
	SD	I										
Choga Mami Transitional	SD	H	2	1		7	4				1	15
	SD	G2	2		1		1			1	5	10
	SD	G1	1	4	2		5	1	1	1	12	27
Surkh	SD	F		3		1	1	1	2		3	11
	SC, SD	E2										
	SC, SD	E1										
	SC	D3										
	SC	D2										
	SC	D1										
	SC	C2										
Sefid	SA	C1										
	SA	B2										
	SA	B1										
	SA	A4										
Mohammad Jaffar	SB	C										
	SB	B										
	SB	A										
Ali Kosh	SA	A3										
	SA	A2										
	SA	A1										
	Totals		5	8	3	8	12	2	3	2	23	66

variety not present at Ali Kosh or Tepe Sabz has an incised rim. One example is from the mixed Sabz Phase deposit at Chagha Sefid and others were found in mixed deposits that contained Uruk sherds; they are probably contemporary with the Uruk sherds. All other examples fit in with our previous findings.

STONE VESSEL FORMS

Bowls with simple, direct rim (Fig. 55*q-r*): The 4 pieces are too fragmentary to determine sizes and overall shapes; however it seems probable that they had flat bottoms. The examples at Chagha Sefid ap-

Table 32
VESSEL FORMS IN SIALK BLACK-ON-RED AT CHAGHA SEFID
by Cultural Phase

Phase	Rims of Open Bowls	Sherds of Open Bowls	Rims of Carinated Bowls	Sherds of Carinated Bowls	Rims of Straight-sided Bowls	Rims of Other Bowls	Rims of Hole-mouth Bowls	Rims of Hemispherical Bowls	Miscellaneous Body Sherds	Total Sherds
Sabz					1				2	3
Choga Mami Transitional	5	5	3	7	10	1	1	2	18	52
Surkh		3		1	1	1	2		3	11
Sefid										
Mohammad Jaffar										
Ali Kosh										
Totals	5	8	3	8	12	2	3	2	23	66

pear to be identical to those from Ali Kosh (Hole, Flannery and Neely, 1969:107). Three examples are Surkh Phase, Zones D2 and E1, and one is Zone B2, Sefid Phase.

Bowls with out-turned or "beaded" rim (Fig. 55s-u): Four small rim sherds are from vessels like the ones at Ali Kosh (Hole, Flannery and Neely, 1969: 107). Previously we found these restricted to the pre-Sabz Phases; the examples from Chagha Sefid are all Sefid Phase, Zones B1, B2 and C1.

Bowls with incised rims (Fig. 55e): One example of Zone J, Sabz Phase has a horizontal groove cut just below the rim on the outside. The vessel, which stands 4 cm high has a flat base. Its diameter was approximately 8 cm.

Trays or shallow bowls (Fig. 55h,i): Two sherds are from relatively small shallow vessels. Both are of Zone B, Sefid Phase.

Ribbed bowl (Fig. 55g): One example, Zone B2, Sefid Phase, is flat-bottomed and has a horizontal rib midway between the base and rim. The overall height is 2.4 cm.

Deep bowl (Fig. 55b): A roughly finished gypsum bowl has a diameter of 20 cm and a height of 9 cm. It has a simple, direct rim and a flat base. The example is from Zone H, Choga Mami Transitional Phase.

Miniature bowl (Fig. 55f): There is one example (Zone B2, Sefid Phase), of a shallow bowl with a flattened rim. The vessel measures about 5.3 cm maximum outside diameters and stands about 1.5 cm high.

Oval bowl (Fig. 55d): A piece of a limestone vessel, Zone E, Surkh Phase, appears to be oval-shaped with a relatively flat bottom. From its present dimensions the vessel was 9 cm wide and perhaps 14 cm long and 4.5 cm high. The surface remains rough with scratches from the shaping. The inside base is also scratched but worn smooth from use.

BASES

Flat bases (Fig. 55n,o): Two sherds, both Sefid Phase, are of vessels whose flat bases join sharply with the sides in the manner of contemporary ceramic bowls.

Rounded bases (Fig. 55l): One example, Zone D2, Surkh Phase, shows a curved junction between vessel wall and base.

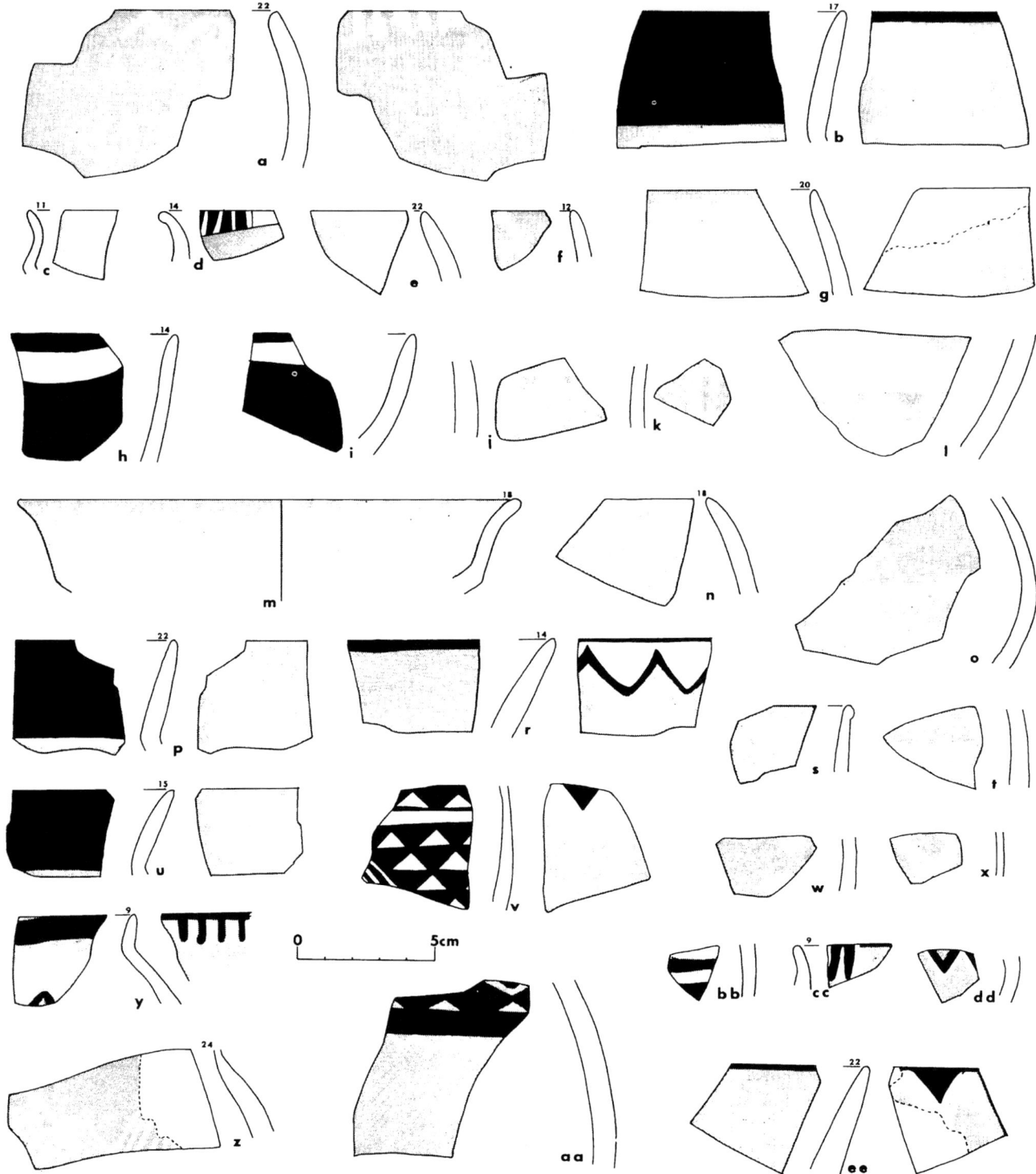

Fig. 54. Sherds With White Paint. *b,d,g,p,u,y,z*, jars; *h,i,r,s*, open or straight-sided bowls; *a,e,f,n*, hole-mouth or hemispherical bowls. All Surkh Phase except *a,c,k*, Choga Mami Transitional; *v,w,ee*, Sefid.

Carinated base (Fig. 55*m*): One example, Zone D2, Surkh Phase.

Out of context examples (Fig. 55*a,c*): Some good examples of stone bowls were found near the surface in disturbed contexts. For purposes of illustrating how the vessels, which are presented by only small fragments in our excavation sample, may have looked, two examples are shown. One has a beaded rim and flat base, the other an incised rim and rounded base.

Plaster Bowls

Sample: 2
Temporal Distribution: Ali Kosh Phase.

Like stone bowls, these vessels typically occur in sites before the introduction of pottery. Although such vessels have not been reported from Khuzistan before, they occur at a number of sites in the Levant (Ras Shamra VB and Ramad) as well as at Bouqras on the Euphrates. In the literature they are referred to as "vaiselle blanche" (Contenson, 1971:282-283).

Examples: One is a body sherd of a bowl wall or base that has the impression of an over-one, under-one basket on the outside (Fig. 55*j*). It may be in this instance that the vessel was molded inside a basket. The interior surface follows the curve of the outside, showing that the fragment does not just represent a hardened lump of plaster that had been mixed in a basket.

The second example is a portion of the wall and base of a large bowl or basin (Fig. 55*k*), of roughly

Table 33
MISCELLANEOUS SHERDS AT CHAGHA SEFID
by Stratigraphic Zone

Phase	Area	Zone	White-on-Red	Hassuna Incised	Black Rim Plain Bowl	Crude Plain Bowl
Sabz	SD	J				
	SD	I				
Choga Mami Transitional	SD	H	1			
	SD	G2	1			
	SD	G1	4			
Surkh	SD	F	1			1
	SC, SD	E2			1	
	SC, SD	E1	4			
	SC	D3				
	SC	D2	4			
	SC	D1	3			
	SC	C2	8			
Sefid	SA	C1	2	1		
	SA	B2	1			
	SA	B1				
	SA	A4				
Mohammad Jaffar	SB	C				
	SB	B				
	SB	A				
Ali Kosh	SA	A3				
	SA	A2				
	SA	A1				
	Totals		29	1	1	1

Table 34
MISCELLANEOUS SHERDS AT CHAGHA SEFID
by Cultural Phase

Phase	White-on-Red	Hassuna Incised	Black Rim Plain Bowl	Crude Plain Bowl
Sabz				
Choga Mami Transitional	6			
Surkh	20		1	1
Sefid	3	1		
Mohammad Jaffar				
Ali Kosh				
Totals	29	1	1	1

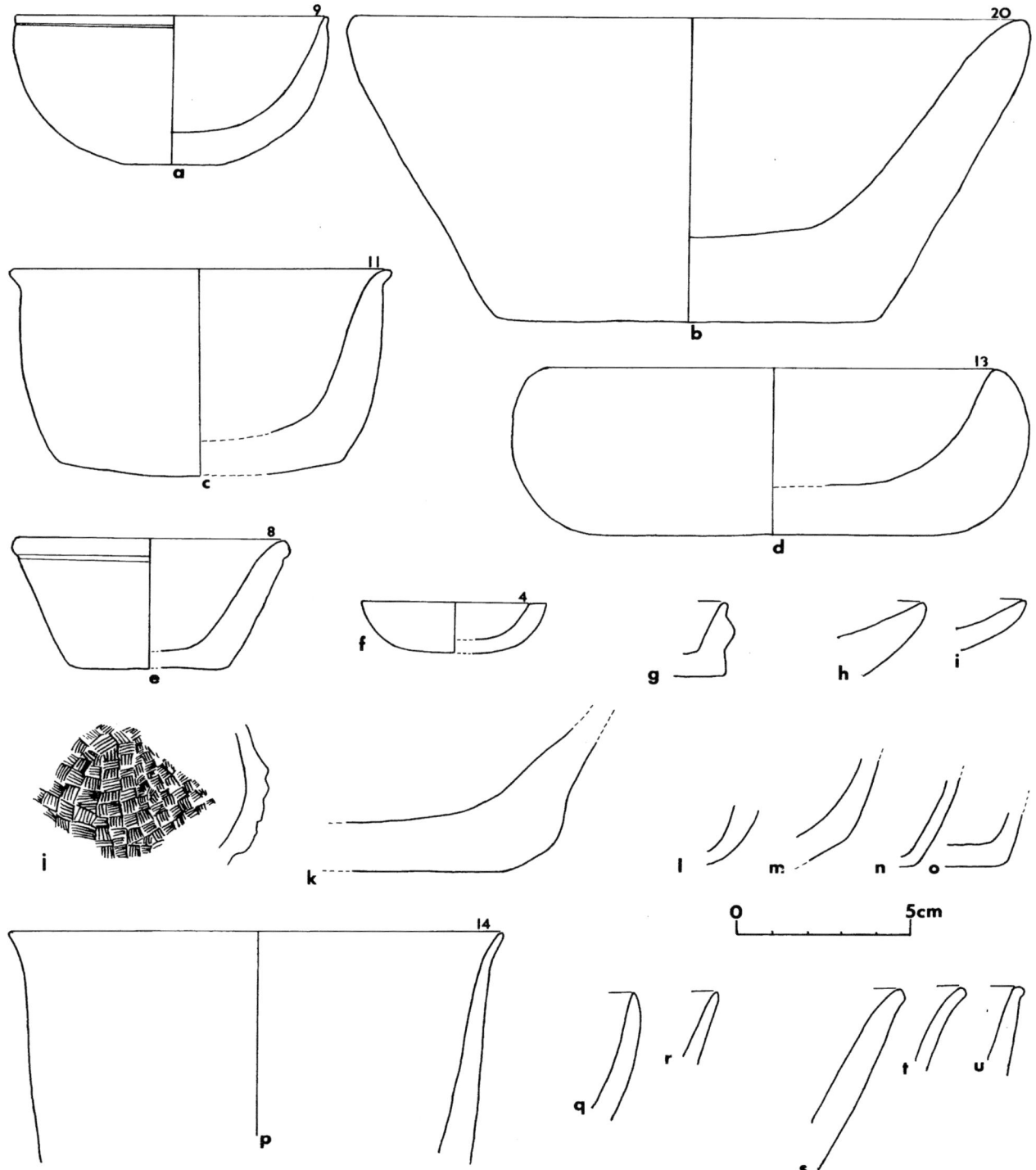

Fig. 55. Stone, Plaster and Asphalt Bowls. Stone Bowls: *a,e,l*, out of context examples; *b*, deep bowl; *e*, incised rim; *f*, miniature bowl; *g*, ribbed bowl: *h,i*, trays or shallow bowls; *l-o*, bases; *q-r*, simple, direct rims: *s-u*, out-turned or beaded rims. Plaster Bowls: *j*, sherd with basket impression; *k*, bowl. Asphalt bowls, *p,a,c,l*, out of context; *b,e*, Choga Mami Transitional; *d,m,p*, Surkh; *f-k, n,o*, Sefid.

the same shape as Jaffar Plain ceramic bowls of the succeeding phase.

Asphalt Bowls

Sample: 2

Temporal distribution: Late Sefid and Surkh phases.

Asphalt vessels have not been reported previously although we found a number of objects made of asphalt in Ali Kosh. Traces of the substance are common in all the sites and they frequently preserve impressions of matting or basketry. In view of the widespread use of asphalt for adhesives and for waterproofing containers it is surprising that it was not used more often for vessels and other containers.

Examples: The most complete example is a crudely molded rectangular shallow box or dish which lay alongside a stone wall foundation in Zone C1, late Sefid Phase. This object was apparently manufactured out of a solid block of asphalt. There are no signs that the sides were built up separately from the base. The dimensions are: 17 cm long, 11.5 cm wide and 6 cm high. The sides are 2-2.5 cm thick and the flat-bottomed interior is about 3 cm deep.

The second example is a sherd of a deep bowl with slightly convex walls and outleaning rim, a form common in contemporary pottery (Fig. 55*p*). The sherd is from Zone E2, Surkh Phase.

Table 35

SHERDS OF STONE, PLASTER & ASPHALT AT CHAGHA SEFID
by Stratigraphic Zone

Phase	Area	Zone	Sherds of Stone Bowls	Sherds of Plaster Bowls	Sherds of Asphalt Bowls	Total
Sabz	SD	J	1			1
	SD	I				
Choga Mami Transitional	SD	H	1			1
	SD	G2	1			1
	SD	G1	1			1
Surkh	SD	F				
	SC, SD	E2	1			1
	SC, SD	E1	4		1	5
	SC	D3				
	SC	D2	3			3
	SC	D1				
	SC	C2				
Sefid	SA	C1	5		1	6
	SA	B2	9			9
	SA	B1	3			3
	SA	A4				
Mohammad Jaffar	SB	C				
	SB	B				
	SB	A				
Ali Kosh	SA	A3	1	2		3
	SA	A2				
	SA	A1				
		Totals	30	2	2	34

Table 36

SHERDS OF STONE, PLASTER & ASPHALT AT CHAGHA SEFID
by Cultural Phase

Phase	Sherds of Stone Bowls	Sherds of Plaster Bowls	Sherds of Asphalt Bowls	Total
Sabz	1			1
Choga Mami Transitional	3			3
Surkh	8		1	9
Sefid	17		1	18
Mohammad Jaffar				
Ali Kosh	1	2		3
Totals	30	2	2	34

VII

CHIPPED STONE ARTIFACTS

INTRODUCTION

At Chagha Sefid, as at Ali Kosh and Tepe Sabz, pieces of chipped stone were the most common artifacts. Some 40,000 tools and pieces of chipping debris, mostly flint, were recovered from the stratified deposits throughout the phases. Since the chipped stone of Chagha Sefid shows few differences from that of Ali Kosh, we can simply repeat most of the type descriptions from our earlier report.

The most important finding is the continuity between the Mohammad Jaffar and Sabz phases as seen in the new phases at Chagha Sefid. When we completed the previous report we were not sure whether we would find a gradual transition between the phases or a rather abrupt change. What is clear now is that the trends we saw beginning in the phases at Ali Kosh continue through the phases at Chagha Sefid and merge with those of Tepe Sabz in an unbroken continuity (Table 37). These trends are discussed more fully with the descriptions of the various groups of tools.

A second finding of importance is that there is little difference between contemporary sites in Deh Luran. While we had postulated that this would be true, it was then an untested assumption. One might have postulated that specialized activities would characterize different sites or strata within sites and that in consequence their contents would not be very comparable. We did not find this to be true. Certain minor differences do exist, chiefly in the very high proportions of plain blades in the Ali Kosh and Mohammad Jaffar phases at Ali Kosh, but these differences in no way contradict our arguments of general trends through time.

Finally, the essential differences between the types of tools present in the Sabz and later phases (as seen at Tepe Sabz) and the earlier phases (as seen at Ali Kosh and Chagha Sefid) are substantiated by our work at Chagha Sefid. It is clear that an early tradition of chipped stone technology and use has run its course by the Sabz Phase. Rather than viewing this as an abrupt change we can now see it as the culmination of trends that are evident as early as the Bus Mordeh and Ali Kosh phases at Ali Kosh.

The reasons for the trends are not immediately apparent. As we had surmised in our earlier report there is evidence of influences from outside Deh Luran. These appear in the Choga Mami Transitional Phase and are marked by the appearance of new ceramics. Their origin unquestionably lies outside Deh Luran, probably in sites in nearby eastern Iraq. Also, by the time of the Sabz Phase we know that agricultural technology had undergone basic changes toward the use of hybrid races of grains and of irrigation, both of which certainly resulted in higher and more dependable yields. With an increase in dependence on cereal agriculture one might expect that the number of tools used for hunting and butchering would decline. Whether the trends we see are related to this factor remains to be tested.

Obsidian

A full discussion of obsidian is in Appendix II where Colin Renfrew considers the sources and quantities of the material in the sites of Deh Luran. He finds that although the proportion of obsidian to flint is low at all the sites (Table 38), there are changes in proportion through time and there are differences between contemporaneous deposits in Ali Kosh and Chagha Sefid. Renfrew relates the small quantities of obsidian to the long distances from the sources (Renfrew, 1969) and the differences between sites to differential access to the limited supply. This

CHIPPED STONE ARTIFACTS 149

Table 37
PERCENTAGES OF CHIPPED STONE TOOL TYPES AT ALI KOSH, CHAGHA SEFID AND TEPE SABZ
by Cultural Phase. Total of tools does not include plain blades.

Site	Phase	Geometric and Other Microliths					Piercing-Reaming Tools					Sickles		Scrapers			Cutting-Scraping Tools								Misc. Tools					Total Tools (Less Plain Blades)
		Trapezes and Triangles	Crescents	Diagonal-ended	Diagonal-ended and Backed	Backed Bladelets	Nibbled Bladelets	Drills	Reamers	End Reduced on Bulbar Side	Pointed Pieces	Frags. of Drills and Reamers	Plain Sickles	Truncated Sickles	Blade, Round-end Scrapers	Flake, Round-end Scrapers	Blade, Misc. End Scrapers	Flakes with Bulbar End Retouch	Plain Blades	Backed Blades	Truncated Blades	Retouched or Used Blades	Notched Blades	Retouched or Used Flakes	Notched Flakes	Denticulated Flake Scraper	Burins	Micro-burins	Scaled Pieces	Blades with Ground Edges	Bifacially Chipped Flakes	Bifacial Picks	
TS	Bayat							5					40	3			1		174	1	4	26	3	7	5								205
TS	Mehmeh							14					26	1					146	1	7	29	1	20	7						3		69
TS	Khazineh							2					21	16					88	2	2	14	4	21	17						2		57
TS	Sabz		2					2					6	17			1	1	70	4	8	10	1	18	29		1				1		104
CS	Sabz	2					2	8	3			9	6	2	2				104		2	23	3	24	2	11	3						66
CS	Choga Mami Transitional	1	1			1	1	4	1			1	5	1	3		4		109	1	1	24	11	25	5	13	1					1		195
CS	Surkh	1						5	1			2	14	1	3	1	3		123	1		33	11	12	2	6	1						961
CS	Sefid	1						7	2		1	2	16		3	1	1	1	214			31	14	15		2	1		1					2,242
CS	Mohammad Jaffar	1		1	3	5	3	3	1	1		1	7		4				314			38	19	6	2	2								232
AK	Mohammad Jaffar				1	1	11	5	2	1			8		2	1	1		668			38	29	1										1,575
CS	Ali Kosh				1	1		4	1		1	2	9		14	1	1		234	1	1	21	31	9										1,045
AK	Ali Kosh					1	7	4	1				5		4	1	2		473			40	33	1										2,071
AK	Bus Mordeh				1	5	6	9	2		1		3		9		2		1,240			35	26											1,216

Table 38

NUMBER AND PERCENTAGE OF CHIPPED STONE RAW MATERIALS TO TOTAL CHIPPED STONE
AT ALI KOSH, CHAGHA SEFID AND TEPE SABZ
by Cultural Phase

Site	Phase	Flint		Obsidian		Crystal		Total
		No.	%	No.	%	No.	%	
TS	Bayat	1,261	99.5	6	0.5			1,267
TS	Mehmeh	710	99.6	3	0.4			713
TS	Khazineh	820	100.0					820
TS	Sabz	1,873	100.0					1,873
CS	Sabz	745	99.7	2	0.3			747
CS	Choga Mami Transitional	2,011	99.0	11	1.0			2,022
CS	Surkh	5,527	98.0	79	1.0	35	1	5,641
CS	Sefid	21,648	95.0	1,041	5.0	40		22,729
CS	Mohammad Jaffar	1,841	92.0	156	8.0	2		1,999
AK	Mohammad Jaffar	23,517	98.2	417	1.7			23,934
CS	Ali Kosh	7,240	99.0	109	1.0			7,349
AK	Ali Kosh	22,757	98.0	474	2.0			23,231
AK	Bus Mordeh	39,767	99.1	347	0.9			40,114

and the fact that different proportions come from different sources suggest changing patterns of exchange, especially as these were mediated by sites along the supply route.

Crystal

Seventy-seven pieces of clear obsidian, or crystal, were chipped into tools and waste flakes, mainly during the Sefid and Surkh phases. The source of this material is not known but it is interesting to note the occurrence of bullet cores and other chipping debris of crystal, suggesting that the material was chipped locally. Crystal was not found at either Ali Kosh or at Tepe Sabz (Table 38) and its distribution at other sites is not known.

Terms Used in Analysis

GENERAL

Flint: As used here, the term refers to a related series of crypto-crystalline quartz rocks for which flint, chert and chalcedony are common names.

Obsidian: A natural glass of volcanic origin, which can be chipped to make sharp but brittle edges.

Core: A prepared piece of flint or obsidian from which flakes were struck.

Blade: A flake which is parallel-sided, and at least twice as long as wide. Blades are relatively thin and have one or more ridges (scars from previously detached blades) running the length of the piece. (Note that this definition is quite at variance with the way American archeologists use the term "blade.")

Bladelet: An unusually small blade. Here, the term is used only if the piece has secondary chipping and falls into one of the geometric or microlith types.

Microlith: Here, the term "microlith" or "microlithic" is used to suggest small tools, but not with the object of distinguishing a type of tool. Microliths can be considered the lower end of a size continuum which also includes large pieces.

Edge: On a blade, edges run parallel to the long axis

of the piece, in the sense of a "knife edge." On a flake, edges are the margins of the piece.

End: Edges which are at right angles to the long axis. Most flakes have no clear long axis, so "end" is considered to be the extremity farthest from the bulb of percussion.

Bulb of percussion: A characteristic convex bulb on one end of a flake, at the point of conchoidal fracture where it was struck from a core.

Bulbar surface: The surface (for "surface," read "face" interchangeably) on which the bulb of percussion is found. The bulbar surface is plain, having no scars from previously struck flakes. It is also called the "reverse" or "ventral" side.

Upper surface: The surface which shows the scars of previously removed blades or flakes. It is opposite the bulbar face, and is sometimes called the "obverse" or "dorsal" side.

TYPES OF CHIPPING

Squamous: Retouch which consists of broad, shallow, and irregular flake scars. It is ordinarily used to shape the edges of flakes to make them into scrapers.

Stepped or resolved: Overhanging flake scars which occur in a series, producing a steep or semi-steep face. These merge typologically with steep and squamous retouch.

Steep: Concentrated stepped and squamous chipping from one or both faces to produce a surface which is nearly perpendicular to the adjoining plain surface. This type of retouch can be used to blunt the edge of a backed blade, shape the end of a broken blade so that it becomes truncated, or shape flakes into various forms of scrapers.

Backing: Steep retouch along an edge, especially of a blade or bladelet.

Nibbling: Tiny, usually uniform-sized flake scars occurring along an edge. Nibbling may be caused by use or by deliberate retouch.

Battering: Concentrated stepped or resolved flaking on a small scale, often ending in a notch, or at least a very dull edge.

Nicking: Deeply concave flake scars, often on alternate opposite (upper and bulbar) faces of the same edge.

Crushing: The process of producing a dulled, pulverized edge by continuous pressure rather than by a sharp blow.

Illustrations

For the most part the stone tools in this report have been illustrated with photographs. In instances where photographs do not show the chipping or form of the tool, line drawings have been used. Readers should consult our earlier report for line drawings of all the types discussed here. The illustrations are intended to show the range of variation within types and are not meant to illustrate assemblages from each of the phases separately. The most accurate and rapid means of determining the components of any zone or phase is to consult the tables that list the numbers and proportions of each type of tool. All illustrations of chipped stone are natural size (i.e., 1:1).

TOOL TYPES

For convenience, the tool types which seem to be related by use are clustered into functional groups. The relationship of the tools within each group is based on the type and location of chipping, the shape of the finished piece, or the use which can be inferred from wear. Tables 39 and 40 summarize the occurrence of all chipped stone tools; Tables 41-46 show the occurrence of tools of flint, obsidian and crystal separately.

Functional Group: Geometrics and Other Microliths

The six types in this group were probably used as arrowheads or as barbs set serially in the heads of spears. Abundant historical evidence, ethnographic parallels, and arrows preserved in archeological sites (Clark, 1963:Figs. 13, 14) testify to the way similar artifacts have been used, but we cannot be very specific as to the type of projectile used in Deh Luran. A drawing on a pot of the Mehmeh Phase (Hole, Flannery and Neely, 1969:Fig. 131a) attests to the use of bows and arrows in Khuzistan, and we know from murals that they were used at Çatal Hüyük at a time contemporary with the Mohammad Jaffar and Sefid phases (Mellaart, 1963, Part II:Fig. 6). 6).

The specific types of microlithic elements change

Table 39

ALL CHIPPED STONE (FLINT, OBSIDIAN, CRYSTAL) TOOL TYPES AT CHAGHA SEFID
by Stratigraphic Zone

Phase	Area	Zone	Trapezes and Triangles	Crescents	Diagonal-ended	Diagonal-ended and Backed	Backed Bladelets	Nibbled Bladelets	Drills	Reamers	End Reduced on Bulbar Side	Pointed Pieces	Frags. of Drills and Reamers	Plain Sickles	Truncated Sickles	Blade, Round-end Scrapers	Flake, Round-end Scrapers	Blade, Misc. End Scrapers	Flakes with Bulbar End Retouch	Plain Blades	Backed Blades	Truncated Blades	Retouched or Used Blades	Notched Blades	Retouched or Used Flakes	Notched Flakes	Denticulated Flake Scraper	Burins	Micro-burins	Scaled Pieces	Blades with Ground Edges	Bifacially Chipped Flakes	Bifacial Picks	Total Tools
Sabz	SD	J	1					1	3	2			4	3						37	1		15		10	1	6	1						89
	SD	I							2	1			2	1	1	1				31				2	6		1	1						45
Choga Mami	SD	H	1						1	1			1	1		1				39			3		15	1	7							71
Transitional	SD	G2	1				1		3	1				5			2		4	47	2		25	5	15	7	13							130
	SD	G1		1		1		1	3					4			3		4	126		1	18	16	19	2	5	1			1			206
Surkh	SD	F	1				1	2	5	1			1	10			5		7	147	3		38	16	24	6	12	2						283
	SC, SD	E2	2		1		5		11	3	1		5	35	7		2		7	164		1	43	15	35	3	18	2	1	2	1			365
	SC, SD	E1	1				2		6	1	6	2	3	21	2		6		4	265		1	77	27	16	4	4	1	1		1	1		446
	SC	D3			1	1	1		1		1		1	6			1		1	62			19	3			3							104
	SC	D2				2			4	2	6	1	3	20	2		8		3	186		1	55	20	10	2	7							328
	SC	D1	2						1		1			14	2		3		5	157	1		24	3	6	1	4			2				225
	SC	C2	3				3		17	6	1	2	3	29			3		3	201	1	1	64	16	21	1	12	3						392
Sefid	SA	C1	10		3	1	2		20	4	1	3	8	74	1		9	6	7	779	1		83	36	100		19	6		1				1,174
	SA	B2	6		1	2	6		97	31	6	8	14	202	8		16	12	6	2,968	3	6	399	175	136		12	10		6	2			4,140
	SA	B1				2	3		35	8	1	3	12	63	2		28	5	9	798	3	1	168	81	74		10	4		7			1	1,321
	SA	A4			1	5			25	4	1	1	2	10			16	7	3	248	1		36	27	32		4							400
Mohammad	SB	C				1	1	1	4		1		1	2			5	1	1	140		1	15	14	4	4	2	1						191
Jaffar	SB	B	2			1	5	6	3	2			1	6			3	3	6	360			37	17	4	2	2							458
	SB	A				2	2	1	1		2		1	9			2	2	9	228			35	13	7	1	3							311
Ali Kosh	SA	A3				5	3	1	4	3	1	1	2	16	1		19		1	144	1	1	39	24	19		2							287
	SA	A2				3	7		16	4	1	2	2	22			44	6	6	601		1	75	102	22		2	1			1			913
	SA	A1			5	7	6	1	23	8	1	5	22	55	2		79	9	9	1,697	4	6	106	194	49		2	1				1		2,287
Totals			30	1	15	35	52	15	262	81	14	28	86	608	29	21	257	39	79	9,425	21	21	1,374	806	628	32	146	34	2	16	5	3	2	14,166

Table 40

ALL CHIPPED STONE (FLINT, OBSIDIAN, CRYSTAL) TOOL TYPES AT CHAGHA SEFID
by Cultural Phase

Phase	Geometric and Other Microliths							Piercing-Reaming Tools					Sickles		Scrapers				Cutting-Scraping Tools								Misc. Tools					Total Tools
	Trapezes and Triangles	Crescents	Diagonal-ended	Diagonal-ended and Backed	Backed Bladelets	Nibbled Bladelets	Drills	Reamers	End Reduced on Bulbar Side	Pointed Pieces	Frags. of Drills and Reamers	Plain Sickles	Truncated Sickles	Blade, Round-end Scrapers	Flake, Round-end Scrapers	Blade, Misc. End Scrapers	Flakes with Bulbar End Retouch	Plain Blades	Backed Blades	Truncated Blades	Retouched or Used Blades	Notched Blades	Retouched or Used Flakes	Notched Flakes	Denticulated Flake Scraper	Burins	Micro-burins	Scaled Pieces	Blades with Ground Edges	Bifacially Chipped Flakes	Bifacial Picks	
Sabz	1										6	4	1	2		8		68		1	15	2	16	1	7	2						134
Choga Mami Transitional	2	1			1	1	5	2			1	10	1	5				212	2	1	46	21	49	10	25	1				1		407
Surkh	9		2	3	12	2	45	13		6	15	135	13	29	30	8		1,182	6	4	320	100	116	17	60	8	2	2	2	1		2,143
Sefid	16		5	9	11	1	154	47	9	15	36	349	11	59	29	25	11	4,793	8	7	686	319	342	45	20	14	2	2				7,035
Mohammad Jaffar	2						8	2	2		2	17		10			1	728		1	87	44	15	4	5	1						960
Ali Kosh			5	15	16	2	43	15	3	7	26	93	3	142	9	16		2,442	5	7	220	320	90		4	2		1		1	1	3,487
Totals	30	1	15	35	52	15	262	81	14	28	86	608	29	257	39	79	20	9,425	21	21	1,374	806	628	32	146	34	2	16	5	3	2	14,166

Table 41
FLINT CHIPPED STONE TOOL TYPES AT CHAGHA SEFID
by Stratigraphic Zone

Phase	Area	Zone	Geometric and Other Microliths						Piercing-Reaming Tools						Sickles		Scrapers				Cutting-Scraping Tools						Misc. Tools						Total Tools
			Trapezes and Triangles	Crescents	Diagonal-ended	Diagonal-ended and Backed	Backed Bladelets	Nibbled Bladelets	Drills	Reamers	End Reduced on Bulbar Side	Pointed Pieces	Frags. of Drills and Reamers	Plain Sickles	Truncated Sickles	Blade, Round-end Scrapers	Flake, Round-end Scrapers	Blade, Misc. End Scrapers	Flakes with Bulbar End Retouch	Plain Blades	Backed Blades	Truncated Blades	Retouched or Used Blades	Notched Blades	Retouched or Used Flakes	Notched Flakes	Denticulated Flake Scraper	Burins	Micro-burins	Scaled Pieces	Blades with Ground Edges	Bifacially Chipped Flakes	Bifacial Picks	
Sabz	SD	J	1					1	3				4	3	1	1				36		1	15	2	10	1	6	1						88
	SD	I							2	2			2	1		1				31					6		1	1						45
Choga Mami Transitional	SD	H	1						1	1			1	1						37			3	5	15	1	7							69
	SD	G2	1					1	3	1				5		2		4		47	2		25	16	14	7	13	1						129
	SD	G1		1					3					4		3		4		123		1	18		19	2	5					1		203
Surkh	SD	F	1					2	5	1			5	10		5		7	1	147	3		35	16	22	6	12	2	1					278
	SC, SD	E2	2				1		11	3		1	3	35	7	2		7	1	160			42	14	35	3	18	2	1	2		1		359
	SC, SD	E1	1				5		6	1		2		21	2	6		4		260	1		77	26	16	4	4	1				1		439
	SC	D3				1	2		1				1	6		2		1		59			19	3			3							101
	SC	D2				2	1		4	2		1	3	20	2	6		3	1	172		1	53	20	10	1	7							312
	SC	D1	2		1				1					14	2	2		5	2	147	1		23	2	6	2	4		1					213
	SC	C2	3				2		17	6		2	3	29		8		3	2	187	1	1	62	15	20	1	12	1						370
Sefid	SA	C1	10		3	1	2		20	4	1	3	8	74	1	9	6	7	8	730	1		77	32	100		19	3	2					1,111
	SA	B2	4		1	1	6		92	31	6	8	14	202	8	11	12	9	3	2,623	3	6	340	162	104	3	12	5	1	1	2			3,668
	SA	B1				2	3	1	33	8	1	3	12	62	2	28	5	9		726	3	1	163	78	69	3	10						1	1,223
	SA	A4			1	5			2	4	1		2	10		16	7	3		239	1		36	27	31	1	4							390
Mohammad Jaffar	SB	C			1	1			4			1		2		5				130		1	13	14	3	1	2	1						178
	SB	B	2		1	5	8	6	3	2		1		6		3	1	1		342	1		34	17	4	2								437
	SB	A			1	2	4	1	1		2			9		2	5	6		213			33	12	7	1	3							292
Ali Kosh	SA	A3				5	3	1	4	3	1	2	2	16		19	1	1	1	141	1	1	39	23	19		2							283
	SA	A2				3	7		16	4	1	2	2	22		44	5	6	1	584	1	1	73	102	22			1				1		894
	SA	A1			5	7	6	1	23	8	1	5	22	55	2	79	3	9	6	1,677	4	6	103	194	49		2						1	2,264
Totals			28	1	15	35	51	15	255	81	14	28	86	607	29	252	39	79	18	8,811	21	20	1,283	780	585	32	146	20	2	3	5	3	2	13,346

Table 42

FLINT CHIPPED STONE TOOL TYPES AT CHAGHA SEFID
by Cultural Phase

Phase	Geometric and Other Microliths						Piercing-Reaming Tools					Sickles		Scrapers				Cutting-Scraping Tools								Misc. Tools						Total Tools
	Trapezes and Triangles	Crescents	Diagonal-ended	Diagonal-ended and Backed	Backed Bladelets	Nibbled Bladelets	Drills	Reamers	End Reduced on Bulbar Side	Pointed Pieces	Frags. of Drills and Reamers	Plain Sickles	Truncated Sickles	Blade, Round-end Scrapers	Flake, Round-end Scrapers	Blade, Misc. End Scrapers	Flakes with Bulbar End Retouch	Plain Blades	Backed Blades	Truncated Blades	Retouched or Used Blades	Notched Blades	Retouched or Used Flakes	Notched Flakes	Denticulated Flake Scraper	Burins	Micro-burins	Scaled Pieces	Blades with Ground Edges	Bifacially Chipped Flakes	Bifacial Picks	Total Tools
Sabz	1					1	5	2			6	4	1	2				67		1	15	2	16	1	7	2						133
Choga Mami Transitional	2	1			1	1	7	2			1	10	1	5		8		207	2	1	46	21	48	10	25	1				1		401
Surkh	9		2	3	11	2	45	13		6	15	135	13	29		32	7	1,132	6	3	311	96	113	17	60	6	2	2	2	2		2,072
Sefid	14		5	9	11	1	147	47	9	15	36	348	11	64	30	28	11	4,318	8	7	616	299	304		45	8		1	2	1		6,392
Mohammad Jaffar	2		3	8	12	8	8	2	2		2	17		10				685		1	80	43	14	4	5	1						907
Ali Kosh			5	15	16	2	43	15	3	7	26	93	3	142	9	16		2,402	5	7	215	319	90		4	2		1	1		1	3,441
Totals	28	1	15	35	51	15	255	81	14	28	86	607	29	252	39	79	18	8,811	21	20	1,283	780	585	32	146	20	2	3	5	3	2	13,346

Table 43

OBSIDIAN CHIPPED STONE TOOL TYPES AT CHAGHA SEFID
by Stratigraphic Zone

Phase	Area	Zone	Geometric and Other Microliths							Piercing-Reaming Tools					Sickles		Scrapers				Cutting-Scraping Tools									Misc. Tools					Total Tools
			Trapezes and Triangles	Crescents	Diagonal-ended	Diagonal-ended and Backed	Backed Bladelets	Nibbled Bladelets	Drills	Reamers	End Reduced on Bulbar Side	Pointed Pieces	Frags. of Drills and Reamers	Plain Sickles	Truncated Sickles	Blade, Round-end Scrapers	Flake, Round-end Scrapers	Blade, Misc. End Scrapers	Flakes with Bulbar End Retouch	Plain Blades	Backed Blades	Truncated Blades	Retouched or Used Blades	Notched Blades	Retouched or Used Flakes	Notched Flakes	Denticulated Flake Scraper	Burins	Micro-burins	Scaled Pieces	Blades with Ground Edges	Bifacially Chipped Flakes	Bifacial Picks	
Sabz	SD	J																		1														1
	SD	I																																
Choga Mami Transitional	SD	H																		2														2
	SD	G2																							1									1
	SD	G1																		3														3
Surkh	SD	F																		2			3											5
	SC, SD	E2																		3			1											4
	SC, SD	E1																		3		1	1											5
	SC	D3																																3
	SC	D2																		10			1											11
	SC	D1																		7			1	1										9
	SC	C2																	1	13			2	1	1			2						20
Sefid	SA	C1																		36			6	4	1			3		1				50
	SA	B2	2						5							5				337			59	13	32			5		6				464
	SA	B1							2					1						72			5	3	5			4		6				98
	SA	A4																		9					1									10
Mohammad Jaffar	SB	C																		9			2		1									12
	SB	B																	1	17			3	1										20
	SB	A																		15			2	1										19
Ali Kosh	SA	A3																		3														4
	SA	A2																		17					2									19
	SA	A1																		20					3									23
Totals			2						7					1		5			2	579		1	90	26	43			14		13				783

Table 44

OBSIDIAN CHIPPED STONE TOOL TYPES AT CHAGHA SEFID
by Cultural Phase

Phase	Geometric and Other Microliths						Piercing-Reaming Tools					Sickles		Scrapers				Cutting-Scraping Tools								Misc. Tools						Total Tools
	Trapezes and Triangles	Crescents	Diagonal-ended	Diagonal-ended and Backed	Backed Bladelets	Nibbled Bladelets	Drills	Reamers	End Reduced on Bulbar Side	Pointed Pieces	Frags. of Drills and Reamers	Plain Sickles	Truncated Sickles	Blade, Round-end Scrapers	Flake, Round-end Scrapers	Blade, Misc. End Scrapers	Flakes with Bulbar End Retouch	Plain Blades	Backed Blades	Truncated Blades	Retouched or Used Blades	Notched Blades	Retouched or Used Flakes	Notched Flakes	Denticulated Flake Scraper	Burins	Micro-burins	Scaled Pieces	Blades with Ground Edges	Bifacially Chipped Flakes	Bifacial Picks	
Sabz																		1														1
Choga Mami Transitional																		5					1									6
Surkh																	1	38		1	8	4	3			2						57
Sefid	2						7					1		5				454			70	20	38			12		13				622
Mohammad Jaffar																	1	41			7	1	1									51
Ali Kosh																		40			5	1										46
Totals	2						7					1		5			2	579		1	90	26	43			14		13				783

Table 45
CRYSTAL CHIPPED STONE TOOL TYPES AT CHAGHA SEFID
by Stratigraphic Zone

Phase	Area	Zone	Geometric and Other Microliths						Piercing-Reaming Tools					Sickles		Scrapers				Cutting-Scraping Tools									Misc. Tools					Total Tools
			Trapezes and Triangles	Crescents	Diagonal-ended	Diagonal-ended and Backed	Backed Bladelets	Nibbled Bladelets	Drills	Reamers	End Reduced on Bulbar Side	Pointed Pieces	Frags. of Drills and Reamers	Plain Sickles	Truncated Sickles	Blade, Round-end Scrapers	Flake, Round-end Scrapers	Blade, Misc. End Scrapers	Flakes with Bulbar End Retouch	Plain Blades	Backed Blades	Truncated Blades	Retouched or Used Blades	Notched Blades	Retouched or Used Flakes	Notched Flakes	Denticulated Flake Scraper	Burins	Micro-burins	Scaled Pieces	Blades with Ground Edges	Bifacially Chipped Flakes	Bifacial Picks	
Sabz	SD	J																																
	SD	I																																
Choga Mami Transitional	SD	H																																
	SD	G2																																
	SD	G1																																
Surkh	SD	F																		2														2
	SC, SD	E2																		2														2
	SC, SD	E1																																
	SC	D3																																
	SC	D2																		4			1											5
	SC	D1																		3														3
	SC	C2					1													1														2
Sefid	SA	C1																		13														13
	SA	B2																		8														8
	SA	B1																																
	SA	A4																																
Mohammad Jaffar	SB	C																		1														1
	SB	B																		1														1
	SB	A																																
Ali Kosh	SA	A3																																
	SA	A2																																
	SA	A1																																
Totals							1													35			1											37

Table 46

CRYSTAL CHIPPED STONE TOOL TYPES AT CHAGHA SEFID
by Cultural Phase

Phase	Geometric and Other Microliths — Trapezes and Triangles	Crescents	Diagonal-ended	Diagonal-ended and Backed	Backed Bladelets	Nibbled Bladelets	Piercing-Reaming Tools — Drills	Reamers	End Reduced on Bulbar Side	Pointed Pieces	Frags. of Drills and Reamers	Sickles — Plain Sickles	Truncated Sickles	Scrapers — Blade, Round-end Scrapers	Flake, Round-end Scrapers	Blade, Misc. End Scrapers	Flakes with Bulbar End Retouch	Plain Blades	Backed Blades	Truncated Blades	Cutting-Scraping Tools — Retouched or Used Blades	Notched Blades	Retouched or Used Flakes	Notched Flakes	Denticulated Flake Scraper	Burins	Micro-burins	Misc. Tools — Scaled Pieces	Blades with Ground Edges	Bifacially Chipped Flakes	Bifacial Picks	Total Tools
Sabz																																
Choga Mami Transitional																																
Surkh				1													12			1											14
Sefid																	21															21
Mohammad Jaffar																	2															2
Ali Kosh																																
Totals				1													35			1											37

during the Deh Luran sequence. First to appear (and confined to the Bus Mordeh, Ali Kosh, Mohammad Jaffar, Sefid and Surkh phases) are the various backed bladelets. Geometric forms—trapezes and crescents—appear first in the late Mohammad Jaffar Phase, and are found as late as the Bayat Phase. This sequence is by no means universal, however. Although many of the bladelets have predecessors in the late Paleolithic of Iran (Hole, 1966), triangles and crescents are found in deposits contemporary with the Bus Mordeh Phase and earlier periods in Iraq (e.g., Zawi Chemi Shanidar) and especially in the Levant (e.g., Kebaran and Natufian sites).

We suggested in an earlier study (Hole, 1961:126-28) that diagonal-ended bladelets may have been set serially on spears to hunt gregarious herd animals on the valley floors, while the trapezes and crescents were used as tranchet arrows to kill lighter game. This hypothesis cannot be supported by our evidence from Deh Luran. The same wild animals were hunted throughout the sequence, although perhaps in diminished numbers as time passes. The shift in type of microlith probably relates, therefore, to the use of different hunting tools and the customary ways of hafting them.

In our type descriptions, we refer to the geographic distribution of our tool types within the general Zagros area; these artifacts, however, have seldom been reported in sufficient detail to allow very precise comparisons. The Jaffarabad report (Dollfus, 1971) covers essentially the same range as our Choga Mami Transitional and Sabz phases, while the Guran (Mortensen and Flannery, 1966) and Shimshara (Mortensen, 1970) reports deal with material contemporary with the earlier phases.

TYPE: Trapezes and Triangles (Figs. 56a-b; 59a-d)

Sample: 28 flint, 2 obsidian
Description: Sections of blades broken and retouched in such a manner that the shape of the finished piece is trapezoidal (Fig. 56a; 59a-c) or triangular (Fig. 56b; 55a-d). The edges of the parent blade remain sharp, but the ends are retouched diagonally to the long axis of the blade. The retouch is steep, and may be directed from either the upper or bulbar face.
Temporal distribution: Mohammad Jaffar through Bayat phases.

Geographic distribution: Tepe Sabz (Hole, Flannery and Neely, 1969:77); Jaffarabad (Dollfus, 1971: Fig. 24:10-11); Jarmo (Braidwood and Howe, 1960:Pl. 18); Sarab (Hole, 1961); Kuhbanan (Huckriede, 1962:Fig. 4); Choga Mami (Mortensen, 1973: Fig. 18k-l). The examples found at Shimshara are considerably longer than the ones from Deh Luran (Mortensen, 1971:Fig. 28).

TYPE: Crescents (Figs. 56c; 59e)

Sample: 1 flint
Description: Sections of blades broken and retouched in such a manner that the shape of the finished piece is crescentic. The two retouched ends merge along one edge to form an unbroken arc. These pieces are probably functional equivalents of trapezes and triangles.
Temporal distribution: Choga Mami Transitional and Sabz phases
Geographic distribution: Tepe Sabz (Hole, Flannery and Neely, 1969:77); Zawi Chemi (Solecki, 1964: 407); Jarmo (Braidwood and Howe, 1960:Pl. 18); Tepe Guran (Mortensen, personal communication); and many other sites.

TYPE: Diagonal-Ended Bladelets (Figs. 56d-f, 59f-g)

Sample: 15 flint
Description: Bladelets which have retouch, diagonal to the long axis of the piece, across one end. The edges have no retouch, and the overall shape is that of a scalene triangle.
Temporal distribution: Bus Mordeh through Surkh phases.
Geographic distribution: Ali Kosh (Hole, Flannery and Neely, 1969:77); Jarmo (Braidwood and Howe, 1960:Pl. 18); Sarab (Hole, 1961); Choga Mami (Mortensen, 1973:Fig. 18h); and other sites.

TYPE: Diagonal-Ended and Backed Bladelets (Figs. 56e; 59h-i) (Figs. 56e; 59h-i)

Sample: 35 flint
Description: Bladelets shaped like scalene triangles, which have steep retouch on an end and an edge. The backing can be from the upper face or from the lower face.
Temporal distribution: Bus Mordeh through Sefid

CHIPPED STONE ARTIFACTS

Fig. 56. Chipped stone tool types from Chagha Sefid: *a*, trapezes; *b*, triangle; *c*, crescents; *d,e*, diagonal-ended bladelets; *e*, diagonal-ended and backed bladelets; *g*, backed bladelets; *h*, drills.

phases with scattered examples in Surkh deposits.
Geographic distribution: Ali Kosh (Hole, Flannery and Neely, 1969:78); Zawi Chemi (Soleki, 1964: 407); Karim Shahir (Braidwood and Howe, 1960:52); Jarmo (Braidwood and Howe, 1960:Pl. 18); Sarab (Hole, 1961).

TYPE: Backed Bladelets (Figs. 56g; 59n,o)

Sample: 51 flint, 1 crystal
Description: Bladelets with backing along one edge. Most are broken, and some could be sections of geometrics.
Temporal distribution: Bus Mordeh through Choga Mami Transitional.
Geographic distribution: Ali Kosh (Hole, Flannery and Neely, 1969:78); Zawi Chemi (Solecki, 1964:407); Karim Shahir (Braidwood and Howe, 1960:52); Jarmo (Braidwood and Howe, 1960:Pl. 18); Sarab (Hole, 1961).

TYPE: Nibbled Bladelets (Figs. 59p-r)

Sample: 15 flint
Description: Bladelets with very shallow chipping along one or both edges. Nibbling is found on both the upper and lower edges. Unremarkable as these pieces may look, chipping of this sort is confined to the microliths, and we suppose that it is related either to some specific use or to ways of hafting.
Temporal distribution: Bus Mordeh through Sefid phases with some examples as late as the Choga Mami Transitional.
Geographic distribution: Ali Kosh (Hole, Flannery and Neely, 1969:78); Kuhbanan (Huckriede, 1962: Fig. 3, no. 7); Choga Mami (Mortensen, 1973:Fig. 18a-b).

Functional Group: Piercing-Reaming Tools

The retouch on the four types included here is always on two edges, and done in such a manner that a point (or strong but blunt working shaft) is produced. Drills and "pointed pieces" have fairly sharp, thin tips which would have been suitable for drilling or piercing, whereas the reamers and the flints with retouch on the bulbar side of one end seem too dull to puncture an object; they were probably used to enlarge holes already made. Any of these objects could have been used on hides, but there would have been no particular advantage in using stone tools rather than bone awls. We suggest, therefore, that these tools were probably most often used to drill stone and pottery (as for beads) and to work wood. Unfortunately no trace of such materials remains in the archeological record.

TYPE: Drills (Figs. 56h; 57a,b; 59j-k)

Sample: 255 flint, 7 obsidian
Description: Pieces on which steep retouch along both edges converges to form a point or tip. The tips are usually symmetrical, but in some cases one edge is straight and the other angles inward. The point is rarely at the bulbar end of the piece. Retouch may be directed from the upper face, the lower face, or from alternate faces. A few pieces have the tip sharply delimited by shoulders.
Temporal distribution: Throughout the sequence.
Geographic distribution: Ali Kosh, Tepe Sabz (Hole, Flannery and Neely, 1969:79); Jaffarabad (Dollfus, 1971:Fig. 24:12-14, 16); Zawi Chemi (Solecki, 1964: 407); Karim Shahir (Braidwood and Howe, 1960:53); Jarmo (Braidwood and Howe, 1960:Pl. 18); Kuhbanan (Huckriede, 1962:Fig. 3); Choga Mami (Mortensen, 1973:Figs. 6d; 8b-e).

TYPE: Reamers (Figs. 57c; 58a; 59m,s,t)

Sample: 81 flint
Description: Similar to drills in having steep bilateral retouch, but reamers have essentially parallel rather than converging edges. The tip, which is usually made on the bulbar—generally the thickest—end, tends to be squared off.
Temporal distribution: Throughout the sequence.
Geographic distribution: Ali Kosh (Hole, Flannery and Neely, 1969:79); Jaffarabad (Dollfus, 1971:Fig. 24: 17-18); Zawi Chemi (Solecki, 1964:407); Jarmo, Sarab (Hole, 1961); Choga Mami (Mortensen, 1973: Fig. 7d).

TYPE: Blades with End Reduced on Bulbar Side (Figs. 58b, 59u-w)

Sample: 14 flint

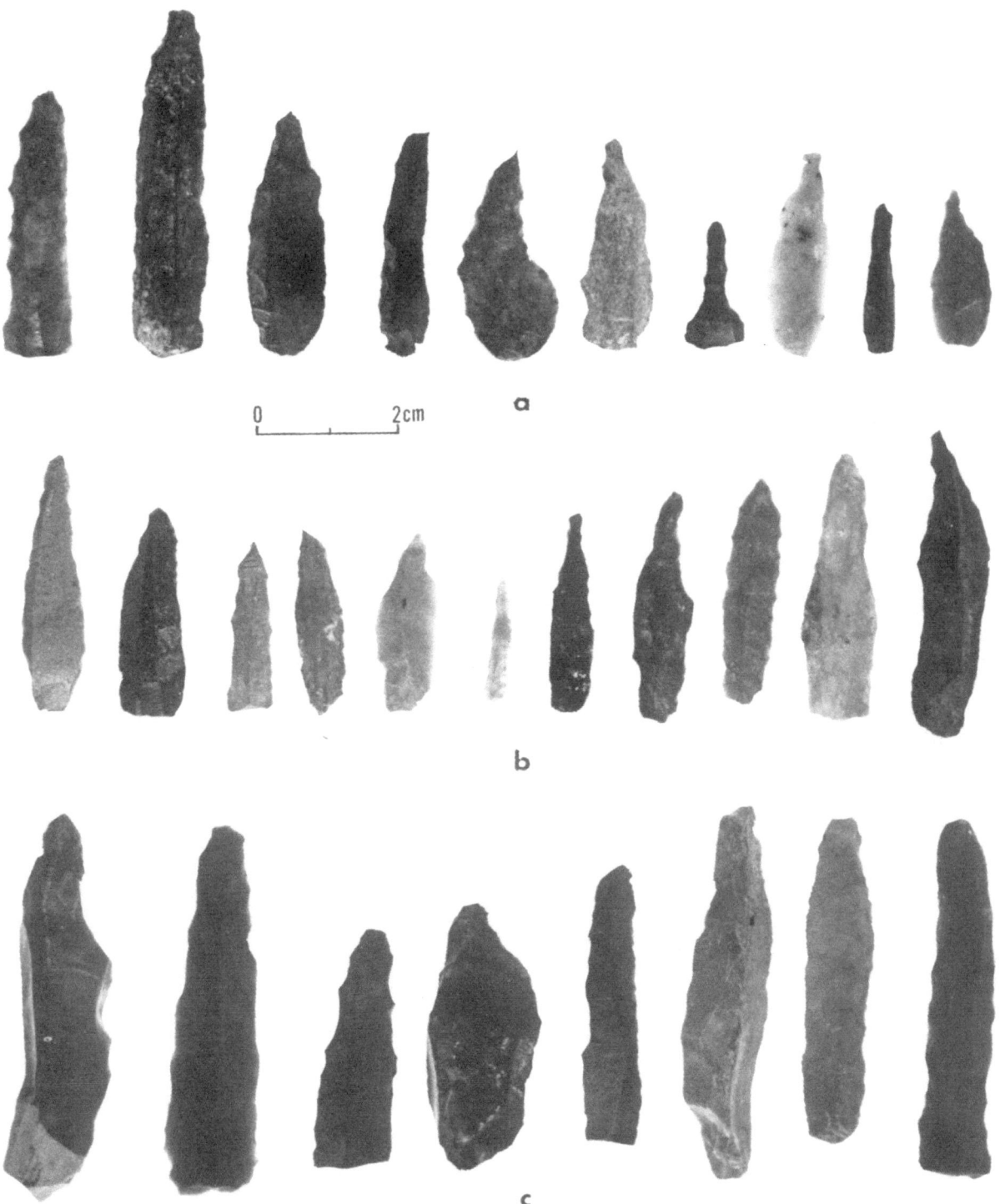

Fig. 57. Chipped stone tool types from Chagha Sefid: *a*, drills (Sefid Phase); *b*, drills (Ali Kosh Phase); *c*, reamers (Sefid Phase).

Fig. 58. Chipped stone tool types from Chagha Sefid: *a*, reamers (Sefid Phase); *b*, blades with end reduced on bulbar side; *c*, pointed pieces.

Description: One end has been reduced in thickness by squamous chipping on the bulbar side. Bulbar ends and broken ends are both treated this way, but not together on the same piece.

Temporal distribution: Bus Mordeh through Sefid phases.

Geographic distribution: Ali Kosh (Hole, Flannery and Neely, 1961:79); Jarmo, Sarab (Hole, 1961).

TYPE: Pointed Pieces (Figs. 58*c*; 59*x-z*)

Sample: 28

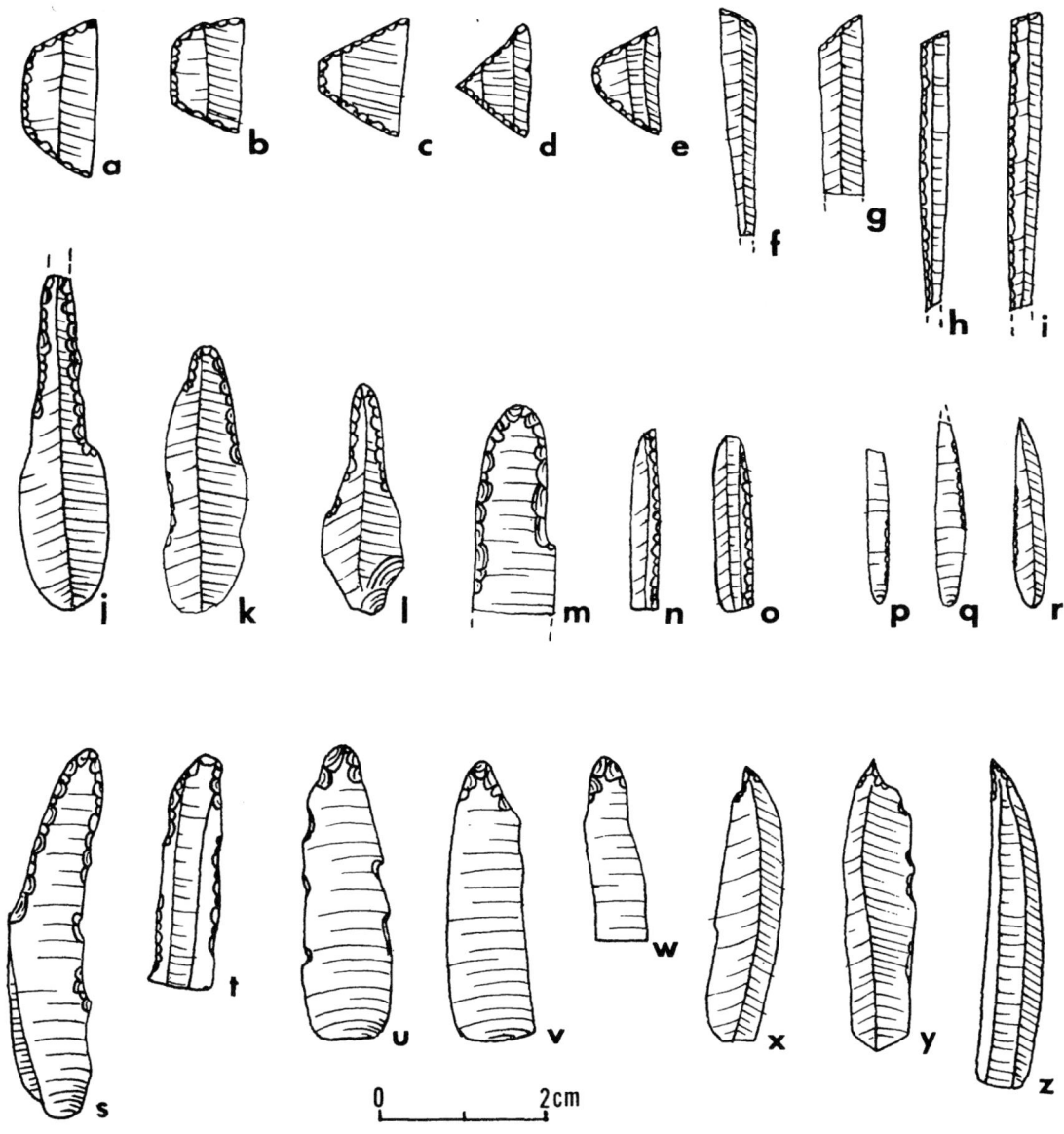

Fig. 59. Chipped stone tool types from Chagha Sefid: *a-c*, trapezes; *d*, triangle; *e*, crescent; *f-g*, diagonal-ended bladelets; *h,i*, diagonal-ended and backed bladelets; *j-l*, drills; *m,s,t*, reamers; *n,o*, backed bladelets; *p-r*, nibbled bladelets; *u-v*, blades with end reduced on bulbar side; *x-z*, pointed pieces.

Description: Blades and flakes which have limited retouch at one end, forming a point or tip. Perhaps functionally equivalent to drills, these may have accidentally resulted from the use of a conveniently-shaped piece of flint which had no prior preparation. Temporal distribution: Bus Mordeh through Surkh phases.
Geographic distribution: Ali Kosh (Hole, Flannery and Neely, 1969:79); Jaffarabad (Dollfus, 1971:Fig. 24:8, 15); Jarmo, Sarab (Hole, 1961); Choga Mami (Mortensen, 1973:Figs. 6*a,c*, 7*f-i*, 8*c*).

FRAGMENTS OF DRILLS OR REAMERS

Sample: 86 flint
Description: Blade fragments that have backing on

both edges suggesting that they are broken from either drills or reamers. While not a tool type, these pieces are included to give an impression of the quantity of piercing-reaming tools in the various phases.

Functional Group: Sickles

Two types—plain sickles without secondary retouch, and sickles which have steep retouch on one edge or on the ends—are included in this group. Sickles by definition have a glossy sheen on the cutting edge. The sheen is probably caused by prolonged rubbing against a fine abrasive—in this case the epidermis of plants whose cells contain silica. Although sheen has not been produced experimentally by reaping with flint sickles, this hypothesis is widely believed by archeologists. Discussions of sheen occur in Vayson (1919), Curwen (1930), Steensberg (1943), and Witthoft (1967). The latter report is of particular interest in that it relates Witthoft's experience as a youth in reaping with a metal scythe to the sheen produced on flints. He found after analysis of both the sheen on flints and the cortex and fibers of plants that it is friction between opal in the plant fibers and the edge of the flint which produces sheen through "frictional fusion of flint and dehydration and fusion of opal to flint surfaces" (Witthoft, 1967: 388). Thus sheen is not a polish or an accretion of silica on the flint, but rather fusion of the crystalline structure of the flint as a result of the heat produced by friction as the grains are cut.

In general sickles follow the pattern found in Ali Kosh where plain sickles greatly outnumber the truncated variety. As expected, there is only one backed sickle in our Chagha Sefid sample. Through time in Deh Luran there is a tendency for sickles to increase in frequency relative to other tools although it is not a simple unvarying relationship of the type we find with some other tools (Table 37).

TYPE: Plain Sickles (figs. 60a-c, 61a,b)

Sample: 607 flint, 1 possible obsidian
Description: Blades and elongated flakes which have sheen on one or both edges, but which are unaltered by deliberate chipping. Most of these implements have minor nicking on the edges, probably as a result of wear. The asphalt mastic used in setting sickles into a handle remains on many of these tools.
Temporal distribution: Throughout the sequence.
Geographic distribution: Ali Kosh, Tepe Sabz (Hole, Flannery and Neely, 1969:81); Jaffarabad (Dollfus, 1971: Fig. 24: Nos. 3, 7); Karim Shahir (Braidwood and Howe, 1960:53); Jarmo (Braidwood and Howe, 1960: Pl. 17); Sarab (Hole, 1961); Choga Mami (Mortensen, 1973: Fig. 11*d-m*); reported from nearly every village site in southwest Asia.

TYPE: Truncated Sickles (Fig. 61*c*)

Sample: 29 flint
Description: Sickles with chipping on one or both ends. The retouching of the ends presumably eases hafting by making a piece fit a predetermined spot in a handle which already contains other sickle elements. One example (Fig. 61*c*, third from left) is also backed.
Temporal distribution: Truncated sickles throughout the sequence although in low frequency before the Sabz Phase; backed sickles appear first in the Choga Mami Transitional.
Geographic distribution: Ali Kosh, Tepe Sabz (Hole, Flannery and Neely, 1969:81); Jaffarabad (Dollfus, 1971: Fig. 24: Nos. 1, 2, 5, 6); Choga Mami (Mortensen, 1973:Fig. 13*h-l* [truncated], Fig. 13*a-g* [backed]).

Functional Group: Scrapers

Most of the scrapers are round-ended and made on blades. This type is especially common in the Ali Kosh Phase and declines in relative proportion as we go through the sequence. The pattern in this respect is similar to that found in Ali Kosh and Tepe Sabz (Table 37). The essential similarity of our findings at Chaga Sefid to those at Ali Kosh is once again striking, and underscores the transitional nature of the new phases at Chagha Sefid. There is a marked lack of scraping tools in the Sabz and later phases. This, coupled with the distinct drop-off in blades, suggests fundamentally different activities than in the earlier phases. That this changeover was not abrupt, however, is demonstrated by the Chagha Sefid data. The overall pattern of decline in types such as blade scrapers was completed at the time of the appearance

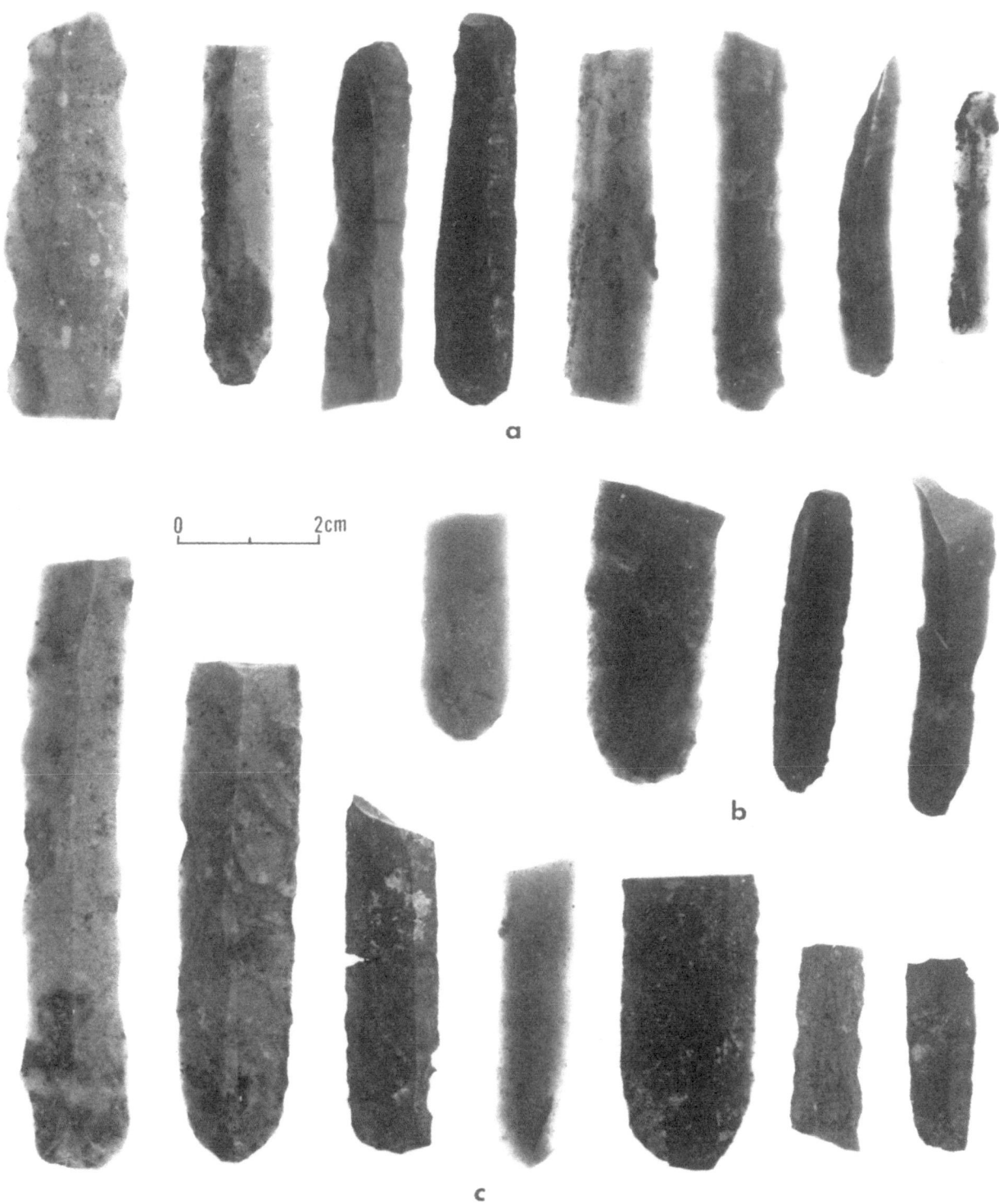

Fig. 60. Plain sickles: *a,b*, Sefid Phase; *c*, Ali Kosh Phase.

Fig. 61. Sickles: *a*, plain sickles (Sefid Phase); *b*, plain sickles (Surkh Phase); *c*, truncated sickles (third example from left is also backed).

of new traditions in the Sabz Phase but not caused by them.

The scrapers listed here are suited, with their regular, smooth ends, for use in skinning or in removing the fatty tissue which adheres to a freshly-skinned hide. Some may also have been used to work "tanning" material into the hides as they were treated, a possibility suggested by the fact that the ends of some of the scrapers are bevelled from use on a soft material. The absence of scrapers from the later phases tends to support an inference that the use of woven cloth had replaced the use of skins for clothing and other artifacts although it does not exclude the possibility that hide working may have been done outside the sites in question after the Sabz Phase.

TYPE: Blade, Round-End Scrapers (Fig. 62)

Sample: 252 flint and 5 obsidian
Description: Blades which have one or both ends convexly rounded, usually by steep retouch which extends to one or both of the edges. A few are double-ended. Some show traces of polishing from prolonged use on soft material. A few are made on sickles which had become too dull for cutting.
Temporal distribution: Principally Bus Mordeh through Sefid phases.
Geographic distribution: Ali Kosh, Tepe Sabz (Hole, Flannery and Neely, 1969:85); Shimshara (Mortensen, 1970: Fig. 24*d-i*); Zawi Chemi (Solecki, 1964: 407); Jarmo (Braidwood and Howe, 1960: Pl. 17); Sarab (Hole, 1961); Kuhbanan (Huckriede, 1962: Fig. 3: No. 22); Choga Mami (Mortensen, 1973: Fig. 5*i-k*).

TYPE: Flake, Round-End Scrapers (Fig. 63)

Sample: 39 flint
Description: Flakes with an edge or end convexly-shaped by relatively steep retouch. The thinner and narrower varieties grade into blade end scrapers. Most of these pieces have the retouch concentrated on an end, but a few are nearly discoidal, having retouch nearly all the way around.
Temporal distribution: Bus Mordeh through early Surkh phases.
Geographic distribution: Ali Kosh (Hole, Flannery and Neely, 1969:85-86); Karim Shahir (Braidwood and Howe, 1960:52); Zawi Chemi (Solecki, 1964: 407); Jarmo (Braidwood and Howe, 1960: Pl. 19); Sarab (Hole, 1961); Kuhbanan (Huckriede, 1962: Fig. 3: Nos. 19, 20, 30); Choga Mami (Mortensen, 1973: Fig. 5*a-b*).

TYPE: Blade, Miscellaneous End Scrapers

Sample: 79 flint
Description: Included are blades whose ends are retouched but not rounded, and others that simply show signs of wear on an otherwise steeply broken edge. The retouched ends are oriented from horizontal to diagonal to the long axis of the blade. A few examples are concave (Fig. 64*a,b*).
Temporal distribution: Sporadically throughout the sequence.
Geographic distribution: Ali Kosh (Hole, Flannery and Neely, 1969:86); Shimshara (Mortensen, 1970: Fig. 24*j-p*); Karim Shahir (Braidwood and Howe, 1960:52); Jarmo (Braidwood and Howe, 1960: Pl. 17); Sarab (Hole, 1961); Choga Mami (Mortensen, 1973: Fig. 14).

TYPE: Flakes with Bulbar End Retouch
(Hole, Flannery and Neely, 1969: Fig. 28*d,e*)

Sample: 18 flint and 2 obsidian
Description: These flakes have secondary retouch on the bulbar end, which results in a smooth edge suitable for scraping. They are thin in section and tend to be crescentic or subround in plan. The trimming may have resulted from the preparation of the core prior to striking blades, a possibility suggested by Bruce Bradley (personal communication). Such pieces are very common at Sarab.
Temporal distribution: sporadically in Ali Kosh through Sabz phases.
Geographic distribution: Ali Kosh, Tepe Sabz (Hole, Flannery and Neely, 1969:87); Jarmo, Sarab (Hole, 1961).

Functional Group: Cutting-Scraping Tools

This is a varied group that includes plain blades and various kinds of flakes and blades with edge retouch. Such tools seem to be related principally to cutting and light-duty scraping.

Fig. 62. Blade, round end scrapers: *a*, Surkh Phase; *b*, Sefid Phase; *c*, Ali Kosh Phase; *d*, Ali Kosh Phase.

Fig. 63. Flake, round end scrapers: examples from various phases.

Fig. 64. Chipped stone tool types from Chagha Sefid: *a,b,* blade, miscellaneous end scrapers with concave ends; *c,* blade, miscellaneous end scrapers; *d,* plain blades (the range of variation in the late Surkh Phase).

By far the most abundant type is the plain blade (some 9,400 of the 14,000 tools recovered), which accounts for more than half of all tools in all except the latest phases, a statistic consistent with our findings at Ali Kosh (Table 37). The sheer quantity of blades, however, is not as impressive as at Ali Kosh.

Table 37 also shows that the deposits in Ali Kosh had nearly three times the relative proportion of blades to other tools as any of our phases at Chagha Sefid. The great number of blades in either site is a measure of the skill of the flint knappers and an indication that blades were a cheap commodity to be used and then discarded as soon as their sharp edges became dull from use. Still, this does not account for the enormous disparity between phases of equivalent age. For example in the Ali Kosh deposits of Chagha Sefid and Ali Kosh, plain blades are 234 and 473 percent of the remaining tools respectively, while in the Mohammad Jaffar Phase at the two sites the figures are 314 and 668 percent. This pattern is continued in the Bus Mordeh Phase at Ali Kosh where blades are a remarkable 1,240 percent of the other tools. Two things are clear from these figures: first, there is a trend toward relatively fewer blades as one advances in time, and second, the deposits at Ali Kosh are extraordinarily rich in blades.

The clue to the different nature of the deposits in the two sites is the "flint dump" at the base of the Bus Mordeh Phase which was the remains of a flint knapper's workshop. It seems likely there was considerably more chipping being done at this site, perhaps for purposes of trade rather than for immediate use, a situation that remains true throughout the phases at Ali Kosh.

Alternatively we might consider that the Ali Kosh villagers were engaged in activities that required far more cutting than was the case at other sites. Unfortunately we have no direct evidence of this, although the lack of evidence is scarcely definitive since blades were evidently used for the most part on perishable, soft material.

The trend toward absolutely fewer blades holds true for all the phases we have excavated where there is no question of local manufacture. After the Sabz Phase at Tepe Sabz blades were apparently imported and, although still low in frequency, are relatively more numerous. The impressive thing about the trend is that at both Chagha Sefid and Ali Kosh, in spite of the great disparity in absolute numbers of blades, there is a gradual decline in their number and in their proportion relative to other tools. It is important to note that this decline took place without a concomitant change in the number of tool types; thus it represents a true trend within a closely homogeneous tradition of manufacturing and use.

TYPE: Plain Blades (Figs. 64d; 65a-b)

Sample: 8,811 flint, 579 obsidian and 35 crystal
Description: Blades which have no deliberate retouch, although the edges may have irregular chips and nicks.
Temporal distribution: Throughout the sequence.
Geographic distribution: Throughout the near East; large quantities are found at Ali Kosh, Jarmo and Sarab.

TYPE: Backed Blades (Fig. 68a)

Sample: 20 flint, 1 obsidian
Description: Blades, or segments of blades, which have one edge blunted by steep retouch.
Temporal distribution: Sporadically, throughout the sequence but relatively more abundant after the Sabz Phase.
Geographic distribution: Ali Kosh, Tepe Sabz (Hole, Flannery and Neely, 1969:87).

TYPE: Truncated Blades (Fig. 67c)

Sample: 21 flint
Description: Blades that have steep retouch on an end but no retouch on the edges. The retouch serves to trim the end of the blade to a sharp diagonal.
Temporal distribution: Throughout the sequence but relatively most common after the Sabz Phase.
Geographic distribution: Ali Kosh, Tepe Sabz (Hole, Flannery and Neely, 1969:87).

TYPE: Retouched or Used Blades (Figs. 65c; 66a-b)

Sample: 1,283 flint, 90 obsidian, 1 crystal
Description: Blades whose edge or edges have zones of chipping, most of which probably resulted from use. In most phases 20-40 percent of the tools are of this type. The retouch is probably not deliberate since the chipping is localized and does not greatly alter the form of the blade.
Temporal distribution: Throughout the sequence.
Geographic distribution: Throughout the Near East, including Ali Kosh and Tepe Sabz (Hole, Flannery and Neely, 1969:88); Jarmo (Braidwood and Howe, 1960:Pl. 17).

TYPE: Notched Blades (Figs. 67a-b; 68b-c)

Sample: 780 flint, 26 obsidian
Description: Blades whose edges have been chipped

Fig. 65. Chipped stone tool types from Chagha Sefid: *a,b*, plain blades (the range of variation in the early Surkh Phase); *c*, used blades (Sefid Phase).

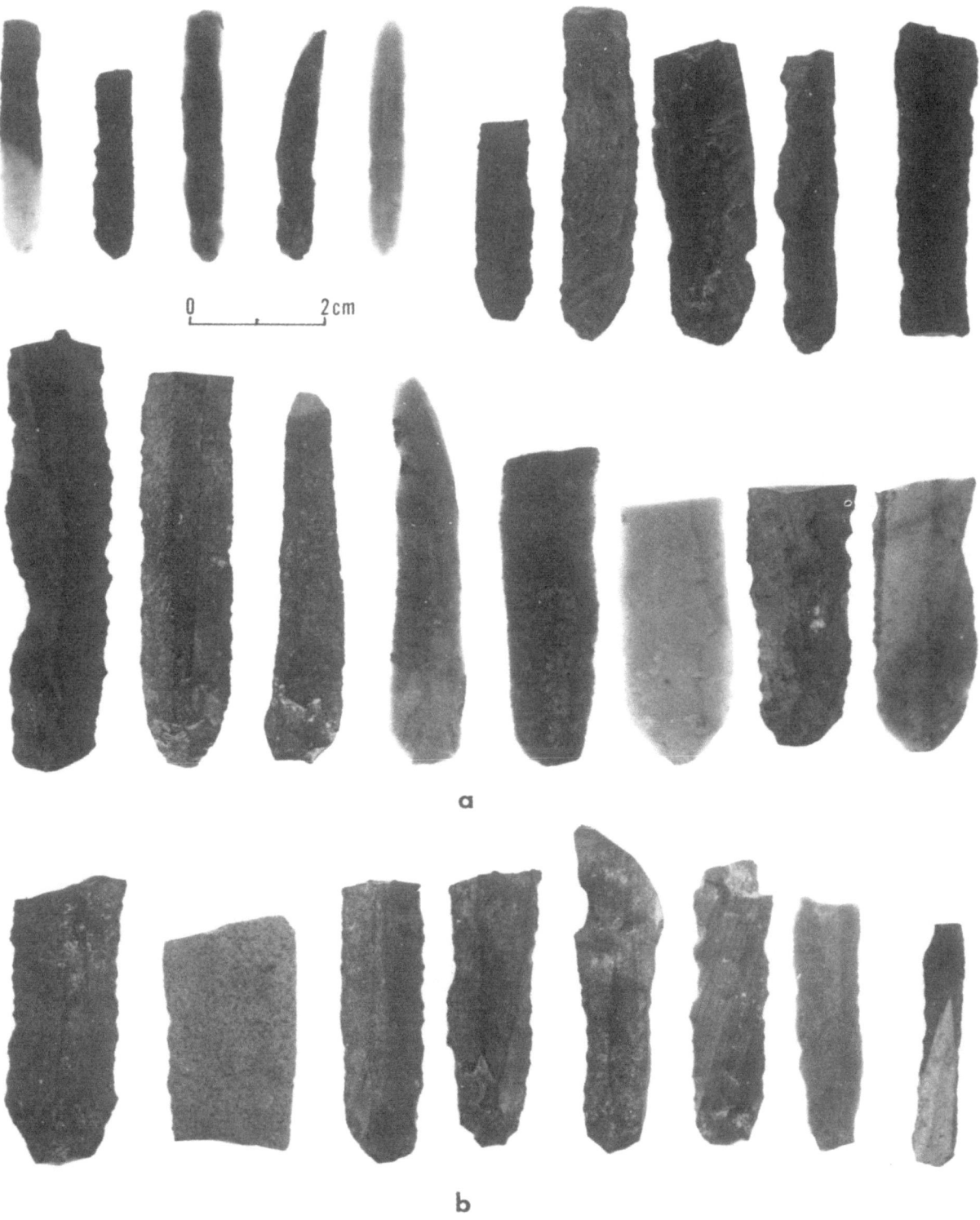

Fig. 66. Used blades: *a*, Sefid Phase; *b*, Ali Kosh Phase.

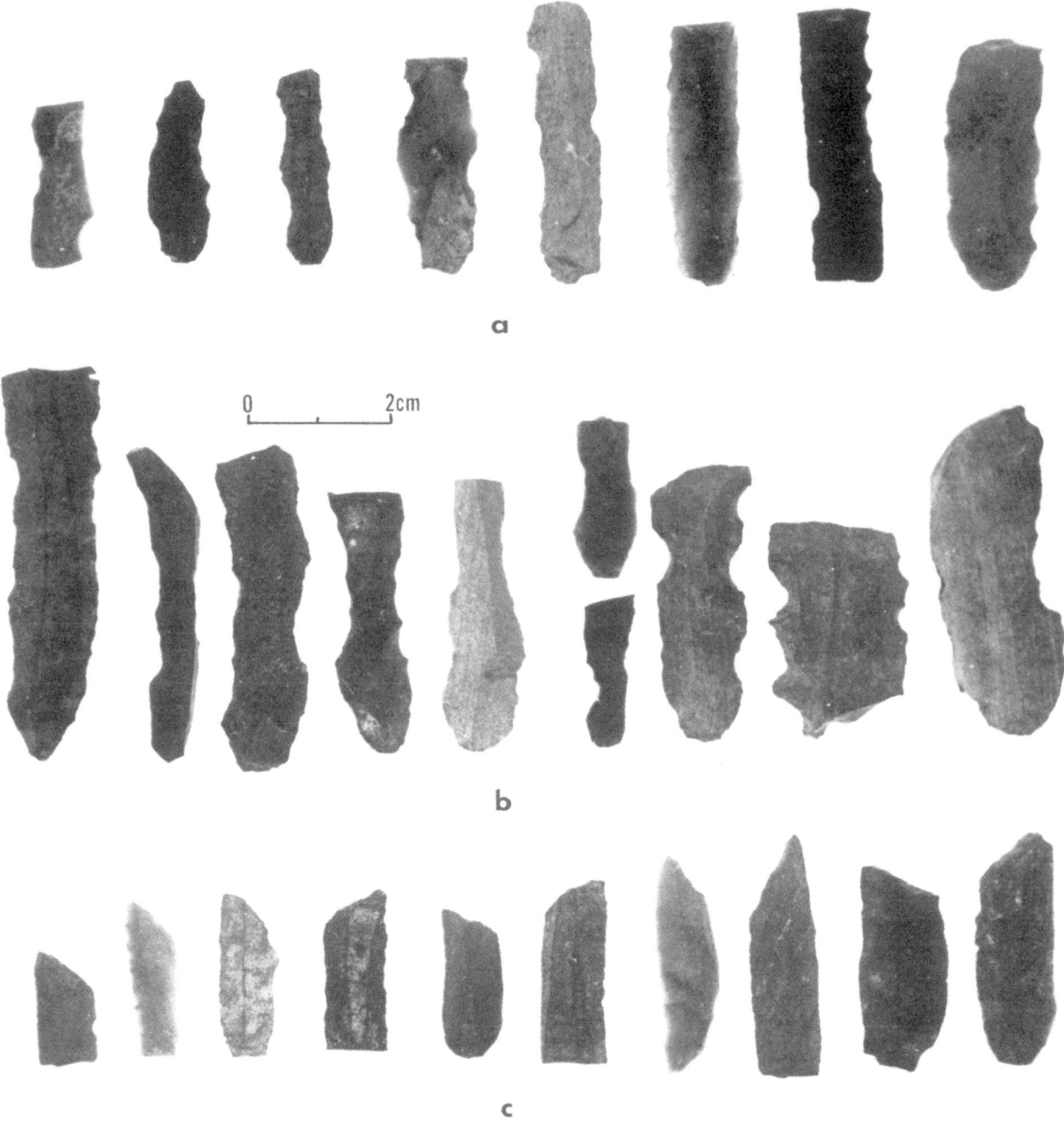

Fig. 67. Chipped stone tool types from Chagha Sefid: *a*, notched blades (late Sefid Phase); *b*, notched blades (early Sefid Phase); *c*, truncated blades.

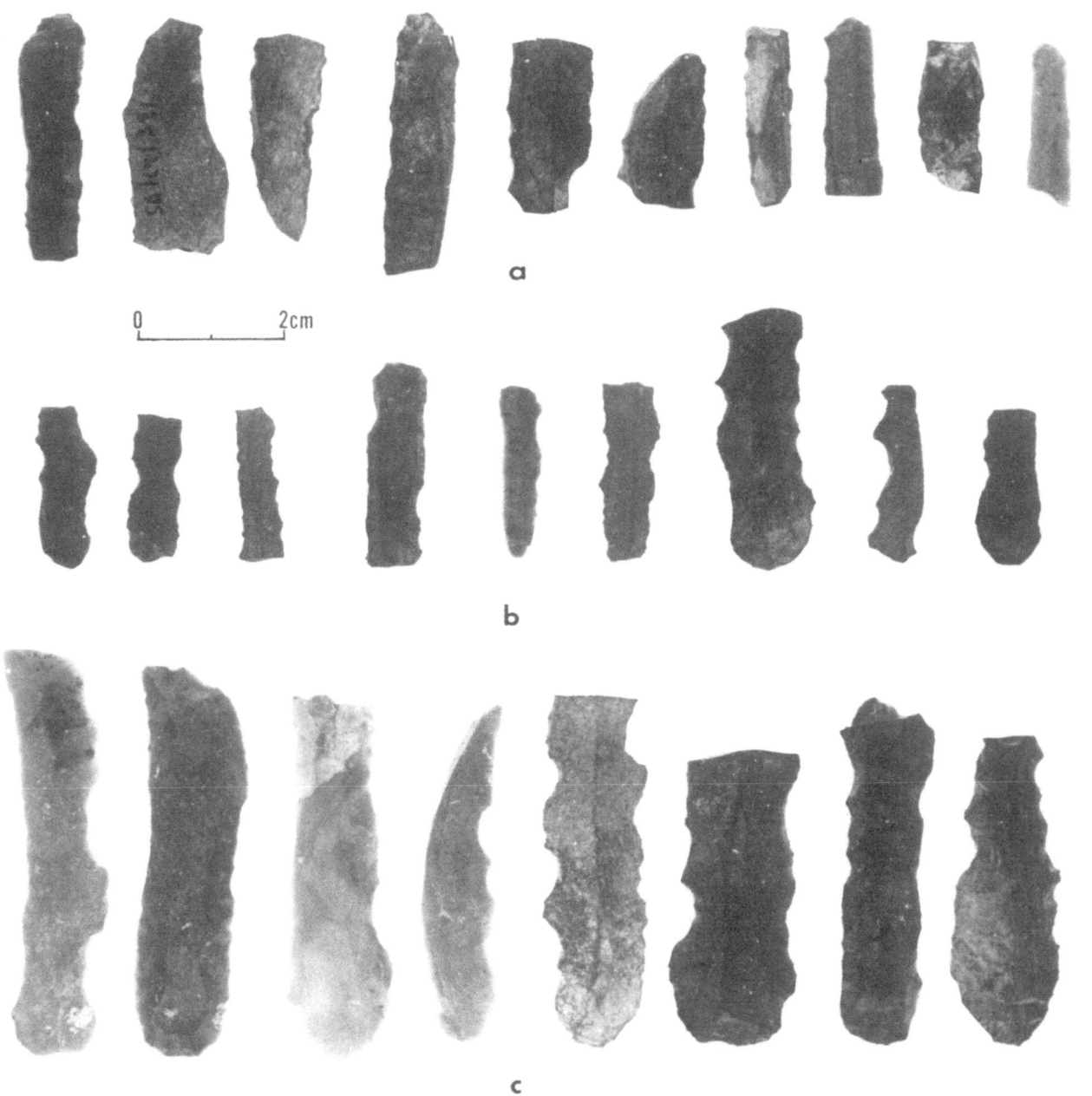

Fig. 68. Chipped stone tool types from Chagha Sefid: *a,* backed blades; *b,c,* notched blades (Ali Kosh Phase).

to produce a notch or notches. Only rarely are the notches regularly enough spaced for them to be called "denticulated." Many of the notches probably were to prepare the flints as spokeshaves for wooden shafts.

Temporal distribution: Throughout the sequence but most common in the Bus Mordeh through Choga Mami Transitional phases.

Geographic distribution: Throughout the Near East, including Ali Kosh and Tepe Sabz (Hole, Flannery and Neely, 1969:88-90); Shimshara (Mortensen, 1970:Fig. 28*a-e*); Jarmo (Braidwood and Howe, 1960:Pl. 17); Choga Mami (Mortensen, 1973:Figs. 10*d-f*, 18*c-e*).

TYPE: Notched Flakes (Figs. 69*a-b*, 70*c*)

Sample: 32 flint, 26 obsidian

Description: Flakes whose edges have been chipped to produce a notch or series of irregularly-spaced notches.

Temporal distribution: Throughout the sequence, but most common in the Surkh and later phases—a reflection of the decline in blade making.

Geographic distribution: Ali Kosh, Tepe Sabz (Hole, Flannery and Neely, 1969:90-91); Karim Shahir (Braidwood and Howe, 1960:52); Choga Mami (Mortensen, 1973:Figs. 5*g*, 10*a-c*); and probably throughout the Near East.

TYPE: Retouched or Used Flakes (Fig. 70*a-b*)

Sample: 585 flint, 41 obsidian

Description: Flakes whose edge or edges have zones of chipping which probably resulted from use. The chipping is localized and does not greatly alter the form of the flake.

Temporal distribution: Throughout the sequence but most common in the Sefid and later phases.

Geographic distribution: Throughout the Near East.

TYPE: Denticulate Flake Scrapers (Figs. 71; 72*a-c*)

Sample: 146 flint

Description: A variety of retouched flake made on thick or chunky flakes. The edges of these pieces are relatively steep and rough and give the piece a denticulate rather than a smooth outline. This type was not distinguished in the analysis of Ali Kosh and Tepe Sabz but some examples occur among the notched flakes.

Temporal distribution: Throughout the sequence but chiefly in the Surkh, Choga Mami Transitional and Sabz phases.

Geographic distribution: Choga Mami (Mortensen, 1973: Fig. 5*c*).

Miscellaneous Tools

TYPE: Burins (Fig. 73*a-g*)

Sample: 20 flint, 14 obsidian

Description: Simple burins, with the burin blow having been struck on a broken end of a blade or flake to produce a sharp, strong chisel or graver edge. Burins were used to cut and engrave stone, bone and wood. These tools were most popular in the Upper Paleolithic, and occur in very low frequency in sites contemporary with our present sequence, except in the Levant. Some examples of engraving on bone that may have been done with the burins are shown in Plate 53.

Temporal distribution: Throughout the sequence but most common in the Sefid through Sabz phases.

Geographic distribution: Ali Kosh, Tepe Sabz (Hole, Flannery and Neely, 1969:91); Shimshara (Mortensen, 1970:Fig. 26*a,e,g*); Zawi Chemi (Solecki, 1964: 407); Jarmo, Sarab (Hole, 1961); Choga Mami (Mortensen, 1973:Fig. 9); probably at other sites of this age.

TYPE: Bifacially chipped flakes (Figs. 72*d*; 73*k*)

Sample: 3

Description: Irregular flakes which have an edge roughly chipped from both faces. These tools were probably used for chopping or cutting, although they are not very large.

Temporal distribution: Late Surkh and Choga Mami Transitional phases and sporadically in Ali Kosh and Tepe Sabz.

Geographic distribution: Ali Kosh, Tepe Sabz (Hole, Flannery and Neely, 1969:91)

Fig. 69. Notched flakes: *a*, early Sefid Phase; *b*, Ali Kosh Phase.

Fig. 70. Chipped stone tool types from Chagha Sefid: *a*, used flakes (late Surkh Phase); *b*, used flakes (early Surkh Phase); *c*, notched flakes (Surkh Phase).

Fig. 71. Denticulate flake scrapers from various phases.

TYPE: Bifacially chipped "Picks" (Fig. 73h,i)

Sample: 2

Description: Broken implements with oval cross-sections and rough flaking on both faces. The edges merge to form a dull point.

Temporal distribution: Ali Kosh, Sefid phases.

Geographic distribution: Jaffarabad (Dollfus, 1971:

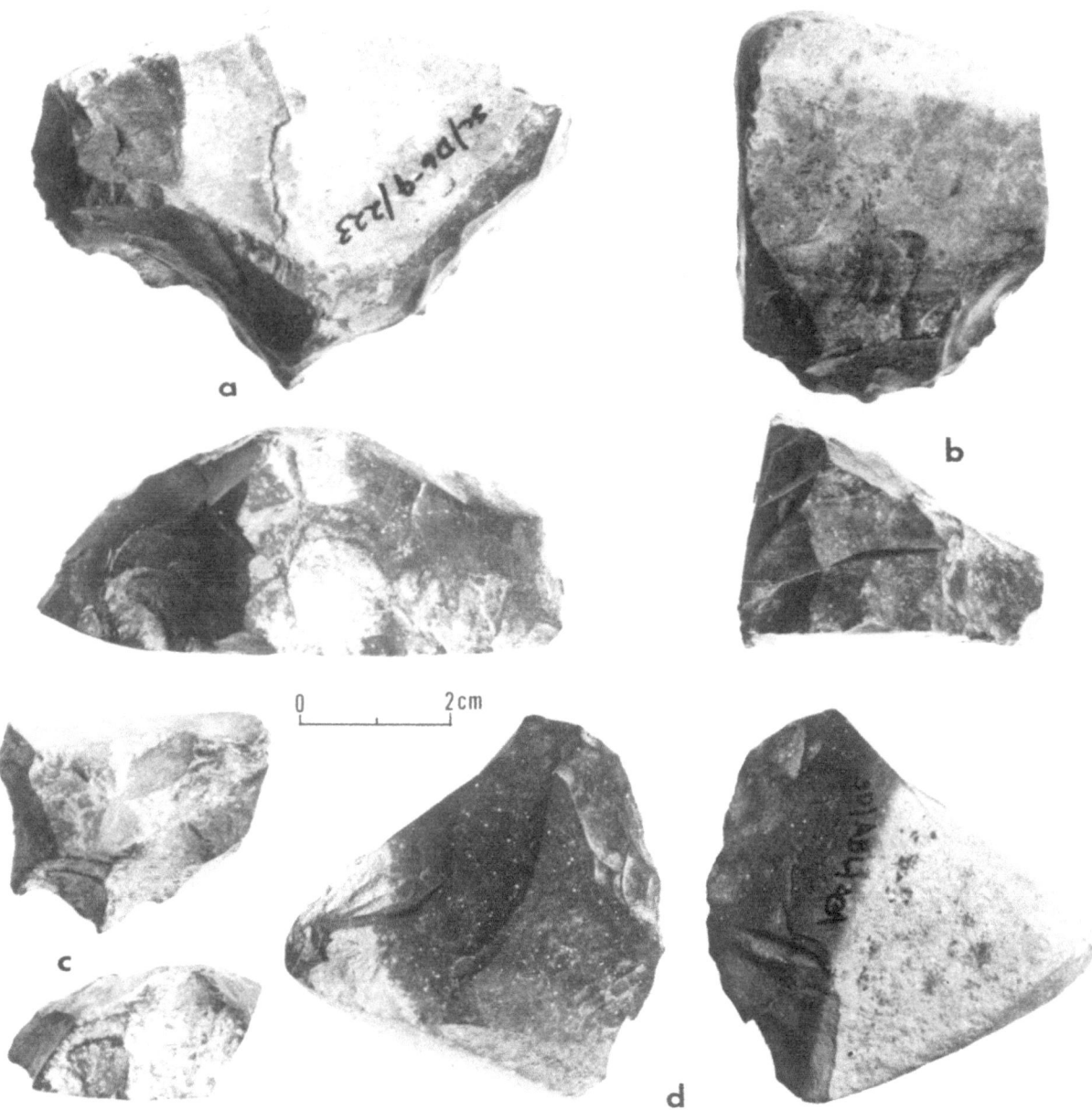

Fig. 72. Denticulate flake scrapers: *a,b,c*, top and front views (Surkh Phase); *d*, bifacially chipped flake (late Surkh Phase).

Fig. 25 No. 9); Choga Mami (Mortensen, 1973: Fig. 16).

TYPE: Scaled Flakes (Fig. 73*j*)

Sample: 13 obsidian

Description: Flakes that have scaling retouch on the bulbar surfaces at the ends. Such pieces were probably produced when the flakes were used as punches.
Temporal distribution: Sefid and Surkh phases.
Geographic distribution: Found occasionally in various sites but not described as a separate type.

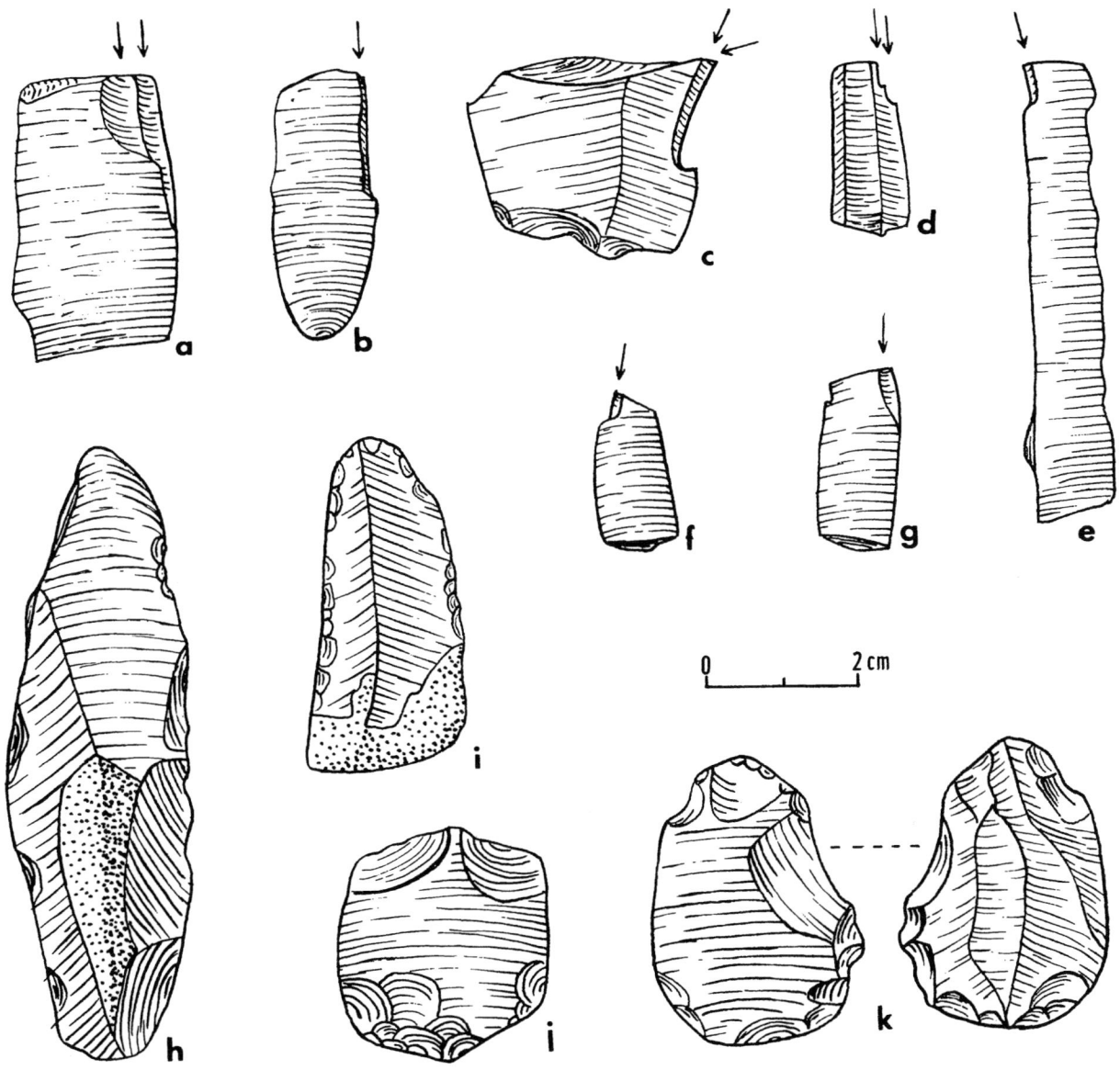

Fig. 73. Chipped stone tool types from Chagha Sefid: *a-g*, burins; *h,i*, bifacially chipped picks; *j*, scaled flake; *k*, bifacially chipped flake.

Chipping Debris

There is much less variety in the cores and chipping debris at Chagha Sefid than we found in the phases at Ali Kosh and Tepe Sabz (Tables 49-51). At the latter site a shift in the raw material resulted in much cruder work than characterized the earlier phases. At Chagha Sefid we find a tendency toward cruder workmanship and the use of inferior raw material but the complete change in raw material presumably occurs in the Sabz Phase, which is poorly represented in our exposure at Chagha Sefid (Tables 47, 48).

In this report we have simplified the description of chipping debris somewhat, taking into account the lesser variety and the fact that we have not found the

Table 47

NUMBER AND PERCENTAGE OF CORES TO TOTAL CORES AT ALI KOSH, CHAGHA SEFID AND TEPE SABZ by Cultural Phase

Site	Phase	Bullet Cores No.	%	Other Blade Cores No.	%	Flake Cores No.	%	Total Cores
TS	Bayat			6	60	4	40	10
TS	Mehmeh			5	23	17	77	22
TS	Khazineh			2	6	29	94	31
TS	Sabz	2	2	3	4	80	94	85
CS	Sabz			1	14	6	86	7
CS	Choga Mami Transitional	3	7	8	17	35	76	46
CS	Surkh	6	4	50	37	79	59	135
CS	Sefid	92	21	203	46	150	34	445
CS	Mohammad Jaffar	8	33	8	33	8	33	24
AK	Mohammad Jaffar	221	74	21	7	55	19	297
CS	Ali Kosh	86	60	28	20	29	20	143
AK	Ali Kosh	182	54	35	10	122	36	339
AK	Bus Mordeh	159	61	64	25	38	15	261

cores and their fragments which are the most informative. Although considerable attention is paid to chipping debris by some workers it was not considered worth the effort for the present report. Of course the material remains available if it becomes clear in the future that more detailed study is warranted. The changes from the earlier report are largely a different division of the cores and the discarding of some of the categories of core fragments. These differences will be clear by comparing this report with the Ali Kosh and Tepe Sabz study.

In general the Chaga Sefid findings substantiate our previous work in showing a tendency toward cruder workmanship and in this sense document the transition from the Mohammad Jaffar to Sabz phases that we had lacked. What we see is much less control and standardization of blade making as we proceed through time. By the time of the late Mohammad Jaffar Phase at Chagha Sefid we find bullet cores for the first time falling below 50 percent of the total cores and after this time their proportion drops rapidly as they are replaced first by other kinds of blade cores and later by flake cores (Table 47).

Further evidence of the slippage in standards of workmanship is seen in the proportion of chipping debris to total chipped stone. Table 48 shows how the proportion of waste flakes and cores to the total of chipped stone increases with time at Chagha Sefid as at other sites. On this basis there is no reason to postulate any sudden changes in the basic technology in use in Deh Luran. It seems more reasonable that there was a gradual lowering of standards which culminated in the change toward poorer raw material that was seen at Tepe Sabz. What these changes in standards of workmanship relate to is a matter that cannot be solved by reference solely to the chipped stone; it must be seen in relation to the uses to which the tools were put and to the prevailing cultural orientation concerning workmanship.

TYPE: Bullet-Shaped Cores (Fig. 74)

Sample: 193 flint, 2 crystal
Description: Small, conical cores with round or slightly oval platforms. The platform, generally unfaceted, is perpendicular to the long axis. Blades were struck around the entire perimeter. The cores are ordinarily widest at the platform, and narrow to a point at the lower end. They range in length from 2 to 5.5 cm and have a rim diameter from 0.3 to 2.5 cm. The majority of the cores have lengths off around 3 cm and diameters between 1 and 1.5 cm.
Temporal distribution: Largely Bus Mordeh through Sefid phases; a few occur as late as Sabz Phase.
Geographic distribution: Ali Kosh (Hole, Flannery and Neely, 1969:93); Shimshara (Mortensen, 1970: Fig. 22a); Karim Shahir (Braidwood and Howe, 1960:53); Jarmo (Braidwood and Howe, 1960: Pl. 19); Sarab (Hole, 1961); Kuhbanan (Huckriede, 1962:Fig. 3, Nos. 23-27); perhaps a few at Tepe Guran (collections of the Danish National Museum); Tamerkhan (Oates, 1968:3-4).

TYPE: Blade Cores, Variety a (Fig. 75)

Sample: 36 flint, 1 crystal
Description: Bullet-shaped cores which have either

Table 48
NUMBER AND PERCENTAGE OF CORES AND DEBITAGE TO CHIPPING DEBRIS, AND OF CHIPPING DEBRIS TO TOTAL CHIPPED STONE AT ALI KOSH, CHAGHA SEFID AND TEPE SABZ
by Cultural Phase

Site	Phase	Blade Cores of All Kinds No.	%	Flake Cores No.	%	Debitage & Core Frags. No.	%	Total Chipping Debris	Chipping Debris / Total Chpd. Stone No.	%
TS	Bayat	6	1	4	1	706	99	716	716/1,267	57
TS	Mehmeh	5	1	17	3	513	96	535	535/713	75
TS	Khazineh	2		29	4	682	96	713	713/820	87
TS	Sabz	5		80	5	1,610	95	1,697	1,696/1,873	91
CS	Sabz	1		6	1	606	99	613	613/747	82
CS	Choga Mami Transitional	11	1	35	2	1,569	97	1,615	1,615/2,022	80
CS	Surkh	56	2	79	2	3,363	96	3,498	3,498/5,641	62
CS	Sefid	295	2	150	1	15,249	99	15,694	15,694/22,729	69
CS	Mohammad Jaffar	16	2	8	1	1,015	97	1,039	1,039/1,999	52
AK	Mohammad Jaffar	242	2	55		11,546		11,843	11,843/23,934	49
CS	Ali Kosh	114	3	29	1	3,719	96	3,862	3,862/7,349	53
AK	Ali Kosh	217	2	122	1	11,052		11,371	11,371/23,231	49
AK	Bus Mordeh	223	1	38		23,555		23,816	23,816/40,114	59

cortex on one side or imperfections in the flint on one side which prevented removal of blades from the entire periphery. These are essentially round in section and of the same shape as bullet cores.
Temporal distribution: Throughout the sequence at Chagha Sefid
Geographic distribution: cf. semi-chipped blade cores (Hole, Flannery and Neely, 1969:93-94); Jaffarabad (Dollfus, 1971:Fig. 25, No. 1).

TYPE: Blade Cores, Variety *b* (Fig. 76)

Sample: 53 flint
Description: In shape the platforms describe a flat-

Table 49
ALL CHIPPING DEBRIS (FLINT, OBSIDIAN AND CRYSTAL) AT CHAGHA SEFID
by Cultural Phase

Phase	Flint									Totals	
	Bullet Cores	Blade Cores a	Blade Cores b	Blade Cores c	Bullet Core Frags.	Blade Core Frags.	Flake Cores	Flake Core Frags.	Debitage	Total Chipping Debris	Total of All Chipped Flint Stone
Sabz		1				5	6	7	594	613	747
Choga Mami Transitional	3	1	2	5		13	35	13	1,543	1,615	2,022
Surkh	6	10	4	36	4	47	79	59	3,253	3,498	5,641
Sefid	92	18	44	141	50	106	150	270	14,823	15,694	22,729
Mohammad Jaffar	8	2	1	5		9	8	19	987	1,039	1,999
Ali Kosh	86	4	2	22	37	13	29	93	3,576	3,862	7,349
Totals	195	36	53	209	91	193	307	461	24,776	26,321	40,487

tened oval that results from the fact that blades were removed from only one side. About one half of the core retains its cortex or is chipped transversely to the axis of the blades.
Temporal distribution: Ali Kosh through Choga Mami Transitional phases
Geographic distribution: cf. tongue-shaped blade cores (Hole, Flannery and Neely, 1969:93); Jaffarabad (Dollfus, 1971:Nos. 3-4); Choga Mami (Mortensen, 1973:Figs. 1*a, c-f*; 2*a,b*).

TYPE: Blade Cores, Variety *c* (Fig. 77)

Sample: 208 flint
Description: A group of pyramidal or relatively straight sided cores with blades removed from only a portion of the periphery. These are not bullet-shaped and tend to be larger and cruder than the other blade cores.
Temporal distribution: Ali Kosh through Choga Mami Transitional phases.
Geographic distribution: cf. semi-chipped blade cores (Hole, Flannery and Neely, 1969:93-94); Jaffarabad (Dollfus, 1971:Fig. 25, Nos. 5-6).

TYPE: Flake Cores (Figs. 78, 79)

Sample: 228
Description: In our previous report we described several varieties of flake cores but the only important differences were related to the raw material used. Accordingly we have simply lumped all flake cores.

Flake cores are nodules from which only flakes have been removed. Included in this group are cores that have been chipped from a single platform or multiple platforms, cores that are entirely chipped or only partially chipped (cf. whole-chipped flake cores and "tea cozy" flake cores, semi-chipped flake cores, and amorphous flake cores [Hole, Flannery and Neely, 1969:95-100]. The chief difference among the varieties we described previously was the amount of chipping and the number of platforms from which flakes were struck.

Flake cores are regarded as blanks or roughouts

Table 50

CHIPPING DEBRIS AT CHAGHA SEFID
by Stratigraphic Zone and Raw Material

Phase	Area	Zone	Flint: Bullet Cores	Blade Cores a	Blade Cores b	Blade Cores c	Bullet Core Frags.	Blade Core Frags.	Flake Cores	Flake Core Frags.	Debitage	Total Chipping Debris	Total of All Chipped Flint	Obsidian: Flake Cores	Flake Core Frags.	Debitage	Total Chipping Debris	Total of All Chipped Obsidian	Crystal: Bullet Cores	Blade Cores	Blade Core Frags.	Debitage	Total Chipping Debris	Total of All Chipped Crystal	Total All Chipping Debris	Total All Chipped Stone
Sabz	SD	J		1				5	4	4	437	451	539			1	1	2							452	541
Sabz	SD	I							2	3	156	161	206												161	206
Choga Mami Transitional	SD	H				1		1	4	3	303	312	381	1		4	5	7							317	388
Choga Mami Transitional	SD	G2	2			4		5	22	7	465	506	635					1							506	636
Choga Mami Transitional	SD	G1	1	1	1			7	8	3	771	792	995					3							792	998
Surkh	SD	F	1	1		5		6	12	14	1,030	1,070	1,348			1	1	6							1,071	1,354
Surkh	SC, SD	E2				12		7	27	12	1,020	1,078	1,437			3	3	7				2	2	4	1,083	1,448
Surkh	SC, SD	E1	1	4	1	5		15	12	14	938	989	1,428			1	1	6				3	3	5	993	1,439
Surkh	SC	D3				2			1		34	38	139			1	1	4							39	143
Surkh	SC	D2	1	2		3	1	4	9	5	69	94	406			2	2	13				2	2	7	98	426
Surkh	SC	D1	2	1		2	2	2	6	3	32	53	266			4	4	13				7	7	10	64	289
Surkh	SC	C2	1	3	3	6	1	7	11	10	91	133	503	1	1	8	10	30		1	1	5	7	9	150	542
Sefid	SA	C1	9	1		12	3	10	44	57	4,231	4,367	5,478	4	34	38	88				10	11	24	4,416	5,590
Sefid	SA	B2	47	14	43	107	25	71	60	109	6,089	6,565	10,223	16	30	269	315	779	1			7	8	16	6,888	11,028
Sefid	SA	B1	20	2		18	18	20	17	52	3,305	3,452	4,675		6	51	57	155	1						3,509	4,830
Sefid	SA	A4	14	1	1	4	4	5	13	11	819	872	1,262		1	8	9	19							881	1,218
Mohammad Jaffar	SB	C	1			3			2	3	198	208	386	1		29	30	42					1	1	238	429
Mohammad Jaffar	SB	B	5	1	1			7	1	9	444	467	904			31	31	51							498	956
Mohammad Jaffar	SB	A	2	1		2		2	4	7	241	259	551			44	44	63						1	303	614
Ali Kosh	SA	A3	4			5	3	3	8	11	628	662	945	1		4	5	9							667	954
Ali Kosh	SA	A2	26				7		2	21	991	1,047	1,941	2	29	31	50							1,078	1,991
Ali Kosh	SA	A1	56	4	2	17	27	10	19	54	1,901	2,090	4,354	4	23	27	50							2,117	4,404
Totals			193	36	53	208	91	192	288	412	24,193	25,666	39,012	19	49	547	615	1,398	2	1	1	36	40	77	26,321	40,487

Table 51

CHIPPING DEBRIS AT CHAGHA SEFID
by Cultural Phase and Raw Material

Phase	Flint											Flint Totals	Obsidian				Obsidian Totals	Crystal					Crystal Totals	Totals	
	Bullet Cores	Blade Cores a	Blade Cores b	Blade Cores c	Bullet Core Frags.	Blade Core Frags.	Flake Cores	Flake Core Frags.	Debitage	Total Chipping Debris	Total of All Chipped Flint	Flake Cores	Flake Core Frags.	Debitage	Total Chipping Debris	Total of All Chipped Obsidian	Bullet Cores	Blade Cores	Blade Core Frags.	Debitage	Total Chipping Debris	Total of All Chipped Crystal	Total All Chipping Debris	Total All Chipped Stone
Sabz		1				5	6	7	593	612	745			1	1	2							613	747
Choga Mami Transitional	3	1	2	5		13	34	13	1,539	1,610	2,011			4	5	11							1,615	2,022
Surkh	6	10	4	35	4	46	78	58	3,214	3,455	5,527	1	1	20	22	79		1	1	19	21	35	3,498	5,641
Sefid	90	18	44	141	50	106	134	229	14,444	15,256	21,648	16	41	362	419	1,041				17	19	40	15,694	22,729
Mohammad Jaffar	8	2	1	5		9	7	19	883	934	1,841	1		104	105	156	2					2	1,039	1,999
All Kosh	86	4	2	22	37	13	29	86	3,520	3,799	7,240		7	56	63	109							3,862	7,349
Totals	193	36	53	208	91	192	288	412	24,193	25,666	39,012	19	49	547	615	1,398	2	1	1	36	40	77	26,321	40,487

Fig. 74. Bullet cores.

Fig. 75. Blade cores, variety *a*.

Fig. 76. Blade cores, variety *b*.

Fig. 77. Blade cores, variety *c*.

CHIPPED STONE ARTIFACTS

Fig. 78. Flake cores.

Fig. 79. Flake cores.

for blade cores although the flakes derived from them may have been used. In many instances the initial trimming did not achieve the results desired for the subsequent removal of blades and the cores were discarded or used as hammerstones.

No discoidal flake cores or thin nodule cores were found at Chagha Sefid.

Temporal distribution: Throughout the sequence.

CORE FRAGMENTS

Sample: Bullet core: 91 flint
　　　　Blade core: 183 flint, 1 crystal
　　　　Flake core: 412 flint, 49 obsidian

Description: The following kinds of fragments are recorded (cf. Hole, Flannery and Neely, 1969:100-102).

Bullet core fragments: Both tablets and sections of these cores are counted.

Blade core fragments: Tablets, edges of striking platforms, faces and sections are counted. These fragments may have come from any of the varieties of blade core.

Flake core fragments: Any tablet, edge of striking platform, face, or section that does not have blade scars is listed in this category.

DEBITAGE

Sample: 24,193 flint, 547 obisidian, 36 crystal

Description: Flakes which have no signs of retouch. We regard these as analogous to sawdust—useless debris left over from the manufacture of tools.

Temporal distribution: Throughout the sequence.

VIII

OTHER ARTIFACTS

INTRODUCTION

Grinding and Pounding Tools

To some extent the occurrence of grinding tools must be considered fortuitous unless they are found on the floors of houses where they were left when the houses were abandoned. At Ali Kosh this seems to have been the case in many instances, whereas at Chagha Sefid all grinding implements were found either incorporated into wall foundations or in the trash filling of abandoned domestic areas. Grinding stones rarely occur in pure midden. Thus the nature of the deposit determines to some extent what will be found, just as the amount dug in each phase bears some relation to the probability that tools of any kind will be found. The prevailing architectural practices are also important. At Chagha Sefid, where walls were founded on stone, discarded grinding stones would probably have been used for this purpose rather than left in place where they were initially discarded. Despite these factors, one can point to clear differences in the occurrence of categories of grinding tools in contemporary phases at the two sites. The basic categories are grinding slabs and mortars, handstones, pestles, and pounders.

The flat-topped boulder grinding slab occurs relatively frequently at Ali Kosh, whereas only one example turned up in the Ali Kosh Phase at Chagha Sefid and none was found in the new phases in spite of the large numbers of grinding stones in general. They are not absent at Chagha Sefid because the type went out of use; they occur in the Sabz and Khazineh phases at Tepe Sabz. Since these are relatively crude grinding stones, perhaps one should not make too much of the distribution.

Far more striking is the fact that there are no combination shallow basin and mortar types at Chagha Sefid although they were the second most frequent type in the Ali Kosh Phase at Ali Kosh. Another difference in the two sites can be seen in bowl mortars which are found only at Chaga Sefid. One was even found in Ali Kosh Phase deposits, where few grinding stones of any kind appear. It is not certain that these objects were used for the preparation of food; all had tar smeared in and around the central depression and they may have served a quite different purpose.

Another difference between sites is seen in handstones. There is a curious lack of the simple discoidal form at Chagha Sefid although this type was found throughout the phases at Ali Kosh and Tepe Sabz. Only in the Surkh Phase do we find these implements at Chagha Sefid. Likewise, irregular elongate handstones are lacking at Chagha Sefid, although their distribution at Ali Kosh suggests that they should have been present.

At Chagha Sefid, only the relatively crude and irregular pestles are at all common, whereas at Ali Kosh both core pestles and combination pestles and rolling handstones are common. In other words, less care was expended on handstones at Chagha Sefid and the manner in which they were used may have been different. The core pestles found at Ali Kosh probably relate to the fact that some unusually large blade cores, of "foreign" origin, made their way to the site in the Ali Kosh Phase.

Other types of ground stone appear in the deposits at Chagha Sefid where one would expect to find them, based on their distributions at Ali Kosh and Tepe Sabz. With the exception of basalt pebbles, the same is true of the types of pounders found at the sites. At Chagha Sefid, as at Ali Kosh, simple spherical pounders are the most common form. The basalt pebbles are of non-local origin and this material does not occur at either Ali Kosh or Tepe Sabz.

Although the maximum diversity in grinding stones at Ali Kosh was in the Ali Kosh and Mohammad Jaffar deposits, relatively few stones were recovered from contemporary deposits at Chagha Sefid. This is not solely because of the sizes of the exposures. There are 16 and 15 types respectively in the two phases at Ali Kosh, whereas the numbers at Chagha Sefid are 7 and 1. What seems to be the case is that the people at Chagha Sefid simply had less variety in their grinding stones, even in phases where they were far more abundant than they were at Ali Kosh.

The divisions in Table 52 suggest functional groupings. If these are accurate, it then appears that people in all phases had at least one type of each essential kind of tool. The greater variety found in some phases is more a reflection of an elaboration on a theme than it is of basic differences in activities.

Miscellaneous Stone Artifacts

It is difficult to ascribe uses to all the implements in the sequence although one may postulate some ways in which they may have been used. We surmised earlier (Hole, Flannery and Neely, 1969:189) that the flint pebble choppers were used to butcher animals. These tools occur with great frequency in the Ali Kosh Phase at Ali Kosh and appear only sporadically thereafter. What is striking is that they do not occur at all in the contemporary phases at Chagha Sefid, although a few were found in the Sefid and Surkh Phases. The differences almost certainly relate to the fact that large animals were being hunted regularly at Ali Kosh, only occasionally at Tepe Sabz, and scarcely at all at Chagha Sefid. The decided drop in the abundance of animal bones of any kind at Tepe Sabz as compared with Ali Kosh is paralleled in the finding that caprines compose about 95 percent of all fauna at Chagha Sefid. Different eating habits in different phases and sites are thus strongly suggested.

Slicing slabs are another artifact probably related to butchering. We have suggested that they were inserted under tendons as an aid in cutting (Hole, Flannery and Neely, 1969:196). Their disappearance after the Sabz Phase and their considerable decline in frequency after the Mohammad Jaffar Phase suggest either the decline of meat eating or different butchering techniques. Likewise, chipped limestone discs, found abundantly at Ali Kosh, are found only in the Sefid Phase at Chagha Sefid. None occurs later. Flannery has suggested that these were used as "anvils" against which long bones of the larger animals were tapped after cooking to drive the marrow out.

Chipped stone hoes were rare at Ali Kosh. (They may be "intrusive" from later deposits which we did not recognize when we dug the site. These later occupations are indicated by sherds found on the surface, especially in 1969.) These crude hoes are relatively common at Chagha Sefid in the Sefid, Surkh and Choga Mami Transitional phases and occur only rarely thereafter. In their stead we find polished celts, certainly a functional counterpart and a more carefully prepared tool that reflects a greater concentration on agriculture, concomitant with the introduction of irrigation. According to historic sources (for example, the Farmer's Almanac; Kramer, 1961: 109-113), hoes are used to break clods in the fields and to dig ditches for the channeling of water. The crude chipped hoes would serve well for the former purpose but would be of little use for the latter. It is probably no coincidence that they disappear with our first evidence of irrigation.

Perforated stones, not found earlier than the Surkh Phase, very likely relate to weaving, as is also suggested by the occurrence of spindle whorls. By this time the eating of meat was becoming rarer and animals were used more for their secondary products like wool than as the basis of subsistence.

Figurines

Models of animals, especially sheep or goats, dogs, pigs, and occasionally cattle are found at nearly every preceramic village and probably at every seventh millenium settlement in southwest Asia. Often crude and usually broken, these figurines constitute one of the most impressive indications of underlying similarities throughout this wide area. It is hard to escape the conclusion that they are found predominantly among people who place a heavy emphasis on keeping animals, although it cannot be demonstrated that herding in the sense of domestication was practiced at all these sites. Nevertheless animal figurines disap-

Table 52

GRINDING AND POUNDING TOOLS AT ALI KOSH (AK), CHAGHA SEFID (CS) AND TEPE SABZ (TS)
by Cultural Phase

		Grinding Slabs and Mortars									Handstones						Pestles					Pounders			
Site	Phase	Flat-topped Boulder	Saddle-shaped Slab	Shallow Basin & Trough Metates	Comb. Shallow Basin and Mortar	Pebble Mortar	Bowl Mortar	Boulder Mortar	Comb. Saddle-shaped Slab and Mortar	Saddle-shaped Slab with Central Depr.	Simple Discoidal	Loaf-shaped	Irregular Elong.	Small Slab Abrader	Irregular Sausage-shaped	Comb. Conical Pestle and Rolling Handstone	Comb. Cylindrical Pestle and Handstone	Stubby Bell-shaped Pestles	Irregular Sausage-shaped Pestles	Core Pestles	Spherical Pounders	Core Pounders	Cuboid Pounder-Rubbing Stones	Basalt Pebbles
TS	Bayat		15						1		7													
TS	Mehmeh		39						5	1	18	1			6			1				6	8		
TS	Khazineh	2	9		1			2			7								2			3	7	1	
TS	Sabz	1	7		1			2	2		3								6			7	18		
CS	Sabz											1													
CS	Choga Mami		6			4	1	3				12							3			17	5		3
CS	Surkh		11			12	2	6			16	56		2				2	13			48	19	3	9
CS	Sefid		226	2		3		9				62		4			1		14			55	6	3	13
CS	Mhd Jaffar											1													
AK	Mhd Jaffar	5	26	16		3		4			7	3	5	2		2	8	2	3			39	9	1	
CS	Ali Kosh	1	5			1	1					2							3			9			
AK	Ali Kosh	2	73	2	13	4					20	5	6	4		4	10		6	8		90	27	1	
AK	Bus Mordeh	1	3								3		2	2		2	2					17	10		

pear in the Deh Luran sequence in the late Surkh Phase and from this time through the 5th millenium we find only isolated examples. The demise of animal figurines occurs at the same time that human figures and faces become common.

Rather than seeing this as a simple replacement in style, we should consider whether entirely different purposes are served by the two forms of figurines. In order to determine this it will be necessary to have considerably more associational data than are now available. The figurines at Chagha Sefid occur almost exclusively in midden deposits, whereas at some sites human figures are found in graves (Oates, 1966), in niches in "shrines or temples" (Oates, 1966; Mellaart, 1967:202-203), or seated on "thrones" flanked by felines as at Çatal Hüyük (Mellaart, 1967:182-184). These human figures sometimes occur in pairs such as mother and child or two adults (Mellaart, 1967:184), and both sexes may be represented (Oates, 1966; Mellaart, 1967:181). This evidence, along with the fact that the more elaborate figurines are sometimes made of stone, strongly points to a ritual rather than a mundane use for the human figurines. Nevertheless, there are few published reports that give enough associational data to enable us to say very much about the uses to which figurines of any kind were put.

While the animal figurines are relatively rare at some sites, they are extremely common at others. For example, the deposits at Ali Kosh and Chagha Sefid together had far fewer figurines than Sarab on the Kermanshah Plain. The latter site may have been a summer herding encampment, yet a high proportion of the figurines are of dogs. By contrast, no dogs were found at either Ali Kosh or Chagha Sefid. Jarmo has some dogs, as well as sheep/goats and human females (Braidwood and Howe, 1960:Pl. 16). Well-modeled female figures occur at both Jarmo and Sarab and at the latter site occur in considerable numbers in the midden. No males have been described at either site. Although there is considerable variation in the occurrence of figurines, we have as yet few clues as to their significance.

Although there is nothing in the figurines themselves to suggest direct links with subsistence, the more elaborate, well-modeled, and sometimes painted human figures appear to occur only at sites where domestication is well advanced and it is at the larger sites, where there is evidence of substantial nondomestic architecture, that the finest examples of human figures are found. At these sites, animal figures continue to be made, if at all, in the same crude style as the earliest examples. Thus there would appear to be a clear difference in the ways these various representations were regarded.

In the early sites there are other kinds of modeled objects that have been called figurines, but whose relationship to the more naturalistic ones can hardly be determined at this time. Among these, the T-shaped and stalk "figurines," which in some respects resemble highly stylized humans, are probably quite different in their uses. In any case it is clear that they are not just crude versions of naturalistic figures; indeed, they are anything but crude and are often made with more attention to detail than either the animal or human figures. Especially notable are incisions, belting, and appliqued "hair" and "eyes." In these respects they resemble stylized or abstract human forms. When we were digging at Chagha Sefid and found these in great numbers, I was able to assemble a very convincing "chess set" on the table one evening. The bases of the T-shaped figurines are usually polished, as if they had been slid across a board countless times. The stalks are less commonly polished but they do stand readily. On none of the figures is the upper portion much worn although for the most part the heads or features had been broken off. There is nothing in the contexts in which we found these figures to suggest other than the most mundane uses for them; nearly all were in middens where they had been discarded. Assuming that they were used in a game, it is curious that they disappear along with the animals; one would hardly expect a game to die out.

The tradition of making objects out of clay has a long history of development which may be significant in relationship to games. The earliest forms of figurines are simple squat cones which are reported from several early sites: Suberde (Bordaz, 1970:51), Jarmo (Braidwood and Howe, 1960:44), and Ganj Darreh (Smith, 1970). The age of the pieces in Jarmo is not stated, but the other two sites are 9th-10th millenium and both show evidence for herding of goats. A head of a stalk figurine was found at Karim Shahir (Braidwood and Howe, 1960: Fig. 23, No. 8), a probable 8th millenium site. The apparent absence of figurines at Zawi Chemi is a striking exception to the general pattern.

Most material reported from early sites consists of tools for agriculture or implements for cooking and eating. Rarely do we find things that may inform on the less tangible aspects of life or of beliefs. Figurines may be in this category but they will not be of much value until we can get some accurate descriptions of the contexts in which they occur, preferably when they are found in situ rather than in middens.

Ornaments

Changing fashions in ornamentation are well attested in southwest Asia from Natufian and probable contemporary sites such as Shanidar B1 through the early villages. As a general rule, the earlier burials are more likely to have ornamentation than are the later ones. It seems to be in almost all sites where burials have been reported that some are more elaborately decorated than others. In earlier times there is abundant use of beads and other personal adornment whereas in later sites there is more use of "status" objects such as well-made figurines and other objects of stone and of finely made flint or obsidian tools. It appears that the widespread use of beads for most persons went out of style shortly after the establishment of large village farming communities. This is particularly striking in Deh Luran where we found most of the burials in Ali Kosh outfitted with beaded skirts, bead necklaces and in some cases with labrets. At Chagha Sefid, by contrast, beads are relatively rare and none was associated with a burial. The two burials at Tepe Sabz had only grinding stones in association. Still, the occurrence of labrets, bracelets, and rings in the site suggests that some personal adornment continued in fashion long after the use of beads went out of style. Labrets are reported at most sites well into the Susiana sequence but they seem to be most common at sites in the Zagros and the lower Mesopotamian plain. In northern Mesopotamia, further elaboration of beads and "amulets" seems to have been the style.

The miscellaneous artifacts from the early villages inform on matters of technology (hunting, butchering, food collecting and processing), of chronology when we can discern changes in types or styles of artifacts, of trade or exchange when we can identify material of "foreign" origin, and of differences among contemporary peoples at different sites. What still escapes us is the significance of the non-utilitarian objects, even though they are readily identifiable and can be placed into traditional categories. The various kinds of figurines are a case in point. Also elusive is the significance of changes and differences in personal ornamentation as we find it on burials as well as scattered throughout the sites.

GRINDING AND POUNDING TOOLS

For the most part the grinding stones and fragments were found incorporated into wall foundations; consequently in zones with substantial architectural remains there are more of these implements. These stones were never found in situ on house floors or work areas, suggesting that when they were discarded they were put to other uses. The proportions of different types of grinding stones are thus not very revealing; what is significant is the types represented.

By far the greatest number of metates are of the type we call saddle-shaped, a relatively flat-surfaced stone for the milling of grain. In our previous work we reported that grinding stones are as characteristic of phases as are ceramics and other artifacts. To the distributional lists given before (Hole, Flannery and Neely, 1969:Table 30) we can add additional types (Table 52). Trough metates, a type similar to the shallow basins found at Ali Kosh, are found in the Sefid Phase at Chagha Sefid. The distribution of this form of grinding stone thus includes the Ali Kosh, Mohammad Jaffar and Sefid phases. Types which ended before the Sabz Phase can now be shown to have a distribution in the Sefid and Surkh phases. These include pebble mortars, small slab abraders, combination pestles and rolling handstones, and stubby bell-shaped mullers. Notably lacking at Chagha Sefid are combination shallow basin and mortar types although they occur both at Ali Kosh and at Chagha Sefid.

Grinding Slabs and Mortars

TYPE: Flat-topped Boulder Grinding Slab

Sample: 1
Material: Limestone

Description: These are river boulders which, in their natural state, had at least one relatively flat surface; that surface has been further flattened and smoothed by grinding. A feature which distinguishes them from other grinding slab types is the fact that the grinding surface is never basin-shaped or saddle-shaped in cross-section, no matter which direction it is viewed from. Examples vary from 25 to 45 cm in length.
Temporal distribution: Ali Kosh Phase.
Geographic distribution: A search of the archeological literature reveals no illustrated specimens of what we call "flat-topped boulder grinding slabs." We feel relatively confident that such must have existed at sites contemporary with Ali Kosh; it is possible that they have simply not been illustrated or even, perhaps, not recognized as tools. Ali Kosh, Tepe Sabz (Hole, Flannery and Neely, 1969:171).

TYPE: Saddle-Shaped Grinding Slab
(Figs. 80, 81a,b,d; Pl. 45a,b,e)

Sample: 248, mostly broken
Material: Limestone
Description: These are slabs or boulders of limestone which have been ground until their upper surface presents a concave appearance. Most are about twice as long as they are wide, and such is the pattern of grinding that only the two ends of the long axis present unground "ridges" preserving the original surface of the rock. There are no ridges along the sides of the long axis, for the associated handstone (frequently our "simple discoidal" type) has been ground over these areas also. This lack of lateral ridges, besides giving the slab its "saddle-shaped" appearance, distinguishes it from our "shallow basin" type, which is completely enclosed by ridges. A few specimens were partially coated with asphalt, and many are stained with red ochre. They vary from 30 to 50 cm in length.
Temporal distribution: Throughout the sequence.
Geographic distribution: Ali Kosh, Tepe Sabz (Hole, Flannery and Neely, 1969:171); Jaffarabad (Dollfus, 1971:Fig. 28:7, 9, 12); Jarmo (Braidwood, 1951: Fig. 11, lower right; Braidwood, 1952:Fig. 14; and possibly also the fragmentary specimen shown in Braidwood, Howe, et al. 1960:Plate 20, No. 6); Hassuna (Braidwood, 1952:Fig. 6); and many other, later sites.

TYPE: Trough Metate (Fig. 81c; Pl. 45c)

Sample: 3
Material: Limestone
Description: Essentially the same size and shape as saddle-shaped grinding slabs, these pieces are deeply worn along the central axis, leaving ridges along the sides. The handstones used with these implements must have been smaller than those usually employed on the saddle-shaped variety.
Temporal distribution: Sefid Phase.
Geographic distribution: Guran (Mortensen and Flannery, 1966:Figs. 9, 10).

TYPE: Boulder Mortar (Figs. 82a,c-e, 83a-d Pl. 45g,h)

Sample: 18
Material: Limestone
Description: These are river boulders which are unmodified except for one, or sometimes two, deep, well-defined sockets which apparently served as mortars. Many seem to have been selected for their weight and stability rather than conformation. Examples vary from 20 to 40 cm in diameter, and from tall to relatively flat.
Temporal distribution: Surkh and Choga Mami Transitional phases.
Geographic distribution: Ali Kosh, Tepe Sabz (Hole, Flannery and Neely, 1969:176); similar boulder mortars occurred at Jarmo (Braidwood,1951:Fig. 11, upper left).

TYPE: Pebble Mortars (Fig. 84a-c, Pl. 46j,p-r)

Sample: 20
Material: Limestone or gypsum
Description: These tiny mortars are only 5 to 10 cm in diameter, and consist of smooth river bed stones, each bearing a socket with evidence of grinding. Some examples contained red ochre, and it is not unreasonable to suppose that most may have been used for grinding pigment.
Temporal distribution: Ali Kosh through Choga Mami Transitional phases.
Geographic distribution: Ali Kosh (Hole, Flannery and Neely, 1969:176); Guran (Mortensen and Flannery, 1966:Fig. 10); Jarmo (Braidwood, 1951:Fig. 11,

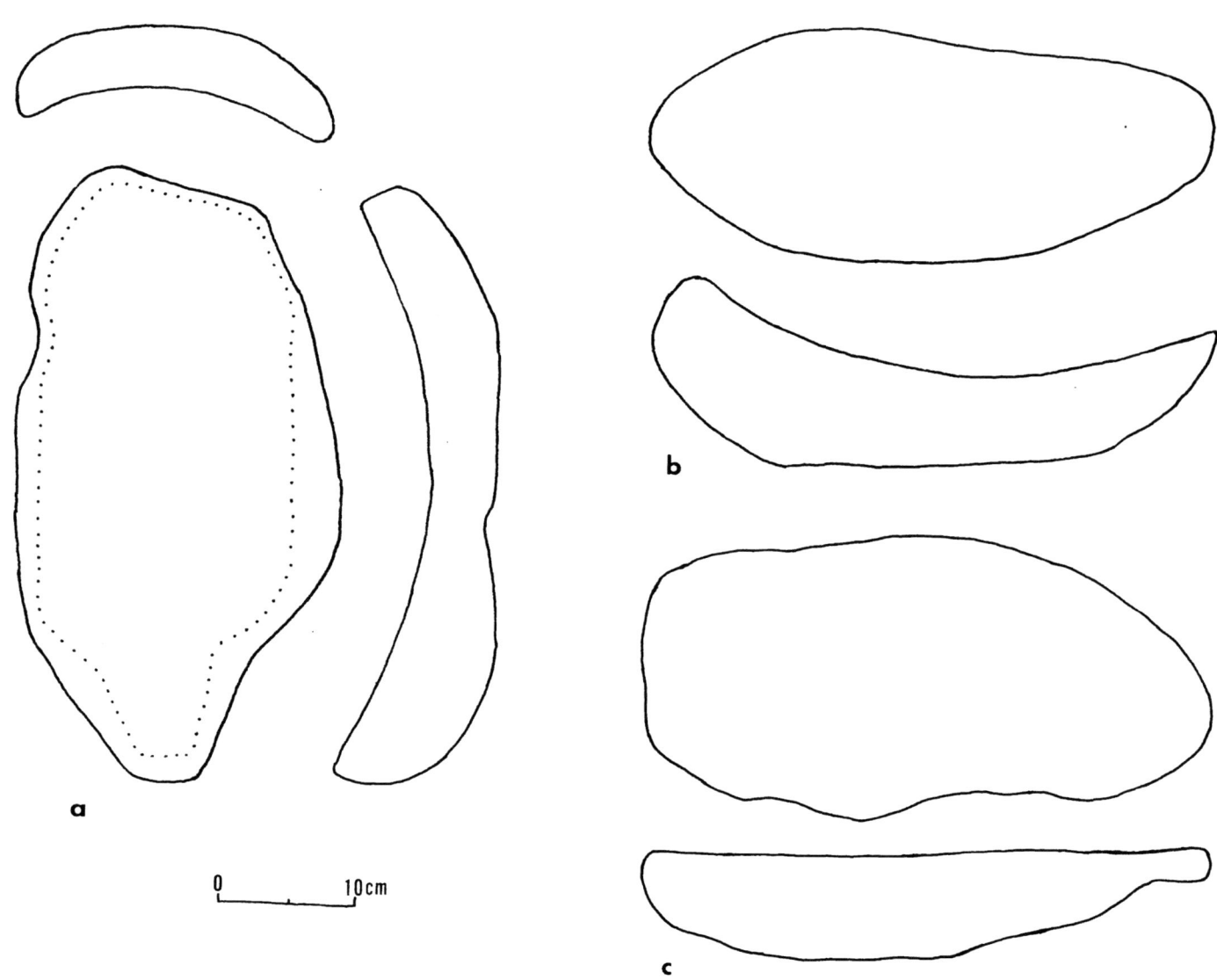

Fig. 80. Grinding tools from Chagha Sefid. *a-c*, saddle-shaped grinding slabs.

lower center; Braidwood, Howe, et al. 1960:Plate 20, No. 3).

TYPE: Bowl Mortars (Fig. 84*d,e*, Pl. 46*e,i*)

Sample: 4
Material: Limestone
Description: These implements, possibly a larger variety of pebble mortars, stand up to 12 cm high and have diameters up to 11 cm with central mortar cups as deep at 6 cm. In contrast with the pebble mortars, tar has been spilled into the holes, although this may have been quite accidental.
Temporal distribution: Ali Kosh through Choga Mami Transitional phases.
Geographic distribution: Unknown.

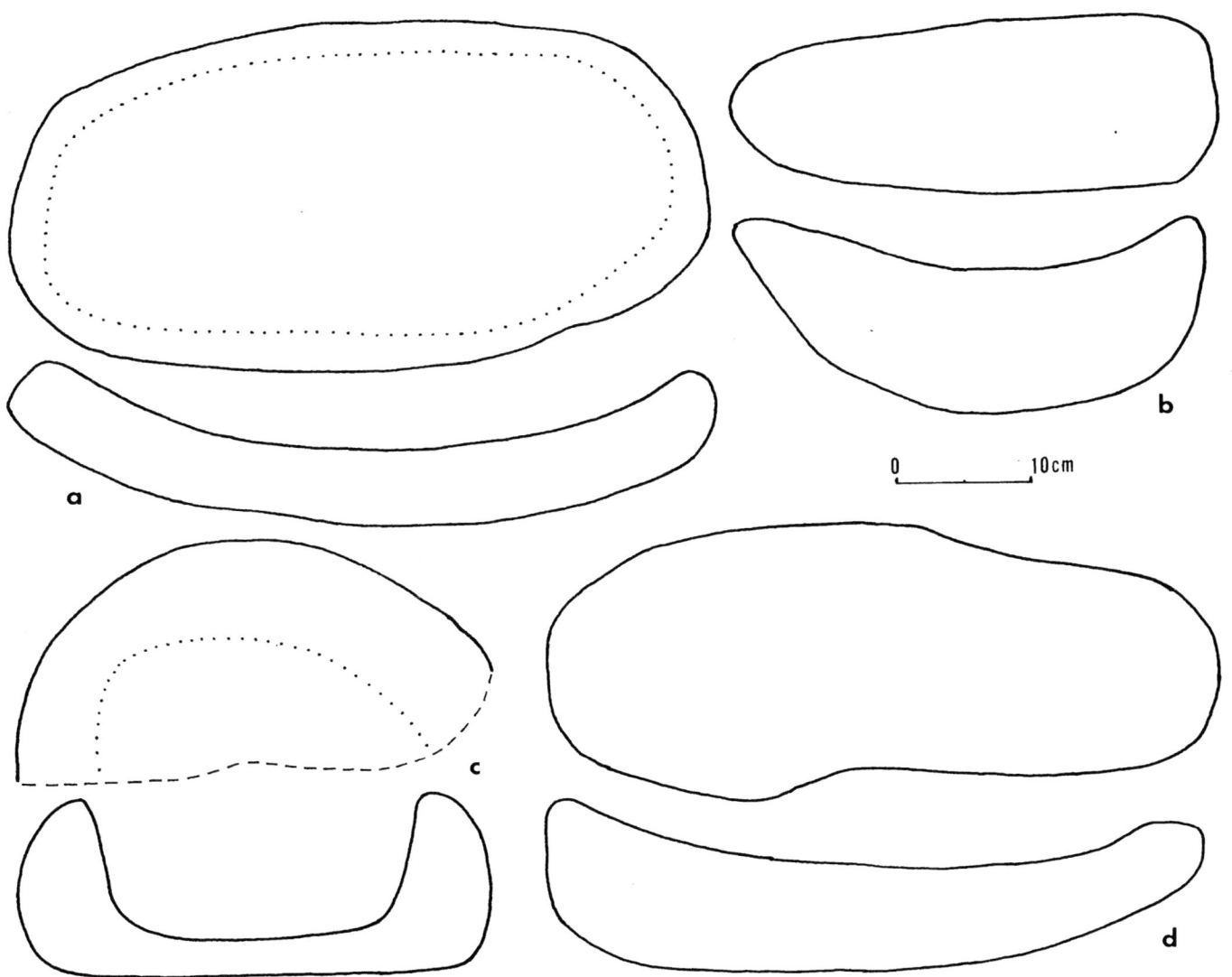

Fig. 81. Grinding tools from Chagha Sefid. *a,b,d,* saddle-shaped grinding slabs; *c,* trough metate.

Handstones

TYPE: Simple Discoidal Handstone
(Fig. 85*c,e,f,h,j,k;* Pl. 46*c,d,f-h*)

Sample: 16
Material: Limestone
Description: As the name implies, these are symmetrical, disc-shaped cobbles which were used as handstones for the grinding slabs already described. They have a lens-shaped cross-section, and no pronounced facets. These handstones range from 15 to 18 cm in diameter and are no more than 1 cm longer than wide. For the most part these stones are wider than the saddle-shaped slabs with which they were used—a fact which helps explain the lack of unground lateral ridges on the latter. In most cases, these handstones are harder and more fine-grained than the slabs on which they were used.
Temporal distribution: Surkh Phase.
Geographic distribution: Throughout Mesopotamia and the Zagros.

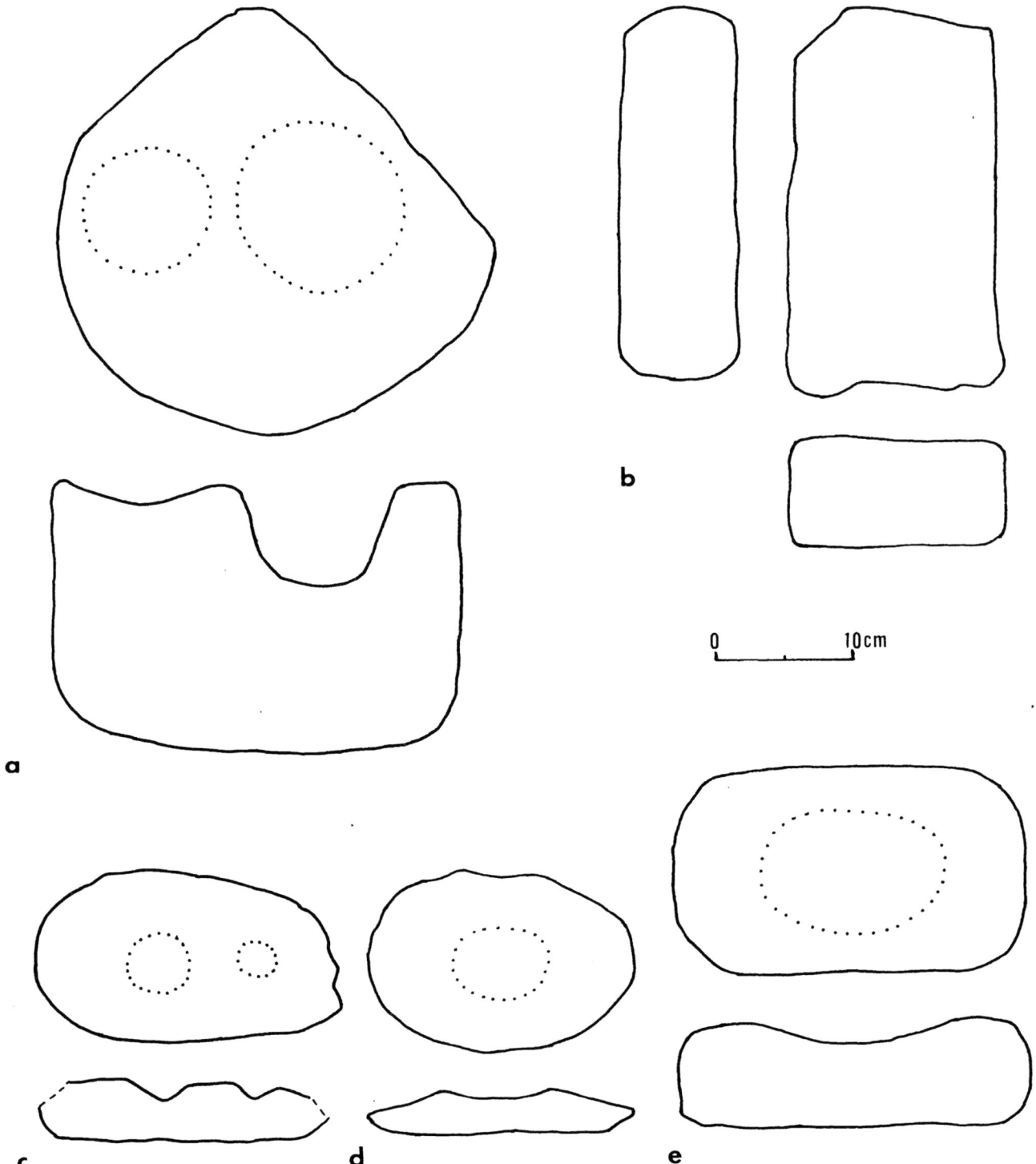

Fig. 82. Grinding tools from Chagha Sefid. *a*, boulder mortar; *c,d,e*, low boulder mortars; *b*, shaped and polished stone of uncertain use.

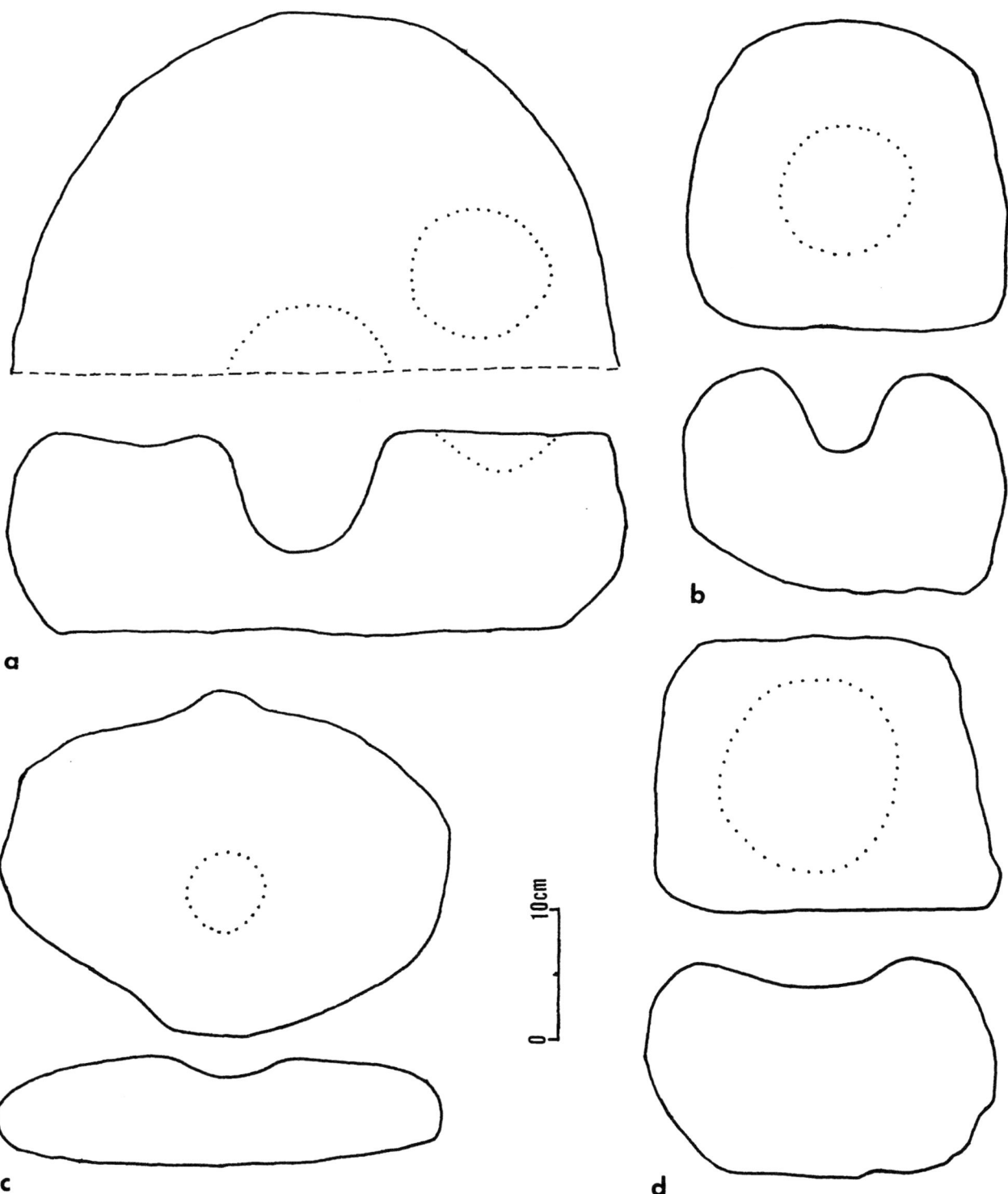

Fig. 83. Grinding tools from Chagha Sefid. *a,b,d*, boulder mortars; *c*, low boulder mortar.

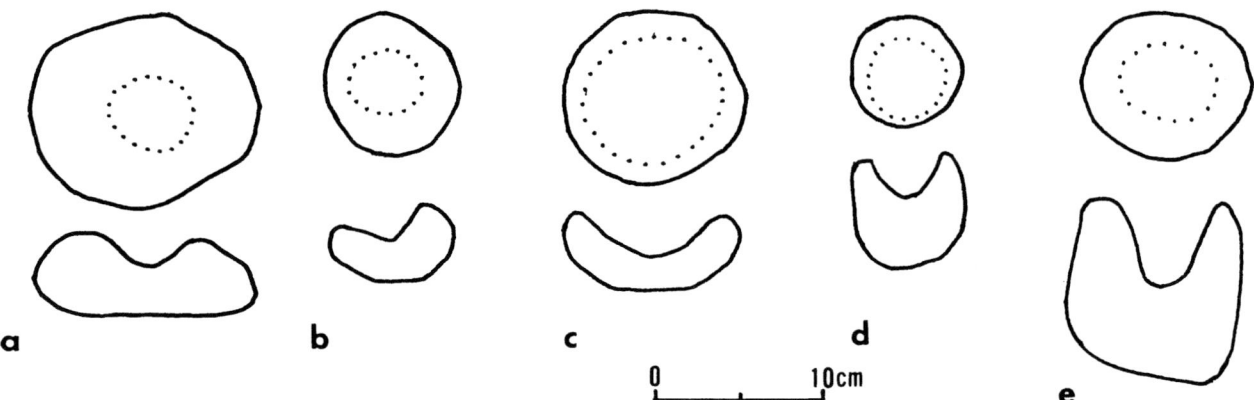

Fig. 84. Mortars from Chagha Sefid. *a-c,* pebble mortars; *d,e,* bowl mortars.

TYPE: Loaf-Shaped (Faceted) Handstone
(Fig. 85*a,b,d,g,i*; Pl. 45*f* 46*a,b*)

Sample: 134
Material: 133 limestone, 1 sandstone
Description: These handstones are plano-convex, resembling loaves of bread. The upper or convex surface is rarely used, while the undersurface displays a very worn, level facet. Evidently these stones were rubbed back and forth over the grinding surface without ever being rolled or having their position shifted. The type of grinding slab with which they were used is unknown. Some of the larger examples may well be considered small metates. The average dimensions for these fairly uniform implements are given in the accompanying table.

Average Dimensions

Phase	Number	Length	Width	Thickness
Choga Mami Transitional	8	17.5	14.0	4.7
Surkh	60	20.1	14.6	5.0
Sefid	1	25	13	3.5

(Measurable examples only)

Temporal distribution: Throughout the sequence.
Geographic distribution: Ali Kosh, Tepe Sabz (Hole, Flannery and Neely, 1969:182-184).

TYPE: Small Slab Abrader

Sample: 6
Material: Limestone
Description: Flat pieces of stone which show signs of abrasion. Some have traces of ochre on their surfaces and minor battering on their edges.
Temporal distribution: Sefid and Surkh phases.
Geographic distribution: Ali Kosh (Hole, Flannery and Neely, 1969:184).

Pestles

TYPE: Combination Conical or Cylindrical
Pestle and Rolling Handstone (Pl. 46*m,n*)

Sample: 2
Material: Limestone
Description: One (Sefid Phase) is a limestone cone 6 cm in diameter at the widest part, with definitely tapered ends which show pounding and grinding through use as a pestle. In addition, the sides of the implement show grinding all the way to the untapered end, which suggests that it was also used as a "rolling" handstone; that is it was rotated as it moved over the surface of the grinding slab so that no facets developed.

The cylindrical pestle-handstone (Sefid Phase) is 6 cm in diameter. One end shows pounding and

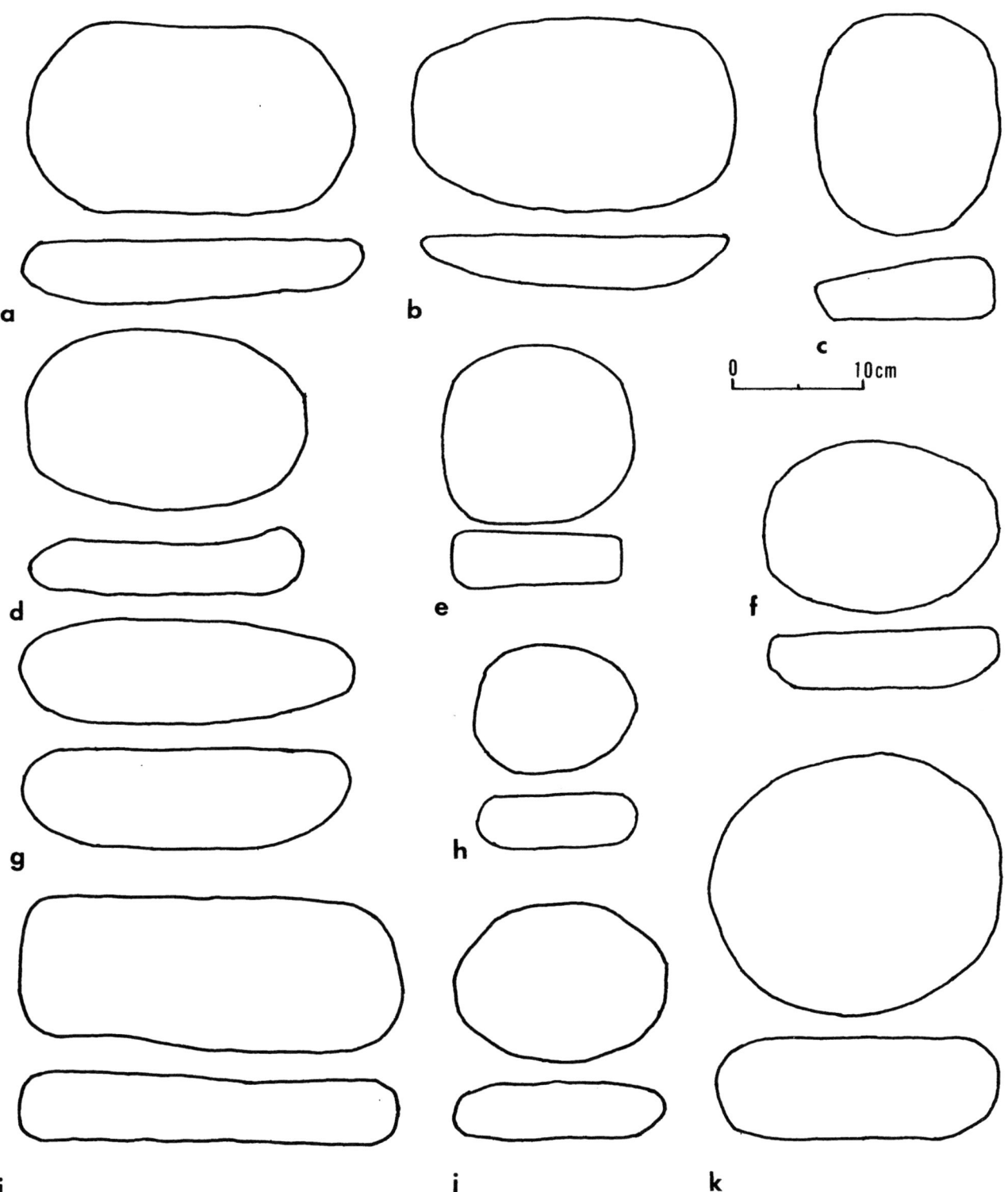

Fig. 85. Grinding tools from Chagha Sefid. *a,b,d,g,i,* loaf-shaped handstones; *b,c,e,f,h,j,k,* simple discoidal handstones.

grinding through use as a pestle. These pestles fit easily into the sockets of most of the mortars.
Temporal distribution: Sefid Phase.
Geographic distribution: Ali Kosh (Hole, Flannery and Neely, 1969:184)

TYPE: Stubby Bell-shaped Muller (Pl. 46*l*)

Sample: 2
Material: Limestone
Description: Short, blunt mullers or pestles 6 to 8 cm in length and 5 to 6 cm in diameter at the maximum, with a gradual widening or "bell-shaped" effect at the end which was used for grinding. These stubby mullers fit comfortably in the palm of the hand.
Temporal distribution: Surkh Phase.
Geographic distribution: Ali Kosh (Hole, Flannery and Neely, 1969:186); Jaffarabad (Dollfus, 1971:Fig. 28:5).

TYPE: Irregular Sausage-shaped Pestle (Pl. 46*o,bb*)

Sample: 33
Material: Limestone
Description: Sausage-shaped cobbles 11 to 20 cm long and about half that in diameter, whose ends show pounding and grinding from use as pestles. There is no evidence that they were ever used as handstones.
Temporal distribution: Ali Kosh through Choga Mami Transitional phases
Geographic distribution: Ali Kosh, Tepe Sabz (Hole, Flannery and Neely, 1969:186); Jaffarabad (Dollfus, 1971:Fig. 28:6).

Pounders

TYPE: Spherical Pounder or Hammerstone
(Pl. 46*y*, 47*a,b,d*)

Sample: 129
Material: Quartz or flint
Description: Stones averaging 6 cm in diameter, battered into a spherical shape by heavy-duty pounding over all or most of the surfaces.
Temporal distribution: Throughout the sequence.
Geographic distribution: Ali Kosh, Tepe Sabz (Hole, Flannery and Neely, 1969:186).

TYPE: Core Pounder (Pl. 46*aa*)

Sample: 30
Material: Flint
Description: Chunky pieces of flint which began as cores and were later used as pounders. The edges of the platforms and distal ends are battered, and in some cases the piece is nearly round in shape as a result of the pounding. The use of blade cores for this purpose is rare. All examples still have traces of scars from the removal of flakes or blades.
Temporal distribution: Sefid, Surkh and Choga Mami Transitional phases.
Geographic distribution: Ali Kosh, Tepe Sabz (Hole, Flannery and Neely, 1969:186).

TYPE: Cuboid Pounder/Rubbing Stone (Pl. 46*s,t,u,z*)

Sample: 6
Material: Limestone
Description: These are small irregular pebbles which (a) have been battered into a roughly cuboid shape by use as a pounder, and (b) bear several flat facets which indicate their use as grinding or rubbing stones (or abraders) as well. Some have traces of ochre on their surfaces.
Temporal distribution: Sefid through Surkh phases.
Geographic distribution: Ali Kosh, Tepe Sabz (Hole, Flannery and Neely, 1969:186-187).

TYPE: Basalt Pebble Pounders (Pl. 46*v,w,cc,dd*)

Sample: 25
Description: Basalt pebbles of irregular shape ranging from 4 to 10 cm in length which show signs of pounding.
Temporal distribution: Sefid through Choga Mami Transitional phases
Geographic distribution: Unknown.

MISCELLANEOUS STONE ARTIFACTS

Miscellaneous stone artifacts include some that are clearly utilitarian and some whose use is uncertain. Some of the objects are represented by only one example but most of the types were found previously in the excavations at Ali Kosh and Tepe Sabz (Table 57). The most striking difference at Chagha Sefid is

Table 53

GRINDING SLAB TYPES (WHOLE AND FRAGMENTARY) AT CHAGHA SEFID by Stratigraphic Zone

Phase	Area	Zone	Flat-topped Boulder	Saddle-shaped Slab	Trough Metate	Pebble Mortar	Boulder Mortar	Bowl Mortar	Totals
Sabz	SD	J							
	SD	I							
Choga Mami Transitional	SD	H					1		1
	SD	G2		2					2
	SD	G1		4		4	3		11
Surkh	SD	F		3		1			4
	SC, SD	E2		2		1		1	4
	SC, SD	E1		3	1	6	2	1	13
	SC	D3		1		2			3
	SC	D2		1		2	1		4
	SC	D1		1			3		4
	SC	C2							
Sefid	SA	C1		196	2	3	9		210
	SA	B2		29					29
	SA	B1							
	SA	A4		1					1
Mohammad Jaffar	SB	C							
	SB	B							
	SB	A							
Ali Kosh	SA	A3	1	3			1		5
	SA	A2		1		1			2
	SA	A1		1					1
		Totals	1	248	3	20	18	4	294

the lack of flint pebble choppers which were abundant on house floors at Ali Kosh. The fact that so few were found at Chagha Sefid probably reflects the fact that we did not excavate a house of Mohammad Jaffar age and that these implements went out of common use in the later phases. On the other hand, chipped hoes, which were rare at Ali Kosh, were abundant at Chagha Sefid. This is a type that appears to precede the polished celts or hoes that begin in the Sabz Phase. It appears that hoe agriculture was well developed by the Surkh Phase. Another type, cut pebbles which are probably the functional equivalent of slicing slabs, first appears in the Sefid Phase at the time slicing slabs are going out of use. Thus we see continuity and change in the miscellaneous stone tools as another example of the transitional nature of the Chagha Sefid phases.

TYPE: Flint Pebble Choppers (Pl. 49a-d)

Sample: 7
Description: These are pebbles or cobbles broken across one end and then chipped with two or three blows from one direction, so that a sharp edge at an angle of 60 degrees to the long axis of the pebble is produced. Most are 7 to 15 cm in their longest dimension. The cutting edge is typically between 6 and 10 cm in breadth.
Temporal distribution: Sporadically in the Mohammad Jaffar and Surkh Phases (cf. Ali Kosh where they were found in clusters).
Geographic distribution: Ali Kosh (Hole, Flannery and Neely, 1969:189).

TYPE: Chipped-Stone Hoes (Pl. 49e-j)

Sample: 36
Material: Flint and limestone
Description: Large flakes struck from cobbles and rudely chipped into T-shaped or pear-shaped hoe blades (a few are more slender), whose bits are usually convex but not polished. The outer edge of the cobble usually forms one face of the blade, and the predominantly unifacial chipping is directed from the bulbar face. The length ranges from 9 to 13 cm, the width of the shaft from 3 to 6 cm, and the bit width from 4 to 14 cm. In some instances, traces of asphalt remain on the shaft as evidence of hafting.
Temporal distribution: Sefid through Sabz phases.
Geographic distribution: Ali Kosh, Tepe Sabz (Hole, Flannery and Neely, 1969:189); Jaffarabad (Dollfus, 1971:Fig. 26); throughout Susiana (Le Breton, 1947: Fig. 17,1-3), Mesopotamia (see Stronach, 1961:105 for summary), and immediately adjacent areas from at least Hassunan times through the Ubaid.

TYPE: Polished Celt (Pl. 50c)

Sample: 1
Material: Fine-grained basalt

Description: A small celt, unlike the implements previously found in Deh Luran (Hole, Flannery and Neely, 1969:189-190). The bit is ground on all surfaces with squared edges and a slightly curved cutting edge. The butt end is not finished and may be broken. Maximum width is 1.7 cm while the overall length is 2.26 cm and the thickness at the butt is .92 cm.
Temporal distribution: Surkh Phase.
Geographic distribution: Jaffarabad (Dollfus, 1971: Fig. 27:19); similar to celts found in the Jarmo period of the Zagros Mountains (Braidwood, Howe, et al., 1960:45).

TYPE: "Sashweight" Stirring Rods or
Asphalt Pounders (Pl. 50a,b)

Sample: 65
Material: Elongate limestone pebbles
Description: These rods are elongate, and rectangular in section like window sashweights, from whence their name is derived. Often the ends are split, broken, and reddened from heat, and smeared with asphalt. The asphalt is usually confined to the ends, as if the implements had been used to pound it, or to stir boiling asphalt as it was being prepared for use as a mastic. These objects range in length from 14 to 25 cm.
Temporal distribution: Throughout the sequence.
Geographic distribution: Ali Kosh, Tepe Sabz (Hole, Flannery and Neely, 1969:192).

TYPE: Slicing Slabs (Pl. 50c-h,k)

Sample: 10
Material: Elongate limestone pebbles
Description: Thin, elongate pebbles whose surfaces, and especially ends, are scarred with cut marks. Frequently the ends are considerably thinned as a result of the repeated cutting. (In some cases sashweight stirring rods were similarly scarred by cutting on their sides.) Lengths are generally in the 10 to 12 cm range.

We suspect that these stones were slipped under sinews to provide a surface against which to cut with a flint knife. It is also possible that these were used as "sharpening" blocks for blade tools which were becoming hard to use because of adherent meat tissues.
Temporal distribution: Throughout the sequence.
Geographic distribution: Ali Kosh, Tepe Sabz (Hole, Flannery and Neely, 1969:192-196).

TYPE: Cut Pebbles (Pl. 50m-o,s)

Sample: 10
Material: Flat, fine-grained limestone pebbles
Description: Waterworn flat pebbles whose surfaces are polished and show many cut marks similar to those found on the slicing slabs with which are probably a functional equivalent. The ends of the pebbles sometimes show signs of pounding.
Temporal distribution: Sefid and Surkh phases.
Geographic distribution: Unknown.

TYPE: Small Ground-stone Chisel (Pl. 50j)

Sample: 1
Material: Fine-grained limestone
Description: The tip of a chisel, convex in cross-section, which is bevelled to a sharp edge. The specimen is 11 mm wide and 26 mm thick.

Table 54

GRINDING SLAB TYPES (WHOLE AND FRAGMENTARY)
AT CHAGHA SEFID
by Cultural Phase

Phase	Flat-topped Boulder	Saddle-shaped Slab	Trough Metate	Pebble Mortar	Boulder Mortar	Bowl Mortar	Totals
Sabz							
Choga Mami Transitional		6		4	3	1	14
Surkh		11	1	12	6	2	32
Sefid		226	2	3	9		240
Mohammad Jaffar							
Ali Kosh	1	5		1		1	8
Totals	1	248	3	20	18	4	294

Table 55
HANDSTONES, PESTLES AND POUNDERS AT CHAGHA SEFID
by Stratigraphic Zone

Phase	Area	Zone	Simple Discoidal Handstones	Loaf-shaped Handstones	Small Slab Abraders	Combination Pestles and Handstones	Stubby Bell-shaped Mullers	Irregular Sausage-shaped Pestles	Spherical Pounders	Core Pounders	Cuboid Pounders-Rubbing Stones	Basalt Pebbles	Totals
Sabz	SD	J											
	SD	I		1									1
Choga Mami Transitional	SD	H											
	SD	G2							1	4		1	6
	SD	G1		12				3	16	1		2	34
Surkh	SD	F		1			1	3	3	3	1	4	16
	SC, SD	E2	1	8					1	6		1	17
	SC, SD	E1	6	39			1	8	17	3		1	75
	SC	D3	5	3					10		1		20
	SC	D2	4	3	2			1	10	5	1	1	27
	SC	D1		2					3	1		2	8
	SC	C2							4	1			5
Sefid	SA	C1		51	1			7	28	2	1	2	92
	SA	B2		11	3			7	20	2	1	6	50
	SA	B1				1			4	2	1	5	13
	SA	A4				1			3				4
Mohammad Jaffar	SB	C											
	SB	B											
	SB	A		1									1
Ali Kosh	SA	A3		1				1	7				9
	SA	A2		1				1	2				4
	SA	A1						1					1
Totals			16	134	6	2	2	33	129	30	6	25	383

Temporal distribution: Sefid Phase.
Geographic distribution: Ali Kosh (Hole, Flannery and Neely, 1961:192).

TYPE: Grooved Rubbing Stones (Pl. 50*p-r*, Fig. 86*i*)

Sample: 4
Material: 2 limestone, 1 sandstone, 1 "brick"
Description: Pebbles or tablets of stone varying from 4 to 7 cm in diameter, each of which bears on its upper surface a centrally placed groove some 3 to 5 mm deep. These grooves may be U-shaped or V-shaped in cross-section, and give evidence of having been used for abrading; one limestone example has a groove which shows high polish. The brick is hard-fired clay with a striated groove.

Comment: These stones have frequently been called "shaft-smoothers" or "arrowshaft straighteners," but obviously those whose groove is V-shaped in cross-section cannot have been used for that purpose. In the Mohammad Jaffar Phase, two such "V-shaped" specimens were found in association with two small stone chisels in a way that suggested they had been used to sharpen the bits of the latter. Other speci-

Table 56

HANDSTONES, PESTLES AND POUNDERS AT CHAGHA SEFID
by Cultural Phase

Phase	Simple Discoidal Handstones	Leaf-shaped Handstones	Small Slab Abraders	Combination Pestles and Rolling Handstones	Stubby Bell-shaped Mullers	Irregular Sausage-shaped Pestles	Spherical Pounders	Core Pounders	Cuboid Pounders-Rubbing Stones	Basalt Pebbles	Totals
Sabz		1									1
Choga Mami Transitional		12				3	17	5		3	40
Surkh	16	56	2		2	13	48	19	3	9	168
Sefid		62	4	2		14	55	6	3	13	159
Mohammad Jaffar		1									1
Ali Kosh		2				3	9				14
Totals	16	134	6	2	2	33	129	30	6	25	383

mens may have been used to sharpen bone or wooden awls, for example.
Temporal distribution: Sefid and Surkh phases.
Geographic distribution: Ali Kosh, Tepe Sabz (Hole, Flannery and Neely, 1969:196); similar grooved rubbing stones are widely distributed in Kurdistan and Luristan, occurring at Jarmo (Braidwood, Howe, et al. 1965:45); Zawi Chemi Shanidar (Solecki, 1963: Fig. 7d,e); Tepe Asiab (Braidwood, 1960:Fig. 4); Tepe Guran (Mortensen, personal communication); and Zarzi Cave (Garrod, 1930:Fig. 11).

TYPE: Small, faceted Rubbing stones (Pl. 46k, 50i,l)

Sample: 16
Material: Limestone pebbles
Description: Twelve pebbles less than 6 cm in maximum diameter, which have facets on one or more faces, probably as a result of rubbing on a palette. Four examples are pencil-like stone rods with facets on their sides.
Temporal distribution: Sefid and Surkh phases.
Geographic distribution: Ali Kosh (Hole, Flannery and Neely, 1969:196).

TYPE: Chipped Limestone Discs (Pl. 47c,e,f)

Sample: 16
Material: Tabular limestone
Description: Flat discs of limestone, bifacially chipped around the periphery to give them a round or oval outline. Diameters range from 6 to 15 cm.
Temporal distribution: Sefid Phase.
Geographic distribution: Ali Kosh (Hole, Flannery and Neely, 1969:196); widespread, occurring at such distant sites as Çayönü in Turkey (Braidwood, personal communication), Zawi Chemi Shanidar in Iraq (Rose Solecki, personal communication), and prehistoric sites near Seistan on the Indo-Iranian border (Fairservis, 1961:Fig. 3e,f). They are also present at Tepe Guran (Mortensen, personal communication).

TYPE: Perforated Stones (Pl. 47g,m)

Sample: 4

Table 57
SELECTED MISCELLANEOUS STONE ARTIFACTS AT ALI KOSH, CHAGHA SEFID AND TEPE SABZ
by Cultural Phase

Site	Phase	Flint Pebble Choppers	Chipped Stone Hoes	Polished Celts	"Sashweight" Stirring Rods	Slicing Slabs	Ground Stone Chisels	Grooved Rubbing Stones	Small, Faceted Rubbing Stones	Chipped Limestone Discs	Perforated Stones	Limestone Cleavers	Pecked Stone Balls
TS	Bayat		1	8	1						5		1
TS	Mehmeh	2		38	5			1			15		6
TS	Khazineh			8	6			1			1		
TS	Sabz	2	1	21	4						5		
CS	Sabz		1			2							1
CS	Choga Mami Transitional			11	3	1							1
CS	Surkh	5	13	1	7	1		2	8		4	1	8
CS	Sefid	2	11		54	5	1	2	8	16			22
CS	Mohammad Jaffar												
AK	Mohammad Jaffar	95	1		85	19		4	1	6			26
CS	Ali Kosh				1	3							3
AK	Ali Kosh	59	1		58	26		2	1	14		1	16
AK	Bus Mordeh	1			8	3				1			4

Material: Limestone
Description: Heavy, flat discs of stone with a lens-shaped cross-section which have been perforated in the center by drilling through from both sides.
Temporal distribution: Surkh Phase.
Geographic distribution: Tepe Sabz (Hole, Flannery and Neely, 1969:196-198); Jaffarabad (Dollfus, 1971:Fig. 27:12-13).

Limestone Cleaver-Rubbing Stone (Pl. 48*a*)

Sample: 1
Material: Limestone
Description: An oblong flat stone object whose handle is broken, showing traces of rubbing or grinding on either side. In addition, there is bifacial chipping around the cutting edge and end producing a cleaver-like cutting edge.
Temporal distribution: Surkh Phase.
Geographic distribution: Ali Kosh (Hole, Flannery and Neely, 1969:198-199).

TYPE: Pecked Stone Balls (Pl. 46*gg,hh*, 47*n-u*)

Sample: 36
Material: Fine-grained limestone
Description: These spherical or nearly spherical balls were carefully pecked from pebbles of irregular shape. Some are highly polished. The average diameter of these artifacts is about 4 cm.

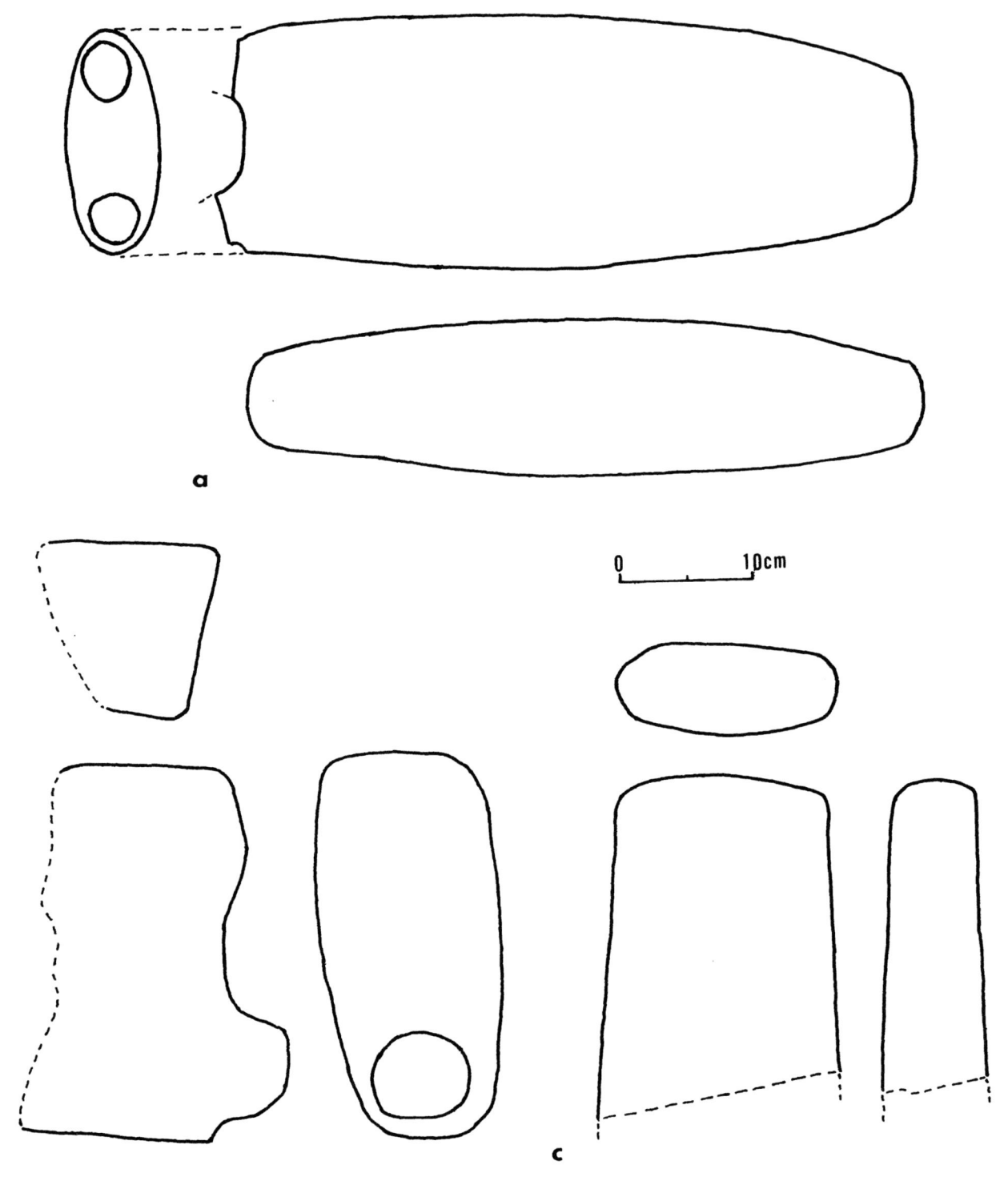

Fig. 86. Shaped and polished stones from Chagha Sefid. *a-c*, (and Fig. 82*b*), all Surkh Phase, found among foundation stones.

Comment: No obvious function can be ascribed to these stones. Possible uses are as gaming pieces, light-duty pounders, weights, or even bolas stones.
Temporal distribution: Throughout the sequence.
Geographic distribution: Ali Kosh, Tepe Sabz (Hole, Flannery and Neely, 1969:200); Jarmo (Braidwood and Howe, et al. 1960:46) and other early village sites in the Zagros Mountains.

TYPE: Sandstone Abraders (Pl. 46x,ee,ff, 48b,c,d)

Sample: 6
Description: Fragments of sandstone that have one or more surfaces ground from various sanding or grinding activities.
Temporal distribution: Sefid through Choga Mami Transitional phases.
Geographic distribution: Unknown.

TYPE: Palette Fragments (Pl. 48e,f)

Sample: 5
Material: 4 limestone, 1 sandstone
Description: Flat polished fragments of larger implements that appear to have been palettes.
Temporal distribution: Sefid and Surkh phases.
Geographic distribution: Unknown.

TYPE: Sandstone Basin (Pl. 48j)

Sample: 1
Description: A fragment of a basin hollowed on both sides that probably broke when the depressions became too deep. One surface is covered with red ochre.
Temporal distribution: Surkh Phase.
Geographic distribution: Unknown.

"GAMING BOARD" (Pl. 48h)

Sample: 1
Description: A gypsum slab with 13 holes or traces of holes arranged in parallel rows. The overall dimensions of the fragment remaining are 17 cm long, 10 cm wide and 5.5 cm thick. The holes are 1 cm in diameter and 1 cm deep.
Temporal distribution: Sefid Phase.
Geographic distribution: This example is similar to objects found at Beidha in DPNB Level II which is dated to about 6500 B.C. (Kirkbride, 1966:34, Fig. 8).

LARGE, SHAPED STONES (Figs. 82b, 86a-c)

Sample: 4, all Surkh Phase
Description: Four stones, evidently shaped with care, but without obvious use, were found among the foundation stones.

Two are from Zone C1 in Area A. The first is a broken, roughly finished but carefully shaped piece of limestone which looks somewhat like a torso (Fig. 86). The body is 30 cm long with a maximum width of 20 cm and a thickness of 3.5 cm. One "arm" stub projects from the unbroken side as a cylinder. This projection may have been socketted into another stone or object; it was, however, not smoothed or worn. The second example is a highly polished and finished piece of limestone which looks as if it had had "legs" or a loop carved at one end (Fig. 86). There now remain only the stumps of the projections. The present dimensions are 52 cm long, 20 cm wide and 13 cm thick. Traces of red ochre covered the other end of the piece.

One piece, also highly polished limestone, is from Zone E1, Area C. This rectangular piece is broken at one end and now measures 27 cm long, 18 cm wide and 8 cm thick (Fig. 86).

The fourth piece, from Zone F in Area D, is a rectangle 30 cm long, 16 cm wide, and 9 cm thick of highly polished limestone. One end is slightly concave from wear and looks as if it had been used as a device over which to draw a rope. The other end is chipped but apparently essentially intact and has patches of red ochre on its surface (Fig. 86).

Since these pieces were found outside their original context and were reused as building material, it can hardly be determined what their use may have been. The high polish and careful workmanship on three examples suggests that they were not originally utilitarian. The fourth example may have been in the process of manufacture when it broke and was discarded.

MISCELLANEOUS POLISHED STONES (Pl. 48g,i,k,l)

Sample: 24

Table 58

MISCELLANEOUS STONE ARTIFACTS
by Stratigraphic Zone

Phase	Area	Zone	Flint Pebble Choppers	Chipped Stone Hoes	Polished Celt	"Sashweight" Stirring Rods	Slicing Slabs	Cut Pebbles	Ground Stone Chisel	Grooved Rubbing Stones	Small, Faceted Rubbing Stones	Chipped Limestone Discs	Perforated Stones	Limestone Cleaver-Rubbing Stone	Pecked Stone Balls	Sandstone Abraders	Palette Fragments	Sandstone Basin	"Gaming Board"	Large, Shaped Stones	Misc. Polished Stones	Totals
Sabz	SD	J																					
	SD	I		1											1							2
Choga Mami Transitional	SD	H				1	1														2	4
	SD	G2		2												1					1	4
	SD	G1		9		2									1						1	13
Surkh	SD	F		3						1	1		1		1	1				1	3	12
	SC, SD	E2		4	1	1							1		2						2	11
	SC, SD	E1		4		1				1	2				3			1		1	1	13
	SC	D3	2	1			1				1				1	1						7
	SC	D2	3			1					3		1	1	1	1	2					13
	SC	D1		1		1							1			1						4
	SC	C2				3		2			1										2	8
Sefid	SA	C1		9		5				2	3	3			9	1	1		1	2	6	42
	SA	B2		2		42	4	7	1		5	12			10	1	1				7	92
	SA	B1				6	1	1							2							10
	SA	A4	2			1						1										4
Mohammad Jaffar	SB	C																				
	SB	B													1							1
	SB	A																				
Ali Kosh	SA	A3													1							1
	SA	A2					1															1
	SA	A1				1	2								2							5
		Totals	7	36	1	65	10	10	1	4	16	16	4	1	35	6	5	1	1	4	24	247

Description: Small pieces of stone that show polish on their surfaces. Some of these pieces were probably being prepared as beads.

MISCELLANEOUS ARTIFACTS

Spindle whorls

The data at Chagha Sefid extend the ranges of types previously discovered at Ali Kosh and Tepe Sabz, but add nothing new in spindle whorls. Although oval-discoidal spindle whorls are not usually found until after the Khazineh Phase, two examples were found in the new phases at Chagha Sefid.

TYPE: Perforated Sherd Discs (Pl. 51*f,g*)

Sample: 57
Material: Khazineh Red sherds

Table 59

MISCELLANEOUS STONE ARTIFACTS
by Cultural Phase

Phase	Flint Pebble Choppers	Chipped-stone Hoes	Polished Celt	"Sashweight" Stirring Rods	Slicing Slabs	Cut Pebbles	Ground Stone Chisel	Grooved Rubbing Stones	Small, Faceted Rubbing Stones	Chipped Limestone Discs	Perforated Stones	Limestone Cleaver-Rubbing Stone	Pecked Stone Balls	Sandstone Abraders	Palette Fragments	Sandstone Basin	"Gaming Board"	Large, Shaped Stones	Misc. Polished Stones	Totals
Sabz		1											1							2
Choga Mami Transitional		11		3	1								1	1					4	21
Surkh	5	13	1	7	1	2		2	8		4	1	8	3	3	1		2	7	68
Sefid	2	11		54	5	8	1	2	8	16			22	2	2		1	2	13	149
Mohammad Jaffar																				
Ali Kosh				1	3								3							7
Totals	7	36	1	65	10	10	1	4	16	16	4	1	35	6	5	1	1	4	24	247

Description: Chipped sherd discs with ground-down edges, each perforated by a single central hole 5-6 mm in diameter, biconically drilled. Most of the discs are slightly concave in cross-section. Diameters range from 2 to 8 cm.
Temporal distribution: Late Sefid through Choga Mami Transitional phases.
Geographic distribution: Ali Kosh, Tepe Sabz (Hole, Flannery and Neely, 1969:205-206).

TYPE: Star-Shaped Spindle Whorl (Fig. 87c,d)

Sample: 1
Material: Susiana Buff
Description: In the shape of a 4-pointed star, it is plano-convex in cross-section. There is no paint on the fragment.
Temporal distribution: Choga Mami Transitional. This may be an intrusive example although such whorls are known from the Sabz Phase and seem to be early in the Susiana sequence.
Geographic distribution: Tepe Sabz (Hole, Flannery and Neely, 1969:206).

TYPE: Oval-Discoidal Spindle Whorls (Fig. 87a)

Sample: 2
Description: Fired ceramic whorls which are discoidal in outline when viewed from above, but oval or lenticular in cross-section. A girdle of incised lines encircles them at the point of their maximum diameter.
Temporal distribution: Late Surkh and Choga Mami Transitional phases.
Geographic distribution: Tepe Sabz (Hole, Flannery and Neely, 1969:206-209); Jaffarabad (Dollfus, 1971:Fig. 21:2,6); these are usually found after the Khazineh Phase.

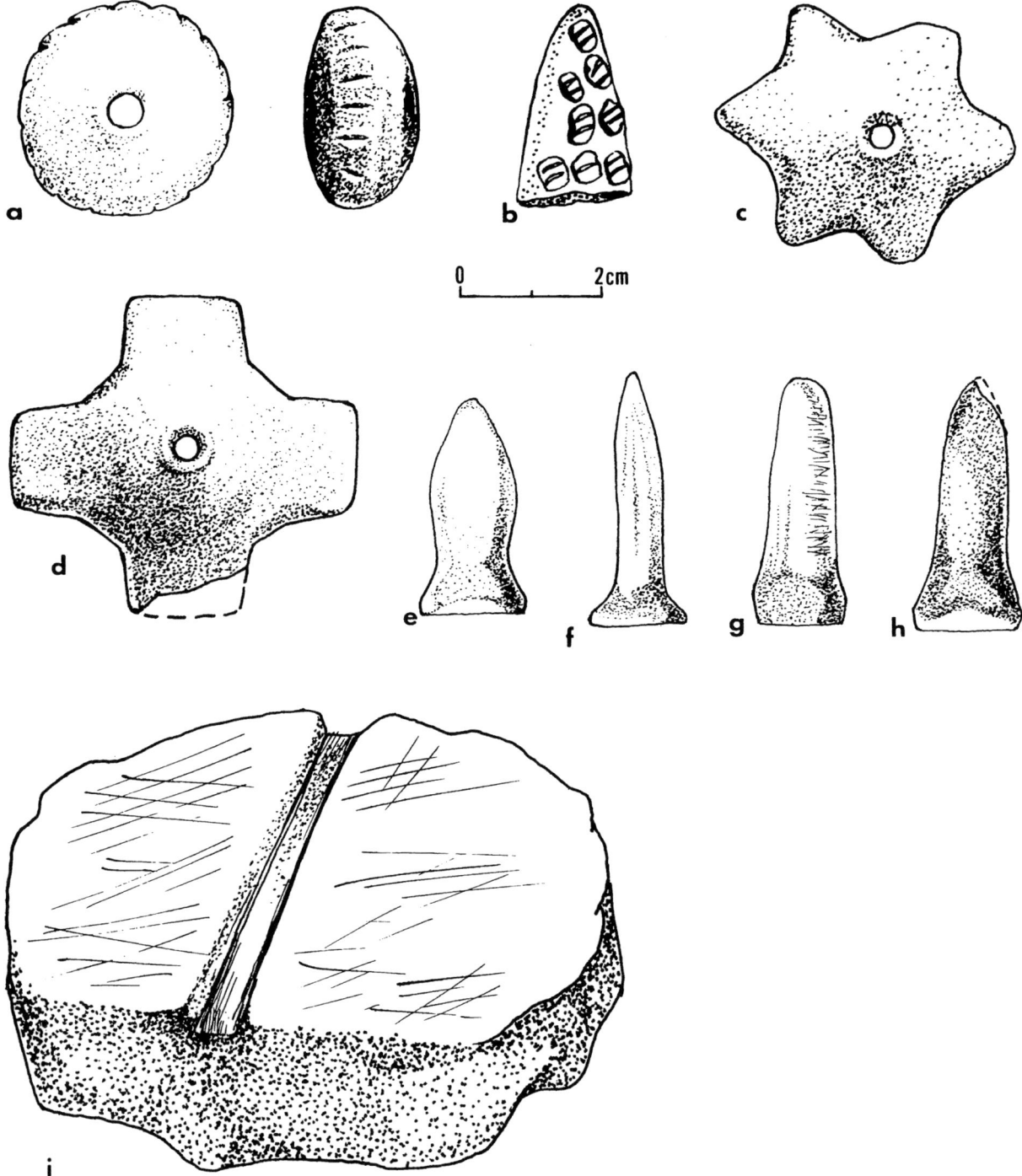

Fig. 87. Miscellaneous ceramic objects. *a*, oval-discoidal spindle whorl (probably intrusive); *b*, appliqued piece; *c,d*, star-shaped spindle whorls (intrusive); *e-h*, clay and stone mullers; *i*, baked ceramic grooved rubbing "stone."

Other Ceramic Artifacts

CHIPPED SHERDS

Sample: 22
Description: Fourteen are roughly chipped into a discoidal form, perhaps as the initial preparation for sherd disc whorls; the others have been ground along the edges, suggesting that they were used as scrapers.
Temporal distribution: Sefid and Surkh phases. This extends the distribution back in time. Previously chipped sherds occurred only in the Sabz and later phases.
Geographic distribution: Tepe Sabz (Hole, Flannery and Neely, 1969:210-212).

Asphalt Artifacts

ASPHALT BALLS (Pl. 52e,f,i,k,p)

Sample: 37
Description: Roughly ball-shaped lumps of asphalt, some of which were formed around stones.
Temporal distribution: Ali Kosh through Choga Mami Transitional phases.
Geographic distribution: Unknown.

ASPHALT HANDLE (Pl. 52n)

Sample: 1, Late Surkh Phase
Description: A cylindrical piece of asphalt about 5 cm long into which a reed(?) with a diameter of 1.2 cm was inserted.

ASPHALT PESTLE? (Pl. 52m)

Sample: 1, Late Surkh Phase
Description: A roughly rectangular piece of asphalt 9.4 cm long, 5.7 cm wide and 3.3 cm thick, with a hole in one end about 2 cm deep and 2x1 cm wide at the opening. The other end of the object is coated with red ochre.

ASPHALT "BASE" (Pl. 52j)

Sample: 1, Sabz Phase
Description: Like similar clay objects at Ali Kosh (Hole, Flannery and Neely 1969:230) this piece resembles a miniature flag staff. The bottom is roughly round and concave. A cone-shaped stick hole penetrates to about 1.5 cm.

BONE ARTIFACTS

Two hundred twenty-five pieces of worked bone, most of them from the Sefid Phase were found at Chagha Sefid. Of these the most abundant were bone awls made from splinters of ungulate long bone. Most of the remainder are unidentifiable fragments of worked or polished bone. Otherwise the assemblage is unremarkable, consisting of needles, spatulas, gouges and possible drilled bone pendants. The latter are the

Table 60

MISCELLANEOUS ARTIFACTS AT ALI KOSH, CHAGHA SEFID AND TEPE SABZ
by Cultural Phase

Site	Phase	Perforated Sherd Disc Spindle Whorls	Star-shaped Spindle Whorls	Worked Sherds (Chipped & Ground)
TS	Bayat	5		7
TS	Mehmeh		3	14
TS	Khazineh	4		4
TS	Sabz	6		23
CS	Sabz			
CS	Choga Mami Transitional	7	1	1
CS	Surkh	30		7
CS	Sefid	20		14
CS	Mohammad Jaffar			
AK	Mohammad Jaffar	2		
CS	Ali Kosh			
AK	Ali Kosh			
AK	Bus Mordeh			

Table 61

MISCELLANEOUS ARTIFACTS AT CHAGHA SEFID
by Stratigraphic Zone

Phase	Zone Area	Zone	Spindle Whorls				Asphalt Artifacts				Totals
			Perforated Sherd Discs	Star-shaped	Oval-discoidal	Worked Sherds	Asphalt Balls	Handle	Pestle	Base	
Sabz	SD	J									
	SD	I								1	1
Choga Mami Transitional	SD	H	1	1			1				3
	SD	G2	2				2				4
	SD	G1	4		1	1	8		1		15
Surkh	SD	F	10			2	7	1			20
	SC, SD	E2	4			3					7
	SC, SD	E1	3		1		3				7
	SC	D3									
	SC	D2	5			1	1				7
	SC	D1	4								4
	SC	C2	4			1	4				9
Sefid	SA	C1	6			9	8				23
	SA	B2	14			5	1				20
	SA	B1									
	SA	A4									
Mohammad Jaffar	SB	C									
	SB	B									
	SB	A									
Ali Kosh	SA	A3									
	SA	A2									
	SA	A1					2				2
	Totals		57	1	2	22	37	1	1	1	122

only type of worked bone not found previously at Ali Kosh or Tepe Sabz, nor, from the reports at any other contemporary site. Neither the metapodial awls nor nipple-like perforators, which were previously found in Deh Luran, occurred at Chagha Sefid.

AWLS (Fig. 88*a-g,l*; Pl. 53*a-i*)

Sample: 97

Description: Most of the Chagha Sefid examples are long-bone splinter awls. These are piercing or perforating tools made by carefully chipping and polishing a long splinter of limb bone from one of the local ungulates. Unbroken specimens range from 4 to 12 cm in length.

Temporal distribution: Throughout the sequence.

Geographic distribution: Ali Kosh, Tepe Sabz (Hole, Flannery and Neely, 1969:214); Jaffarabad (Dollfus, 1971:Fig. 29:2-7).

Table 62
MISCELLANEOUS ARTIFACTS AT CHAGHA SEFID
by Cultural Phase

Phase	Spindle Whorls				Asphalt Artifacts				Totals
	Perforated Sherd Discs	Star-shaped	Oval-discoidal	Worked Sherds	Asphalt Balls	Handle	Pestle	Base	
Sabz								1	1
Choga Mami Transitional	7	1	1	1	11				21
Surkh	30		1	7	15	1	1		55
Sefid	20			14	9				43
Mohammad Jaffar									
Ali Kosh					2				2
Totals	57	1	2	22	37	1	1	1	122

NEEDLES (Fig. 87h, Pl. 53m,n)

Sample: 7
Description: Carefully polished, slender long-bone splinters some 3 to 4 mm in diameter, with an eye drilled in one end and the other end worked to a point. No complete examples were found.
Temporal distribution: Sporadically from Ali Kosh to Choga Mami Transitional phases.
Geographic distribution: Ali Kosh, Tepe Sabz (Hole, Flannery and Neely, 1969:214); Jaffarabad (Dollfus, 1971:Fig. 29:13-15); Guran (Mortensen and Flannery, 1966:Fig. 11).

SPATULAS (Pl. 53j-l)

Sample: 8
Description: Long slats of polished bone which resemble a physician's tongue depressor. No complete specimens were found.
Temporal distribution: Sporadically throughout the sequence.
Geographic distribution: Ali Kosh, Tepe Sabz (Hole, Flannery and Neely, 1969:217); Jaffarabad (Dollfus, 1971:Fig. 29:9).

GOUGES (Pl. 53o,p)

Sample: 8
Description: Trough-shaped sections of bone from an ungulate metapodial (preserving the ridges of the medullar canal) with one end sharpened as a gouge.
Temporal distribution: Sefid and early Surkh phases.
Geographic Distribution: Tepe Sabz (Hole, Flannery and Neely, 1969:217-218); similar bone gouges appeared in Phase A of the Amuq (Braidwood and Braidwood, 1960:Fig. 38-44); and at Tepe Gawra in all strata (Tobler, 1950:214).

DRILLED BONES (Pl. 53r-t, w-aa)

Sample: 9
Description: All are phalanges of ungulates drilled longitudinally through the distal ends. They have also

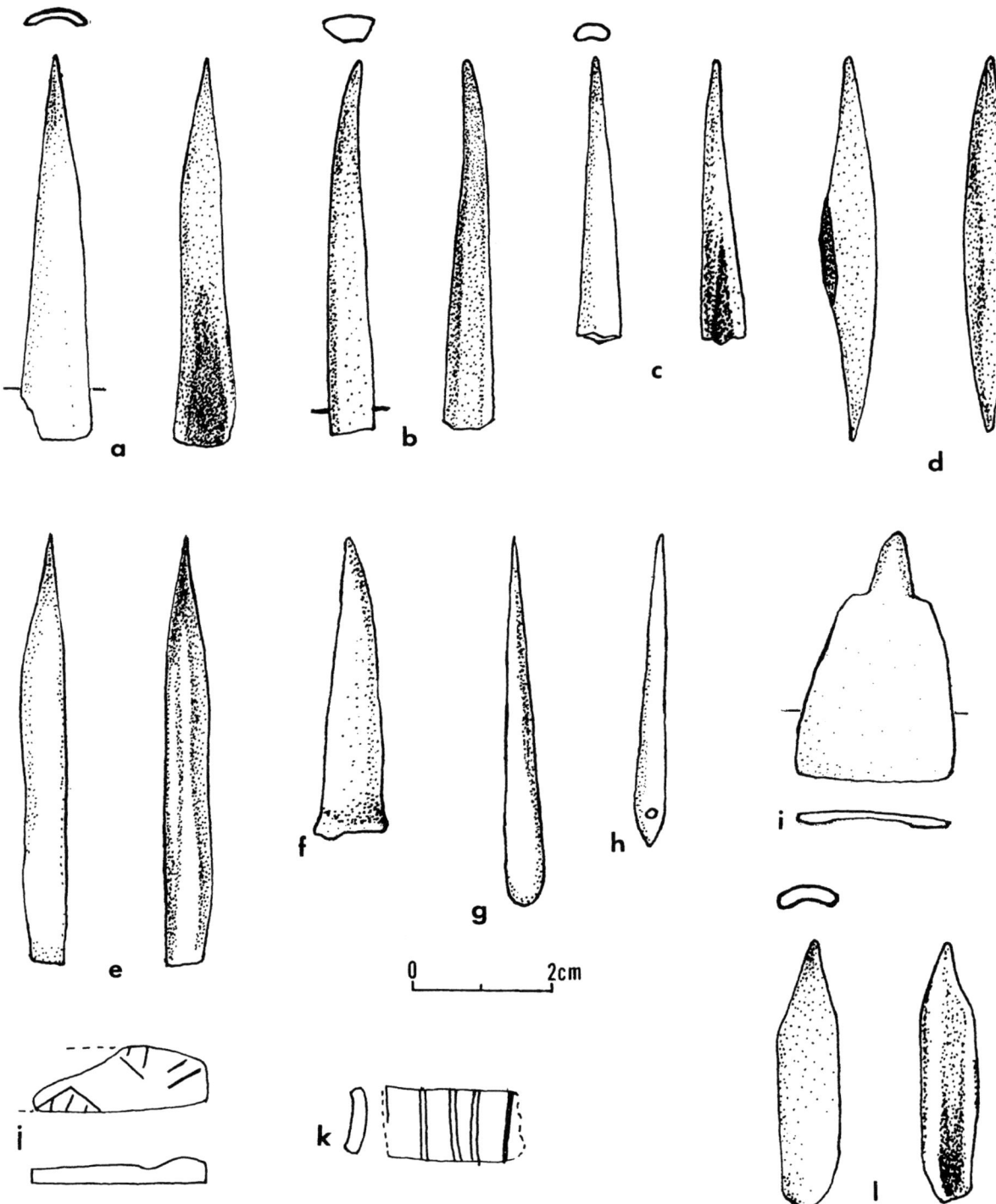

Fig. 88. Bone Objects. *a-g,l*, bone awls; *h*, needle; *i*, bone scoop; *j,k*, engraved bones.

been ground down somewhat to flatten the ventral surface and all surfaces are polished. Some were drilled along the axis as well and the interiors filled with asphalt. One example has faint zig zag lines that are apparently traces of paint.

Temporal distribution: 6 of 8 in the Surkh Phase, but apparently of greater temporal range elsewhere.

Geographic distribution: Commonly found in Natufian sites where they sometimes occurred with burials as if they had been stitched to a cap. e.g., El Wad (Garrod, 1957:221) and Mallaha (Perrot, 1968: Fig. 839); also found at Arpachiyah (Mallowan, 1935:99, Pl. 10, Fig. 51) where human finger bones were either used or modeled in stone; Saudi Arabian Ubaid sites (Burkholder, 1972: 266-267).

BONE HANDLE (Pl. 53u)

Sample: 1 (Sefid Phase)

Description: A fragment of the junction of shaft and handle of an implement of unknown use. The shaft is oval, measuring .95 by 1.6 cm. The handle was apparently carved from the long bone of a bovid.

BONE SCOOP (Fig. 88i)

Sample: 1

Description: The blade end of a shovel-shaped scoop cut from a long bone. A short tang may have been socketted into a handle. The object, which is in Iran, measures approximately 2 cm across the widest part of the blade and has an overall length of about 3 cm.

ENGRAVED BONES (Fig. 88j,k)

Sample: 2

Description: Both pieces are small fragments. One, from the Sefid Phase, is a spatulate-shaped section of long bone with four deeply incised grooves running across the surface transverse to the axis of the bone (Fig. 88k).

The second piece, from the Surkh Phase, is a small fragment of long bone that was carved as well as incised. The incisions are simple triangles filled with lines (Fig. 88j).

CUT LONG BONES (Pl. 53q,u,v).

Sample: 2

Description: One, from the Choga Mami Transitional Phase, may have been a form of pipe. The bone was neatly cut near the end and the cut smoothed and polished. The interior of the bone is cleaned out and there is evidence of burning at the cut end. The other end was broken. The shaft shows use polish. Several other fragments of long bones counted among the polished fragments appear to be of similar type.

The second cut bone, from the Ali Kosh Phase, is the distal end of an ungulate metapodial (sheep) which was scored with an encircling groove 3.1 cm from the end and then snapped off. Two longitudinal grooves suggest that a groove and splinter technique was employed to obtain material for awls, needles and similar tools. Other pieces of long bone fragments showed similar isolated longitudinal grooves.

ANTLER FLAKER (Pl. 52l)

Sample: 1

Description: The basal portion of an antler cut about 5 cm. from the base. The cut end is beveled and polished from use on one side and roughly flaked on the other.

Temporal distribution: Ali Kosh Phase.

Geographic distribution: Unknown.

FRAGMENTS OF WORKED BONE

Sample: 92

Description: Miscellaneous fragments of bone that show evidence of polish, grinding or cutting.

MATTING AND BASKETRY

Among the hundreds of pieces of asphalt that were found at Chagha Sefid, 59 bore large enough impressions of matting and basketry to identify the weave. Most of these were of floor mats although some impressions of baskets that had been reinforced with asphalt were also recovered. One basket had evidently been lined with plaster, perhaps as a mold for a plaster vessel, a fragment of which bore the impression and shape of the container.

There is nothing new among the finds at Chagha Sefid. Simple over two—under two reed mats are the

Table 63
BONE ARTIFACTS AT CHAGHA SEFID
by Stratigraphic Zone

Phase	Area	Zone	Awls	Needles	Spatulas	Gouges	Drilled Bones	Handles	Scoop	Engraved Bone	Cut Bone	Antler Flaker	Fragments of Worked Bone	Total
Sabz	SD	J												
	SD	I			1								1	2
Choga Mami Transitional	SD	H	1	1									7	9
	SD	G2	1											1
	SD	G1	2				1				1		2	6
Surkh	SD	F	4	1	1								4	10
	SC, SD	E2	1										1	2
	SC, SD	E1	1										2	3
	SC	D3					1							1
	SC	D2	1				5						2	8
	SC	D1	3	1									3	7
	SC	C2											4	4
Sefid	SA	C1	7	1	1	1				1			9	20
	SA	B2	57	2	2	7	1		1	1			38	109
	SA	B1	11		2			1					9	23
	SA	A4	1										2	3
Mohammad Jaffar	SB	C	1											1
	SB	B												
	SB	A	1											1
Ali Kosh	SA	A3	2	1									1	4
	SA	A2	1										1	2
	SA	A1	2		1						1	1	4	9
		Totals	97	7	8	8	8	1	1	2	2	1	90	225

most common type; they are also commonly found as "silica ghosts" on the floors of houses. No coiled baskets were found. We had surmised earlier (Hole, Flannery and Neely, 1969:220) that the latter appeared first in the Sabz Phase. This supposition is not contradicted by our work at Chagha Sefid.

OVER-ONE, UNDER-ONE TWILLED MAT
OR BASKET-WALL FRAGMENTS

Sample: 13 fragments
Material: Reeds or club-rushes (?) varying from 4 mm to 2 cm in width

Comment: It is difficult to tell which of these fragments are from twilled mats and which are from the walls of shallow, tray-like baskets.
Temporal distribution: Sporadically throughout the sequence.
Geographic distribution: Ali Kosh, Tepe Sabz (Hole, Flannery and Neely, 1969:220).

OVER-TWO, UNDER-TWO TWILLED MATS (Pl. 52d,h)

Sample: 34 fragments
Material: Reeds or club rushes (?) ranging from 5 mm to 2 cm in width.

Table 64
BONE ARTIFACTS AT CHAGHA SEFID
by Cultural Phase

Phase	Awls	Needles	Spatulas	Gouges	Drilled Bones	Handles	Scoop	Engraved Bone	Cut Bone	Antler Flaker	Fragments of Worked Bone	Total
Sabz			1								1	2
Choga Mami Transitional	4	1			1				1		9	16
Surkh	10	2	1		6						16	35
Sefid	76	3	5	8	1	1	1	2			58	155
Mohammad Jaffar	2											2
Ali Kosh	5	1	1						1	1	6	15
Totals	97	7	8	8	8	1	1	2	2	1	90	225

Comment: This is the most common type of weave in our sequence, as it was at Ali Kosh and Tepe Sabz. Most of the fragments are clearly from mats, and we suspect the larger weaves (rushes 2 cm in width) were from floor mats like those at Jarmo, Hassuna, and similar sites.
Temporal distribution: Sefid through Choga Mami Transitional phases.
Geographic distribution: Ali Kosh, Tepe Sabz (Hole, Flannery and Neely, 1969:220); over-two, under-two mats appear on the floors of prehistoric villages in Mesopotamia and Kurdistan (Braidwood, 1952:Figs. 7 and 14).

TWINED BASKETS WITH FLOORS (Pl. 52a-c)

Sample: 5 fragments
Material: Reeds or club-rushes (?)
Description: These are actually composite baskets or "carrying trays." The floor of the basket is twilled matting (over-two, under-two), and has a diameter up to 10 cm; near the edges, this gives way to a different construction. Some of the reeds from the floor extend upright like radii, forming the warps of the basket wall, and wefts are interwoven through them in the over-one, under-one style called "randing" by Hodges (1964:Fig. 38, No. 1). What results is a wide, shallow basket perhaps 40 cm in diameter. It is worth noting that all the examples we found which clearly showed both walls and floor appeared to have been purposely coated with strips of asphalt, as if to strengthen the juncture between wall and floor. At the base the asphalt is as much as 4 mm thick while it tapers to some 2 mm toward the top. Strips of reeds composing the floor and sides are .7 cm to 1 cm in width.

The example in the Ali Kosh Phase is a plaster impression of the side of a basket. Evidently the basket served as a mold in making a plaster bowl. The weave is an over-one, under-one made of reeds about 5 mm wide (Pl. 52g).
Temporal distribution: Ali Kosh, Surkh, and Choga Mami Transitional phases.
Geographic distribution: Ali Kosh (Hole, Flannery and Neely, 1969:221).

FIGURINES AND OBJECTS OF LIGHTLY BAKED CLAY

The excavation at Chagha Sefid illustrates very well the essential continuity in figurines following the Mohammad Jaffar Phase and corroborates the conclusions we reached earlier. The proportions of the various types of figurines (Table 67) are sensitive to the passage of time as are the specific attributes of the different types (Tables 68-72). Animal figurines are found up through the Surkh Phase at which time they disappear from the *local* sequence, although they are known to be present in Susa A (post Bayat Phase) in Khuzistan. Whether there is continuity of this type between the Surkh and Bayat phases may be discovered when results from sites such as Choga Mish are published. Human figurines are rare and always crude; they are found so far only in the Ali Kosh through Choga Mami Transitional phases. T-shaped figurines increase sharply in percentage from the Ali Kosh through the Sefid and Surkh phases at which time they are by far the most common type. Stalk figurines, by contrast, decrease in frequency from the Bus Mordeh through Surkh phases.

It is striking that figurines of all types, with the exception of possibly redeposited examples, disappear from all post-Surkh phases at Chagha Sefid and Tepe Sabz. This change coincides with the intrusion of many new traits, especially in pottery, and may reflect changes in the local population as well.

Table 65

MATS AND BASKETRY AT CHAGHA SEFID
by Stratigraphic Zone

Phase	Area	Zone	Over One–Under One Fragments	Over Two–Under Two Fragments	Twined Baskets with Floors	Twined Fragments	Totals
Sabz	SD	J					
	SD	I					
Choga Mami Transitional	SD	H		1		2	3
	SD	G2					
	SD	G1	4	1	2		7
Surkh	SD	F		7	2	1	10
	SC, SD	E2	1	6			7
	SC, SD	E1		1			1
	SC	D3					
	SC	D2		2			2
	SC	D1		2			2
	SC	C2					
Sefid	SA	C1	3	13		1	17
	SA	B2	4	1		3	8
	SA	B1					
	SA	A4				1	1
Mohammad Jaffar	SB	C					
	SB	B					
	SB	A					
Ali Kosh	SA	A3	1		1		2
	SA	A2					
	SA	A1					
		Totals	13	34	5	8	60

Table 66

MATS AND BASKETRY AT CHAGHA SEFID
by Cultural Phase

Phase	Over One–Under One Fragments	Over Two–Under Two Matting Fragments	Twined Baskets with Floors	Twined Fragments	Totals
Sabz					
Choga Mami Transitional	4	2	2	2	10
Surkh	1	18	2	1	22
Sefid	7	14		5	26
Mohammad Jaffar					
Ali Kosh	1		1		2
Totals	13	34	5	8	60

Table 67
NUMBER AND PERCENT OF TYPES OF FIGURINES (INCLUDING FRAGMENTS) IN THE PHASES AT TEPE SABZ (TS), CHAGHA SEFID (CS) AND ALI KOSH (AK)

Site	Phase	Animal		Human		T-shaped		Stalk		Large Stalk		Total
		No.	%	No.	%	No.	%	No.	%	No.	%	
TS	Bayat	1										1
TS	Mehmeh											
TS	Khazineh											
TS	Sabz					1						1
CS	Sabz							4				4
CS	Choga Mami Transitional			1	11			7	78	1	11	9
CS	Surkh	3	6	1	2	37	69	12	22	1	2	54
CS	Sefid	29	15	7	4	111	56	42	21	8	4	197
CS	Mohammad Jaffar											
AK	Mohammad Jaffar	4	7	4	7	10	19	36	67			54
CS	Ali Kosh	10	8			4	3	104	87	2	2	120
AK	Ali Kosh	8	6	1	1	1	1	130	93			140
AK	Bus Mordeh	20	6					299	94			319

Of the remaining objects of lightly-baked clay, only the ceramic strips deserve mention here. These enigmatic artifacts appear abruptly in the latest Sefid Phase and continue through the Choga Mami Transitional although they are most abundant in the early Surkh Phase. Whatever they may be, these objects constitute a convenient chronological marker for the new phases at Chagha Sefid.

Figurines

TYPE: Animal Figurines (Fig. 89)

Sample: 42
Material: Clay
Description: Stylized figurines of animals, mostly fragmentary, showing general form rather than the details of anatomy. Heads are generally knobs of clay although on some ears, "pinprick" eyes and a slit mouth are present. Two examples of horns were found detached from heads. Bodies, legs and tails are modeled with a minimum of detail and have no suggestion of hair, wool, or hooves. From the form of the body, one can guess that sheep or goats are most commonly represented. One well-modeled head of a cow may have been attached to a pot; it is made of red slipped ceramic (Fig. 88a).
Temporal distribution: Sporadically through the Surkh Phase.
Geographic distribution: Ali Kosh (Hole, Flannery and Neely, 1969:224); Jaffarabad (Dollfus, 1971: Fig. 22:5, 8, 10, 11, 13); Kurdistan (Braidwood, Howe, et al. 1960:Plate 16); Luristan (Mortensen, 1964); and Khuzistan.

TYPE: Fragments of Human Figurines (Fig. 90)

Sample: 9
Material: Clay
Description: All are fragmentary although one can be reconstructed in its entirety (Fig. 90a).
Breasts: 3 examples (Sefid Phase), 2 with holes

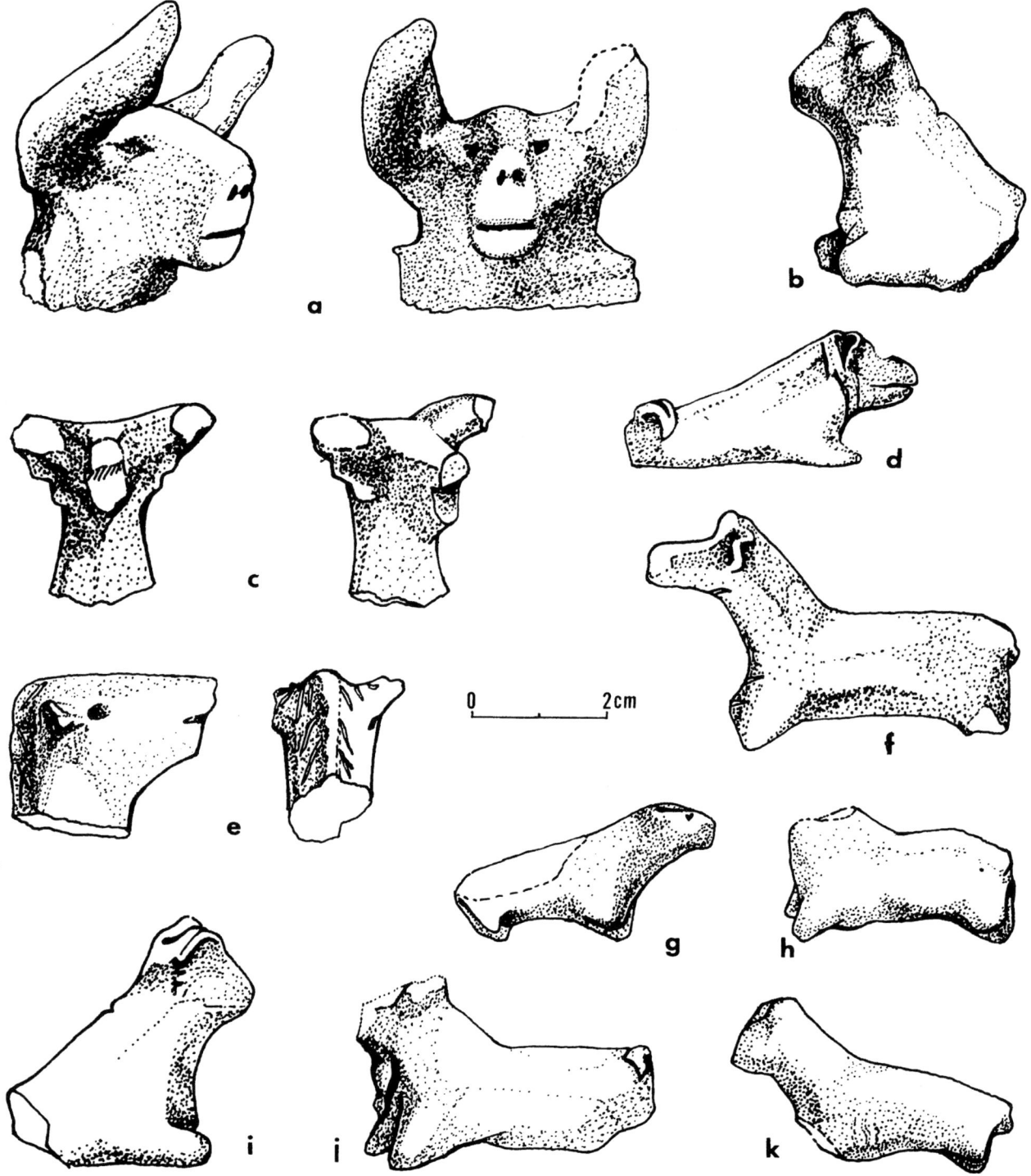

Fig. 89. Animal figurines. *a*, ceramic head of cow that was probably attached to a red ware vessel; *b-k*, miscellaneous lightly baked clay figurines of animals.

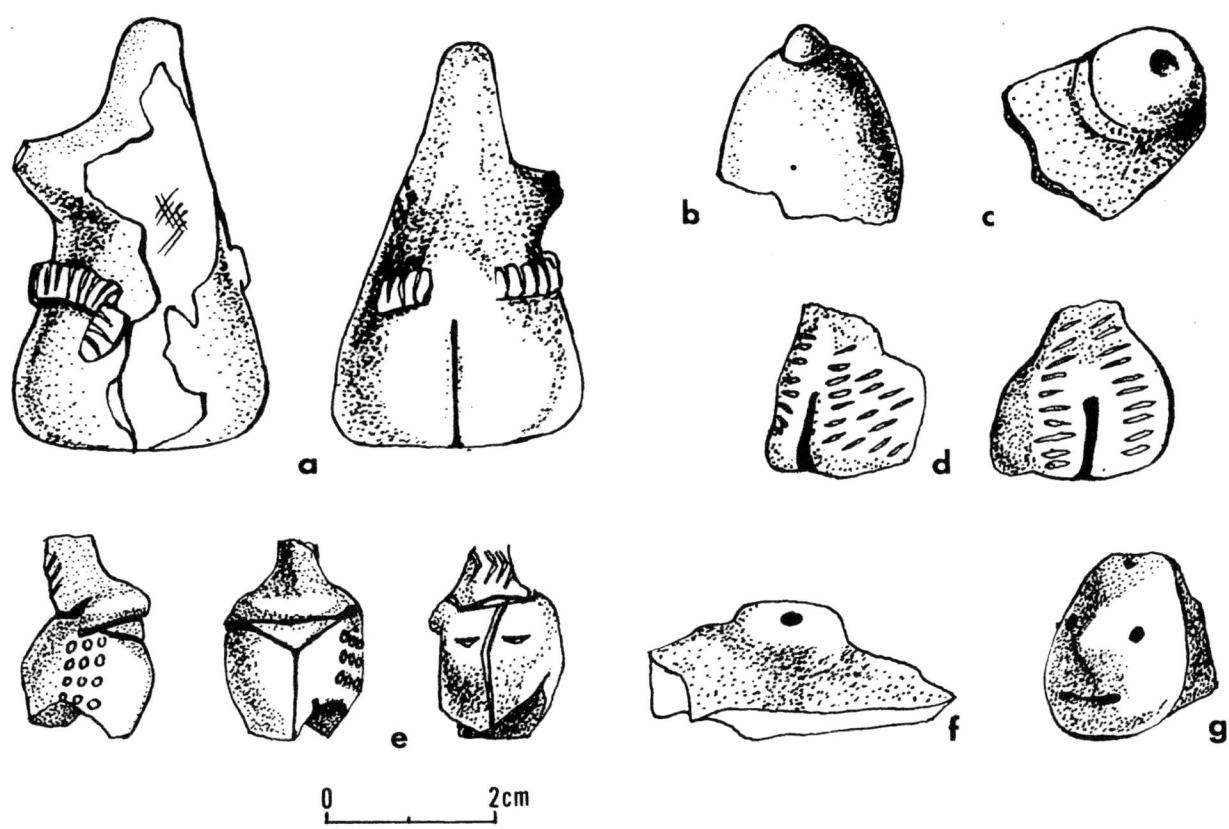

Fig. 90. Human figurines. *a*, stalk with belt and stumps of arms; *b,c,f*, breasts; *d,e*, portions of figures with incisions and punctations; *g*, face.

and one with an appliqued nipple, all from the Sefid Phase (Fig. 90*b,c,f*). These pieces are evidently broken from large figurines.

Face: 1 example (Sefid Phase) crudely modeled with pinprick eyes and a simple slash mouth (Fig. 90*g*).

Seated (?) stalk figures: 2 examples (Surkh and Choga Mami Transitional phases) both seem to show the buttocks and legs by means of slashes in the base (Fig. 90*d*) In both cases there are punctations and incised lines suggesting ornamentation or clothing. In neither case is the sex obvious.

Large stalk female: 1 example (Sefid Phase). The base has a slit indicating the buttocks, there is a belt around the waist and there are breasts or arm stumps. The head and neck are simply indicated by a tapering stalk (Fig. 90*a*).

Possible human figurine fragments: 2 examples (Sefid Phase). Both appear to be one half of the basal part of large stalk figurines. In each case the base is concave and fingernail impressions indicate decoration. Both have large buttocks and one retains the left breast with a hole at the nipple (Fig. 90*e*).

TYPE: T-shaped Figurines (Fig. 97*g-n*)

Sample: 152
Material: Clay
Description: Clay stalks centered on an elongate, and often slightly concave, base. Most of the bases are burnished suggesting they were rubbed or moved about on a surface either before or after their firing.

Considerable variety is evident in the Chagha Sefid sample and while most are broken, enough pieces are present to permit an accurate reconstruction of the principal changes in style.

Let us consider three parts of the figurines: the

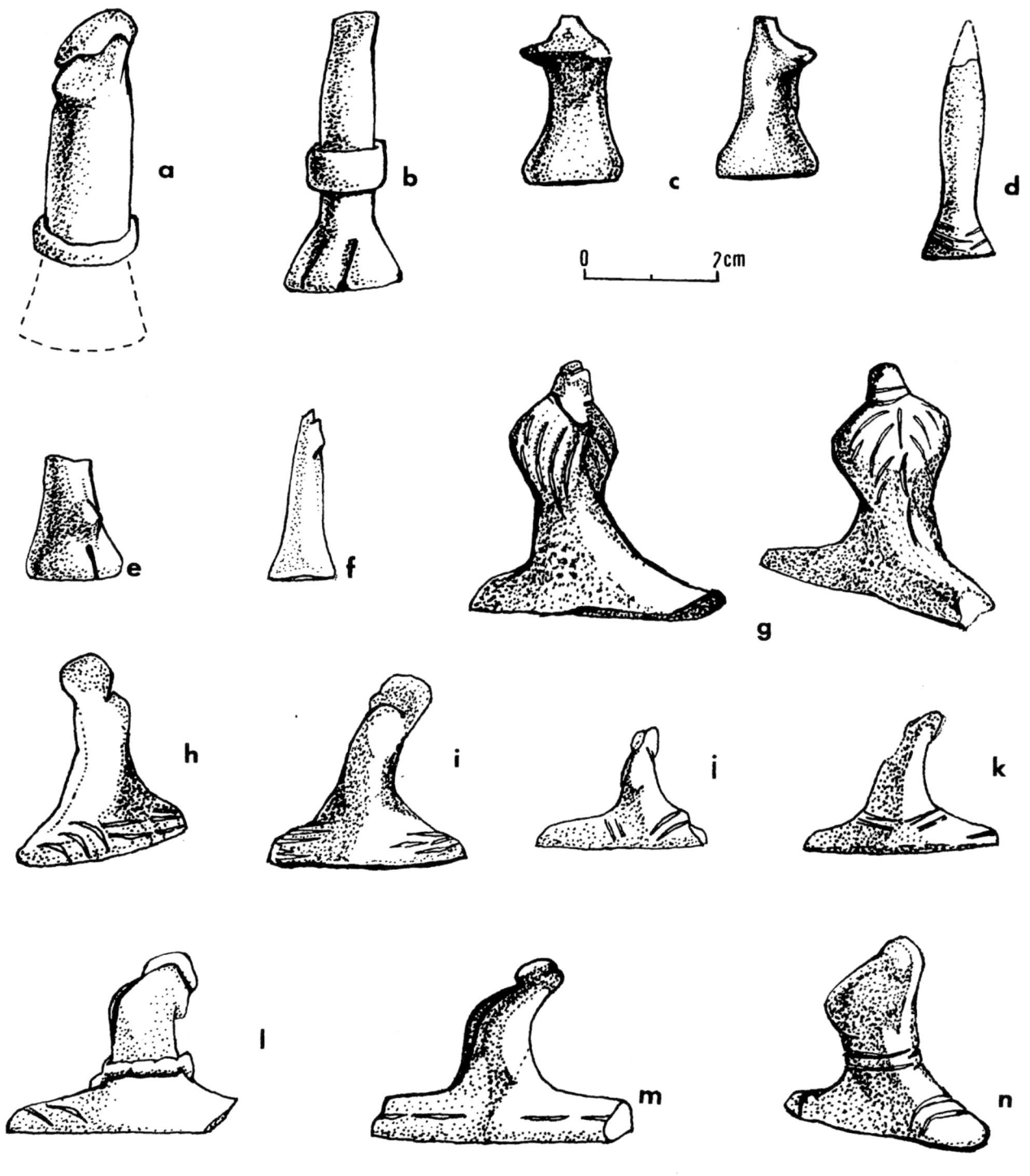

Fig. 91. Stalk and T-shaped figurines. *a-f,* stalk figurines; *g-n*, T-shaped figurines.

OTHER ARTIFACTS

Table 68
ATTRIBUTES OF T-SHAPED FIGURINES AT CHAGHA SEFID
by Stratigraphic Zone

Phase	Area	Zone	Bases						Stalks							Heads				
			All Examples	Plain	Oblique Incision	Horiz-Oblique Incision	Appliqued	Painted	All Examples	Plain	Incised at Base	Belted	Vertical Incision	Slashed	Painted	All Examples	No Face	Pinched	Flared	Appliqued
Sabz	SD	J																		
	SD	I																		
Choga Mami Transitional	SD	H																		
	SD	G2																		
	SD	G1																		
Surkh	SD	F	2	1		1		1	3	1	1		2			2	1			1
	SC, SD	E2	1			1			3		1		1			2	2			2
	SC, SD	E1	4			4	1	2	3				3			2	1	1		
	SC	D3																		
	SC	D2	5	1	1	2	2	2	5	1	1	1	4			2	2			2
	SC	D1	6	4		2		2	5	1	1		4			3	2			2
	SC	C2	4		2	3	1	2	4				2	2		1				
Sefid	SA	C1	14	7		5	1	6	16		9		8		5	1		1		1
	SA	B2	64	20	23	13	5	5	54	21	22	4	11	2	4	18	1	10	5	5
	SA	B1	6	3	2			1	4	1		2	1			1		1		
	SA	A4																		
Mohammad Jaffar	SB	C																		
	SB	B																		
	SB	A																		
Ali Kosh	SA	A3																		
	SA	A2							1				1			1	1			
	SA	A1	1	1					3	1	2		1							
		Totals	107	37	28	31	10	21	101	26	37	9	38	2	21	29	3	12	5	13

bases, the stalks and the heads. Tables 68, 69 show the attributes related to the three parts.

Bases: Plain bases and those with oblique incisions are restricted to the Sefid and early Surkh phases. Bases with horizontal incisions, applique and paint are found in the later Sefid and throughout the Surkh Phase.

Stalks: Plain and belted stalks are found in the Sefid and early Surkh phases while the incised and painted begin in the late Sefid and continue through the Surkh Phase.

Heads: Heads are rare but it is evident that the simple pinched variety is confined to the Sefid and earliest Surkh phases while the appliqued and painted varieties begin in late Sefid and continue throughout the Surkh Phase.

In summary we find a sequence that begins with simple plain, incised, and belted T-shaped figurines in the Sefid and early Surkh phases, and shifts to an emphasis on more elaborately incised, appliqued and painted varieties in the late Sefid and Surkh phases.

These trends are in accord with our findings at

Table 69

ATTRIBUTES OF T-SHAPED FIGURINES AT CHAGHA SEFID
by Cultural Phase

Phase	Bases						Stalks							Heads				
	All Examples	Plain	Oblique Incision	Horiz-Oblique Incision	Appliqued	Painted	All Examples	Plain	Incised at Base	Belted	Vertical Incision	Slashed	Painted	All Examples	No Face	Pinched	Flared	Appliqued
Sabz																		
Choga Mami Transitional																		
Surkh	22	6	3	13	4	9	23	3	4	3	16		12	8	1			7
Sefid	84	30	25	18	6	12	74	22	31	6	20	2	9	20	1	12	5	6
Mohammad Jaffar																		
Ali Kosh	1	1					4	1	2		2			1	1			
Totals	107	37	28	31	10	21	101	26	37	9	38	2	21	29	3	12	5	13

Ali Kosh where we recovered only a few examples of simple T-shaped figurines in situ in the Ali Kosh and Mohammad Jaffar deposits. The combined data also show that stalk figurines precede the T-shaped varieties (cf. Hole, Flannery and Neely, 1969:227-230: Miscellaneous objects of unfired clay).

Temporal distribution: Ali Kosh through Surkh phases. Geographic distribution: Ali Kosh (Hole, Flannery and Neely, 1969:226); in the upper part of Jarmo, similar objects with "double-wing bases" were found, (Braidwood, Howe, et al., 1960:44 and Plate 16:14, 15).

TYPE: Stalk Figurines (Fig. 91a-f)

Sample: 181

Comment: Previously we described stalk figurines under a number of related types (Hole, Flannery and Neely, 1969:227-230). At Chagha Sefid we found enough intact examples to demonstrate that they are of one type and that they are probably functionally related to T-shaped figurines which they resemble in some respects and which occur in inverse proportions to the stalks.

Description: These are clay stalks that stand on a flared or bell-shaped base. The upper portion of the stalk may be pinched to suggest a head or have appliqued features. The attributes of stalk figurines are given in more detail below (Tables 70, 71).

Bases: Sixty examples, of which 40 are plain and 20 incised. In 11 instances there is a plain belt around the junction of the base and the stalk. With one exception incised bases and belted stalks are restricted to the Ali Kosh Phase.

Stalks: The cylindrical stalks are usually plain; 4 have traces of red fugitive paint and 2 have incisions.

Heads: Fifty-six examples, of which 37 have the upper end pinched to create the suggestion of a face, 16 have appliqued pieces of clay to indicate hair, and 13 examples are merely drawn to a rounded cone at the tip.

Temporal distribution: Apparently confined to the Ali Kosh, Mohammad Jaffar, Sefid and early Surkh phases; probably redeposited examples occur in later phases. The distribution is borne out in Tables 67 and 73 which shows the distribution of figurines at the three Deh Luran sites.

Geographic distribution: Ali Kosh (Hole, Flannery

Table 70

ATTRIBUTES OF STALK FIGURINES AT CHAGHA SEFID
by Stratigraphic Zone

Phase	Area	Zone	Plain Base	Incised Base	Plain Belt	Pinched Face	Appliqued Face	No Face	Painted Stalk	Incised Stalk	Stalk Fragments Only (Both Ends Broken)
Sabz	SD	J									1
	SD	I	1								2
Choga Mami Transitional	SD	H									4
	SD	G2	1								1
	SD	G1	1								
Surkh	SD	F	3							1	
	SC, SD	E2									
	SC, SD	E1	1								
	SC	D3									
	SC	D2									
	SC	D1									2
	SC	C2							1		5
Sefid	SA	C1				1	2			1	2
	SA	B2	6			4	2	2	1		18
	SA	B1	1	1		1					3
	SA	A4	2			3					
Mohammad Jaffar	SB	C									
	SB	B									
	SB	A									
Ali Kosh	SA	A3	1			1					2
	SA	A2	11	13	7	17	1				5
	SA	A1	12	6	4	10	5		2	1	20

and Neely, 1969:227-230); Jarmo and Sarab (Oriental Institute collections).

Miscellaneous Objects of Lightly Baked Clay

TYPE: Clay Balls (Pl. 47*h-l*)

Sample: 19
Description: Spherical balls of clay whose average diameter is 1.5 cm.
Temporal distribution: Sporadically in the Ali Kosh through Sabz phases.
Geographic distribution: Ali Kosh (Hole, Flannery and Neely, 1969:203).

CLAY PELLETS

Sample: 15
Description: Thirteen plano-convex pellets 1.5-2 cm in diameter came from the Sefid Phase. Two other flat pellets were found in the Ali Kosh Phase.
Geographic distribution: Unknown.

SLING MISSLES (Pl. 51*c-e*)

Sample: 2
Description: Ovoid or teardrop-shaped pieces of fired clay. The two examples in context measured 4 x 2.8 cm and 6.2 x 3.5 cm; one out of context example measured 4 x 2.5 cm.

Table 71
ATTRIBUTES OF STALK FIGURINES AT CHAGHA SEFID
by Cultural Phase

Phase	Plain Base	Incised Base	Plain Belt	Pinched Face	Appliqued Face	No Face	Painted Stalk	Incised Stalk	Stalk Fragments Only (Both Ends Broken)
Sabz	1								3
Choga Mami Transitional	2								5
Surkh	4					1	1		7
Sefid	9	1		9	4	2	1	1	23
Mohammad Jaffar									
Ali Kosh	24	19	11	28	6		2	1	27

Temporal distribution: Sefid and Surkh phases.
Geographic distribution: Tepe Sabz (Hole, Flannery and Neely, 1969:213).

DOMED STALK

Sample: 1, Ali Kosh Phase
Description: A squat clay object with a flaring concave base and an incised, dome-shaped top.
Geographic distribution: Unknown.

APPLIQUED PIECE (Fig. 87*b*)

Sample: 1, Ali Kosh Phase
Description: A cone-shaped fragment of a larger object, possibly a figurine, which has oval pellets appliqued to one side. The pellets are each impressed with one or more marks.
Geographic distribution: Unknown.

TYPE: Clay or Stone Mullers (Fig. 87*e-h*, Pl. 54*a-c*)

Sample: 7 stone, 2 clay
Description: Cone or nail shaped objects whose bases are polished from rubbing. The shafts also show polish from use.

Temporal distribution: Mohammad Jaffar through early Surkh phases.
Geographic distribution: Ras al Amiya (Stronach, 1961:Pl. 43:8-10).

STRIPS OF LIGHTLY BAKED CLAY (Pl. 51*a,b*)

Sample: 12,656
Comment: The ceramic strips occur in large concentrations in Zone C of Area A along with calcined ash/plaster between walls of houses. They are also found in quantity between building levels where trash was evidently thrown in to level areas for new structures. All of these pieces seem to occur among trash.

The uses to which these objects may have been put are hard to imagine, although their manner of manufacture is obvious. The impressions on many of them show that they are associated with matting in some way but they have no obvious function since they are always broken, show no signs of wear, and are only associated with trash contexts. With the possible exception of Jowi, nothing like them has been reported elsewhere. This is all the more surprising in view of the extraordinary numbers in which they occur; in total number of pieces they rank behind only flint and pottery, suggesting that they

Table 72

FIGURINES AT CHAGHA SEFID
by Stratigraphic Zone

Phase	Zone Area	Zone	Animal	Human Fragments	T-shaped	Stalk	Large Stalks and Fragments	Totals
Sabz	SD	J				1		1
	SD	I				3		3
Choga Mami Transitional	SD	H				4	1	5
	SD	G2				2		2
	SD	G1		1		1		2
Surkh	SD	F	1		3	3		7
	SC, SD	E2			3			3
	SC, SD	E1			8	1		9
	SC	D3						
	SC	D2	1	1	10		1	13
	SC	D1	1		8	2		11
	SC	C2			5	6		11
Sefid	SA	C1	4		20	3	2	29
	SA	B2	23	6	83	28	6	146
	SA	B1	1		7	7		15
	SA	A4	1	1	1	4		7
Mohammad Jaffar	SB	C						
	SB	B						
	SB	A						
Ali Kosh	SA	A3	1			4		5
	SA	A2	4		1	57	1	63
	SA	A1	5		3	43	1	52
	Totals		42	9	152	169	12	384

are both useful and cheap. Their possible use in roasting is suggested in the description of fireplaces, Chapter IV.

Description: Strips of clay which usually show mat impressions on one side while the other side often bears finger impressions where the strips were pressed against the matting. The number of pieces with impressions is unknown because the strips usually were covered with solidified ash (Pl. 51b) and the sheer quantity of examples precluded cleaning in acid; consequently most were simply counted and discarded.

Virtually all examples are broken. Lengths range up to 10 cm; the range in width is 2.1 to 5.8 cm, with most between 3 and 4 cm; the range of thickness is .4 to 1.8 cm with most between .6 and .8 cm. Virtually all the strips are slightly curved along the length.

Temporal distribution: Late Sefid through Surkh phases. By far the greatest number are in the Late Sefid deposits of Area A.

Geographic distribution: Unknown. An object similar in appearance is illustrated from Jowi (LeBreton, 1947:Fig. 17:15). It is described as one of many fired clay objects with broken parallel lines suggesting the imitation of basketry (LeBreton, 1947:149). Although the illustrated object is painted and has a hole in one end, it is not clear whether all are similarly treated. The deposits at Jowi are of Khazineh-Mehmeh age.

ORNAMENTS

Changing styles in ornaments are well documented at Chagha Sefid. Types present in the Ali Kosh and Mohammad Jaffar phases at Ali Kosh are usually represented at Chagha Sefid, while a number of new types and varieties are introduced (Table 76). Among the labrets we find the cuff-link variety of Ali Kosh giving way to a "domed" variety that continues through the Choga Mami Transitional. T-shaped labrets continue as expected through the new phases. Nail-shaped labrets have been found as far back as the Sefid Phase. A new type, studs, appears only in the Surkh Phase and is found contemporaneously in the Samarran at Choga Mami. Other ornaments, although not found in great numbers, likewise fit well with our previous findings and add a number of varieties, chiefly of rings and beads, not seen at either Ali Kosh or Tepe Sabz. Unfortunately the smaller ornaments, which are difficult to recover without screening, are seldom reported at other sites so we do not have an accurate impression of the geographic distribution of most types.

Labrets

TYPE: Domed, Cufflink-Shaped Labrets
(Pl. 54*n-r,t-bb*; Fig. 92*o,q-t*)

Sample: 73
Material: 44 crystal, 20 ceramic, 5 stone, 4 asphalt
Description: Except for two examples from the early Surkh Phase these are different from most of the labrets found at Ali Kosh and Tepe Sabz. The examples at Chagha Sefid have domed, almost ball-shaped top surfaces backed by a two-pronged flange. The flanges may be parallel to the plane of the face of the labret or may swing back away from it.
Temporal distribution: Sefid through Choga Mami Transitional phases.
Geographic distribution: Ali Kosh, Tepe Sabz (Hole, Flannery and Neely, 1969:237); in various styles found at many other sites.

TYPE: T-Shaped Labret (Fig. 92*m,n,p*; Pl. 54*k-m,s*)

Sample: 12
Material: 1 crystal, 9 ceramic, 1 stone, 1 asphalt
Description: Long, narrow, pointed labrets with a sharply defined T-shaped flange. They range in length from 1.7 to 3.5 cm. The shafts, which have their maximum diameter at the junction with the flange, taper gradually to a point.
Temporal distribution: Ali Kosh through Surkh phases.
Geographic distribution: Ali Kosh, Tepe Sabz (Hole, Flannery and Neely, 1969:237); Choga Mami (Oates, 1969: Fig. 30:*a,b*).

TYPE: Nail-Shaped Labrets (Pl. 54*h-j*)

Sample: 11
Material: 1 crystal, 3 ceramic, 7 stone

Table 73

FIGURINES AT CHAGHA SEFID
by Cultural Phase

Phase	Animal	Human Fragments	T-shaped	Stalk	Large Stalk and Fragments	Totals
Sabz				4		4
Choga Mami Transitional		1		7	1	9
Surkh	3	1	37	12	1	54
Sefid	29	7	111	42	8	197
Mohammad Jaffar						
Ali Kosh	10		4	104	2	120
Totals	42	9	152	169	12	384

Table 74

MISCELLANEOUS OBJECTS OF LIGHTLY-BAKED CLAY AT CHAGHA SEFID
by Stratigraphic Zone

Phase	Zone Area	Zone	Clay Balls	Clay Pellets	Sling Missles	Domed Stalk	Appliqued Piece	Mullers	Strips of Clay	Totals
Sabz	SD	J								
	SD	I	1							1
Choga Mami Transitional	SD	H							12	12
	SD	G2							48	48
	SD	G1	1						244	245
Surkh	SD	F	2		1				390	393
	SC, SD	E2	2						373	375
	SC, SD	E1	1						696	697
	SC	D3							259	259
	SC	D2	1						665	666
	SC	D1	1						233	234
	SC	C2						1	1,546	1,547
Sefid	SA	C1		4	1			1	7,875	7,831
	SA	B2	4	8				6	308	326
	SA	B1	1						3	4
	SA	A4							1	1
Mohammad Jaffar	SB	C								
	SB	B								
	SB	A						1		1
Ali Kosh	SA	A3		1		1			1	3
	SA	A2	3	1			1			5
	SA	A1	3						2	5
	Totals		19	15	2	1	1	9	12,606	12,653

Description: These labrets have a long conical shaft, with the base of the cone expanding into a discoidal flange (like the head of a nail). The shaft is round in cross-section. The two whole examples measured 1.7 and 1.9 cm long; broken examples suggest larger ones as well.
Temporal distribution: Scattered throughout the sequence.
Geographic distribution: Tepe Sabz (Hole, Flannery and Neely, 1969:237); scattered occurrences in Khuzistan and Mesopotamia (Stronach, 1961:Plate XLIII, Nos. 8, 9; Tobler, 1950:Fig. XCIIa, Nos. 11, 12) and the Iranian plateau (Ghirshman, 1938:Pl. LII:28-30).

TYPE: Stud-Shaped Labrets (Fig. 92k,l; Pl. 54d,e,f)

Sample: 2
Material: 1 ceramic, 1 stone
Description: Shaped like shirt studs. These are very small labrets, measuring less than 1 cm in overall height. An asphalt example was found out of context.
Temporal distribution: Surkh Phase.

Table 75
MISCELLANEOUS OBJECTS OF LIGHTLY-BAKED CLAY AT CHAGHA SEFID
by Cultural Phase

Phase	Clay Balls	Clay Pellets	Sling Missles	Domed Stalk	Appliqued Piece	Mullers	Strips of Clay	Totals
Sabz	1							1
Choga Mami Transitional	1						304	305
Surkh	7		1			1	4,162	4,171
Sefid	4	13	1			7	8,137	8,162
Mohammad Jaffar						1		1
Ali Kosh	6	2		1	1		3	13
Totals	19	15	2	1	1	9	12,606	12,653

Geographic distribution: Choga Mami (Oates, 1969:Fig. 30:*b*).

Pendants

TYPE: Boar Tusk Pendants (Fig. 92*a*, Pl. 55*o*)

Sample: 4
Material: The lower canine tooth of wild boar, *Sus scrofa*
Description: The pieces found at Chagha Sefid are fragmentary. At Ali Kosh the examples were more complete and included holes drilled at one or both ends.
Temporal distribution: Ali Kosh and Sefid phases.

Geographic distribution: Ali Kosh (Hole, Flannery and Neely, 1969:233); Jaffarabad (Dollfus, 1971: Fig. 29:10).

TYPE: Flat Pebble and Sherd Pendants
(Fig. 92*b,d,e,i*; Pl. 55*h,r,t*)

Sample: 3 pebble, 1 sherd
Description: Miscellaneous flat pebbles with a hole drilled. The pebbles are also polished.

Temporal distribution: Sefid, and Choga Mami Transitional phases.
Geographic distribution: Ali Kosh (Hole, Flannery and Neely, 1969:233); and many other early village sites.

TYPE: Bone Pendants (Fig. 92*c,h*; Pl. 55*s*)

Sample: 6
Description: Flat slivers of ungulate bone pierced at one end, with polished or smoothed surfaces. A carefully carved "frog"-shaped pendant is from Zone D, Surkh Phase (Fig. 92*h*).
Temporal distribution: Sefid and Surkh phases.
Geographic distribution: Ali Kosh (Hole, Flannery and Neely, 1969:235).

TYPE: Crab Claw Pendants or Beads

Sample: 5
Description: Pincers of river crab, *Potamon* sp., which have been polished. Examples at Ali Kosh were perforated at one end; at Chagha Sefid they lack all but the central hole.
Temporal distribution: Ali Kosh, and Sefid phases.

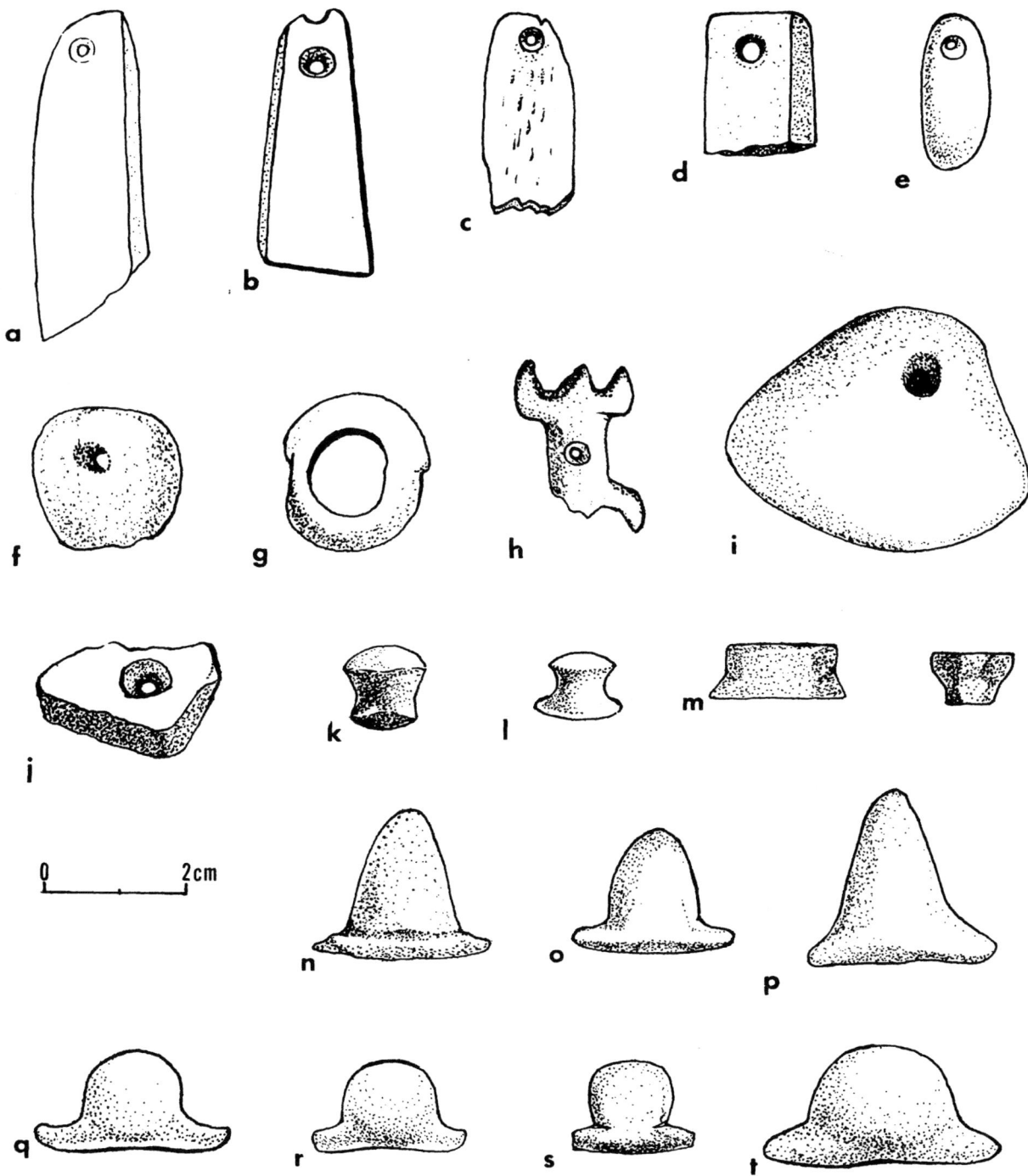

Fig. 92. Miscellaneous ornaments. *a*, boar tusk pendant; *b,d,e,i*, flat pebble and sherd pendants; *c,h*, bone pendants; *j*, ceramic bead blank; *g*, shell ring; *k,l*, stud-shaped labrets; *m,n,p*, T-shaped labrets; *o,q-t*, domed cufflink-shaped labrets.

Table 76
MISCELLANEOUS ORNAMENTS AT ALI KOSH, CHAGHA SEFID AND TEPE SABZ
by Cultural Phase

Site	Phase	Pendants			Labrets			Bracelets			Rings		
		Boar's Tusk	Pebble	Crab Claw	Cufflink	T-shaped	Nail-shaped	Smooth Surface	Incised	Ceramic (Susiana Buff)	Shell	Stone	Bone
TS	Bayat				1	2			1	1			
TS	Mehmeh					1				1			
TS	Khazineh				2		3			3			
TS	Sabz				1	3	5		6	1			
CS	Sabz					1							
CS	Choga Mami Transitional		1		8			1	1				
CS	Surkh				30	5	6						2
CS	Sefid	1	3	4	35	6	2	3		(3)	2	1	1
CS	Mohammad Jaffar												
AK	Mohammad Jaffar		1	2	10	1		5					
CS	Ali Kosh	3		1		1	1						1
AK	Ali Kosh	2	1		1	1							
AK	Bus Mordeh	5	1										

Geographic distribution: Ali Kosh (Hole, Flannery and Neely, 1969:235).

Bracelets

TYPE: Smooth-Surfaced Stone Bracelets
(Pl. 55a,b)
Sample: 4
Description: Rings of polished limestone with diameters of 7 cm or larger. They may be round or plano-convex in cross-section. The surfaces are smooth and unstriated.
Temporal distribution: Sefid and Choga Mami Transitional phases.
Geographic distribution: Ali Kosh (Hole, Flannery and Neely, 1969:237); and at many other contemporary sites.

Other Ornaments

TYPE: Rings (Fig. 92g; Pl. 55c-f)

Sample: (3) ceramic, 2 shell, 1 stone, 4 bone
Description: The three ceramic rings are like the ones found at Tepe Sabz but are out of context in strata of Surkh Phase where they were found because the buff ware pottery of which they are made does not appear until the Sabz Phase.

The shell and stone rings are essentially the same; a disc was prepared and a hole drilled and enlarged to form the center.

The bone rings are sections of long bone about 1 cm long which have been polished on the exterior and ends.
Temporal distribution: Sefid Phase.

Geographic distribution: Unknown.

TYPE: Ceramic Spool (Pl. 54g)

Sample: 1
Description: About 2.4 cm in diameter and 1.5 cm thick, with a groove .4 cm deep encircling the body. The ends are flat and one is polished. This is probably an ear spool.
Temporal distribution: Sefid Phase.
Geographic distribution: Ali Kosh (Hole, Flannery and Neely, 1969:240).

Beads

All finds at Chagha Sefid were isolated occurrences, unlike at Ali Kosh where strings of beads were found with burials (Table 78). Surprisingly the burials at Chagha Sefid did not contain beads or other ornamentation.

TYPE: Disc Beads (Fig. 92f Pl. 55q)

Sample: 3 ceramic, 10 stone, 8 shell
Description: Between 3 and 7 mm in diameter and up to 2.5 mm thick.
Temporal distribution: Ali Kosh through Surkh phases.
Geographic distribution: Ali Kosh (Hole, Flannery and Neely, 1969:243).

TYPE: Tubular Beads (Pl. 55g)

Sample: 2 ceramic, 5 stone, 3 bone
Description: Ranging from .8 to 1.6 cm long these beads were probably used as spacers in necklaces.
Temporal distribution: Sefid through Choga Mami Transitional phases.

Table 77

LABRETS AT CHAGHA SEFID
by Stratigraphic Zone

Phase	Area	Zone	Domed Cufflink-shaped	T-shaped	Nail-shaped	Studs	Totals
Sabz	SD	J			1		1
	SD	I					
Choga Mami Transitional	SD	H					
	SD	G2	3		1		4
	SD	G1	5				5
Surkh	SD	F	3				3
	SC, SD	E2	3	1	1		5
	SC, SD	E1	2	1	1		4
	SC	D3					
	SC	D2	5				5
	SC	D1			1	1	2
	SC	C2	1				1
Sefid	SA	C1	16	3	3	1	23
	SA	B2	30	4	2		36
	SA	B1	5	2			7
	SA	A4					
Mohammad Jaffar	SB	C					
	SB	B					
	SB	A					
Ali Kosh	SA	A3		1	1		2
	SA	A2					
	SA	A1					
	Totals		73	12	11	2	98

Table 78

LABRETS AT CHAGHA SEFID
by Cultural Phase

Phase	Domed Cufflink-shaped	T-shaped	Nail-shaped	Studs	Totals
Sabz			1		1
Choga Mami Transitional	8		1		9
Surkh	30	5	6	2	43
Sefid	35	6	2		43
Mohammad Jaffar					
Ali Kosh		1	1		2
Totals	73	12	11	2	98

Table 79

DISTRIBUTION OF STYLES OF BEADS AT ALI KOSH, CHAGHA SEFID AND TEPE SABZ
by Cultural Phase

Site	Phase	Flat Stone Disc	Thick Stone Disc	Tubular Stone	Tubular Shell	Ceramic Disc	Shell Disc	Tubular Ceramic	Tubular Bone	Spherical Ceramic	Spherical Stone	Barrel Ceramic	Cowrie
TS	Bayat												
TS	Mehmeh												
TS	Khazineh												
TS	Sabz												
CS	Sabz												
CS	Choga Mami Transitional			x						x			
CS	Surkh	x		x		x	x			x	x	x	
CS	Sefid	x		x	x	x	x	x	x	x	x	x	x
CS	Mohammad Jaffar				x		x				x		
AK	Mohammad Jaffar	x	x	x									x
CS	Ali Kosh	x					x						
AK	Ali Kosh	x	x	x									x
AK	Bus Mordeh	x		x									

Geographic distribution: Ali Kosh (Hole, Flannery and Neely, 1969:243).

TYPE: Spherical Beads

Sample: 7 ceramic, 1 stone
Description: Essentially flattened balls with a hole through the short diameter.
Temporal distribution: Mohammad Jaffar through Choga Mami Transitional phases.
Geographic distribution: Unknown.

TYPE: Barrel-Shaped Ceramic Beads

Sample: 3
Description: Squat barrel-shaped cylinders whose greatest diameter is at the center. Lengths range from 1 to 1.3 cm.

Temporal distribution: Sefid and Surkh phases.
Geographic distribution: Unknown.

TYPE: Small White Shell Bead

Sample: 1
Description: A segment of a tubular shell whose ends were cut to make a bead. The exterior of the shell has parallel ribbing. The example remains in Iran and the species could not be determined, although it appears to be *Dentalium* sp.
Temporal distribution: Sefid Phase.
Geographic distribution: Ali Kosh (Hole, Flannery and Neely, 1969:244).

TYPE: Cowrie Shell Beads

Sample: 2

Table 80

MISCELLANEOUS ORNAMENTS AT CHAGHA SEFID
by Stratigraphic Zone

			Pendants				Bracelet	Rings					Beads											Blanks		
Phase	Area	Zone	Boar's Tusk	Pebble and Sherd	Bone	Crab Claw	Smooth-surfaced Stone	Ceramic	Shell	Stone	Bone	Spool	Ceramic Disc	Stone Disc	Shell Disc	Tubular Ceramic	Tubular Stone	Tubular Bone	Spherical Ceramic	Spherical Stone	Barrel-shaped Ceramic	Shell	Cowrie Shell	Discoidal Bead Blanks	Tubular Blanks	Totals
Sabz	SD	J																									1
	SD	I																									2
Choga Mami Transitional	SD	H		1																							4
	SD	G2																							1		3
	SD	G1					1										2		1					1	1	8
Surkh	SD	F			1									1										1	1	5
	SC, SD	E2												1				1	1							3
	SC, SD	E1												2	1		1	1	1					3		8
	SC	D3									1																1
	SC	D2												1							1						2
	SC	D1			1																						1
	SC	C2			1								1	1	1										1		5
Sefid	SA	C1		1		1	1	(3)	1		1	1		2		1	1	1	1		1		1	3		15
	SA	B2		2	3	2			1				2	2		1		1	2			1	1		2	18
	SA	B1				1	1			1	1				1		1				1					9
	SA	A4					1					1													1	3
Mohammad Jaffar	SB	C			1										1											2
	SB	B													2					1						3
	SB	A													1											1
Ali Kosh	SA	A3	2			1								1												4
	SA	A2	1		1						1				1									1		1
	SA	A1																								3
		Totals	4	4	6	5	4	(3)	2	1	4	1	3	10	8	2	5	3	7	1	3	1	2	11	4	91

Table 81

MISCELLANEOUS ORNAMENTS AT CHAGHA SEFID
by Cultural Phase

Phase	Pendants				Bracelet	Rings				Spool	Beads												Blanks		Totals
	Boar's Tusk	Pebble and Sherd	Bone	Crab Claw	Smooth-surfaced Stone	Ceramic	Shell	Stone	Bone		Ceramic Disc	Stone Disc	Shell Disc	Tubular Ceramic	Tubular Stone	Tubular Bone	Spherical Ceramic	Spherical Stone	Barrel-shaped Ceramic	Shell	Cowrie Shell	Discoidal Bead Blanks	Tubular Blanks	
Sabz																								
Choga Mami Transitional		1			1										2		1					2		7
Surkh			2						2		1	5	2		1	2	3		1			5	1	25
Sefid	1	3	3	4	3	(3)	2	1	1	1	2	4	1	2	2	1	3		2	1	2	3	3	45
Mohammad Jaffar			1										4					1						6
Ali Kosh	3			1					1			1	1									1		8
Totals	4	4	6	5	4	(3)	2	1	4	1	3	10	8	2	5	3	7	1	3	1	2	11	4	91

Description: Cowrie shells with holes for suspension.
Temporal distribution: Sefid Phase.
Geographic distribution: Ali Kosh (Hole, Flannery and Neely, 1969:244).

BEAD BLANKS (Pl. 55*j-n,p*; Fig. 92*j*)

Sample: 11 discoidal, 4 tubular
Description: Stone and ceramic which has been shaped like beads but not perforated. In a few cases drill holes had been started.
Temporal distribution: Thoughout the sequence.

COPPER

Only three of the eight pieces of copper recovered from Chagha Sefid are in good stratigraphic context, although three others may be of prehistoric age. Only one identifiable object is clearly prehistoric. This is a copper crochet which was found beneath wall foundation stones in a Late Sefid Phase context in Area A. A cold-hammered copper bead was found in Ali Kosh Phase deposits (Cyril Smith in Hole, Flannery and Neely, 1969: Appendix II) and copper occurs in some quantity at Çayönü in Turkey, a site slightly older than the Sefid Phase (Braidwood et al., 1971). Copper is rare in sites of the 7th-8th millenium, probably in part because it occurs in such small bits that it is difficult to recover. The following pieces of copper were recovered at Chagha Sefid.

CROCHET (Pl. 55*w*)

Description: A rod of copper about 6.5 cm long and 2 mm in diameter with one end turned up to form a hook. This object was found beneath wall foundation stones of Late Sefid Phase and appears to be in unequivocal context.

RINGS (Pl. 5 5*u,v*)

Sample: 3
Description: Two examples, both fragmentary, are rectangular in section. According to a preliminary analysis, one of these, which contained only superficial corrosion, is "of a brass containing tin, or bronze containing zinc, and minor additions of lead and iron. Probably it is a bit of 19th century extruded wire, filed to shape" (Cyril Smith, personal communication). Unfortunately this example was found in Zone A1, near the base of Area A. The explanation for this occurrence seems to be the rodent burrows that also brought sherds down from the surface.

A very small fragment of a ring with flattened edges came from a mixed Surkh Phase deposit at the top of Area A. This fragment is only 4 mm long. There is no reason to doubt that this ring is also intrusive.

A third ring, not yet analyzed in detail by Professor Smith, is from Zone B1, Sefid Phase. This fragment (Pl. 55*v*) does not appear to have filed edges but it is very corroded; it may be prehistoric.

LUMPS OR FLAKES OF COPPER

Sample: 4
Description: Two are flat flakes which are too corroded for analysis and two are chunks, perhaps melted copper or slag. These examples have not been analyzed. One of the small chunks, 9 mm long, with a diameter of about 4 mm, is from Zone F, Late Surkh Phase and appears to be in good prehistoric context. The other three examples are from mixed contexts.

BIBLIOGRAPHY

Abu Al-Souf, Behnam
    1968   Tell es-Sawwan. Sumer, vol. 24:3-15.

Adams, Robert McC.
    1962   Agriculture and urban life in early southwestern Iran. Science, vol. 136:109-122.

Adams, Robert McC., and H. J. Nissen
    1972   The Uruk countryside. Chicago, The University of Chicago Press.

Al-A'dami, K. A.
    1968   Excavation at Tell es-Sawwan. Sumer, vol. 24:57-60.

Ammerman, A. J., and L. L. Cavalli-Sforza
    1973   A population model for the diffusion of early farming in Europe. *In* The explanation of culture change: models in prehistory, C. Renfrew, ed. London, Duckworth. pp. 343-357.

Barth, Fredrik
    1956   Ecologic relations of ethnic groups in Swat, North Pakistan. American Anthropologist, vol. 58:1079-1089.

Bordaz, Jacques
    1970   The Suberde excavations, southwestern Turkey. An interim report. Türk Arkeoloji Dergisi, vol. 17:43-71.

Braidwood, R. J.
    1951   From cave to village in prehistoric Iraq. Bulletin American Schools of Oriental Research, no. 124:12-18.
    1952   The Near East and the foundations for civilization. Eugene, Oregon.
    1960   Seeking the world's first farmers in Persian Kudistan; a full-scale investigation of prehistoric sites near Kermanshah. The Illustrated London News, October 22:695-697.
    1975   Prehistoric men. 8th Edition. Scott, Foresman, and Co., Glenview, Ill.

Braidwood, R. J., and L. S. Braidwood
    1960   Excavations in the Plain of Antioch I. The earlier assemblages. Phases A-J. Oriental Institute Publication 61. Chicago, The University of Chicago Press.

Braidwood, R. J., Bruce Howe, et al.
    1960   Near Eastern prehistory. Science, vol. 131:1536-1541.

Braidwood, R. J., et al.
    1952   Matarrah: a southern variant of the Hassunan assemblage, excavated in 1948. Journal of Near Eastern Studies, vol. 11:1-75.
    1953   Symposium: Did man once live by beer alone? American Anthropologist, 55:515-26.
    1971   Beginnings of village-farming communities in southeastern Turkey. Proceedings of the National Academy of Science, vol. 68:1236-1240.

Burkholder, Grace
    1972   Ubaid sites and pottery in Saudi Arabia. Archaeology, vol. 25:264-269.

Clark, J. G. D.
    1963   Neolithic bows from Somerset, England and the prehistory of archery in Northwest Europe. Proceedings of the Prehistoric Society for 1963, vol. 29:50-98.

Colton, Harold S.
    1953   Potsherds: an introduction to the study of prehistoric Southwestern ceramics and their use in historical reconstruction. Museum of Northern Arizona Bulletin, no. 25. Flagstaff.

Contenson, H. de
1971 Tell Ramad, a village of Syria of the seventh and sixth millenia B.C. Archaeology, vol. 24, pp. 278-285.

Contenson, H. de, and Willem J. van Liere
1966 Seconde campagne à Tell Ramad, 1965. Rapport Préliminaire. Annales Archéologiques Arabes Syriennes XIV:167-174.

Curwen, C. E.
1930 Prehistoric flint sickles. Antiquity, vol. 4:179-186.

Dollfus, Geneviève.
1971 Les fouilles à Djaffarabad de 1969 à 1971. Cahiers de la Délégation Archéologique Française en Iran, vol. Vol. 1:17-162.
1974 Jaefarabad. Proceedings of the 2nd Annual Symposium on Archaeological Research in Iran, Muzeh-e Iran-e Bastan, Tehran. pp. 1-14.

Delougaz, P. P., and H. J. Kantor
1971 The fourth season of excavations at Chogha Mich in Khuzestan (1969-70). Preliminary report. Bastan Chenassi va Honar-e Iran. 7/8:36-41.
1972 The 1971 season of excavation of the joint Iranian expedition. Bastan Chenassi va Honar-e Iran, 9/10:88-96.

Dorrell, Peter
1972 A note on the geomorphology of the country near Umm Dabaghiyah. Iraq 34:69-72.

Edelberg, Lennart
1966/67 Seasonal dwellings of farmers in north-western Luristan. Folk, vol. 8-9:373-401.

El-Wailly, Faisal
1963 Tell as-Sawwan. Sumer, vol. 19:1-2.
1964 Tell as-Sawwan. Sumer, vol. 20:1-2.

Fairservis, Walter A., Jr.
1961 Archeological studies in the Seistan Basin of southwestern Afghanistan and eastern Iran. Anthropological Papers, American Museum of Natural History, vol. 48, Part 1. New York.

Garrod, Dorothy A. E.
1930 The paleolithic of southern Kurdistan: excavations in the caves of Zarzi and Hazar Merd. American School of Prehistoric Research, Bulletin no. 6:8-43, New Haven.
1957 Digging up Jericho. London, Ernest Benn Ltd.

Gautier, J. E., and G. Lampre
1905 Fouilles de Moussian. Mémoires de la Mission archéologique en Iran, No. 8, pp. 59-148.

Ghirshman, Roman
1938 Fouilles de Sialk, près de Kashan. I. Paris, Musée du Louvre, Département des antiquites orientales. Série archéologique IV, Paris.

Helbaek, Hans
1969 Plant collecting, dry-farming, and irrigation agriculture in prehistoric Deh Luran. In Prehistory and human ecology of the Deh Luran Plain, by Frank Hole, Kent V. Flannery and James A. Neely. Memoirs, no. 1. Ann Arbor, The University of Michigan Museum of Anthropology.
1972 Traces of plants in the early ceramic site of Umm Dabaghiyah. Iraq 34:17-19.

Hodges, H. W. M.
1964 Artifacts; an introduction to primitive technology. New York, F. A. Praeger.

Hole, Frank
1961 Chipped stone analysis and the early village farming community. Ph.D. Dissertation, University of Chicago.
1966 Investigating the origins of Mesopotamian civilization. Science, vol. 153:605-611.
1974 Tepe Tula'i, an early campsite in Khuzistan, Iran. Paleorient 2:219-242.
1975 The Sondage at Tappeh Tula'i. Proceedings IIIrd Annual Symposium on Archaeological Research in Iran, November 1974. Muzeh-e Iran-e Bastan, Tehran, pp. 63-76.

Hole, Frank, editor
　1969　Preliminary reports of the Rice University Project in Iran 1968-69. Unpublished reports circulated among participants in the project and other archeologists doing related work.

Hole, Frank, and Kent V. Flannery
　1962　Excavations at Ali Kosh, Iran, 1961. Iranica Antiqua, vol. 2:97-148.
　1968　The prehistory of southwestern Iran: a preliminary report. Proceedings of the Prehistoric Society fo 1967, vol. 33:147-206.

Hole, Frank and Bonnie Hole
　n.d.　Survey of early prehistoric sites in Khuzistan. manuscript in preparation.

Hole, Frank, Kent V. Flannery, and James A. Neely
　1969　Prehistory and human ecology of the Deh Luran Plain. Memoir No. 1. Ann Arbor, University o Michigan Museum of Anthropology.

Huckriede, Reinhold
　1962　Jung-Quartär und End-Mesolithikum in der Provinz Kerman (Iran). Eiszeitalter und Gegenwart, vol 12:25-42.

Kantor, H. J.
　1974　The Čoqa Mis excavations. Proceedings of the IInd Annual Symposium on Archaeological Research in Iran. Muzeh-e Iran-e Bastan, Tehran, pp. 15-22.

Kirkbride, Diana
　1966　Five seasons at the pre-pottery Neolithic village of Beidha in Jordan. Palestine Exploration Quarterly pp. 8-274.
　1972　Umm Dabaghiyah 1971: a preliminary report. Iraq 34:3-15.

Kirkby, M. and A. V. T. Kirkby
　1969　Provisional report on geomorphology and land use in Deh Luran and Upper Khuzistan. In Preliminary report of the Rice University Project in Iran 1968-1969. Houston, Texas, Department of Anthropology, Rice University, pp. 1-8.

Kramer, S. N.
　1961　History begins at Sumer. Revised edition. London, Thames and Hudson.

LeBreton, Louis
　1947　Note sur la céramique peinte aux environs de Suse et à Suse. Mémoires de la Mission archéologique en Iran, vol. 30:193-217.

Löffler, von Reinhold, and Erika Friedl
　1967　Eine ethnographische sammlung von den Boir Ahmad, Südiran. Archive fur Völkerkunde 21:95-207

Lorimer, D. L. R.
　1908　A report on Pusht-i-Kuh. Unpublished military and political assessment of Luristan.

Mallowan, M. E. L., and J. Cruikshank Rose
　1935　Excavations at Tell Arpachiyah, 1933. Iraq, vol. 2:1-178.

Matson, F. R.
　1971　A study of temperatures used in firing ancient Mesopotamian pottery. In Science and archaeology R. H. Brill, ed. Cambridge, Mass., MIT Press.

Meadow, R. H.
　1971　The emergence of civilization. In Man, Culture, and Society, H. L. Shapiro, ed. Oxford University Press.

Mellaart, J. A.
　1963　Çatal Hüyük in Anatolia: excavations which revolutionize the history of the earliest civilizations Illustrated London News, 9 Feb., p. 196.
　1967　Çatal Hüyük. A neolithic town in Anatolia. London, Thames and Hudson.

Mortensen, Peder
　1964　Early village-farming occupation. In Excavations at Tepe Guran, Luristan, by J. Meldgaard, P Mortensen, H. Thrane. Acta Archaeologica, vol. 39:110-121.
　1970　Tell Shimshara. The Hassuna Period. Hist. Filos. Skr. Dan. Yid. Selsk., vol. 5:1-148.
　1971　A preliminary study of the chipped stone industry from Beidha. Acta Archaeologica, vol. 41:1-54.
　1973　A sequence of Samarran flint and obsidian tools from Choga Mami. Iraq, vol. 35:37-55.
　1975　A survey of prehistoric settlements in northern Luristan. Acta Archaeologica 45:1-47.

Mortensen, Peder, and Kent V. Flannery
    1966   En af aveden's aeldste landsbyer. Nationalmuseets Arbejdsmark, 1966, pp. 85-96.

Munsell, Albert H.
    1961   A color notation. An illustrated system defining all colors and their relations by measured scales of hue, value, and chroma. 11th Edition. Munsell Color Co., Baltimore.

Nissen, Hans Jörg
    1968   Survey of an abandoned modern village. Sumer, vol. 24:107-114.

Oates, Joan
    1960   Ur and Eridu, the prehistory. Iraq, vol. 22:32-50.
    1966   The baked clay figurines from Tell es-Sawwan. Iraq, vol. 28:146-153.
    1968   Prehistoric investigations near Mandali, Iraq. Iraq, vol. 30:1-20.
    1969   Choga Mami 1967-68: a preliminary report. Iraq, vol. 31:115-152.
    1973   The background and development of early farming communities in Mesopotamia and the Zagros. Proceedings of The Prehistoric Society 39:147-181.

Perrot, J.
    1968   Premiers villages de Syrie et de Palestine. Compte rendus de l'Academie des Inscriptions et Belles Lettres, April-June 1968. pp. 161.

Reed, Charles A.
    1969   The pattern of animal domestication in the prehistoric Near East. In The domestication and exploitation of plants and animals. P. J. Ucko and G. W. Dimbleby, eds. Chicago, Aldine, pp. 361-380.

Renfrew, Colin
    1969   The obsidian from Ali Kosh and Tepe Sabz. In Prehistory and human ecology of the Deh Luran Plain, by Frank Hole, Kent V. Flannery, and James A. Neely. No. 1. Ann Arbor, Museum of Anthropology, University of Michigan.

Shepard, A. O.
    1956   Ceramics for the archaeologist. Carnegie Institution of Washington, Publication 609.

Smith, P. E. L.
    1970   Ganj Dareh Tepe. Iran, vol. 8:178-180.

Solecki, Ralph S.
    1952   A paleolithic site in the Zagros mountains of northern Iraq, report on a sounding at Shanidar Cave. Sumer 8:127-161.
    1963   Prehistory in Shanidar Valley, Northern Iraq. Science, vol. 139:179-193.
    1964   Shanidar Cave, a late Pleistocene site in Northern Iraq. Report of the VIth International Congress on Quaternary, vol. 4:413-423.
    1969   Milling tools and the epi-paleolithic in the Near East. In Etudes sur le Quaternaire dans le Monde. VIIIe Congres INQUA, Paris, 989-994.

Steensberg, A.
    1943   Ancient harvesting implements: a study in human geography. Copenhagen, Nationalmuseets skrifter. Arkoolegisk-historisk Roekke I.

Stronach, David
    1961   The excavations at Ras al-Amiya. Iraq, vol. 23:95-137.

Stuiver, M.
    1970   Long-term C14 variations. Proceedings of the Twelfth Nobel Symposium, Uppsala, Sweden, August 11-15, 1969. Ingrid U. Olsson, ed. New York, Wiley-Interscience Division, John Wiley & Sons.

Tauber, H.
    1970   The Scandinavian varve chronology and C14 dating. Proceedings of the Twelfth Nobel Symposium, Uppsala, Sweden, August 11-15, 1969. Ingrid U. Olsson, ed. New York, Wiley-Interscience Division, John Wiley & Sons.

Tobler, A. J.
    1950   Excavations at Tepe Gawra, II. Museum Monographs. Philadelphia, University of Pennsylvania.

van Loon, Maurits
    1966   First results of the 1965 excavations at Tell Mureybit near Meskene. Annales Archéologiques Arabes Syriennes XVI. pp. 211-217.
    1968   The Oriental Institute excavations at Mureybit, Syria: preliminary report on the 1965 campaign. Part I: architecture and general finds. Journal of Near Eastern Studies, vol. 27, pp. 265-290.

Vayson de Pradenne, A.
    1919   Faucille préhistorique de Solferino. L'Anthropologie, Vol. 29:393-422.

Witthoft, John
    1967   Glazed polish on flint tools. American Antiquity, vol. 32:383-388.

APPENDIX I

LAND AND WATER RESOURCES OF THE DEH LURAN AND KHUZISTAN PLAINS

by Michael J. Kirkby
Department of Geography
The University of Leeds, England

ACKNOWLEDGEMENTS

This study has been carried out as a part of a National Science Foundation project, administered by Rice University, Houston, Texas. This particular part of the study was, however, directly supported by a grant from Rice University. The author wishes to thank the University for its sponsorship; Professor Frank Hole, of the Department of Anthropology for his support as director of the project; Dr. James Neely and Dr. Anne Kirkby for their especial help in the field and since; Mr. Alan Craig, then of the Khuzistan Water and Power Authority, for his hospitality, help and advice based on long experience of the area; and the University of Bristol, England, for leave of absence to take part in the project.

INTRODUCTION

This report forms a part of the results of the archeological project centered on Chagha Sefid, near Deh Luran, which follows from previous work in the Deh Luran plain (Hole, Flannery and Neely, 1969). The study serves not only as a fairly detailed account of the physical geography of the plain, but also as a model of the larger area of the Khuzistan plain, which has been examined at a reconnaissance level.

The Khuzistan Plain System

The Tigris-Euphrates River valley forms a trough of low-lying land which drains southeast towards the head of the Persian Gulf. Khuzistan, with its geographic extension in Deh Luran, is on the north side of this trough near the Gulf, and the only part of the trough in Iran. The plain of Khuzistan slopes less than 0.1 percent mainly towards the Shatt-al-Arab (the combined lower Tigris and Euphrates) rather than towards the Gulf. Across this plain flow the Karun, with its tributary, the Diz, the Karkheh, and some smaller streams, which together drain 100,000 km^2 of the Zagros Mountains and bring perennial water to the plain.

The contrast between the plain and the Zagros Mountains is dramatic. The mountains stand as a backdrop, faulted and folded above the flat alluvial stage along its northern and northeastern flanks. Above Ahwaz several low folds of the Zagros have been almost buried beneath the plains sediments, but still survive as low ridges, through gaps in which the rivers must flow (Fig. 93). The Zagros not only provide a topographic contrast which highlights the even surface of the plain, but also provide an area of slightly higher rainfall (400-800 mm) which is able to recharge aquifers and maintain year-round flows in the Khuzistan rivers which would otherwise dry up in the summer, during which no rain falls for almost four months and temperatures reach 40°C.

Khuzistan is the largest lowland area in Iran, and has been an important agricultural area for 10,000 years. The rivers have played a vital part by providing a source of irrigation water. Canal and qanat systems became more complex over the years, reaching a peak in Sasanian or Early Islamic times which modern construction is only beginning to rival. Without some

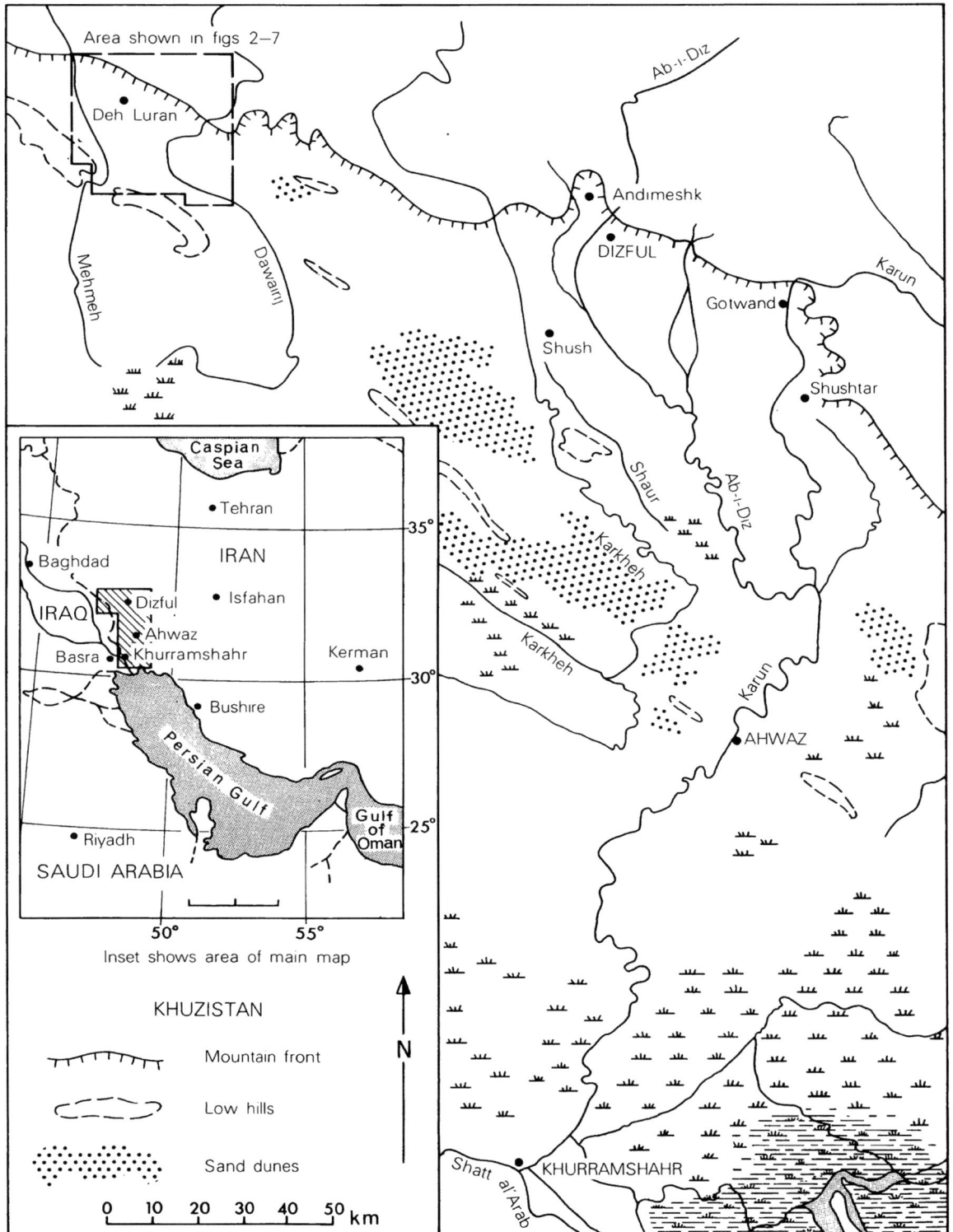

Fig. 93. Location map for the Khuzistan Plain, Iran.

form of additional water supply, rainwater farming is marginal even in the rainy winter months. With effective irrigation, large areas of the plain receive sufficient water to more or less guarantee winter crops of wheat and barley, while market gardening can be practiced over a smaller area in the summer.

Rivers dissolve minerals from the rocks, and in Khuzistan, where the rocks contain highly soluble common salt, gypsum and calcium carbonate, the river waters generally contain high concentrations of dissolved material. In a semi-arid area, evaporation increases these concentrations still further. During irrigation, the evapo-transpiration of the irrigation water by crop plants commonly raises the concentrations to such a high level that the minerals are precipitated in the soil. Over time the mineral content of the soil may become so high that crop plants can no longer grow. If excess irrigation water is applied, however, concentrations of minerals in soil water need not become high enough for them to build up in the soil; while sufficient water draining through the soil can slowly reverse the effects of previous salinization, provided that sodium salts have not been abundantly deposited in the soil. If sodium salts are present, they give the soil such poor drainage characteristics that the salinization process can no longer be reversed. Some land in Khuzistan (and much more in the Tigris-Euphrates valley) appears to have been ruined in this way by inadequate irrigation. The problem appears to have been most severe in southern Khuzistan, where irrigation water is initially more saline and more scarce and where the water need per square kilometer is greatest, so that there is none to spare for drainage to prevent salts from accumulating.

The Persian Gulf is a geosynclinal area of long-continued subsidence, whereas the Tigris-Euphrates valley, including Khuzistan, is an area of rapid sedimentation which tends to build the land surface upwards and outwards as deltas into the Gulf. At the same time, uplift of the Zagros Mountains, and their outliers on the Khuzistan plain, may still be continuing, though the evidence is somewhat equivocal. In such a dynamic situation, the position of the coastline might either advance or retreat, though the evidence suggests (Lees and Falcon, 1952) that it has been more or less stationary since the Pliocene. Alluviation and subsidence have had the most influence close to the sea, and the area north of Ahwaz, with which this report is most concerned, has been partially decoupled from these effects by the outlying low ridges of the Zagros (especially the Ahwaz ridge). It will, however, be seen below that considerable alluviation has occurred, allowing river courses to change over time. The resulting changes of river regime from down-cutting to aggradation, and vice-versa, have had a considerable effect on local conditions with regard to flood frequency and ease of irrigation.

The Deh Luran Plain

If the line of the low ridge which passes through Ahwaz is followed to the northwest, it gradually converges with the main Zagros mountain front, crossing first the Karkheh River, and then two smaller, but still considerable and perennial streams, the Dawairij and the Mehmeh. The area around these two rivers, and contained between this ridge and the Zagros front is the Deh Luran plain, an area about 25 by 25 km. The ridge, the Jebel Hamrin, partially isolates the Deh Luran plain from the sedimentation and subsidence of the Tigris-Euphrates valley in the same way that the Ahwaz ridge isolates the Upper Khuzistan plains from events in the Persian Gulf. The Deh Luran plain can thus be considered, for most purposes, as a microcosm of Upper Khuzistan.

An exploration of this analogy will help describe the Deh Luran plain. Like Khuzistan, the plain has a low gradient of monotonous uniformity, although the actual gradient is distinctly higher, more like 1 percent than 0.1 percent because it is closer to the mountains. As in Khuzistan, the mountains appear to rise abruptly from the plains. Rainfall is not fully adequate for a winter crop, with similar rainfalls (350-400 mm) to those at the same elevation (150 m) in Khuzistan. The perennial streams are able to supply enough water to ensure winter crops, but in the Deh Luran plain the smaller drainage areas of the two main streams (2400 km^2 together) result in relative lower summer flows with much higher salinities, so that conditions for summer irrigation are exceedingly marginal. Salinization problems may therefore be more marked than in most of Upper Khuzistan, though nothing like as severe and with no signs of the irreversible damage that is evident in some soils of Lower Khuzistan or parts of the main Tigris-Euphrates valley.

SURFACE PROPERTIES OF THE DEH LURAN PLAIN

Deposition and Erosion

The plain is composed of a series of overlapping low-gradient alluvial fans. Each stream flows out from the steep mountains in its own valley. On leaving the mountain front, the flow is able to spread laterally and, on the much lower gradient, begins to deposit the solid debris which it carries when in flood. The stream deposits first large stones, and then in turn small stones, sand, and finally silt or clay. At the same time, the long profile of the fan develops a concave upward form, gradients decreasing from $5°$ (10 percent) or more near the fan apex, in conjunction with stones 20 cm or more in diameter, down to gradients of $0.3°$ (0.6 percent), in conjunction with silts, 20 km from the apex. Over a period, the form of the surface comes into equilibrium with the hydraulic forces acting on it, and aggradation ceases, so that the fan surface passively transports the debris from the mountains. This equilibrium is, however, a very delicate one in semi-arid areas and small changes in conditions can produce large changes in the regime of the fan, either towards renewed aggradation, or towards down-cutting into the fan.

During an aggradational phase, streams flowing over silt or coarser material, as in the Deh Luran plain, characteristically have a braided channel pattern, the flow splitting into a number of distributaries which separate and rejoin repeatedly. As each channel deposits its load, it blocks its own path, and raises its own level until it overflows to the side into one or more new channels. The fan is thus covered with many small channels, each flowing within a few centimeters of the fan surface, and many of them shifting in position in each storm. The whole of the fan is characterized by a very high frequency of flooding, though it is rarely severe, and by a seasonally high water table. Conditions are therefore very suitable for floodwater farming, or farming which relies on a shallow water table, over a large area. Shallow, temporary wells and small canals are sufficient to ensure that the available water is spread laterally and is never concentrated enough to erode the fields. At the same time, conditions are very unsuitable for living at the plain level. Even a *tepe* of modest height, however, would allow farming groups to live close to their fields, and there would be a strong incentive to continue occupation of such sites.

During an erosional phase, streams cut down into the fan surface, and thus stabilize their position. The largest streams cut down the most, and so drain all others into the same course. Over a period, meandering of the stream within its trench leads to erosion of the trench sides, and the gradual widening of a floodplain at a level below that of the main plain. At the present time, the main rivers of the Deh Luran plain are incised in this way, 5-10 m below the plain surface. On the floodplains, the water table is high year-round, because the channelling of the flow reduces evaporation losses and so maintains flows throughout the summer in rivers the size of the Mehmeh or Dawairij. Flooding, however, is more severe within the floodplain, and absent, or very rare, outside the floodplain. Farming is therefore more or less impossible on the floodplain, because of the severity of flooding. On the main plain, however, settlement is possible almost anywhere, but farming must either rely solely on rainfall, or else use relatively sophisticated canal systems to raise water from the river to the plain above.

For example, a canal or qanat, to raise water through 10 meters on a plain sloping at $1°$ must be at least 1 km long. Against this difficulty must be set the greater control over exactly where the water is applied, and the possibility of some summer irrigation from the now perennial stream.

Although the present time is characterized by erosion over the Deh Luran plain, it will be seen below that much of the archeological period was characterized by aggradation. Figure 94 shows the positions of the fans deposited by the Mehmeh and Dawairij, which can still be seen in the direction of drainage lines on the main plain. Between these two large fans are a series of smaller fans, which have not been separately delimited in the figure. On these smaller fans, the aggradation which produced them appears to have resulted from the erosion of older fans, so that the younger fans spread out of, and bury the toes of, older fans. The boundary between older and younger fans is also shown in Figure 94. Erosion of these older fans has gradually produced a gently rolling landscape with 5-20 meters of local relief, as the slopes between lower floodplain and upper plain have been reduced in gradient until the two levels are connected by smooth convexo-concave profiles. In this area the surface is more stony, because it is close to the mountain front, and canal irrigation is difficult. Dry farming is barely possible, making use of the very slight increase of rainfall with elevation, and terracing may be of advantage, both to minimize surface erosion and to hold fine material and rainwater.

The sequence from coarse to fine material, and from rolling to smooth surface may be traced in Figures 95 and 96. Figure 95 shows the number of stones larger than 25 mm per square meter of surface, an indication of the progressive reduction in grain size away from the mountains. Figure 96 shows the depths of dissection of the landscape, with relief of 5 m or more in the older fan areas progressively reducing to almost no relief in a central area.

Salinity

The salinity of the near-surface soils (Fig. 97) is a characteristic which originally derives from the topographic position of each site with respect to the fans, but which can be greatly modified through irrigation. As water spreads out across and down the length of a fan, the flows become less, partly because of downward percolation, and partly because of evaporation, which progressively concentrates the salts, so that the soils, like the river waters, become more and more saline downslope (downstream). Irrigation will tend to overlay this natural picture with areas of unusually high salinity in, and immediately downslope from, the cultivated area. Plant yields are much reduced at salinities in excess of 0.2-0.4 percent, so that favored areas for cultivation tend to be a little upslope—where the soil is moist but does not have salinity problems—from the area which naturally has these salinities. If cultivation is uneven, then areas of former cultivation may be revealed as areas of anomalously high salinity, but if cultivation is uniform within the optimum zone, then its effect will merely be to increase the high-salinity area, the boundaries of which will still be accordant with other features of the environment. Such features will also gradually be obliterated by natural water flows, and more rapidly if the surface is buried by new deposits.

In fact such anomalies appear to be slight, and are not enough to give clear evidence of the destruction of cultivable land at the present time or in the past. The extent of anomalies is discussed further below, but there is the problem that very old fields have been buried under new sediment (as will also be seen below). It is perhaps more pertinent to note, therefore, that the levels of salinity in this area are only very locally severe enough to prevent cultivation, and are not associated with the high sodium content, such as is found in parts of the Tigris-Euphrates valley, which leads to irreversible changes in the soil. It is thus thought that salinization has not been a major factor in the agricultural history of the Deh Luran plain, although it cannot be ruled out as a reason for local redistribution of land near the saline limit of 0.35 percent shown in Figure 97.

Vegetation

The distribution of uncultivated vegetation is even more of an artifact than soil salinity, because of the continuing pressures of cultivation and of grazing. If, however, the land use is in harmony with variations in the environment, then the vegetation pattern will equally reflect the variation in both; whereas anomalies between vegetation and environment might, if present, show discordance between land use and environment. As with salinity, no discordance has been detected. Since vegetation is able to adjust rather rapidly to a change in environment, this agreement would refer primarily to present-day patterns of land use, whereas salinity changes more slowly.

The vegetation zones of Figure 98 have been ranked from 1 to 7 according to their salinity tolerance with zone 1 being least tolerant, although the boundaries shown are the vegetation boundaries. It can be seen that, using this ranking, the zones show a very similar pattern of environment to that shown by other factors discussed above. Vegetation zones have been defined on the basis of presence or absence of indicator species. These, which have been identified by Dr. Jane Renfrew, are listed in Table 82. Most of the species chosen are shrubs because of their greater permanence, so that they refer to conditions over a period of several years. The indicator species generally show a continuous gradation from plants with higher drought tolerance and lower salt tolerance to

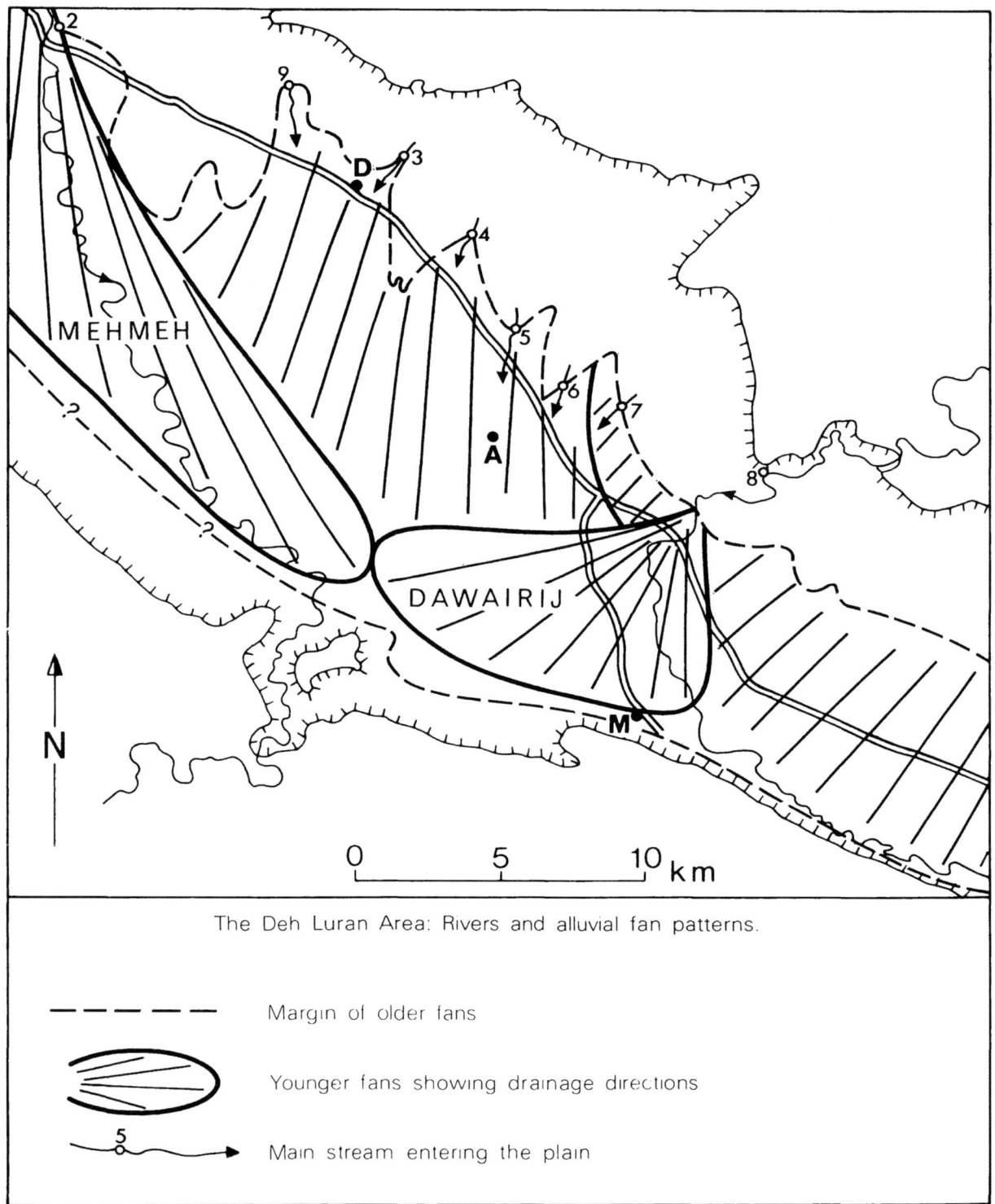

Fig. 94. The Deh Luran area: rivers and alluvial fan patterns.

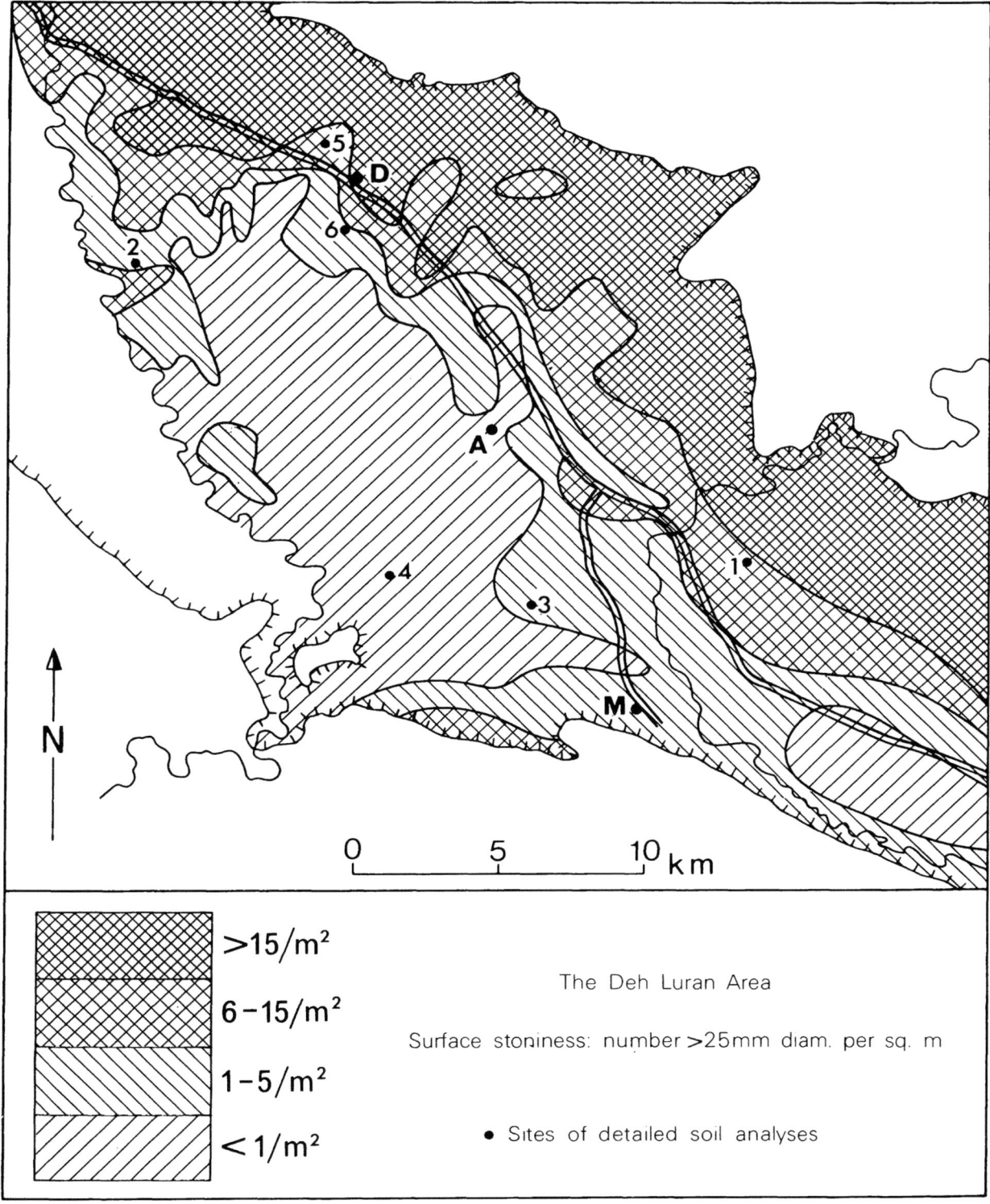

Fig. 95. The Deh Luran area: surface stoniness—number stones per m² of more than 25mm diameter.

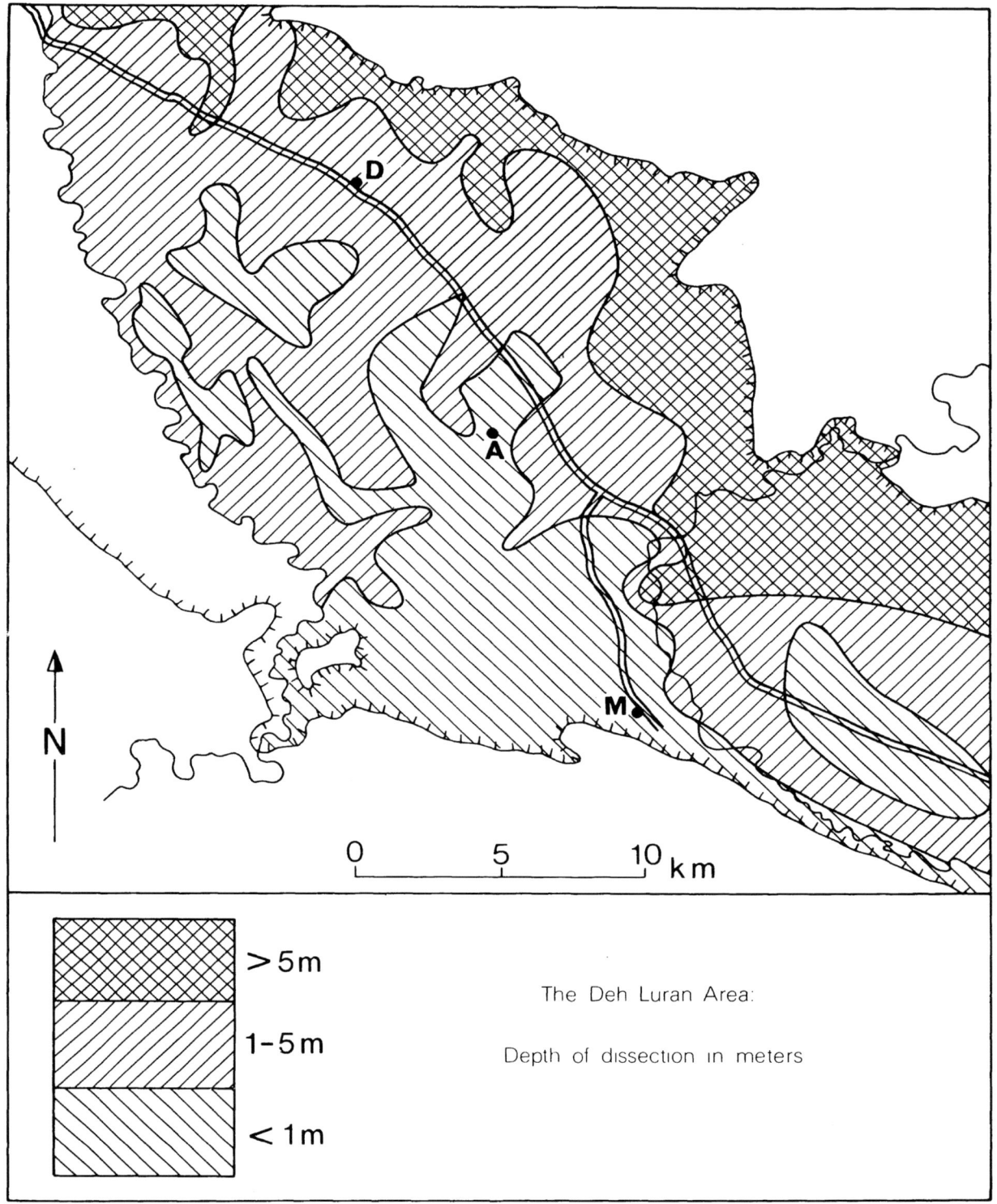

Fig. 96. The Deh Luran area: depth of dissection in meters.

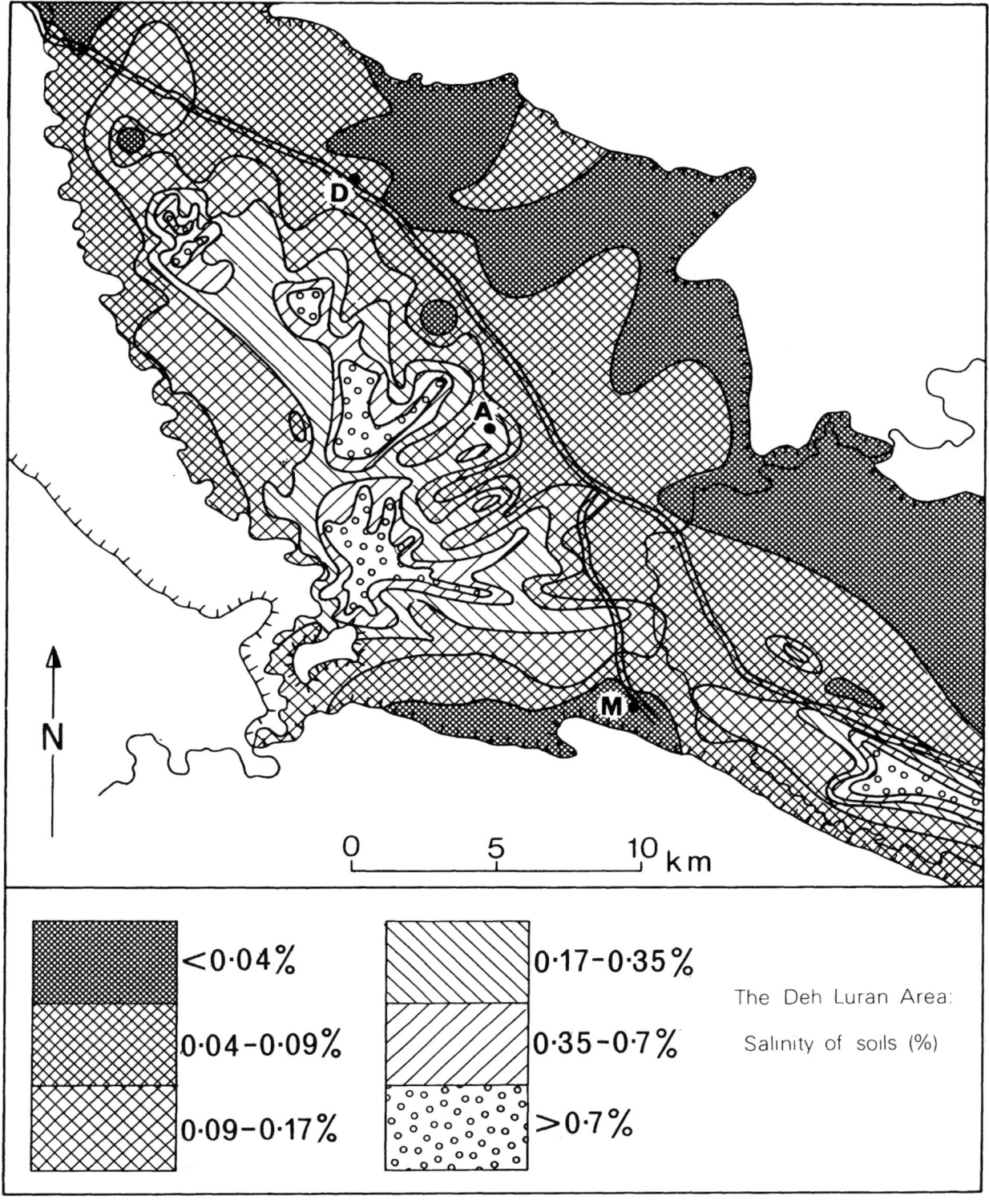

Fig. 97. The Deh Luran area: percentage salinity of soils.

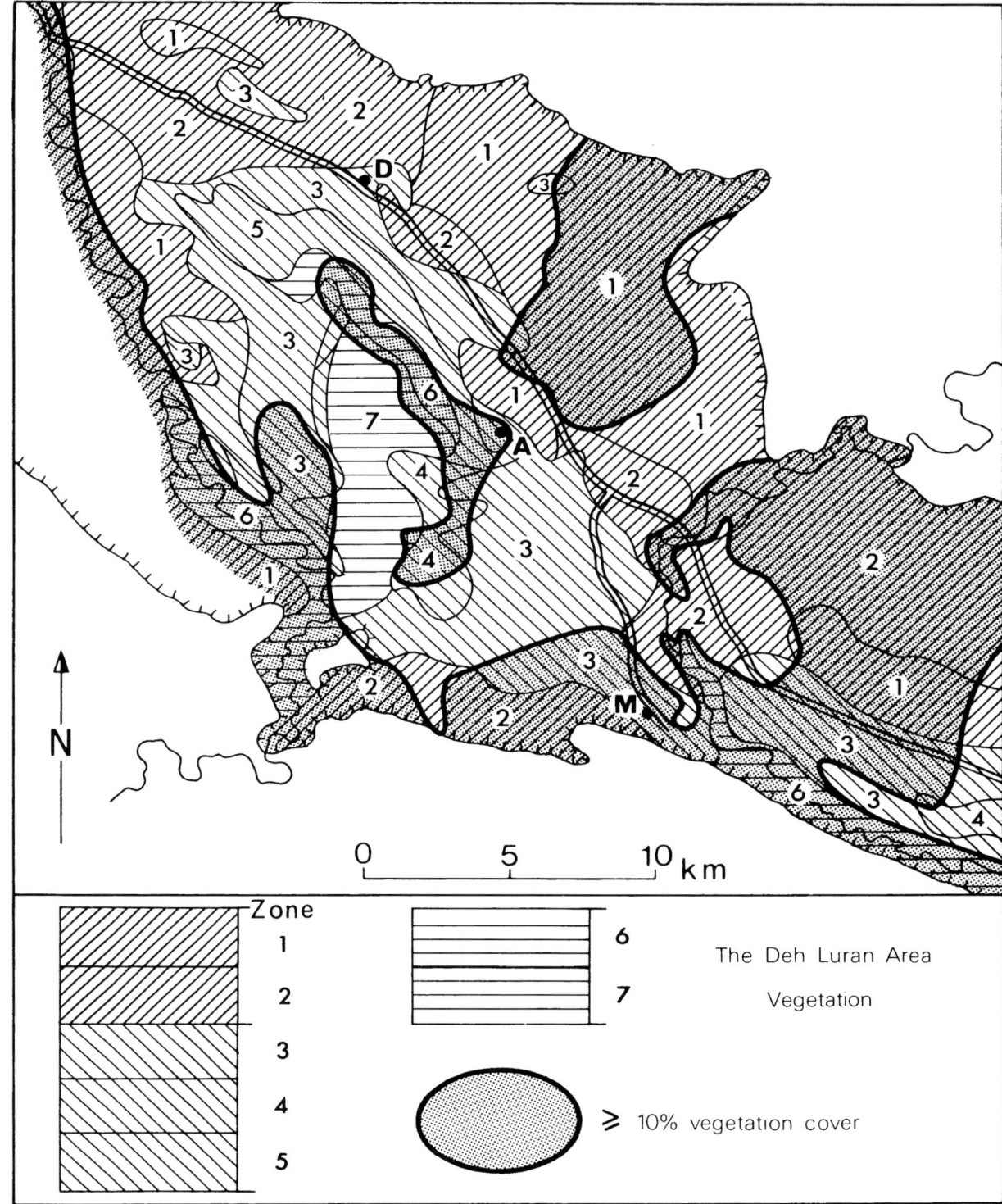

Fig. 98. The Deh Luran area: vegetation zones, based on presence or absence of indicator species which a listed in Table 82.

Table 82

INDICATOR PLANTS FOR VEGETATION MAPPING

Plant	Zone						
	1	2	3	4	5	6	7
Gramineae	+	+	+	+	+	+	+
Zizyphus spina-christi	−	a	+	−	−	−	−
Prosopis stephaniana/Alhagi maurorum	−	+	a	+	+	−	−
Limonium	−	−	−	+	+	+	−
Suaeda vera	−	−	−	−	+	+	−
Tamarix galliea	−	−	−	−	−	+	−
Thymelaea hirsuta	−	−	−	−	−	−	+

− Indicates absence from zone.
+ Indicates presence in zone.
a Indicates dominance in zone.

plants with lower drought and higher salt tolerances, but zone 6 stands somewhat apart from this sequence. It is indicated by *Tamarix* (salt-cedar), which is a noted phreatophyte, with deep roots to groundwater, and is relatively resistant to flood flows, so that it is characteristic of two main areas: (1) along the parts of the river of flood plain which are wide enough for floods not to destroy it; and (2) in a band along the base of cultivated fields south of Deh Luran, where excess irrigation water drains from the fields. This area of relatively frequent flooding is characterized by a large number of collapsed sinkhole features which make travel somewhat hazardous. The area's characteristics are thought to be produced by the concentration of flood waters in the cultivated area, but they do not appear to include any corresponding increase in salinity. It is therefore judged to be an area of very recent origin, probably formed since the resettlement of Deh Luran earlier this century. Figure 98 also shows the areas of denser (although still sparse) vegetation, which provide the better areas for grazing. These include the western part of the upper fans, the drier flood plains and a band between the most saline area and the cultivated area.

Analysis of Surface Features

Figures 94-97 show different, though related, features of the plain surface, and it is apparent that the patterns have a good deal in common. Because only ranked data is available, a conventional factor analysis has not been attempted. Instead a procedure has been adopted to give an approximation to a set of first-factor scores, and residuals from this factor have been examined to look for anomalies which might be the result of human interference with the natural environment. The properties of the plain surface at 232 sites have been ranked on a 1-7 scale for the four variables shown in Figures 94-97, namely surface stoniness, depth of dissection, salinity and vegetation, and also for surface slope. In each case, rank 1 is assigned to the zone nearest to the mountains, and it is clear that the first factor is a positive combination of all the ranks, taken in this sense. The overall 'factor score' has therefore been calculated as the mean rank, again with a possible range of 1-7, and this rank is mapped in Figure 99. A strong family resemblance may be seen with the previous figures, and it is suggested that this figure should be used as a basis for stratified sampling of the environment, since it shows the principal overall pattern of environmental variation in the Deh Luran plain.

In brief, Figure 99 shows a continuous transition from the mountains in the north, and to a lesser extent from the Jebel Hamrin in the south, towards a central low gradient area, which is most notably characterized by frequent flooding and high salinity, with associated halophytic vegetation. The present positions of the main rivers have surprisingly little impact on this pattern, reinforcing the idea that their positions are somewhat arbitrarily superimposed within the area of their fans. Indeed, comparison with the positions of the fans, shown in Figure 94, shows that the lowland area lies essentially between the fans of the Dawairij and the Mehmeh, and between the fan of the Mehmeh and the fans of the smaller streams flowing down around Deh Luran. A less important lowland area lies between the mountains and the Jebel Hamrin in the east. Near the mountains, two areas with anomalously high scores are found around saline springs (Ab-i-Garm at Deh Luran, and the Bitumen Spring). It should be noted that the lowland area of high salinity, although of very low gradient and therefore frequently flooded during the wet season, could never be described as a lake, and it is very doubtful whether such alluvial fan formations could ever have formed a true lake, as has been suggested by Helbaek (1969).

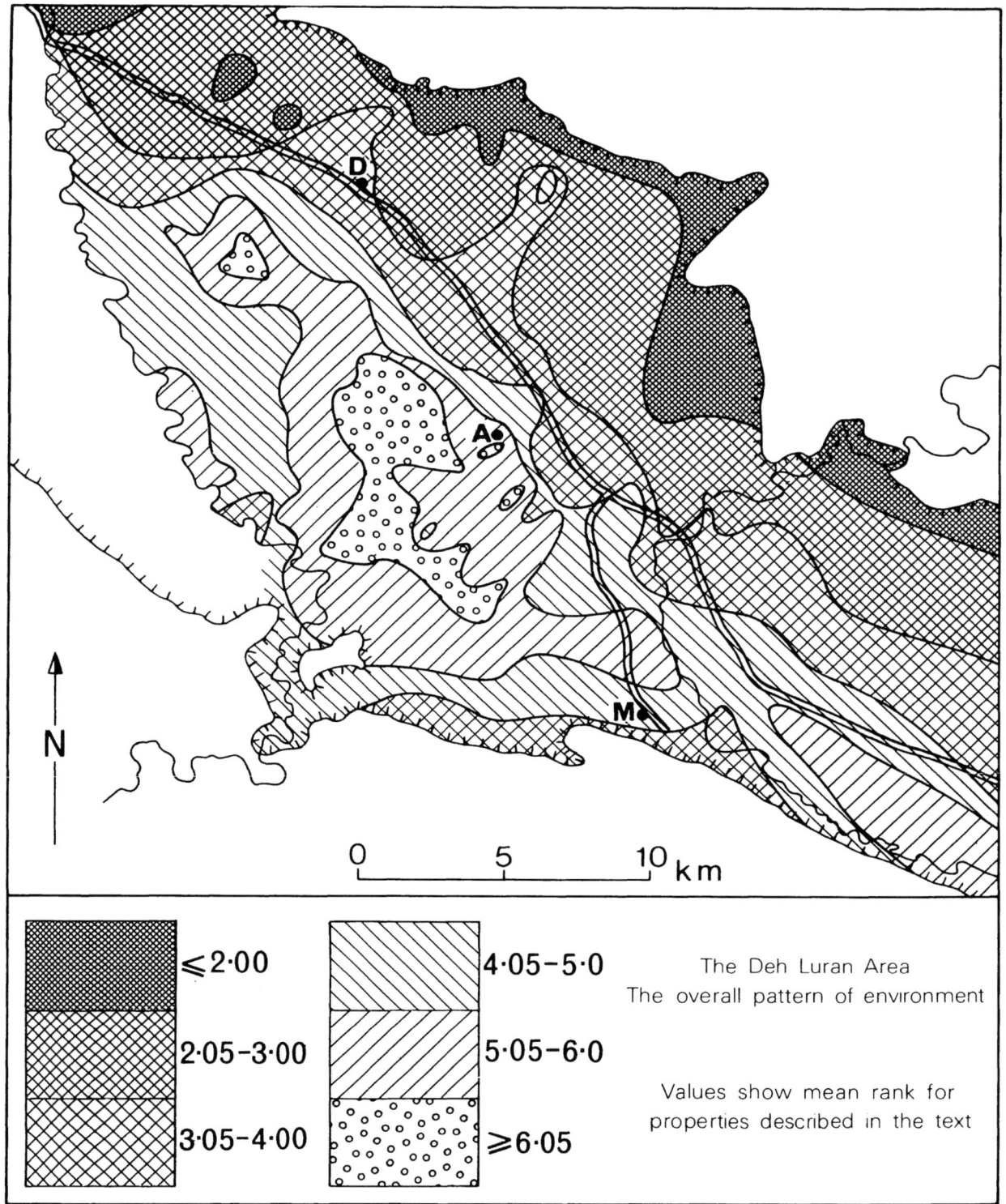

Fig. 99. The Deh Luran area: the overall pattern of environment. Values show the mean rank for properties described in the text.

Residuals from the mean rank score shown in Figure 99 were calculated as the sum of the differences between individual ranks and the mean rank, calculated for each site. Their magnitudes were fairly small, supporting the choice of the factor mapped in Figure 99, and casting doubt on the importance of a second, independent factor. Examination of the types of common residual, and their areal distribution, showed that the two commonest patterns of residual, which could be identified with subsidiary factors, were: (1) Low ranks for vegetation and perhaps salinity; high ranks for a slope, dissection and perhaps stoniness.(2) Low ranks for dissection; high ranks for slope.

The first of these residuals represents a site which is flat, but does not have saline vegetation. It occurs commonly in a ring around the high score area. At first sight this might appear to represent man's intervention in the agricultural zone, but the residual nearly always has the wrong sign (that is too low, rather than too high salinity), and it is instead thought to be a result of the non-linear relationship between the sets of ranks. In other words, the plain reaches the highest rank for slope and stoniness rather sooner than for vegetation and salinity. Thus, in the flattest area, distinctions of rank can still be applied to vegetation and salinity, although no further distinctions in slope or gradient can be made.

The second type of residual represents an area which is flat but dissected. These residuals appear to represent a more genuinely anomalous situation, but usually one of very local significance. For example, sites near one of the main rivers may be close to an incised channel leading down to the river. A more interesting location for such anomalies is, in a few instances, below an area of cultivated land, where the concentration of flood water is tending to initiate local soil erosion, as a direct result of man's influence. However, the freshness of such gullies and their small areal extent again suggest a very recent origin.

The high degree of accordance of the different surface variables and the insignificance of the anomalies from this accordance therefore suggest either that man's use of the environment has had no appreciable effect on it, or that land use has been in close accord with the environment. These conclusions apply most strictly to the rather recent past, and certainly to no period before the Sasanian. The absence at present of irreversible changes, however, especially in soil salinity, suggests that normal land use is unlikely to have produced irreversible changes in earlier periods.

The present accordance of the areal distributions of these semi-natural features suggests that the present correlations with land use may be extended into the past, at least for the period since plains aggradation ceased. Agriculture is probably associated with ranks of 4-5 in Figure 99, indicating a compromise between low slope and good moisture retention and a tendency towards flooding and high salinities. The best grazing land is in a band on either side of the cultivated land and along the river flood plain, where it is wide enough to support dense vegetation. Extrapolation to a period of plain aggradation is more difficult. During aggradation, the higher flows on the plain surface, instead of being confined within the floodplains of the Mehmeh and Dawairij, would lead to more frequent flooding, but to a greater flushing downwards of salts, and to addition of new, less saline material to the ground surface. At the same time the additional flood water might increase the area liable to seasonal flooding. The overall effect on farming is discussed more fully in the concluding section below, but it is clear that movements of arable land could arise from changes in the natural environment, and not only through a destruction of land through irrigation and hence salinization.

Extension to the Upper Khuzistan Plain

The analyses applied in detail to the Deh Luran plain have also been applied to 53 points in the much larger area of Upper Khuzistan (Fig. 100). Although it is impossible to map the resulting environmental zones in detail, a broad overall pattern of surface properties can be seen. Figure 100 shows the same overall environmental parameter for Upper Khuzistan as that shown for the Deh Luran plain in Figure 99. In Khuzistan, there is a much more marked gradation from northeast to southwest, that is from the mountains to the central Mesopotamian plain of the Tigris-Euphrates. Individual ridges, and the Shaur depression, interrupt this pattern, adding details which only partly register at the sampling density used. It is apparent from the pattern that the area between

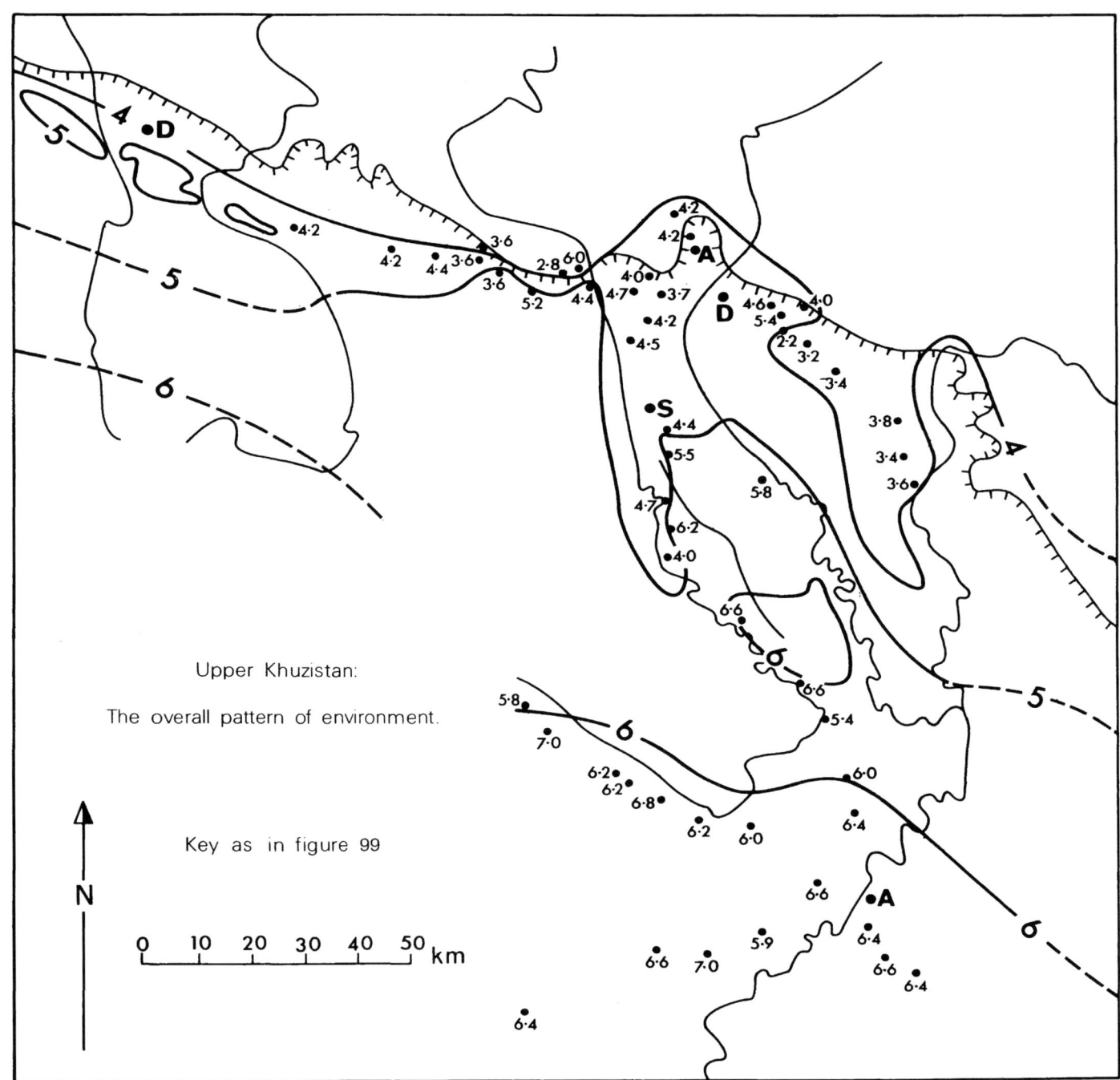

Fig. 100. Upper Khuzistan: the overall pattern of environment. Numbers and isolines refer to the mean ranks, as in Fig. 99.

Dizful and Shush in particular contains a larger area than can be found on the Deh Luran plain, of land which is neither too saline nor too hilly for irrigation.

The surface characteristics shown in Figure 100 are, however, not the only variables which control land use and settlement. At least as important are the availability of irrigation water, which in turn means not only the proximity of non-saline water but also the possibility of applying it to the fields, usually along gravity canals. Clearly the whole of the

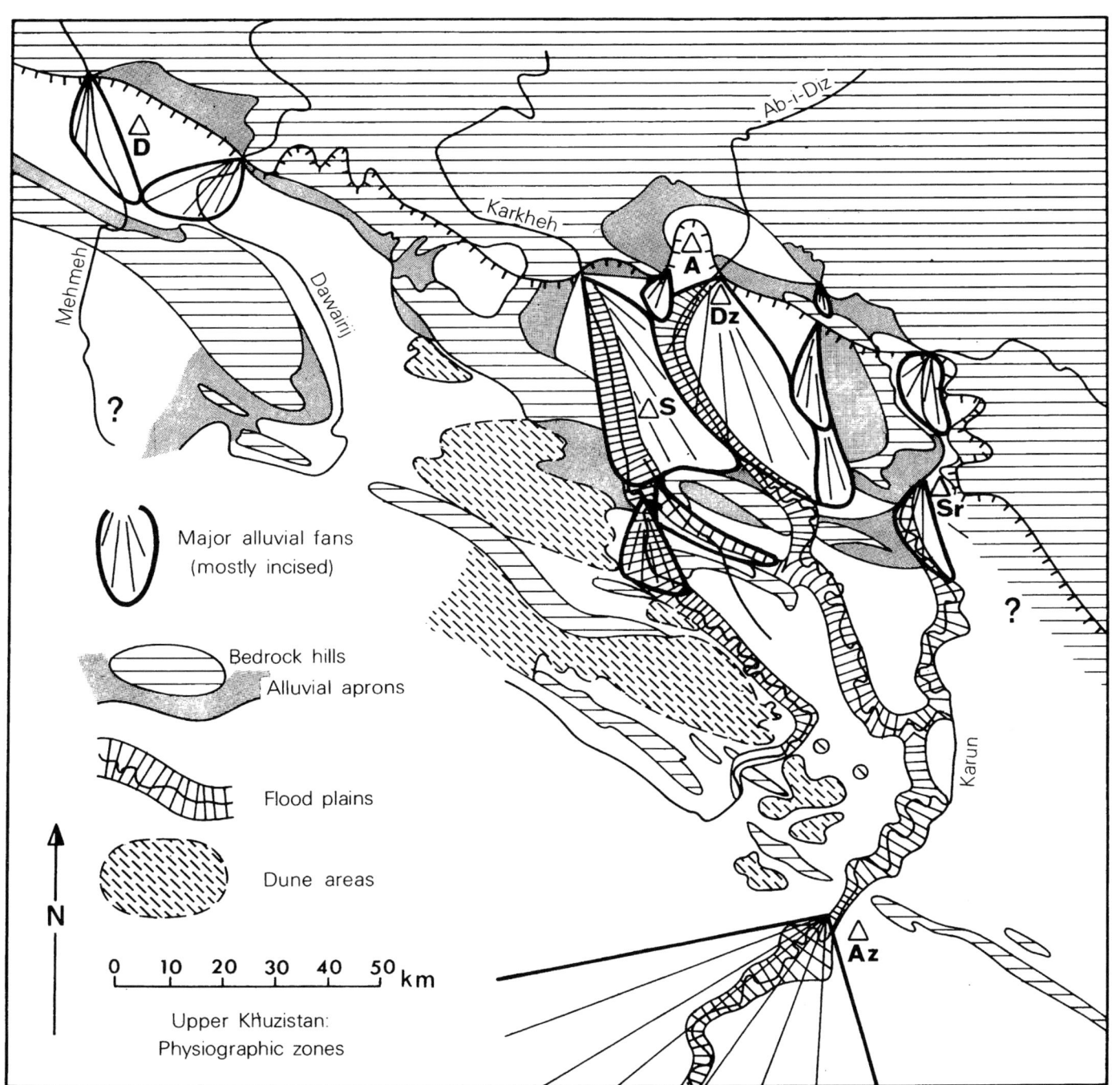

Fig. 101. Upper Khuzistan: principal physiographic zones and features.

Khuzistan plain is close to excellent perennial water supplies, but the problem of channelling it to the fields is slightly more limiting. To the north of the central Haft Tappeh ridge, which runs across the rivers immediately south of Shush and north of the Shaur River, the main surfaces of the plains are readily accessible, each from the river which formed them before incision of the present rivers into them (Fig. 101). Thus canals or qanats can be used to raise water to the plain surface, 5 or 10 meters above the present river level, close to the point at which the river flows out from the mountains and mountain fans, so that the whole of the plains can be irrigated. Between the Haft Tappeh and Ahwaz ridges, however, the units of plain area are somewhat smaller, so that more complicated canal systems are needed. Only in Sasanian or Early Islamic times have such canals, running across the Haft Tappeh and Shaur ridges, been constructed. At earlier periods, and again today, this area has been only scantily settled except along the rivers.

Still further downstream, south of the Ahwaz ridge, the plain surface is younger than farther north, with a continuing history of changing river courses. Channels are only shallowly incised, and a high density of settlement has been maintained to the present day, although once more mainly along river and canal courses. This pattern occurs in spite of the poor surface conditions indicated in Figure 100; that is, despite high soil salinity and poor drainage. This southern area is, however, as stated above, analogous to other parts of the Tigris-Euphrates plain, in maintaining settlement despite severe salinity problems. As such, its use of the available resources is so different from that of the Deh Luran area that it is rash to compare the two areas without closer study. By the same token, the problems of Upper Khuzistan are closely similar to those of Deh Luran, and may be satisfactorily compared with it.

In the northern region, the most important area for irrigation is on the fan formed by the Ab-i-Diz when it was at a higher level. The fan, which is almost entirely on the east side of the river, can be irrigated with a minimum of effort. The Diz has the additional advantages of relatively low salinity and a relatively high summer flow (even greater since construction of the Pahlavi Dam), allowing summer irrigation. The area of intensive summer irrigation is mostly on the upper part of the fan, close to Dizful (Fig. 102). The Karun also has high enough summer flows, with low salinity, to allow summer cropping, but there are not such large areas of flat land along the upper Karun, most of the water from which is used for irrigation farther south. The Karkheh flow is much less in summer, and more saline, so that only a small area is suitable for summer irrigation. Below these areas of year-round growth are larger areas in which the river waters are used to augment and more or less guarantee a winter crop (the only possible role for irrigation in Deh Luran). This area extends south of Shush across the full width of the fans, and farther south in a band running close to the rivers, but widening out again south of Ahwaz. Very recently the area of year-round irrigation from the Diz has been extended to the area immediately north of the Haft Tappeh ridge. An area which was formerly used less intensively now makes use of the higher summer flows of the Diz resulting from construction of the Pahlavi dam to grow sugar cane. This project, however, appears to have no ancient analogues.

Periods of aggradation in northern Khuzistan would have had similar effects on farming conditions as in Deh Luran. That is to say that on the surface of a fan, the water table is high everywhere in winter, but summer flows are much reduced. Minor floods occur every year, but major floods less frequently. The addition of sediment to the surface reduces salinity problems by burying the saline surface, if one is present. Conditions therefore favor winter cultivation at the expense of summer crops. They also strongly encourage settlement on areas above the plain surface, such as tepes. There may also be a tendency to cultivate at the downstream end of the fan into more saline areas, but this tendency appears to be less marked in Khuzistan than in Deh Luran.

HYDROLOGY AND CLIMATE

Precipitation and Evaporation

The climate is of primary concern because it determines whether farming is possible with the available rainfall. In considering this possibility, two cases will be discussed: first the water requirement for growing a dense crop, which transpires approximately 80 percent of the open-water evaporation during its growing period, and, second, the water requirement for a dry farmed crop, growing at about half the plant density, and having somewhat less than half the yield. This type of growth, which is able to tap the water falling on a larger area of ground, requires approximately half the open-water evaporation for its survival. From these water needs, it is possible to calculate water deficiencies which must be supplied under irrigation, and make comparisons with the available river flows.

Rainfall increases with elevation above sea level,

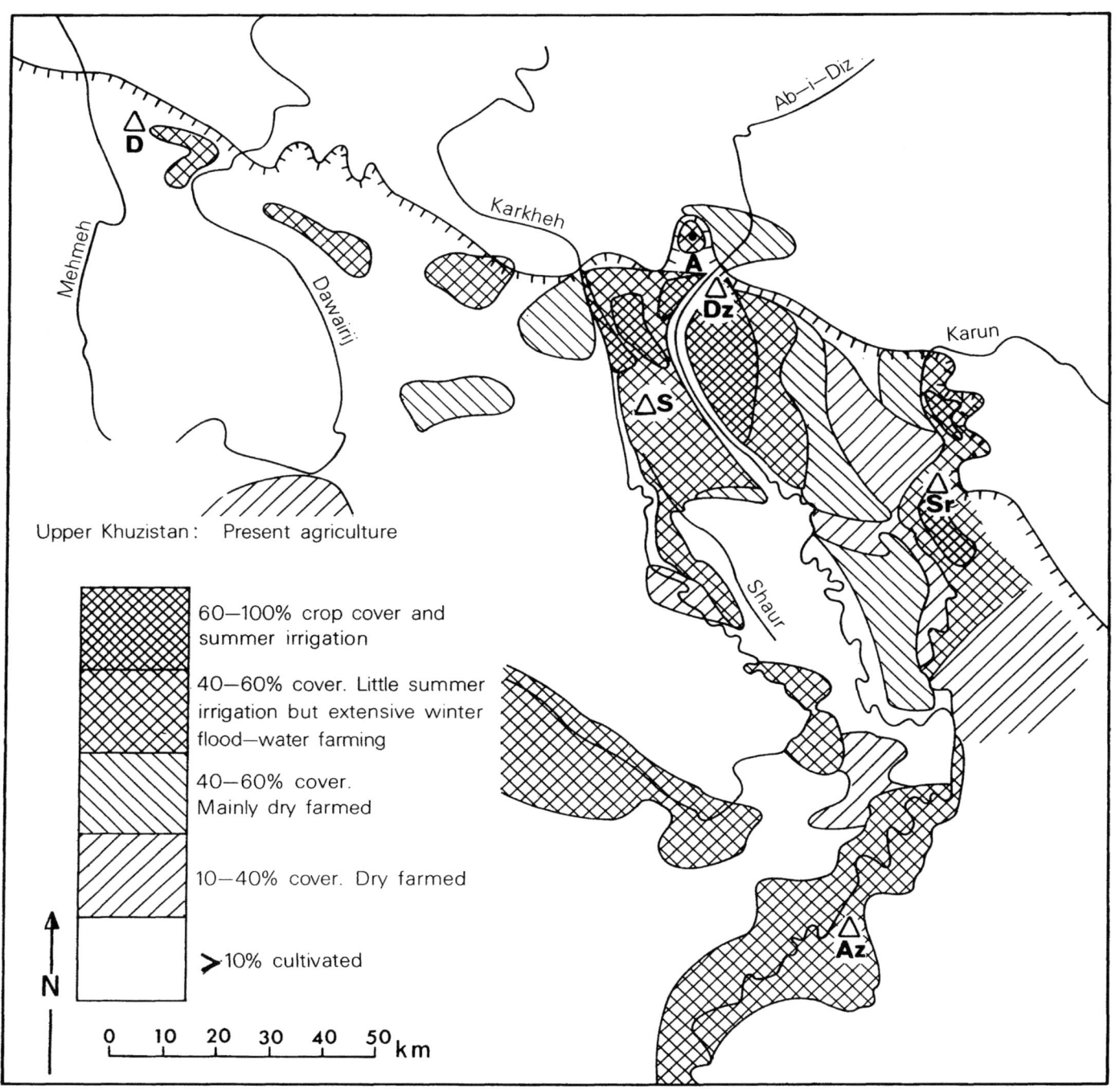

Fig. 102. Upper Khuzistan: present agricultural land use.

but the relationship is not a simple linear one. Rainfall tends to show two peaks, one in December and one in March, and the strengths of these two vary. At low elevations the December peak is more marked, whereas at higher elevations both peaks increase and the March peak becomes the greater. Averaging available rainfall records for southwest Iran, synthetic average rainfalls have been generated in Table 83 to show the overall variation of rainfall with elevation. Looking at annual totals it may be seen that rainfall is low on the lower Khuzistan plains, and almost twice as high between Ahwaz and Dizful, close to the

Table 83

SYNTHETIC RAINFALL RECORDS IN MILLIMETERS

Elevation (m)	Month												Total
	J	F	M	A	M	J	J	A	S	O	N	D	
0	37	31	19	15	3	0	--	--	--	5	31	49	190
200	72	52	51	43	27	5	--	--	--	16	64	80	410
400	75	58	59	50	33	6	--	--	--	17	66	83	445
600	78	65	68	58	36	7	--	--	--	17	68	85	478
800	79	70	76	64	42	7	--	--	--	17	68	85	504
1000	78	73	81	69	45	8	--	--	--	17	66	83	516
1200	77	76	86	73	47	8	--	--	--	16	66	81	526
1400	76	78	91	77	50	9	--	--	--	16	63	78	534
1600	76	79	93	80	52	9	--	--	--	15	62	76	538

Table 84

ESTIMATED OPEN-WATER EVAPORATION IN MILLIMETERS

Elevation (m)	J	F	M	A	M	J	J	A	S	O	N	D	Yearly Total
0	101	112	151	258	415	540	605	590	515	380	180	108	3955
200	92	102	133	237	380	513	581	577	490	340	171	101	3717
400	87	93	118	200	335	462	538	535	443	303	156	92	3362
600	80	85	106	170	290	412	496	493	396	266	139	82	3015
800	70	78	92	138	250	364	454	452	349	229	122	73	2671
1000	50	60	85	120	210	318	412	411	302	192	105	64	2329
1200	35	40	80	108	170	270	370	370	255	155	88	55	1996
1400	25	28	78	98	147	235	325	318	219	131	82	40	1726
1600	12	20	50	91	124	200	280	267	183	107	77	25	1636

mountain front. Thereafter the increase of rainfall with elevation is much less, although the increase with horizontal distance remains large.

These rainfall values must be compared with those for evaporation. The best available sources appear to be open-water tanks at Safiabad and Haft Tappeh in Khuzistan, and these values have been correlated with monthly temperatures in Figure 103. This correlation has then been used to transpose to other elevations, making use of measured monthly mean temperatures, and interpolating at a mean environmental lapse rate of 0.65°C per 100 meters of elevation. The final evaporation estimates are listed in Table 84, indicating a reduction from almost 4000 mm a year at sea level to less than half that at 1600 m elevation.

In Table 85 monthly average water surpluses are calculated for a dense vegetation cover, which is assumed to use 80 percent of the estimated open-water evaporation calculated above (Table 84). Total surpluses (+) or deficits (-) are calculated for the year, and for the four-month period of minimum deficit, that is, December to March inclusive. This period is the most suitable, and usual, for winter crop growth. It can be seen that conditions are only wet enough

APPENDIX I

Table 85
EXCESS OF RAINFALL OVER CROP WATER NEEDS
(in millimeters), = R - 0.8E

Elevation (m)	J	F	M	A	M	J	J	A	S	O	N	D	Yearly Total	Dec.-Mar.
0	-43	-61	-102	-191	-329	-432	-484	-472	-412	-299	-113	-37	-2974	-243
200	-2	-30	-55	-147	-277	-405	-465	-462	-392	-256	-73	-1	-2564	-88
400	+5	-16	-35	-110	-235	-364	-430	-428	-354	-225	-59	+9	-2245	-37
600	+14	-3	-16	-78	-196	-323	-397	-395	-317	-176	-44	+17	-1934	+12
800	+23	+8	+2	-46	-158	-284	-363	-362	-279	-166	-30	+27	-1633	+60
1000	+38	+25	+13	-27	-123	-246	-330	-329	-241	-137	-18	+32	-1347	+108
1200	+49	+44	+22	-13	-89	-208	-296	-296	-204	-108	-4	+37	-1071	+152
1400	+56	+55	+29	-1	-68	-179	-260	-254	-175	-89	-3	+46	-847	+176
1600	+66	+63	+53	+7	-47	-151	-224	-213	-146	-71	0	+56	-771	+238

for a good winter crop at 600 m or above. Since the elevation of Deh Luran is only 200 m, of Dizful 150 m and of Ahwaz 20 m, it is clear that good crops can only be grown in winter with some irrigation. Using dry farming methods, however, with lower crop densities, it is possible to obtain a winter crop at elevations of 150 m or above, though at sea level the water deficit, even for this type of farming, is 100 mm for the growing period.

It should however be remembered that these figures refer to average conditions. Perhaps a more realistic way of looking at the statement that dry farming is, on average, possible at 150 meters elevation is to say that the crop will succeed 50 percent of the time. A farmer who is relying on rainfall cannot plant until the first month of water surplus, and his crop will only survive if the accumulated surplus remains positive for a period of at least three months. Figure 104 shows the accumulated surplus of rainfall over 50 percent open-water evaporation for Safiabad, near Dizful, at an elevation of 150 meters for the growing seasons beginning in December of 1964 to 1968. In this example, only two out of the five years were wet enough for crop production on a dry farming basis. In the other three years, it would have been impossible to plant until February, giving a very slim chance of success.

Strategies of Land Use

The marginality of dry farming suggests several possible strategies for minimizing the risks. The most direct is to restrict cultivation to areas which are generally more favorable—that is to areas close to the mountain front, or even above it. The need for water then conflicts with the need for flat land, both to limit erosion and to hold the available water. The later requirement is met by flat land in two ways: (1) because low slopes lose less water by lateral drainage, and (2) because, in mainly alluvial material, flat slopes are associated with fine-grained material, which provides slower vertical drainage down from the surface soil. Within this zone the detailed local topography can also be very important, because small hollows collect lateral water flows and fine debris, and so contain much moister soils. Fields may therefore be confined to local hollows or depressed former water courses to make the most of their additional moisture. This set of strategies is very important both for pre-irrigated agriculture and for nomadic groups today, who are not organized to maintain irrigation structures, but wish to grow a winter crop in their lowland winter grazing area.

Farming without canal irrigation is also possible in the south of Khuzistan, and in the Tigris-Euphrates valley, in areas where the water table is seasonally high enough to supply plants with water directly. Between the southern area and the mountain front area, conditions for cultivation without irrigation canals are least good, with substantial water deficits, and high enough water tables only on low river ter-

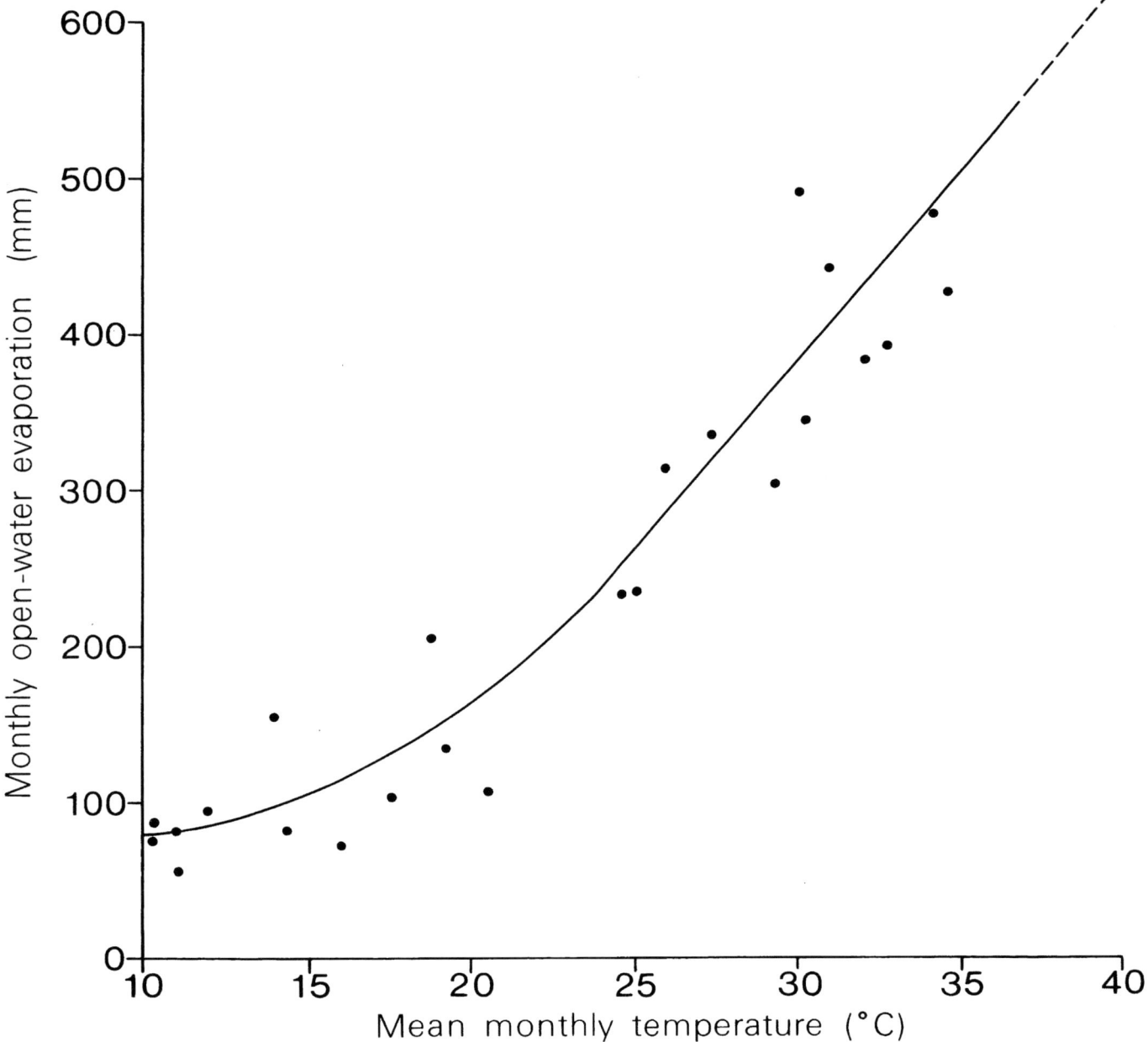

Fig. 103. Correlation between monthly evaporation and monthly mean temperatures, from pan data for individual months at Safiabad (near Dizful) and Haft Tappeh (Southeast of Shush).

races, so that settlements must rely on canal systems.

Irrigation depends on the major rivers. Winter irrigation only needs to supply the winter water deficit shown in Table 85. For summer irrigation, the September water deficit must be supplied from the summer minimum river flows, which also occur in September, at the end of the dry season. In each case, the area which could be irrigated may be calculated from the available river flow data (Khuzistan Water and Power Authority records). The results are shown in Table 86.

What is immediately apparent is that present irrigation systems are matched closely to summer requirements. The discrepancy between actual and potential areas of summer irrigation for the Diz and Karkheh is explained partly by flows not abstracted for irriga-

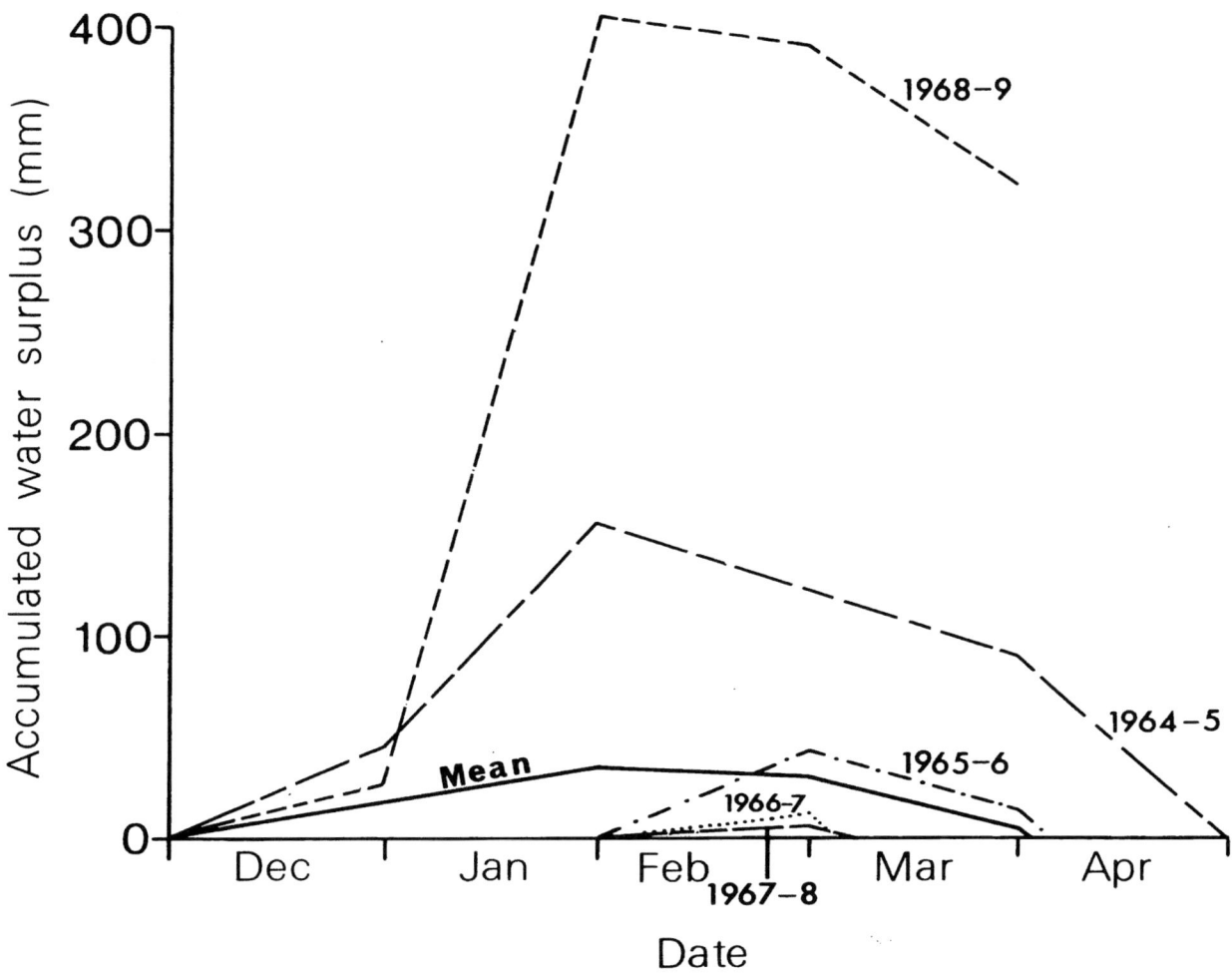

Fig. 104. Accumulated water surplus for dry farming (R−0.5 E) at 150m elevation in Deh Luran and Khuzistan areas. Data for 5 individual years, and estimated for 20 year mean.

tion, but mainly by the very high (up to 60 percent) losses from primitive canals during conveyance to the fields. For the Karun, irrigation is limited by the scarcity of enough flat land north of Ahwaz, and it is only in the south that water is available for irrigation. The actual areas served by canal systems are about five times greater than the areas irrigated at any one time, because of the rotation of summer and winter cropping which is followed.

Sasanian and Early Islamic canal systems appear to have been approximately twice as extensive as present ones for both the Karkheh-Shaur and the Diz systems, and more than twice as extensive in the Deh Luran plain. The inference is that these systems were constructed primarily for winter irrigation (although for the larger rivers they might alternatively imply a different fallowing system). Under present economic and population conditions, the increased winter yields resulting from irrigation are not sufficient to justify the costs of canal maintenance in the absence of summer cropping. It may be argued however that the combination of high population and efficient central canal organization might be sufficient to increase crop values and decrease irrigation costs to a point where canals used only in the winter could be worthwhile. Such conditions may have existed in Sasanian or Early Islamic times.

In periods when only the bonus of summer cropping makes canal irrigation worthwhile, there has always been a strong incentive to concentrate the irrigation as near as possible to the mountains. This gives a marginal benefit in reduced summer water deficits

Table 86
AREAS IRRIGABLE BY MAJOR RIVERS IN UPPER KHUZISTAN AND DEH LURAN

River	Area for Winter Irrigation (km^2)			Area for Summer Irrigation (km^2)		
	Estimated Maximum		Actual	Estimated Maximum		Actual
	Sea Level	200 m.		Sea Level	200 m.	
Mehmeh	–	190	1	–	1.3	0
Dawairij	–	110	7	–	0	0
Karkheh (Pa-i-Pol)	3,100	6,000	310	149	155	63
Diz (Dizful)	4,900	9,100	410	280	290	130
Karun (Gotwan)	10,100	19,100	c.40	840	880	c.10

(Table 85), and greater advantages in reducing losses in the natural river channels, thus maximizing the irrigated area and minimizing salinity. The latter, however, despite several thousand years of irrigation, appears to be only a slight problem in Upper Khuzistan. Settlement will always tend to be concentrated first into areas favorable for summer irrigation, and second into areas suitable for dry farming. Both of these coincide within the strip of land below the mountain front, although only the area close to the major rivers has sufficient water for effective summer irrigation.

Figure 105 illustrates the difference in water quality between the major rivers, a secondary factor influencing the distribution of irrigated agriculture. On the figure, the concentrations of chloride and sulphate ions, in milli-equivalents per liter, are plotted against one another. The third main anion, carbonate, remains much more constant, at 2-3 m.e.q. per liter. This diagram therefore shows not only the total concentration of dissolved material, high concentrations occurring at the top and right of the figure, but also the composition of the water. Almost all of the chloride ion occurs in the form of NaCl (salt) and the sulphate occurs mostly as $CaSO_4$ (gypsum). It is apparent that all of the waters are derived from similar environments in which these two salts are present in similar, rather large, amounts which are typical of evaporate deposits formed in enclosed basins under arid conditions. There are, however, differences in the measured concentrations of salts, which influence the suitability for irrigation. It is clear that the waters of the Diz are the least saline, and therefore best for irrigation, but all of the large rivers are much better than the Mehmeh and Dawairij in the Deh Luran plain. For these two rivers, most of the measurements are for low flows, so that it is apparent that even these rivers can be used for winter irrigation, but the Mehmeh in particular is highly unsuitable for summer irrigation. It has not only unacceptable total salt concentrations, but creates a severe risk of causing sodium alkalinity, that is, irreversible damage to the soil. The absence of such damage, and the evidence of former canal systems on this river further support the view that these canal systems must have been used for winter irrigation only.

HISTORY OF CHANNEL CHANGES IN KHUZISTAN

The major rivers of Khuzistan not only bring vital irrigation water, the most critical positive resource to the area, but also bring the risk of floods, a significant negative resource. Information on flood flows is very scarce, with good records only for the Karun at Ahwaz, and shorter records for the Karkheh (Hamidieh) and the Diz (Dizful). It has therefore been necessary to extrapolate these records to the Dawairij and Mehmeh, and the most satisfactory

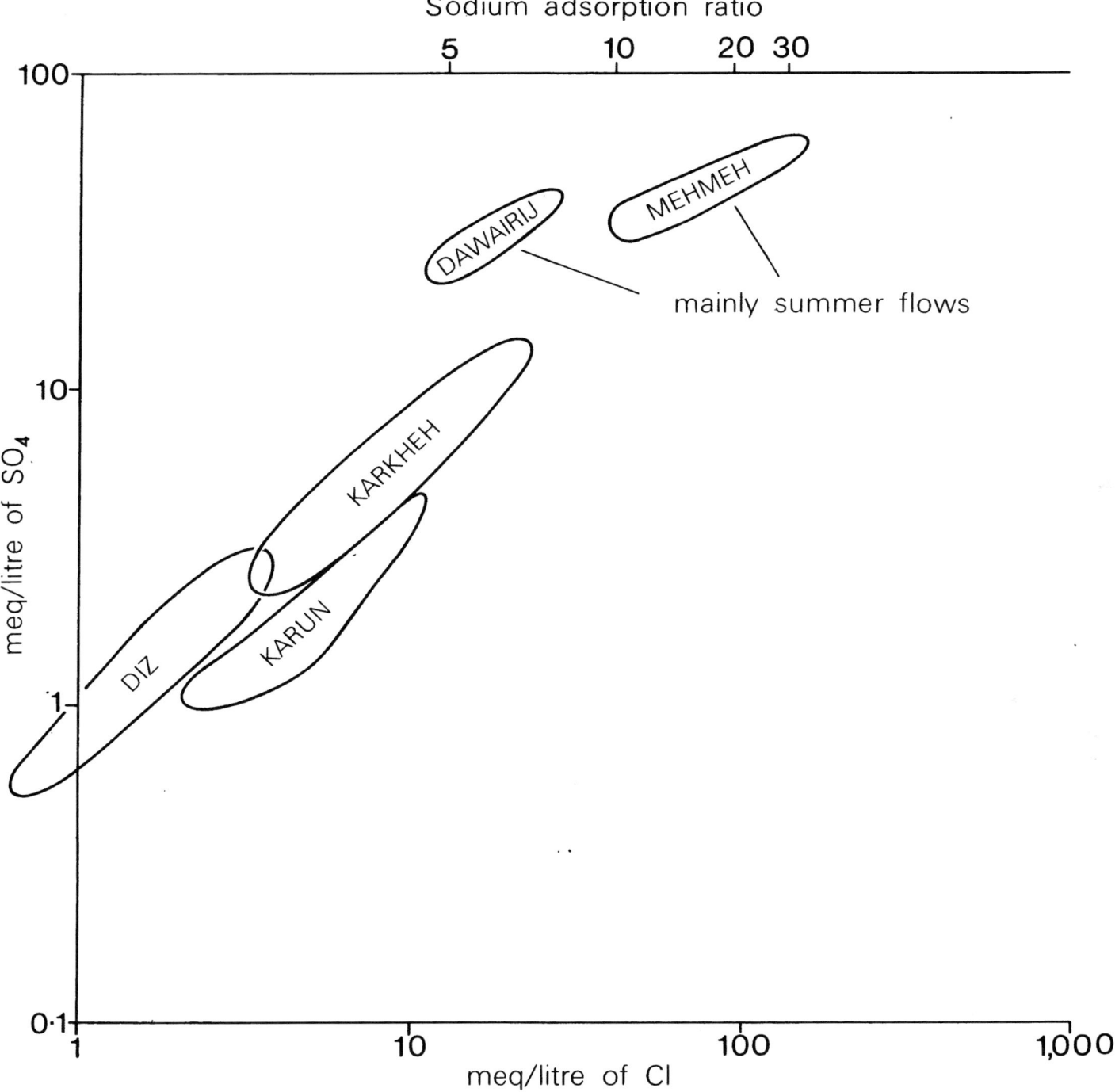

Fig. 105. Chemical composition of Khuzistan rivers at various stages of flow, expressed in milli-equivalents per liter of Cl and SO_4 ions. Composition of third major constituent, CO_3, was less variable. Data from K.W.P.A. records.

method available works from the meander pattern. There is a well-established relationship between bankfull discharge (the flow which just fills the channel to the top of its banks and, on average, occurs every 1.5 years) and the wavelength of the meanders formed by the river (Leopold and Wolman, 1957). This best-fit line is shown in Figure 106. On the same figure, the two reliable data points for Khuzistan (1.5 year floods from Khuzistan Water and Power Authority records) are plotted, indicating a parallel, but slightly

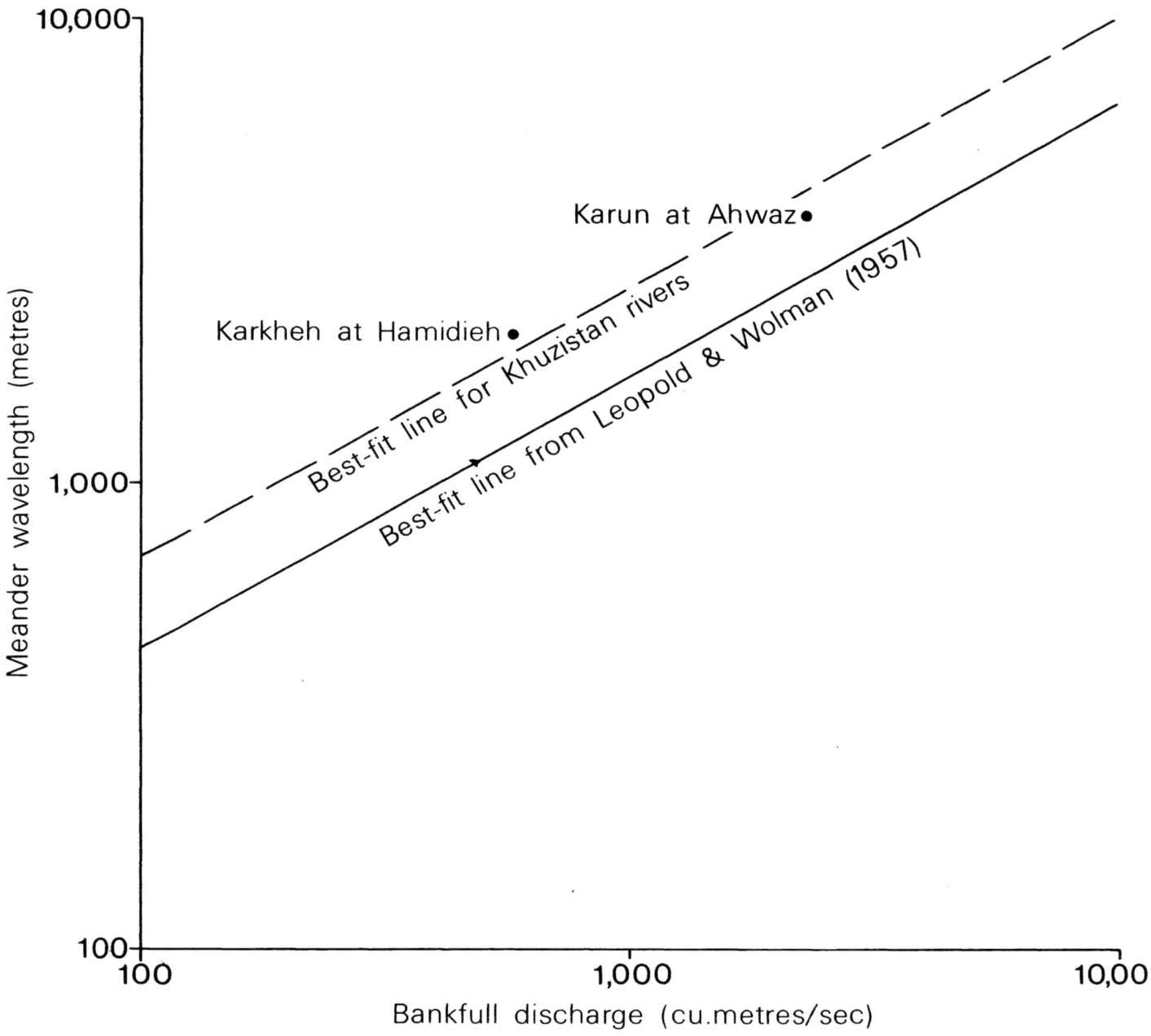

Fig. 106. Relationships between meander wavelength and bankfull discharge for U.S. rivers (Leopold and Wolman, 1957) and for Khuzistan rivers (plotted points from K.W.P.A. records).

different line. This line is preferred for estimating flows in other Khuzistan rivers, because it takes account of flow frequency distributions in these semi-arid rivers which are not typical of Leopold and Wolman's original sample.

In examining the meander patterns of the Khuzistan rivers, it became apparent that meander wavelengths could be measured, not only at several points along existing river courses, but also along a number of former, or largely abandoned, river channels, which have some bearing on the history of land use in Khuzistan. Such former patterns only survive for a restricted period, and so appear to represent the last channel courses prior to the present ones in the areas

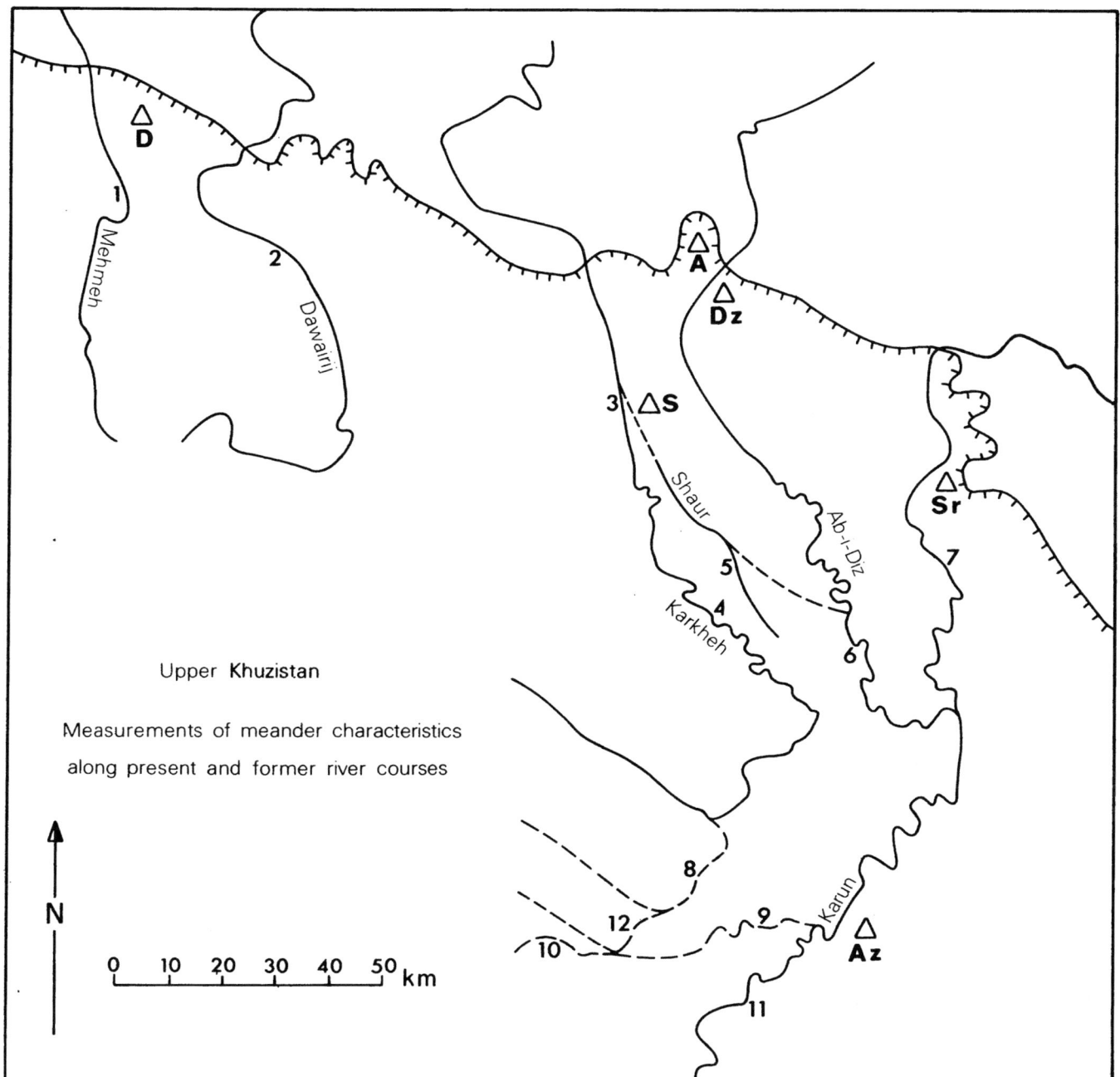

Fig. 107. Upper Khuzistan: sites for which air photograph measurements of present and former meander characteristics have been analyzed.

where they occur. The history of these channel changes is discussed below in terms of the deduced flows.

Meander patterns were measured in the twelve reaches shown in Figure 107, and Table 87 lists the meander wavelengths and bankful discharges esti-mated from Figure 106, for each reach. Following the geometry of the systems in Figure 107, there can be no doubt that only the Karkheh can have flowed past sites (8) and (12); only the Karun past site (9), and either of these, or both, past site (10). In the possible Karun system (Fig. 107):

Table 87

MEANDER WAVELENGTHS AT ESTIMATED BANKFULL DISCHARGES FOR KHUZISTAN RIVERS

Site	Meander Wavelengths in Meters	Estimated Bankfull Discharge (m^3/sec.)
1	1360	320
2	900	160
3	1400	340
4	2100	580*
5	2800	1100
6	3000	1280
7	2400	850
8	1700	470
9	3800	1850
10	4400	2600
11	3800	2300*
12	2400	850

*Measured.

Site (7) indicates 850 cumecs (cubic meters per second) from the Upper Karun only.

Site (11) indicates 2300 cumecs, derived from the Upper Karun (850), and the Diz (1280 cumecs at site 6). This shows an agreement within 10 percent.

Site (9) indicates 1850 cumecs, indicating a similar flow for the Diz + Upper Karun.

Site (10) indicates 2600 cumecs, which may not be significantly larger than at site (9), but matches better a flow for site 9 (1850 cumecs) + site 12 (850 cumecs).

In the possible Karkheh system:

Site (3) indicates 340 cumecs.

Site (4) indicates 580 cumecs, a discrepancy which cannot be simply explained.

Site (8) indicates 470 cumecs, an intermediate value.

Site (12) indicates 850 cumecs.

Site (10) indicates 2600 cumecs, and so must have been formed by either the Karun alone, or by the Karkheh and Karun combined.

The final site which is relevant to a discussion of former river courses is that along the Shaur at site (5), with an indication of 1100 cumecs, a value which is quite out of proportion with the present size of the Shaur. Since this river rises on the flood plain of the Karkheh, it can only be assumed that it represents a previous course of the Karkheh. The meander patterns indicate that this course did not follow the present (partly artificial) course, but a more northerly one flowing into the Diz. It is clear that this course must be older than that at site (12), which must be older than that at site (8) which must, in its turn, be older than the present lower course.

If a river course is altered, then the meander pattern will also alter, but while a large discharge will eradicate a small meander pattern rapidly, small meanders may persist for some time within larger meanders, especially if the two patterns are of very different sizes. This effect may be seen very clearly for the present Shaur along the ancient meander path to the Diz, but is perhaps also relevant for site (10), which may have been occupied by the Karkheh alone after abandonment by the Karun to near its present lower course. This suggestion is supported by the much less fresh condition of the ancient course near site (9) than near site (10). On the basis of these purely hydrologic arguments, a sequence of former river courses is put forward in Figure 108.

Dating of these river courses must call on other types of evidence, but it will be argued in the section on stratigraphy that all of these courses must be later than the second millenium B.C., although all old courses within this period may not be preserved as meander traces on air photographs. All that are preserved are the most recent ones. Air photographs also show ancient canal traces with great clarity. Once more the most recent are clearest, and most of these appear to date, in the region under discussion, from the Sasanian and Early Islamic periods. This is evident from their massive form and from associated pottery remains (John Hansman, oral communication). These canal traces (Fig. 109) show major canal systems from the Upper Karkheh and from the Shaur, but not from the Karkheh below its divergence with the Shaur, even though canals from the Shaur run very close to it. Canal lines also run from the former course of the Karun, but run along and intersect its present course. It is therefore deduced that at some time during the first millenium A.D., the river courses of the area were as shown in the first diagram of Figure 108. On the basis of degree of

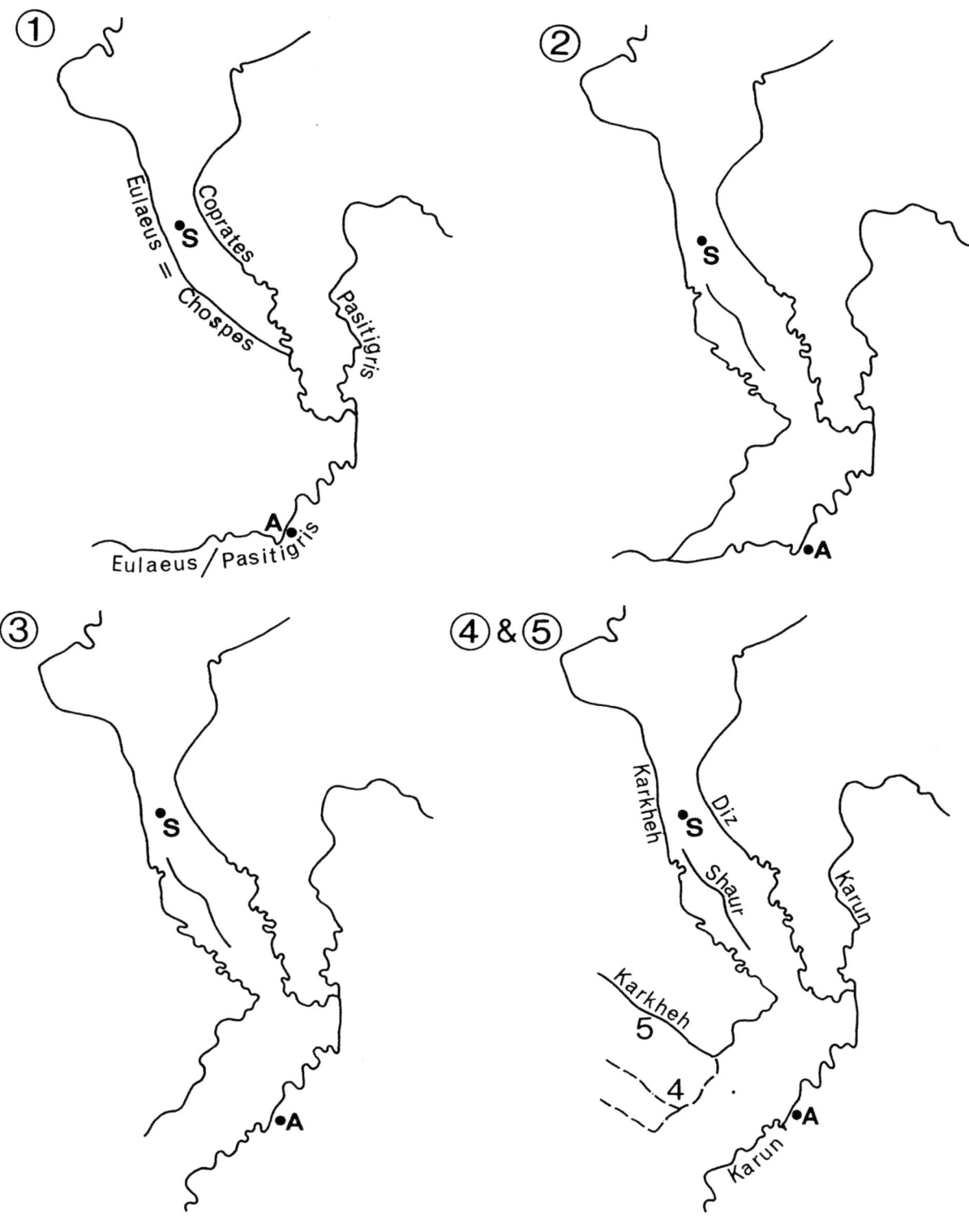

S—Shush A—Ahwaz

Fig. 108. Sequence of river courses in Khuzistan, based on freshness and wavelength of meander patterns. Stage 1 shows the ancient names of the rivers if they are consistent with this sequence.

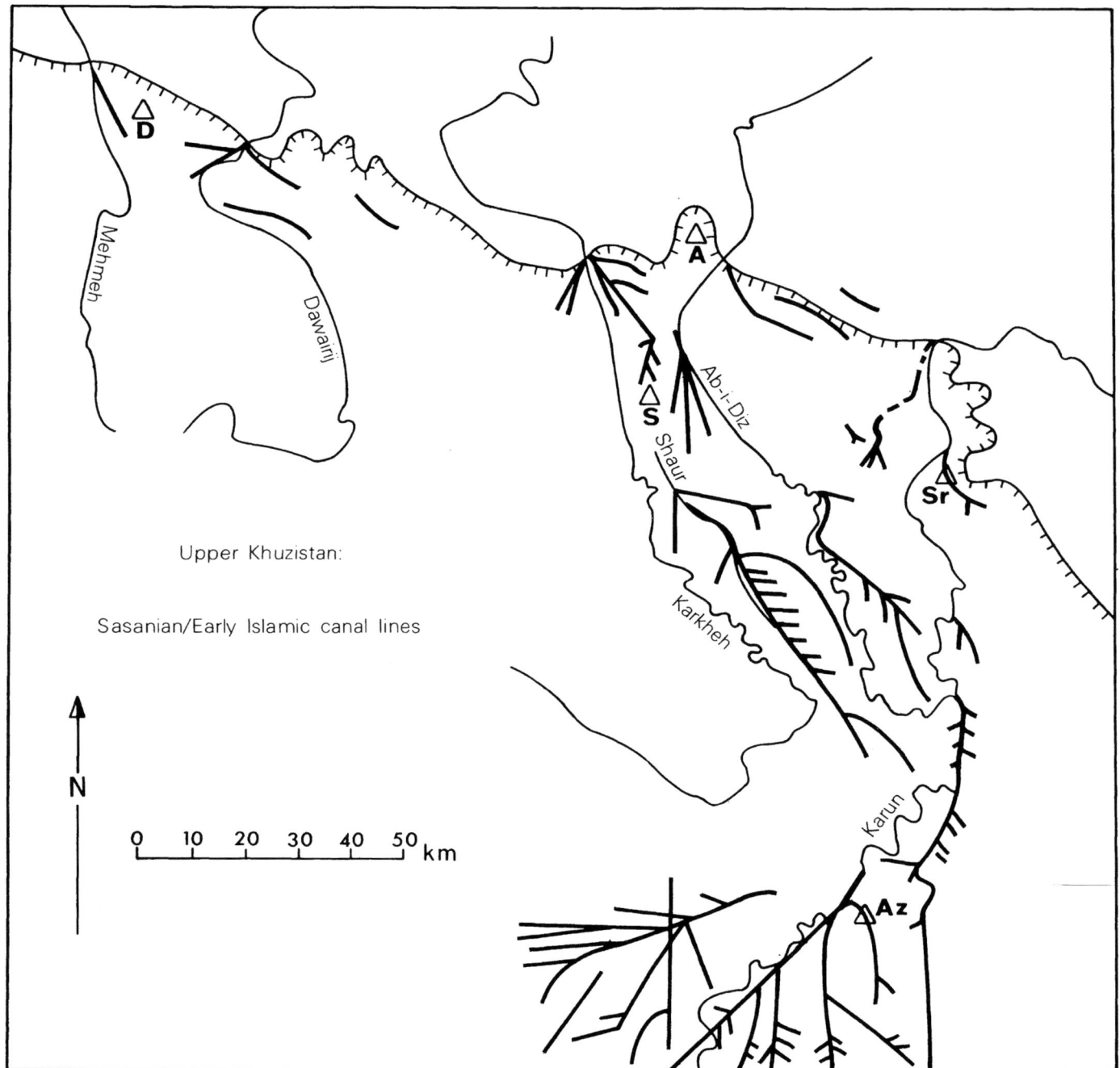

Fig. 109. Upper Khuzistan: Sasanian or Early Islamic canal lines (bold). Note cases where river now follows an original canal line, and where canal lines cross early courses of lower Karkheh and Karun.

preservation of the various channels, but without additional corroborative evidence, the author surmises that the dates of stages 1-5 in figure 108 are approximately:

State 1: 1500 B.C. – 500 A.D.
Stage 2: 500 A.D. – 1200 A.D.
Stage 3: 1200 A.D. – 1450 A.D.
Stage 4: 1450 A.D. – 1700 A.D.
Stage 5: 1700 A.D. – present.

These figures represent only orders of magnitude for the relative ages.

The sequence of river courses suggested conflicts to some extent with that proposed by Hansman (1967) based on historical evidence for the period of stage 1 above, though this in no way detracts from his major conclusion about the location of Charax Spasinou on the Tigris. It is noted here that the evidence which he presents might be considered consistent with the present proposals if the Choaspes and Eulaeus are both taken to refer to the former Karkheh course (Fig. 108). Later changes of river course would tend to confuse the historical record, and might give rise to much of the difficulty in separately identifying the Choaspes and Eulaeus. It may be noted that the present proposal simplifies the journey of Nearchus from the Pasitigris (Karun) to Shush (Hansman, 1967:30-31), and explains the alternative use of the names Eulaeus and Pasitigris for the lower Karun (Ibid: 33).

The sequence of old meanders of the Karkheh not only helps to identify the rivers to which they belong, but also provides a history of discharge over the period. For the Karkheh, the bankfull discharges are:

Stage 1 (Site 5 on the Shaur)	1100 cumecs
Stages 2 & 3 (Site 12)	850 cumecs
Stage 4 (Site 8)	470 cumecs
Stage 5 (Sites 3 and 4)	460 cumecs (average).

This sequence is most complete for the Karkheh, but it is clearly not paralleled by the Karun at least, which shows comparable discharges near Ahwaz at Stage 2 (1850 cumecs) and the present (2300 cumecs). If bankfull discharge is plotted against drainage area (Fig. 110), the Karkheh is also seen to be discrepant in having an unusually low discharge for its drainage area. This would have been true, though to a lesser extent, for even the highest former discharge listed above. How, then, is the Karkheh different from the other large rivers? In terms of hydrology, its drainage basin differs from the other large rivers in passing through a number of large cultivated highland valleys, and in having a slightly lower average rainfall within its basin area. Explanations for the declining discharge of the Karkheh can therefore be sought either in climatic change, a hypothesis which seems untenable over the period involved, and which should have induced comparable changes in the Karun, or else in a history of changing land use. Increasing abstraction for irrigation is one possibility, and judging by the available measurement points, the abstraction might have occurred at any point north of Shush: that is, either in northern Khuzistan or in the highland valleys. Since current water use in northern Khuzistan is inadequate to explain such a large decline in peak flows, it must be assumed that the abstraction results from changes in water use in the highland areas.

Abstraction of water for irrigation, even winter irrigation, normally relies on low flows, since high flows come after rain when the land needs no irrigation. Canal abstraction systems thus seem unlikely to account for a fall in *peak* flows. Only a reservoir system, which stored peak flows for distribution to the land in drier times, would adequately explain the reduction of peak flows in terms of water use in the highland valley floor areas. Such a system was within the technical competence of the Sasanian period, but has not been reported for this area in ancient times. Peak flows may also be reduced by good land use practices, which encourage water retention within the soil. This may be achieved by afforestation, but a more likely cause is a gradual change towards greater cultivation, with careful soil management, at the expense of grazing animals, which tend to encourage soil erosion (see below). This can be no more than a hypothesis without direct evidence from the highland valleys. The reasons for the reduction of peak flows in the Karkheh over the last 1500 years therefore remain something of a mystery, and the effect on Karkheh lowflows is quite uncertain. Irrigation abstraction with dam storage would certainly lead to lower low flows. A switch from grazing would, on its own, tend to *increase* low flows, but if (as probable) it was associated with summer irrigation, the additional summer flows might all have been used in the highland valleys.

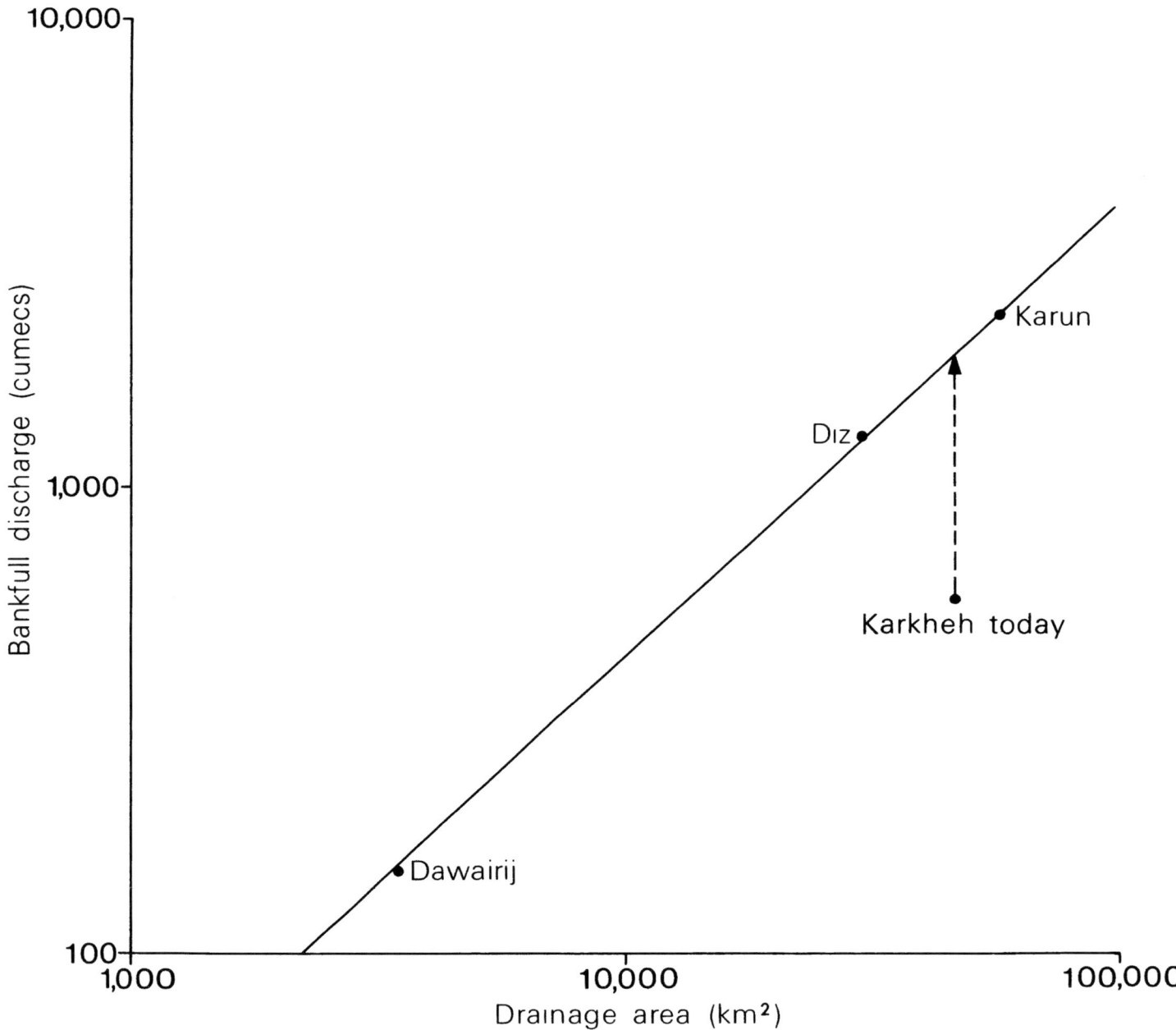

Fig. 110. The relationship between bankfull discharge and drainage area for Khuzistan rivers today. Arrow shows the extent to which the Karkheh flow falls below the expected value. Earlier flow estimates, based on meander wavelengths, though higher, were still below the line.

CHANGES IN THE SURFACES OF THE PLAINS

During excavation of many of the large mounds in the Deh Luran plain and in Upper Khuzistan, cultural layers are seen to extend below the present surface of the plain, which itself consists of sterile alluvial material. The surface of the plain must therefore have been aggraded by running water, and new cultural layers have continually kept the surface of the mound above the plain level. Basal layers of the mound must postdate the sterile material on which they rest, and hence the elevation of the plain at the time when the mound was begun. High layers of cultural material must be older than alluvium beside them at the same level, but it is impossible to know by how much. The only criterion is that living levels must have been high enough to keep above most of the flood flows which deposited the alluvium.

Although alluvium is necessarily deposited by running water, it cannot with certainty be assumed natural. The possibility that the aggradation is produced by flow along irrigation canals has to be considered, but the depth, widespread distribution and date of the deposits appears to make this highly unlikely. If it may be assumed that the aggradation of the plain surface is produced by natural floods, then conditions for farming must have been very different from those of today, as noted above. In addition, mound tops would have had great advantages as dwelling sites because of their protection from flooding while they still provided access to fields. In a period of generally increasing village and town population, the desirability of living on mounds must have encouraged high population densities on the mounds, because of the work required to enlarge them or to build new ones.

Stream regimes during aggradation may be of two types: meandering with levees or braided. An aggrading meandering river gradually builds up its flood plain as it overtops its levees in flood, depositing silt on the levee itself and clays in a back-swamp area. At low flows it is entirely confined to a single channel. After many floods not only are the floodplain and levee raised, but also the river bed itself, until it approaches a condition in which the river bed is higher than parts of the flood plain. At this time, a particularly large flood can erode a cut in the levee and an entirely new channel beyond it, causing a catastrophic and permanent change in the river course. Very severe river floods, such as those experienced on the Hwang Ho river, often have this effect. This type of regime however, can only occur if the sediment available is sufficiently fine-grained, with no gravel and a high proportion of clay. In coarser materials, such as those of Khuzistan, meanders develop without appreciable levees, as can be seen today. Such meander systems exhibit frequent small changes of course as individual meanders cut back their banks, but no aggradation. The absence of levee features on the aggraded plains of Khuzistan, therefore, confirms that river regimes during aggradation were not meandering, but must have been braided.

Braided patterns, with many distributaries (described above), commonly produce aggradation all over extensive plains in silts or coarser material, and at higher surface slope angles than for meanders. It therefore appears likely that braided patterns once covered the whole of the Deh Luran and Khuzistan plains, depositing 5 meters or more of sediment since the last glaciation. The history of deposition and erosion raises several questions, few of which can be fully answered. It is important to know when the aggradation occurred, and if at the same time for all the major rivers; and, a more difficult question, why the aggradations occurred.

The evidence for rates of aggradation lies in a series of dates and levels of basal cultural material in mounds which were excavated during the present project (Chagha Sefid), during the previous Deh Luran project (Hole, Flannery and Neely, 1969), at Djafarabad (Dollfus, 1971), at Haft Tappeh (Ezat Negahban, personal communication), and at sites surveyed by Adams (n.d.) in Khuzistan. One site is based on a sherd found in the river bank of the Mehmeh near Tell El Ramon, which was in good enough condition to be assumed contemporary with the natural alluvium around it. Evidence from all of these points is plotted in Figure 111, which shows how far each dated level is below the main surface of the surrounding plain.

From Figure 111, some simple conclusions may be drawn, although their simplicity is not enough to demonstrate their truth. It is inferred tentatively that aggradation was simultaneous in all the river systems, and that the amount of aggradation was very similar in each, though perhaps slightly less on the Karkheh. It is surprising that the rivers should have such similar rates of aggradation, since each is an almost separate system, but it is not surprising that the rates are of the same order of magnitude, since a very high rate of aggradation in one river would raise it enough to overflow across the fan of a neighboring river. In this way some rough balance between fan areas and aggradation rates must be maintained.

In Figure 111, two curves are drawn though the data points, which illustrate different possible interpretations which might be placed on the data. At the earliest period there might appear to be a low rate of aggradation, or indeed no aggradation, until about 6500 B.C., but this interpretation depends on the exact position of one point. Local differences in plain

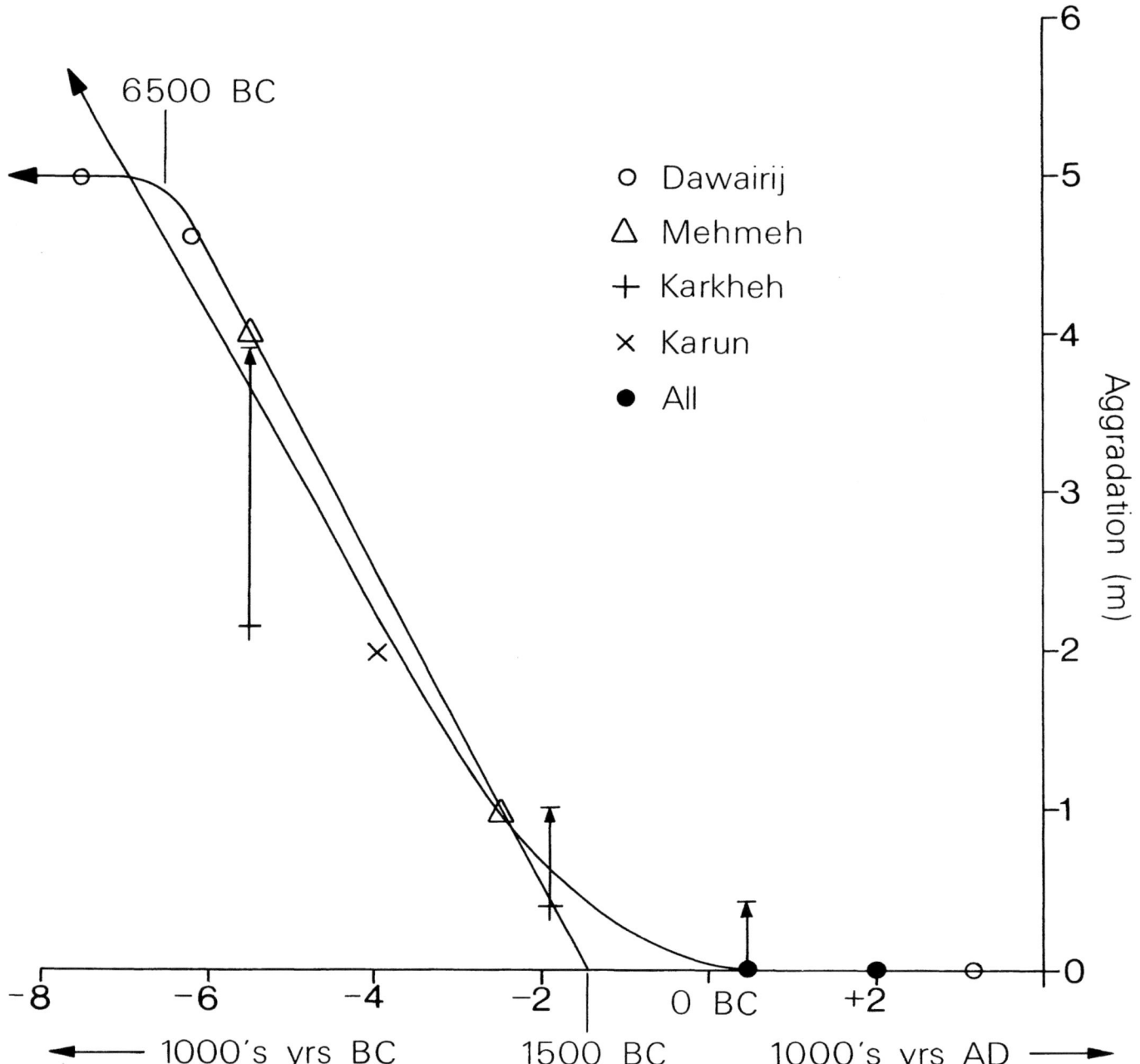

Fig. 111. Total aggradation of the main plains level since dates shown. Evidence mainly from dating of mound-base archeological levels. Symbols refer to drainage basins within which the site lies. Lines show two possible interpretations from data points.

elevation do not justify this sort of reliance on single points, and, on this evidence, the simpler interpretation is of continuous aggradation, which had already started by 8000 B.C.

Since 2000 B.C. aggradation has ceased, and has now been replaced by down-cutting into the plain alluvium to form stable channel positions within a floodplain which is several meters below the plain surface. Thus, at the present time there is no aggradation because the plain surface very rarely floods. Figure 111 shows two possible alternatives, representing a sudden or a gradual abandonment of aggradation, and its replacement by incision. All that can be said is that aggradation stopped at some date between about 1500 B.C. and A.D. 500. Historical evidence (the ancient Choaspes-Eulaeus discussed above) reduces this range of uncertainty somewhat, because Alexander the Great was able to sail down a river from Shush in 335 B.C. To do this, the river must have had a well-defined single course, or, in other words, a meandering regime associated with incision of the plains. Thus aggradation must have ceased by about 500 B.C., suggesting a relatively sudden change of regime on the scale indicated on Figure 111.

The relative timing of aggradation in the distinct river systems is uncertain, but the argument about levels and rates of aggradation also applies, indicating approximate synchrony between major rivers in a lateral sense. Similarly Figure 111, given the simplest interpretation, can be taken as evidence for simulteneous aggradation in all river systems. If this conclusion is accepted, it has important implications for the cause of aggradation, which must be sought in widespread events: in tectonic, climatic or broad cultural events, rather than in purely local sequences of events.

Broadly, the mountain area is one of erosion, the plains area one of transportation or deposition, and the Persian Gulf area one of steady deposition. These basic regimes are determined by the geometry and tectonics of the area, over time and space scales which are much greater than those relevant to the immediate discussion. What is relevant is the small changes in conditions which have altered the role of the plains rivers from aggradation to passive transportation, or even erosion, within the recent archeological period. Briefly, a change to aggrading conditions may arise in one of four ways, which are discussed in turn below:

(1) A reduction in the rate of subsidence of Gulf sediments.
(2) A change to a wetter climate, in association with aggradation upstream.
(3) A change to a drier climate, in association with erosion upstream.
(4) A change in human land or water use.

Tectonic Movements

The Khuzistan shoreline is determined as a dynamic equilibrium between deposition of stream sediments, and subsidence of the Gulf area. Geological evidence (Lees and Falcon, 1952) suggests that the shoreline has been more or less stationary since the Pliocene, and archeological work substantiates this in greater detail for the more recent period (Hansman, 1967). There seems, therefore, to be no reason to assume a change in shore line circumstances which might cause aggradation to change to erosion or viceversa. Furthermore, the Ahwaz ridge, and the corresponding rapids on the Karun serve to decouple the Khuzistan plain from possible changes in conditions for sedimentation at the coast. Aggradation might arise from uplift further inland, along one or more of the hill ridges which intersect the plain, and Lees and Falcon (1952) have suggested that a canal across the Shaur ridge indicates post-Sasanian uplift. Examination of this canal by the author, however, leaves this question very open. The canal line undoubtedly goes up across the top of the ridge, but the line is now composed of infilled material, not the original canal bed. In the center of the ridge, the canal would require a deeper cutting, so that subsequent infill has been greater, and has raised the canal line more than at less incised sites. The elevation of the canal line across the ridge is no greater than can be explained by such a differential infill, but, in the absence of detailed borings, the case must remain unproven. Although the overall case for aggradation resulting from tectonic movements must remain open, there appears to be no other evidence to support such a change. Taking into account also the lateral uniformity of aggradation, tectonic movements are not considered to be the most probable cause of aggradation.

Climatic Changes

Climatic change is a well-established possible cause of alternating aggradation and erosion in rivers in semi-arid areas. Most authors consider that in semi-arid areas, aggradation is associated with wetter periods, and down-cutting with drier periods. In a slightly drier period, plant cover is sparser, so that rain compacts and seals the unprotected soil surface. The effect is to reduce infiltration into the soil, and increase surface runoff, which carries with it a greatly increased sediment load. To accommodate these changes, more channels are formed and existing ones incised. These changes occur first of all in headwater areas, and then progressively downstream, though with some delay. The first effect of the headwater erosion on downstream areas is to increase the sediment supply greatly, but to influence the flood flows only slightly. The upstream erosion is, therefore, commonly associated with some downstream aggradation. There is thus a transition point between upstream erosion and downstream deposition; and, as headwater erosion settles down to equilibrium, the transition point tends to migrate downstream—that is in the opposite direction to an erosional knick-point generated by changes at the mouth of the river.

In the context of Khuzistan, this climatic change theory provides a simple fit to the available data, if it is assumed that the post-glacial increase of temperature or reduction in rainfall (pollen studies indicate that the climate was cooler *and drier* during the late Pleistocene) has led to drier conditions, and that the effects of this change are still working downstream. Thus the initial effect of the drier conditions was to increase the rate of headwater erosion as hillside vegetation became sparser. To begin with, this erosion led to an increase of sediment downstream, causing aggradation all over the plains. Over the last ten thousand years, however, the continued drier climate (overall) has allowed the area of erosion to spread downstream into the Khuzistan plains, which are now more or less stable, although 'wetter' conditions since the 4000 B.C. climatic optimum might have assisted this stabilization. It is suggested that at a slightly earlier stage the partly natural changes of course, recorded in Figure 108, showed the last changes of course as the rivers became effectively established in their present positions by incision.

Water and Land Use

Aggradation might also be attributed to cultural causes, via changes in land or water use over the archeological period. The most likely changes of this sort are an increase in abstraction of water for irrigation, and an increase in the intensity of grazing. The first of these possibilities is an attractive one, for which evidence has been seen in other areas of the world. However, because the regime of a river depends most strongly on its high flows, takeoffs must be great enough to significantly reduce them. This requirement is at variance with normal irrigation practice, which does not require water when the river is highest, because rainfall is also highest. As a result the flood flows are usually the least affected, in both relative and absolute amounts, by normal irrigation, although contrary possibilities have been noted above. Passing over this problem, however, it can be seen that irrigation takeoffs increase the number of channels, and decrease the flow in each. All, including the natural stream, are therefore less able to carry their share of the sediment load, which is consequently deposited. The difficulty with this theory is that aggradation began at a time when irrigation played little or no part; and aggradation stopped at the time when irrigation expanded most rapidly. Thus irrigation is presumably not a main cause of aggradation.

An increase in grazing intensity, associated with more intensive dependence on herding, presumably at the expense of sedentary cultivation, has effects somewhat similar to those of a drier climate. Sheep and especially goats can reduce vegetation cover, and so encourage erosion. This erosion will occur as an increase in the number of gullies. As a result of increased gullying, flash floods tend to become more common, with higher flood peaks, and lower low flows. The effect on sedimentation in the Khuzistan plains would be the same as for a dry period: that is, increased grazing would lead first to aggradation, and then to incision within the deposited material as the system settled down to its new equilibrium. Both aggradation and incision will follow from a single change to more intense grazing, and although a reverse change to less intense grazing could accelerate and intensify the change-over to incision, it is not absolutely necessary to make the change-over occur.

Grazing as an instigator of aggradation or erosion is a concept with more to support it than other possible cultural causes. The onset of aggradation by around 8000 B.C. (Fig. 111) appears to coincide with the period in which man grew to depend on domestic animals (as well as with a period of increasing aridity). The period around 1000 B.C. appears to correspond tolerably well with the period of Achaemenian canal building, and hence with a period of increasing cultivation and decreasing animal use. This association of events for the latter period, however, presents some problems. First, the effect on the river should be delayed by at least several centuries from the onset of a land-use change, whereas the canal building is a necessary sequel to river down-cutting, so that the causal chain appears to be reversed, unless the canals can merely be taken as symptomatic of intensive cultivation which was already going on. Secondly, changes in river sedimentation are most responsive to changes in headwater conditions, and the implications of intensive cultivation on the plains could well be increased grazing in the mountains—again a reverse effect. As with climatic change, it appears simplest to associate the cessation of aggradation with the initial major change of climate or grazing, as the 7000-year-plus wave of sedimentation passes through Khuzistan. However, evidence has been presented above of declining peak flows in the Karkheh, but not in other major rivers, over the last 2,500 years, suggesting a change of land use away from grazing in the highland valleys.

There are thus two workable hypotheses to explain the widespread aggradation and its cessation in the Khuzistan and Deh Luran plains. The major cause is probably the increase in aridity following the Pleistocene, but increases in grazing intensity may be an important subsidiary cause.

ARCHEOLOGICAL IMPLICATIONS

Environmental Zones

The Deh Luran plain has been described as containing a continuous range of environments. As one proceeds from the mountains of the Kuh-i-Siah towards the center of the valley, a number of factors change more or less together, clearly demonstrating their physiographic interdependence. The surface slope declines from 5° to less than 0.5°; the dense spread of large boulders near the mountains gradually thins, until eventually the only stones are in archeological sites; the landscape changes from rolling hills 5-10 meters high to an almost featureless plain; the soil becomes progressively more saline and more liable to floods in the winter; and the vegetation mirrors these differences as it changes from scattered jujube (*Zizyphus*) trees, via *Prosopis* and *Alhagi* bushes, to salt-tolerant and phreatophyte species in the center flats and along the river floodplains.

Although these changes are continuous, it is perhaps worthwhile to identify four key environmental zones: near the mountains the 'dry steppe,' next the more heavily used 'alluvial plain,' and, in the center, the 'seasonal marsh' and 'floodplain' areas. It is important to think of these environments not only as they are today, but as they may have changed over the last 10,000 years.

Today the dry steppe has sandy soils, moderate surface slopes and some dissection by stream courses, all of which combine to make it exceedingly well-drained. Although this good drainage avoids any problem of salinization, it also provides the worst possible conditions for dry farming in an area where water is, at best, marginally sufficient for agriculture. This land, with its characteristic *Zizyphus* cover and some seasonal grass, is therefore given over almost entirely to grazing, although there are some possible sites for farming in a narrow channel-side strip close to the mountains.

The alluvial plain has finer soils, less incision, and generally low enough slopes to conserve rainwater better and to allow distribution of tributary flood waters with simple techniques. There is, however, enough through passage of water to minimize salinity problems. The wetter fringes of this area are the best for agriculture, allowing use of all the rainfall augmented by flood water to provide an adequate supply in most years, without any of the problems which arise from excessive water. This zone is characterized by the *Prosopis* and *Alhagi*, especially on the mountain side of the cultivated belt.

The seasonal marsh is the small central area towards which all the tributaries between the Mehmeh and the Dawairij flow. In winter it commonly floods, and is characterized by highly calcareous silts with distinct plastic properties, which make them difficult to work, slow to drain, and liable to salinization. In this area, salt levels in the soil are high enough to seriously inhibit cultivation, although there is no evidence of a harmful build-up of sodium salts which would lead to irreversible loss of soil fertility, as has occurred in the main Tigris-Euphrates valley. The conformity of salinity patterns with other physiographic variables strongly suggests that salinization has occurred more or less naturally in the Deh Luran plain. That is to say, salinity is not a result of over-intensive land use associated with irrigation. This conclusion is tentatively applied to past periods.

These environments parallel many in northern Khuzistan, north of the Shaur ridge, but the possibility of summer irrigation from the major rivers introduces a new factor of major importance in the latter plain. South of the Shaur ridge, the environment of Khuzistan differs significantly in its lower rainfall, which makes farming too hazardous an occupation without properly organized irrigation. It appears that only in the Sasanian-Early Islamic periods did it seem worthwhile to construct such irrigation systems primarily for winter use (the same applies to the systems of the Deh Luran plain). Still farther south in Khuzistan, high water-tables and high salinity become the dominant conditions, which vary in intensity from the rather mild problems of Deh Luran to the irreversible sodium alkalinity of parts of the Tigris-Euphrates valley.

Environmental Changes through Time

On these environments must be imposed the dimensions of changes over time, which are by no means simple or certain in their interpretation. Two main components are present: first, the overall pattern of post-Pleistocene climatic change, and, second, the local history of sedimentation which has been described above. Since the Pleistocene, higher temperatures and lower rainfalls have changed the hydrologic balance considerably, so that between about 6000 and 1000 B.C., conditions for dry farming were appreciably more hazardous than today. An even more sensitive response to the changing climate might be expected in the response of a wet area (a marsh or a lake). Such an area evaporates water at a maximum rate, whereas evapo-transpiration is very restricted in other parts of a semi-arid basin. The area of such a wetland is proportional to the ratio of run-off to potential evaporation, so that a decrease in rainfall produces a more than proportional decrease in the wetland area. This argument may be applied to the seasonal or perhaps permanent marsh of the Deh Luran plain to infer that its area perhaps halved between 8000 and 4000 B.C., and then experienced a partial recovery.

It should be remembered that, in this period, the Mehmeh and Dawairij rivers were not incised as at present, but that their waters contributed directly to the marsh. This means that prior to incision the marsh would have been proportionately bigger for a given climate, and that its shape would have been somewhat different, spreading around towards the present major river courses. This complex of factors already complicates the problem too much for reliable quantification, but offers some pointers on the course of environmental change in the marsh area.

The alluvial plain area of today was the locus of sedimentation in the period from pre-8000 B.C. until about 1000 B.C. Following the major post-Pleistocene climatic change, aggradation passed downstream as a wave, and at any moment there were distinct zones along the length of a river system: (1) a headwater area of erosion, (2) an alluvial area which had been deposited previously, but which was now being incised, (3) an area of active aggradation, where stream levels were close to the surface and changes of course frequent, and (4) a downstream area in which the distributaries which had formed during aggradation gradually came together, usually reuniting in the old downstream river bed. The present alluvial plain is like area (2), with little incision between major rivers. Area (3) has no parallel today, but was suited to irrigation with the very simplest diversion systems, though liable to flood. It was therefore particularly suitable for primitive cultivation in a drier period, and, because there was active aggradation, salinity was kept in check by renewed deposition of sediment. The upper part of area (4) was one of rather disorganized drainage, and appears to be particularly suitable for marsh conditions, given sufficient water.

Thus the marsh area first contracted, and then tended to expand again after the climatic optimum of about 4000 B.C. Meanwhile the wave of sedimentation moved steadily downstream through the area until 1000 B.C. For the first part of this period, therefore, from 8000 until 4000 B.C., the marsh and sediment wave moved together, so that agriculture was continually able to make use of the aggrading area (3), in which the water table was high without salinity problems, and crops could obtain the advantages of irrigation without the need for more than the most primitive irrigation techniques. Nevertheless, this cultivation belt was moving inwards through time, separating areas of dry plant gathering (area (2)) from areas of marsh plant gathering (area (4)). In the second part of this period, from 4000 to 1000 B.C., the sedimentation continued to move downstream, as is shown by the stratigraphic evidence, while the marsh area expanded again. This means that the marsh area may have expanded into the dissected part of the alluvial plain. It could only do this along the incised river courses, so that at some time within this period, and there is no way of being sure of the date on present evidence, the present dichotomy of wetland areas in the marsh and floodplain began to develop, along with the present shape of the marsh area. At the same time, the potential area which was best for cultivation was, for the first time, a dissected area. For the smaller tributaries, the dissection was small enough to require no appreciable change of irrigation technique, and cultivation patterns could have been similar to those of today; but near the two major streams, larger canal systems were needed to raise water from the rivers a kilometer or so upstream.

In the steppe area, the already marginal conditions for crop growth must have completely prevented cultivation from about 6000-1000 B.C., so that this zone could not have been more than a plant gathering area, but greater use of the zone for cultivation was possible both before and since. Clearly, this zone has always been available for grazing, but better pasture was to be found next to the farming belt, in the marshes, and along floodplains when these started to develop.

As well as sites which depend directly on these moving resource belts, other sites may have been dependent on the position of the major rivers, once these began to stabilize from the mountains down. In the early stages of stablilization, river courses, although undivided, were less incised and therefore much more liable to major changes of course, of the sort that has been described above for Khuzistan in more recent times. Of particular relevance is the possibility that the Dawairij once flowed across its fan to join the Mehmeh at Bayat. Changes of course from the fourth to second millennia B.C. would be expected to show no trace on the present landscape, but the position of Tepe Garan especially seems to raise the possibility that it was exploiting the position of a former course of the Dawairij towards Bayat; whereas Tepes Musiyan and Farukhabad are relatively close to the present stable river courses. Such changes should, however, have been finally stabilized by the first millennium B.C. on the Deh Luran plain.

The evidence on site use presented in the previous archeological report on Deh Luran (Hole, Flannery and Neely, 1969) can readily be interpreted in the light of the above model of environmental change, although in ways which are somewhat at variance with the suggestions in that report. A major problem of archeological sites is that they are in different environmental zones, as well as representing different periods. At Ali Kosh, the replacement of marsh plants in the Bus Mordeh Phase by a dominance of agricultural material in the Ali Kosh Phase, and by steppe plants, including *Prosopis* in the Mohammad Jaffar Phase seems to indicate clearly the gradual contraction of the marsh, so that the site environment changed from marsh to alluvial plain to the edge of the steppe area over a 1250-year time span. The absence of *Zizyphus* throughout suggests that it never became very much of a steppe area. At Tepe Sabz, in the Sabz Phase, there is evidence that the site is within the agricultural belt, as might be expected for a somewhat later period at a site which is closer to the center of the marsh. It is likewise to be expected that abandonment of Tepe Sabz in the Bayat Phase is associated with a similar movement to steppe plants, like *Prosopis*, as that which occurred at Ali Kosh 2000 years earlier. The position of Chagha Sefid, appears to be intermediate between these two, although even its *position* relative to the marsh in pre-incision times cannot be certain. The quoted evidence for irrigation at Tepe Sabz can be taken to indicate an abundant water supply, but it seems likely that this could have been supplied by direct reliance on a high water table, rather than through specific water control techniques.

In this perspective, the history of the Deh Luran plain is seen as a slow movement, up to about 4000 B.C., of sites towards the center of the marsh as it gradually contracted, in a period when rainfall was scarcer than today, and with a dependence on a high water table and simple flood-spreading methods rather than more complex techniques of water control. Subsequently, as the climate became less arid, the best sites for agriculture were on the plain above incised rivers, so that farming had to rely on more and more complex irrigation methods to raise water from the rivers. This would favor the establishment of larger sites, dependent on the two major rivers, such as Musiyan. Later still, reduced aridity allowed expansion into the dry steppe in Achaemenian era, as cultivation became possible with a minimum of water control, and the situation has remained similar up to the present day.

BIBLIOGRAPHY

Adams, Robert McC.
   1962   Agriculture and urban life in early southwestern Iran. Science 136:109-122.
   n.d.   Unpublished field notes of survey of Khuzistan, Iran. 1960-1961.

Dollfus, G.
   1971   Djaffarabad 1967-1970 Rapport préliminaire sur les deux premierès campagnes de fouilles. Syria 48:61-84.

Hansman, John
   1967   Charax and the Karkheh. Iranica Antiqua 7:21-58.

Helbaek, Hans
   1969   Plant collecting, dry-farming and irrigation agriculture in prehistoric Deh Luran. *In* Hole, Flannery and Neely, 1969.

Hole, Frank, Kent V. Flannery and James A. Neely
   1969   Prehistory and human ecology of the Deh Luran Plain. Memoir No. 1. Ann Arbor, University of Michigan Museum of Anthropology.

Lees, G. M. and N. L. Falcon
   1952   The geographical history of the Mesopotamian plains. Geographical Journal 118:24-39.

Leopold, L. B. and M. G. Wolman
   1957   River Channel Patterns: Braided, Meandering and Straight. U.S. Geological Survey, Professional Paper 282-B.

APPENDIX II

THE LATER OBSIDIAN OF DEH LURAN—THE EVIDENCE OF CHAGHA SEFID

by Colin Renfrew
Department of Archaeology
University of Southampton,
England

ACKNOWLEDGEMENTS

I am grateful to Dr. Frank Hole for inviting me to study the Chagha Sefid obisidian, and to both him and Barbara Hole for their generous hospitality to my wife and myself in Deh Luran. Dr. John Dixon, now of the Grant Institute of Geology, University of Edinburgh, was kind enough to undertake the analyses reported in Table 89 as part of our obisidan research program reported in a number of papers. We are grateful to Mr. R. S. Allen of the Department of Mineralogy, University of Cambridge, for reading the spectrograph plates and for much helpful cooperation. Professors Jean Perrot and Henry Wright, and Dr. and Mrs. David Stronach, have afforded useful information and advice.

Already by 1966 a qualititative picture was emerging of the early obsidian trade in the Near East. By 1968 a general quantitative picture could be offered (Renfrew, Dixon and Cann, 1968) of the supply of obsidian in the 'early Neolithic' period—that is to say, during the time of occupation of Ali Kosh and of sites such as Jarmo and Tepe Guran over a time range from about 7500 B.C. to 6000 or 5500 B.C. in radiocarbon years. The excavations at Ali Kosh allowed some aspects of this trade, as it affected southwestern Iran, to be studied more closely, and the position was surveyed in detail in the first Deh Luran report (Renfrew, 1969).

At that time the excavations at Tepe Sabz already offered insight into the 'chalcolithic' or Halaf-Ubaid period in the area, but the very scanty obsidian obtained from that site had not been subjected to analysis. Now, with the excavations at Chagha Sefid, the gap is bridged between the early period revealed at Ali Kosh and the later materials of Tepe Sabz, and the gradual decline of the obsidian supply in Deh Luran from the early to the late phase can more clearly be seen and studied. Before reporting in detail on the analyses from Chagha Sefid it will be useful to review briefly the information available from previous work.

THE EVIDENCE OF ALI KOSH AND TEPE SABZ

Analyses of obsidian from these sites have already been reported: they are summarized in Table 88. They have contributed to a clear picture of the early obsidian supply in Deh Luran, which can now be set within a wider context (Renfrew and Dixon, n.d.).

The second variety is characteristically grey in color (although identifications on the basis of appearance are not reliable unless backed up by chemical analysis). Such analysis permits attribution of this material to group 1g, which characteristically has over 500 ppm of barium and between 160 and 270 ppm of zirconium. Early in the program of obsidian analyses it became clear that the source of the group 1g obsidian must lie in the same general region as the 4c source at Nemrut Dağ, an area sometimes loosely termed 'Armenia,' which will here be designated Van-Armenia-Azerbaijan (abbreviated VAA) to stress its extension across the territorial boundaries of modern Turkey, USSR and Iran. Further consideration of the distribution of finds of group 1g obsidian (Renfrew and Dixon, n.d.) suggests that its source may lie many kilometers to the west or southwest of the Nemrut Dağ source.

The general picture of the obsidian trade in

Table 88

SUMMARY OF ANALYSES FROM ALI KOSH AND TEPE SABZ

No.	Site	Phase	Publication	Color	Group
187	Ali Kosh	Ali Kosh	Renfrew, Dixon and Cann, 1966	Clear (white)	1g
323	Ali Kosh	Mohammad Jaffar	Renfrew, Dixon and Cann, 1966	Grey	1g
333	Ali Kosh	Mohammad Jaffar	Renfrew, Dixon and Cann, 1966	Grey	1g
186	Ali Kosh	Ali Kosh	Renfrew, Dixon and Cann, 1966	Green	4c
206	Ali Kosh	Ali Kosh	Renfrew, Dixon and Cann, 1966	Green	4c
322	Ali Kosh	Mohammad Jaffar	Renfrew, Dixon and Cann, 1966	Green	4c
334	Ali Kosh	Mohammad Jaffar	Renfrew, Dixon and Cann, 1966	Green	4c
414	Ali Kosh	Ali Kosh	Table 89, below	Grey	1g
415	Ali Kosh	Ali Kosh	Table 89, below	Grey	1g
416	Ali Kosh	Bus Mordeh	Table 89, below	Grey	1g
399	Tepe Sabz	Mehmeh	Renfrew and Dixon, n.d.	Green	4c
400	Tepe Sabz	Bayat	Renfrew and Dixon, n.d.	Grey	3a
401	Tepe Sabz	Bayat	Renfrew and Dixon, n.d.	Green	4c
402	Tepe Sabz	Bayat	Renfrew and Dixon, n.d.	Clear (white)	2b
406	Susa Acropolis	Susa A	Renfrew and Dixon, n.d.	Green	4c
407	Susa Acropolis	Susa A	Renfrew and Dixon, n.d.	Grey	3a
408	Susa Acropolis	Susa A	Renfrew and Dixon, n.d.	Grey	3a
409	Susa Acropolis	Susa A	Renfrew and Dixon, n.d.	Clear (white)	3a

western Asia during this period is given in Figure 112. Three interaction zones may be identified—an obsidian interaction zone being defined as the area within which sites derived 30 percent or more of their obsidian from the same specific source. In the west are the Konya and Levant zones, which do not concern us here, since no group 1e-f or group 2b obsidian reached Deh Luran at this time. In the east is the Zagros zone, based on the supply of group 4c obsidian. Crosses on the map show the findspots of group 1g obsidian, which has been reported as in excess of 30 percent of the total of obsidian found only at Bouqras.

During the early period, represented by the Bus Mordeh, Ali Kosh and Mohammad Jaffar phases, obsidian was reaching Deh Luran from two sources. The greater part has trace element characteristics, notably more than 300 parts per million of zirconium and fewer than 30 ppm of barium, which permit its attribution to group 4c. Obsidian of this group, which

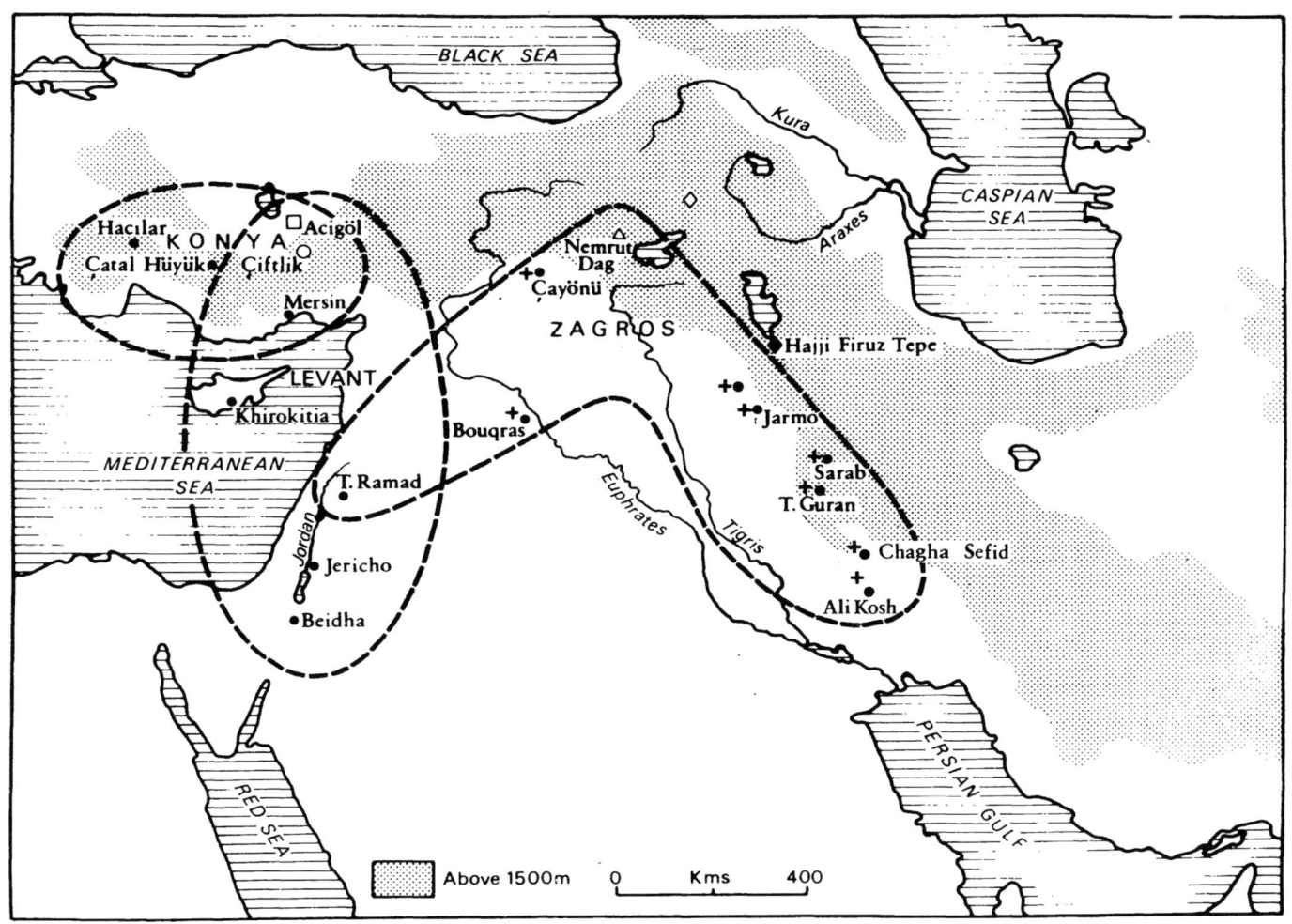

Fig. 112. The obsidian trade in western Asia, c. 7500-5500 B.C. In the Levant interaction zone the obsidian is predominantly of group 2b, from Çiftlik; in the Konya zone of group 1e-f; in the Zagros zone of group 4c (from the Nemrut Dağ area) and of group 1g. Findspots of group 1g obsidian are indicated by a cross. The only known findspot of group 3 obsidian at this period is indicated by a lozenge.

characteristically has a greenish tinge when seen in transmitted light, derives from the source at Nemrut Dağ on the north-west side of Lake Van, in the Van vilayet of eastern Turkey.

The changing pattern in the Deh Luran area will be reviewed again below. The analysis of number 416, reported in Table 88 and detailed in Table 89 merits comment, however, since this is the first indication that group 1g obsidian was already reaching Deh Luran in the Bus Mordeh Phase.

Turning now to the later phase, documented at Tepe Sabz, we see a very much diminished supply of obsidian. Group 4c obsidian still plays a significant role, but group 1g obsidian is no longer seen. Instead a new variety, group 3a (with a sub-group 3a" at Susa) is present. The source of the group 3 obsidians is again not precisely known, although it clearly lies in the VAA region. The preponderance of group 3 obsidian among the artifacts analyzed in the Lake Urmia region makes a location at the north of Lake Urmia seem likely. A single piece of obsidian from Tepe Sabz is of group 2b, indicating for the first time the presence of obsidian from the central Anatolian source.

The general picture at this time, broadly contemporary with the Halaf-Ubaid-Uruk phases, from c. 5000 to c. 3000 B.C., is seen in Figure 113. The picture in the west is little altered, and a new inter-

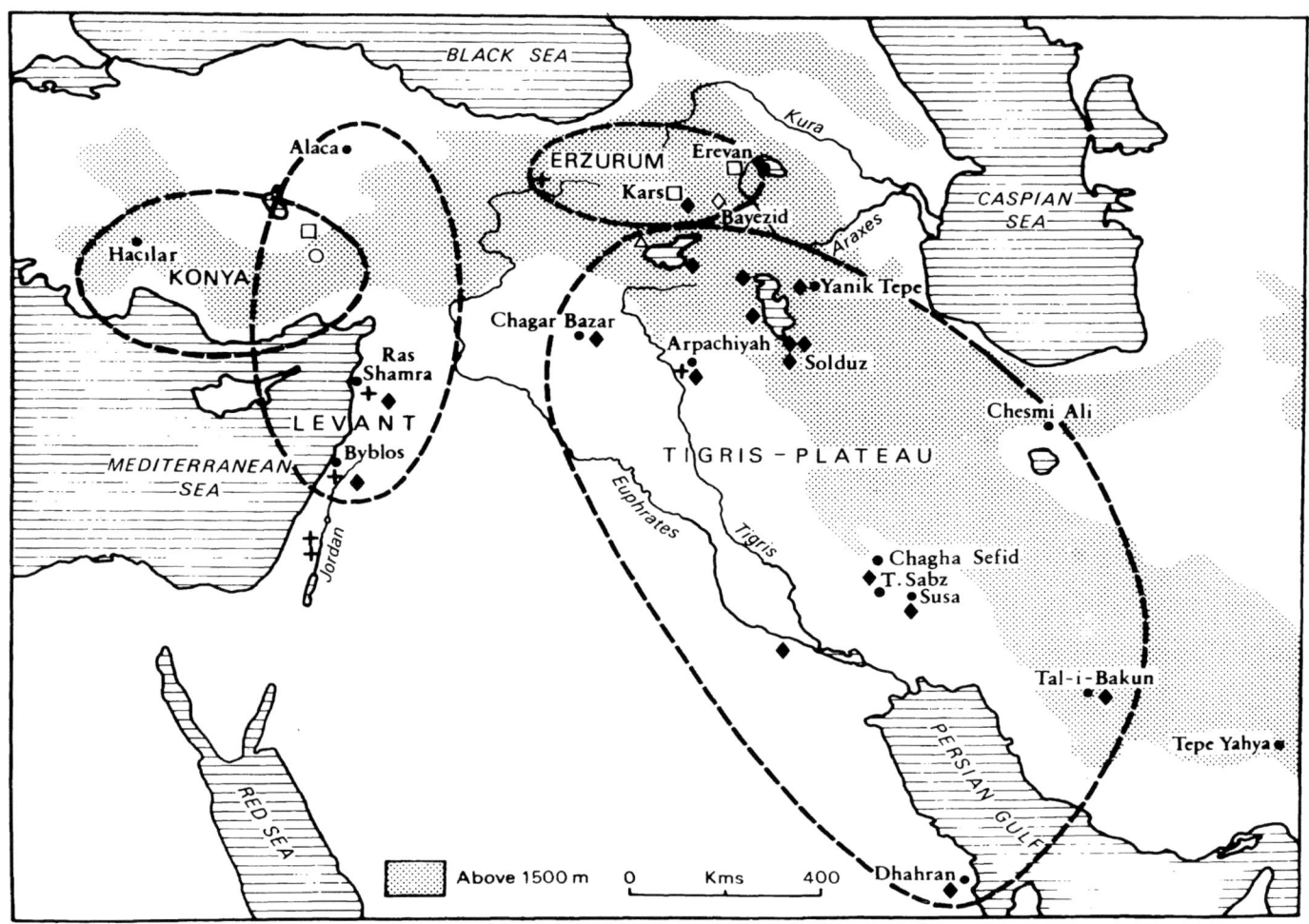

Fig. 113. The obsidian trade in western Asia, c. 5000–3000 B.C. In the Tigris-Plateau zone the obsidian is predominantly of group 4c and of group 3. Findspots of group 1g obsidian are shown by crosses, of group 3 obsidian by lozenges (see text for details of Deh Luran finds).

action zone has emerged in northeastern Anatolia. For Khuzistan, however, the main development is the reorientation of what may now be termed the Tigris-Plateau interaction zone. Group 3 obsidian now plays an important role along with group 4c, and has effectively displaced group 1g.

The interest of the Chagha Sefid material is that it bridges the time interval between the periods represented in these two maps, and allows some insight into the changing trading patterns over time.

THE CHAGHA SEFID ANALYSES

In all, some 1400 fragments of obsidian were recovered during the excavation at Chagha Sefid. All of these were examined for the present study, and the visual characteristics of the material carefully noted.

The experience of previous programs of analysis indicated that variations in translucency and transparency do not in general correlate with composition in any marked way, nor does the presence of striations, cloudiness, or small spots in the material. The single feature which has in the past consistently correlated with composition (and hence with provenience) is the presence of a green color, as seen in the obsidian from Nemrut Dağ.

The purpose of the sampling of specimens for subsequent trace-element analysis was, of course, to establish the full range of obsidian sources serving the site. A sampling procedure drawing on the full range of variability of the obsidian was therefore desired. The obvious policy to follow was to sample the full range of variation in appearance (color, transparency, etc.) on the assumption that variation in appearance might well correlate to some extent with that in composition, and at worst could only vary randomly with respect to composition.

Since the early phase had already been sampled fairly thoroughly at Ali Kosh (and three more grey samples from that site were included in the new run), it seemed appropriate to sample material from a later phase. Accordingly a large quantity of material was examined from stratigraphic zone B2 of the Sefid Phase. Most of the samples selected were unretouched blades.

Among the pieces classed as 'green' (indicated as 'E' in the appropriate column of Table 89), were several with minor variations in appearance. Two pieces were absolutely clear bottle green (nos. 425 and 426), and two somewhat fuzzy in appearance due to the presence of numerous very small black spots (nos. 427 and 428). One piece had light striations (no. 429) and one was cloudy (no. 430).

It should be noted that the green color is seen only in transmitted light and is not easy to detect in thin pieces; daylight was used in all cases. In each instance a group 4c attribution was predicted.

Two pieces were almost entirely opaque, so that only at the extreme edge was any color visible (nos. 422 and 423). This thin edge was dark treacle-brown in color, and the color is indicated 'Br' in the appropriate column. Both pieces are assigned to group 1g.

Among the grey or clear-white pieces the variation in appearance was more striking, and I felt that they might include material from more than one source. Indeed, the almost crystal clear obsidian with a very faint rosy tinge seen in nos. 412, 413, 417 and 424 was reminiscent of the appearance of some of the group 2b obsidian of central Anatolia. The other pieces were all grey in transmitted light, either striated (nos. 418 and 419), cloudy (nos. 420 and 421) or almost entirely opaque (nos. 410 and 411) in appearance. These different pieces encompass the whole range of variation in appearance of the Chagha Sefid obsidian. Just one other piece, of an unusual brown color (no. 431), was selected, which on analysis and subsequent examination turned out to be not obsidian but flint. The results of the analyses are seen in Table 89. The analyses were carried out by Dr. J. E. Dixon at the Department of Mineralogy and Petrology, University of Cambridge, using the Hilger-Littrow E 478 spectrograph (see Cann and Renfrew, 1964).

Among the results, only one, no. 422, presents any difficulties in interpretation. It has some rather weak claims to unique status, being low in Zr (and also in Ga, Pb, Ca and Fe), and high in La and Li, relative to other members of group 1g. As a single anomalous specimen it should probably be regarded as a 'sport' or 'joker': several comparable analyses would be needed before it could be considered significant. It is closest to the analyses of group 1g, with which it has been entered.

Setting this one specimen aside, the results are extremely clear. All the 'green' pieces, for which a group 4c attribution was predicted, and only those pieces, are assigned to group 4c. All the grey or clear-white pieces are assigned to group 1g. No other groups are represented.

Two consequences flow from these results. First, in the Sefid Phase, as in previous phases in Deh Luran, obsidian from two and only two sources was reaching the area. None was coming across from central Anatolia, and none at this time was coming down from the Lake Urmia-Solduz area, where group 3 obsidian was already in use. All the material came from the VAA area, either from the group 4c source at Nemrut Dağ and nearby, or from the group 1g source thought to lie to the south or southwest.

Secondly, the very high correlation between green color and group 4c, and between grey or clear-white and group 1g, already discussed in previous papers (Renfrew, Dixon and Cann, 1966; Renfrew, 1969) is strongly confirmed for the Sefid and, by implication, for preceding periods in Deh Luran. This is an important result, for it permits the formulation of quantitative conclusions based on the careful study of the appearance of hundreds of specimens from Chagha Sefid, whereas it would have been quite impracticable to analyze them all. The discussion which follows is thus based upon this visual criterion, but put forward for consideration only after the test described above. I would repeat that, in general, appearance is not a good test for the provenience of obsidian unless preceded and supported by a coherent program of trace-element analysis.

Table 89
TRACE ELEMENT COMPOSITION OF THE OBSIDIANS ANALYZED
(In Parts per Million)

Serial No.	Site	Group	Ba	Sr	Zr	Y	Nb	La	Rb	Li	Mo	Ga	V	Pb	Ca*	Fe*	Mg*	Color	Translucency/Transparency	Remarks
410	Sefid	1g	880	100	160	13	16	70	320	35	<3	7	<3	36	36	70	370	G	0	
411	Sefid	1g	880	75	160	13	16	70	250	47	<3	11	<3	36	36	83	540	G	0	
412	Sefid	1g	880	100	160	13	16	100	320	47	<3	7	<3	36	36	70	450	W	6	R
413	Sefid	1g	520	54	160	13	10	100	200	47	<3	7	<3	22	36	56	300	W	6	R
417	Sefid	1g	680	75	160	24	16	100	200	35	<3	11	<3	36	36	83	370	G	6	R
418	Sefid	1g	680	54	220	24	16	70	200	80	<3	7	<3	36	48	70	450	G	5	S
419	Sefid	1g	520	54	220	24	16	130	200	63	<3	7	<3	22	48	70	370	G	4	S
420	Sefid	1g	680	43	160	24	22	250	200	47	<3	17	<3	36	42	70	540	G	5	C
421	Sefid	1g	520	54	160	18	10	70	200	47	<3	7	<3	22	36	70	370	G	4	C
423	Sefid	1g	680	54	160	18	10	70	200	63	<3	7	<3	22	36	70	370	Br	0	
424	Sefid	1g	520	43	160	18	10	190	160	63	<3	7	<3	10	36	70	370	W	6	R
422	Sefid	?1g	680	75	120	18	10	250	200	80	<3	7	<3	10	32	70	370	Br	0	
425	Sefid	4c	4	<10	800	63	50	130	160	47	<3	25	<3	22	18	100	33	E	6	
426	Sefid	4c	4	<10	800	63	40	190	200	80	4	25	<3	36	15	120	33	E	6	
427	Sefid	4c	6	<10	800	50	40	190	400	100	4	25	<3	22	15	180	33	E	5	F
428	Sefid	4c	6	<10	690	50	40	130	320	100	<3	17	<3	10	18	120	33	E	4	C, F
429	Sefid	4c	6	<10	800	50	40	190	320	100	<3	25	<3	22	15	150	33	E	5	S
430	Sefid	4c	9	<10	800	50	22	190	125	125	<3	25	<3	36	15	120	33	E	5	C
431	Sefid	--	40	10	<8	<5	50	<50	<28	<13	<3	<2	<3	5	36	<20	670	Br	4	C (flint)
414	Ali Kosh	1g	520	43	160	10	16	70	200	35	<3	7	<3	36	36	70	450	G	5	S
415	Ali Kosh	1g	400	43	160	13	16	100	320	47	<3	11	<3	22	36	70	300	G	5	S
416	Ali Kosh	1g	680	54	220	24	16	100	200	47	<3	11	<3	22	36	100	450	G	3	

*Times 10^{-2}
Color: G=grey, E=green, W=white, B=treacle-brown at edge. Translucency/Transparency: coded as in Cann and Renfrew, 1964. Remarks: R=rosy clear, S=striations, C=cloudy, F=fuzzy.

Table 90
QUANTITIES OF OBSIDIAN RECOVERED FROM SUCCESSIVE PHASES AT CHAGHA SEFID

Phase	No. of Obsidian	Total Chipped Stone	Percent Obsidian	Mean Weight Per Obsidian Fragment (gms. approx.)	Est. Total Obsidian Excavated (gms.)
Sabz	2	747	0.27 }	1.25	3
Choga Mami Transitional	11	2,022	0.54 }		14
Surkh	79	5,641	1.40	0.90	71
Sefid	1,041	22,666	4.59	0.85	885
Mohammad Jaffar	156	1,999	7.80	0.72	112
Ali Kosh	109	7,349	1.48	0.87	95
	1,398	40,487	3.45	0.85	1,180

THE CHAGHA SEFID OBSIDIAN INDUSTRY

The position of the obsidian industry in the culture as a whole can best be understood by stressing its relatively minor role even within the context of the chipped stone industry. In all phases at Chagha Sefid obsidian constituted less than 10 percent of the total industry, the remainder being flint, with a little crystal. Its most frequent occurrence in a single stratigraphic zone was in Zone A of the Mohammad Jaffar Phase, where it constituted 10.3 percent of the total chipped stone. The changing proportions are seen in Table 90. The percentages are based on the total number of pieces recovered, including debitage and core fragments. In all cases the soil was screened through sieves with a mesh aperture of 3 to 4 mm.

In general, the nature of the obsidian industry, judged solely on the basis of the waste materials, did not differ markedly from phase to phase at Chagha Sefid. A study of the forms of artifacts showing secondary working is presented elsewhere in this volume (Ch. VIII). From the standpoint of obsidian supply and utilization, however, the waste material itself gives a rather coherent picture. It may be considered in terms of blades, cores, and debitage since it is very much a blade industry, like other Zagros industries and those of the Aegean early bronze age. It is unlike the obsidian of Çatal Hüyük or the Saliagos culture of the Neolithic Aegean (Evans and Renfrew, 1968:46-62) where reworking by flat flaking is an important feature and where the proportion of blades is very much lower.

The occurrence of chipping debris by zone and phase is seen in Table 50. In general, the percentage of flake cores in the total collection is on the order of 1.5 percent, and there is no significant variation in this proportion, although the absolute figures are too small, except in Zone B2 of the Sefid Phase, to allow the variation to be investigated.

In studying variation in the waste material, given that its character does not greatly vary during the occupation of the site, two factors merit study in addition to the obvious one of the quantity of obsidian represented from different sources. The first is the size of the various materials, which will be significant, especially when compared with other sites in the Near East, in understanding the form in which the obsidian was traded. The second question is the extent to which the two different obsidians present (group 4c and group 1g) are preferred for different forms of artifacts.

The mean weight per fragment by phase is given in Table 90. Clearly this is heavily dependent on the recovery procedure used: as stated above all the soil was screened through a mesh of 3 to 4 mm aperture. In view of the small number of pieces from the later phases, the slightly larger mean weight (1.25 gms) is probably not significant. The overall mean of 0.85 grams will clearly be of interest for comparison with industries in other areas, when suitable data are available. In general terms it is my experience that mean weight of fragment should decrease monotonically with distance from source, just as does the abundance of obsidian. It has been shown that abundance does

Table 91

QUANTITIES AND WEIGHTS OF OBSIDIAN WASTE CATEGORIES IN ZONE B2 OF THE SEFID PHASE AT CHAGHA SEFID
(Weights to Nearest 5 gms.)

Material	Grey Obsidian (Group 1g)			Green Obsidian (Group 4c)			Total Obsidian		
	No. in Sample	Wt. (gms.)	Wt. Per Piece (gms.)	No. in Sample	Wt. (gms.)	Wt. Per Piece (gms.)	No. in Sample	Wt. (gms.)	Wt. per Piece (gms.)
Flakes	73	45	0.51	41	30	0.73	124	75	0.65
Retouched and Used Flakes	13	30	2.3	10	25	2.5	23	55	2.4
Blades and Blade Fragments	93	50	0.53	47	30	0.65	140	80	0.58
Retouched and Used Blades	24	30	1.3	13	15	1.2	37	45	1.2
Cores and Core Fragments	19	45	2.4	4	15	3.8	23	60	2.6
Total	222	200	0.90	115	115	1.0	337	310	0.92

indeed decrease exponentially (Renfrew, Dixon and Cann, 1966). Clearly, however, size and weight are closely governed by functional criteria, so that scarcity of obsidian will be reflected more obviously by decreased frequency than by decreased weight of individual artifacts. The whole question of the decrease in mean weight with distance from source clearly merits investigation of the kind that decrease in abundance has received. Two factors, however, do make the study more difficult. The first is the critical dependence upon screen mesh size, since we are dealing here with an absolute quantity rather than with a ratio which, being dimensionless, is less vulnerable to difference in recovery procedure. The second is that the size of artifact is not governed solely by availability of obsidian (even if we make the assumption that obsidian will be used where possible in preference for flint), but also by functional and stylistic criteria related only in part to the nature of the raw material.

The figure of 0.85 grams as the mean weight of waste fragments (including blades) at Chagha Sefid may be compared with the range at Çayönü, much nearer to the natural sources. There the average for phase 4 (1.2 gms) is greatly exceeded by that for phase 5 (3.8 gms) (Redman, 1973:719). The only other site in the Zagros area where such a figure is available is Jarmo where I obtained a figure of 0.2 gms per piece on a sample made available by Professor R. J. Braidwood. However, in light of the figures given above I now look on this figure with suspicion, and prefer to await the publication in the Jarmo report of the full data.

Of course the mean weight per fragment is itself only a rather crude measure of size, and *a fortiori* of abundance, since it lumps together both blades, whose size may be determined by function or by constraints of manufacture, and core fragments and other waste which may much more accurately reflect the abundance of material. Unfortunately the size of sample at Chagha Sefid was too small for a phase-by-phase analysis of mean weights for the different categories of waste, with the available apparatus for weighing. Only in the Sefid Phase could these figures be established. They are given in Table 91, with green (group 4c) and grey (group 1g) obsidian weighed separately. It should be noted that weighings were made to the nearest five grams.

Predictably, the mean weight of cores and core fragments is considerably greater than the overall average, and that of blades and blade fragments is very much less, only 0.6 grams. The mean weight of retouched and used blades and flakes is high, but this may partly be explained by the difficulty of recognizing retouching or use except in the larger fragments. Clearly in some ways these figures are more meaningful than the overall mean of 0.92 grams per fragment for this deposit. But while overall mean is an objective figure, dependent only on the mesh size for the sieve, the attribution of fragments on the basis of their shape into different categories is in part a subjective procedure. In retrospect the most appropriate presentation of the data would be by means of a frequency distribution of fragments by weight. But to compile this would be laborious, involving the weighing of each piece separately, and would be dependent on the availability of a balance able to weigh rapidly to the nearest 0.1 gram.

The presentation in Table 91 also allows comparison of the mean weights by color. In each category except that of retouched and used blades group 4c obsidian artifacts are a little heavier, and hence larger, than those of group 1g. It is not clear if much significance should be attached to this: it would have been interesting to test the effect in other phases where group 1g obsidian was much rarer. But if the difference is real it need not reflect abundance of supply, since the mechanical properties of group 4c obsidian may facilitate the production of larger blades and other artifacts. This is a question which has not been investigated, nor can it be until the group 1g source is precisely located, since experiments would require material fresh from the source.

The frequency distribution of blade widths of group 1g and group 4c obsidian for the same period is seen in Figure 114. There is no striking difference between the two distributions. The data will, however, be useful for comparison with sites in other areas such as Jarmo and Çayönü.

In this discussion of the waste material, its small size—already implied in Table 91—must be stressed. For part of the sample examined, a record was kept of all pieces greater than 4 cms in length, of all greater than 4 mm in thickness, and of blades greater than 1.5 cms in width: the total of such exceptionally large pieces ran around 4 percent. Cores were typically from 2 to 4 cms in length, and were thus entirely worked out. No large cores, longer than 6 or 7 cms, were noted.

Clearly the available obsidian was fully utilized, and no fragments greater than about 3 cms in length were allowed to go to waste. It is clear that much of the obsidian was worked on site, and the question arises as to the form in which it originally reached the site. I observed only one fragment showing cortex in the sample examined, and clearly the obsidian did not travel in the form of unworked lumps. It must therefore have travelled either as ready-made artifacts or as roughed-out cores. Large artifacts have not been found on the site, but since they would have been reworked on breakage this does not document their nonexistence. However, had they existed, they would clearly have been greatly valued. One would expect to recover such objects, like the daggers of Çatal Hüyük, from burials or from caches. In the absence of contrary evidence, exchange in the form of roughed-out cores seems the most likely: this was certainly the practice in the prehistoric Aegean.

THE CHANGING OBSIDIAN SUPPLY IN DEH LURAN

Using the figures now available from the successive phases at Chagha Sefid (Table 92) together with those for Ali Kosh and Tepe Sabz (Hole, Flannery and Neely, 1969) and for Tepe Farukhabad (Wright, 1972:101), it becomes possible to compile Table 93. (Figures for the volume of material excavated in each phase at Chagha Sefid are given in this volume, Table 4; for Ali Kosh, see Renfrew, 1969:431. Excavated volumes by phase at Tepe Sabz have been estimated as follows: Saba, 90 cu m; Khazineh, 16 cu m Mehmeh, 15 cu m; Bayat, 26 cu m). These and other data are presented graphically in Figures 114 to 118 inclusive, in the first three cases on a logarithmic scale.

The percentage of obsidian to total chipped stone in the successive stratigraphic zones at Chagha Sefid is seen in Figure 115 (broken line), and the average of these to give a figure for each phase in histogram form (continuous line). The scale is a logarithmic one, indicating a range from 0.16 percent in Zone G2

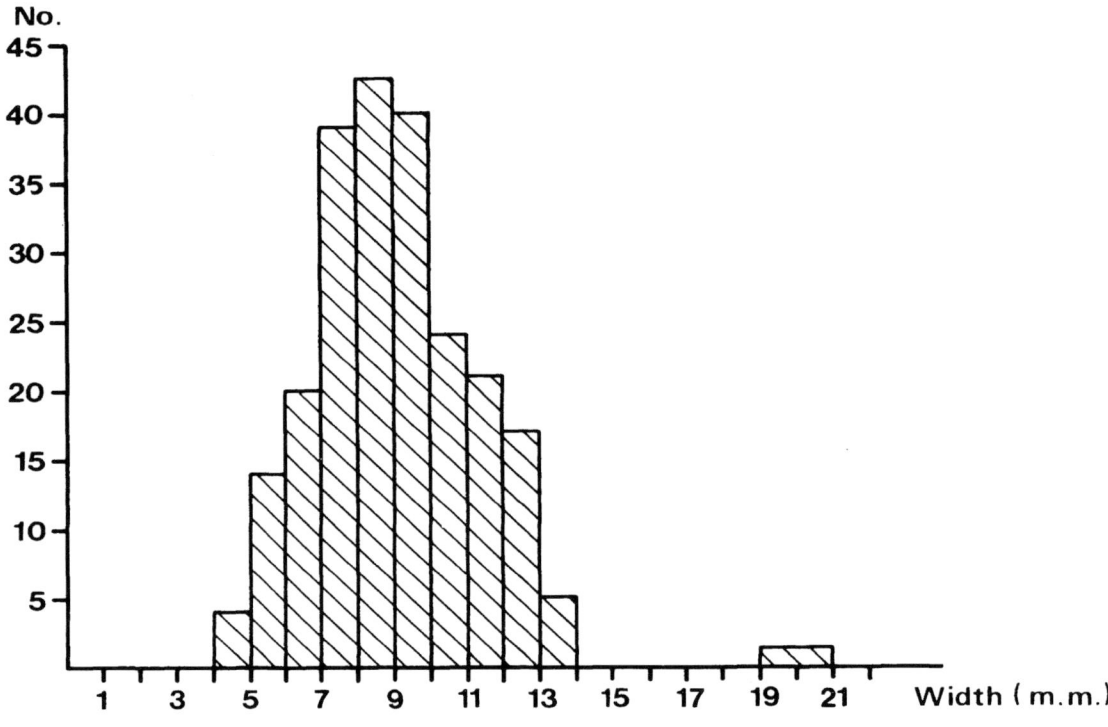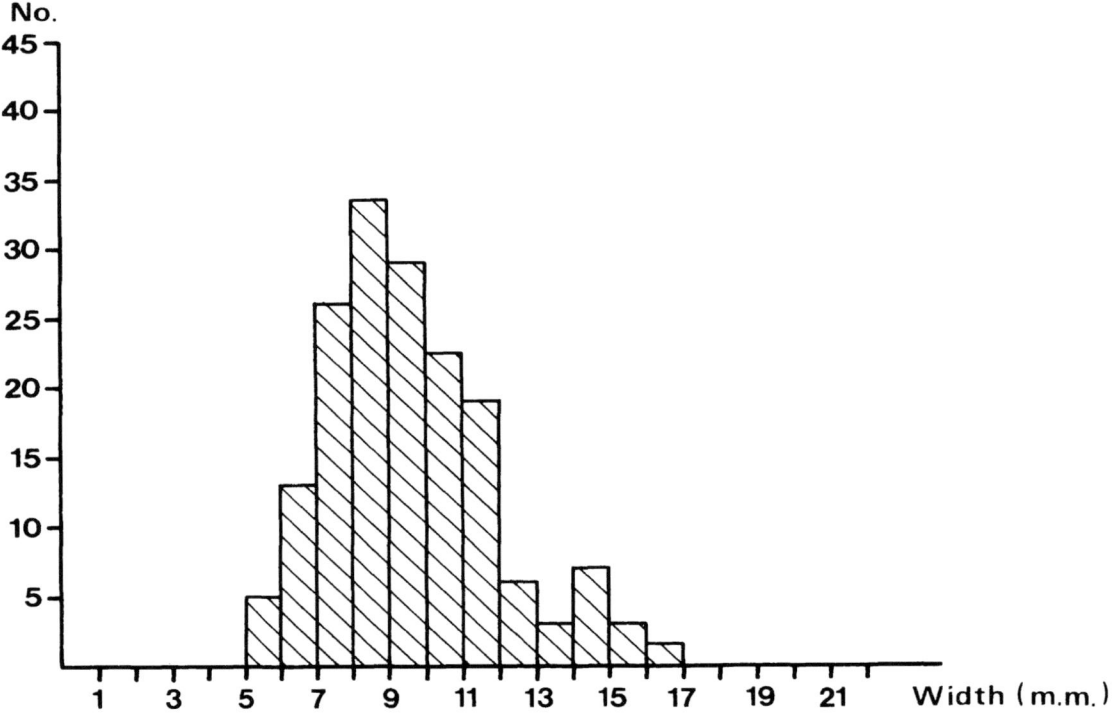

Fig. 114. Blade widths from the Sefid phase at Chagha Sefid (from SA level 4): group 1g obsidian (above), group 4c obsidian (below).

Table 92
FREQUENCY OF GREY (GROUP 1g) OBSIDIAN IN SUCCESSIVE PHASES AT CHAGHA SEFID

	Total in Sample	No. Grey	Percent Grey	Blades That Are Grey	No. Grey Per 100 cu.m.	No. Green Per 100 cu.m.
Sabz	2	1	(50)	--	(27.7)	(27.7)
Choga Mami Transitional	11	4	36.4	--	4.8	8.3
Surkh	39	13	33.3	--	6.29	12.6
Sefid C1	81	41	50.6	50.0	93.8	91.5
Sefid B2	740	423	57.2	58.0	661.9	496.1
Sefid B1	143	16	12.6	17.6	52.8	419.1
Sefid A4	20	5	25.0	30.0	45.4	136.3
Mohammad Jaffar	155	23	14.8	15.0	102.2	586.6
Ali Kosh	109	7	6.9	5.1	9.9	144.5

(Choga Mami Transitional Phase) to 10.3 percent in Zone A (Mohammad Jaffar Phase). Evidently the proportion is about 1.5 percent obsidian for the Ali Kosh Phase and falls down to 0.5 percent during the Surkh Phase (Zone E1), and lower in subsequent phases. The great increase comes during the Mohammad Jaffar Phase when the proportion rises to around 8 percent, and then there is some oscillation in the Sefid Phase with a high of 7 percent (Zone B2) and a low of 1.5 percent (zones A4 and 01).

At the outset, however, it should be stressed that the total obsidian recovered at Chagha Sefid was small, some 1400 pieces, amounting to little more than 1 kilogram in weight altogether. Taking the excavator's estimate that about 0.5 percent by volume of the site at Chagha Sefid was excavated, we obtain an approximation of 200 kgm for the obsidian recovered from the mound as a whole over its entire period of settlement. (At present I see no way of estimating the volume of deposit on a phase-by-phase basis, as Redman (1973) has suggested.) The total is thus about one fifth of a metric ton. This may be compared with an estimate of about 8 tons for the total flint, which is probably an underestimate since the same figure for average weight per fragment was used as for obsidian.

To set this figure of 200 kilos in perspective, it is worth remarking that in Deh Luran today a donkey can carry 4 five-gallon cans of water, equivalent to a volume of about 90 liters and hence to some 90 kilos. In other words the total obsidian contained at Chagha Sefid is of the same order as that which could be carried by a couple of fully-laden donkeys. Now of course the evidence indicates that beasts of burden were not domesticated in the Near East until about the very end of the time period with which we are concerned. But the image serves to remind us that the obsidian trade, as it concerns Deh Luran, was never a bulk trade.

Signal or Noise?

The important question which at once arises is the extent to which these figures, based on limited excavation in just one or two areas, are to be regarded as typical of the site. Do they arise from local conditions within that stratum of the trench—for instance from the presence during certain time-zones of waste debris in that trench from specific obsidian or flint chipping episodes? It is in this connection that the absolute figures, expressing number of finds per cubic meter, give a further insight (Fig. 116). The use of chipped stone at the site may be divided into two segments: from the beginning to Zone C1 of the Sefid Phase the number of pieces of chipped stone runs between 50 and 170 per cubic meter. After that it runs between 10 and 50. It is against this fairly coherent background that the changing absolute

Table 93

QUANTITATIVE CHANGE OF THE DEH LURAN OBSIDIAN INDUSTRY THROUGH SUCCESSIVE PHASES AT ALI KOSH (AK), CHAGHA SEFID (CS), TEPE SABZ (TS) AND TEPE FARUKHABAD (F): AVERAGING THE FARUKH AND URUK PERIODS

Phase	No. Chipped Stone per cu.m.				No. Obsidian per cu.m.				Percent Obsidian in Chipped Stone				Percent Grey Obsidian in Obsidian				Total Obsidian			
	AK	CS	TS	F	AK	CS	TS	F	AK	CS	TS	F	AK	CS	TS	F	AK	CS	TS	F
'Susa A'				2.56				0.04				1.43								5
Bayat		25.1				0.12				0.47								6		
Mehmeh		18.0				0.08				0.42								3		
Khazineh		17.8				0				0								0		
Sabz	207.5	97.0			0.56	0			0.27	0				(50)				2	0	
Choga Mami Transitional	24.1				0.13				0.54				36.4				11			
Surkh	27.3				0.38				1.40				33.3				79			
Sefid	152.2				6.99				4.59				49.2				1041			
Mohammad Jaffar	145.0	88.8			2.52	6.93			1.74	7.80			29.4	14.8			417	156		
Ali Kosh	161.3	104.0			3.29	1.54			2.04	1.48			12.4	6.9			474	109		
Bus Mordeh	573.1				4.96				0.86				0.0				347			

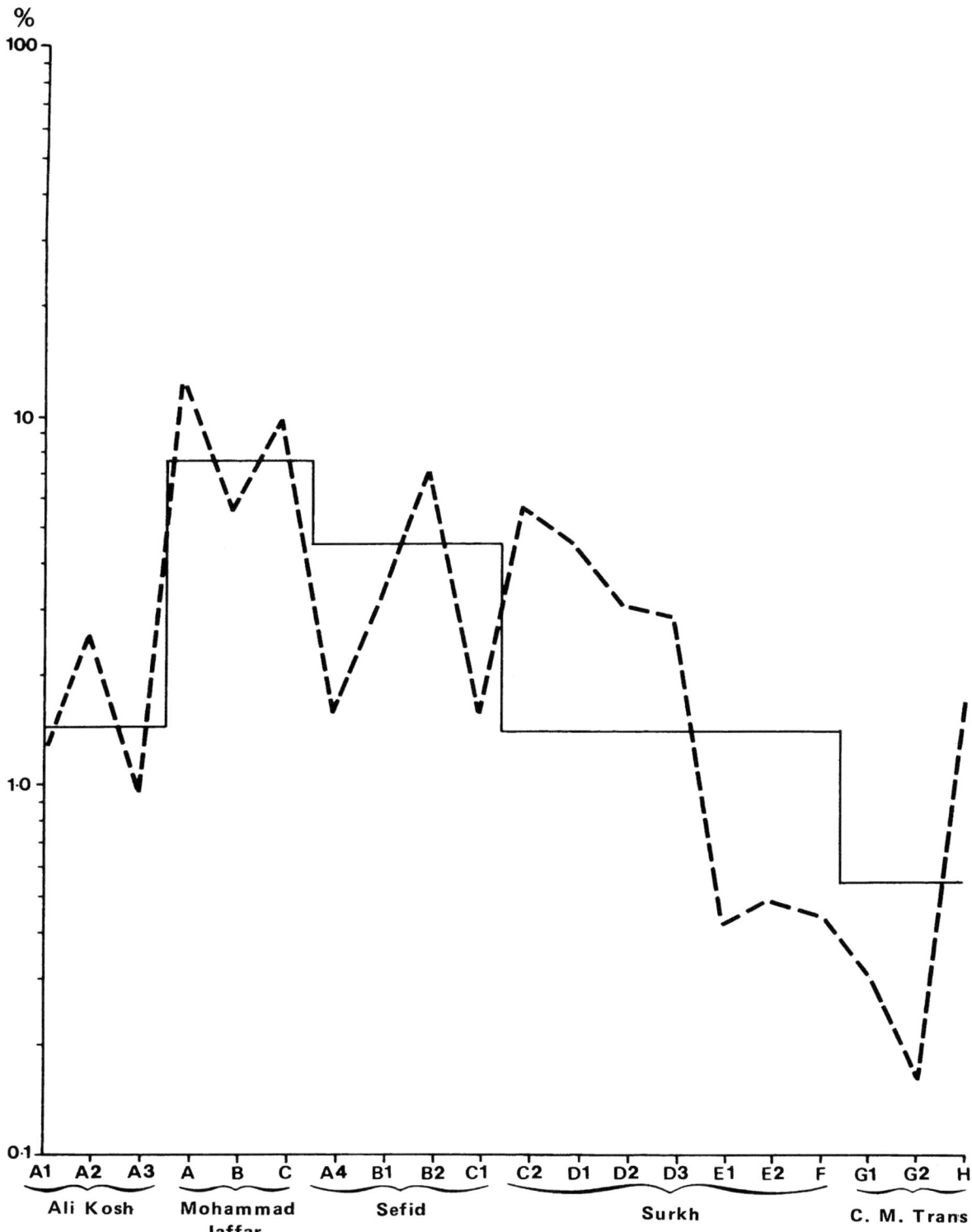

Fig. 115. Percentage of obsidian in the chipped stone industry at Chagha Sefid in successive phases (continuous line) with details for each stratigraphic zone (broken line).

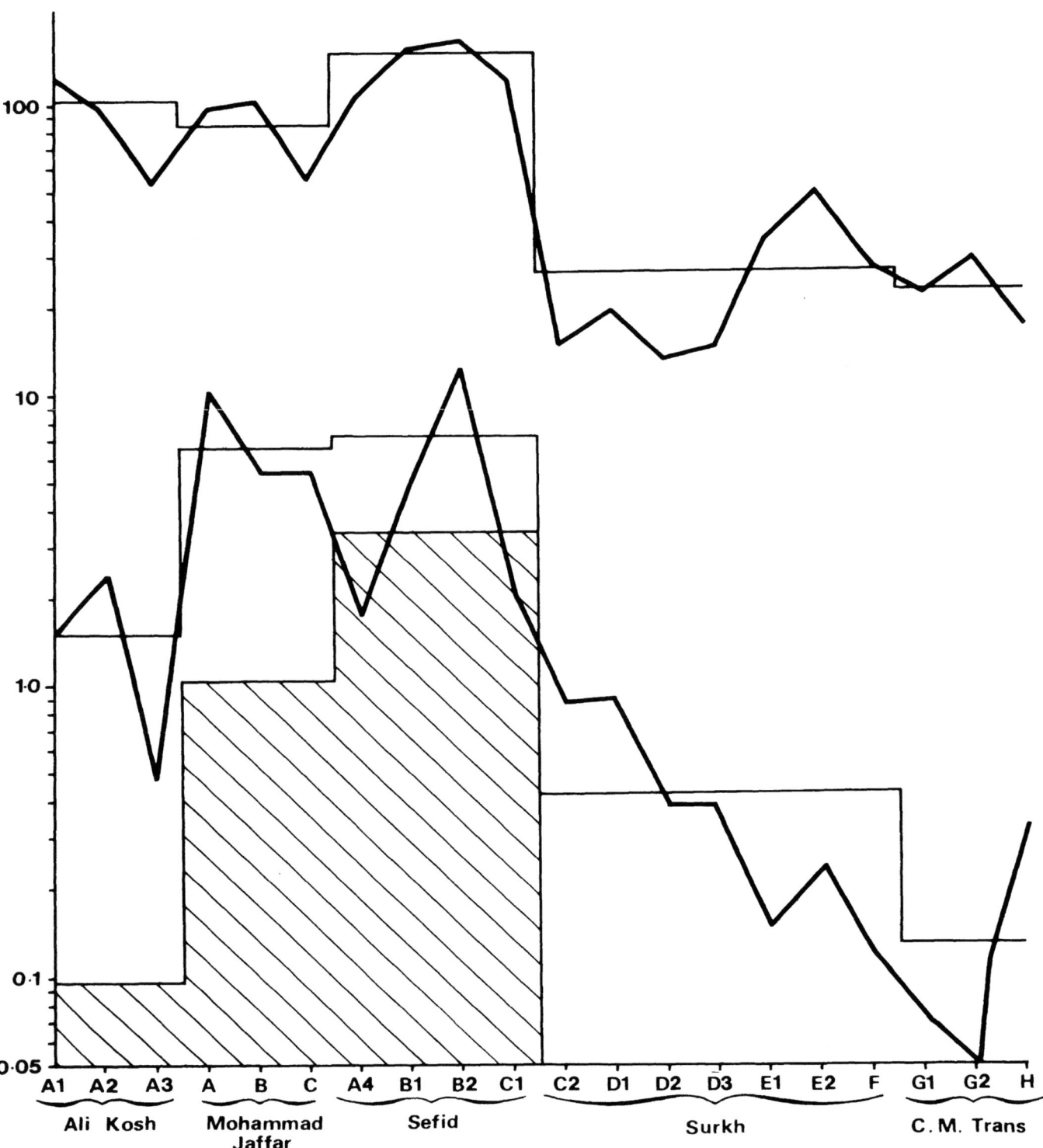

Fig. 116. Number of pieces of chipped stone per cubic meter at Chagha Sefid in successive phases and stratigraphic zones (above), indicating also the number of pieces of all obsidian per cubic meter (below), and of grey, group 1g obsidian (shaded).

figures for the obsidian must be viewed. Varying between 0.5 and 3 per cubic meter in the Ali Kosh Phase, the range goes up from 2 to 12 in the Mohammad Jaffar Phase and Sefid phases, falling thereafter to well below 1.0, and subsequently below 0.1 pieces per cubic meter.

Consideration of Figures 115 and 116 suggests that the absolute figures (Fig. 116) are more informative than the ratio, since the sharp decline in the proportion of obsidian in Zone A4 of the Sefid Phase, for instance, is revealed as in part the consequence of the abundance of flint in this zone. This does not in itself, however, document for us that the figure for each zone is unhesitatingly to be accepted as a reflection of the level of supply throughout the period occupied by the zone. First, the strata assigned to that zone at the site may occupy only a portion of the time-range of the zone itself (i.e., the site may not be continuously occupied). Second, there is the possibility that the deposits, formed over a limited period of time, may be simply the reflection of special activities carried out locally in them during that time.

To the first question, the analysis of obsidian data can itself give no answer. The figures may or may not accurately reflect the site as a whole, but in any case cannot inform us whether the levels representing the zone at that site give a complete or a partial representation of its duration. The second point, however, can be examined further. Figures for the variation *within* the zone will show whether the frequency is continuously high within it, or whether the high mean for the zone is the result of a freakishly high figure over a very limited depth of deposit. When we are dealing with a zone represented by well over one meter of deposit, a consistently high figure implies a high frequency of obsidian in that particular area over a considerable period. And while this might still be explained by the use of that area for obsidian-working during that period, with a subsequent shift in the locus of working, the possibility that the high frequency is valid for the site as a whole is considerably enhanced. In other words we are seeking to identify (in order to discount) specific localized functional episodes (obsidian working) by sampling, not in different parts of the site, since this was not practical, but at successive times in the same spot.

Table 94 presents relevant data from within Zone B2 of the Sefid Phase. Within this zone the obsidian was collected by area and depth, and the figures are presented by absolute depth rather than by stratigraphic stratum. Despite this, however, they may be taken as giving an indication of the variation in occurrence of obsidian within the Sefid B2 time period. This was precisely the time when obsidian at the site was at its most abundant. Inspection of the figures indicates that the obsidian per cubic meter during this time remained at a high level, between 9 and 15, a figure well in excess of the average of 7 for the Sefid Phase as a whole. (The sample here in question is derived from 54 cubic meters of deposit, some 36 percent of the total deposit for the phase). There is no pronounced fluctuation to suggest that the figure was abnormally high over short time periods, and this argues against the material deriving directly from a local area of chipping debris, unless the excavation trench SA happened to be the locus of a special area of this kind over a considerable period of time.

It is interesting, moreover, to consider the proportion of grey (group 1g) obsidian in the total (column 4). In column 6 the mean for three successive values (including the value from the depth range immediately above and below the one in question) is given. There is no overall trend in the obsidian per cubic meter. But when similar averages are calculated for group 4c and group 1g obsidian (columns 10 and 8), two very striking trends are seen. The quantity of grey obsidian rises markedly throughout (from an absolute low of 4.3 to a high of 9.5 pieces per cubic meter). And at the same time the quantity of group 4c obsidian declines from an absolute maximum of 8.0 to a figure well below 4. The moving averages in columns 8 and 10 indicate that this is indeed a progressive and general trend in each case. The importance of this point for the obsidian supply is considered below. Here it is sufficient to suggest that internally consistent figures of this kind could not be obtained if there were significant and major disturbance due to local specialist functional effects (e.g., chipping floors). Either the figures are to be taken as reasonably typical of the site as a whole, or the area of the SA trench contained an area of special obsidian working throughout this part of the Sefid Phase. Against the latter hypothesis is the circumstance that the average of obsidian per cubic meter for the phase as a whole is more than

Table 94

OCCURRENCE OF OBSIDIAN BY 20 CM LEVELS IN AREA A AT CHAGHA SEFID
(Covering approximate time range of Zone B2 of the Sefid phase)

Depth (meters)	No. of Grey Obsidian	Total Obsidian	Percent Grey Obsidian	No. obs./cu.m.	Travelling Mean for 3 Values of 5	No. of Grey obs./cu.m.	Travelling Mean for 3 Values of 7	No. of Green obs./cu.m.	Travelling Mean for 3 Values of 9
1	2	3	4	5	6	7	8	9	10
2.10-2.30	57	82	69.5	13.7	--	9.5	--	4.1	--
2.30-2.50	46	66	69.6	11.0	12.4	7.7	8.6	3.3	3.7
2.50-2.70	52	75	69.3	12.5	11.3	8.7	7.7	3.8	3.6
2.70-2.90	41	63	65.1	10.5	10.6	6.8	6.7	3.7	3.9
2.90-3.10	28	53	52.8	8.8	11.4	4.7	6.9	4.2	4.6
3.10-3.30	56	91	61.5	15.1	11.8	9.3	6.6	5.8	5.3
3.30-3.50	35	70	50.0	11.7	12.9	5.8	6.7	5.8	6.2
3.50-3.70	30	72	41.7	12.0	12.0	5.0	5.0	7.0	6.9
3.70-3.90	26	74	35.1	12.3	--	4.3	--	8.0	--
2.10-3.90	371	646	57.4	12.0	--	6.9	--	5.1	--

APPENDIX II

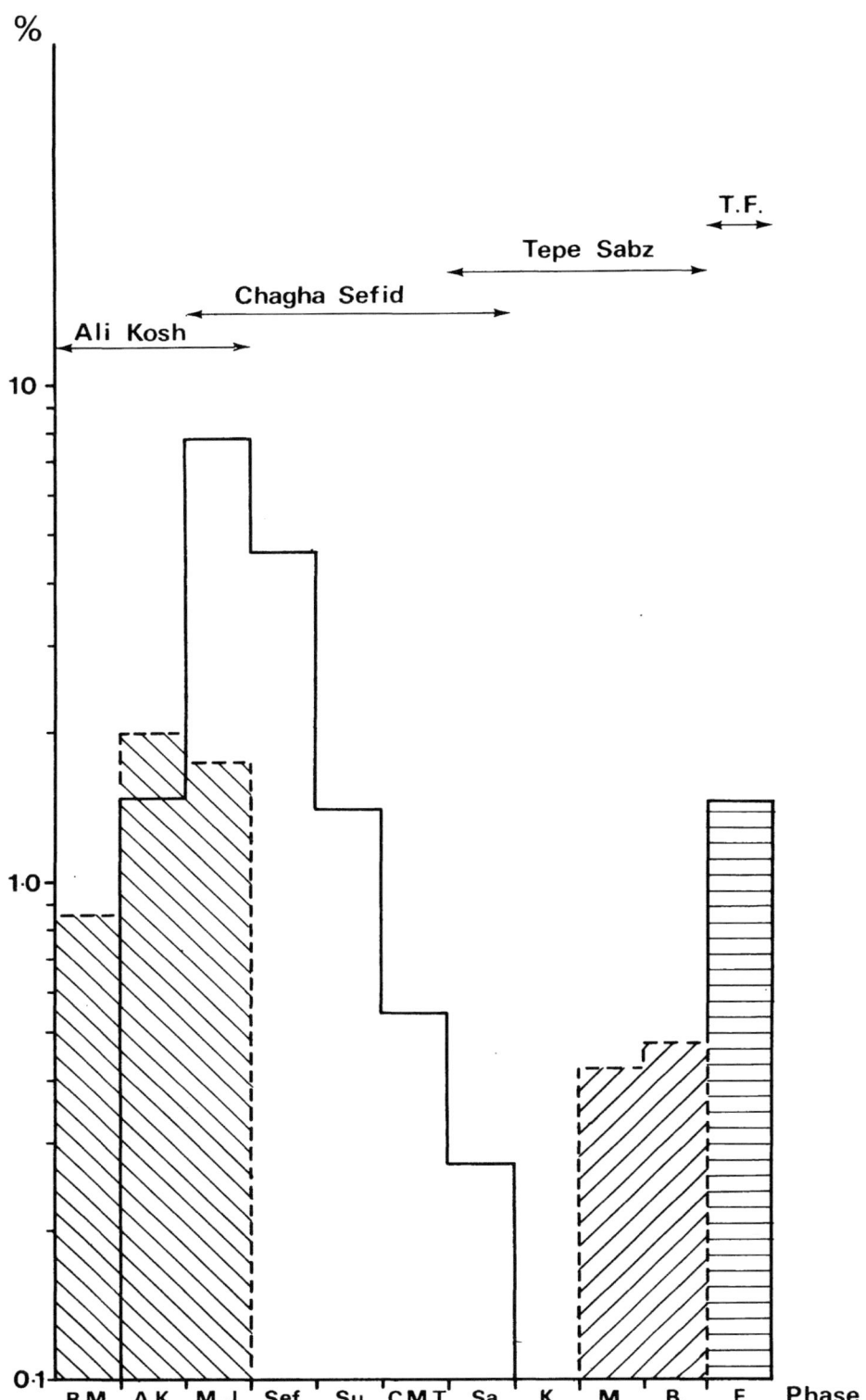

Fig. 117. Phase-by-phase variation in the percentage of obsidian in the chipped stone industry in successive phases at four sites in Deh Luran (T.F. indicates Tepe Farukhabad). Phases: Bus Mordeh, Ali Kosh, Mohammad Jaffar, Sefid, Surkh, Choga Mami Transitional, Sabz, Khazineh, Mehmeh, Bayat, Farukh.

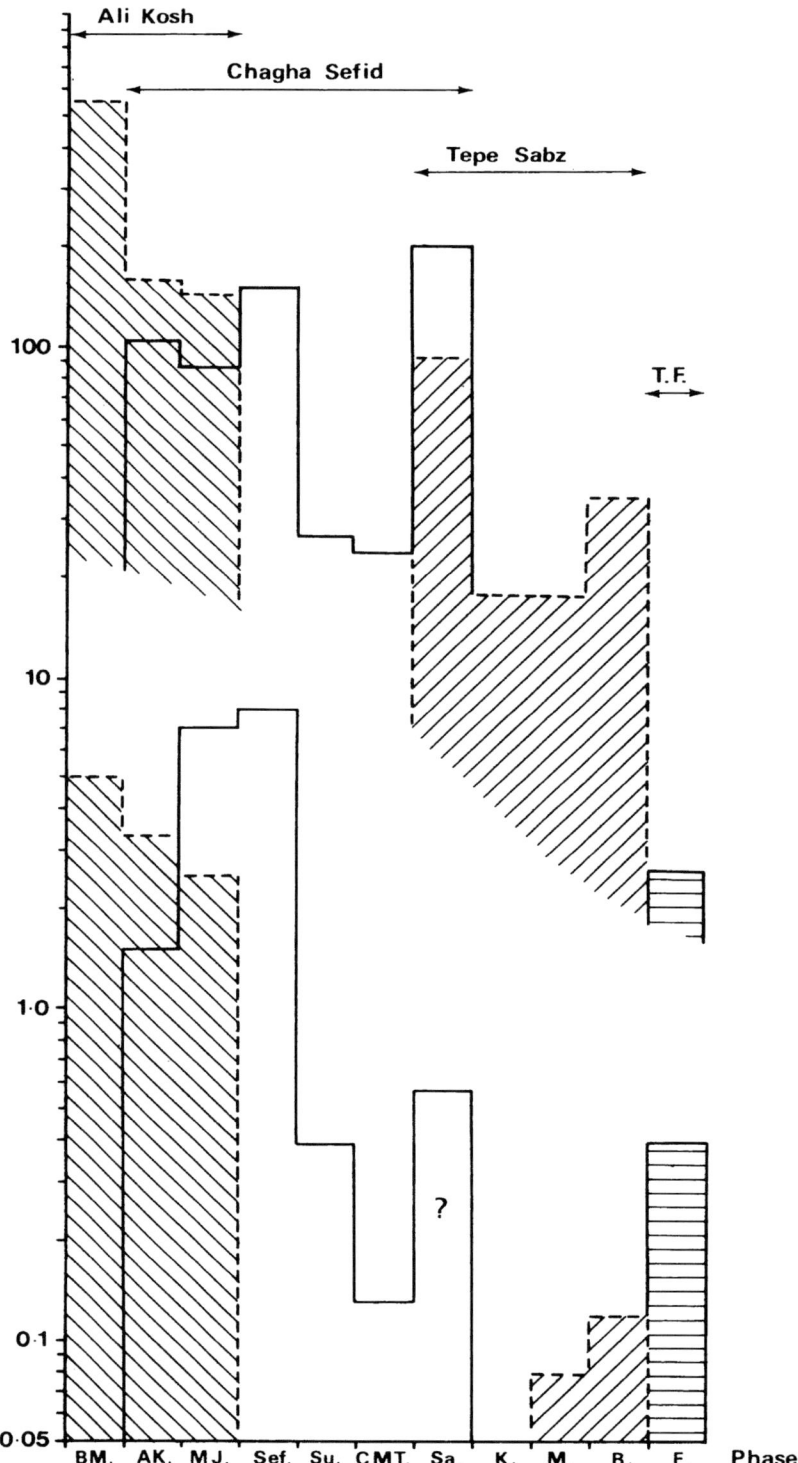

Fig. 118. Phase-by-phase variation in the number of pieces of chipped stone per cubic meter (above), and of obsidian per cubic meter (below) in the lithic industry at four sites in Deh Luran. Abbreviations as for Fig. 117.

half the average over this zone of particular abundance, as indeed is the average for the preceding Mohammad Jaffar Phase. It is concluded, therefore, that the average for the zone gives an adequate indication of the obsidian use, and that special disturbing factors have not been observed during the Sefid Phase The regularities seen in the successive twenty centimeter levels in Table 94 suggest that variations within zones may also be of real significance, and that the background of random 'noise' is lower than might have been imagined.

Chronological Variation

The phase-by-phase pattern of variation in the obsidian supply is seen in Figures 117 and 118, where the results for the sites of Ali Kosh and Tepe Sabz (as well as Tepe Farukhabad) are added to those of Chagha Sefid to give a composite picture of the entire time range from c. 7500 to c. 3000 B.C. It should be noted, however, as the last column of Table 93 makes clear, that the absolute quantities after the Surkh Phase, are exceedingly small, being less than a dozen obsidian fragments per phase. No reliance can be put on the results after that phase.

As a test of consistency it is interesting to compare the figures in the three cases where the same phase is documented from two excavated sites. This occurs at the beginning of the Chagha Sefid sequence where the Ali Kosh and Mohammad Jaffar phases are represented both at that site and at Tepe Ali Kosh. The presentation of the figures on a logarithmic scale in Figures 117 and 118 brings out the main difference, which is the greater concentration of obsidian per cubic meter during the Mohammad Jaffar Phase at Chagha Sefid (6.93) than at Ali Kosh (2.52). The detailed zone-by-zone figures seen on Figure 116 confirm that this is a real increase at Chagha Sefid.

During both overlap phases, flint is more abundant at Ali Kosh than at Chagha Sefid, but it should be noted that the concentration of flint is much higher in the preceding Bus Mordeh period. This may either be an indication of abundance of flint in that period, or of a slower rate of deposition of building debris, due to the use of less substantial buildings or their slower replacement rate.

It is possible that the fall in abundance of obsidian at Ali Kosh during precisely the period that it is first supplied to Chagha Sefid is a direct reflection of competition between the two sites for a relatively inelastic supply. The increase in the number of settlements at this time in Deh Luran may have placed demands on the down-the-line supply system which it could not entirely fulfill. If we think in terms of competition during the Ali Kosh Phase, it is clear that in succeeding Mohammad Jaffar Phase Chagha Sefid is winning the competition since both in absolute terms and in the proportion of obsidian to total chipped stone it is more adequately supplied than Ali Kosh, while Ali Kosh still has more flint.

At the later end of the Chagha Sefid sequence when there is an overlap with the Tepe Sabz sequence in the Sabz Phase, we see again that the longer established site has the more effective supply of flint, by a factor of two. Tepe Sabz has no obsidian whatever in this phase, in a total excavated volume of about 19 cubic meters. Chagha Sefid produced only two pieces, although admittedly in an excavated volume of only 3.6 cubic meters. In the circumstances these could very easily have found their way in from earlier materials, perhaps through the re-use of mud for pisé. We may regard the quantity of obsidian as exceedingly small at both sites during this phase.

Figure 118 may thus be interpreted as giving a coherent picture of an obsidian supply rising in the Mohammad Jaffar period to a figure of about 7 pieces per cubic meter of deposit, forming between 4 and 8 percent of the total chipped stone industry. With the Surkh period it falls to well under one piece per cubic meter, on the order of one percent of the chipped stone industry, and effectively to zero in the Sabz Phase, although flint is in good supply at this time.

Subsequently the flint supply itself is much more limited, but a small amount of obsidian is found, in the Mehmeh and Bayat phases, and at Tepe Farukhabad, in circumstances suggesting that it is not merely a contamination from an earlier phase, so that some resumption of the trade network must be contemplated after 4500 B.C.

The more detailed zone-by-zone picture seen in Figure 116 confirms this picture, stressing the abundance in the Mohammad Jaffar and Sefid phases, and the pronounced decline in the Surkh Phase, which sees a fall from one piece per cubic meter to less than 0.1.

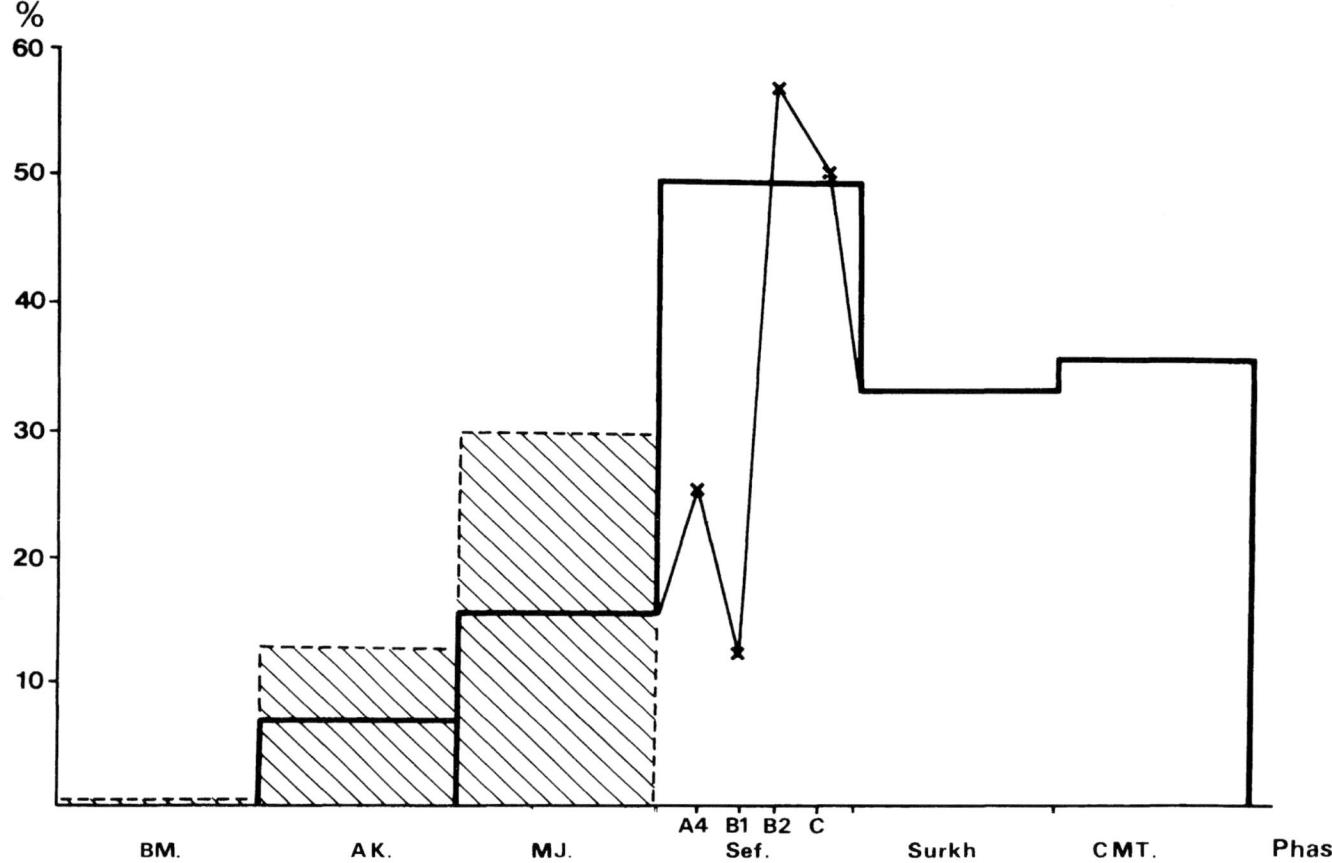

Fig. 119. The percentage of group 1g obsidian in the total obsidian industry in successive phases at Ali Kosh (shaded) and Chagha Sefid (heavy line). The percentage in successive stratigraphic zones within the Sefid Phase at Chagha Sefid is also indicated.

The same picture is seen in Figure 115. One interesting aspect here is that the decline in the Surkh Phase is so steady that the quantities in that phase cannot be explained simply as material deriving from earlier phases as a result of digging for soil to make pisé. The decline in absolute quantity of obsidian is seen already in Zone C1 of the Sefid Phase, followed by a marked decline in flint in the next phase (which makes Figure 114 rather misleading).

The discussion above of the data in Table 94 suggests the conclusion that the fluctuation in supply between zones should be taken seriously, not dismissed as mere noise. We must thus reckon with a peak in supply during Zone A of the Mohammad Jaffar Phase, and a second peak in Zone B2 of the Sefid Phase.

Competing Sources?

It is at this point that a comparison of the ratios of grey to green obsidian (Fig. 119), and especially of the absolute quantities (Table 92, and shaded portion of Fig. 116) of the two obsidian varieties is particularly interesting. The maximum abundance of the green, group 4c, obsidian is precisely during the Mohammad Jaffar Phase, with a concentration of 5.8 per cubic meter. It will be recalled that group 4c obsidian predominates to the exclusion of group 1g obsidian during the Bus Mordeh Phase, the earliest yet found in settlement mounds in Deh Luran. After reaching this early peak, the number falls to an average of 3.5 in the succeeding Sefid Phase, before falling substantially to around 0.1 as part of the general decline in the Surkh Phase. It is this relative abundance of group 4c obsidian which is responsible for the maximum during the early part of the Mohammad Jaffar Phase.

Turning now to the grey, group 1g, obsidian, we find it is present in only extremely small amounts (under one percent of the total obsidian, under 0.05 per cubic meter) in the early Bus Mordeh Phase. The supply still amounts to a mere 0.09 per cubic meter in the Ali Kosh. It is in the Mohammad Jaffar Phase that the group 1g obsidian is present in more significant quantity, around one piece per cubic meter, forming 15 percent of the total obsidian. But in the succeeding Sefid Phase the quantity increases very markedly to a striking 3.5 per cubic meter, rising to a peak during Zone B2 of 6.6 per cubic meter (and in one 20 cm level of that zone to 9.5 per cubic meter, cf. Table 94). It is this increase, and this increase alone, which accounts for the supply maximum during Zone B2 of the Sefid Phase, for the quantity of group 4c obsidian is not notably greater than previously.

The interesting bi-modal pattern in the obsidian/time plot on the lower part of Figure 116, is thus a result of the superimposition of two supply curves. The first, of group 4c obsidian, peaks during the Mohammad Jaffar Phase, and then persists at a lower but still significant level during the Sefid Phase, at the end of which it declines sharply. The second, of group 1g obsidian, emerges effectively only during the Mohammad Jaffar Phase, then peaks strikingly in the Sefid Phase, declining markedly thereafter.

CONCLUSIONS

The evidence of Chagha Sefid has contributed significantly to our understanding of the changing obsidian supply in the Deh Luran area. At the very beginning of settled village life, as Tepe Ali Kosh documents, group 4c obsidian from the Nemrut Dağ source in eastern Anatolia was reaching Deh Luran in significant quantities, yielding some 5 pieces per cubic meter on excavation, and forming 0.9 percent of the total chipped stone industry. Some 20 kilos may have reached Tepe Ali Kosh during this period.

In the next, Ali Kosh Phase, the site of Chagha Sefid was also settled, and perhaps for this reason the concentration per cubic meter falls slightly at Ali Kosh. In the succeeding Mohammad Jaffar Phase at Chagha Sefid, the supply of group 4c obsidian reaches its maximum, with a concentration of 5.9 per cubic meter.

Already during the Bus Mordeh Phase one or two pieces of group 1g obsidian are found in Deh Luran. It derives from a source probably some tens of kilometers west or southwest of the Nemrut Dağ source. In the next two phases it plays a minor role, being 7 percent and 15 percent respectively of the total obsidian. But then in the Sefid Phase the concentration increases to a maximum in Zone B2 of 6.6 per cubic meter. Group 1g obsidian is now, for a brief spell, actually more abundant on the site than group 4c obsidian, and together with group 4c obsidian brings the concentration for the phase as a whole up to its maximum of 7 pieces per cubic meter, although this is still less than 5 percent of the total lithic assemblage.

In this interaction of two distant sources we have a fascinating picture of competing efficiencies, either in transmission effectiveness by the down-the-line trade network, or effectiveness in access to that network of the two sources. Since we hypothesize that these are no more than 100 km distant from each other, the path travelled by obsidian from one cannot differ very substantially from that travelled by obsidian from the other to a location as distant as Deh Luran, some 900 km to the southeast. So it seems more likely that the difference lies in access of the sources to the network, although whether this change is due to practical factors (for instance a development of new transport facilities such as beasts of burden, boats on Lake Van or a river), or on political factors, is not at present clear.

What is clear, however, is that the change seems to indicate a shift in the supply situation, not in the demand situation, since there is no evidence that either variety of obsidian was used preferentially for any specific purpose.

Clearly it would be fascinating to examine this competition between sources at other sites which are located nearer to the VAA area. However, only a fairly long time sequence, like that now available for Deh Luran, can be expected to give the necessary data.

Before the end of the Sefid Phase the quantities of obsidian available in Deh Luran begin to fall, and continued to fall throughout the Surkh Phase, so that by the end of that phase the quantities recovered are very small, and may indeed derive from earlier levels at the site. By the Sabz Phase there is effectively no obsidian trade.

This is a result of great interest, since the decline in the obsidian trade has not been dated before, although it has for some time been clear that there was a decline sometime between the periods of occupation of Tepe Ali Kosh and Tepe Sabz. We can now see that, as the zone-by-zone figures for the Surkh Phase document, this decline, although fairly rapid, was not sudden. Why did it happen? Again I suggest it was a question of supply rather than of demand. For the Surkh Phase is probably too early for the use of metal to have had much impact on the use of stone tools, and the quantity of flint tools found in the Sabz Phase indicates that the chipped stone industry still had a major role to play.

The decline in obsidian in Deh Luran can only be a political phenomenon. And it is to be explained in terms either of political developments in the source area, or of changes in the nature of the down-the-line supply network. For it seems that the demand still existed in Deh Luran.

I have tentatively offered a general explanation for this phenomenon (Renfrew and Dixon, n.d.) which I think harmonizes well with the Deh Luran data. It is that the essentially reciprocal nature of the down-the-line trade was disrupted at this time by the emergence of *redistributive* exchange, that is to say by the emergence of central places. I have suggested that in these circumstances, the steady flow of obsidian down the line through a network of relatively undifferentiated villages, would be replaced by its movement into the central place of each territory and then out again. This in itself would lead to a preferential supply to the central persons located at the central places. But for more distant areas like Deh Luran, the supply would now be dependent upon relations between the central places of successive adjacent territories, rather than on more numerous links between adjacent villages in the original down-the-line chain.

At first sight the smaller number of links required in a reciprocal exchange between central places might favor an increased supply. But it is a feature of reciprocity of the kind hypothesized at the village level that exchange takes place readily, to some extent for its own sake. It was a feature of the proto-urban states of the Near East, which these central places soon became, that competition and hostility were frequent, and there is no reason to suppose that the basis for reciprocity would be the same as previously.

A relevant factor here could likewise be the attempt by nearby territories to secure physical control of the sources, or of specialist merchants to exploit them. The foundation of Tepe Tilki on the east coast of Lake Van, which was certainly flourishing during the Halaf period may be of relevance here.

Whatever the nature of these changes, they certainly took place just prior to and during the Surkh period, during the sixth millennium B.C. There are indications that small quantities of obsidian were reaching Deh Luran again from about 4500 B.C. onwards, however, and this must surely have been by way of some kind of central place trade. The evidence of the Near East in general, supported by the group 3a and 2b analyses from the Bayat Phase at Tepe Sabz, suggests a less single-minded concentration on just one or two sources. At this time group 1g obsidian is scarcely found in the Zagros area, but is replaced by obsidian of group 3 from the area of Lake Urmia. It is clear that trade routes were now opening across the Zagros. But it should always be remembered that the absolute quantities of obsidian reaching sites in Deh Luran were small, measured in kilograms rather than tons. Obsidian is significant for us not as a commodity of great economic importance, but as a sensitive indicator of changing patterns of exchange, communication and social interaction.

BIBLIOGRAPHY

Cann, J. R. and C. Renfrew
    1964   The characterisation of obsidian and its application to the Mediterranean region. Proceedings of the Prehistoric Society 30:111-133.

Evans, J. D. and C. Renfrew
    1968   Excavations at Saliagos near Antiparos. London, British School of Archaeology at Athens and Thames & Hudson.

Hole, Frank, Kent V. Flannery and James A. Neely
    1969   Prehistory and human ecology of the Deh Luran plain. Memoir No. 1. Ann Arbor, University of Michigan Museum of Anthropology.

Redman, C. L.
1973 Multivariate approach to understanding changes in an early farming community in southeast Anatolia. *In* The explanation of culture change, ed. by C. Renfrew. London, Duckworth.

Renfrew, C.
1969 The sources and supply of the Deh Luran obsidian. *In* Hole, Flannery and Neely, 1969. Appendix III.

Renfrew, C. and J. E. Dixon
n.d. Obsidian in western Asia—a review. *In* Problems in economic and social archaeology, ed. by I. H. Longworth and G. Sieveking. London, Duckworth.

Renfrew, C., J. E. Dixon and J. R. Cann
1966 Obsidian and early culture contact in the Near East. Proceedings of the Prehistoric Society 32:30-72.
1968 Further analysis of Near Eastern obsidians. Proceedings of the Prehistoric Society 34:319-31.

Wright, Gary A.
1969 Obsidian analysis and prehistoric Near Eastern trade 7500 to 3500 B.C. Anthropological Paper No. 37. Ann Arbor, University of Michigan Museum of Anthropology.

Wright, Henry T.
1972 A consideration of interregional exchange in Greater Mesopotamia: 4000-3000 B.C. *In* Social Exchange and Interaction, ed. by E. N. Wilmsen. Anthropological Paper No. 46. Ann Arbor, University of Michigan Museum of Anthropology.

PLATES 1-55

PLATE 1

Plate 1a. Chagha Sefid from the south early in the autumn. Excavation Area B is on the right flank of the mound and areas A, C and D are on the left flank. 1b. Chagha Sefid from the northwest after crops have begun to grow. The main trench (areas A, C and D) is on the lower slope of the site.

Plate 2. Chagha Sefid from the west showing the early stages in the excavation of areas A and C. The wadi in the foreground has cut into archeological deposits below the present surface of the plain on the north side of the site.

PLATE 3

Plate 3. View of Deh Luran at the base of the mountains. *a.* In early October. *b.* In January after crops have begun to grow. Both photographs were taken from the top of Chagha Sefid. An eroded portion of a brick outbuilding of the fort is in the foreground.

a

b

Plate 4a. The Ab-i-garm, which is normally only a meter-wide stream flowing from the hot sulphur spring above Deh Luran, widens into a raging torrent after heavy rains and serves as one of the sources of water for irrigating the fields around Chagha Sefid. 4b. During flash floods water courses through Deh Luran, often seriously eroding wall foundations and causing walls to collapse. The walls pictured have stones placed at their base, sometimes covered with a batter of earth to deflect water.

a

b

Plate 5a. The initial 3x5 meter pit in Area A revealed the stone foundation of a house of Sefid Phase immediately below the surface. 5b. The main trench at Chagha Sefid showing the location of the three areas before they were linked to form a continuous trench 45 meters long.

Plate 6. At the end of the excavation, areas A, C and D were linked into a continuous step trench that has the deep pit of Area A at the lower end. The line of stones and the ditch outlining the trench are to prevent erosion.

Plate 7. Photograph of the gully cut into the sterile sands and gravels that underlie the archeological deposits in the lower portion of Area A. Midden debris and brickbats eventually filled the gully.

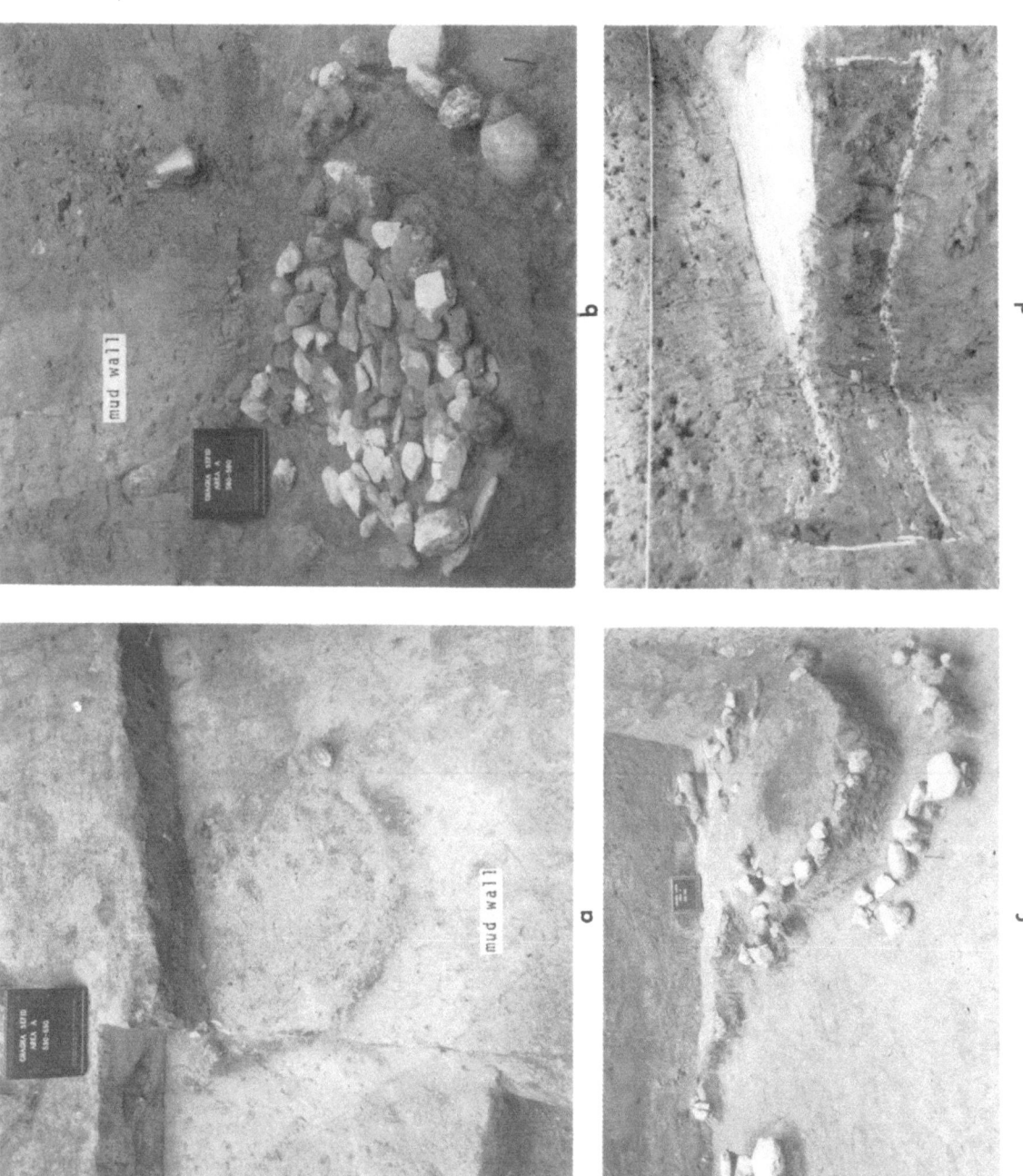

Plate 8a. The top of the fireplace in the corner of a brick walled room in Zone A3 shows as a dark oval in the center of the picture. The outline of the walls can be seen as lighter clay against the darker fill.

8b. The base of the fireplace is a layer of flat stones. The outside of the mud walls is outlined by a row of stones.

8c. The lowest level of the fireplace shows an encircling row of stones, stones at the base of the brick walls (which have been removed in this photograph), and remnants of a plaster floor.

8d. A section through the plaster floor showing two distinct stages of resurfacing and the curving of the plaster up the sides of the walls.

PLATE 9

a

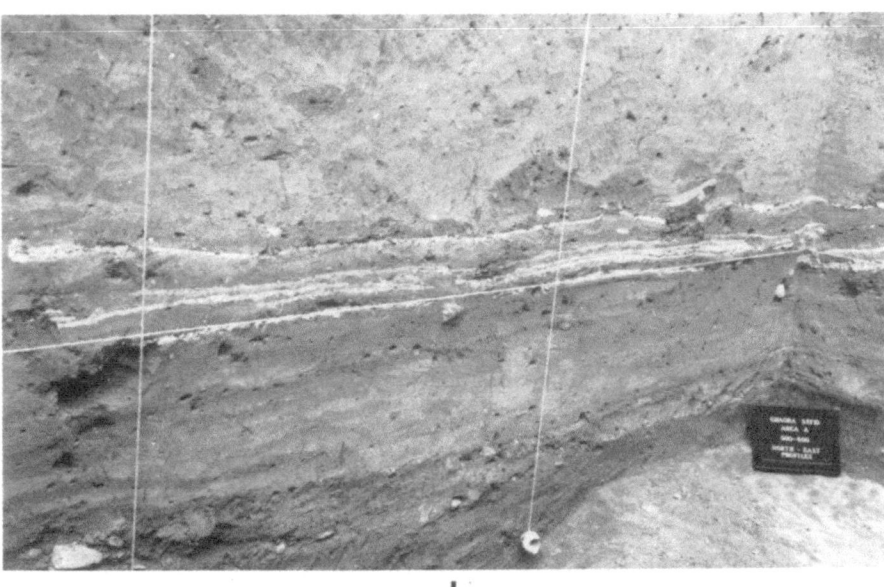

b

Plate 9a. The position of burial No. 4 with respect to the broken plastered floor of Zone A4. The burial consists of a skull and the thoracic section of the body placed upon flat stones.

9b. The plaster floor showing above was resurfaced 4-5 times as seen in this section along the west wall of the pit. The strings are at one meter intervals.

Plate 10. Event No. 1 of Zone C contained a stone rectangle with a plastered basin set into one end. The floor of the rectangle was paved with mud bricks. Under the basin were the bones of burial No. 3.

PLATE 11

a

b

Plate 11a. The lower platform in Zone C was composed of large, soft, ashy black bricks.
11b. The limits of the platform are approximately outlined by the stone foundations that lie above it. Area A shows at the pit at the lower end of the excavation trench.

Plate 12a. Exposing the bricks of the platform required careful work with trowels.
12b. The platform in the early Surkh Phase in the process of being exposed. Architecture of Zone D1, Surkh Phase, is seen in the foreground.

Plate 13a. Subsequent to the building of the platform in Zone C, brick walls were placed against its west side.
 13b. The plano-convex bricks used in the walls are laid alternately along the length of the wall and across its width. The pit of Area A truncates the upper wall.
 13c. Outside one of the walls are piled broken manos and metates.

a

b

Plate 14a. The stone pavement of Event No. 3 in Zone C is inside the heavy stone wall foundations.
14b. A rebuilding of the pavement and a lateral extension of it to the east is denoted Event No. 4. Bricks of Event No. 5, a small mud brick platform, can be seen in the rear wall overlying the stone pavement.

PLATE 15

a

b

Plate 15a. The plano-convex ashy mud bricks of the platform designated Event No. 5 can be seen in the east profile of Area A.

15b. Brick pavement and plaster basin of Event No. 4 from the northwest side. The bricks of the platform in Event No. 5 are seen in the walls of the pit as is the pit of burial No. 1 that cuts through it.

PLATE 16

a

b

Plate 16a. Walls of Zone D1 showing stones and other trash filling the room.
16b. The same area with trash removed and bricks of the Zone C platform being exposed under the level of the Zone D1 walls.

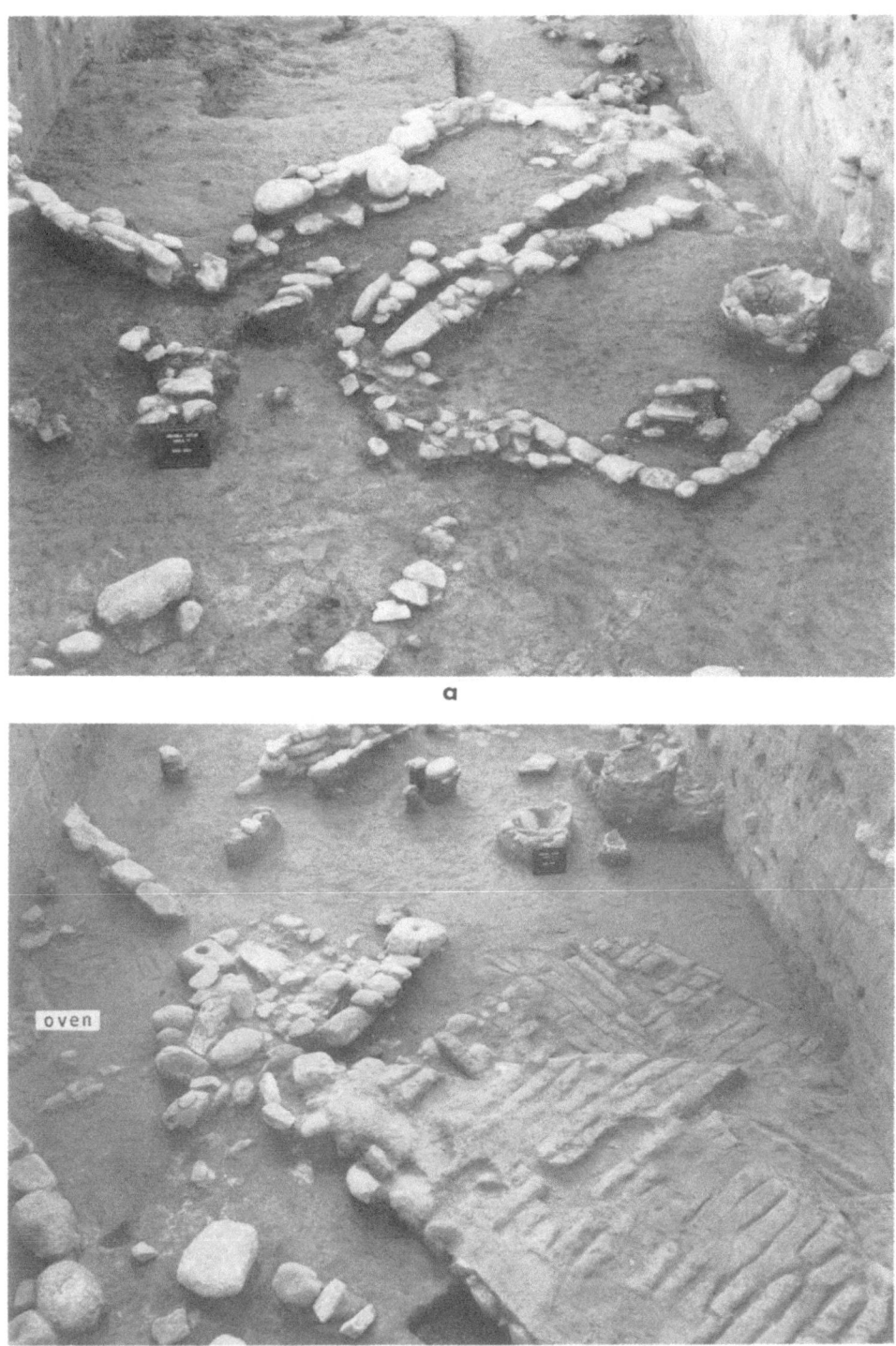

Plate 17a. House walls and plaster basins in Zone D1 with the west end of this architectural level removed (see Fig. 19 for complete plan).

17b. The east end of the same zone. Note the rectangular brick platform, the tumbled and moved foundation stones and the base of a fireplace against the east side of the trench. The stone wall foundations surrounding the basins have been removed and that area dug slightly deeper than in Plate 17a.

Plate 18a. The brick platform in Zone D1 was founded on a single row of stones.

18b. An oven with vertical clay sides was found in Zone D3. Other ovens of the same size and foundation which were heavily eroded probably were of this type.

18c. The base of the same fireplace is paved with flat stones. The slab to the right of the base is part of a wall that was built after the fireplace had gone out of use.

Plate 19. The final rebuilding in Zone D4. A plaster basin set at the end of a "walkway" at the lower right of the picture.

Plate 20a. The initial 3x5 meter pit in Area C revealed the stone-founded walls and partially paved room of Zone E2. The corridor shown on Figure 22 lies to the left of the stone wall.

20b. After Area C was enlarged heavy rains filled the initial pit with mud and severely eroded the sides of the excavation, in which there were heavy ash layers.

Plate 21a. The platform in Zone F showing the foundation stones and the trench cut into its interior.
21b. The trench cut into the platform clearly shows the dark, ashy brick core and the capping of buff clay bricks lying within and upon the foundation stones.

Plate 22a. Following the primary use of the platform, its corner was cut and used as part of a brick-walled house. A plaster basin is incorporated into the edge of the platform as part of the post-platform construction. 22b. Detail of the northeast corner of the platform after it had been cut by the wall of the house.

PLATE 23

Plate 23a. A stone-founded house or work area lying adjacent to the platform in Zone G1. The level of this structure is above the base of the platform and well below its top.
23b. Detail of the plaster and mud basin inside the structure, with a pile of stones alongside.
23c. Detail of the base of the fireplace paved with flat rocks. The upper part of the fireplace was broken by the construction in Zone G2.

a

b

Plate 24a. Wall of house in Zone H with pile of broken manos and metates lying at its base outside.
24b. Remaining foundation stones of house in Zone I after it had been cut by the plaster kiln and its associated ash pit.

PLATE 25

a

b

Plate 25a. Mud-sided oven in Zone I. This oven had a base of flat stones.
25b. The plaster kiln that cut the wall of the house in Zone I. The pit into which ash and bits of burned plaster was dumped lies in front of the entrance to the kiln. The entrance is behind the sign board. The oven can be seen in section against the rear wall of the excavation.

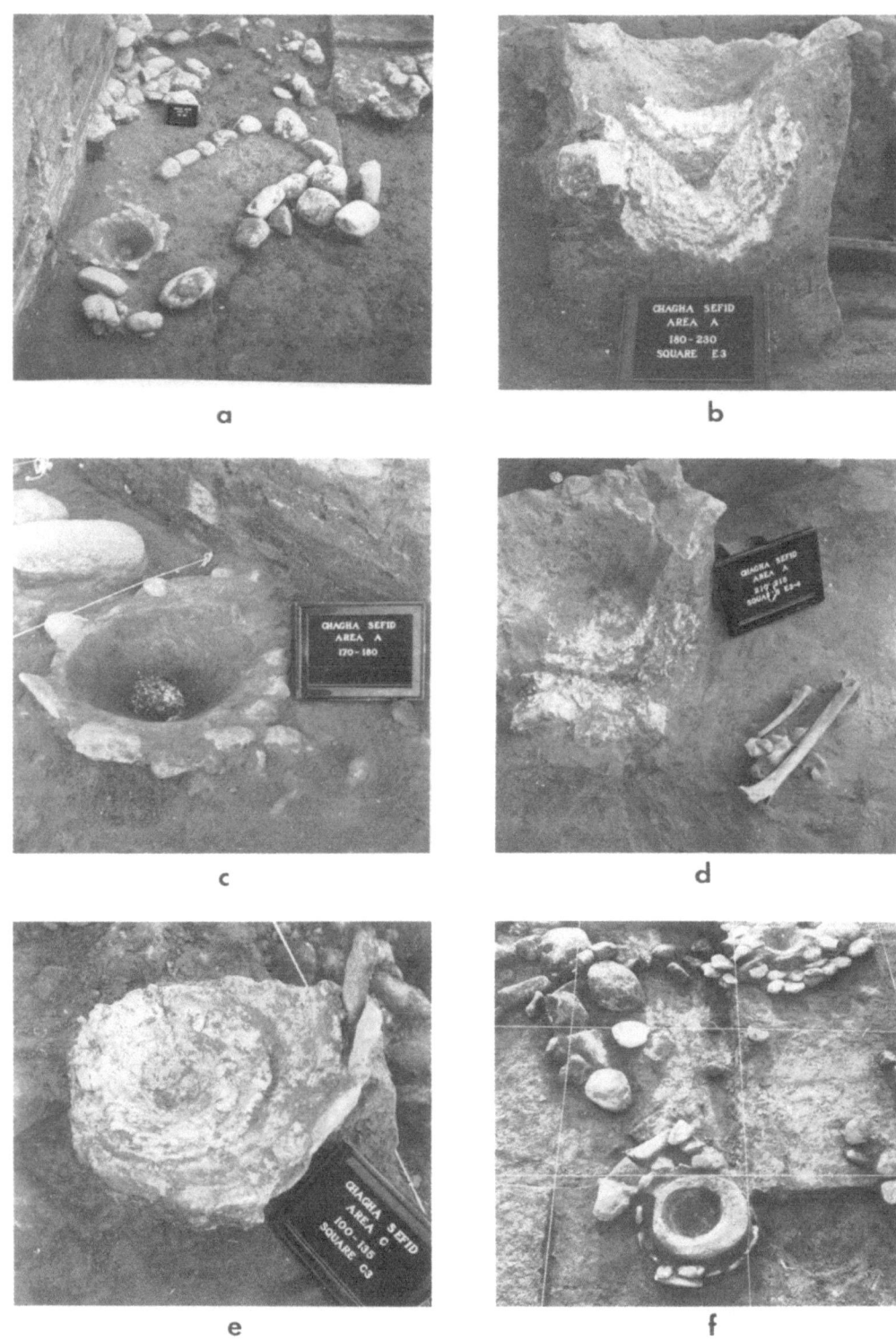

Plate 26a. Stone rectangle with plaster basin in late Sefid deposits, Zone C, Event 1.
26b. The repeated replastering of the basin shows in this section.
26c. Detail of plaster basin set into bricked floor.
26d. Bones of burial No. 3 lie adjacent to the base of the plaster basin.
26e. A plaster basin in Zone E1, Surkh Phase.
26f. A mud-lined basin in Zone D4, Surkh Phase.

PLATE 27

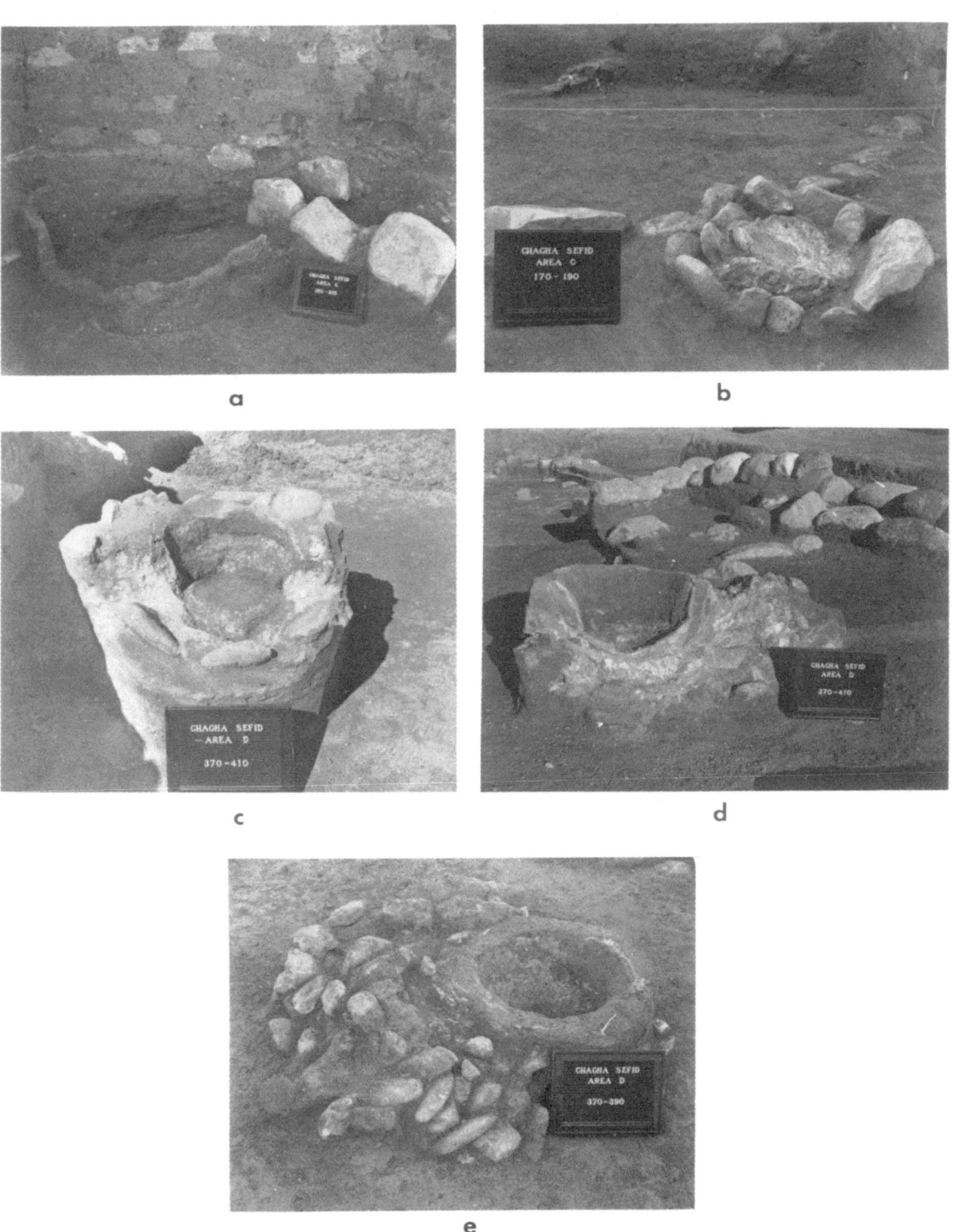

Plate 27a. Mud walled oven or fireplace in Zone D3, Surkh Phase.
27b. The base of a plaster basin in Zone D4, Surkh Phase.
27c. A plaster basin with a handstone set in its base in Zone F, late Surkh Phase.
27d. A section through a mud-lined basin in Zone F, late Surkh Phase.
27e. A mud-lined basin in Zone F, late Surkh Phase.

PLATE 28

a

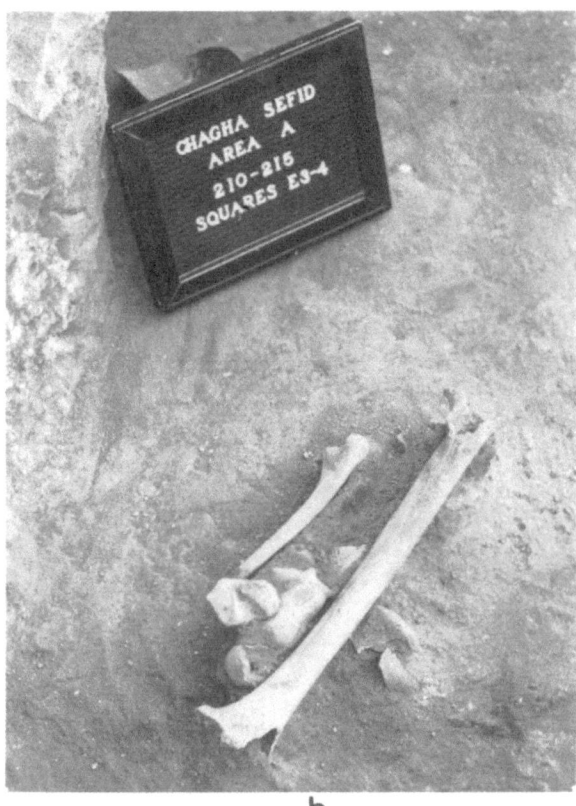

b

c

d

Plate 28*a*. Burial No. 5, Early Sefid Phase(?). Redeposited bundle of human and caprine bones. Skull with cranial deformation lies upside down among other human and many sheep/goat bones.

28*b*. Burial No. 3, Sefid Phase. Redeposited leg bones in small pit.

28*c*. Burial No. 4, Early Sefid Phase(?). Skull lies upside down, detached from thoracic section of body which lies on flat stones.

28*d*. Burial No. 4, Early Sefid Phase(?). Flat stones under burial lie on prepared clay surface. Stones appear to be from base of fireplace.

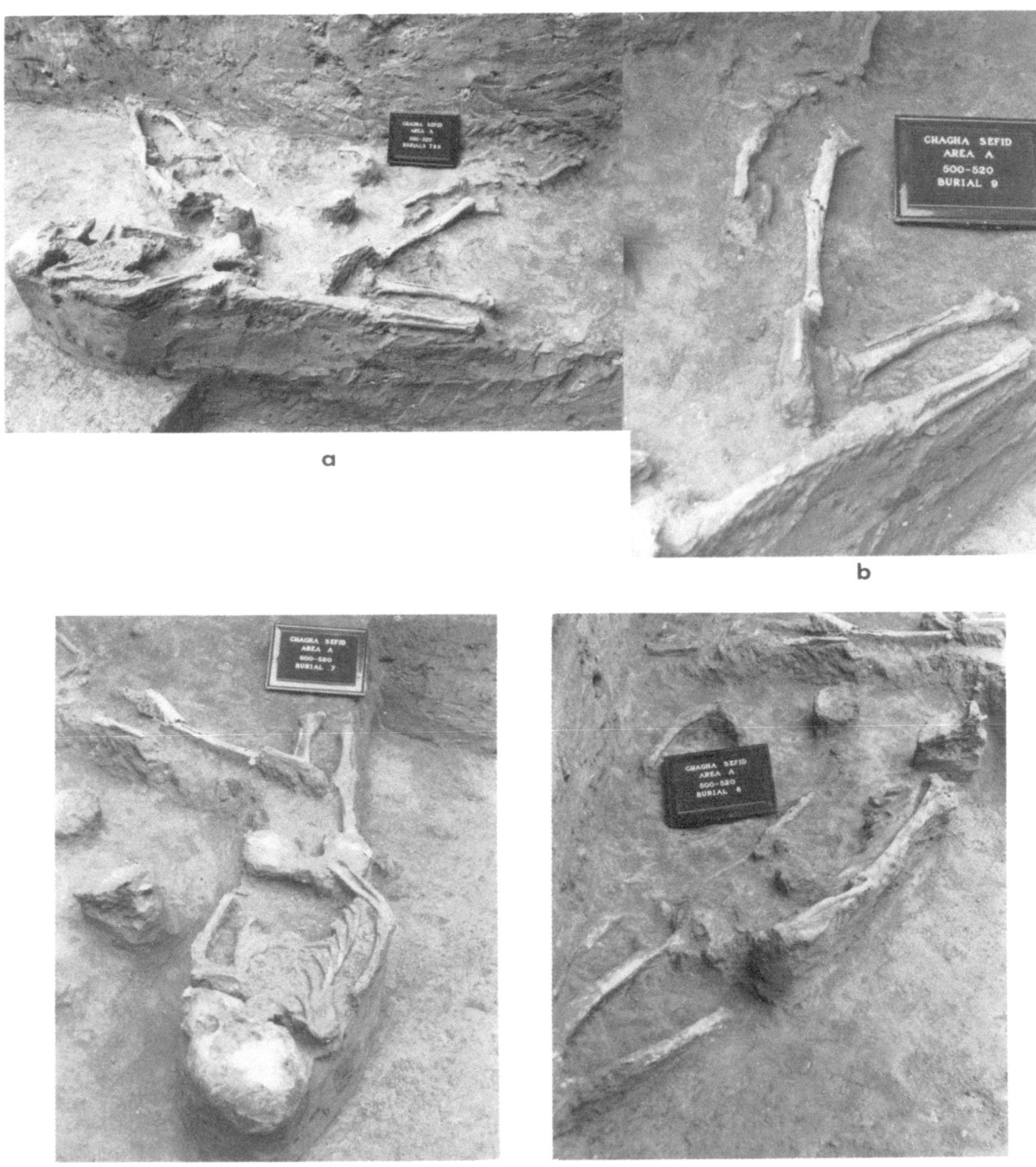

Plate 29a. Burials Nos. 7, 8, 9, Early Sefid Phase(?). Burial No. 7 is cut by later burials No. 9, and No. 8.

29b. Legs of burial No. 8 cut into left femur and pelvis of burial No. 7. The skull of this burial remains under the north wall of our excavation.

29c. Burial No. 7.

29d. Burial No. 9. The skull of this burial is broken and scattered, probably disturbed when burial No. 8 was interred. The pit for this burial seems to have cut into the left arm of burial No. 7.

Plate 30a. Skull of burial No. 7. Note deformation.
30b. Head and upper torso of burial No. 7.

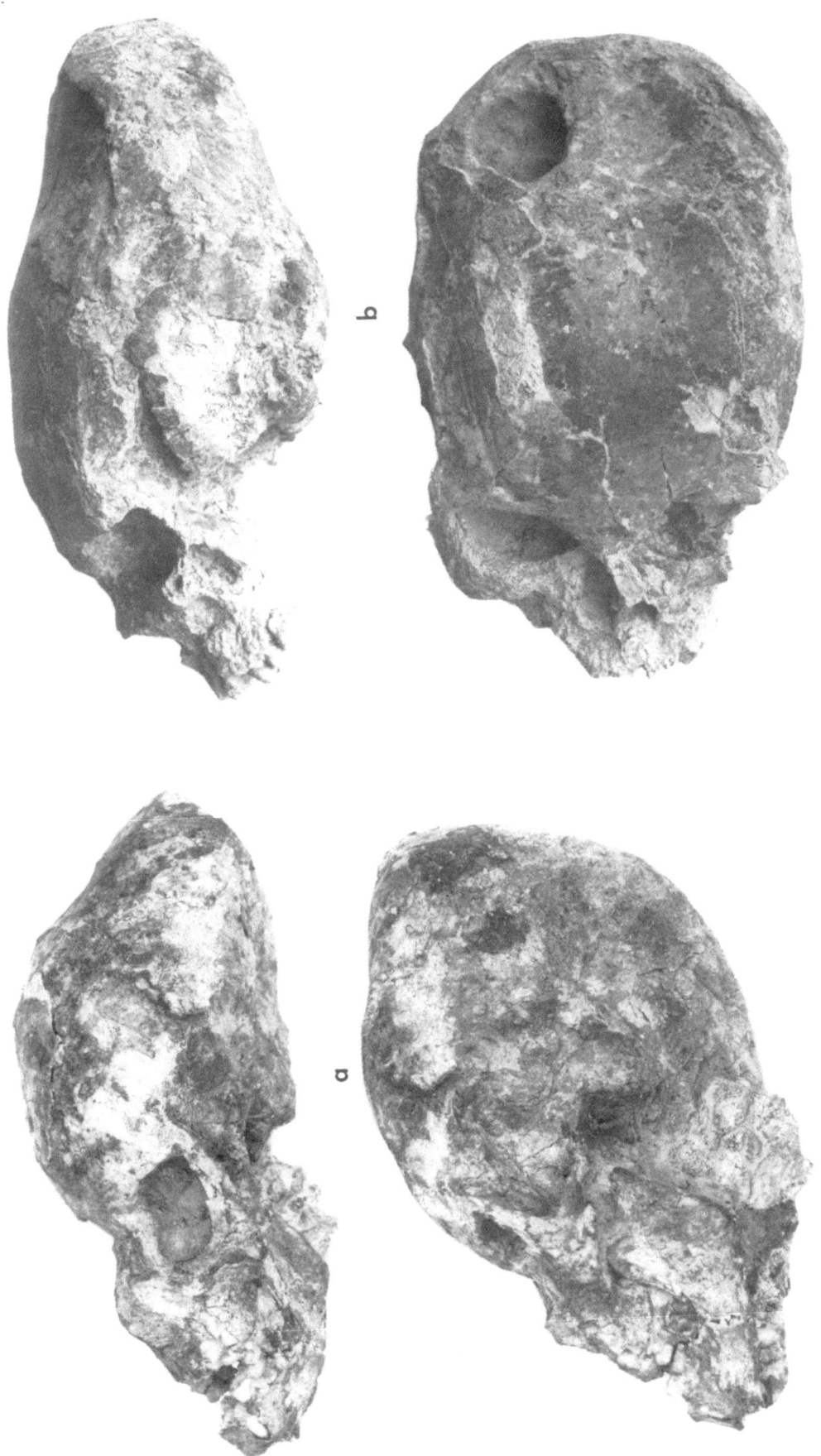

Plate 31a. Two views of skull of burial No. 7.
31b. Two views of skull of burial No. 5.

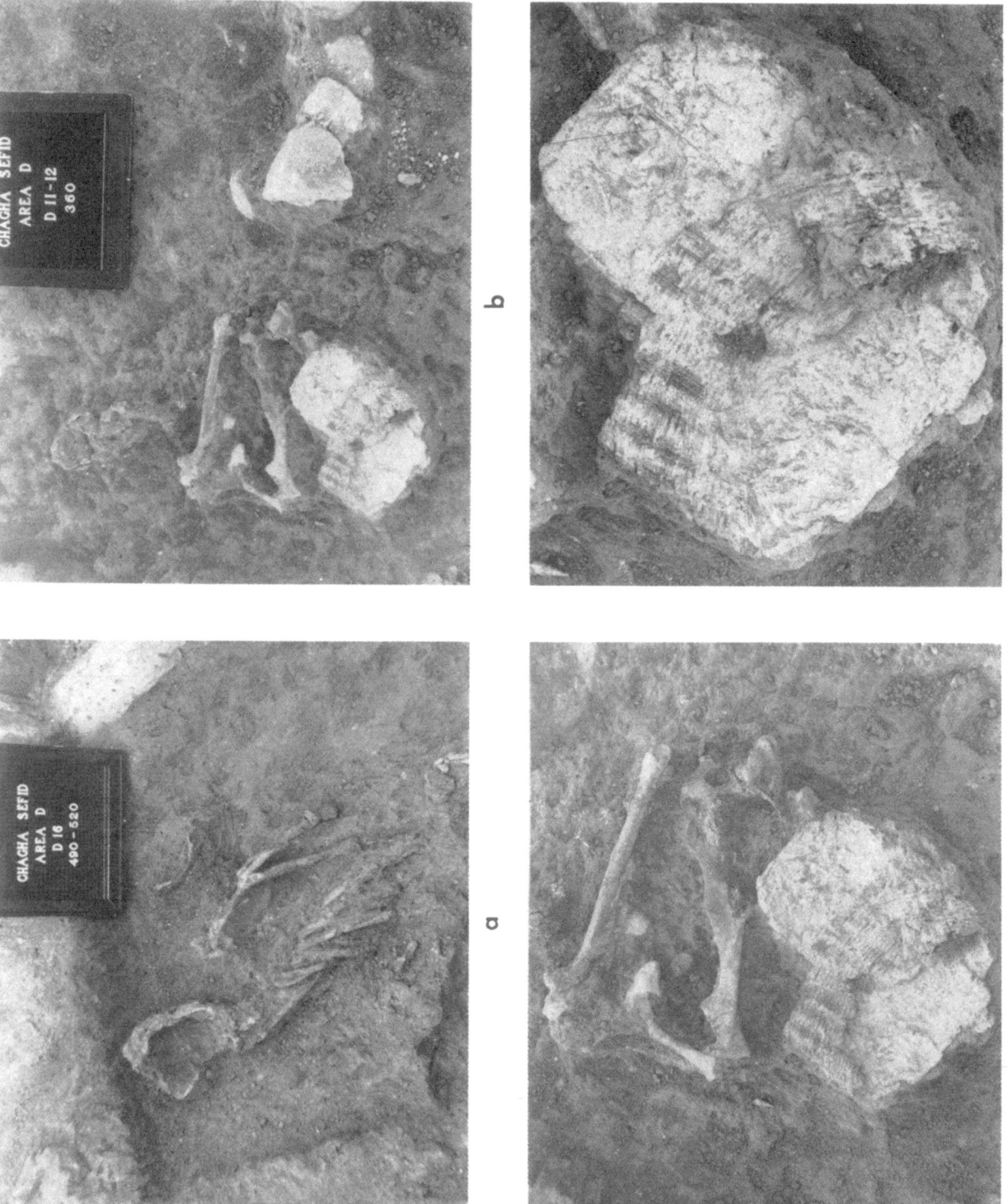

Plate 32a. Burial No. 10. Surkh Phase. Badly disturbed burial, with only the left side of the skeleton relatively intact. Burial pit contains many wheat seeds.
32b. Burial of dog, Zone G2, Choga Mami Transitional Phase. Skull and long bones of dog in association with asphalted remnant of basket.

PLATE 33

Plate 33a. Burial No. 1, Age Unknown. Burial lies in pit dug into Sefid Phase deposits.
33b. Burial No. 2, Age Unknown. Burial lies in pit dug into Sefid Phase deposits. A large metate lies upside down over the skull.
33c. Burial No. 2. Burial pit nearly cut into plaster basin of Sefid Phase.
33d. Burial No. 2. Skeleton with metate removed.

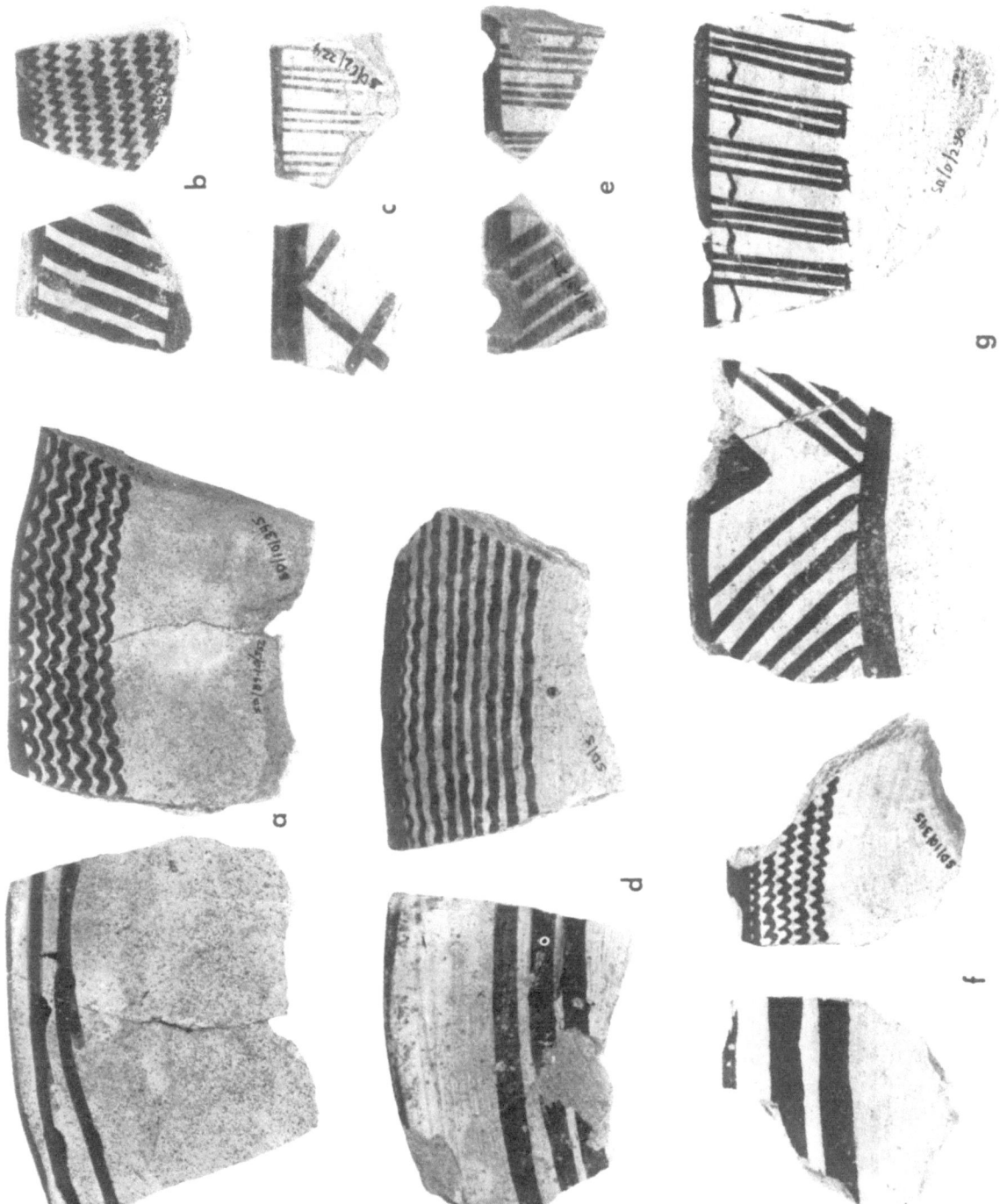

Plate 34. Susiana Black-on-Buff. *a,b,d,f*, open bowls, variety A; *c,e,g*, open bowls, variety B. *a,b,f*, out of context; *c,d,e,g*, Choga Mami Transitional.

PLATE 35

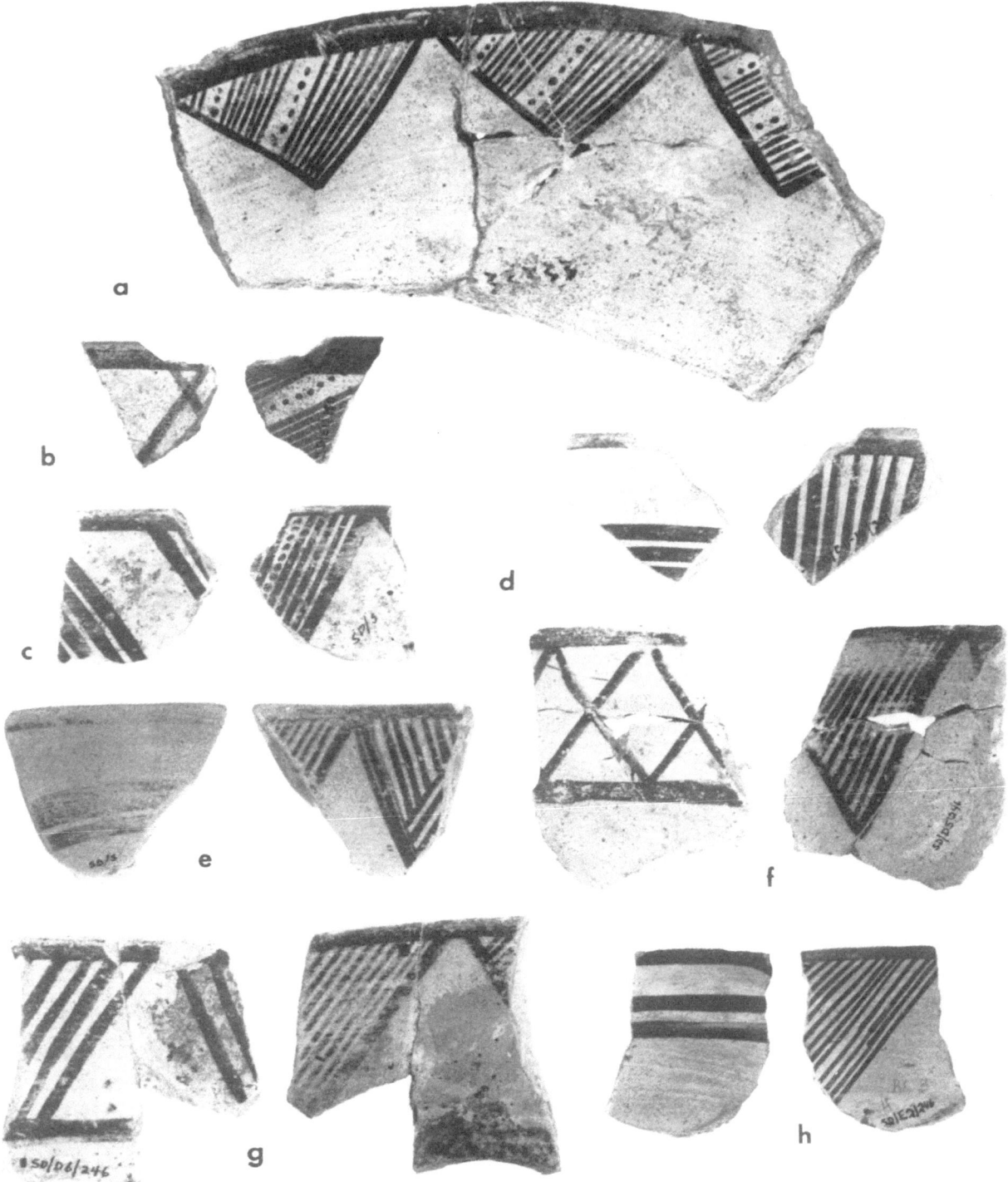

Plate 35. Susiana Black-on-Buff. All sherds are open bowl variety B. *c,d,e*, out of context; *b,d,f,g,h*, Choga Mami Transitional.

Plate 36. Susiana Black-on-Buff. *a-e*, open bowls, variety E; *f-o*, open bowl interiors. *a-d,f,g,k*, out of context; *h-j,m-o*, Choga Mami Transitional.

Plate 37. Susiana Black-on-Buff. *a-g,i*, unique open bowls; *j*, miscellaneous open bowl; *h*, Susiana Plain Buff. All out of context except *h*, Sabz and *a*, Choga Mami Transitional.

Plate 38. Susiana Black-on-Buff. *a-l*, hemispherical bowls; *m-x*, miscellaneous bowls, variety A. *b,c,d,e,k,m-o, q,u*, out of context; *a,f,g-i,l,p,r,s,t,v,w,x*, Choga Mami Transitional.

Plate 39. Susiana Black-on-Buff. *a-h*, miscellaneous bowls, variety A; *i-q*, miscellaneous bowls, variety B. *a-d,g,i,j,l,n,q*, out of context; *e,f,h,k,m,o,p*, Choga Mami Transitional.

Plate 40. Susiana Black-on-Buff. Miscellaneous bowls and jars. *a,i-k,l,m,r*, out of context; *b,f,n,o*, Sabz; *d,e,g,h,p,q*, Choga Mami Transitional.

Plate 41. Susiana Black-on-Buff. Miscellaneous bowl sherds. *a,c,d,k,i,j,l,m-o,* out of context; *b,e,f,g,* Choga Mami Transitional.

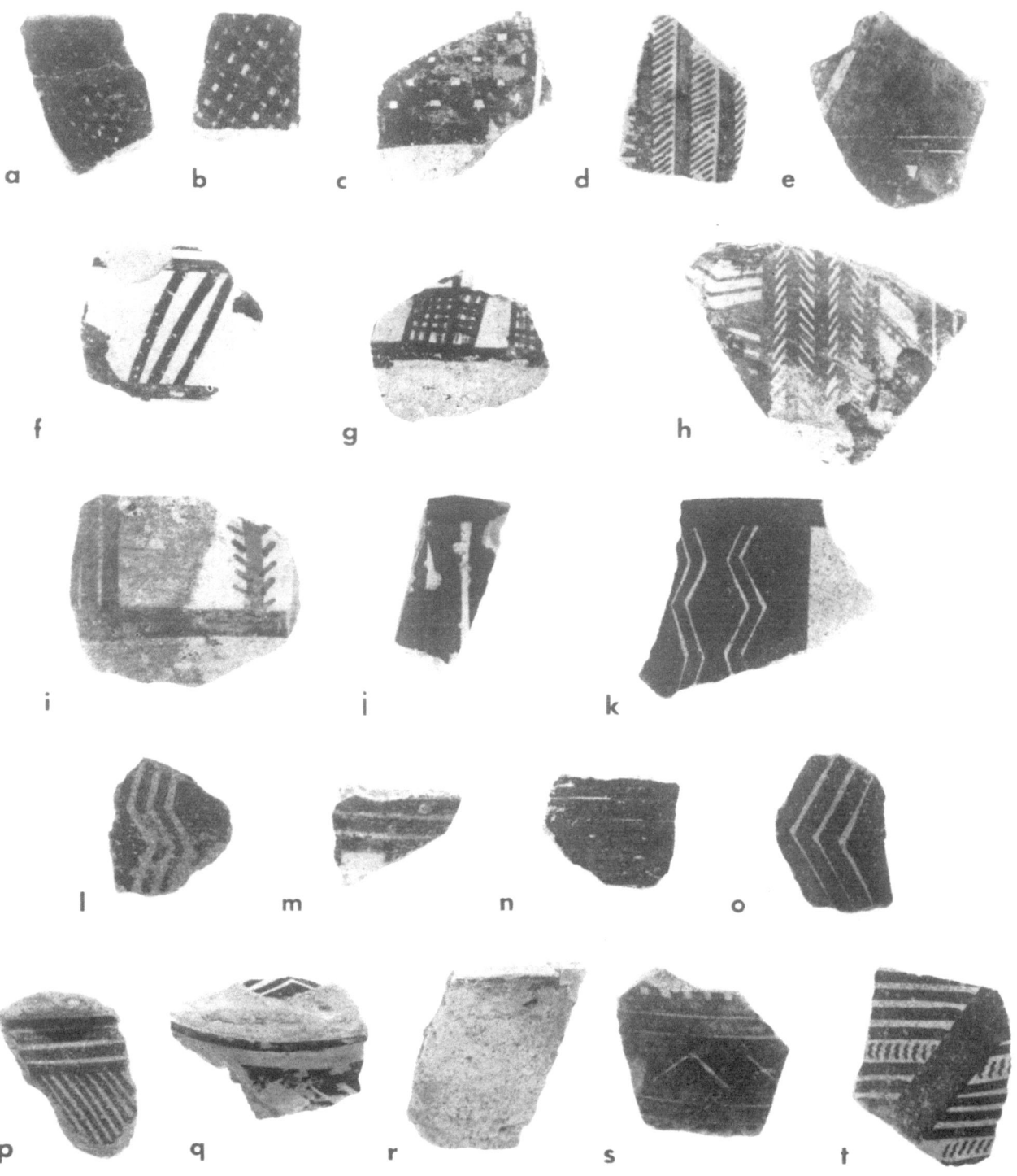

Plate 42. Susiana Black-on-Buff. *a-i,k*, Sabz pots; *j*, basin; *l-t*, pedestals. *a,c,h-j,l-p,r-t*, out of context; *b,d-g,q*, Choga Mami Transitional.

Plate 43. Susiana Black-on-Buff. Miscellaneous unique bowls. *b,c,e,h,i,l,m,n,p,r*, out of context; *j*, Sabz; *a,d,f,g,k,o,q,t*, Choga Mami Transitional.

Plate 44. Susiana Black-on-Buff. *a-i*, jars; *j-k*, handles; *l,m*, spouts. *e,f,i,k,l*, out of context; *a-d,j,m*, Choga Mami Transitional.

PLATE 45

Plate 45. Ground stone tools from Chagha Sefid. *a,b,e*, saddle-shaped grinding slabs; *c*, trough metate; *g,h*, boulder mortars; *f*, loaf-shaped handstone; *d*, stone bowl.

Plate 46. Grinding and pounding tools from Chagha Sefid. *a,b*, loaf-shaped handstones; *c,d,g-h*, simple discoidal handstones; *e,i*, bowl mortars; *j,p-r*, pebble mortars; *m,n*, combination cylindrical pestles and rolling handstones; *l*, stubby, bell-shaped muller; *o,bb*, irregular, sausage-shaped pestles; *y*, spherical pounder or hammerstone; *aa*, core pounder; *s,t,u,z*, cuboid pounder/rubbing stone; *v,w,cc,dd*, basalt pebble pounders; *gg,hh*, pecked stone balls; *x,ee,ff*, sandstone abraders; *k*, small, faceted rubbing stone.

PLATE 47

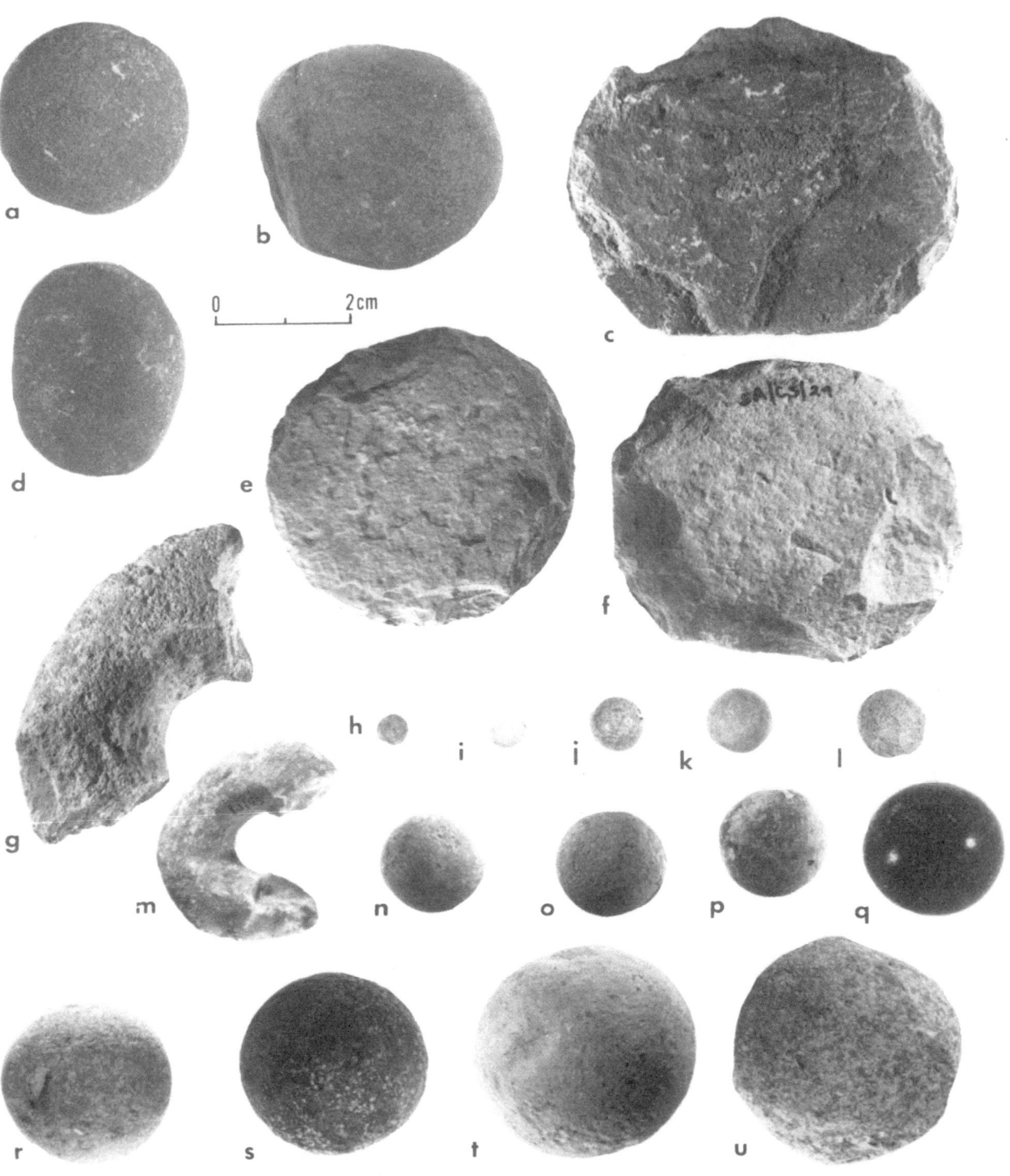

Plate 47. *a,b,d,* spherical pounders or hammerstones; *c,e,f,* chipped limestone discs; *g,m,* perforated stones; *h-i,n-u,* pecked stone balls (entire range of variation).

Plate 48. *a*, limestone cleaver/rubbing stone; *b-d*, sandstone abraders; *e,f*, palette fragments; *g,i,k,l*, miscellaneous polished stones; *h*, "gaming board"; *j*, sandstone basin.

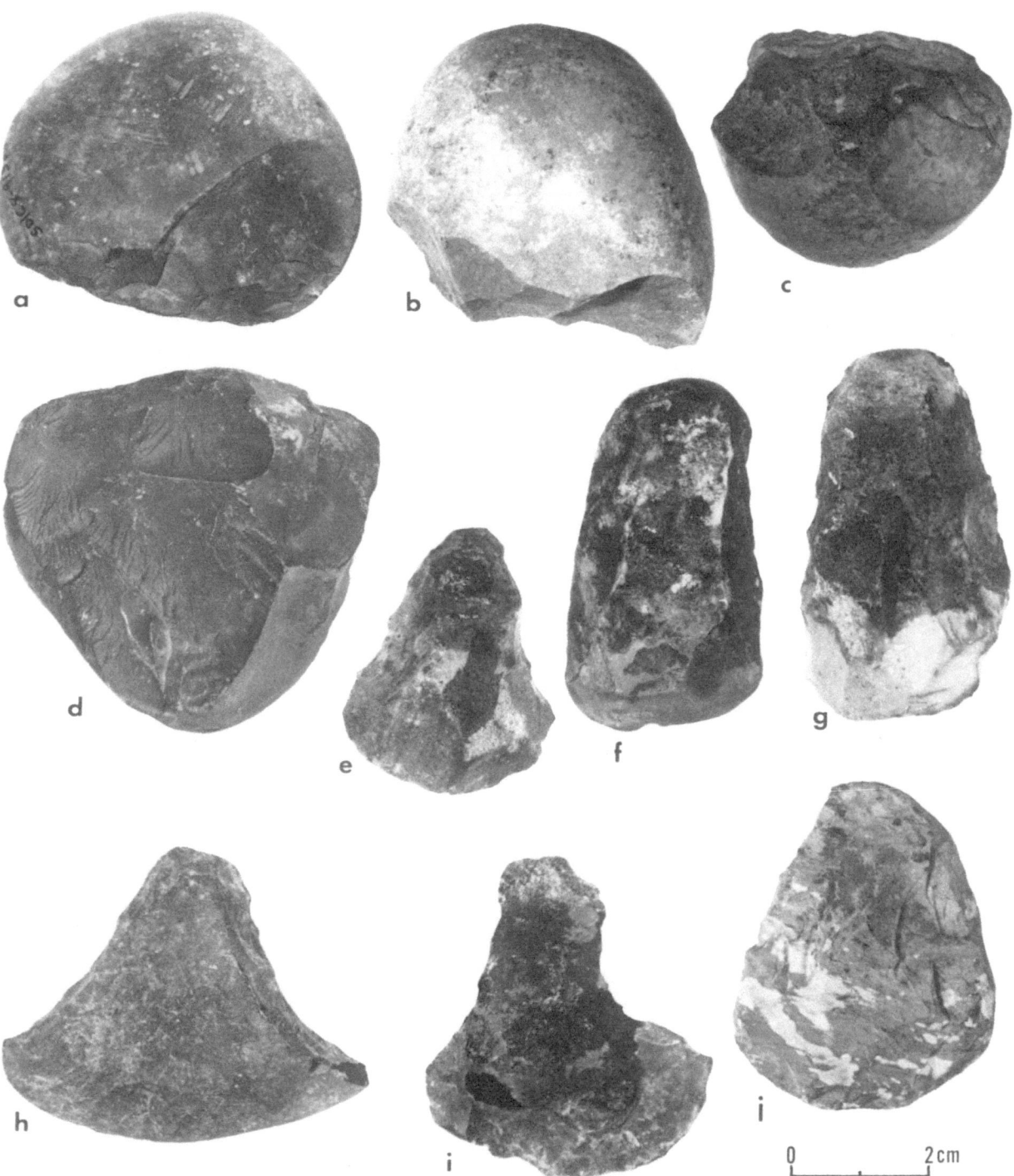

Plate 49. *a-d*, pebble choppers; *e-j*, chipped stone hoes.

Plate 50. *a,b*, sashweight stirring rods; *c*, celt; *d-h,k*, slicing slabs (*k* is enlarged 2 times); *i,l*, small faceted rubbing stones; *j*, chisel; *m-o,s*, cut pebbles; *p-r*, grooved rubbing stones.

Plate 51. *a*, impressed ceramic strips; *b*, ceramic strips before cleaning; *c-e*, sling missles; *f,g*, perforated sherd discs.

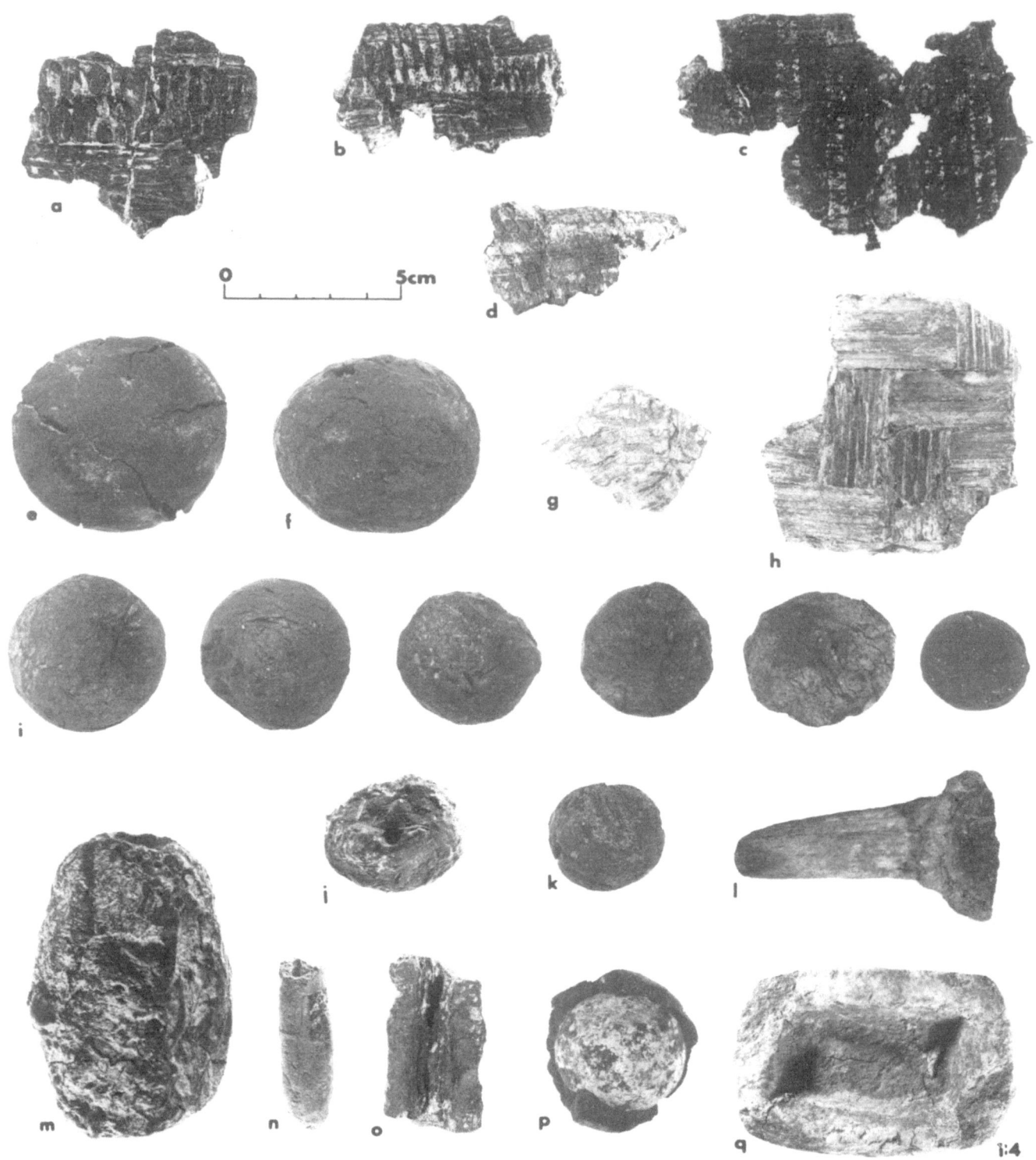

Plate 52. Asphalt and other artifacts. *a-c,* asphalt impressions of twined baskets with floors; *d,h,* asphalt impressions of over-two, under-two twilled mats; *g,* plaster impression of basket; *e,f,i,k,p,* asphalt balls; *j,* asphalt "base"; *m,* asphalt pestle(?); *n,* asphalt handle; *o,* asphalt with impression of stick; *l,* antler flaker; *q,* asphalt box.

Plate 53. Bone tools. *a-i;* bone awls; *j-l*, spatulas; *m,n*, needles; *o,p,* gouges; *q,v,* cut long bones; *u,* bone handle; *r-t,w-aa,* drilled bone pendants(?).

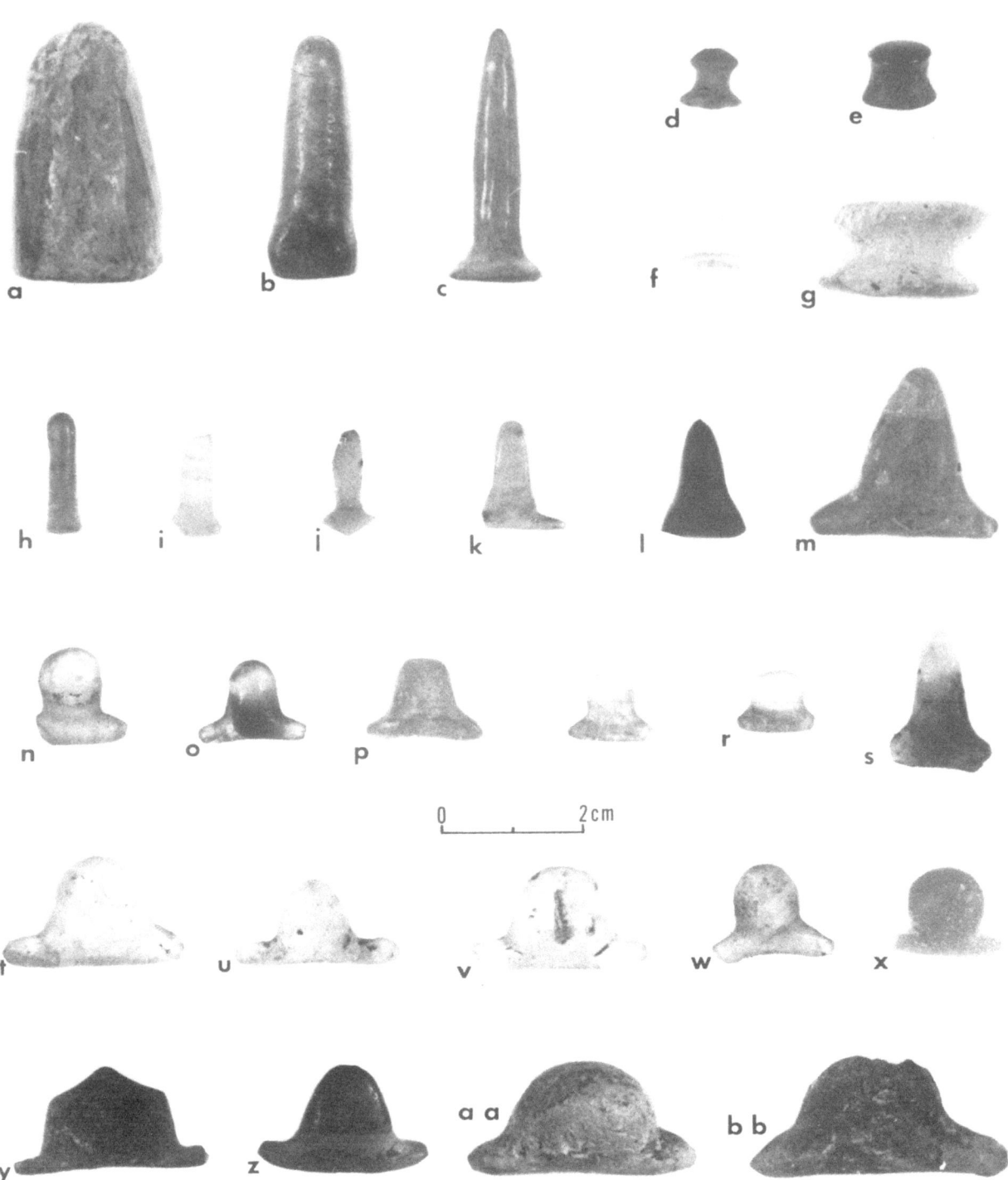

Plate 54. Miscellaneous ornaments and other artifacts. *a-c*, stone mullers; *d-f*, stud-shaped labrets; *g*, ceramic spool; *h-j*, nail-shaped labrets; *k-m,s*, T-shaped labrets; *n-r,t-bb*, domed cufflink-shaped labrets.

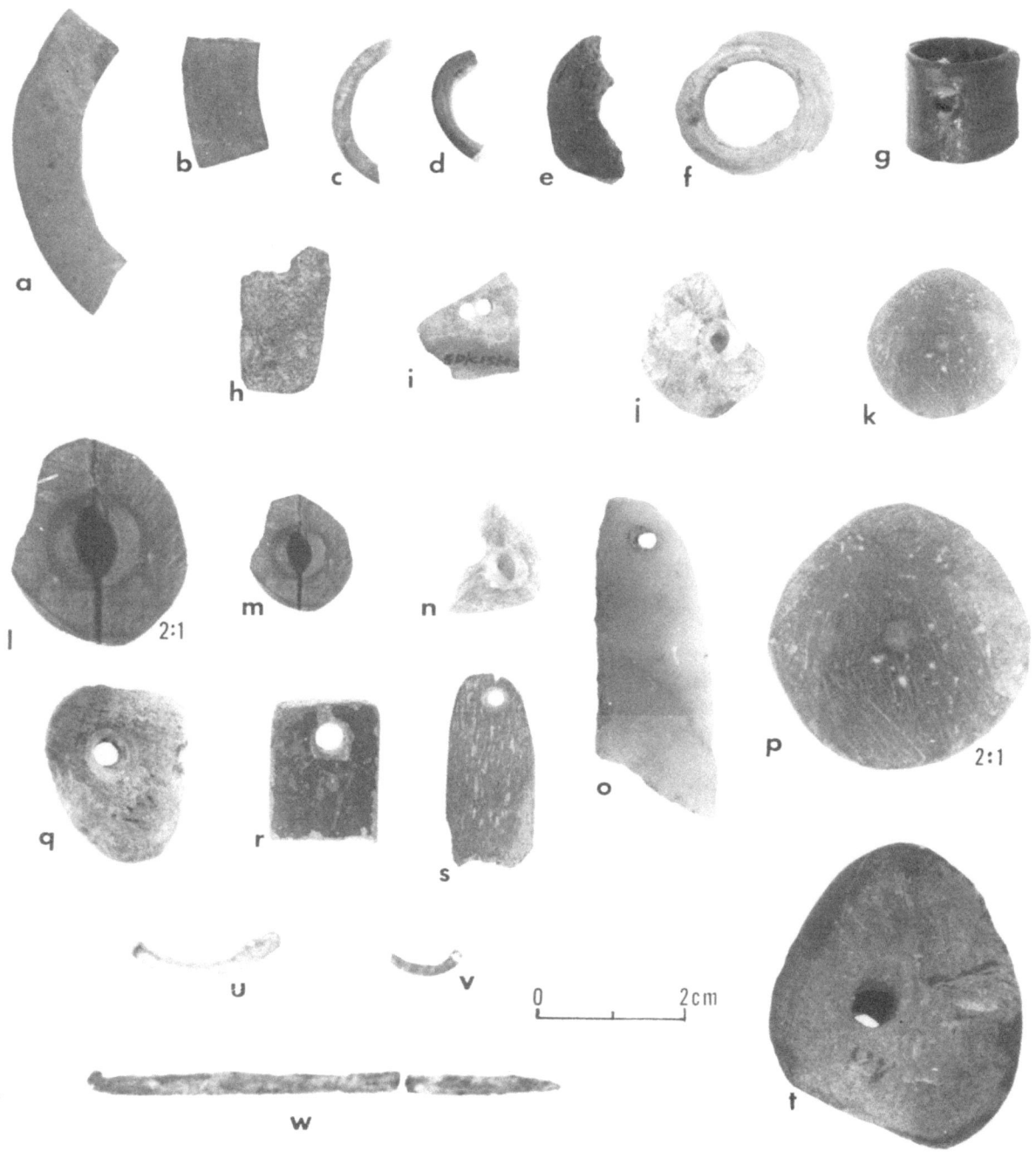

Plate 55. Miscellaneous ornaments and other artifacts. *a,b,* fragments of stone bracelets; *c,d,* fragments of stone rings; *e,* bone ring; *f,* shell ring; *g,* tubular bone bead; *h,r,t,* flat pebble pendants; *s,* bone pendant; *j-n,p,* bead blanks (scale of *l* is 2 times *m*, and scale of *p* is 2 times *k*); *o,* boar tusk pendant; *u,v,* fragments of copper rings; *w,* copper crochet.